Getting Started is as EASY as 1, 2, 3 . . . 4!

 **W9-BEP-928**

1. Sign Up

Instructors register with myBusinessCourse.com

2. Setup Your Course

Add your class details and additional materials.

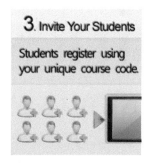

3. Invite Your Students

Students register using your unique course code.

4. Manage Your Course

Study, test, and grade assignments. It's simple!

Provide Instruction and Practice 24/7

◆ Assign homework from your Cambridge Business Publishers textbook and have myBusinessCourse grade it for you automatically.

◆ With our eLectures, your students can revisit accounting topics as often as they like or until they master the topic.

◆ Guided Examples show students how to solve select problems.

◆ Make homework due before class to ensure students enter your classroom prepared.

◆ Additional practice and exam preparation materials are available to help students achieve better grades and content mastery.

STUDENT SELF-STUDY OPTION

Not all instructors choose to incorporate **myBusinessCourse** into their course. In such cases, students can access the Self-Study option for MBC. The Self-Study option provides most of the learning tools available in the Instructor-Led courses, including:

◆ eLectures
◆ Guided Examples
◆ Practice Quizzes

The Self-Study option does not include homework assignments from the textbook. Only the Instructor-Led option includes homework assignments.

Want to learn more about myBusinessCourse?

Contact your sales representative or visit **www.mybusinesscourse.com**.

STUDENTS: Find your access code on the myBusinessCourse insert on the following pages. If you have a used copy of this textbook, you can purchase access online at **www.mybusinesscourse.com**.

my BusinessCourse

FREE WITH NEW COPIES OF THIS TEXTBOOK*

Scratch here for access code

EB8tCCmvxJ2Wb4Ðp

Start using myBusinessCourse Today: www.mybusinesscourse.com

myBusinessCourse is a web-based learning and assessment program intended to complement your textbook and faculty instruction.

Student Benefits

- **eLectures**: These videos review the key concepts of each Learning Objective in each chapter.
- **Guided examples**: These videos provide step-by-step solutions for select problems in each chapter.
- **Auto-graded assignments**: Provide students with immediate feedback on select assignments. **(with Instructor-Led course ONLY)**.
- **Quiz and Exam preparation**: myBusinessCourse provides students with additional practice and exam preparation materials to help students achieve better grades and content mastery.

You can access myBusinessCourse 24/7 from any web-enabled device, including iPads, smartphones, laptops, and tablets.

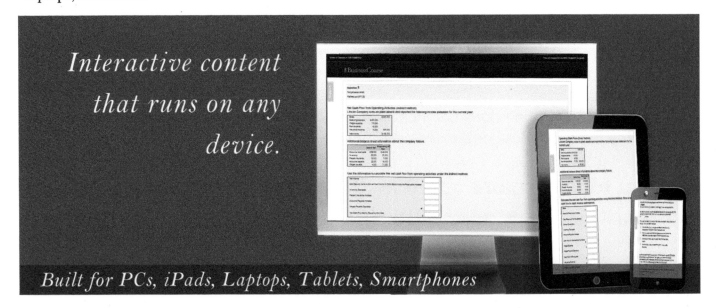

Interactive content that runs on any device.

Built for PCs, iPads, Laptops, Tablets, Smartphones

Each access code is good for one use only. If the textbook is used for more than one course or term, students will have to purchase additional myBusinessCourse access codes. In addition, students who repeat a course for any reason will have to purchase a new access code. If you purchased a used book and the protective coating that covers the access code has been removed, your code may be invalid.

Access to myBusinessCourse is free ONLY with the purchase of a new textbook.

Managerial Accounting
for Undergraduates

First Edition

Theodore E. Christensen
J.M. Tull School of Accounting
University of Georgia

L. Scott Hobson
The Marriott School of Management
Brigham Young University

James S. Wallace
The Peter F. Drucker and Masatoshi Ito
Graduate School of Management
Claremont Graduate University

Photo Credits

Chapter 1: © istockphoto.com
Chapter 2: © istockphoto.com
Chapter 3: © istockphoto.com
Chapter 4: © istockphoto.com
Chapter 5: © istockphoto.com
Chapter 6: © istockphoto.com
Chapter 7: © istockphoto.com
Chapter 8: © istockphoto.com
Chapter 9: © istockphoto.com
Chapter 10: © istockphoto.com
Chapter 11: © istockphoto.com
Chapter 12: © istockphoto.com
Chapter 13: © istockphoto.com
Chapter 14: © istockphoto.com

Permissions Statement:

Materials from the Certified Management Accountant Examinations, Copyright © 2015 by the Institute of Certified Management Accountants, are reprinted and/or adapted with permission.

All Fezzari photos courtesy of Fezzari Bicycles.

Cambridge Business Publishers

MANAGERIAL ACCOUNTING FOR UNDERGRADUATES, First Edition, by Theodore E. Christensen, L. Scott Hobson, and James S. Wallace

ISBN 978-1-61853-112-4

Bookstores & Faculty: To order this book, contact the company via email **customerservice@cambridgepub.com** or call 800-619-6473.

Students & Retail Customers: To order this book, please visit the book's website and order directly online.

Printed in the United States of America.
10 9 8 7 6 5 4 3

THEODORE E. CHRISTENSEN is director and Terry Distinguished Chair of Business in the J. M. Tull School of Accounting at the University of Georgia (UGA). Prior to coming to UGA, he was on the faculty at Brigham Young University from 2000–2015 and at Case Western Reserve University from 1995–2000. He was a visiting professor at the University of Michigan (2013–2014) and the University of Utah (2012) and has taught at Santa Clara University in a summer program since 2005. He received a B.S. degree in accounting from San Jose State University, an M.Acc. degree in tax from Brigham Young University, and a Ph.D. in accounting from the University of Georgia. Professor Christensen has authored and coauthored articles published in many journals, including *The Accounting Review*; the *Journal of Accounting and Economics*; the *Journal of Accounting Research*; *Review of Accounting Studies Contemporary Accounting Research*; *Accounting Organizations and Society*; the *Journal of Business Finance & Accounting*; the *Journal of Accounting, Auditing, and Finance*; *Accounting Horizons*; and *Issues in Accounting Education*. He is also the author of an advanced financial accounting textbook. Professor Christensen has taught financial accounting at all levels, financial statement analysis, business valuation, both introductory and intermediate managerial accounting, and corporate taxation. He is the recipient of numerous awards for both teaching and research. He has been active in serving on various committees of the American Accounting Association and is a CPA.

L. SCOTT HOBSON is a Teaching Professor of Accounting at Brigham Young University (BYU), where he joined the faculty in 2003. He received his B.S. in accounting and Master of Accountancy degrees from BYU in 1983. Prior to his career in academics, Professor Hobson was the founder and owner of Hilton Farnkopf & Hobson (now HFH Consultants), a management consulting firm headquartered in Walnut Creek, California, for 14 years. He also worked in public accounting at Price Waterhouse for 5.5 years in both audit and consulting. While at Price Waterhouse, he taught for 2 years as an adjunct faculty at San Jose State University. He has taught accounting at all levels, from principles to M.B.A. courses, including managerial accounting, financial accounting, governmental and not-for-profit accounting, and management consulting. Professor Hobson is licensed as a CPA (inactive) in California. Professor Hobson has published a case titled "Managing the CPA Firm at Dodge Company" in *Issues in Accounting Education*.

JAMES S. WALLACE is an Associate Professor at The Peter F. Drucker and Masatoshi Ito Graduate School of Management at The Claremont Graduate University. He received his B.A. from the University of California, Santa Barbara; his M.B.A. from the University of California, Davis; and his Ph.D. from the University of Washington. Professor Wallace also holds a CPA certification from the state of California. He previously served on the faculty of the University of California, Irvine and has served as a visiting professor at the University of California, San Diego. Professor Wallace's work has appeared in leading academic journals, including the *Journal of Accounting and Economics*, the *Journal of Corporate Finance*, and *Information Systems Research*, along with leading applied journals such as the *Journal of Applied Corporate Finance*, the *Journal of Accountancy*, *Issues in Accounting Education*, and *Accounting Horizons*. Prior to his career in academics, Professor Wallace worked in public accounting and in industry with a Fortune 500 company. He has done consulting work with numerous companies in multiple industries.

Preface

Welcome to *Managerial Accounting for Undergraduates*. We have written this book to introduce future business professionals to management accounting concepts and decision-making tools that will help them manage their companies in an increasingly competitive global market. While working for both small and large service firms and teaching in a university setting, we observed that some business professionals, although possessing a technically sound knowledge of accounting principles and methods, had difficulty understanding how the "answer" applied in the context of real business issues faced by these firms. Although a business professional may be able to calculate the materials efficiency variance, for example, determining who might have been responsible for the variance and what should be done to address the variance requires a broader understanding of the overall business. We want young professionals to be better prepared to make good business decisions and contribute to the overall strategy of the companies for which they work.

Many undergraduate managerial accounting textbooks focus primarily on calculations and formulas and how to apply these accounting skills in a manufacturing environment. However, business professionals must be able to apply their technical accounting knowledge and expertise in a broader context in making good business decisions. Moreover, because the U.S. market is increasingly service oriented, professionals must develop experience in applying these skills to decision making in a service environment. Having spent several years supplementing existing textbook problems with more real-world and service industry examples, we saw a need for a new approach. Hence, we focus on helping students to (1) develop strong analytical skills and (2) apply them in realistic decision-making contexts. Finally, we have written the book with a heavy emphasis on managerial decisions in service and merchandising enterprises.

TARGET AUDIENCE

Managerial Accounting for Undergraduates is intended for use in the first managerial accounting course at the undergraduate level—one that balances the development of management accounting tools with their implementation in decision making. This book teaches future business professionals how to read, analyze, and interpret accounting and other company, industry, and economic data to make informed business decisions.

We believe students become more engaged in the course when they see how the course content pertains to their future careers. Once engaged in the course, students perform much better and enjoy the class more. Furthermore, we believe accounting is a discipline best learned by doing. Unlike some other disciplines, accounting needs to be practiced. Consequently, we have taken great care to incorporate a number of pedagogical devices and real company examples that illustrate the relevance of managerial accounting to professional careers.

RELEVANCE

Business professionals know that the economy has changed dramatically over the last two decades and that the demands placed on professionals now require an understanding of broad business disciplines, including finance, marketing, organizational behavior, supply chain management, operations management, and strategy. By exposing students to real-world companies and the challenges that they face, they can begin to understand the need to integrate accounting information with other business information in making good decisions.

One of the authors is a former founder, owner, and chief financial officer of a very successful regional consulting firm, HFH Consultants, LLC. The author was intimately involved in the strategy, marketing, human resource management, finance, and accounting of this service firm from its founding with three partners and a secretary to its growth to include four offices, approximately two dozen professionals and staff, and over $3.5 million in annual revenue. His extensive experience managing this firm for 14 years is reflected throughout the textbook in the form of a continuous problem based on a fictitious service firm. This practical experience is also reflected in other real-world examples and problems based on real companies.

The following features are used throughout the textbook to help students understand how managerial accounting principles are used in real businesses today.

Real Company Examples

Students are more likely to engage in the learning process and retain the concepts taught if the examples used are real companies with which they are familiar. Throughout the textbook, we incorporate a wide range of examples using real companies such as **Microsoft**, **Amazon**, **Google**, and **Waste Management**. In addition, the **Service Industry in Focus** section in the assignments of each chapter requires the students to use the financial and operational data of a fictitious consulting company, Environmental Business Consultants, LLC, to address real business issues.

Most chapters also include real-world examples from Fezzari, a custom bike manufacturer.

Environmental Business Consultants

Accounting in Practice

These boxed inserts help students bridge the gap between the classroom and what students encounter in the real world. Accounting in Practice illustrations document situations a student will likely encounter and present choices that companies face in making decisions.

Factory Supplies versus Indirect Materials	ACCOUNTING IN PRACTICE
Factory supplies are different from indirect materials. Factory supplies are used in the factory but are not part of the product itself. Lubricant used on the machine that stamps the sheet metal used in a laptop computer would be a factory supply. Indirect materials are part of the product, but are difficult to trace to each individual product. Solder used to attach computer chips to a motherboard would be an indirect material. Both factory supplies and indirect materials can become part of manufacturing overhead.	

Service Industry in Focus

The service sector is the fastest growing segment of the U.S. economy. The Service Industry in Focus inserts help students understand how managerial accounting is applied to improve the competitiveness of service companies.

Environmental Business Consultants, LLC (EBC) worked on and completed two projects during June 2016: a review of appropriate rates for solid waste and recycling collection within Klamath County, and a competitive procurement of landfill disposal services for the City of Redding. The following information relates to these two projects:

	Rate Review Project—Klamath	Procurement Project—Redding
WIP Inventory balance at June 1, 2016	$46,320	$85,318
Hours worked during June.	100	74
Payroll cost per hour:		
Partner	$ 60	$ 60
Manager	$ 38	$ 38
Staff	$ 24	$ 24
Overhead rate per labor hour.	$ 25	$ 25

During June, the partner charged 10 hours to the rate review project and 20 hours to the

Decision Time

Often, companies are faced with a choice among alternative courses of action where the correct choice is not apparent. The Decision Time inserts help students look beyond the accounting numbers to see the importance of other business information in making the best decision.

DECISION TIME

The solution is on page 109.

Because the estimated manufacturing overhead and/or the estimated activity level used in the predetermined overhead rate will differ from actual manufacturing overhead and/or actual activity, the manufacturing overhead applied to work in process will be under- or overapplied. What should management do with this under- or overapplied overhead amount?

a. Add/subtract from cost of goods sold.

b. Allocate among work in process inventory, finished goods inventory, and cost of goods sold.

c. Either a or b, depending on the significance of the amount.

STUDENT SUCCESS

Managerial accounting is often challenging—especially for students lacking business experience or previous exposure to business courses. To help students succeed in the course and better prepare for a career in business management, we include many features that provide direction to students and require them to recall and apply the managerial accounting techniques and tools described in each chapter.

Putting Each Chapter in Context

Often, students lose sight of the big picture. The **Past/Present/Future** feature provides students with an overview of where the chapter fits within the whole course.

 PAST

Chapter 1 introduced managerial accounting. It explored career opportunities in managerial accounting, its objectives, and professional

 PRESENT

Chapter 2 defines basic costing terminology and introduces different types of manufacturing inventories. It illustrates how costs flow through the

 FUTURE

Chapter 3 introduces and explains job costing in more detail for both manufacturing and service industries. It also explains overhead allocation.

Mapping Each Chapter

Each chapter begins with an overview that visually depicts the layout of the chapter.

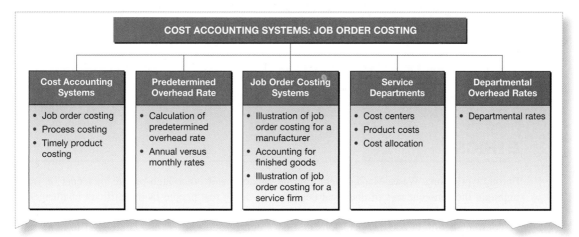

Your Turn!

Your Turn boxes are integrated throughout each chapter as a means of reinforcing the material just presented. Solutions are provided at the end of the chapter so students can check their work.

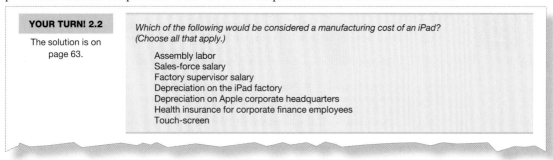

A.K.A. Boxes

A.K.A. (Also Known As) boxes inform students of commonly used alternative terms that they may encounter in practice.

A.K.A. Manufacturing overhead has several other names that are commonly used in practice, such as **factory overhead**, factory burden, or indirect manufacturing costs.

3. **Manufacturing overhead** consists of all manufacturing costs not included in direct material and direct labor. Manufacturing overhead includes indirect material, indirect labor, factory supplies used, factory payroll tax and fringe benefits costs, factory utilities, and factory building and machinery costs (such as depreciation, insurance, property taxes, and repairs and maintenance). Manufacturing overhead specifically *excludes* selling and non-factory administrative expenses because these expenses are not incurred in the manufacturing process.

Hints

Helpful suggestions are inserted in the margin as **Hints** to help students understand difficult concepts.

When the under- or overapplied amount is significant, it should be allocated to all of the jobs that were worked on during the year. This is accomplished by a journal entry that transfers the amount to Work in Process Inventory, Finished Goods Inventory, and Cost of Goods Sold. An overapplied amount is transferred by debiting Manufacturing Overhead and crediting Work in Process Inventory, Finished Goods Inventory, and Cost of Goods Sold. An underapplied amount is transferred by debiting Work in

Hint: After the disposition of over- or underapplied overhead, the balance in the overhead account should be $0.

Takeaways

These in-chapter summaries ensure that students grasp key concepts before proceeding to the next topic.

> **TAKEAWAY 2.2**
>
> The three manufacturing inventory accounts (direct materials, work in process, and finished goods) comprise the inventory balance reported on a company's balance sheet. The expense associated with producing the inventory (cost of goods sold) is reported on the income statement when the product is sold, which may be in a period after the product was manufactured. The purpose of journal entries 1–8 in **Exhibit 2-15** is to determine these amounts as accurately as possible.

ETHICS

Enron, WorldCom, Waste Management, Bernie Madoff, and other high-profile incidents of fraud highlight the consequences of unethical decisions made by real people facing difficult challenges in businesses today. Although most students will not face such significant decisions, they will certainly be confronted with day-to-day decisions that have ethical implications and could lead to more serious challenges. For example, students may be tempted to inflate chargeable hours when performance evaluations and bonuses are based on achieving a target level of chargeability. We discuss ethics where appropriate in the textbook, including an assignment in most chapters that raises an ethical issue. Assignments involving ethics are identified by the icon in the margin.

>
>
> **EYK2-3. Ethics Case** Great Cakes is a large bakery known for its quality "boxed cake" products. Its motto is "We Use Only the Best Ingredients." Ralph Sands, the purchasing supervisor, is responsible for ordering the ingredients for all the bakery products. He is being considered for a promotion based on his proven ability to purchase ingredients at the best price available.
>
> The cost of all the ingredients has risen substantially over the past few months. Sands decides to purchase 25% of the ingredients at a lower quality than Great Cakes normally uses because the cost is significantly less. Without relying on the company's test kitchens, he believes this substitution will not be noticed by the customers and the lower cost will counterbalance the increased costs of the other ingredients.
>
> Sands explains this decision to his friend, Lynn Pall, the company's accountant, one day at lunch. He also tells her that he does not intend to inform management of the inclusion of the lower-quality ingredients in the bakery's products.
>
> *Required*
> What ethical considerations arise from Ralph Sands' decisions? What problems face Lynn Pall because of his actions?

SUPPLEMENT PACKAGE

For Instructors

myBusinessCourse: A web-based learning and assessment program intended to complement your textbook and classroom instruction. This easy-to-use course management system grades homework automatically and provide students with additional help when you are not available. In addition, detailed diagnostic tools assess class and individual performance. myBusinessCourse is ideal for online courses or traditional face-to-face courses for which you want to offer students more resources to succeed. Assignments with the  in the margin are available in myBusinessCourse.

Solutions Manual: Created by the textbook authors, the Solutions Manual contains complete solutions to all the assignment material in the text.

PowerPoint: The PowerPoint slides outline key elements of each chapter.

Test Bank: Created by the textbook authors, the Test Bank includes multiple-choice items, matching questions, short essay questions, and problems.

Website: All instructor materials are accessible via the book's website (password protected) along with other useful links and marketing information: www.cambridgepub.com.

Instructor CD-ROM: This convenient supplement provides the text's ancillary materials on a portable CD-ROM. All the faculty supplements that accompany the textbook are available, including Power-Point, Solutions Manual, Test Bank, and Computerized Test Bank.

For Students

BusinessCourse: A web-based learning and assessment program intended to complement your textbook and faculty instruction. This easy-to-use program grades homework automatically and provides you with additional help when your instructor is not available. Assignments with the MBC in the margin are available in myBusinessCourse. Access is free with new copies of this textbook (look for the page containing the access code toward the front of the book). If you buy a used copy of the book, you can purchase access at **www.mybusinesscourse.com**.

Website: Useful links are available to students free of charge on the book's website: www.cambridge-pub.com.

ACKNOWLEDGMENTS

This text benefited greatly from the valuable feedback of focus group attendees, reviewers, students, and colleagues. We are extremely grateful to them for their help in making this project a success.

We are particularly grateful for the help of Niels Bybee, our graduate assistant and friend, whose timely and accurate work was so crucial.

Thanks, too, to our families (Ted's wife, Donna, and children, Tyler and Hannah Christensen, Scott and Hannah Christensen, Dallin, Matthew, Joshua, and Stephanie; Scott's wife, Kay Lani, and children, Ryan and Megan Hobson, Kellie and Callen Bagley, Todd and Chelsea Hobson, Jessica and Kyle Kubal, Daniel, and Kaitlyn; and Jim's wife, Debra Lester) for their love, encouragement, and support.

Permission has been received from the Institute of Certified Management Accountants (CMA) to use questions and/or unofficial answers from past CMA examinations.

Wagdy Abdallah, *Seton Hall University*

Ira Abdullah, *Robert Morris University*

Nasrollah Ahadiat, *California State Polytechnic University*

Natalie Allen, *Texas A&M University*

Michael Alles, *Rutgers University*

Bridget Anakwe, *Delaware State University*

Lisa Banks, *Mott Community College*

Vernon Bell, *Marshall University*

Jason Bergner, *University of Nevada—Reno*

Diane Biagioni, *Indiana University*

Timothy Biggart, *Berry College*

Rada Brooks, *University of California—Berkeley*

Eugene Bryson, *University of Alabama—Huntsville*

Marci Butterfield, *University of Utah*

James Cannon, *Iowa State University*

Rodney Carmack, *Arkansas State University*

Jackie Casey, *University of North Carolina—Wilmington*

John Cergnul, *St. Mary's College—IN*

Yu Chen, *Texas A&M International*

Julie Chenier, *Louisiana State University*

Scott Collins, *Penn State University*

Carolyn Conn, *St. Edwards University*

Sue Convery, *Michigan State University*

David Cook, *Calvin College*

James Crumbacher, *West Liberty University*

Somnath Das, *University of Illinois—Chicago*

Tom Determan, *University of Wisconsin—Parkside*

Patricia Doherty, *Boston University*

Raymond Elson, *Valdosta State University*

James Emig, *Villanova University*

Lili Eng, *Missouri University of Science & Technology*

Connie Fajardo, *National University*

Kurt Fanning, *Grand Valley State University*

Charles Fazzi, *St. Vincent College*

David Folsom, *Lehigh University*

Dennis George, *University of Dubuque*

Brian Gilligan, *Morton College*

Glen Greencorn, *St. Mary's University Canada*

Tom Guarino, *Plymouth State University*

Judy Harris, *Nova Southeastern University*

Patricia Hart-Timm, *Northwood University*

Hassan Hefzi, *California State Polytechnic University*

Cassy Henderson, *Sam Houston State University*

Maggie Houston, *Wright State University*

Connie Hylton, *George Mason University*

Mark Judd, *University of San Diego*

Kathy Kapka, *University of Texas—Tyler*

Suzanne Kiess, *Jackson College*

Christine Kloezeman, *Glendale Community College*

Phillip Korb, *University of Baltimore*

Donald Ladd, *University of Southern Maine*

John Long, *Jackson College*

Susan Lynn, *University of Baltimore*

Lois Mahoney, *Eastern Michigan University*

Joseph Manzo, *Lehigh University*

Annie McGowan, *Texas A&M University*

Cathryn Meegan, *Chipola College*

Michael Meyer, *The University of Notre Dame*

Sue Minke, *Indiana University Purdue University—Fort Wayne*

Bruce Neumann, *University of Colorado—Denver*

Wayne Nix, *Jackson State University*

Hossein Noorian, *Wentworth Institute of Technology*

Angela Pannell, *Mississippi State University*

Elizabeth Pierce, *Saginaw Valley State University*

Claudia Qi, *University at Buffalo*

Kamala Raghavan, *Texas Southern University*

Kathleen Rankin, *Duquesne University*

Paul Recupero, *Newbury College*

Reed Roig, *Queens University of Charlotte*

Pamela Rouse, *Butler University*

Bernadette Ruf, *Delaware State University*

Robert Schweikle, *Blackburn College*

Barbara Scofield, *Washburn University*

Daniel Selby, *University of Richmond*

Randy Serrett, *University of Houston Downtown*

Dan Sevall, *Hult International University*

Mehdi Sheikholeslami, *Bemidji State University*

Ken Sinclair, *Lehigh University*

James Smith, *University of San Diego*

Liang Song, *University of Massachusetts—Dartmouth*

George Starbuck, *McMurray University*

Randall Stone, *East Central University*

Jeff Strawser, *Sam Houston State University*

Kent Swift, *University of Montana*

Kim Tan, *California State University—Stanislaus*

Jenny Teruya, *University of Hawaii—Manoa*

Eric Typpo, *University of the Pacific*

Robert Walsh, *University of Dallas*

Randi Watts, *Jackson College*

Valerie Williams, *Duquesne University*

Jim Williamson, *San Diego State University*

Paula Wilson, *University of Puget Sound*

Jia Wu, *University of Massachusetts—Dartmouth*

In addition, we are extremely grateful to George Werthman, Marnee Fieldman, Beth Nodus, Jill Sternard, Debbie McQuade, Terry McQuade, and the entire team at Cambridge Business Publishers for their encouragement, enthusiasm, and guidance. Feedback is always welcome. Please feel free to contact us with your suggestions or questions.

Ted Christensen   Scott Hobson   Jim Wallace

January 2016

Brief Contents

Contents

CHAPTER 7

Variable Costing: A Tool for Decision Making **240**

CHAPTER 8

Relevant Costs and Short-Term Decision Making **262**

CHAPTER 9

Planning and Budgeting **296**

CHAPTER **10**

Standard Costing and Variance
Analysis **338**

CHAPTER **11**

Flexible Budgets, Segment Reporting, and
Performance Analysis **374**

APPENDIX A

Accounting and the Time Value of Money A-1

1 Overview of Managerial Accounting

Past/Present/Future provides an overview of where the chapter fits within the whole course.

Learning Objectives identify the key learning goals of the chapter.

PAST

Most students will have taken an introductory financial accounting class. This book builds upon many of the concepts you have likely seen in prior accounting and management courses.

PRESENT

Chapter 1 introduces managerial accounting. Moreover, it presents an overview of two companies used throughout the book to illustrate various concepts and procedures common to managerial accounting and decision making.

FUTURE

Chapter 2 defines basic costing terminology and introduces different types of manufacturing inventories. It illustrates how costs flow through the inventories and explains the schedule of cost of goods manufactured.

LEARNING OBJECTIVES

1. **Define** managerial accounting and **describe** its objectives. *(p. 4)*

2. **Describe** the three types of business entities. *(p. 5)*

3. **Discuss** major trends in business and managerial accounting. *(p. 6)*

4. **Describe** important characteristics of two companies used throughout the book to illustrate key concepts and processes. *(p. 9)*

5. **Describe** career options in managerial accounting. *(p. 11)*

6. **Understand** differences between various professional certifications available to managerial accountants. *(p. 13)*

amazon.com®

AMAZON.COM: THREE COMPANIES UNDER ONE ROOF

*A **Focus Company** introduces each chapter and illustrates the relevance of accounting in everyday business.*

Amazon.com (Amazon) is the world's largest online retailer. Amazon claims to offer "Earth's Biggest Selection," offering millions of unique products through its website. If you have ever purchased something online, you have most likely visited Amazon's retail website.

What you may not know is that Amazon offers much more than retail consumer products. For example, it is a major provider of cloud computing services, known as "Amazon Web Services." Companies (including the U.S. Department of Health and Human Services) may "rent" online computing resources to develop business applications, host corporate data, and run data analyses. The market for these public cloud services was $45.7 billion in 2014, with Amazon leading two of the three major product groups in the public cloud services market. Within the third group, Amazon competes with **Microsoft Corp.** and **Google, Inc.** for the bulk of the market.

In addition to being a retailer and a service provider, Amazon is also a manufacturer. It produces an e-book reader, the Amazon Kindle; a tablet computer, the Kindle Fire HD; and, a smartphone, the Fire Phone. Despite these manufactured products, Amazon is very focused on making profits on its digital content, not its hardware. Chief Executive Jeff Bezos says: "We want to make money when people use our devices, not when they buy our devices."

So, although most people think of Amazon as an online retailer, you now know better—Amazon is a retailer, a service firm, and a manufacturer all in one!

Chapter Organization charts
visually depict the key topics and
their sequence within the chapter.

OVERVIEW OF MANAGERIAL ACCOUNTING				
Introduction to Managerial Accounting	**Types of Business Entities**	**Major Trends in Business and Managerial Accounting**	**Introducing Two New Companies**	**Careers in Managerial Accounting**
• Managerial accounting versus financial accounting • Objectives of managerial accounting	• Manufacturing firms • Merchandising firms • Service firms	• Outsourcing • Factory automation • Just-in-time inventory systems • Lean manufacturing • Customer profitability • Big data and predictive analytics	• Fezzari • Environmental Business Consultants	• Alternative career paths • Work/life balance • Professional certifications

eLecture *icons identify topics for which there are instructional videos in*
myBusinessCourse *(MBC). See the Preface for more information on MBC.*

INTRODUCTION TO MANAGERIAL ACCOUNTING

LO1 **Define** managerial accounting and **describe** its objectives.

*Learning Objectives are
repeated at the start of
the section covering that
topic.*

Businesses make decisions every day that impact their competitiveness in the market. What is our target market? What products or services should we offer? How should we price our goods or services to compete effectively with our competitors? How much should we pay our employees to attract and retain great talent? Where should we locate our office or fulfillment center to minimize delivery time and cost? How do we build awareness of our firm and products or services within our target market? How do we achieve our objectives with limited resources? How many employees do we need to hire in the coming year to meet anticipated demand for our products or services? Which employees should we assign to work on this project?

These questions, and many others, require an understanding of broad business disciplines, including finance, marketing, organizational behavior, supply chain management, operations management, and strategy. However, a common element to all of these questions is the need to have a clear understanding of the financial implications of each alternative course of action. For example, in setting the price of a good or service, management needs to not only understand the customers' needs and expectations, competitors' positions in the marketplace, and the anticipated demand for the product or service, but also the business's costs of providing them.

Managerial Accounting versus Financial Accounting

Key Terms *are highlighted
in bold, red font.*

This book focuses on **managerial accounting**, which plays a vital role in *internal* decision making. Many students will have previously taken a **financial accounting** course, which focuses on reporting a company's financial performance to *external* parties. Whereas financial accountants are typically engaged in measuring and reporting the financial results of a business's *past* actions and activities, management accountants utilize data from many different sources, such as financial, operational, sales, and human resources, to help top management make decisions regarding *future* performance. Financial accountants report the results of past transactions in accordance with a set of standards known as generally accepted accounting principles (GAAP). Management accountants provide information to management in a form that is timely, relevant, decision-useful, and in a format that is easily accessible to management but not determined by any external organization. Thus, whereas financial accountants prepare financial reports to assist external stakeholders, such as investors, creditors, and regulators, management accountants provide information to managers (internal users) so that they can plan, manage, and make strategic decisions regarding the growth and profitability of the business.

Objectives of Managerial Accounting

Management accountants are professionals who work in business, across all areas of an organization, in decision support, planning, and control functions. They partner with personnel from their firm's executive management to its line employees to make strategic business decisions. Management accountants must capture, analyze, and report critical data in a timely manner. To address important strategic questions like those mentioned previously, management accountants will identify data needed to answer those questions. Such data will usually include financial information, but often include non-financial information from both inside and outside the company. If the necessary data aren't readily available, management accountants may help design systems to capture the data. Sometimes, the data are available, but must be summarized in a form that is useful to management. Management accountants can help develop reports that allow management to make sense of the data. They are also proactive in identifying relevant information to help recommend needed improvements in all aspects of their firm's business.

Hints *help explain difficult concepts.*

Hint: Because the information management accountants provide managers is so important, they must ensure that it is both accurate and relevant.

TYPES OF BUSINESS ENTITIES

eLectures
MBC

LO2
entities.

Describe the three types of business

Manufacturing firms are companies that convert materials such as sheets of steel and coils of wire and components such as electric motors and microprocessors into finished products. The manufacturer utilizes human labor; utilities such as electricity, natural gas, and water; and factory assets such as buildings, machinery, and computers to convert the materials and components into sellable products.

Merchandising firms are companies that purchase finished products from manufacturers for warehousing, display, and sale to consumers. Wholesalers typically buy finished products in large quantities and store them in large warehouses until they can be sold and shipped in smaller quantities to local retailers. The retailer utilizes human labor or electronic advertising to sell products from a "brick-and-mortar" store or through an online store available through a website.

Service firms are companies that provide services to customers. Examples include companies in health care, legal, and accounting services. The types of costs incurred by these firms are generally similar to those of other types of firms except they don't sell a product. Hence, they normally do not carry inventory.

Accounting for manufacturing operations is usually more complex because more activities are involved in producing a product than in purchasing and selling merchandise or providing a service.

Each year, *Forbes* magazine ranks the worlds "most reputable" companies. The 2013 ranking[1] indicates that roughly 77% of the world's most reputable, and presumably best known, companies are manufacturing firms. You probably recognize most of them and are likely familiar with their products. For example, BMW, Rolex, Daimler (Mercedes-Benz), Sony, Microsoft, Canon, Nestlé, Lego Group, Intel, Apple, and Adidas are among the most reputable manufacturing firms in the world. Interestingly, only 9% of the most reputable firms are retailers. You're familiar with retailers like Amazon.com, Giorgio Armani, eBay, and Starbucks. Notably missing from this list are some of the world's largest retailers, such as Walmart, Target, Costco, Home Depot, and

[1] Jacquelyn Smith, "The World's Most Reputable Companies," *Forbes*, April 9, 2013.

Lowe's. A slightly higher percentage of the world's most reputable firms, about 14%, are service companies. This list contains well-known companies like Google, Marriott International, FedEx, the BBC, UPS, and several airlines (Deutsche Lufthansa, Qantas Airways, Air France-KLM, SAS [Scandinavian Airlines], Singapore Airlines, and British Airways), whereas the U.S.-based airlines are all noticeably absent.

YOUR TURN! 1.1

The solution is on page 17.

For each of the following companies, identify whether they are a manufacturing, merchandising, or service firm.

Exxon Mobil Co.	Walmart
Southwest Airlines	Hershey Co.
Costco	Boston Consulting Group

Guided Example *icons denote the availability of a demonstration video in* **myBusinessCourse** *(MBC). See the Preface for more on MBC.*

CORPORATE SOCIAL RESPONSIBILITY

More Than the Bottom Line

Being a good corporate citizen means more than just providing large returns to a company's shareholders; it means considering all the company's stakeholders. In addition to shareholders, other stakeholders include employees, customers, suppliers, the environment, and the community—essentially, all of society. But does a company have to sacrifice shareholder returns in order to provide for these other stakeholders? Enlightened companies are learning that the answer is no. In fact, providing for all stakeholders can enhance shareholder returns.

Amazon.com, the top retailer on Forbes' list of the world's 100 most reputable companies, has learned that being a good corporate citizen is good for business. One example of this is Amazon's Frustration-Free Packaging program that eliminates hard plastic clamshell cases that prove so difficult to open and replaces the plastic cases with 100 percent recyclable packaging that is not only less frustrating but also better for the planet and less costly to the manufacturer.

As Amazon explains on its website:

> At Amazon, if we do our job right, our greatest contribution to the good of society will come from our core business activities: lowering prices, expanding selection, driving convenience, driving frustration-free packaging, creating Kindle, innovating in web services, and other initiatives we'll work hard on in the future.
>
> We also contribute to the communities where our employees and customers live. Our contributions can be seen in many ways—through our donations to dozens of nonprofits across the United States, through the disaster relief campaigns that we host on our homepage, through our employees' volunteer efforts, through the grants that we make to the writing community, and through the Amazon Web Services credits that we provide to educators.

MAJOR TRENDS IN BUSINESS AND MANAGERIAL ACCOUNTING

Outsourcing

LO3 **Discuss** major trends in business and managerial accounting.

Many companies have ceased trying to maintain a general focus. Instead, they have increasingly tried to identify their strengths and focus on these activities. **Outsourcing** occurs when a business hires or contracts with another business to provide a product or service that had previously been provided within the business. Examples might include the hiring of a third party to handle a company's customer service call center, hiring a landscaping service, and hiring an expert to develop and maintain the company website. One advantage is that it allows the company to focus on its core competency (e.g., the manufacturing of a product or provision of a service). Also, it may allow the company to pay for only the level of service that it needs, without having to worry about hiring and training staff, paying for excess capacity, or staffing to meet seasonal demand.

The growth and development of the Internet has allowed companies to provide specialized business services virtually from anywhere in the world. For example, many firms outsourced their customer service centers to India and other countries around the world. A call to your Internet service provider for technical support may be answered by someone in India, who is able to test your Internet connection and even reprogram your modem remotely over the Internet.

The anticipated cost savings that result from outsourcing do not always materialize as expected, however. Deloitte Consulting found in a 2005 survey that one-quarter of the companies that had outsourced tasks had reversed their strategy and brought the task back inside the company. There are many reasons for this, including miscommunication, lower quality of intermediate products or services, and unexpected delays in the production process.

Factory Automation

Factory automation is a widely recognized trend in modern manufacturing facilities. Factory automation exists in many forms. **Stand-alone automation** incorporates a robot or computer-controlled machine into an existing manufacturing process to perform a single function, such as welding. Stand-alone automation is usually undertaken to reduce both labor and material costs.

Flexible-manufacturing-system automation involves multiple cells of two or more automated machines. All of the machines in each cell are controlled by a computer. The machines in each cell are interconnected to allow an automated flow of product through the **manufacturing cell**. This type of automated system produces the product from start to finish. The functions performed within the cell can be changed quickly by changing the program in the computer that controls the process.

When deciding whether to automate all or part of a manufacturing process, a manufacturer must compare the costs associated with the automation with the benefits to be derived from the automation. The costs may include the cost of the automated equipment, the costs of eliminating direct labor workers, and the costs of reorganizing the manufacturing operation. The benefits may include lower direct labor costs, better product quality, and fewer defective units. In general, automation should reduce direct labor costs and increase factory overhead costs. However, the increase in factory overhead should be less than the decrease in direct labor costs.

Just-in-Time Inventory Systems

Manufacturing firms typically maintain inventories (materials, work in process, and finished goods) as buffers against unforeseen delays. For example, a manufacturer would keep a supply of various materials on hand to protect against a supplier's being late in the delivery of materials needed to produce a particular product. This approach is sometimes referred to as maintaining **just-in-case inventories** (just-in-case the supplier does not deliver when scheduled), or **safety stocks**. Safety stocks create carrying costs for the manufacturer, including casualty insurance, warehousing costs, and the cost of capital on the investment in the inventory. Higher levels of inventory create higher levels of carrying costs.

Just-in-time (JIT) inventory systems seek to eliminate the safety stock balances. A company operating under a complete just-in-time philosophy would have no inventories at the end of each day of operations, that is, zero balances of materials, work in process, and finished goods. Materials would be ordered so that only the materials needed for production each day would be received each morning. Production would be scheduled so that all products started during the day would be completed by the end of the day (resulting in no work in process inventory) and shipped to customers by the end of the day (resulting in no finished goods inventory). Just-in-time means that materials are received just in time to be placed into production and that products are completed just in time to be shipped to customers.

Most manufacturing companies have been unable to reach the ideal zero balance level of all three manufacturing inventories. To guard against delayed shipments due to inclement weather or other problems, manufacturers may order materials so they arrive one or two days before they are actually needed. Even with this approach, the true just-in-case quantities are still minimized. In addition, manufacturers may be subject to seasonal demand for their products, so that they may be required to build finished goods inventory during low-demand periods of the year so they can meet customer demand during high-demand periods of the year.

Lean Manufacturing

Henry Ford is credited with integrating an entire production process by combining interchangeable parts with a moving conveyance system to produce the Model T Ford. His approach allowed the Ford Company to significantly reduce the production time and cost of producing an automobile. However, initially he was only able to provide one model in one color—black. Even when additional body styles became available, they were drop-on features from outside suppliers that were added at the very end of the production line. All models used the same chassis.

As demand for more variety increased, U.S. car manufacturers responded, but production times increased. Attempts to reduce the time to deliver an automobile meant larger and faster fabrication machines, larger parts inventories, and more complex operational and accounting information systems.

Mr. Kiichiro Toyoda studied the U.S. car manufacturing process and identified innovations that would improve the process flow and the variety of model offerings. He called this approach the Toyota Production System. By focusing on the flow of product through the entire manufacturing process, Toyota reduced the number of fabrication machines, lined up the machines in process sequence, reduced setup times, and introduced a system whereby a product was "pulled" through the process by demand from the subsequent step in the process.[2] This is the basis of **lean manufacturing**.

Lean manufacturing concepts have been adopted by manufacturers all over the world and have begun to be applied to other disciplines, including logistics and distribution, services, retail, health care, and construction. Lean manufacturing has also impacted companies' business information systems, performance measures, reports, and decisions.

Customer Profitability

In the past, companies focused their efforts on the development and standardization of products and services. As discussed previously, management attention was given to wringing all reasonable cost savings from the production process through the automation of manufacturing processes, the modification of product flow to improve efficiencies, the improvement of product quality, and the streamlining of production and delivery systems to minimize inventory on hand.

As markets have become more competitive and available products more homogeneous, companies have shifted to trying to differentiate themselves from their competitors through service. Customers have access to a tremendous amount of information about product features, prices, and quality via the Internet and have become more demanding of quality customer service.

Likewise, companies have a tremendous amount of information about their customers, including the frequency and volume of product purchases by type, their history of

---

[2] http://www.sae.org/manufacturing/lean/

change orders, special handling and delivery requests, product returns, and customer service calls. Companies have begun to distinguish among their high-demand and low-demand customers relative to the cost of service to the customer and to focus on ways to increase customer profitability, not just product margin.

Big Data and Predictive Analytics

Bernard Marr, CEO and Director of Research at Advanced Performance Institute, posted an article in the blog "The Big Data Guru"[3] on Amazon.com's use of customer data to predict who will order what and when. In the article, he notes that Amazon has obtained a patent for what it calls "Anticipatory Shipping." The concept is that Amazon believes that its customer data will allow it to predict what you want and ship it to your door even before you order it. Already, Amazon customizes your online shopping experience by remembering what you bought previously, what you have on your wish list, what you have previously rated and reviewed, and what other customers who searched for similar items bought.

Amazon is not the only company trying to read your mind. The development of new and faster ways of analyzing the data trail that you leave behind following every online search, purchase, and social media interaction is allowing companies of all sizes to anticipate your desires and customize their products and services to better meet those needs.

INTRODUCING TWO NEW COMPANIES

Throughout the textbook we will highlight two companies to explain key concepts and illustrate how real companies implement different managerial accounting practices. To provide a real-world view of manufacturing and retail sales, we frequently highlight Fezzari Performance Bicycles. Although it is important for students to understand the manufacture and sale of inventory, the U.S. economy has evolved into a much more service-oriented network of businesses. Hence, we will focus significant attention on how managerial accounting practices are used in the service sector and provide illustrations based on a consulting business, Environmental Business Consultants, LLC. Both of these companies will become very familiar to you throughout the various chapters of the book.

LO4 **Describe** important characteristics of two companies used throughout the book to illustrate key concepts and processes.

Fezzari—A U.S. Bicycle Manufacturer and Distributor

Fezzari is a manufacturer and distributor located in Lindon, Utah, that designs, engineers, manufactures, and builds both mountain and road bikes. Fezzari's business model uses primarily a consumer-direct approach, with the vast majority of its sales completed through web-based, direct orders. This direct-order approach allows Fezzari to cut out the middleman (the local bike shop) and provide its customers with a higher-quality product at a lower cost than the brand-name bike manufacturers. Fezzari provides a 23-point custom setup with each bike sold, allowing the company to provide customers with a custom fit.

Fezzari's business model is not without risk. Most cyclists, particularly those who want to purchase a higher-end bike for

---

[3] http://smartdatacollective.com/bernardmarr/182796/amazon-using-big-data-analytics-read-your-mind.

several thousand dollars, want to be able to see, touch, and even ride the bike before purchase. Almost three-quarters of all bikes are sold in the United States through mass merchandisers (department, discount, and chain toy stores), and local bike shops account for an additional 15% of bike sales. However, according to the National Bicycle Dealers Association, the local bike shops' 14% unit sales are equivalent to 50% of the dollar value of bikes sold in 2013. Fezzari competes primarily with the local bike dealers for sales. By using a consumer-direct, web-based sales model, most Fezzari customers are unable to "kick the tires" before purchase like they can in a mass merchandiser or local bike shop.

Nevertheless, Fezzari's growth has been impressive. Fezzari sold its first bike in 2006 and now sells thousands of bikes each year. The company achieved a 20% year-over-year annual growth rate and is looking to expand its current facility to better service its growing customer base.

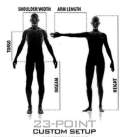

Although transactions are typically begun through the company's website, virtually all transactions involve one or more phone calls to gather information from the customer that is needed in the custom-build process. Not only does Fezzari gather body measurements (e.g., height, weight, inseam length, torso length, arm length, etc.), it also asks about the customer's age, the type of riding that the customer plans to do, and injuries that the customer may have experienced that might impact range of motion or flexibility.

Once the specific bike model and components are selected, Fezzari orders the required parts from its suppliers. A minimal quantity of parts is kept in inventory so that the bike assembly can be started without waiting for the parts to arrive. A technician assembles the bike to the customer's specifications, tunes it up, and then test rides it to ensure that it works properly. A second technician then checks the assembly, testing every screw and component, then checks the tune, and performs a second test

ride. The bike is then sent to packing to be prepared for shipment by a packer. A second packer checks the pack for completeness. The bike is then sent to the shipping bay, where a final check is performed. The assembly and packaging process can take up to 8 to 12 hours for one of Fezzari's high-end bikes, depending on the degree of customization.

The bicycle manufacturing business is seasonal, with sales picking up in the early spring and not slowing down until the early fall. As a result, Fezzari's employee headcount varies from winter to summer, almost doubling from its low point to its high point.[4]

Environmental Business Consultants, LLC—A U.S. Service Firm

Environmental Business Consultants, LLC (EBC) is a fictitious management consulting firm headquartered in Los Angeles, California, based on an actual company. It was formed in 1984 by three individuals who had worked together at one of the large international accounting firms. EBC provides consulting services to the local government market, including cities, counties, and special districts, in the areas of recycling and solid waste and water/wastewater management services.

---

[4] We are grateful to Fezzari Performance Bicycles for providing significant access to its business model and management philosophy. Moreover, the company has given us access to management and many company resources.

In the western United States, most local governments contract with private companies for garbage, recycling, and water services. Wastewater, or sewer, services are often provided by a regional sewer district created by the local governments utilizing the service. In many cases, the local governments do not have the necessary personnel resources or expertise to manage these services effectively. They frequently turn to outside consultants to assist them. These outside consultants include engineering firms, large international and regional accounting firms, and local consulting firms. Competition is fierce and success is largely based on relationships and reputation.

EBC has performed thousands of consulting projects for hundreds of municipal agencies, assisting them with the procurement, management, and delivery of solid waste, water, and wastewater services. With a focus on west coast agencies, EBC offers its clients a breadth of experience coupled with responsiveness, accountability, and personal commitment. EBC has an excellent reputation within its chosen market.

EBC has grown from the three founders and a secretary in 1984 to six owners located in offices in both northern and southern California with a staff of over 30 accountants, economists, engineers, and management consultants.

EBC obtains its client work primarily through requests from clients for whom the firm has worked for many years and also by responding to competitive requests for proposals issued by other municipal agencies. In most instances, EBC will meet with the client to discuss the project and gain an understanding of the client's needs. EBC will then prepare a written proposal outlining a scope of work to be performed for a specified fee. Competitive proposals typically require a presentation of the proposal to the client, where the client has the opportunity to ask questions and discuss the details of the proposed approach.

CAREERS IN MANAGERIAL ACCOUNTING

Alternative Career Paths

LO5 Describe career options in managerial accounting.

Some college students believe that graduating with a degree in accounting leads to one thing: a career in public accounting, often with one of the "Big 4" accounting firms. This may be particularly true at one of the top 5 or 10 college accounting programs in the United States, because the Big 4 spend considerable time and money recruiting students from these schools. A 2013 study published by the American Institute of Certified Public Accountants reported that just over 61,000 bachelor's and almost 21,000 master's students graduated from accounting degree programs in the United States. Approximately 40,000, or 49%, of these students began their careers in public accounting. Regardless of where they begin their careers, it is clear that most accountants will eventually work as management accountants in industry. The U.S. Bureau of Labor Statistics reports that approximately 75% of all U.S. accountants and auditors work in management accounting and academic roles.[5]

A start in public accounting can be advantageous for some students because of the ongoing training and experience that can be obtained as these graduates are exposed to different companies and business functions. Audit or tax attestation experience is often required to be licensed as a certified public accountant (CPA), as discussed further in the next section. Many students want to be certified as CPAs because they believe this professional designation can open doors for future job opportunities. However, upwards of 90% of those who begin their careers in public accounting will leave public accounting and

---

[5] American Institute of Certified Public Accountants, Inc., 2013 Trends in the Supply of Accounting Graduates and the Demand for Public Accounting Recruits," 2013, http://www.aicpa.org/InterestAreas/AccountingEducation/NewsAndPublications/DownloadableDocuments/2013_TrendsReport.pdf.

join a company in business or industry within a few years of graduation. Thus, the study of managerial accounting is critical for the success of virtually all accountants.

One of the reasons for this migration from public accounting to private industry is the myriad of opportunities for accountants. Accounting careers may be forged in government, public accounting, private business, and academia. Every business, from the small "mom-and-pop" store to the multinational conglomerate, needs the skills and expertise of an accountant. Accountants fill many roles, with titles such as accounting manager, controller, chief financial officer, treasurer, budget analyst, finance director, internal auditor, forensic accountant, environmental accountant, trustee in bankruptcy, Internal Revenue Service (IRS) criminal investigation special agent, tax consultant, small business owner, and management accountant. A management accountant might:

- be involved in evaluating the relative costs and benefits of outsourcing certain elements of a business;

- be involved in evaluating whether to "insource" services that have previously been outsourced;

- conduct an analysis and help management decide whether or not to automate a manufacturing process;

- be part of the team that determines the appropriate level of safety stock and seasonal inventory required to ensure that the company can meet customer demand;

- be part of the team that helps to implement lean manufacturing at the company;

- be charged with analyzing customer profitability by determining which customers should be offered special incentives to increase the size and reduce the frequency of their orders and which customers are unprofitable and should either be dropped or receive a reduced level of customer service, or

- help to develop a program that implements anticipatory shipping, similar to that which is under development by Amazon.

Work/Life Balance

Beginning a career in accounting entails a commitment to client service—although the "clients" may be either internal management or external entities. Because accounting typically involves the reporting of results of operations, accountants are regularly working under a deadline—reports are due by a certain date or within a certain number of days of the end of a period. To make the deadline often requires accountants to work whatever hours are needed, resulting in periods of late nights and weekends from time to time. Certain positions or career choices tend to require more overtime than others, although all accountants should expect to work more than a 40-hour work week on a regular basis. Employees of large accounting firms that audit publicly traded companies typically work an average of 55–60 hours per week. Management-level finance professionals, including management accountants, work an average of 47 hours per week, and non-management finance professionals work an average of 42 hours per week.[6] Government accountants probably have the most reliable work schedules, typically working 40 hours per week.

Takeaways summarize the key concepts before proceeding to the next topic.

TAKEAWAY 1.1

Although your college diploma may say "Accounting," your services are not limited to working for accounting firms. An accounting degree is extremely flexible, and will continue to provide value as you progress through the world of business.

---

[6] Thomas Thompson Jr., Financial Executives Research Foundation, Paul McDonald, and Robert Half, *Benchmarking the Finance Function: 2013* (Morristown, NJ: Financial Executives Research Foundation, 2014).

PROFESSIONAL CERTIFICATIONS

Certified Public Accountant (CPA)

The CPA is the most widely recognized and respected professional accounting certification in the United States. The CPA professional certification has been administered by the American Institute of CPAs (AICPA) or its predecessors since 1887. The AICPA is the largest member association representing the accounting profession. It has more than 412,000 members worldwide. The AICPA administers the CPA exam, a four-part exam that covers Auditing and Attestation, Business Environment and Concepts, Financial Accounting and Reporting, and Regulation.

LO6 Understand differences between various professional certifications available to managerial accountants.

Passing the CPA exam is only the first step to obtaining a CPA license. Licensure is handled by each of the 55 State/Territory Boards of Accountancy. Licensure requirements vary slightly from state to state; however, most states require 150 hours of college credit plus a year or more of real-world work experience. Once licensed, CPAs are required to follow a strict Professional Code of Conduct and to complete a certain number of hours of continuing professional education.

Certified Management Accountant (CMA)

The CMA is a professional certification administered by the Institute of Management Accountants (IMA) intended to indicate a level of knowledge and proficiency with accounting and financial management skills, including financial planning, analysis, control, decision support, and professional ethics. CMA candidates are required to hold a bachelor's degree from an accredited college or university, hold membership in the IMA, pass a two-part exam, and have at least two continuous years of professional experience in management accounting or financial management. The exam consists of two four-hour parts, with Part 1 covering Financial Reporting, Planning, Performance, and Control and Part 2 covering Financial Decision Making.

The IMA reports that in 2013 more than 40,000 professionals held the CMA certificate. According to a 2013 IMA salary survey, professionals who have earned the CMA earn almost $36,000 more in average annual compensation than noncertified peers.

Other Professional Certifications

There are numerous other professional certifications that indicate specialized skill or experience. These include certified fraud examiner, certified financial planner, certified internal auditor, and enrolled agent.

Exhibit 1-1 shows the URL where you can find additional information regarding each of these professional certifications.

Exhibit 1-1	Information Regarding Professional Certifications
Certified Public Accountant	www.aicpa.org
Certified Management Accountant	www.imanet.org
Certified Fraud Examiner	www.acfe.com
Certified Financial Planner	www.cfp.net
Certified Internal Auditor	https://na.theiia.org
Enrolled Agent	www.irs.gov/Tax-Professionals/Enrolled-Agent/Enrolled-Agent-Information

Summaries *review key bullet points for each Learning Objective and summarize each section's Takeaway.*

SUMMARY OF LEARNING OBJECTIVES

LO1 **Define managerial accounting and describe its objectives. (p. 4)**
- Managerial accounting focuses on internal decision making.
- Managerial accounting utilizes both financial and operational information.
- Managerial accounting provides information that is timely, relevant, decision-useful, and in a format that is easily accessible to management.
- Management accountants partner with personnel to plan, manage, and make strategic business decisions.

LO2 **Describe the three types of business entities. (p. 5)**
- Manufacturing firms convert materials into finished products.
- Merchandising firms purchase finished products from manufacturers for warehousing, display, and sale to consumers.
- Service firms are companies that perform services for customers.

LO3 **Discuss major trends in business and managerial accounting. (p. 6)**
- Outsourcing occurs when a business hires or contracts with another business to provide a product or service that had previously been provided within the business with the objective of reducing cost and allowing the business to focus on its core competencies.
- Stand-alone automation of a factory incorporates a robot or computer-controlled machine into an existing manufacturing process. Flexible-manufacturing-system automation of a factory operation involves the use of multiple cells of two or more automated machines. Each cell produces a product from start to finish.
- Traditional manufacturing inventories are used as buffers against unforeseen delays.
- Just-in-time inventory systems (rather than just-in-case inventory systems) minimize the amount of inventory that is on hand.
- Lean manufacturing focuses on the flow of the entire production process and uses customer demand to "pull" the product through production, thereby reducing setup times and inventory costs.
- Managerial accounting can help companies distinguish between high-demand and low-demand customers relative to their cost of service. This allows them to focus on ways to increase customer profitability.
- The development of new and faster ways of analyzing the data trail that customers leave behind following every online search, purchase, and social media interaction is allowing companies of all sizes to anticipate customers' desires and customize company products and services to better meet those needs.

LO4 **Describe the important characteristics of two companies used throughout the book to illustrate key concepts and processes. (p. 9)**
- Fezzari is a manufacturer and distributor of bikes.
- Fezzari primarily sells direct to the customer through web-based transactions.
- Environmental Business Consultants (EBC) is a fictitious management consulting firm.
- EBC provides services to local government clients in California.

LO5 **Describe career options in managerial accounting. (p. 11)**
- Careers in managerial accounting might lead to or include titles such as management accountant, accounting manager, controller, chief financial officer, treasurer, budget analyst, finance director, internal auditor, forensic accountant, environmental accountant, trustee in bankruptcy, IRS criminal investigation special agent, tax consultant, and small business owner.
- Almost 90% of those accountants who begin their careers in public accounting will leave for a position in business or industry.

LO6 **Understand differences between various professional certifications available to managerial accountants. (p. 12)**
- The CPA is the most widely recognized and respected professional accounting certification in the United States.
- The CPA is administered by the American Institute of Certified Public Accountants (AICPA).
- The CMA is a professional certification intended to indicate a level of knowledge and proficiency with accounting and financial management skills, including financial planning, analysis, control, decision support, and professional ethics.
- The CMA is administered by the Institute of Management Accountants (IMA).
- There are numerous other professional certifications that indicate specialized skill or experience.

KEY TERMS

Key Terms are listed for each chapter with references to page numbers within the chapter.

Financial accounting (p. 4)

Flexible-manufacturing-system automation (p. 7)

Just-in-case inventories (p. 7)

Just-in-time (JIT) inventory systems (p. 7)

Lean manufacturing (p. 8)

Managerial accounting (p. 4)

Manufacturing cell (p. 7)

Manufacturing firms (p. 5)

Merchandising firms (p. 5)

Outsourcing (p. 6)

Safety stocks (p. 7)

Service firms (p. 5)

Stand-alone automation (p. 7)

Self-Study Questions in multiple choice format with answers provided at the end of each chapter.

Assignments with the ⓜ logo in the margin are available in **ₘᵧBusinessCourse.**
See the Preface of the book for details.

LOs link assignments to the Learning Objectives of each chapter.

SELF-STUDY QUESTIONS

(Answers to Self-Study Questions are at the end of this chapter.)

1. **Which of the following group of terms best describes the role of managerial accounting?**   **LO1**
    a. Internal decision-making, future-focused
    b. Internal decision-making, past-focused
    c. External reporting, future-focused
    d. External reporting, past-focused

2. **A company that sells finished products that it has acquired from a manufacturer to consumers is a**   **LO2**
    a. Manufacturer
    b. Merchandiser
    c. Service firm

3. **What business model does Fezzari follow to sell its products to its customers?**   **LO4**
    a. Sales through local bike shops.
    b. Sales through large mass merchandisers.
    c. Sales direct to customers through web-based orders.
    d. Sales of bike components to other bike manufacturers.

4. **Approximately what percentage of accountants who begin their careers in public accounting will leave for positions in businesses and corporations?**   **LO5**
    a. 50%
    b. 75%   *Homework icons indicate which assignments are available in **myBusinessCourse** (MBC). This feature is only available when the instructor incorporates MBC in the course.*
    c. 90%
    d. 95%

5. **Which of the following is the professional certification intended to indicate a level of knowledge and proficiency with accounting and financial management skills, including financial planning, analysis, control, decision support, and professional ethics?**   **LO6**
    a. CPA
    b. CMA
    c. CFE
    d. CIA

QUESTIONS

1. How does managerial accounting differ from financial accounting?   **LO1**
2. Which type of accounting would produce reports relevant to stockholders?   **LO1**
3. Name the three types of business entities and briefly describe the nature of each.   **LO2**
4. In what way do manufacturing firms and merchandising firms work together to provide end consumers with products?   **LO2**
5. Pick any large company and identify which type of business entity it is.   **LO2**
6. Describe a manufacturing cell and contrast a cell to the equipment arrangement in a traditional manufacturing operation.   **LO3**

LO3   **7.** Describe and contrast stand-alone automation and flexible-manufacturing-system automation.

LO4   **8.** Which type of business model does Fezzari use?

LO4   **9.** What are the advantages of Fezzari's business model?

LO4   **10.** From where does Environmental Business Consultants, LLC, primarily obtain its client work?

LO5   **11.** List five job titles that an individual with an accounting degree may have during a career.

LO5   **12.** Why is managerial accounting relevant to accounting majors and their future careers?

LO6   **13.** Describe the process an accounting graduate takes to obtain the CPA certification.

LO6   **14.** Can an individual with an accounting degree obtain only one professional certification?

LO6   **15.** Use the Internet to explore different career paths that an individual with the CMA certification can take.

Extending Your Knowledge assignments require use of the real world financial statements and critical thinking skills.

EXTENDING YOUR KNOWLEDGE

LO2   **EYK1-1.** **Model Manufacturing** is a company that specializes in producing model cars, trains, and airplanes for customers of all ages. Model has been in business for over 50 years, and has provided generations of detailed models which can be customized by color, type of metal, size, and numerous other features. The company sells its completed models to merchandising companies, which then advertise and sell the products to the end consumer. Because Model produces mass quantities of models, it requires efficient operations to ensure timely delivery of quality products to merchandisers.

      a.   Model can obtain varying qualities of metal and other materials that it uses to produce models. Why would the company choose to spend more for materials of higher quality when it can produce cheaper, similar models with lower-quality materials?

      b.   Model's customers are mainly merchandising companies. Is Model more or less likely to enter into long-term contracts with these companies than Model would with an end consumer? Why?

Service Company *Assignments are included in each chapter.*

LO2   **EYK1-2.** **Masterful Merchandising** is a company that specializes in obtaining large quantities of products from multiple manufacturing companies and sells these products to end consumers. Its products include clothing, athletic equipment, electronics, home and kitchen products, groceries, and many other products. It prides itself in being a one-stop-shop where consumers can fill all their shopping needs without having to travel to multiple stores.

      a.   Masterful receives daily shipments of goods from manufacturers to stock its shelves. From a cost perspective, is it cheaper to buy manufactured goods in small or large quantities? What incentives would a manufacturer provide in order to facilitate ordering large quantities?

      b.   Why would a merchandiser choose to operate online instead of through a brick-and-mortar store? Do you think an online presence eliminates the need to have a physical store for consumer shopping?

LO2   **EYK1-3.** **Superior Services** is a firm that provides audit, tax, and advisory services to over 100 companies in the western United States. It employs thousands of professionals who have obtained accounting, finance, economics, and business degrees, and who focus on providing value and enhancing the operations of their clients. The firm has been in existence for nearly 70 years, and many of its clients are loyal to Superior and look nowhere else for services.

      a.   Superior does not sell physical products, but it does need to consider how to price its services in order to make a profit. What costs will the company consider when deciding how much to charge clients for its services?

      b.   How is accounting for Superior's operations different from accounting for Model's and Masterful's operations? Are there costs that Superior will incur that the other two will not?

LO2   **EYK1-4.** **Peach Inc.** is a manufacturer of consumer electronic devices, including computers, tablets, and phones. Peach has earned a reputation of providing reliable high-quality products at affordable prices. The company has also earned a reputation of being a good corporate citizen with many environmental and social initiatives. For example, the company uses far more recycled materials in its products than any of its competitors. The company is also known for its charity work with educational institutions.

      In an effort to control costs, Peach outsources manufacturing of its hardware to many overseas factories; however, it closely monitors each facility to make sure quality is maintained. Tom Peach, the company CEO, was recently approached by Young, Inc., a company that asserts it can significantly reduce Peach's manufacturing costs by overseeing Peach's manufacturing. Young will find factories that it claims can maintain the same level of quality at lower costs. In addition, Young will do all the monitoring so that Peach can save the costs of monitoring and auditing the manufacturing facilities.

Jorge Workman, Peach's director of accounting, became quite concerned when he learned of the potential deal with Young. Jorge immediately went to Tom with his concerns. In particular, Jorge did not want to turn over the responsibility of monitoring the facilities to another company. Tom, however, feels that the quality control testing done locally is enough to assure that quality can be maintained, and the cost savings are very important to the company's efforts to keep its prices affordable. In addition, Tom felt that under this arrangement, anything that might go wrong at one of the facilities would be Young's responsibility and not the responsibility of Peach.

Jorge was still not convinced. He knew how labor problems in the supply chain of Nike in the 1990s had caused significant reputational and financial damage to Nike, and he did not want to risk the same thing happening to Peach.

What do you think Peach should do?

ANSWERS TO SELF-STUDY QUESTIONS:

1. a (p. 4)   2. b (p. 5)   3. c (p. 9)   4. c (p. 11)   5. b (p. 13)

YOUR TURN! SOLUTIONS

Solution 1.1

Exxon Mobil Co.	Manufacturing
Walmart	Merchandising
Southwest Airlines	Service
Hershey Co.	Manufacturing
Costco	Merchandising
Boston Consulting Group	Service

2 Managerial Accounting Concepts and Cost Flows

PAST

Chapter 1 introduced managerial accounting. It explored career opportunities in managerial accounting, its objectives, and professional certifications for managerial accountants.

PRESENT

Chapter 2 defines basic costing terminology and introduces different types of manufacturing inventories. It illustrates how costs flow through the inventories and explains the schedule of cost of goods manufactured.

FUTURE

Chapter 3 introduces and explains job costing in more detail for both manufacturing and service industries. It also explains overhead allocation.

LEARNING OBJECTIVES

1. **Identify** the key objectives of a managerial accounting system and **define** product costs and period costs; variable, fixed, and mixed costs; direct and indirect costs; and cost control. *(p. 20)*

2. **Describe** the three manufacturing inventories—materials, work in process, and finished goods—and **discuss** the categories of manufacturing costs and how these costs flow among the inventories and cost of goods sold. *(p. 24)*

3. **Define** total manufacturing costs, cost of goods manufactured, and cost of goods sold, and **illustrate** the schedule of cost of goods manufactured and sold and the income statement. *(p. 31)*

4. **Illustrate** the journal entries to record product cost flows using a perpetual inventory system. *(p. 35)*

5. Appendix 2A: **Present** the year-end accounting procedures, including the preparation of a worksheet, adjusting entries, financial statements, closing entries, the schedule of cost of goods manufactured, and cost of goods sold. *(p. 45)*

APPLE INC.: INNOVATIVE CONSUMER ELECTRONICS

At 37 years old, **Apple Inc.** is the world's second largest information technology company by sales revenue ($264 billion in 2015)[1] and the largest publicly traded corporation by market capitalization ($608 billion in 2015).[2] Although it started as a seller of personal computers (PCs), it has expanded its products to include consumer electronics, consumer software, and commercial servers. Apple's PC line includes the Mac computer and the iPad tablet. It added a consumer electronics line, which includes the iPod music player and the iPhone smartphone. Its consumer software line includes the OS X and iOS operating systems, the iTunes media browser, the Safari web browser, and iLife and iWork creativity and production software.

How did Apple grow from a garage-based start-up to overtake companies like Commodore, Tandy, IBM, Microsoft, Sun Microsystems and Xerox? There is no single answer to that question, and many books have been written describing Apple's growth and success. Talented, creative leaders and employees provided the vision. Certainly, innovative products designed with the consumer experience in mind were critical. So too were strategic alliances with Intel for processors and EMI for digital music titles, not to mention the purchase of numerous companies to acquire their technology and software.

Perhaps equally important to Apple's success was the development of management processes and approaches, such as assigning a "directly responsible individual" for each project, an efficient and effective supply chain, and the strategic creation of international subsidiaries to minimize the amount of taxes paid. Each of these management processes and approaches has one element in common—the need for detailed financial and other business information. Without this information, Apple would not be able to compensate its employees fairly, price its products competitively, or determine an appropriate price to pay for new technology companies. The development and maintenance of this information is largely the responsibility of management accountants, who use managerial accounting systems to capture, summarize, and report critical data to be used in making strategic business decisions.

[1] 2015 Apple Form 10-K.
[2] https://ycharts.com/companies/AAPL/market_cap

MANAGERIAL ACCOUNTING CONCEPTS AND COST FLOWS				
Objectives of a Managerial Accounting System	**Inventories and Cost Categories**	**Product Cost Flows**	**Illustration of Product Cost Accumulation**	**Year-End Accounting Procedures (Appendix 2A)**
• Product costing in a manufacturing environment • Product costing in a service and merchandising environment • Cost control	• Inventories • Manufacturing product cost categories	• Raw materials • Labor • Manufacturing overhead • Cost of goods manufactured • Cost of goods sold	• Introduction of T-accounts • Schedule of cost of goods manufactured • Calculating cost of goods sold • Income statement for a manufacturing firm • Illustration of product cost journal entries	• Year-end accounting procedures for a manufacturing firm • Worksheet for a manufacturing firm

KEY OBJECTIVES OF A MANAGERIAL ACCOUNTING SYSTEM

eLectures
MBC

LO1 **Identify** the key objectives of a managerial accounting system and **define** product costs and period costs; variable, fixed, and mixed costs; direct and indirect costs; and cost control.

Hint: A cost object is anything to which costs may be traced. Examples for Apple include everything from an mp3 file to a tablet PC to a service department.

Business operations vary widely in complexity. However, all managerial accounting systems have the objective of providing management with financial and other business information that is useful in analyzing and making business decisions.

Product Costing in a Manufacturing Environment

Business managers need information about the cost of their products and services in order to control costs and set prices that will result in a profit to the owners and provide the ability to grow the business. For example, Apple is clearly interested in knowing its costs and market share for its manufactured products (such as the iPhone and the iPad) for determining merchandise prices.

Product costing involves accumulating and allocating the costs of all inputs in the manufacturing or acquisition process to individual products. The individual products represent a type of **cost object**, which may be anything for which business managers must determine a cost. The manufacturer must know its product costs in order to measure inventory values and calculate the profitability of its products for reporting on its financial statements. Using product costing information, management can also determine which products to continue producing and which products to drop. This chapter introduces product costing.

Product versus Period Costs

Exhibit 2-1 indicates that costs can be classified into two broad categories for companies that sell products. **Product costs** include all costs necessary to bring a product to completion, regardless of the period in which they are incurred. For a manufacturer, product costs include material and components, human labor, utilities, and the use of factory assets. These costs are all recorded initially in inventory accounts.

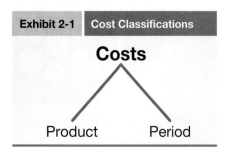

Exhibit 2-1 | **Cost Classifications**

Costs

Product   Period

Period costs are expensed in the period incurred and not assigned to products. The benefits associated with these costs are assumed to expire in the period incurred rather than in the period in which the product is sold. For manufacturers, selling expenses and non-factory administrative expenses are considered period costs. These are reported on the income statement. Some departments in a manufacturing firm, such as personnel, may benefit both factory and non-factory activities. The costs of these departments are therefore partly product cost and partly period cost.

Exhibit 2-2 presents Apple's partial income statement for its 2014 fiscal year, illustrating its product and period costs:

Exhibit 2-2	Apple's Partial Income Statement

APPLE INC. Income Statement For the Year Ended September 27, 2014 (in $millions)		
Sales.		$182,795
Cost of goods sold *(Product costs)*		112,258
Gross profit on sales.		$ 70,537
Operating expenses *(Period costs)*		
Selling, general and administrative expenses	$11,993	
Research and development	6,041	18,034
Income from operations.		$ 52,503

Variable, Fixed, and Mixed Costs

Another way to classify costs that can be helpful to decision makers is to classify them based on their behavior (see **Exhibit 2-3**). A **variable cost** is a cost that *varies in total but is fixed per unit* for a certain period of time and range of activity. In total, variable costs change proportionately with changes in the volume of activity. The cost of a microprocessor chip used in an iPad and the hourly wage paid to the iPad assembly employees are variable costs. To illustrate, assume the cost of the microprocessor chip used in producing one Apple iPad is approximately $30. If Apple produces 100,000 iPads during a period, the total cost of the chips used would be $3,000,000. Alternatively, if Apple produces 1,000,000 iPads, the total cost of the chips would be $30,000,000, still $30 per iPad. In **Exhibit 2-4**, total variable costs increase by $30 for each additional iPad produced. Yet, the cost per iPad is a constant $30 per unit.

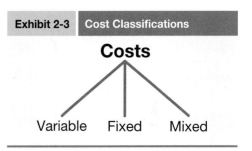

Exhibit 2-3	Cost Classifications

Costs

Variable   Fixed   Mixed

A **fixed cost** is *fixed in total but variable on a per-unit basis* for a particular period of time and range of activity. Fixed costs do not change when the volume of activity changes. Examples are depreciation on buildings and property taxes. Assume that the depreciation on the iPad manufacturing facility is $5 million per month, as shown in **Exhibit 2-4**. If only 100,000 iPads are produced in a month, the depreciation per unit is $50. If 1,000,000 iPads are produced, the depreciation per unit is $5. As we will discuss later, making decisions based on fixed costs per unit can be problematic.

Mixed costs—sometimes called **semi-variable costs**—have both fixed and variable components. A mixed cost changes linearly with changes in activity, but there is still a positive cost when the activity level is zero, as shown in **Exhibit 2-4**. As an example of a mixed cost, consider Apple's utility expense at the factory that produces the iPad. Assume that even if Apple shuts down production for one month, it still incurs a minimum amount for utilities, say $200,000. When production resumes, the costs of heating, air conditioning, lighting, and water increase with usage as production increases. We discuss

A.K.A. Mixed costs are sometimes called semi-variable costs as they have both fixed and variable components.

Hint: The classification of costs into these three distinct groups can often be more difficult than it may appear at first glance.

how to determine the variable and fixed portions of a mixed cost in Chapter 6. **Exhibit 2-4** presents a graphic illustration of these three different types of costs.

Exhibit 2-4	Comparison of Variable, Fixed and Mixed Costs*

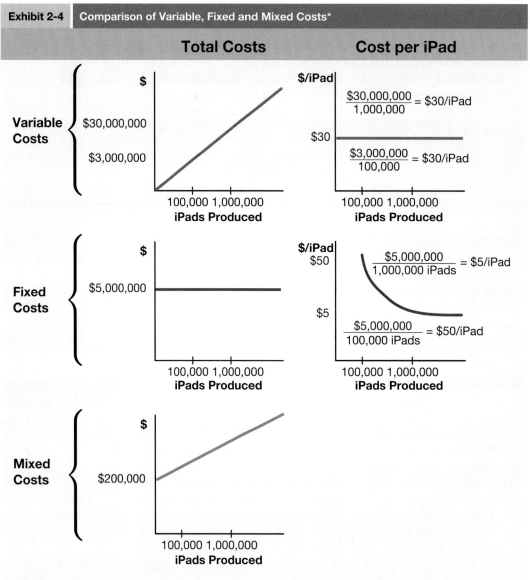

*Assumes all costs are linear

Product costs may be variable (direct material and direct labor), fixed (some overhead costs such as depreciation on assets employed in producing the good or service), or mixed (some overhead costs such as utilities).

Direct and Indirect Costs

Finally, costs can also be classified as *direct* or *indirect* costs (see **Exhibit 2-5**). A **direct cost** is a cost that can be easily and cost-effectively traced to a specific cost object, such as a unit of product. In a manufacturing company, two obvious direct costs are the main materials and labor used to produce a unit of product. However, other costs may be directly traced as well. For example, in determining the cost of an iPad, Apple would attempt to trace as many costs as possible directly to each iPad unit.

Clearly, the main materials such as the liquid crystal display (LCD) screen and the microprocessor and the labor involved in assembly would be traced directly to each iPad. However, in a highly automated process, it is possible that Apple could also trace some robotic assembly costs directly to each iPad.

An **indirect cost**, therefore, is a cost that cannot be easily and cost-effectively traced to a specific cost object. If Apple were interested in the cost of one of the thousands of products shipped from one of its warehouses, the depreciation expense for that warehouse would be an indirect cost, because it is not easily traced to any one unit of product that passes through the warehouse. It would be considered a common cost for all products of the warehouse. As noted in the previous examples, a particular cost may be considered direct or indirect, depending on the cost object.

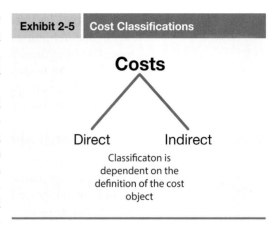

Exhibit 2-5 Cost Classifications

Costs

Direct   Indirect

Classificaton is dependent on the definition of the cost object

---

Which of the following would be considered a direct cost of an iPad? (Choose all that apply.)

Assembly labor
iPad case
CEO salary
Microprocessor
Depreciation on Apple corporate headquarters
Health insurance for factory workers
Touch-screen
Adhesive on the serial number label

YOUR TURN! 2.1

The solution is on page 63.

Product Costing in a Service and Merchandising Environment

SERVICE AND MERCHANDISING

Product versus Period Costs

Like manufacturers, service firms need to understand the cost of providing their services to customers. Although these firms do not produce a tangible product, they must know the cost of their services to determine the proper fee for those services and ensure a return to their owners. Service firms may include labor and other directly traceable costs in determining the **cost of jobs or projects**. Merchandising companies record the cost of acquired inventory as a product cost, whereas items such as salaries and wages, utilities, and depreciation are recorded immediately as operating expenses.

Service firms expense **period costs** in the period the costs are incurred. The benefits associated with these costs are assumed to expire in the period incurred rather than in the period in which the product is sold. Like manufacturers, selling expenses and non-factory administrative expenses are considered period costs.

Variable, Fixed, and Mixed Costs

The definitions of variable, fixed, and mixed costs are the same for service and merchandise firms as those given previously for manufacturers. An example of a variable cost in a consulting firm would be office supplies expense, which would increase with the number of consulting projects performed. The consulting firm's office lease expense would be considered a fixed cost because it would not vary with the number of projects performed. The firm's contribution to the employee 401(k) profit-sharing retirement plan would be a mixed cost assuming that the plan required a minimum contribution of 3%, and that additional contributions would be made based on the level of profit earned in a year.

Direct and Indirect Costs

Again, the definitions of direct and indirect costs are the same as given previously for a manufacturing firm. In a service company, wages or salaries are the most common direct cost. However, costs such as photocopying, postage, and travel can be traced to a particular job. Service companies would typically consider marketing costs and costs associated with employee continuing education classes as indirect costs.

Cost Control

Business managers also need information that will assist them in competing effectively in their chosen market. As information becomes more easily available to customers in a global market, price competition can become more intense. For example, because customers can instantly compare prices for products and services on their smartphones, tablets, and computers, businesses might have little or no control over the prices that they can charge. Therefore, business managers must control their costs to ensure a reasonable profit. **Cost control** involves the accumulation of information to measure management performance and evaluate operational efficiency. Subsequent chapters present cost control approaches and techniques that are used by businesses of all types. For example, Chapter 9 illustrates how business managers use budgets to evaluate actual versus expected performance. Chapter 10 introduces the use of standard costs as a way of identifying where and why operations deviate from management's expectations.

INVENTORIES AND COST CATEGORIES

Inventories

LO2 Describe the three manufacturing inventories—materials, work in process, and finished goods—and **discuss** the categories of manufacturing costs and how these costs flow among the inventories and cost of goods sold.

Manufacturing Firms

At any point in time, manufacturing operations typically have units of product at various stages of completion. Three inventories are usually maintained on a perpetual basis to reflect these stages—materials, work in process, and finished goods.

The **materials inventory** includes factory materials and components that have been purchased but not yet placed into production. Some of the items in the materials inventory, such as sheets of steel or microprocessors, were finished products to the supplying company but are materials and components to the purchasing company. All items in the materials inventory account are recorded at their net delivered cost (i.e., product cost plus in-bound shipping).

The **work in process inventory** of a manufacturing firm includes units of product that have been placed in production but have not yet been completed. All the costs of material and components, direct human labor, utilities, and use of factory assets (overhead costs) are included in the work in process inventory. All items in the work in process inventory account are recorded at cost.

The **finished goods inventory** of a manufacturing firm includes all units of product that have been completed but have not been sold. All items in the finished goods inventory account were recorded at cost in the work in process inventory account and transferred to the finished goods inventory account.

Many manufacturing firms also maintain an inventory of factory and office supplies for the manufacturing operation. **Factory supplies** are consumable items, such as cleaning supplies and machinery lubricants, used in the factory but not incorporated into the product; **office supplies** include copy paper, toner, and paper clips, items used in the office but not charged to a particular job. The inventory of factory and office supplies is usually maintained on a periodic basis, so the cost of factory and office supplies used during a period is determined at period-end after the supplies on hand are counted.

Merchandising and Service Firms

SERVICE AND MERCHANDISING

Merchandising firms have only one inventory account—merchandise inventory. This is similar to the finished goods inventory account at a manufacturer because it contains finished products that are available for immediate sale. As discussed previously, manufacturing firms usually have three primary inventory accounts: materials, work in process, and finished goods.

Service firms typically have only one inventory account—work in process inventory. This account represents the service firm's partially completed projects. Service firms would include the cost of direct labor and overhead in work in process inventory. Although service firms may utilize office supplies on their projects, these costs are usually immaterial and not considered a materials inventory. Because completed projects are billed to the customer immediately upon completion, there is no need for a finished goods inventory. These inventories are reported in the current assets section of the balance sheet, as illustrated in **Exhibit 2-6**.

Exhibit 2-6	Comparison of Merchandising, Service, and Manufacturing Inventories

Merchandising Firm		Service Firm		Manufacturing Firm	
Cash	$ 10,000	Cash	$ 10,000	Cash	$ 10,000
Short-term investments . .	20,000	Short-term investments . .	20,000	Short-term investments . .	20,000
Receivables	45,000	Receivables	45,000	Receivables	45,000
Merchandise inventory . . .	80,000	Work in process inventory	80,000	Inventories:	
Prepaid expenses	15,000	Prepaid expenses	15,000	Materials	35,000
Total current assets	$170,000	Office supplies	5,000	Work in process	55,000
		Total current assets	$175,000	Finished goods	25,000
				Prepaid expenses	15,000
				Factory supplies	5,000
				Total current assets	$210,000

Factory Supplies versus Indirect Materials	ACCOUNTING IN PRACTICE

Factory supplies are different from indirect materials. Factory supplies are used in the factory but are not part of the product itself. Lubricant used on the machine that stamps the sheet metal used in a laptop computer would be a factory supply. Indirect materials are part of the product, but are difficult to trace to each individual product. Solder used to attach computer chips to a motherboard would be an indirect material. Both factory supplies and indirect materials can become part of manufacturing overhead.

Manufacturing Product Cost Categories

Product costs in a manufacturing setting can be classified into three subcategories (see **Exhibit 2-7**):

1. **Direct materials** include all of the important materials and components that physically make up the product (such as sheets of steel and electric motors). Incidental material items, such as glue and fasteners, are considered **indirect materials** and are included in manufacturing overhead. Both direct material items and indirect material items are included in the materials inventory. Therefore, all items in the materials inventory will be used as either direct material or indirect material.

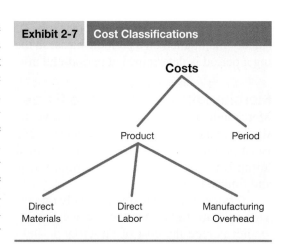

Exhibit 2-7 | **Cost Classifications**

Costs

Product — Period

Product: Direct Materials — Direct Labor — Manufacturing Overhead

Hint: "Manufacturing product costs" include all direct materials, direct labor, and manufacturing overhead for a period of time and represent the additions to work in process inventory. "Manufacturing costs" should not be confused with "manufacturing overhead costs," although both terms have the word "manufacturing" in them.

2. **Direct labor** includes the salary and wage cost of factory employees who work directly on the product (such as machine operators, assemblers, and painters). The salary and wage cost of factory employees who do not work directly on the product (such as supervisors, inspectors, and material handlers) is considered **indirect labor**, which is included in manufacturing overhead. The total amount of factory labor (direct and indirect) is identified on a manufacturing firm's factory payroll.

© istockphoto.com

Apple Inc. Corporate Headquarters | **iPad Factory**

A.K.A. Manufacturing overhead has several other names that are commonly used in practice, such as **factory overhead**, factory burden, or indirect manufacturing costs.

3. **Manufacturing overhead** consists of all manufacturing costs not included in direct material and direct labor. Manufacturing overhead includes indirect material, indirect labor, factory supplies used, factory payroll tax and fringe benefits costs, factory utilities, and factory building and machinery costs (such as depreciation, insurance, property taxes, and repairs and maintenance). Manufacturing overhead specifically *excludes* selling and non-factory administrative expenses because these expenses are not incurred in the manufacturing process.

YOUR TURN! 2.2

The solution is on page 63.

Which of the following would be considered a manufacturing cost of an iPad? (Choose all that apply.)

Assembly labor
Sales-force salary
Factory supervisor salary
Depreciation on the iPad factory
Depreciation on Apple corporate headquarters
Health insurance for corporate finance employees
Touch-screen

Combined Costs

Manufacturing Firms

Manufacturing cost categories are frequently combined for convenience. As illustrated in **Exhibit 2-8**, the sum of direct material and direct labor for a particular product is known as prime cost. **Prime cost** is made up of the elements of product cost that are easily and directly traceable to individual products. **Conversion cost** is the sum of direct labor and manufacturing overhead. Conversion cost represents the elements of product cost necessary to convert the materials and components to the final finished products.

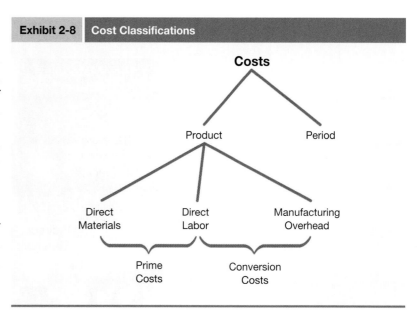

| Exhibit 2-8 | Cost Classifications |

Service Firms

Prime cost and conversion cost can also apply to a service firm. A service firm's prime cost is limited to direct labor cost (because no direct materials are typically used). A service firm's conversion cost is the sum of direct labor and applied general overhead.

Although Apple is not primarily a service firm, it has a technical support department that assists customers with hardware and software questions that arise in the normal operation of Apple products. Prime costs for the technical support department would simply include the wages and salaries of support personnel because the service department would have no direct materials. Conversion costs for the technical support department would include both the wages and salaries of support personnel in addition to overhead costs such as depreciation on office equipment, employee health insurance premiums, the costs associated with janitorial services, and utilities.

SERVICE AND MERCHANDISING

PRODUCT COST FLOWS

Raw Materials

The materials inventory frequently contains both direct and indirect materials. As direct materials are used in production, they are traced directly to specific units of product. Thus, the cost of direct materials flows from raw materials inventory directly into work in process inventory. On the other hand, indirect materials cannot be traced to particular units of product. As a result, as they are used in the production process, their cost is transferred from raw materials inventory to manufacturing overhead. For example, it may not be cost effective for Apple to trace the cost of screws to each iPad. As a result, screws are likely classified as indirect materials and their cost would be transferred from raw materials inventory to manufacturing overhead as they are used in production. Overhead costs are then allocated (applied) to particular jobs. **Exhibit 2-9a** illustrates the flow of both direct and indirect materials from raw materials inventory to the work in process and manufacturing overhead, respectively.

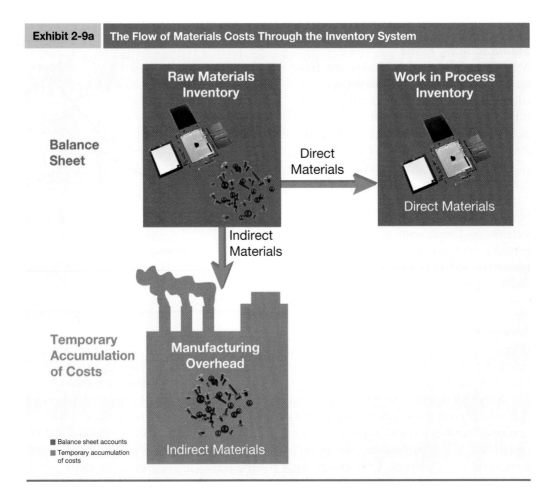

Exhibit 2-9a   The Flow of Materials Costs Through the Inventory System

Labor

Both direct and indirect labor costs are incurred in the manufacturing process. The wages of employees who work directly on units of product are traced directly to specific units. Therefore, when these labor costs are incurred, they are recorded in work in process inventory. On the other hand, the wages of factory employees not working directly on the product cannot be traced directly to particular units. They are recorded as manufacturing overhead and allocated to jobs based on a predetermined overhead application rate. In the iPad manufacturing facility, the costs of employees directly involved in the assembly of iPads are recorded directly in work in process inventory. On the other hand, the salaries and wages of supervisors, maintenance personnel, and quality inspectors in the iPad factory would be classified as indirect labor and recorded as manufacturing overhead. **Exhibit 2-9b** illustrates how both direct and indirect labor flow into work in process and manufacturing overhead, respectively.

Exhibit 2-9b	The Flow of Labor Costs Through the Inventory System

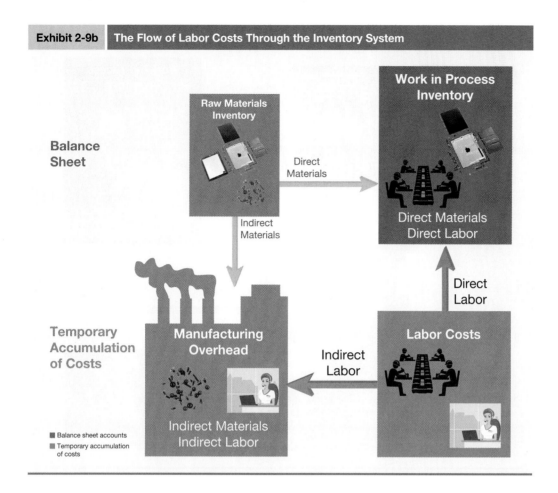

Manufacturing Overhead

Because overhead costs are, by definition, indirect costs that can not be traced to a particular unit of product, they are accumulated in manufacturing overhead during the accounting period. Indirect materials and indirect labor are just two examples of indirect costs accumulated in manufacturing overhead. Other examples include costs that cannot be traced to a particular unit of product, such as depreciation on the factory and factory equipment, factory utilities, insurance on production facilities, property taxes related to the factory, and so forth. The problem accountants face is that it is impossible to know with certainty how much manufacturing overhead will accumulate during a particular period. Rather than waiting until the end of the period to divide the actual manufacturing overhead costs by the number of units actually produced to allocate the costs to jobs passing through the production process, accountants use their knowledge from past periods to calculate an estimated overhead rate at the beginning of the period to allocate overhead to jobs as they pass through the production process. We discuss the process for estimating and allocating manufacturing overhead in more detail in Chapter 3. However, **Exhibit 2-9c** illustrates the flow of overhead costs from manufacturing overhead to the work in process inventory.

Hint: Actual indirect costs are recorded on the debit side of the manufacturing overhead account, whereas overhead applied to units produced is recorded on the credit side because overhead is allocated to jobs (in the work in process inventory account).

Exhibit 2-9c	The Flow of Manufacturing Overhead Costs Through the Inventory System

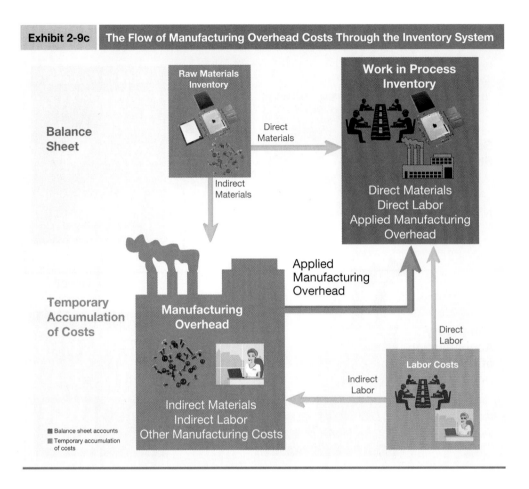

Cost of Goods Manufactured

Total manufacturing costs consist of direct materials, direct labor, and manufacturing overhead. **Exhibit 2-9d** summarizes how all of these costs flow into work in process inventory.

The product costs that flow from work in process to the finished goods during an accounting period are known as **cost of goods manufactured (COGM)**. The schedule of cost of goods manufactured (which we demonstrate in the next section) summarizes all of the different costs incurred in the production of inventory: (1) direct materials, (2) labor costs, and (3) manufacturing overhead. All of these costs flow into work in process inventory. The total cost of goods manufactured is transferred to finished goods inventory, as illustrated in **Exhibit 2-9e**.

Exhibit 2-9d	The Flow of Total Manufacturing Costs Through the Inventory System

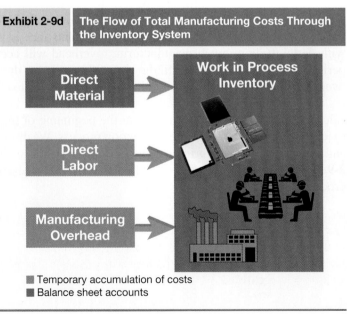

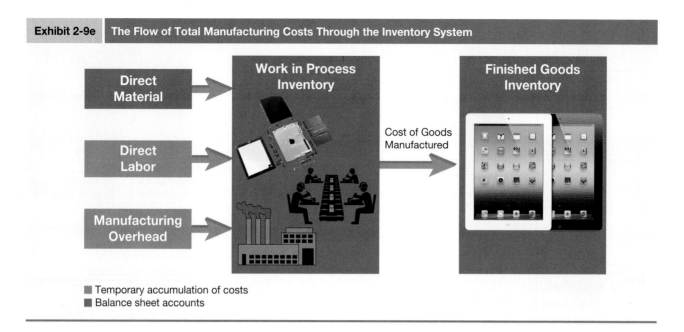

Exhibit 2-9e | The Flow of Total Manufacturing Costs Through the Inventory System

■ Temporary accumulation of costs
■ Balance sheet accounts

Cost of Goods Sold

Exhibit 2-9f illustrates the flow of all product costs through the inventory system of a manufacturing firm. All costs that are accumulated in work in process eventually flow to finished goods and, when the products are sold, are recognized as **cost of goods sold** (**COGS**).

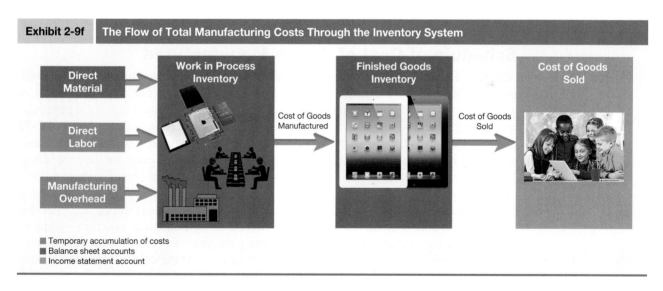

Exhibit 2-9f | The Flow of Total Manufacturing Costs Through the Inventory System

■ Temporary accumulation of costs
■ Balance sheet accounts
■ Income statement account

ILLUSTRATION OF PRODUCT COST ACCUMULATION

Introduction of T-Accounts

Exhibit 2-9f illustrates the flow of all product costs through the inventory accounts. As you learn in financial accounting, each account can be represented by a T-account, which is a visual illustration of the flow of dollars into and out of the account. **Exhibit 2-10** illustrates the T-accounts associated with each item in **Exhibit 2-9f**.

LO3 **Define** total manufacturing costs, cost of goods manufactured, and cost of goods sold, and **illustrate** the schedule of cost of goods manufactured and sold and the income statement.

Exhibit 2-10   The Flow of Total Manufacturing Costs Through the Inventory Accounts

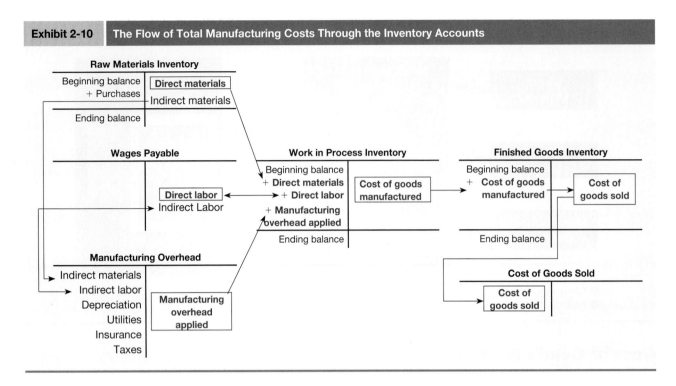

Real-World Manufacturing Example

We introduced Fezzari Performance Bicycles in Chapter 1. Fezzari is a manufacturer of road and mountain bikes. Using estimates of sales and manufacturing costs at Fezzari, **Exhibit 2-11** shows how the costs of manufacturing bikes flow through the inventory accounts.

Schedule of Cost of Goods Manufactured

Although **Exhibit 2-11** is helpful in visualizing the flow of costs through Fezzari's accounts, it is not very useful for management decision making. The schedule of cost of goods manufactured presents information about an entity's product cost for a particular accounting period in a format that is more suitable for decision making. **Exhibit 2-12** presents Fezzari's 2016 schedule of cost of goods manufactured. The schedule has two sections. The first section summarizes the **total manufacturing costs** for the year: direct material, direct labor, and manufacturing overhead incurred in the manufacturing process during the year. These are all of the costs that flow into the work in process inventory account during the year. In the calculation of direct material used during the year, the net delivered cost of materials purchased is added to the beginning materials inventory to determine the cost of material available during the year. The cost of material not used (ending materials inventory) is then subtracted to identify the cost of all material used during the year. This total represents both direct material used and indirect material used. We subtract indirect material used to determine the direct material used. Direct labor is presented on a single line. The detail of manufacturing overhead is calculated by summing all of the individual components of manufacturing overhead.

Exhibit 2-11 The Flow of Fezzari's Costs Through the Inventory Accounts

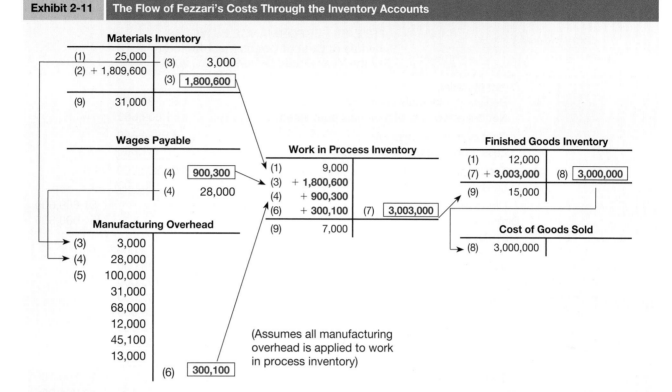

(Assumes all manufacturing overhead is applied to work in process inventory)

(1) Beginning inventory balances.

(2) $1,809,600 of materials inventory is purchased and received.

(3) Materials inventory is used in the production process. $1,800,600 of direct materials is used and transferred to work in process inventory. $3,000 of indirect materials is used and transferred to and accumulated in the manufacturing overhead account.

(4) Factory wages are incurred in the production process. $900,300 of direct labor is incurred and recorded in both the work in process inventory and wages payable accounts. $28,000 of indirect labor is incurred and recorded in both the manufacturing overhead and wages payable accounts.

(5) Additional indirect manufacturing costs are incurred during the production process and accumulated in the

manufacturing overhead account. These costs include the lease on the factory of $100,000, factory utilities of $31,000, factory insurance of $68,000, property taxes on the factory of $12,000, depreciation on factory machinery of $45,100 and other factory overhead of $13,000.

(6) At the end of the period, the $300,100 of costs accumulated in manufacturing overhead are applied to work in process inventory.

(7) As bikes are completed, their total manufacturing costs of $3,003,000 are transferred from the work in process inventory to the finished goods inventory.

(8) When bikes are sold, their total manufacturing costs of $3,000,000 are transferred out of finished goods inventory and recognized as a cost of goods sold expense. This entry is recorded along with the related sales entry.

(9) Ending inventory balances.

The second section of the schedule of cost of goods manufactured determines the cost of goods manufactured—the cost of goods completed during the year and transferred to finished goods. In this section, total manufacturing costs for the year are added to the amount representing the work in process at the beginning of the year to determine the total cost of work in process during the year. The cost of incomplete units (ending work in process inventory) is then subtracted to determine the cost associated with the completed units (cost of goods manufactured). These are all of the numbers that appear in the work in process inventory account.

Exhibit 2-12	Schedule of Cost of Goods Manufactured

FEZZARI PERFORMANCE BICYCLES
Schedule of Cost of Goods Manufactured
For the Year Ended December 31, 2016

Direct material:		
Beginning materials inventory.	$ 25,000	
Net delivered cost of materials purchased.	1,809,600	
Cost of material available	$1,834,600	
Less: Ending materials inventory	(31,000)	
Total material used	$1,803,600	
Less: Indirect material used	(3,000)	
Direct material used		$1,800,600
Direct labor.		$ 900,300
Manufacturing overhead:		
Indirect material	$ 3,000	
Indirect labor.	28,000	
Lease—factory	100,000	
Factory utilities	31,000	
Factory insurance	68,000	
Factory property taxes	12,000	
Depreciation—factory machinery.	45,100	
Other factory overhead.	13,000	
Total manufacturing overhead		$ 300,100
Total manufacturing costs for the year		**$3,001,000**
Add: Beginning work in process inventory.		$ 9,000
Total cost of work in process during the year		3,010,000
Less: Ending work in process inventory.		(7,000)
Cost of goods manufactured		**$3,003,000**

DECISION TIME 2.1

The solution is on page 63.

How might understanding these cost components help Fezzari management? For example, if you were Fezzari management and wanted to reduce the cost of its bikes, what actions might you take?

a. Negotiate lower costs for the bike components with Fezzari's suppliers.

b. Increase training of assembly technicians so that they can assemble each bike more quickly.

c. Consider relocating the manufacturing facility to reduce the facility lease cost.

d. All of the above.

e. None of the above.

Calculating Cost of Goods Sold

Exhibit 2-13 presents Fezzari's cost of goods sold summary for 2016. The calculation of cost of goods manufactured is an important step in determining cost of goods sold. The cost of the beginning finished goods inventory is added to cost of goods manufactured to report the cost of goods available for sale during the year. The cost of unsold units (ending finished goods inventory) is then subtracted to identify the cost associated with the units that were sold during the year (cost of goods sold).

Exhibit 2-13	Summary of Goods Sold

FEZZARI PERFORMANCE BICYCLES
Summary of Cost of Goods Sold
For the Year Ended December 31, 2016

Cost of goods manufactured.	$3,003,000
Add: Beginning finished goods inventory	12,000
Cost of goods available for sale.	$3,015,000
Less: Ending finished goods inventory	(15,000)
Cost of goods sold.	$3,000,000

The schedule of cost of goods manufactured and the calculation of cost of goods sold provide useful information about product costs in support of the income statement. They are not, however, required financial statements.

Income Statement for a Manufacturing Firm

Exhibit 2-14 presents the income statement for 2016 for Fezzari. The format is virtually the same as the income statement for a merchandising firm that uses the perpetual inventory system. Because Fezzari uses the perpetual inventory system for its finished goods inventory, the cost of goods sold amount is available in a general ledger account. The schedule of cost of goods manufactured (see **Exhibit 2-12**) and the cost of goods sold calculation (see **Exhibit 2-13**) lead to the cost of goods sold amount in the income statement and provide additional information about the flow of product costs.

Exhibit 2-14	Income Statement

FEZZARI PERFORMANCE BICYCLES
Income Statement
For the Year Ended December 31, 2016

Sales.		$4,500,000
Cost of goods sold.		3,000,000
Gross profit on sales.		$1,500,000
Operating expenses:		
Selling expenses.	$400,000	
Non-factory administrative expenses.	340,000	740,000
Income from operations.		$ 760,000
Other income and expense:		
Interest expense.		5,000
Income before income tax		$ 755,000
Income tax expense.		264,250
Net income.		$ 490,750

ILLUSTRATION OF PRODUCT COST JOURNAL ENTRIES

The following illustration for **Apple Inc.** presents hypothetical summary transactions and adjustment entries for 2014 related to the accounts used to accumulate product costs. Assume that Apple Inc. uses the perpetual inventory system and had the following manufacturing inventory account balances (in millions) at September 28, 2013 (the beginning of its 2014 fiscal year):

eLectures
MBC

LO4   **Illustrate** the journal entries to record product cost flows using a perpetual inventory system.

Materials inventory..	$ 3
Work in process inventory	680
Finished goods inventory	1,081

When a manufacturing firm uses the perpetual inventory system for Materials Inventory, Work in Process Inventory, and Finished Goods Inventory, cost of goods sold can be determined directly by reference to the Cost of Goods Sold account in the general ledger. Total manufacturing costs and cost of goods manufactured, however, are not directly available in a general ledger account. Assume Apple's subsidiary records for 2014 contain the following data:

1. Net delivered cost of materials purchased was $45,228.
2. Direct labor totaled $10,270.
3. The cost of direct materials used in production was $41,223.
4. Manufacturing overhead consists of the following:

Indirect material	$ 4,000
Indirect labor	3,000
Various costs	50,107
Year-end adjustments	4,000*
	$61,107

*This is composed of $1,000 for manufacturing supplies and $3000 for depreciation on factory machinery.

Based on this information, assume Apple records the following entries for 2014:

1. Acquisition of materials

Materials inventory	45,228	
Accounts payable		45,228
To record the delivered cost of materials purchased.		

2. Use of direct material and indirect material

Work in process inventory	41,223	
Manufacturing overhead	4,000	
Materials inventory		45,223
To record the transfer of direct material ($41,223) to the work in process inventory and the transfer of indirect material ($4,000) to manufacturing overhead.		

3. Incurrence of factory payroll

Work in process inventory	10,270	
Manufacturing overhead	3,000	
Wages payable		13,270
To record the factory payroll as direct labor ($10,270) to the work in process inventory and as indirect labor ($3,000) to manufacturing overhead.		

4. Incurrence of manufacturing overhead costs during year

Manufacturing overhead	50,107	
Accounts payable or cash		50,107
To record various factory costs incurred during the year as manufacturing overhead.		

5. Recognition of certain manufacturing overhead costs with year-end adjustments

Manufacturing overhead	4,000	
Manufacturing supplies		1,000
Accumulated depreciation—factory machinery		3,000
To record cost of supplies used for and depreciation on factory machinery.		

6. Application of manufacturing overhead

Work in process inventory	61,107	
Manufacturing overhead		61,107
To record the application of manufacturing overhead to the work in process inventory. (The procedures for determining this application will be described in a subsequent chapter.)		

Cost Flows

Exhibit 2-15 presents T-accounts to which these summary entries have been posted. The arrows in **Exhibit 2-15** indicate the flows of product cost. Direct material flows from Materials Inventory to Work in Process Inventory, whereas indirect material flows from Materials Inventory to Manufacturing Overhead. Direct labor flows from Wages Expense to Work in Process Inventory, whereas indirect labor flows from Wages Payable to Manufacturing Overhead. Actual manufacturing overhead comes from several sources, and manufacturing overhead applied flows to Work in Process Inventory.

Hint: In practice, applied manufacturing overhead rarely equals the actual manufacturing overhead incurred during a period, as illustrated in this example. Chapter 3 explains how to deal with over- or underapplied overhead.

Exhibit 2-15	Apple Inc. Flow of Manufacturing Costs

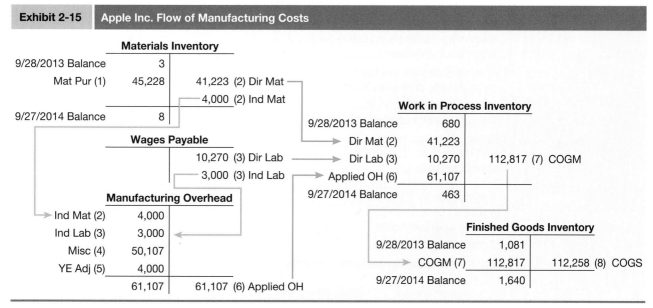

Cost of goods manufactured (the product cost of goods completed during the accounting period) flows from Work in Process Inventory to Finished Goods Inventory. The cost of goods sold flows from Finished Goods Inventory to the Cost of Goods Sold account. These cost flows are represented by the following journal entries:

7. Recognition of cost of goods manufactured

Finished goods inventory	112,817	
Work in process inventory		112,817
To record the transfer of the cost associated with goods completed from the work in process inventory to the finished goods inventory.		

8. Recognition of cost of goods sold

Cost of goods sold	112,258	
Finished goods inventory		112,258
To record the transfer of the cost associated with goods sold to customers from the finished goods inventory to cost of goods sold—recorded with the related sales entry.		

The three manufacturing inventory accounts (direct materials, work in process, and finished goods) comprise the inventory balance reported on a company's balance sheet. The expense associated with producing the inventory (cost of goods sold) is reported on the income statement when the product is sold, which may be in a period after the product was manufactured. The purpose of journal entries 1–8 in **Exhibit 2-15** is to determine these amounts as accurately as possible.

Based on the information in these journal entries and as summarized in the T-accounts in **Exhibit 2-15**, **Exhibit 2-16** presents Apple Inc.'s schedule of cost of goods manufactured for 2014.

Exhibit 2-16	**Schedule of Costs of Goods Manufactured**

APPLE INC.
Schedule of Cost of Goods Manufactured
For the Year Ended September 27, 2014
(in $millions)

Direct material:		
Beginning materials inventory................	$ 3	
Materials purchased....................	45,228	
Cost of materials available.............	$45,231	
Less: Ending materials inventory........	8	
Total materials used.................	$45,223	
Less: Indirect materials used..........	4,000	
Direct materials used................		$ 41,223
Direct labor.........................		$ 10,270
Factory overhead:		
Indirect material....................	$ 4,000	
Indirect labor.....................	3,000	
Various costs.....................	50,107	
Year-end adjustments..............	4,000	
Total factory overhead.............		$ 61,107
Total manufacturing costs for the year		**$112,600**
Add: Beginning work in process inventory........		$ 680
Total cost of work in process during the year......		113,280
Less: Ending work in process inventory........		(463)
Cost of goods manufactured		**$112,817**

Financial Statements

Exhibit 2-17 presents Apple Inc.'s 2014 income statement.

Exhibit 2-17	Income Statement

APPLE INC.
Income Statement
For the Year Ended September 27, 2014
(in $millions)

Sales.		$182,795
Cost of goods sold.		112,258
Gross profit on sales.		$ 70,537
Operating expenses:		
Selling, general, and administrative expenses	$11,993	
Research and development	6,041	18,034
Income from operations.		$ 52,503
Other income/(expense).		980
Income before income tax		$ 53,483
Income tax expense.		13,973
Net income.		$ 39,510
Basic earnings per share of common stock.		
(6,085.572 weighted average shares).		$ 6.49

Exhibit 2-18 shows the retained earnings statement for Apple Inc., given that it declared cash dividends of $11,215 during 2014.

Exhibit 2-18	Statement of Retained Earnings

APPLE INC.
Statement of Retained Earnings
For the Year Ended September 27, 2014
(in $millions)

Retained earnings, September 28, 2013	$123,549
Add: Net income for 2014	39,510
Less: Dividends declared.	(11,215)
Less: Repurchase of common stock	(45,399)
Retained earnings, September 27, 2014	$ 87,152

Exhibit 2-19 presents the September 27, 2014, balance sheet for Apple Inc. Note that the multiple inventory accounts are combined into a single line in the current assets section for presentation purposes.

Exhibit 2-19	Balance Sheet

APPLE INC.
Balance Sheet
As of September 27, 2014
(in $millions)

Assets
Current assets

Cash...		$ 25,077
Accounts receivable......................	$17,546	
Allowance for uncollectible accounts.....................	(86)	$ 17,460
Inventories		2,111
Other current assets....................		23,883
Total current assets		$ 68,531

Long-term assets

Long-term marketable securities		$130,162
Property, plant, and equipment	$39,015	
Less: Accumulated depreciation	(18,391)	20,624
Other long-term assets		12,522
Total assets		$231,839

Liabilities
Current liabilities

Accounts payable..................................		$ 30,196
Other current liabilities		33,252
Total current liabilities		$ 63,448

Long-term liabilities

Noncurrent liabilities...........................		$ 56,844
Total liabilities....................................		$120,292

Stockholders' equity

Common stock, no par value, 5,866,161,000 shares outstanding.....................................	$23,313	
Retained earnings	87,152	
Accumulated other comprehensive income...............	1,082	$111,547
Total liabilities and stockholders' equity		$231,839

Environmental Performance Reporting at Apple

There are probably few companies as secretive as Apple. The company is very careful to control any leaks on its upcoming products. Apple uses this strategy of keeping things secret in order to increase the anticipation before new product announcements. The strategy seems to be working well, based on the excitement surrounding these new product events.

One area that Apple is not secretive about is its environmental responsibility. Apple uses its detailed managerial accounting system to measure the environmental impact of how every product is manufactured. Unlike the secrecy surrounding what the next new product will be, Apple believes in full transparency regarding its environmental performance and reports on this performance in its comprehensive Product Environmental Reports. Every Apple product is measured and rated in four categories: climate change, restricted substances, energy efficiency, and material efficiency.

As stated on Apple's website, "We strive to create products that are the best they can be in every way. . . . the same passion for innovation goes into how we think about environmental responsibility. It's why we work tirelessly to reduce our impact on climate change, find ways to use greener materials, and conserve the resources we all need to thrive."

A famous expression in business is that you can't manage what you can't measure. For Apple to be a leader in both product development and environmental responsibility, the company depends on its managerial accounting systems to provide the information needed to properly manage everything the company does.

SERVICE INDUSTRY IN FOCUS

Environmental Business Consultants, LLC (EBC), is a consulting firm that specializes in the areas of recycling and solid waste and water/wastewater management services. The firm has offices located in northern and southern California. EBC has serviced hundreds of municipal agencies since 1984. Both the firm's executives and consultants work on client projects. EBC's 2016 adjusted trial balance is shown below.

SERVICE AND MERCHANDISING

Description	Trial Balance Debit	Trial Balance Credit
Cash	390,000	
Accounts receivable.	474,000	
Allowance for uncollectible accounts.		—
Work in process inventory	247,000	
Other current assets.	32,000	
Furniture and fixtures	150,000	
Accumulated depreciation—furniture		150,000
Office equipment	277,000	
Accumulated depreciation—equipment.		198,000
Accounts payable.		—
Other current liabilities		37,500
Non-current liabilities		3,000
Owners' capital		90,000
Retained earnings		573,000
Sales.		4,146,000
Reimbursable costs	431,000	
Executive salaries.	844,500	
Clerical salaries	217,500	
Consultant salaries.	1,050,000	
Employee benefits	145,500	
Payroll taxes.	123,000	
Employee bonuses.	126,000	
Marketing expenses.	48,000	
Employee continuing education expenses.	27,000	
Office lease expense	202,500	
Office supplies expense.	64,500	
Other general administrative expense	355,500	
Other income/(expense).		7,500
	5,205,000	5,205,000

Required

1. Classify each of the expense line items in the trial balance as:
   a. Direct or indirect. Assume that the cost object is a consulting project.
   b. Fixed or variable. Assume that the cost object is one of EBC's two offices.
   c. Product or period. Assume that the cost object is a consulting project.
2. Prepare a schedule of cost of services for EBC for the year ended December 31, 2016. Assume that the beginning Work in Process Inventory balance was $223,000. Regardless of your classification in Requirement 1, assume that all executive and consultant salaries, benefits, and taxes are product costs and that EBC treats all bonuses and continuing education expenses as period costs.
3. Prepare an income statement for EBC for the year ended December 31, 2016.

Solution

1a.

Line Item	Direct Cost	Indirect Cost
Reimbursable costs	X	
Executive salaries.	X	X
Clerical salaries		X
Consultant salaries.	X	
Employee benefits	X	X
Payroll taxes.	X	X
Employee bonuses.	X	X
Marketing expenses.		X
Employee continuing education expenses.		X
Office lease expense		X
Office supplies expense.		X
Other general administrative expenses		X

1b.

Line Item	Fixed Cost	Variable Cost
Reimbursable costs		X
Executive salaries.	X	
Clerical salaries	X	
Consultant salaries.	X	
Employee benefits	X	
Payroll taxes.	X	
Employee bonuses.		X
Marketing expenses.		X
Employee continuing education expenses.		X
Office lease expense	X	
Office supplies expense.		X
Other general administrative expenses	X	X

1c.

Line Item	Product Cost	Period Cost
Reimbursable costs	X	
Executive salaries.	X	
Clerical salaries		X
Consultant salaries.	X	
Employee benefits	X	X
Payroll taxes.	X	X
Employee bonuses.		X
Marketing expenses.		X
Employee continuing education expenses.		X
Office lease expense	X	
Office supplies expense.	X	X
Other general administrative expenses	X	X

2.

Environmental Business Consultants, LLC Statement of Cost Services As of December 31, 2016		
Direct Labor		$2,380,500
General Overhead:		
Office lease expense	$202,500	
Office supplies expense	64,500	
Total General Overhead		267,000
Total Manufacturing Costs for the Year		2,647,500
Add: Beginning Work in Process Inventory		223,000
Total Cost of Work in Process during the Year		2,870,500
Less: Ending Work in Process Inventory		(247,000)
Cost of Services		$2,623,500

3.

Environmental Business Consultants, LLC Income Statement For the Year Ended December 31, 2016		
Gross Sales		$4,146,000
Less Reimbursable Costs		$ (431,000)
Net Sales		$3,715,000
Cost of Services		2,623,500
Gross Profit on Sales		1,091,500
Operating Expenses:		
Employee bonuses	126,000	
Marketing expenses	48,000	
Employee continuing education expenses	27,000	
Other general administrative expenses	355,500	
Total Operating Expenses		556,500
Income from Operations		535,000
Other Income/(Expense)		7,500
Net Income		$ 542,500

COMPREHENSIVE PROBLEM

At December 31, 2016, the end of its fiscal year, Perez Manufacturing Corporation collected the following data for 2016:

Materials inventory, January 1	$ 80,000
Materials inventory, December 31	60,000
Work in process inventory, January 1	100,000
Work in process inventory, December 31	140,000
Finished goods inventory, January 1	120,000
Finished goods inventory, December 31	110,000
Net delivered cost of materials purchased	180,000
Direct labor	280,000
Indirect material	15,000
Indirect labor	75,000
Factory supplies used	16,000
Factory depreciation	30,000
Factory repairs and maintenance	22,000
Selling expenses	64,000
Non-factory administrative expenses	58,000

Required

Prepare a schedule of cost of goods manufactured and sold for Perez Manufacturing Corporation for the year ended December 31, 2016, assuming that there were no other manufacturing overhead items than those listed above.

Solution

PEREZ MANUFACTURING CORPORATION
Schedule of Cost of Goods Manufactured
For the Year Ended December 31, 2016

Direct material:		
Beginning materials inventory	$ 80,000	
Net delivered cost of materials purchased	180,000	
Cost of materials available	$260,000	
Less: Ending materials inventory	60,000	
Total material used	$200,000	
Less: Indirect material used	15,000	
Direct material used		$185,000
Direct labor		280,000
Manufacturing overhead:		
Indirect material	$ 15,000	
Indirect labor	75,000	
Manufacturing supplies used	16,000	
Manufacturing depreciation	30,000	
Manufacturing repairs and maintenance	22,000	
Total manufacturing overhead		158,000
Total manufacturing costs for the year		**$623,000**
Add: Beginning work in process inventory		100,000
Total Cost of work in process during the year		$723,000
Less: Ending work in process inventory		140,000
Cost of goods manufactured		**$583,000**
Add: Beginning finished goods inventory		120,000
Cost of goods available for sale		$703,000
Less: Ending finished goods inventory		110,000
Cost of goods sold		**$593,000**

APPENDIX 2A: Year-End Accounting Procedures

Year-End Accounting Procedures for a Manufacturing Firm

The following **worksheet** illustrates the year-end accounting procedures for Apple Inc. and includes the preparation and use of a worksheet to adjust the general ledger accounts, the preparation of financial statements from worksheet data, and the closing of the temporary accounts. The worksheet illustrates the typical processes used by businesses at the end of their fiscal year. Most businesses (large and small) now employ accounting software packages that facilitate the development of the trial balance and financial statements—the worksheet shows what goes on within these accounting software packages.

Worksheet for a Manufacturing Firm

As previously discussed, a worksheet illustrates the processes used by businesses at year-end to adjust the general ledger accounts and prepare financial statements:

- It includes the debit and credit balances of all general ledger accounts.
- It shows the effects of all necessary adjustments.
- It allows for the grouping of all adjusted balances for the preparation of each financial statement.

LO5 Present the year-end accounting procedures, including the preparation of a worksheet, adjusting entries, financial statements, closing entries, the schedule of cost of goods manufactured, and cost of goods sold.

The following basic year-end closing procedures are similar for all firms:

1. Prepare the unadjusted trial balance from the general ledger (this is illustrated in Columns B and C of the worksheet shown in **Exhibit 2A-1**).
2. Formulate appropriate year-end adjustments (this is shown in Columns D and E, with dollars of debits equal to dollars of credits).
3. Prepare the adjusted trial balance by combining the unadjusted trial balance with the year-end adjustments (this is shown in Columns F and G).
4. Extend amounts from the adjusted trial balance columns to either the income statement (Columns H and I) or the balance sheet (Columns J and K).
5. Ensure that the debit and credit columns of each financial statement are equal to ensure the accuracy of the worksheet.

Exhibit 2A-1 presents the worksheet for Apple Inc. for the year ended September 27, 2014. The unadjusted trial balance reflects the summary journal entries recorded earlier in this chapter. (Note that all numbers are given in millions.)

Exhibit 2A-1	Apple Inc. 2014 Worksheet

	Unadjusted Trial Balance		Adjustments		Adjusted Trial Balance		Income Statement		Balance Sheet	
Description	Debit	Credit	Debit	Credit	Debit	Credit	Debit	Credit	Debit	Credit
Cash....................................	25,077				25,077				25,077	
Accounts receivable.....................	17,546				17,546				17,546	
Allowance for uncollectible accounts.........		41		(1) 45		86				86
Materials inventory......................	8				8				8	
Work in process inventory	463				463				463	
Finished goods inventory..................	1,640				1,640				1,640	
Other current assets.....................	23,883				23,883				23,883	
Long-term marketable securities	130,162				130,162				130,162	
Property, plant, and equipment	39,015				39,015				39,015	
Accumulated depreciation.................		15,947		(2) 2,444		18,391				18,391
Other long-term assets	12,522				12,522				12,522	
Accounts payable........................		30,196				30,196				30,196
Other current liabilities		19,279				19,279				19,279
Non-current liabilities		56,844				56,844				56,844
Common stock—no par value		23,313				23,313				23,313
Retained earnings		58,857				58,857				58,857
Accumulated other comprehensive income....		1,082				1,082				1,082
Dividends	11,215				11,215				11,215	
Sales..................................		182,795				182,795		182,795		
Manufacturing overhead			(2) 2,444							
Cost of goods sold......................	109,814				112,258		112,258			
Research and development expense.........	6,041				6,041		6,041			
Selling, general, and administrative expense...	11,948		(1) 45		11,993		11,993			
Other income/(expense)..................		980				980		980		
	389,334	389,334								
Income tax expense.....................			(3) 13,973		13,973		13,973			
Income tax payable				(3) 13,973		13,973				13,973
			16,462	16,462	405,796	405,796	144,265	183,775	261,531	222,021
Net income............................							39,510			39,510
							183,775	183,775	261,531	261,531

Exhibit 2A-2 summarizes the balances (in millions) of Apple Inc.'s three primary inventories at the beginning and end of fiscal 2014.

Exhibit 2A-2		
	September 24, 2013	September 29, 2014
Materials...	$ 3	$ 8
Work in process....................................	680	463
Finished goods....................................	1,081	1,640

Because we assume that Apple Inc. uses a perpetual inventory system, the September 27, 2014, balances will appear in the trial balance columns of the worksheet.

Adjusting Entries

Adjusting entry data for Apple Inc. at September 27, 2014, are as follows:

1. Uncollectible accounts expense is estimated to be $45.
2. Depreciation on factory machinery for 2014 is $2,444.
3. Estimated income tax expense for 2014 is $13,973.

Following are the entries to record these adjustments, with each adjustment keyed to the number of the data item listed above.

1.	Selling, general, and administrative expense	45	
	Allowance for uncollectible accounts		45
	To estimate uncollectible accounts expense.		

2.	Manufacturing overhead	2,444	
	Accumulated depreciation		2,444
	To record depreciation on factory machinery.		
3.	Income tax expense	13,973	
	Income tax payable		13,973
	To record estimated income taxes for 2014.		

The preceding adjusting journal entries are listed in Columns D and E of the worksheet in Exhibit 2A-1. The total of the debits ($16,462) equals the total of the credits ($16,462) in the adjustments columns of the worksheet.

Unadjusted account balances from Columns B and C are combined with the adjustments from Columns D and E to determine the adjusted trial balance. These combined amounts are shown in Columns F and G. The adjusted trial balance is then extended to either the income statement columns (H and I) or the balance sheet columns (J and K). The data in these columns are used to prepare the income statement, retained earnings statement, and balance sheet.

Closing Entries

Four closing entries are needed for Apple Inc. at September 27, 2014. These closing entries may be taken directly from the worksheet shown in Exhibit 2A-1.

1.	Sales	182,795	
	Income summary		182,795
	To close the sales revenue account.		
2.	Income summary	143,285	
	Other income	980	
	Cost of goods sold		112,258
	Research and development expense		6,041
	Selling, general, and administrative expense		11,993
	Income tax expense		13,973
	To close the other revenue and expense accounts.		
3.	Income summary	39,510	
	Retained earnings		39,510
	To close the income summary account.		
4.	Retained earnings	11,215	
	Dividends		11,215
	To close the dividends account.		

SUMMARY OF LEARNING OBJECTIVES

Identify the key objectives of a managerial accounting system and define product costs and period costs; variable, fixed, and mixed costs; and direct and indirect costs; and cost control. (p. 20)   **LO1**

- The primary objectives of managerial accounting systems are to provide management with financial and other business information that is useful in analyzing and making business decisions.
- Product costs include all costs necessary to bring a product to completion.
- Period costs are expensed in the period incurred and not assigned to products.
- A variable cost varies in total but is fixed per unit for a certain range of activity. A fixed cost is fixed in total but varies per unit for a certain range of activity. Mixed costs have both fixed and variable cost components.
- A direct cost can easily be traced to a cost object. An indirect cost cannot be easily traced to a cost object.

LO2 **Describe the three manufacturing inventories—materials, work in process, and finished goods—and discuss the categories of manufacturing costs and how these costs flow among the inventories and cost of goods sold. (p. 24)**

- Materials inventory includes all factory materials and components that have been purchased but not yet placed into production.
- Work in process inventory includes all units of product that have been placed into production but not yet completed.
- Finished goods inventory includes all units of product that have been completed but not yet sold.
- Total product costs consist of direct material, direct labor, and manufacturing overhead (which includes indirect material and indirect labor).
- Prime cost is direct material plus direct labor. Product costs are easily and directly traceable to individual products. Conversion cost is direct labor plus manufacturing overhead. Conversion cost represents the elements of product cost necessary to convert the materials and components to the final finished products.
- Product cost flows from the Materials Inventory account to the Work in Process Inventory account to the Finished Goods Inventory account and finally to the Cost of Goods Sold account.

LO3 **Define total manufacturing costs, cost of goods manufactured, and cost of goods sold, and illustrate the schedule of cost of goods manufactured and sold and the income statement. (p. 31)**

- Total manufacturing costs is the sum of direct material, direct labor, and manufacturing overhead incurred during the accounting period.
- Cost of goods manufactured (cost of product transferred to finished goods inventory during the accounting period) is total manufacturing costs plus beginning work in process inventory minus ending work in process inventory.
- Cost of goods sold is cost of goods manufactured plus beginning finished goods inventory minus ending finished goods inventory.
- The schedule of cost of goods manufactured and sold has subtotals that reveal total manufacturing costs, cost of goods manufactured, and cost of goods sold.

LO4 **Illustrate the journal entries to record product cost flows using a perpetual inventory system. (p. 35)**

- Direct material, direct labor, and manufacturing overhead costs are accumulated in the Work in Process Inventory account.
- When manufacturing is completed, product costs are transferred from the Work in Process Inventory account to the Finished Goods Inventory account.
- When goods are sold, product costs are transferred from the Finished Goods Inventory account to Cost of Goods Sold.

LO5
(Appendix 2A) **Appendix 2A: Present the year-end accounting procedures, including the preparation of a worksheet, adjusting entries, financial statements, closing entries, the schedule of cost of goods manufactured, and cost of goods sold. (p. 45)**

- The manufacturing worksheet has five pairs of amount columns: trial balance, adjustments, adjusted trial balance, income statement, and balance sheet.
- Revenues, expenses, and Cost of Goods Sold are closed to the Income Summary account.
- The schedule of cost of goods manufactured and sold is prepared using data from the worksheet and subsidiary records.

KEY TERMS

Conversion cost (p. 27)	Direct costs (p. 22)	Indirect labor (p. 26)
Cost control (p. 24)	Direct labor (p. 26)	Indirect materials (p. 26)
Cost object (p. 20)	Direct materials (p. 26)	Manufacturing overhead (p. 26)
Cost of goods manufactured (COGM) (p. 30)	Factory overhead (p. 26)	Materials inventory (p. 24)
	Factory supplies (p. 24)	Mixed costs (p. 21)
Cost of goods sold (COGS) (p. 31)	Finished goods inventory (p. 24)	Office supplies (p. 24)
	Fixed cost (p. 21)	Period costs (p. 21, 23)
Cost of jobs or projects (p. 23)	Indirect cost (p. 23)	Prime cost (p. 27)

Product costing (p. 20)
Product costs (p. 20, 25)
Semi-variable costs (p. 21)

Total manufacturing
costs (p. 30, 32)
Variable cost (p. 21)

Work in process
inventory (p. 24)
Worksheet (p. 45)

Assignments with the 🌐 logo in the margin are available in 🎓BusinessCourse.
See the Preface of the book for details.

SELF-STUDY QUESTIONS

(Answers to Self-Study Questions are at the end of this chapter.)

1. Which of the following is never an element of product cost?   **LO1**
   - *a.* Insurance
   - *b.* Utilities
   - *c.* Advertising
   - *d.* Supplies

2. Which of the following is not an element of manufacturing overhead?   **LO2**
   - *a.* Factory office salaries
   - *b.* Plant manager's salary
   - *c.* Product inspector's salary
   - *d.* Company president's salary

3. The sum of direct materials, direct labor, and manufacturing overhead plus beginning work in process inventory minus ending work in process inventory computes   **LO3**
   - *a.* total manufacturing costs.
   - *b.* cost of goods manufactured.
   - *c.* cost of goods sold.
   - *d.* total cost of work in process.

4. The journal entry to record the distribution of the factory payroll requires   **LO4**
   - *a.* a debit to Work in Process Inventory for direct labor.
   - *b.* a debit to Work in Process Inventory for indirect labor.
   - *c.* a debit to Manufacturing Overhead for direct labor.
   - *d.* a credit to Manufacturing Overhead for direct labor.

5. A manufacturer incurred $20,000 of direct material, $10,000 of direct labor, and $15,000 of manufacturing overhead during 2016. Beginning work in process inventory was $8,000. If cost of goods manufactured was $47,000, what was the amount of the ending work in process inventory?   **LO3**
   - *a.* $55,000
   - *b.* $6,000
   - *c.* $10,000
   - *d.* $53,000

QUESTIONS

1. How are product costs accounted for differently from period costs? Give examples of each.   **LO1**
2. What is the basic format of the income statement of a manufacturing firm?   **LO3**
3. Name the three inventory accounts maintained by manufacturing firms and briefly describe the nature of each.   **LO2**
4. Name and briefly describe the three major categories used to account for manufacturing costs.   **LO2**
5. Define prime cost and conversion cost.   **LO2**
6. List six examples of manufacturing overhead costs.   **LO2**
7. In what way is total manufacturing cost different from cost of goods manufactured?   **LO3**
8. If the cost of work in process during the year is $480,000 and ending work in process inventory is $50,000, what is the amount of cost of goods manufactured?   **LO3**
9. If beginning and ending finished goods inventories are $55,000 and $45,000, respectively, and the cost of goods sold is $420,000, what is the cost of goods manufactured?   **LO3**
10. What journal entry would be made to record the transfer of $12,000 of direct material and $2,500 of indirect material from the material inventory?   **LO4**
11. What journal entry would be made to record the distribution of a factory payroll consisting of $11,000 of direct labor and $4,000 of indirect labor?   **LO4**
12. What journal entry would be made to record the payment of $1,500 cash for factory utilities?   **LO4**
13. What journal entry would be required to record the transfer of completed products costing $15,000?   **LO4**

EXERCISES—SET A

LO3   **E2-1A.** **Schedule of Cost of Goods Manufactured and Sold** At December 31, 2016, the end of its fiscal year, Lederman Manufacturing Corporation collected the following data for 2016:

Materials inventory, January 1	$ 25,000
Materials inventory, December 31	15,000
Work in process inventory, January 1	30,000
Work in process inventory, December 31	41,000
Finished goods inventory, January 1	51,000
Finished goods inventory, December 31	36,000
Net delivered cost of materials purchased	125,000
Direct labor	148,000
Indirect material	12,000
Indirect labor	37,000
Factory supplies used	10,000
Factory depreciation	65,000
Factory repairs and maintenance	21,000
Selling expenses (total)	62,000
Non-factory administrative expenses (total)	58,000

Prepare a schedule of cost of goods manufactured and sold for Lederman Manufacturing Corporation for the year ended December 31, 2016, assuming that there were no other manufacturing overhead items than those listed above.

LO3   **E2-2A.** **Income Statement** Lederman Manufacturing Corporation (see E2-1A) sold 15,000 units of product for $40 each during 2016. During the year, 5,000 shares of common stock were outstanding. Prepare an income statement for the year (ignore income taxes).

LO3   **E2-3A.** **Cost of Goods Manufactured and Cost of Goods Sold** For each of the following unrelated companies, compute the cost of goods manufactured and the cost of goods sold.

	A	B	C
Selling expenses	$ 500	$ 800	$ 600
Factory insurance	260	245	140
Ending finished goods inventory	810	750	515
Non-factory administrative expenses	250	450	350
Direct labor	2,560	2,760	2,120
Beginning materials inventory	520	670	350
Beginning work in process inventory	1,120	840	1,070
Indirect material used	390	420	230
Factory utilities	240	275	150
Factory depreciation	730	760	380
Ending work in process inventory	1,360	790	950
Ending materials inventory	440	710	410
Indirect labor	425	280	160
Beginning finished goods inventory	850	725	480
Factory repairs and maintenance	215	230	175
Net delivered cost of materials purchased	3,140	4,410	2,870
Factory supplies used	330	310	210

LO2   **E2-4A.** **Prime Cost and Conversion Cost** Piper Consulting Company incurred the following during 2016:

Direct labor	$30,000
Overhead	45,000
Selling expenses	40,000
Administrative expenses	35,000

Calculate prime cost and conversion cost for Piper Consulting Company during 2016.

E2-5A. **Entries for Product Cost Flow** The following transactions occurred during January 2016 for Richards Manufacturing Company: **LO4**

Jan. 5 Acquired $3,000 of material on account that will be used to produce product for resale.

11 Requisitioned $2,500 of material for use as direct material in the factory.

16 Completed the manufacturing of products with a total product cost of $11,000 and transferred them to the warehouse.

Record these transactions in general journal form. Assume that Richards Manufacturing Company uses the perpetual inventory system.

E2-6A. **Entries for Product Cost Flow** Record the following transactions that occurred during March 2016 for Harris Manufacturing Company, which uses the perpetual inventory system: **LO4**

Mar. 12 Transferred $10,000 of completed goods from the factory to the warehouse.

15 Requisitioned $6,000 of material for use in the factory as direct material and $1,000 for indirect material.

18 Sold goods costing $8,000 for $12,000 on account.

EXERCISES—SET B

E2-1B. **Schedule of Cost of Goods Manufactured and Sold** At December 31, 2016, the end of its fiscal year, Kelly Metal Products Corporation collected the following data for 2016: **LO3**

Materials inventory, January 1	$ 32,000
Materials inventory, December 31	22,000
Work in process inventory, January 1	34,000
Work in process inventory, December 31	45,000
Finished goods inventory, January 1	21,000
Finished goods inventory, December 31	18,000
Net delivered cost of materials purchased	210,000
Direct labor	135,000
Indirect material	13,000
Indirect labor	25,000
Factory supplies used	12,000
Factory depreciation	78,000
Factory repairs and maintenance	28,000
Selling expenses (total)	63,000
Non-factory administrative expenses (total)	57,000

Required
Prepare a schedule of cost of goods manufactured and sold for Kelly Metal Products Corporation for the year ended December 31, 2016, assuming that there were no other manufacturing overhead items than those listed above.

E2-2B. **Income Statement** Kelly Metal Products Corporation (see E2-1B) sold 20,000 units of product for $35 each during 2016. During the year, 10,000 shares of common stock were outstanding. Prepare an income statement for the year (ignore income taxes). **LO3**

E2-3B. **Cost of Goods Manufactured and Cost of Goods Sold** For each of the following unrelated columns of data for the year, compute the cost of goods manufactured and the cost of goods sold. **LO3**

	A	B	C
Selling expenses	$ 600	$ 700	$ 900
Factory insurance..	180	270	300
Ending finished goods inventory	620	660	930
Non-factory administrative expenses........................	300	400	800
Direct labor...	2,130	2,850	3,160
Beginning materials inventory	425	575	850
Beginning work in process inventory.......................	840	920	1,290
Indirect material used.....................................	270	325	520
Factory utilities..	350	360	500
Factory depreciation	820	740	965
Ending work in process inventory	790	985	1,425
Ending materials inventory................................	385	610	820
Indirect labor	225	410	365
Beginning finished goods inventory........................	565	680	950
Factory repairs and maintenance..........................	330	250	415
Net delivered cost of materials purchased.................	2,780	3,620	8,170
Factory supplies used	210	230	260

LO2 **E2-4B.** **Prime Cost and Conversion Cost** Benton Engineering Services Company incurred the following during 2016:

Direct labor..	$47,000
Overhead	63,000
Selling expenses	56,000
Administrative expenses	51,000

Calculate prime cost and conversion cost for Benton Engineering Services Company during 2016.

LO4 **E2-5B.** **Entries for Product Cost Flow** The following transactions occurred during February 2016 for Thompson Manufacturing Company:

Feb. 10 Acquired $5,000 of material on account that will be used to produce product for resale.

11 Requisitioned $4,000 of material for use as direct material in the factory.

16 Completed the manufacturing of products with a total product cost of $24,000 and transferred them to the warehouse.

Record these transactions in general journal form. Assume that Thompson Manufacturing Company uses the perpetual inventory system.

LO4 **E2-6B.** **Entries for Product Cost Flow** Record the following transactions that occurred during April 2016 for Boyd Manufacturing Corporation, which uses the perpetual inventory system:

Apr. 21 Transferred $16,000 of completed goods from the factory to the warehouse.

25 Requisitioned $9,000 of material for use in the factory as direct material and $2,000 for indirect material.

28 Sold goods costing $6,000 for $10,000 on account.

PROBLEMS—SET A

LO3 **P2-1A.** **Schedule of Cost of Goods Manufactured and Sold** The following amounts are available for 2016 for Bourne Manufacturing Company:

Administrative salaries (non-factory)	$ 70,000
Administrative rent (non-factory)	35,000
Advertising and promotion expense	41,000
Depreciation—administrative	22,000
Depreciation—factory	30,000
Depreciation—selling	17,000
Direct labor	175,000
Factory rent	18,000
Factory supplies used	12,000
Finished goods inventory (January 1)	57,000
Finished goods inventory (December 31)	52,000
Indirect material used	14,000
Indirect labor	19,000
Materials inventory (January 1)	13,000
Materials inventory (December 31)	20,000
Net delivered cost of materials purchased	138,000
Other factory overhead	26,000
Sales	845,000
Sales salaries expense	72,000
Work in process inventory (January 1)	18,000
Work in process inventory (December 31)	31,000

Required

Using the above data, prepare a schedule of cost of goods manufactured and sold.

P2-2A. **Cost of Goods Manufactured and Sold** The following data relate to three independent production periods of Riverside Manufacturing Company. Missing data are indicated by question marks. **LO3**

	A	B	C
Materials:			
Beginning inventory	$ 52	$ 164	$110
Purchases	?	700	500
Ending inventory	74	100	?
Total material used	330	?	440
Direct labor	580	960	800
Manufacturing overhead:			
Indirect material	96	?	120
Indirect labor	160	150	350
Other	?	200	340
Total manufacturing overhead	520	480	?
Work in process inventories:			
Beginning	?	90	260
Ending	70	?	100
Finished goods inventories:			
Beginning	?	400	80
Ending	335	120	330
Cost of goods manufactured	1,384	?	?
Cost of goods sold	1,339	2,324	?

Required

Using the above data, determine the missing amounts. (You should set up a schedule of cost of goods manufactured and sold, fill in the known data, and calculate the missing amounts.)

P2-3A. **Journal Entries** Taylor Manufacturing Company uses the perpetual inventory system to record **LO4** transactions related to its manufacturing inventories. The following transactions occurred during March 2016:

Mar.   6   Recorded the payroll: $10,000 of direct labor and $2,000 of indirect labor.

      8   Received $14,000 of materials and components that had been ordered on account.

    10   Completed product costing $22,000 and transferred it to the warehouse. Requisitioned $5,000 of material for use in the factory; $4,000 was used as direct material and the remainder was used as indirect material.

    12   Sold on account product costing $3,000 for $4,500.

    15   Applied $6,000 of manufacturing overhead cost to the product currently being worked on.

    21   Paid $500 cash for a special material component that was shipped via overnight delivery.

    27   Sold product costing $2,900 for $5,000 cash.

Required

Prepare general journal entries to record these transactions.

LO4   **P2-4A.**   **Journal Entries** Paulson Manufacturing Company uses the perpetual inventory system to account for its manufacturing inventories. The following are Paulson's transactions during July 2016:

July   5   Received material costing $2,000 from a supplier. The material was purchased on account.

     9   Requisitioned $6,000 of material for use in the factory, consisting of $5,000 of direct material and $1,000 of indirect material.

    11   Recorded the factory payroll: $13,500 of direct labor and $1,500 of indirect labor.

    17   Incurred various overhead costs totaling $14,000. (Credit Accounts Payable.)

    20   Applied $20,000 of manufacturing overhead to the products being manufactured.

    23   Completed product costing $16,000 and moved it to the warehouse.

    26   Sold goods with a product cost of $3,000 on account for $5,000.

Required

a.   Set up T-accounts for the following four accounts and post the July 1, 2016 balances: Materials Inventory, $7,000; Work in Process Inventory, 25,000; Finished Goods Inventory, $10,000; and Cost of Goods Sold, $30,000.

b.   Record the transactions listed above in general journal form, post relevant portions to the four T-accounts, and balance the four accounts.

LO3   **P2-5A.**   **Total Manufacturing Cost, Income Statement, Unit Cost, and Selling Price** Two inventors, recently organized as Innovation, Inc., consult you regarding a planned new product. They have estimates of the costs of materials, labor, overhead, and other expenses for 2016 but need to know how much to charge for each unit to earn a profit in 2016 equal to 15% of their estimated total long-term investment of $400,000 (ignore income taxes). Their plans indicate that each unit of the new product requires the following:

Direct material	4 lb. of a material costing $5/lb.
Direct labor	2 hrs. of a metal former's time at $11/hr.
	0.6 hr. of an assembler's time at $8/hr.

Major items of production overhead would be annual rent of $46,460 for a factory building, $28,660 rent for machinery, and $21,700 of indirect material. Other production overhead is estimated to be $233,280. Selling expenses are an estimated 30% of total sales, and non-factory administrative expenses are 20% of total sales.

The consensus at Innovation is that during 2016 10,000 units of product should be produced for selling and another 2,000 units should be produced for the next year's beginning inventory. Also, an extra 3,000 pounds of material will be purchased as beginning inventory for the next year. Because of the nature of the manufacturing process, all units started must be completed, so work in process inventories are negligible.

Required

a.   Incorporate the above data into a schedule of estimated total manufacturing costs and compute the unit production cost for 2016.

b.   Prepare an estimated income statement that would provide the target amount of profit for 2016.

c.   What unit sales price should Innovation charge for the new product?

P2-6A. **Worksheet, Financial Statements, and Schedule of Cost of Goods Manufactured and Sold** The **LO5** trial balance for Newton Manufacturing Corporation at the end of 2016 follows: **(Appendix 2A)**

	Debit	Credit
Cash.	$ 40,000	
Accounts receivable.	248,000	
Allowance for uncollectible accounts.		$ 5,600
Materials inventory.	136,000	
Work in process inventory	80,000	
Finished goods inventory.	64,000	
Land	140,000	
Factory buildings	800,000	
Accumulated depreciation—Factory buildings		184,000
Factory equipment.	700,000	
Accumulated depreciation—Factory equipment		68,000
Accounts payable.		168,400
Long-term notes payable—8%		224,000
Common stock, $40 par value		
(All outstanding)		1,120,000
Retained earnings		228,000
Sales.		1,680,000
Manufacturing overhead		72,000
Cost of goods sold.	1,194,800	
Selling expenses	203,200	
Non-factory administrative expense	144,000	
	$3,750,000	$3,750,000

The following information is available (adjusting entries have not been recorded):

1. Annual amounts of depreciation are factory buildings, $44,000 and factory equipment, $28,000.
2. Uncollectible accounts expense, 1/2% of sales. (Debit this expense to Selling Expenses.)
3. Estimated income taxes, $26,000.
4. January 1 inventories were materials, $164,000; work in process, $72,000; and finished goods, $92,000.
5. Additional data needed for schedule of cost of goods manufactured and sold:

Net delivered cost of materials purchased	$380,000
Direct labor.	512,400
Indirect, material.	47,000
Indirect labor	126,800
Factory utilities.	21,600
Factory repairs and maintenance.	16,000
Factory property taxes.	18,000

Required

a. Prepare a worksheet for 2016.
b. Prepare an income statement.
c. Prepare a balance sheet.
d. Prepare a schedule of cost of goods manufactured and sold.

LO5
(Appendix 2A)

P2-7A. **Worksheet, Income Statements, and Schedule of Cost of Goods Manufactured and Sold** The following is the trial balance of Hyde Company at December 31, 2016, together with the worksheet adjustments. Hyde Company uses perpetual inventory procedures.

	Trial Balance		Adjustment	
	Debit	Credit	Debit	Credit
Cash.	$ 28,000			
Materials inventory.	52,000			
Work in process inventory	30,000			
Finished goods inventory.	42,000			
Prepaid insurance	2,800			(1) $ 1,400
Factory machinery	240,000			
Accumulated depreciation—				
Factory machinery		$ 50,000		(2) 17,000
Patents.	40,800			(3) 3,200
Accounts payable.		66,200		
Common stock, $17 par value.		170,000		
Retained earnings		25,400		
Sales.		620,000		
Manufacturing overhead		17,000	(2) $17,000	
Cost of goods sold.	414,000			
Sales salaries expense.	52,000			
Advertising expense.	13,600			
Non-factory			(1) 1,400	
Administrative expenses.	33,400		(3) 3,200	
	948,600	948,600		
Income tax expenses			(4) 20,000	
Income tax payable				(4) 20,000
			41,600	41,600

Additional information:

1. January 1, 2016, inventories were materials, $36,000; work in process, $27,800; and finished goods, $42,000.
2. Net delivered cost of materials purchased was $142,800.
3. Direct labor was $180,800.
4. Manufacturing overhead included the following:

Indirect labor	$61,000
Factory utilities.	8,200
Repairs and maintenance.	4,400
Factory buildings rent.	18,000
Indirect material	15,000

Required

a. Complete the worksheet.
b. Prepare an income statement.
c. Prepare a schedule of cost of goods manufactured and sold.

PROBLEMS—SET B

P2-1B. Schedule of Cost of Goods Manufactured and Sold The following amounts are available for 2016 for Bishop Manufacturing Company: **LO3**

Administrative salaries (non-factory)	$ 85,000
Administrative rent (non-factory)	47,000
Advertising and promotion expense	93,000
Depreciation—administrative	77,000
Depreciation—factory	95,000
Depreciation—selling	36,000
Direct labor	325,000
Factory rent	68,000
Factory supplies used	23,000
Finished goods inventory (January 1)	61,000
Finished goods inventory (December 31)	63,000
Indirect material used	27,000
Indirect labor	44,000
Materials inventory (January 1)	22,000
Materials inventory (December 31)	30,000
Net delivered cost of materials purchased	210,000
Other factory overhead	55,000
Sales	938,000
Sales salaries expense	71,000
Work in process inventory (January 1)	33,000
Work in process inventory (December 31)	29,000

Required
Using the above data, prepare a schedule of cost of goods manufactured and sold.

P2-2B. Cost of Goods Manufactured and Sold The following data relate to three independent production periods of Randolph Manufacturing Company. Missing data are indicated by question marks.   **LO3**

	A	B	C
Materials:			
Beginning inventory	$ 78	$ 410	$ 220
Purchases	?	1,750	1,000
Ending inventory	111	250	?
Total material used	495	?	880
Direct labor	870	2,400	1,600
Manufacturing overhead:			
Indirect material	144	?	110
Indirect labor	240	375	700
Other	?	500	680
Total manufacturing overhead	780	1,100	?
Work in process inventories:			
Beginning	?	225	520
Ending	105	?	200
Finished goods inventories:			
Beginning	?	1,000	160
Ending	495	300	660
Cost of goods manufactured	2,076	?	?
Cost of goods sold	2,016	5,275	?

Required
Using the above data, determine the missing amounts. (You should set up a schedule of cost of goods manufactured and sold, fill in the known data, and calculate the missing amounts.)

LO4   **P2-3B.**   **Journal Entries** Travis Manufacturing Company uses the perpetual inventory system to record transactions related to its manufacturing inventories. The following transactions occurred during August 2016:

Aug.   5   Received $9,000 of materials and components that had been ordered on account.
       7   Recorded the payroll: $6,500 of direct labor and $1,500 of indirect labor.
      11   Sold on account product costing $3,500 for $5,200.
      16   Completed product costing $16,000 and transferred it to the warehouse.
      20   Requisitioned $7,000 of material for use in the factory; $5,900 was used as direct material and the remainder was used as indirect material.
      25   Applied $10,000 of manufacturing overhead cost to the product currently being worked on.
      29   Paid $400 cash for a special material component that was shipped via overnight delivery.
      31   Sold product costing $1,000 for $1,700 cash.

Required
Prepare general journal entries to record these transactions.

LO4   **P2-4B.**   **Journal Entries** Porter Manufacturing Company uses the perpetual inventory system to account for its manufacturing inventories. The following are Porter's transactions during September 2016:

Sept.   5   Received material costing $3,000 from a supplier. The material was purchased on account.
        9   Requisitioned $7,000 of material for use in the factory, consisting of $5,600 of direct material and $1,400 of indirect material.
       11   Recorded the factory payroll: $14,000 of direct labor and $2,000 of indirect labor
       17   Incurred various overhead costs totaling $15,000. (Credit Accounts Payable.)
       20   Applied $21,000 of manufacturing overhead to the products being manufactured.
       23   Completed product costing $17,000 and moved it to the warehouse.
       26   Sold goods with a product cost of $4,000 on account for $6,000.

Required
a.   Set up a T-account for the following four accounts and post the September 1, 2016, balance listed after the account title: Materials Inventory, $8,000; Work in Process Inventory, $26,000; Finished Goods Inventory, $11,000; and Cost of Goods Sold, $32,000.
b.   Record the transactions listed above in general journal form, post relevant portions to the four T-accounts, and balance the four accounts.

LO3   **P2-5B.**   **Total Manufacturing Costs, Income Statement, Unit Cost, and Selling Price** You are consulted by Investors, Inc., a group of investors planning a new product. They have estimates of the costs of materials, labor, overhead, and other expenses for 2016 but need to know how much to charge for each unit to earn a profit in 2016 equal to 10% of their estimated investment of $500,000 (ignore income taxes).

Their plans indicate that each unit of the new product requires the following:

Direct Material	4 lb. of a material costing $6 per lb.
Direct Labor	3 hrs. of a die cutter's time at $9 per hr.
	2 hrs. of an assembler's time at $8 per hr.

Major items of production overhead would be annual rent of $40,000 on the factory building and $25,000 on machinery as well as indirect material of $21,000. Other production overhead is an estimated 60% of total direct labor costs. Selling expenses are an estimated 20% of total sales, and non-factory administrative expenses are 10% of total sales.

The consensus at Investors is that during 2016 4,000 units of product should be produced for selling and another 1,000 units should be produced for the next year's beginning inventory. Also, an extra 6,000 pounds of material will be purchased as beginning inventory for the next year. Because of the nature of the manufacturing process, all units started must be completed, so work in process inventories are negligible.

Required

a. Incorporate the above data into a schedule of estimated total manufacturing costs and compute the unit production cost for 2016.

b. Prepare an estimated income statement that would provide the target amount of profit for 2016.

c. What unit sales price should Investors charge for the new product?

P2-6B. **Worksheet, Financial Statements, and Schedule of Cost of Goods Manufactured and Sold** The trial balance for the Niagara Boat-builders Corporation at the end of 2016 follows:

LO5
(Appendix 2A)

	Debit	Credit
Cash.	$ 40,000	
Accounts receivable.	151,200	
Allowance for uncollectible accounts.		$ 7,200
Materials inventory.	50,000	
Work in process inventory	44,000	
Finished goods inventory.	54,000	
Land	104,000	
Factory buildings	550,000	
Accumulated depreciation—Factory buildings		148,000
Factory machinery	740,000	
Accumulated depreciation—Factory machinery		108,000
Accounts payable.		128,400
Long-term notes payable—8%		216,000
Common stock, $100 par value		
(All outstanding)		360,000
Retained Earnings		510,000
Sales.		1,476,000
Factory Overhead.		58,000
Cost of Goods Sold	988,800	
Selling Expenses	175,600	
Non-factory Administrative Expense	114,000	
	$3,011,600	$3,011,600

The following information is available (adjusting entries have not been recorded):

1. Annual amounts of depreciation are factory buildings, $32,000 and factory machinery, $26,000.
2. Uncollectible accounts expense, 1% of sales. (Debit this expense to Selling Expenses.)
3. Estimated income taxes, $38,840.
4. January 1 inventories were materials, $64,000; work in process, $32,000; and finished goods, $80,000.
5. Additional data needed for schedule of cost of goods manufactured and sold:

Net delivered cost of materials purchased.	$416,000
Direct labor.	302,000
Indirect material	37,000
Indirect labor	111,000
Factory utilities.	31,800
Factory repairs and maintenance.	18,000
Factory property taxes.	24,000

Required

a. Prepare a worksheet for 2016.

b. Prepare an income statement.

c. Prepare a balance sheet.

d. Prepare a schedule of cost of goods manufactured and sold.

LO5
(Appendix 2A)

P2-7B. Worksheet, Income Statement, and Schedule of Cost of Goods Manufactured and Sold The following trial balance is of Hunter Company at December 31, 2016, together with the worksheet adjustments. Hunter Company uses perpetual inventory.

| | Trial Balance | | Adjustment | |
	Debit	Credit	Debit	Credit
Cash...........................	$ 34,000			
Materials inventory.................	78,000			
Work in process inventory...........	34,000			
Finished goods inventory............	66,000			
Prepaid insurance	10,000			(1) $ 5,000
Factory machinery	570,000			
Accumulated depreciation—				
Factory machinery		$ 48,000		(2) 22,400
Copyright	98,000			(3) 6,000
Accounts payable..................		154,000		
Common stock, $20 par value.........		224,000		
Retained earnings		156,000		
Sales...........................		1,900,000		
Factory overhead..................		22,400	(2) $22,400	
Cost of goods sold.................	1,294,400			
Sales salaries expense..............	134,000			
Advertising expense................	62,000			
Non-factory			(3) 6,000	
Expenses	124,000		(1) 5,000	
	2,504,400	2,504,400		
Income tax expenses...............			(4) 52,840	
Income tax payable				(4) 52,840
			86,240	86,240

Additional information:

1. January 1, 2016, inventories were materials, $68,000; work in process, $50,000; and finished goods, $84,000.
2. Net delivered cost of materials purchased was $504,000.
3. Direct labor was $490,000.
4. Manufacturing overhead included the following:

Indirect labor	186,000
Factory utilities..	26,000
Repairs and maintenance.......................................	12,000
Factory building rent	30,000
Indirect material	42,000

Required

a. Complete the worksheet.
b. Prepare an income statement.
c. Prepare a schedule of cost of goods manufactured and sold.

CERTIFIED MANAGEMENT ACCOUNTANT (CMA®) EXAM SAMPLE QUESTIONS

CMA2-1. All of the following would appear on a schedule of cost of goods manufactured except for

   a. ending work-in-process inventory.
   b. beginning finished goods inventory.
   c. the cost of raw materials used.
   d. applied manufacturing overhead.

CMA2-2. Given the following data for Scurry Company, what is the cost of goods sold?

Beginning inventory of finished goods....................	$100,000
Cost of goods manufactured............................	700,000
Ending inventory of finished goods	200,000
Beginning work-in-process inventory	300,000
Ending work-in-process inventory.......................	50,000

   a. $500,000
   b. $600,000
   c. $800,000
   d. $950,000

CMA2-3. Which one of the following items would not be considered a manufacturing cost?

   a.   Cream for an ice cream maker
   b.   Sales commissions for a car manufacturer
   c.   Plant property taxes for an ice cream maker
   d.   Tires for an automobile manufacturer

CMA2-4. Which one of the following refers to a cost that remains the same as the volume of activity decreases within the relevant range?

   a.   Average cost per unit
   b.   Variable cost per unit
   c.   Unit fixed cost
   d.   Total variable cost

CMA2-5. Taylor Corporation is determining the cost behavior of several items in order to budget for the upcoming year. Past trends have indicated the following dollars were spent at three different levels of output.

	Unit Levels		
	10,000	12,000	15,000
Cost A....................	$25,000	$29,000	$35,000
Cost B	10,000	15,000	15,000
Cost C	15,000	18,000	22,500

In establishing a budget for 14,000 units, Taylor should treat Costs A, B, and C, respectively, as

   a.   mixed, fixed, and variable.
   b.   variable, fixed, and variable.
   c.   mixed, mixed, and mixed.
   d.   variable, mixed, and mixed.

EXTENDING YOUR KNOWLEDGE

EYK2-1. **Business Decision Case** James Alvarez, an engineer, needs some accounting advice. In their spare time during the past year, Alvarez and his college-aged son, Robert, have manufactured a small weed-trimming sickle in a rented building near their home. Robert, who has had one accounting course in college, keeps the books.

    Alvarez is pleased about the results of their first year's operations. He asks you to look over the following income report prepared by Robert before they leave on a well-deserved vacation to Hawaii, after which they plan to expand their business significantly.

Sales (34,000 units at $10 each)		$340,000
Costs of producing 35,000 units:		
Materials:		
Precast blades at $1.50 each.	$ 57,000	
Preturned handles at $1 each.	40,000	
Labor costs of hired assemblers	26,600	
Labor costs of hired painters	33,000	
Rent on building	14,900	
Rent on machinery	7,100	
Utilities for production	8,000	
Other production costs	11,900	
Advertising expense.	26,200	
Sales commissions.	35,700	
Delivery of products to customers.	14,350	
Total costs	$274,750	
Less: Ending inventory of 1,000 units at average production		
costs of $7.85 (or $274,750/35,000 units)	7,850	
Cost of goods sold.		266,900
Net income.		$ 73,100

After you examine the income report, Alvarez responds to your questions and assures you that (1) no theft or spoilage of materials has occurred, (2) no partially completed units are involved, and (3) he and son Robert have averaged 30 hours each per week in the business for 50 weeks. Ignore income taxes in this situation.

Required

a. Identify any apparent discrepancy in the income report in the cost of materials used.

b. Recalculate the cost of goods manufactured, the average cost per unit produced, and the net income for the year.

c. What factors should James consider regarding the profitability of his venture before deciding to expand it significantly?

EYK2-2. **Apple's 2014 Environmental Responsibility Report can be found at the following link:** http://images.apple.com/environment/reports/docs/apple_environmental_responsibility_report_0714.pdf

Skim this report. Why do you think Apple is so transparent with regard to its environmental activity but so secretive regarding its product development?

EYK2-3. **Ethics Case** Great Cakes is a large bakery known for its quality "boxed cake" products. Its motto is "We Use Only the Best Ingredients." Ralph Sands, the purchasing supervisor, is responsible for ordering the ingredients for all the bakery products. He is being considered for a promotion based on his proven ability to purchase ingredients at the best price available.

The cost of all the ingredients has risen substantially over the past few months. Sands decides to purchase 25% of the ingredients at a lower quality than Great Cakes normally uses because the cost is significantly less. Without relying on the company's test kitchens, he believes this substitution will not be noticed by the customers and the lower cost will counterbalance the increased costs of the other ingredients.

Sands explains this decision to his friend, Lynn Pall, the company's accountant, one day at lunch. He also tells her that he does not intend to inform management of the inclusion of the lower-quality ingredients in the bakery's products.

Required

What ethical considerations arise from Ralph Sands' decisions? What problems face Lynn Pall because of his actions?

ANSWERS TO SELF-STUDY QUESTIONS:

1. c, (p. 20) 2. d, (p. 26) 3. b, (p. 33) 4. a, (p. 36) 5. b, (p. 33)

YOUR TURN! SOLUTIONS

Solution 2.1
Assembly labor
iPad case
Microprocessor
Touch screen

Solution 2.2
Assembly labor
Factory supervisor salary
Depreciation on the iPad factory
Touch-screen

DECISION TIME SOLUTION

Solution 2.1
d. All of the above.
Negotiating lower costs for the bike components with Fezzari's suppliers would likely be the most productive choice, since materials comprise approximately 60% of the total product cost. However, increasing the training of assembly technicians could result in increased productivity and reduced direct labor costs. Relocating the manufacturing facility might allow Fezzari to reduce the facility lease cost, thereby reducing overhead costs.

Cost Accounting Systems: Job Order Costing

PAST

Chapter 2 defined basic costing terminology and introduced different types of manufacturing inventories. It illustrated how costs flow through the inventories and explained the schedule of cost of goods manufactured.

PRESENT

Chapter 3 introduces and explains job costing in more detail for both manufacturing and service industries. It also explains overhead allocation.

FUTURE

Chapter 4 introduces process costing and how it differs from job order costing. It illustrates equivalent units and the flow of costs through the inventory accounts, as well as introduces the production cost report.

LEARNING OBJECTIVES

1. **Describe** the two basic types of cost accounting systems, **discuss** how they may be used in both manufacturing and nonmanufacturing environments, and **explain** the need for the timely determination of product costs. *(p. 66)*

2. **Explain** the need for a predetermined overhead rate, **demonstrate** its calculation, and **compare** annual and monthly rates. *(p. 69)*

3. **Describe** and **explain** a job order costing system, **identify** types of records used in job order costing, and **demonstrate** the journal entries that accompany the flow of product costs. *(p. 71)*

4. **Discuss** the procedures and journal entries used to account for finished goods and the sale of finished goods. *(p. 77)*

5. **Describe** the procedures for cost allocation for service departments. *(p. 82)*

6. **Contrast** plant-wide overhead rates and departmental overhead rates. *(p. 85)*

CH2M HILL: GLOBAL SERVICE PROVIDER

CH2M Hill is a U.S.-based consulting, design, construction, operation, and program management service firm that provides services to clients worldwide. In 2013, it ranked 415th on the Fortune 500 list of the largest U.S. companies. CH2M Hill has performed thousands of projects on six continents and in more than 180 countries.

CH2M Hill's projects are typically very large and complex. For example, CH2M Hill was hired for the Panama Canal Expansion Program. This project is intended to double the canal's capacity and allow it to accommodate the larger ships now used to transport goods around the world. CH2M Hill has responsibility to assist the Panama Canal Authority with construction management oversight, risk management, quality, and safety; to advise on design/engineering oversight; and to interface with the designer/builder of the new locks on both the Atlantic and Pacific sides of the canal.

Another massive project is CH2M Hill's task to replace the entire sanitary sewer system for the country of Singapore. CH2M Hill's role includes managing the installation of 90 kilometers of large conveyance tunnels under the entire island nation that will collect wastewater from multiple sewers for treatment at one of two treatment plants. The company is also responsible for the design and construction management of the first (and larger) of the two treatment plants.

Some of CH2M Hill's projects involve not just construction of massive facilities, but deconstruction as well. The Maine Yankee Atomic Power Company hired CH2M Hill to assist with the decommissioning of its nuclear power facility in Wiscasset, Maine. The decommissioning of a nuclear power facility involves complex challenges due to a variety of contaminants, including numerous radioactive isotopes. The decommissioning includes the demolition and removal of most structures on the site as well as the construction of a dry cask storage facility for used nuclear fuel.

CH2M Hill's client contracts typically take one of three forms: fixed-price contracts, where clients pay an agreed amount negotiated in advance for a specific scope of work; cost-plus contracts, where clients pay CH2M Hill's actual costs (direct and indirect) plus a fixed fee (profit); and time and materials contracts, where clients pay a negotiated hourly billing rate for the actual time spent on the project plus CH2M Hill's actual out-of-pocket costs.

As you think about the massive scale of these projects, you might wonder how CH2M Hill keeps track of all of the costs (materials, labor, and overhead) incurred over weeks, months, and even years. To properly track the costs and customer billings associated with each of its projects, CH2M Hill must use some very sophisticated job order costing systems!

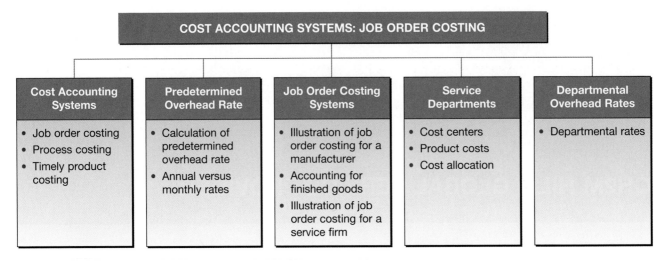

COST ACCOUNTING SYSTEMS

LO1 **Describe** the two basic types of cost accounting systems, **discuss** how they may be used in both manufacturing and nonmanufacturing environments, and **explain** the need for the timely determination of product costs.

Virtually all manufacturing and service firms have a cost accounting system consisting of forms, procedures, and records used to develop and report timely information about product and service costs. Any orderly method of developing product or service cost information constitutes a cost accounting system. Typically, some amount of cost is accumulated and related to some unit of activity or accomplishment. Examples include accumulating the cost of cutting and forming materials, assembling parts, and painting the final product that results in a completed unit of product such as a lawnmower, a computer, or a custom-designed executive jet aircraft, or the costs associated with CH2M Hill's overseeing the widening of the Panama Canal. Although a cost accounting system could be maintained independently of a firm's formal accounting system, most comprehensive cost accounting systems are integrated into the formal accounting system.

Cost accounting systems are usually illustrated for manufacturing situations involving product costs per unit. Note, however, that reliable cost-per-unit-of-production information is vital to managerial decision making in all types of entities, including service firms and governmental units. For example, a hospital may need to know the cost per patient of providing a specific surgical procedure, an insurance company may want to know the cost of providing health care insurance to a particular group, and a city may need to know the cost per ton of trash removal. Many of the cost accounting concepts and techniques that we discuss in this and subsequent chapters therefore apply to nonmanufacturing as well as manufacturing entities.

Two Basic Types Of Cost Accounting Systems

Job order costing systems and process costing systems are designed to develop timely information about product and job costs, manufacturing inventories, and per-unit costs.

A **job order costing system** is used for *customized* products and services. Therefore, job order costing is characterized by a series of *unique products* or *jobs* undertaken either to fill specific orders from customers or to produce a general stock of products from which future customer orders are filled. In a job order costing system, the costs of direct material, direct labor, and manufacturing overhead are accumulated separately for each job or product, as illustrated in **Exhibit 3-1**.

Job order costing is used by construction companies (to accumulate the cost of each construction project), printing companies

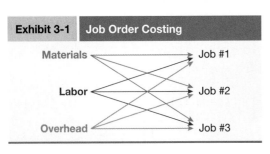

Exhibit 3-1 **Job Order Costing**

Materials → Job #1
Labor → Job #2
Overhead → Job #3

(to track the cost of each printing job), manufacturers of consumer products (to determine the cost per unit of each product manufactured), and hospitals (to determine the cost per patient). For example, CH2M Hill keeps track of the costs associated with its Singapore project separately from those associated with its Panama project.

A **process costing system** (**Exhibit 3-2**) lends itself to the production of a *large volume* of *homogenous products* manufactured in a continual flow operation, such as the distillation of fuels or manufacture of paint or wire. In these manufacturing contexts, the materials and operations are involved repetitively during each manufacturing period. Direct material, direct labor, and manufacturing overhead are accumulated by a production department or process for a period and then divided by the units produced during that period to calculate a per-unit cost. Assembly-line operations of entities such as breweries or flour mills and mass-production operations such as power plants and chemical companies would use process costing.

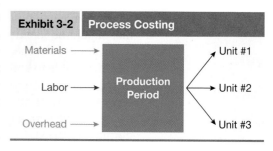

| Exhibit 3-2 | Process Costing |

Job order costing and process costing are two extremes along the spectrum of costing systems. A company will design its own accounting system to fit its particular needs. Many companies blend ideas from both job order costing and process costing systems.

Choosing a Cost Accounting System ACCOUNTING IN PRACTICE

Both job order and process costing systems allocate materials, labor, and overhead costs to determine unit costs. In a job order system, costs are identified with specific jobs or products, but a process costing system identifies costs with production processes and averages them over all jobs completed or products made during the period. The type of cost accounting system used by a particular company depends on the nature of the company's operations. One company may, in fact, use job order costing to account for one part of its operation and use process costing to account for another part of its operation. For example, Fezzari Performance Bicycles (introduced in Chapter 1) uses job costing for each unique bike order received. Yet, the manufacture of bicycle frames is accounted for using process costing because each frame of a particular size and model is identical.

Which costing system (job order or process) would most likely be used by the following industries?

Chemicals	Paints
Printing	Glass
Aircraft	Furniture
Oil refining	Machinery

YOUR TURN! 3.1

The solution is on page 109.

Timely Product Costing

Manufacturing Firms

A cost accounting system—either job order costing or process costing—must provide for the timely determination of product costs. Companies need to calculate product costs to determine work in process and finished goods inventory balances, which they report in periodic financial statements. In order to accurately calculate income, companies must develop a way to identify product costs for products sold and for products that remain on hand, either finished or unfinished.

Managers use engineering studies and cost analyses to establish budgets. They then compare actual product costs to budgets so that problems can be identified and remedial action can be taken when necessary. Managers also use product costs as one of the considerations in setting product prices.

To identify costs with a product or group of products, a manufacturer must trace production costs—direct material, direct labor, and manufacturing overhead—to products. To account for materials used, a company may keep track of the costs of materials requisitioned for production by job, product, or department. Labor costs can similarly be accounted for based on timekeeping records or by identifying a particular product or job with total payroll costs of personnel in the factory production departments. A manufacturing firm cannot, however, directly determine the amount of manufacturing overhead that should be identified with particular products or a group of products. The reason is quite simple: Overhead costs are accumulated during a particular accounting period, but it is impossible to know exactly how much overhead cost will accumulate until the *end* of the period. The problem is that companies need to assign product costs *during* the period *before* total overhead costs can be determined for the period. It isn't feasible to wait until the end of the period to determine total product costs to bill customers for jobs completed during the period. Consequently, firms typically assign manufacturing overhead costs to products during the period based on estimates by using predetermined overhead rates.

Service Firms

The same principles apply to a service company like CH2M Hill. CH2M Hill is also interested in the timely determination of the costs of its projects (or jobs) in order to prepare periodic financial reports and determine income or loss on each project.

Because CH2M Hill's projects typically extend more than a year in length, it is likely that it will have many projects that are in process at the end of each reporting period. Project managers may help to establish budgets, compare budgets to actual results, and take action to control project costs.

For example, the Panama Canal Expansion Program required CH2M Hill to trace labor costs for assigned project managers, engineers, and other consultants to this project over the course of several years. These individuals' salaries and benefits were assigned directly to the project for the period of their involvement on the project team. In addition, CH2M Hill traced other direct project costs to the project as well, such as team member travel, lodging, and meals incurred while working on the project. Corporate overhead was assigned to the project on a monthly basis to allow management to determine project profitability at any point in time.

YOUR TURN! 3.2

The solution is on page 109.

Why is manufacturing overhead assigned to products by using a predetermined overhead rate?

CORPORATE SOCIAL RESPONSIBILITY

Shortage of Highly Trained Engineers

As was noted in the opening vignette, CH2M Hill manages some massive engineering projects. Projects of this size and complexity involve many highly trained engineers. A problem that companies like CH2M Hill face is the acute shortage of engineering talent, especially among women, Hispanics, and African Americans, groups that will comprise a large percentage of the future workforce. As part of its corporate responsibility initiative, CH2M Hill is doing something about this pressing problem.

CH2M believes that "today's children are tomorrow's leaders" is a core tenet of sustainability. The company also understands how important it is to invest in future generations and to mentor them toward careers in engineering and science. CH2M Hill offers summer programs at no cost to the families that introduce their children to these important fields of study. As John Madia, CH2M Hill's chief human resources officer, states, "For most kids, particularly children of color and girls, STEM [Science, Technology, Engineering, and Mathematics] learning opens minds and doors where they have few role models. In helping to grow a diverse pool of future talent, our firm benefits by putting into practice our values of creating partnerships to help sustain and build better communities."

Source: CH2MHILL 2014 Sustainability and Corporate Citizenship Report

PREDETERMINED OVERHEAD RATES

Predetermined manufacturing overhead rates are so named because (1) they are calculated prior to the beginning of each accounting period; (2) they deal with production overhead, that is, all production costs other than direct material and direct labor; and (3) they are usually stated in terms of a rate, such as $20 per direct labor hour. Before the beginning of each year, management normally prepares budgets. Included in the total budget is a production budget, which estimates utilization of the firm's productive capacity in terms of a common measure of activity. Traditionally, firms have used volume measures that are already being recorded for other purposes, such as direct labor hours (recorded for payroll) and machine hours (recorded for depreciation). More recently, more sophisticated and detailed measures have been implemented by some firms, as discussed briefly later in this chapter and in more detail in Chapter 5. Also included in the total budget is an estimate of overhead costs for the year.

LO2 Explain the need for a predetermined overhead rate, **demonstrate** its calculation, and **compare** annual and monthly rates.

TAKEAWAY 3.1

If a company's predetermined manufacturing overhead rate is $20 per direct labor hour, this means that every time an actual direct labor hour is incurred, $20 in overhead is added or applied to work in process inventory and removed from the overhead account.

Multiple Predetermined Overhead Rates   **ACCOUNTING IN PRACTICE**

Often, companies calculate more than one predetermined manufacturing overhead rate for a given period. For example, some firms will calculate a predetermined variable overhead rate and a predetermined fixed overhead rate. Why? Doing so allows management to evaluate a production department's control of costs that are expected to vary with the level of production (often within the control of local management) separately from those costs that are related to the capacity to do work (often fixed in nature and largely out of local management's hands).

Calculation of Predetermined Overhead Rate

A **predetermined manufacturing overhead rate** is computed by dividing the budgeted or estimated total overhead cost for the year by the budgeted or estimated level of the application base. The application base is simply the activity used to assign overhead. This application base is generally the **cost driver** most closely related to the accumulation of overhead costs. This cost driver is typically the utilization of the facility's productive capacity for the year (such as total estimated direct labor hours or total estimated machine hours). Calculations of predetermined rates are typically based on one-year production periods, but they could be calculated based on shorter horizons, such as quarterly or monthly production periods. Companies should choose the application base that corresponds to the period over which activity decisions are typically made.

Assume that the most appropriate measure of activity for applying overhead at CH2M Hill is direct labor hours. If CH2M's management estimates 50 million direct labor hours for 2016 and the estimated total manufacturing overhead cost for 2016 is $2,200 million, the overhead rate for 2016 may be calculated as follows:

$$\text{2016 Predetermined manufacturing overhead rate} = \frac{\text{Estimated overhead cost for 2016}}{\text{Estimated direct labor hours for 2016}}$$

$$= \frac{\$2,200 \text{ million}}{50 \text{ million hours}}$$

$$= \$44 \text{ per direct labor hour}$$

Hint: *Applied overhead is a product of the predetermined overhead rate and actual hours for that job, not budgeted hours.*

If, during March 2016, a particular project requires 1,000 direct labor hours, $44,000 of manufacturing overhead (1,000 × $44) would be assigned to this project.

Before selecting the allocation base for applying overhead to products or projects, a firm should carefully analyze the relationship between overhead incurred and various alternative measures of activity. Direct labor hours or direct labor costs would be used as the measure of activity in a service company that has labor-intensive projects. However, in a factory in which automation has replaced many of the production workers, machine hours may be a more appropriate measure.

Using a predetermined overhead rate, management can estimate the overhead costs of any job at any stage of production, computing "costs to date" both for control purposes and for inventory costing. This method also eliminates wide fluctuations in unit costs that might result if actual recorded overhead costs were assigned to products during short interim periods when production departed markedly from normal levels.

TAKEAWAY 3.2

The total estimated overhead divided by the total estimated activity level of the application base (such as machine hours or direct labor hours) equals the predetermined overhead rate. Management tries to select an activity base that is common to all of the jobs that the company produces.

YOUR TURN! 3.3

The solution is on page 109.

Assume you own a manufacturing company that budgets an estimated $250,000 in overhead for the coming year and 10,000 direct labor hours. Also assume your manufacturing overhead application base is direct labor hours. Actual overhead during the year amounts to $216,000 and employees work 9,000 actual direct labor hours. Compute the predetermined overhead rate and the amount of overhead that is applied to work in process inventory.

Annual versus Monthly Rates

Assume, for example, that normal production is 100,000 direct labor hours per year and that production fluctuates seasonally throughout the year. Suppose also that a large share of actual manufacturing overhead cost is spread fairly evenly over the year. (Such costs as depreciation, maintenance, utilities, and supervisory costs remain fairly constant from month to month.) **Exhibit 3-3** illustrates the possible differences between assigned

Exhibit 3-3	Comparison of Actual Monthly and Predetermined Annual Overhead Rates			
	Manufacturing Overhead Costs Incurred Each Month*	**Direct Labor Hours Worked Each Month**	**Actual Monthly Overhead Rates**	**Predetermined Annual Overhead Rate**
January.......	$ 9,900	4,000	$2.48	$1.50
February......	$ 9,300	3,000	$3.10	$1.50
March........	$ 10,500	5,000	$2.10	$1.50
April	$ 12,300	8,000	$1.54	$1.50
May..........	$ 14,100	11,000	$1.28	$1.50
June	$ 14,700	12,000	$1.23	$1.50
July.........	$ 16,500	15,000	$1.10	$1.50
August	$ 15,300	13,000	$1.18	$1.50
September	$ 13,500	10,000	$1.35	$1.50
October	$ 12,300	8,000	$1.54	$1.50
November.....	$ 11,100	6,000	$1.85	$1.50
December.....	$ 10,500	5,000	$2.10	$1.50
	$150,000	100,000		

*Assumed to be $7,500 each month plus 60 cents per direct labor hour.

overhead costs based on actual monthly overhead rates and those based on an annual overhead rate. The predetermined annual rate in this example is $1.50 per direct labor hour ($150,000/100,000 direct labor hours). The actual monthly rates vary from $3.10 in February to $1.10 in July, with only the months of April and October close to the annual average of $1.50 per direct labor hour. Using actual monthly rates and assuming that a particular unit of product requires 3 direct labor hours, a unit produced in July when production activity was highest would be assigned overhead costs of $3.30 (3 × $1.10). In contrast, a unit produced in February when production activity was lowest would be assigned overhead costs of $9.30 (3 × $3.10). The $6 difference is hardly defensible, especially when the two units of product may be virtually identical. The use of a predetermined overhead rate employing a yearly average produces more meaningful unit-cost figures.

JOB ORDER COSTING SYSTEMS

Job order costing systems are designed to accumulate product costs—direct material, direct labor, and manufacturing overhead—by job and in total. **Exhibit 3-4** illustrates the flow of the documents in a job order costing system that might be used by Fezzari for an order of a high-end triathlon/time-trial bike.

LO3 Describe and explain a job order costing system, **identify** types of records used in job order costing, and **demonstrate** the journal entries that accompany the flow of product costs.

When the customer places the order for the bike, Fezzari would create a **sales order** specifying the bike model and customer-specified options. Based on this sales order, the assembly department would create a **production order** directing the assembly employees to build the bike in accordance with the customer's specifications. Before assembly can begin, the assembly technician must gather the correct parts together. This is done based on a **bill of materials**, or list of each required part for the particular bike model. The technician creates a **materials requisition**,

Exhibit 3-4	Flow of Documents in a Job Costing System

Sales Order → Production Order and Bill of Materials → Materials Requisition / Time Record / Manufacturing Overhead Application Rates

Job Order Cost Sheet

Customer —————— Job No. ——————
Product —————— Date Promised ——————
Quantity —————— Date Started ——————
    Date Completed ——————

Direct Materials		Direct Labor			Manufacturing Overhead			
Req No	Amount	Time Sheet Date	Department	Amount	Time Sheet Date	Hours	Rate	Amount

Cost Summary	
Direct material	
Direct labor	
Manufacturing overhead	
Direct packaging costs	
Total cost	
Units	
Unit cost	

requesting that the bike components on the bill of materials be pulled from inventory and brought to the assembly station. As the technician assembles the bike, she would keep track of her time on a **time record**, either in written form on a timesheet or electronically through a time clock. As the job progresses, the materials used, labor expended, and overhead applied would be accumulated on a **job order cost sheet**. A job order cost sheet is a record of the materials, labor, and overhead for each job and serves as a subsidiary record or subset of the work in process account. When the bike is finished, the job order cost sheet would be closed.

Illustration of Job Order Costing for a Manufacturer

Almost 40 million Americans age seven and older ride a bike six times or more in a given year. The U.S. bicycle industry has been remarkably stable at $6 billion in sales since 2003, with a slight dip in 2013 due to the U.S. recession. Approximately 11.3 million bicycles of wheel sizes over 20" were imported or produced domestically in 2013. It is estimated that 99% of these bikes were imported from China and Taiwan. Domestic bike manufacturers, over 100 in all, produce approximately 56,000 units per year. Department, discount, and chain toy stores sell approximately 74% of the bikes sold, followed by specialty local bike shops (LBSs) at 15%, chain sporting goods stores at 6.5%, outdoor specialty retailers at 2.5%, and "other" at 2%.[1]

Fezzari Performance Bicycles is a U.S. bike manufacturer that builds both mountain bikes and road bikes. Located in Lindon, Utah, it sells a few thousand bikes per year, from a $500 entry-level mountain and hybrid bike to a high-end full-suspension mountain bike and triathlon bike that sells for over $10,000. As described in Chapter 1, once a customer selects a specific bike model and components, Fezzari orders the required parts from its suppliers. Fezzari maintains a minimal quantity of parts in inventory so that the bike assembly can be started without waiting for ordered parts to arrive. A technician assembles the bike to the customer's specifications, tunes it up, and then test rides it to ensure that it works properly. A second technician then checks the assembly, testing every screw and component, then checks the tune-up, and performs a second test ride. The bike is then sent to packing to be prepared for shipment.

We now turn to a comprehensive illustration of job order costing, which provides a conjectural example of how Fezzari's job costing system works. In this illustration, we make the following assumptions:

Hint: A bill of materials is a list of all parts or components needed for the manufacture of the finished product.

1. Fezzari receives a sales order for a high-end triathlon/time-trial bike, the T5.

2. A production order is then issued, along with the related bill of materials necessary to produce the T5.

3. The bill of materials, or list of parts, for the T5 is as shown in **Exhibit 3-5**.

4. It takes one Fezzari technician eight hours to assemble and test the bike and a second technician two hours to perform a quality check.

5. Fezzari uses a predetermined overhead rate of $17 per hour based on annual direct labor hours to assign overhead to products.

---

[1] http://nbda.com/articles/industry-overview-2013-pg34.htm

Exhibit 3-5	Bill of Materials - T5			
Item	**Description**	**Quantity**	**Cost**	**Extension**
Frame	Fezzari Racing Design FA1 3K Monocoque Carbon Aero TT Frame...	1	$4,000	$4,000
Fork	Fezzari Racing XrA 3K Aero Fork, Carbon Steerer Tube............	1	integrated	
Headset	Cane Creek Orbit IS-2 7075/T6 Crown Race, 1⅛" Steerer Tube......	1	integrated	
Shifters	Shimano Dura-Ace 9000, 22 Speed.........................	2	$ 350	$ 700
Shift cables		2	$ 15	$ 30
Front Derailleur	Shimano Dura-Ace 9000, Brazed On	1	$ 70	$ 70
Rear Derailleur	Shimano Dura-Ace 9000, short cage (22 speed)	1	$ 140	$ 140
Cassette	Shimano Dura-Ace 9000	1	$ 175	$ 175
Crank	Vision Trimax Carbon	1	$ 350	$ 350
Chainrings	FSA BB30 Trimax 54/39t	1	$ 60	$ 60
Bottom Bracket	FSA BB30 Ceramic	1	$ 30	$ 30
Chain	Shimano Dura-Ace 9000	1	$ 35	$ 35
Handlebars	Vision Trimax Carbon	1	$ 190	$ 190
Stem	Fezzari Ultra Light	1	$ 90	$ 90
Tape/Grips	Fizik	1	$ 18	$ 18
Saddle	Fizik Arione Tri 2.....................................	1	$ 100	$ 100
Seatpost	Fezzari Racing Design XrTT Aero 3K Carbon	1	integrated	
Rims	Reynolds 90 Areo, Carbon Clinchers.......................	2	$1,200	$2,400
Hubs	Reynolds 90 Areo, Carbon Clinchers.......................	2	included	
Spokes	Reynolds 90 Areo, Carbon Clinchers.......................	36	included	
Tires	Maxxis Xenith Hors Categorie M-201, 700 x 23c, race tire..........	2	$ 90	$ 180
Tubes	Fezzari Performance Road Tubes	2	$ 7	$ 14
Brakes	Shimano Dura-Ace 9000	2	$ 15	$ 30
Brake Levers	Vision Metro Cargon...................................	2	$ 50	$ 100
Brake Cables		2	$ 13	$ 26
				$8,738

Accounting for Materials

For a high-end bike like the T5, Fezzari orders the frame from its Taiwanese supplier and the tires and other components from other local suppliers upon receipt of the order. Thus, the first transaction to record is the *purchase* of materials. Fezzari purchased parts listed on the bill of materials for a total cost of $8,738. Following is the entry to record this purchase:

1	Materials inventory	8,738	
	Accounts payable		8,738
	To record the purchase of materials.		

The next transaction is the *requisition* of the following materials from the materials inventory for use in the production of the T5: $4,000 for the frame, $700 for the shifters, $30 for the shift cables, and so forth. **Exhibit 3-6** shows a sample requisition for a Fezzari T5.

Assume that in addition to the direct materials listed on the bill of materials, the assembly of the T5 requires $30 of indirect materials (lubricants, bar end plugs, etc.). The entry to record the requisitioning and use of both direct and indirect materials is as follows:

2	Work in process inventory	8,738	
	Manufacturing overhead	30	
	Materials inventory		8,768
	To record the requisitioning of materials—both direct and indirect.		

Hint: A materials requisition form is a list of items to be pulled from inventory for use in manufacturing a product.

Exhibit 3-6	Materials Requisition Form			

Date 8/5		Job. No. 372		Requisition No. 567

	Quantity			
Item	Authorized	Issued	Unit Price	Amount
Frame	1	1	$4,000	$4,000
Fork	1	1	integrated	
Headset	1	1	integrated	
Shifters	2	2	$ 350	$ 700
Shift cables.	2	2	$ 15	$ 30
Front Derailleur.	1	1	$ 70	$ 70
Rear Derailleur	1	1	$ 140	$ 140
Cassette	1	1	$ 175	$ 175
Crank	1	1	$ 350	$ 350
Chainrings	1	1	$ 60	$ 60
Bottom Bracket	1	1	$ 30	$ 30
Chain	1	1	$ 35	$ 35
Handlebars.	1	1	$ 190	$ 190
Stem.	1	1	$ 90	$ 90
Tape/Grips	1	1	$ 18	$ 18
Saddle	1	1	$ 100	$ 100
Seatpost.	1	1	integrated	
Rims	2	2	$1,200	$2,400
Hubs.	2	2	included	
Spokes	36	36	included	
Tires	2	2	$ 90	$ 180
Tubes	2	2	$ 7	$ 14
Brakes	2	2	$ 15	$ 30
Brake Levers	2	2	$ 50	$ 100
Brake Cables	2	2	$ 13	$ 26
Total				$8,738

Authorized by: TC   Issued by: GAP   Received by: CB

The effect of the various postings of these transactions is shown in **Exhibit 3-7**. The amount of direct materials used would also be recorded on the job order cost sheet for Job 372 (see **Exhibit 3-11**).

Exhibit 3-7	Entries for Recording the Acquisition and Use of Materials

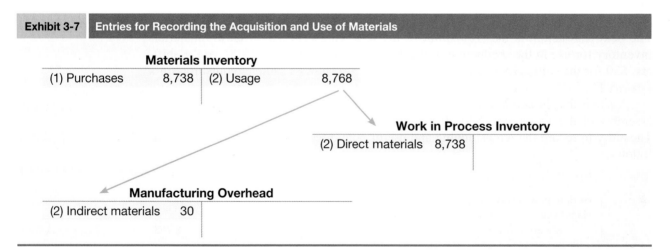

Materials Inventory

(1) Purchases   8,738 | (2) Usage   8,768

Work in Process Inventory

(2) Direct materials   8,738 |

Manufacturing Overhead

(2) Indirect materials   30 |

Accounting for Labor

Manufacturing firms (including Fezzari) typically use **time clocks** or time records to collect the total amount of time that each employee worked during a particular pay period. **Exhibit 3-8** shows a sample time record for a Fezzari employee.

Exhibit 3-8	Time Record						
Employee Name: Robert						Employee No. 42	
Skill Specification:		Technician			Date:	8/5	
Time Started	Time Stopped	Total Time	Hourly Labor Rate	Department	Job No.	Total Cost	
8:00	12:00	4	$25	Assembly	372	$100	
1:00	5:00	4	$25	Assembly	372	$100	
Total		8				$200	
Approved by *LSH*							

Hint: A time record is a method of recording and organizing time spent on a product or job.

Time clocks collect only total time worked; time records collect hours worked on particular jobs. Time clocks and computer time records are used to prepare the payroll recorded in Wages Payable.

Tracking Time   ACCOUNTING IN PRACTICE

In practice, companies use various methods to track employees' time. Where employees are paid on an hourly-rate basis for hours worked, time clocks are used. In some firms, employees place a small paper card in the time clock at the beginning and end of their work shift, and the card is imprinted (or "punched") with the date and time. More commonly, employees slide or wave an employee ID card through or in front of a card reader that records the date and time information. The most recent innovation in tracking employees' time involves a device that recognizes an employee's fingerprint, iris, or face, eliminating the need for a physical card of any kind. Where employees are salaried, but there is a need to attribute hours worked to a particular job or product for costing purposes, time records are used. Employees record the amount of time that they spend each day working on a particular job or jobs so that customers can be billed the appropriate amount for labor.

Assume that Fezzari uses time records to identify labor costs with specific jobs. Hourly wage rates are used to compute the labor costs for the various products assembled. The sum of the amounts calculated using the time records should equal the total wages payable for the period. In fact, the amounts calculated from the time records are used to distribute the wages payable to the individual jobs. To assemble the T5, $200 (8 hours × $25 per hour) of direct labor was incurred. The entry to record the distribution of the wages payable is as follows:

3	Work in process inventory	200	
	Wages payable		200
	To distribute the wages payable.		

The effect of the posting of this transaction is shown in **Exhibit 3-9**. The amount of direct labor incurred would also be recorded on the job order cost sheet for Job 372 (see **Exhibit 3-11**).

Exhibit 3-9 | Entries for Recording and Distributing Labor

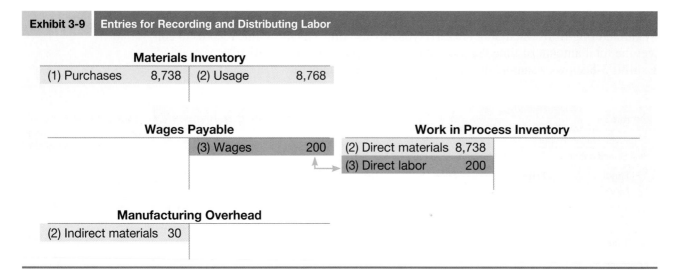

Accounting for Manufacturing Overhead

Factory costs are routinely charged to manufacturing overhead as incurred or through adjusting entries at the end of the accounting period. One of the elements of manufacturing overhead—indirect materials—has already been recorded through the transactions related to materials. Other general manufacturing overhead costs incurred by Fezzari during the period are recorded as they are incurred: indirect labor, $28,000; factory utilities, $31,000; factory lease, $100,000; factory insurance, $68,000; factory property taxes, $12,000; and other manufacturing overhead, $13,000. Manufacturing overhead to be recorded as a year-end adjustment is depreciation on the factory equipment of $45,100. The following are the journal entries to record these items:

4	Manufacturing overhead	252,000	
	Cash, Accounts payable, or Wages payable		252,000
	To record elements of manufacturing overhead as incurred.		

5	Manufacturing overhead	45,100	
	Accumulated depreciation—factory equipment		45,100
	To record depreciation on factory equipment.		

As explained previously, actual manufacturing overhead costs are not assigned directly to individual jobs. Instead, through the use of a predetermined overhead rate, the work in process inventory account is charged with manufacturing overhead applied. During the budgeting process, Fezzari determined its predetermined overhead rate to be $17 per direct labor hour. The T5 order accumulated 8 hours of direct labor. As a result, $136 of manufacturing overhead is applied to the job.

The journal entry to record the application of manufacturing overhead to Job 372 is as follows:

6	Work in process inventory	136	
	Manufacturing overhead		136
	To record the application of manufacturing overhead to the work in		
	process inventory using the predetermined overhead rate.		

The effect of the various postings of these transactions is shown in **Exhibit 3-10**. The amount of overhead applied would also be recorded on the job order cost sheet for Job 372 (see **Exhibit 3-11**).

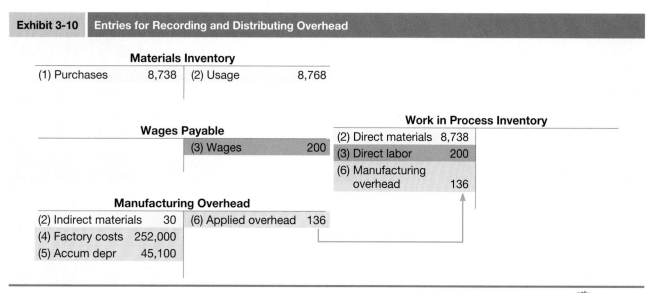

| Exhibit 3-10 | Entries for Recording and Distributing Overhead |

Materials Inventory

| (1) Purchases | 8,738 | (2) Usage | 8,768 |

Wages Payable

| | | (3) Wages | 200 |

Manufacturing Overhead

(2) Indirect materials	30	(6) Applied overhead	136
(4) Factory costs	252,000		
(5) Accum depr	45,100		

Work in Process Inventory

(2) Direct materials	8,738
(3) Direct labor	200
(6) Manufacturing overhead	136

Accounting For Packaging and Finished Goods

When products are finished, they are transferred from Work in Process Inventory to Finished Goods Inventory. The costs transferred from Work in Process to Finished Goods Inventory include all manufacturing costs. However, these costs also include packaging costs.

LO4 **Discuss** the procedures and journal entries used to account for finished goods and the sale of finished goods.

| Treatment of Packaging Costs | ACCOUNTING IN PRACTICE |

A product is not complete or finished until it is packaged in the container in which it will be sold. Packaging costs are part of the product cost transferred to the Finished Goods Inventory account.

Fezzari spends two hours to inspect, partially dissemble, and package the T5 for shipment to the customer. The two hours of inspecting are recorded in a time record at a pay rate of $25 per hour. Approximately $75 is required for the shipment container and packing materials. The packing materials are purchased on account and immediately placed into Work in Process. Remember that Fezzari applies overhead based on direct labor hours. Thus, Fezzari would also record $34 (2 hours × $17 per hour) to Work in Process Inventory. The total packaging costs applied to Work in Process is $125.

7	Work in process inventory	50	
	Cash and wages payable		50
	To record the packaging labor for Job 372.		
8	Work in process inventory	75	
	Accounts payable		75
	To record the cost of packing material for Job 372.		
9	Work in process inventory	34	
	Manufacturing overhead		34
	To record the application of manufacturing overhead to the work in process inventory using the predetermined overhead rate.		

When the T5 bike order is completed, the unit cost of the T5 is obtained by summing the costs charged to the job. **Exhibit 3-11** shows the completed job cost sheet for Fezarri's Job 372. The job cost sheet accumulates all product costs for the job including; direct material, direct labor, manufacturing overhead and packaging. The report also identifies the total unit cost of $9,233. Notice that this amount also matches the total of the debits to the work in process inventory account in **Exhibit 3-12**. The accountant credits Work in Process Inventory and debits Finished Goods Inventory for the total cost of the job completed. The journal entry to record the completion of the T5 is as follows:

10	Finished goods inventory	9,233	
	Work in process inventory		9,233
	To record the completion of Job 372.		

Exhibit 3-11	Fezzari's Job Cost Sheet for Job No. 372

Fezzari Job Cost Sheet

Customer	Ryan Hobson		Job No.	372
Product	T5		Date Promised	5/15
Quantity	1		Date Started	8/1
			Date Completed	8/6

Direct Materials		Direct Labor			Manufacturing Overhead			
Req No	Amount	Time Sheet Date	Department	Amount	Time Sheet Date	Hours	Rate	Amount
567	$8,738	8/5	Assembly	$200	8/5	8	$17/DLH	$136

Cost Summary	
Direct material	$8,738
Direct labor	$200
Manufacturing overhead	$136
Total packaging costs	$159*
Total cost	**$9,233**
Units	1
Unit cost	$9,233

*Total packaging costs include materials of $75, labor of $50, and overhead of $34.

When the T5 is delivered to the customer, the cost of the bike is removed from the finished goods subaccount. Two journal entries are recorded. The first entry is a debit to Accounts Receivable and a credit to Sales for the selling price of the bike. The second entry is a debit to Cost of Goods Sold and a credit to Finished Goods Inventory for the cost of the bike. The entries to record the sale of the T5 are as follows:

11	Accounts receivable	10,500	
	Sales		10,500
	To record the sale of Job 372.		

12	Cost of goods sold	9,233	
	Finished goods inventory		9,233
	To record the cost of Job 372.		

The effect of the various postings of these transactions is shown in **Exhibit 3-12**. Note that entry 11 is not shown in this exhibit because it involves the revenue associated with the sale, not the cost of the job. The job order cost sheet for Job 372 would also be closed.

Exhibit 3-12	Entries for Completing the Job and Recording the Sale

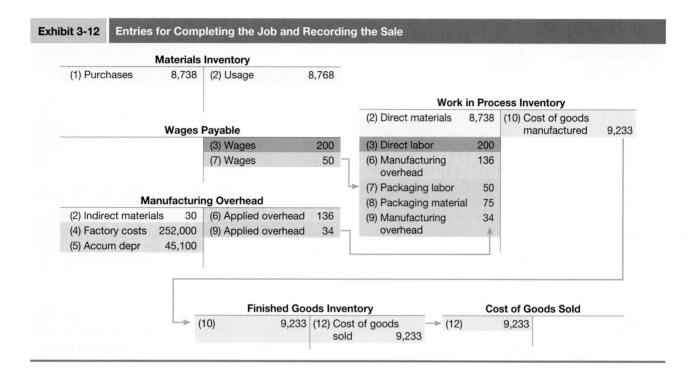

Disposition of Under- and Overapplied Overhead

As introduced in Chapter 2 and described earlier in this chapter, overhead costs are accumulated in the manufacturing overhead account during an accounting period (usually a year). During the same period, overhead costs are being applied to products or jobs based on a predetermined overhead rate. It is not until the end of the period, after all actual overhead costs have been recorded and all overhead has been applied to products and jobs, that management determines whether the amount of overhead applied to products and jobs is greater or less than the amount of actual overhead costs recorded. If more has been applied than recorded, overhead is said to be **overapplied**. If less has been applied than recorded, overhead is said to be **underapplied**.

At year-end, a journal entry is made to dispose of the underapplied or overapplied amount of manufacturing overhead. If the amount of underapplied or overapplied overhead is insignificant, an entry is made to transfer the amount to the cost of goods sold account. The under- or overapplied overhead is almost always immaterial in practice. An overapplied amount is transferred by debiting Manufacturing Overhead and crediting Cost of Goods Sold. An underapplied amount is transferred by debiting Cost of Goods Sold and crediting Manufacturing Overhead.

When the under- or overapplied amount is significant, it should be allocated to all of the jobs that were worked on during the year. This is accomplished by a journal entry that transfers the amount to Work in Process Inventory, Finished Goods Inventory, and Cost of Goods Sold. An overapplied amount is transferred by debiting Manufacturing Overhead and crediting Work in Process Inventory, Finished Goods Inventory, and Cost of Goods Sold. An underapplied amount is transferred by debiting Work in Process Inventory, Finished Goods Inventory, and Cost of Goods Sold sold and crediting Manufacturing Overhead. The amount transferred is allocated proportionately among Work in Process Inventory, Finished Goods Inventory, and Cost of Goods Sold based on the amount of Applied Overhead that is in each of the three accounts at the end of the year.

Hint: After the disposition of over- or underapplied overhead, the balance in the overhead account should be $0.

Because the estimated manufacturing overhead and/or the estimated activity level used in the predetermined overhead rate will differ from actual manufacturing overhead and/or actual activity, the manufacturing overhead applied to work in process will be under- or overapplied. What should management do with this under- or overapplied overhead amount?

  a. Add/subtract from cost of goods sold.
  b. Allocate among work in process inventory, finished goods inventory, and cost of goods sold.
  c. Either *a* or *b*, depending on the significance of the amount.

TAKEAWAY 3.3

After the disposition of over- or underapplied overhead to cost of goods sold or cost of goods sold and the inventory accounts, cost of goods sold should be the correct amount. Management may apply overhead during the year in an amount that differs from what the company actually incurs, but at the end of the year, the cost of the company's products as reported on the income statement is as accurate as management can make it.

Exhibit 3-13 reflects the various postings of the journal entries related to manufacturing overhead. Items from entries 4, 5, 6, and 9 are highlighted in bold type. In addition, assume that an additional $292,280 in manufacturing overhead was applied to other jobs throughout the year. Note that the sum of the debits in manufacturing overhead is $297,130 but that the sum of the credits is $292,450. In other words, actual factory costs were $297,130, but only $292,450 of manufacturing overhead was applied to the work in process inventory account. Therefore, overhead was underapplied by $4,680. Assume that this amount is insignificant.

The journal entry to record the transfer of the underapplied overhead is as follows:

13	Cost of goods sold	4,680	
	Manufacturing overhead		4,680
	To record the disposition of underapplied overhead.		

When perpetual inventory procedures are used in cost accounting systems, the ending balances in Materials Inventory, Work in Process Inventory, and Finished Goods Inventory reflect all the transactions of the accounting period that increase and decrease inventories. These ending balances are adjusted only if a discrepancy is discovered when the year-end physical counts of inventory are taken.

Exhibit 3-13	Entries for Closing Underapplied Overhead

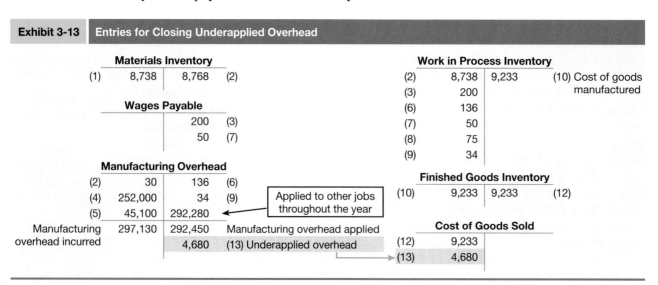

As illustrated in the Fezzari example in **Exhibits 2-12, 13**, and **14** of Chapter 2, the entries shown in the accounts in **Exhibit 3-13** could be used to create a Schedule of Cost of Goods Manufactured and a Schedule of Cost of Goods Sold for the T5. Together with other information about sales and costs of Fezzari's other products and selling and administrative expenses, Fezzari management could then prepare an Income Statement for the period.

Illustration of Job Order Costing for a Service Firm

Job order costing is also used by service companies. An abbreviated illustration using a CH2M Hill project will demonstrate the use of job order costing in a service environment.

One of the services that CH2M Hill provides to clients is assistance with implementation of lean enterprise solutions. Essentially, CH2M Hill utilizes proven approaches and methods to streamline client manufacturing and office processes. One such client was the Perrier Group of America. The objective of the CH2M Hill project was to determine the optimal location for a new bottling facility needed for projected five-year sales growth in the company's Northeast Region. CH2M Hill evaluated Perrier's entire supply chain, from the spring to the customer. The result of the project was the determination of new raw materials requirements to support projected growth, the optimal location of the bottling facility, and the amount and location of additional warehouse facilities to support increased sales during peak periods of the year.

Accounting for Materials

Because this project was for services, no materials were used. This is typical of service projects.

Accounting for Labor

CH2M Hill's project manager, engineers, and consultants recorded their time working on the Perrier project on a time record or timesheet. These employees also worked on other projects during the same period and recorded the time worked on those projects separately. Assume that during one period, the assigned employees worked a total of 40 hours on the Perrier project and that the portion of their salaries associated with the time spent on the Perrier project was $5,000. This would have been recorded as follows:

Work in process—Perrier	5,000	
Salaries payable		5,000
To record salaries on the Perrier project.		

Accounting for Overhead

Assume that CH2M Hill uses a predetermined overhead rate for consulting engagements of $150 per hour. Because 40 hours of labor was charged to the Perrier project for the period, a total of $6,000 ($150 × 40 hours) of overhead would have been applied to the project. The entry to record the application of overhead is the same as shown earlier for Fezzari:

Work in process—Perrier	6,000	
Overhead		6,000
To record the application of overhead to the Perrier project using the		
predetermined overhead rate.		

Recording the Sale

Recall that with the completion of a product, the accumulated cost of the product is moved from work in process inventory to finished goods inventory. However, service companies do not have a finished goods inventory. Instead, when a project is completed, the accumulated cost of the service is removed from work in process inventory as the final project invoice is prepared. In our illustration, assume that when CH2M Hill completed the project, the Work in Process—Perrier account had a total balance of $245,000 and that the contract between CH2M Hill and Perrier was for $300,000. CH2M Hill would have recorded the following journal entries in its financial records:

Accounts receivable	300,000	
Sales		300,000
To record the final billing for the Perrier project.		
Cost of goods sold	245,000	
Work in process—Perrier		245,000
To record the cost of the Perrier project.		

ACCOUNTING FOR SERVICE DEPARTMENTS

LO5 **Describe** the procedures for cost allocation for service departments.

Most factories are so large and so complex that a high degree of organizational specialization naturally exists in their operations. Production usually involves a series of specialized departments, such as cutting, reshaping, grinding, subassembly, final assembly, painting, and packaging. In addition to these production departments, a typical factory also has highly specialized service departments, which may be involved with purchasing, materials handling, personnel, warehousing, inspection, maintenance, and even food service (cafeterias). Whereas production departments work directly on products, service departments provide production departments with support services that contribute indirectly to the completion of products.

Service Departments as Cost Centers

Service departments are often viewed by management as cost centers. That is, the costs of each service department are accumulated separately so management can identify the total cost of such services. Also, unit costs for each service—such as maintenance cost per square foot of floor space—can be derived for comparison with other operating periods and/or other sources of the service such as outside contractors. Most accounting systems account for service departments as cost centers.

Service Department Costs as Product Costs

Although service departments do not perform actual work on specific products, they do provide essential services to the production departments. Thus, service department costs are appropriately considered among the related production department costs and are included in final product costs as part of manufacturing overhead.

TAKEAWAY 3.4

Departments can be divided into two broad classes:

1. Operating or production departments where the main purpose of the organization is carried out, such as the machining department
2. Service departments that assist the activities of operating or production departments, such as maintenance or emergency medical services

By their nature, service departments do not use direct materials or direct labor. Their costs are part of manufacturing overhead. These departments do not work directly on a product, so overhead rates, in the strict sense, are not computed for them. Instead, service department costs become part of product costs by being allocated among several production departments, according to the approximate benefits received by each production department. Service department costs become part of each production department's overhead to be applied to Work in Process.

The T-account diagram (with typical titles and amounts) in **Exhibit 3-14** illustrates how service department costs (1) are accumulated on a cost center basis, (2) are allocated to one or more production departments, and (3) become part of the product costs when manufacturing overhead is applied to work in process for each production department. To simplify this illustration, we assume that these amounts result in no over- or underapplied overhead.

Exhibit 3-14	Allocation of Service Department Costs to Production Departments' Overhead Accounts

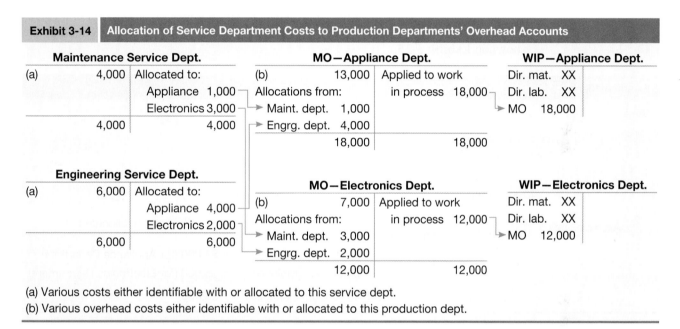

(a) Various costs either identifiable with or allocated to this service dept.
(b) Various overhead costs either identifiable with or allocated to this production dept.

Note that $4,000 is accumulated as the total cost for the Maintenance Department; then $1,000 and $3,000 are allocated to the Appliance and Electronics Departments (manufacturing departments), respectively. The allocated service department costs are in turn included in the totals of $18,000 and $12,000 of overhead costs applied from the respective production departments. Similar observations can be made for the Engineering Department.

Method of Cost Allocation

Costs are allocated among various departments on a basis that reflects the proportion of the service or activity that benefits each department. Some examples of allocated costs and their possible allocation bases are as follows:

Service Cost	Possible Allocation Basis
Personnel salaries	Number of employees in each department
Building depreciation	Square feet of floor space used
Utilities	Machine hours used
Building maintenance	Square feet of floor space used
Machine maintenance	Machine hours used
Heat and light	Cubic feet of building space used

Choosing an Allocation Basis

Once an allocation basis is chosen, it could remain unchanged for a long period of time. The selection of an allocation basis represents a policy decision that is typically reviewed only when major inequities exist.

The concern for cost control may justify the use of elaborate devices and schemes to measure service benefits. Some examples are departmental electric meters, timekeeping systems reflecting actual hours of service requested and used, and weighting techniques in which requests for rush or peak-hour services are assigned higher costs than requests honored at the convenience of the service department.

To allocate a particular cost, we simply divide the total cost among a series of departments in proportion to departmental shares of the appropriate base activity. For example, suppose that $8,000 of personnel department cost is allocated between the Appliance Department (manufacturing department) with 15 employees and the Electronics Department (manufacturing department) with 25 employees. The number of production employees is the allocation basis. The two distinct steps involved and illustrative calculations are shown in **Exhibit 3-15**.

Exhibit 3-15	Service Department Allocation

Step

1.

$$\frac{\text{Total cost to be allocated}}{\text{Total allocation base}} = \text{Allocation rate}$$

$$\frac{\$8,000}{40 \text{ employees}} = \$200 \text{ per employee}$$

2. $\text{Allocation rate} \times \dfrac{\text{Actual amount of allocation}}{\text{basis for the department}} = \text{Specific amount allocated}$

$\$200 \times 15 \text{ employees} = \$3,000 \text{ (for Appliance Department)}$

$\$200 \times 25 \text{ employees} = \underline{\$5,000} \text{ (for Electronics Department)}$

Total amount allocated $\$8,000$

ACCOUNTING IN PRACTICE	Service Department Allocation

The allocation procedure should be simple and easily understood by all involved. If the allocation computations become too complex, their cost may exceed any benefits.

As a final step, we should check allocations and verify that the sum of allocated amounts equals the total amount allocated.

Exhibit 3-16 illustrates a worksheet that could be used to accumulate and allocate manufacturing overhead in a multidepartment manufacturing operation that includes service departments. Note the following:

1. Three categories of costs are involved:
   a. Those directly identifiable with departments
   b. Those requiring allocations to production and service departments
   c. Service department costs allocated to production departments
2. A total overhead amount is first accumulated for each service department and each production department.
3. After service department costs are allocated, the total overhead is assigned to the production departments only.

4. The final amounts assigned to each production department are used to calculate departmental overhead rates for each production department. (See the footnotes to **Exhibit 3-16**.)

The amounts, proportions, and variety of costs shown in **Exhibit 3-16** have been chosen for simplicity of presentation to stress the basic concepts.

We might ask why service department costs are not allocated to other service departments. More sophisticated allocation techniques may involve allocations of some service department costs to other service departments and even mutual assignment of all of one or more service department costs to all other service departments. Discussions of these techniques are for a more advanced text.

Exhibit 3-16	Overhead Distribution Worksheet for the Year Ended December 31, 2016					
		Service Depts.		Production Depts.		
		Maint.	Engin.	Appl.	Elect.	Allocation Basis
(a) Directly identifiable with depts.						
Indirect labor		$ 8,000	$20,000	$38,500	$18,500	Wages payable analysis
Factory supplies used		3,000	2,000	9,000	10,000	Requisition forms
(b) Allocated to production and service depts.						
Building depreciation		600	1,200	3,000	1,200	Square feet of floor space
Personal property taxes		400	800	1,500	1,300	Assessed value of equip. used
Total overhead cost to be allocated		$12,000	$24,000	$52,000	$31,000	
(c) Allocation of service depts.						
Maint. (assumed as 2/3 for Appl. and 1/3 for Elect.)		(12,000)		8,000	4,000	Sq. ft. of factory area used
Engin. (assumed as 1/6 for Appl. and 5/6 for Elect.)			(24,000)	4,000	20,000	Machine hours
Totals		–0–	–0–	$64,000*	$55,000†	

* Assuming an overhead allocation basis of 20,000 machine hours, the overhead rate for the Appl. Dept. is $3.20 per machine hr ($64,000/20,000 machine hrs).

† Assuming an overhead allocation basis of $110,000 direct labor (DL), the overhead rate for the Elect. Dept. is 50 cents per DL dollar ($55,000/$110,000 DL).

DEPARTMENTAL OVERHEAD RATES

Manufacturing companies that use traditional overhead rates typically use either a plant-wide (or company-wide) overhead rate or departmental overhead rates. A **plant-wide (or company-wide) overhead rate** is determined by dividing estimated total plant (or company) overhead for the year by estimated utilization of the total plant (or company) productive capacity for the year. The discussions and illustration in this chapter have incorporated a plant-wide overhead rate. When a plant-wide overhead rate is adopted, the cost accounting system uses a single predetermined rate for applying overhead to work done in all the producing departments, such as bending, drilling, welding, assembling, and painting.

LO6 Contrast plant-wide overhead rates and departmental overhead rates.

Departmental Overhead Rates

Some manufacturing companies have adopted a cost accounting system that uses **departmental overhead rates**. When departmental overhead rates are used, a separate overhead rate is predetermined for each producing department in the factory by dividing the estimated overhead associated with each department by the estimated utilization of the capacity of that department.

A manufacturer would use departmental overhead rates for two primary reasons. First, the predetermined overhead rate in one department may be significantly different from the rate in another department. For instance, in department 1, the overhead rate might be $5 per direct labor hour, whereas the overhead rate in department 2 might be $20 per direct labor hour. Second, the capacity measure in one department may be different from the capacity measure in another department. For example, if department 1 is highly automated, then machine hours would be an appropriate measure of capacity for department 1. However, if department 2 is direct-labor intensive, then direct labor hours would be an appropriate measure of capacity for department 2.

When departmental overhead rates are used, the manufacturer accumulates the appropriate measure of capacity for each department for each job so that the appropriate overhead rates can be applied. Assume that a particular manufacturer has three producing departments: machining, painting, and assembling.

The capacity measure for machining and painting is machine hours, whereas the capacity measure for assembly is direct labor hours. For Job 368, the factory accumulated 30 machine hours of machining, 20 machine hours of painting, and 40 direct labor hours of assembling. Machining has a predetermined overhead rate of $4 per machine hour, painting has a predetermined overhead rate of $3 per machine hour, and assembling has a predetermined overhead rate of $2 per direct labor hour. Manufacturing overhead would be applied to Job 368 as follows:

Machining (30 machine hours × $4)	$120
Painting (20 machine hours × $3)	60
Assembling (40 direct labor hours × $2)	80
Total manufacturing overhead applied to Job 368	$260

Departmental overhead rates usually provide a more equitable application of manufacturing overhead to individual jobs than do plant-wide rates. However, when there are significant variations in volume or complexity among the individual jobs, neither plant-wide nor departmental overhead rates may provide an equitable application of manufacturing overhead among the individual jobs. Instead, **activity-based costing** may be more appropriate. Activity-based costing is discussed in detail in Chapter 5.

YOUR TURN! 3.4	
The solution is on page 109.	*Why would a company use a departmental overhead rate rather than a plant-wide overhead rate?*

SERVICE INDUSTRY IN FOCUS

SERVICE AND MERCHANDISING

Environmental Business Consultants, LLC (EBC) worked on and completed two projects during June 2016: a review of appropriate rates for solid waste and recycling collection within Klamath County, and a competitive procurement of landfill disposal services for the City of Redding. The following information relates to these two projects:

	Rate Review Project—Klamath	Procurement Project—Redding
WIP Inventory balance at June 1, 2016	$46,320	$85,318
Hours worked during June	100	74
Payroll cost per hour:		
Partner	$ 60	$ 60
Manager	$ 38	$ 38
Staff	$ 24	$ 24
Overhead rate per labor hour	$ 25	$ 25

During June, the partner charged 10 hours to the rate review project and 20 hours to the procurement project; the manager charged 30 hours to the rate review project and 24 hours to the procurement project; and the staff charged 60 hours to the rate review project and 30 hours to the procurement project.

On June 30, EBC billed its clients for the completed projects. The invoice for the rate review project was for $60,000 and for the procurement project was $105,000.

Required

1. Prepare the journal entry to distribute the payroll to the projects during June. (Assume that the correct entry was made when the payroll was paid.)

2. Prepare the journal entry to apply the overhead to the projects during June.

3. Prepare the journal entry(ies) to record the completion of the projects as of the end of June. (Hint: Don't forget the work that was performed on the jobs prior to June, which is reflected in the beginning WIP balance. Also, don't forget that there is no finished goods inventory in a service firm—once the project is complete, it is billed to the client.)

4. Determine the amount of profit or loss that EBC earned on each of the two projects.

Solution

1.

WIP—Klamath	3,180	
WIP—Redding	2,832	
Payroll expense		6,012

Klamath: ($60 × 10 hours) + ($38 × 30 hours) + ($24 × 60 hours) = $3,180
Redding: ($60 × 20 hours) + ($38 × 24 hours) + ($24 × 30 hours) = $2,832

2.

WIP—Klamath	2,500	
WIP—Redding	1,850	
Overhead		4,350

Klamath: (10 + 30 + 60) × $25 = 2,500
Redding: (20 + 24 + 30) × $25 = 1,850

3.

Accounts receivable—Klamath	60,000	
Sales revenue		60,000
Cost of sales	52,000	
WIP—Klamath		52,000
(46,320 + 3,180 + 2,500)		
Accounts receivable—Redding	105,000	
Sales revenue		105,000
Cost of sales	90,000	
WIP—Klamath		90,000
(85,318 + 2,832 + 1,850)		

4.

Klamath:		
	Sales revenue..............	$ 60,000
	Cost of goods sold..........	52,000
	Gross profit...............	$ 8,000

Redding:		
	Sales revenue..............	$105,000
	Cost of goods sold..........	90,000
	Gross profit...............	$ 15,000

COMPREHENSIVE PROBLEM

The annual budget for Diamond Corporation for 2016 included the following costs and expenses:

Direct material	$ 30,000
Direct labor ($8 per hour)	120,000
Sales commissions	28,000
Factory supervision	16,000
Indirect labor	27,000
Factory depreciation	25,000
Factory taxes	7,000
Factory insurance	6,000
Factory utilities	9,000

Required

a. Compute the plant-wide predetermined manufacturing overhead rate for 2016 using direct labor hours as the activity measure.

b. Determine the amount of manufacturing overhead that would be applied to jobs during March 2016 when 1,100 direct labor hours were actually incurred.

Solution

a.   Budgeted manufacturing overhead:

Factory supervision	$16,000
Indirect labor	27,000
Factory depreciation	25,000
Factory taxes	7,000
Factory insurance	6,000
Factory utilities	9,000
Budgeted manufacturing overhead	$90,000

Budgeted direct labor hours:

$$\frac{\$120,000}{\$8/hour} = 15,000 \text{ budgeted direct labor hours}$$

Predetermined overhead rate

$$\frac{\text{Budgeted manufacturing overhead}}{\text{Budgeted direct labor hours}} = \frac{\$90,000}{15,000} = \$6 \text{ per direct labor hour}$$

b.   1,100 hours × $6 = $6,600 applied manufacturing overhead

SUMMARY OF LEARNING OBJECTIVES

LO1   **Describe the two basic types of cost accounting systems, discuss how they may be used in both manufacturing and nonmanufacturing environments, and explain the need for the timely determination of product costs. (p. 66)**

- A costing system is an orderly process for tracking product or service cost information.
- In a manufacturing environment, materials, labor, and overhead costs are accumulated and assigned to specific jobs and products.
- In a nonmanufacturing (service) setting, labor and overhead costs are accumulated and assigned to specific customers.
- A job order costing system is used when production is characterized by a series of unique products or jobs undertaken either to fill specific orders from customers or to produce a general stock from which future orders will be filled.

- A process costing system lends itself to the production of a large volume of homogeneous products manufactured in a continual flow operation.
- A cost accounting system must trace, on a timely basis, direct materials, direct labor, and manufacturing overhead to products or jobs.

Explain the need for a predetermined overhead rate, demonstrate its calculation, and compare annual and monthly rates. (p. 69) **LO2**

- The predetermined overhead rate is calculated by dividing the estimated total manufacturing overhead cost for the year by the estimated utilization of the factory productive capacity during the upcoming year.
- The overhead rate should be calculated on an annual basis. Monthly overhead rates may fluctuate significantly from month to month.
- Companies should choose the application base that corresponds to the period over which activity decisions are typically made.

Describe and explain a job order costing system, identify types of records used in job order costing, and demonstrate the journal entries that accompany the flow of product costs. (p. 71) **LO3**

- Materials requisitions authorize issuance from the materials inventory.
- Time records document the labor time by job.
- The *job order cost sheet* summarizes the product costs—direct materials, direct labor, and manufacturing overhead applied—for one job; the predetermined overhead rate is used to apply manufacturing overhead.
- When material is requisitioned from the materials inventory, the Work in Process Inventory account is debited for the cost of direct material and the Manufacturing Overhead account is debited for the cost of indirect material.
- When the wages payable is distributed, the Work in Process Inventory account is debited for the cost of direct labor and the Manufacturing Overhead account is debited for the cost of indirect labor.
- Actual manufacturing overhead costs are recorded by debiting the Manufacturing Overhead account.
- Manufacturing overhead is applied to jobs by debiting the Work in Process Inventory account and crediting the Manufacturing Overhead account.

Discuss the procedures and journal entries used to account for finished goods and the sale of finished goods. (p. 77) **LO4**

- A product is not complete or finished until it is packaged in the container in which it will be sold. Packaging costs are part of the product cost transferred to the Finished Goods Inventory account.
- The cost of finished goods is recorded by debiting the Finished Goods Inventory account and crediting the Work in Process Inventory account.
- The sale of finished goods is recorded by debiting the Cost of Goods Sold account and crediting the Finished Goods Inventory account for the cost of the goods sold and by debiting the Accounts Receivable account and crediting the Sales account for the selling price.
- At year end, a journal entry is made to dispose of the **underapplied** or **overapplied** amount of manufacturing overhead. If the amount of **underapplied** or **overapplied** overhead is significant, an entry is made to transfer the amount to the Cost of Goods Sold Account.

Describe the procedures for cost allocation for service departments. (p. 82) **LO5**

- Service department costs are overhead costs that are allocated to production departments and eventually assigned to products as part of the production department's overhead.
- Each different service cost may be allocated using a different allocation basis.
- Departments can be divided into two broad classes, operating or production departments where the main purpose of the organization is carried out, and service departments that assist the activities of operating or production departments.

Contrast plant-wide overhead rates and departmental overhead rates. (p. 85) **LO6**

- When departmental overhead rates are used, a separate rate is calculated for each producing department in the factory.
- A plant-wide (or company-wide) overhead rate is determined by dividing estimated total plant (or company) overhead for the year by estimated utilization of the total plant (or company) productive capacity for the year.

KEY TERMS

Activity-based costing (p. 86)	Job order cost sheet (p. 72)	Process costing system (p. 67)
Bill of materials (p. 71)	Materials requisition (p. 71)	Production order (p. 71)
Cost driver (p. 69)	Overapplied (p. 79)	Sales order (p. 71)
Departmental overhead rates (p. 85)	Plant-wide (or company-wide) overhead rate (p. 85)	Time clocks (p. 75) Time record (p. 72)
Job order costing system (p. 66)	Predetermined manufacturing overhead rate (p. 69)	Underapplied (p. 79)

Assignments with the ⊕ logo in the margin are available in BusinessCourse.
See the Preface of the book for details.

SELF-STUDY QUESTIONS

(Answers to Self-Study Questions are at the end of this chapter.)

LO2   **1. Predetermined manufacturing overhead rates should be**
  a.   higher than actual manufacturing overhead rates.
  b.   lower than actual manufacturing overhead rates.
  c.   based on monthly budgets.
  d.   based on annual budgets.

LO3   **2. Which account is debited to record the issuance of material to production for incorporation into the product?**
  a.   Direct Materials   *c.*   Work in Process Inventory
  b.   Materials Inventory   *d.*   Factory Supplies

LO4   **3. Which of the following is usually *not* found on a job order cost sheet?**
  a.   Manufacturing overhead   *c.*   Direct materials
  b.   Finished units currently on hand   *d.*   Unit cost

LO4   **4. When should the balance of the manufacturing overhead account be zero?**
  a.   At the end of each month   *c.*   Never
  b.   After year-end closing   *d.*   Each time a job is completed

LO5   **5. Which of the following is *not* one of the categories of cost involved in the allocation of service department costs?**
  a.   Service department costs allocated to production departments
  b.   Costs directly identifiable with departments
  c.   Costs requiring allocation to departments
  d.   Selling department costs

QUESTIONS

LO1   1. Briefly describe a cost accounting system.

LO1   2. What types of entities, other than manufacturers, use cost accounting systems?

LO1   3. Contrast a job order costing system and a process costing system.

LO1   4. Give three examples of types of companies that would use job order costing.

LO2   5. Why do we name it a *predetermined* manufacturing overhead rate?

LO2   6. How is a predetermined manufacturing overhead rate determined?

LO2   7. Briefly justify the use of an annual predetermined manufacturing overhead rate as opposed to actual monthly manufacturing overhead.

LO2   8. Wesley Manufacturing Company uses a predetermined plant-wide manufacturing overhead rate of $25 per direct labor hour. During April, Job 541 had $3,000 of direct materials assigned to it; 60 hours of direct labor at $10 per hour were incurred for the job. What is the total product cost accumulated on Job 541 during April?

LO2   9. Parker Manufacturing, Inc., employs an overhead rate of 140% of direct labor cost. The Job 783 cost sheet shows that $5,000 in direct materials has been used and that $8,000 in direct labor has been incurred. If 1,000 units of product have been produced on Job 783, what is the unit cost of the product?

10. Briefly explain the sequential flow of product costs through a cost accounting system. **LO3**

11. What type of records would be used or maintained for the following manufacturing activities? **LO3**

    a. Determining the amount of a specific material on hand
    b. Issuing direct material for production
    c. Assigning the direct labor costs for a particular worker
    d. Accumulating the cost of a particular product or batch of products

12. Explain the general format and give examples of the data that would appear on (a) a sales order, (b) a bill **LO3** of materials, and (c) a job order cost sheet.

13. Why can we say that the sale of a manufactured product is recorded at two different amounts? **LO4**

14. Slaton Company records both actual overhead and applied overhead in one account, Manufacturing Over- **LO4** head. On January 31, the account has a credit balance. Has overhead been under- or overapplied during January?

15. Lyle Manufacturing Company applies manufacturing overhead at the rate of 150% of direct labor cost. **LO4** During October 2016, Lyle incurred $82,000 of direct labor costs and $120,000 of manufacturing overhead costs. What is the amount of over- or underapplied manufacturing overhead for October 2016?

16. Contrast service departments with production departments. Give three examples of a service department. **LO5**

17. Why might service departments be treated as cost centers? **LO5**

18. Explain what each of the following statements means: **LO5**

    a. Service departments do not work directly on products.
    b. Service department costs are manufacturing overhead costs.
    c. Overhead rates are not used for service departments.
    d. In spite of part (c), service department costs become part of product costs.

19. How do we choose a basis for allocating a cost to several departments? **LO5**

20. How is an allocation rate calculated? How is the specific amount allocated to a department calculated? **LO5**

21. Briefly describe the general format, data, and calculations that would appear on an overhead distribution **LO5** worksheet for a company with a number of production and service departments.

EXERCISES—SET A

E3-1A. **Calculate and Use Overhead Rate** Selected data for the consulting department of Austin Consulting, **LO3, 5** Inc., follow:

Estimated consulting overhead cost for the year.	$270,000
Estimated direct labor cost for the year (@ $9/hr.).	180,000
Actual manufacturing overhead cost for January	16,000
Actual direct labor cost for January (1,200 hours).	11,000

Assuming that direct labor cost is the basis for applying consulting overhead,

    a. Calculate the predetermined overhead rate.
    b. Prepare a journal entry that applies consulting overhead for January.
    c. By what amount is consulting overhead over- or underapplied in January?

E3-2A. **Calculate and Use Overhead Rate** Using the data in Exercise 3-1A, but assuming that the basis for **LO3, 5** applying consulting overhead is direct labor hours, complete requirements (a) through (c).

E3-3A. **Calculate and Use Overhead Rate** During the coming accounting year, Baker Manufacturing, Inc., **LO3** anticipates the following costs, expenses, and operating data:

Direct material (16,000 lb.)	$ 80,000
Direct labor (@ $10/hr.).	140,000
Indirect material	12,000
Indirect labor	22,000
Sales commissions.	34,000
Factory administration	16,000
Non factory administrative expenses.	20,000
Other manufacturing overhead*	48,000

*Provides for operating 35,000 machine hours.

    a.   Calculate the predetermined manufacturing overhead rate for the coming year for each of the following application bases: (1) direct labor hours, (2) direct labor costs, and (3) machine hours.

    b.   For each item in requirement *a*, determine the proper application of manufacturing overhead to Job 63, to which 16 direct labor hours, $150 of direct labor cost, and 40 machine hours have been charged.

LO4 **E3-4A.** **Applied vs. Actual Manufacturing Overhead** Davis Manufacturing Corporation applies manufacturing overhead on the basis of 150% of direct labor cost. An analysis of the related accounts and job order cost sheet indicates that during the year total manufacturing overhead incurred was $315,000 and that at year-end Work in Process Inventory, Finished Goods Inventory, and Cost of Goods Sold included $40,000, $20,000, and $140,000, respectively, of direct labor incurred during the current year.

    a.   Determine the underapplied manufacturing overhead at year-end (assume it is significant).

    b.   Prepare a journal entry to record the disposition of the underapplied manufacturing overhead.

LO3 **E3-5A.** **Flow of Product Costs through Accounts** Assuming a routine manufacturing activity, present journal entries (account titles only) for each of the following transactions:

    a.   Purchased material on account.

    b.   Recorded wages payable earned but not paid.

    c.   Requisitioned both direct material and indirect material.

    d.   Assigned direct and indirect labor costs.

    e.   Recorded factory depreciation and accrued factory property tax.

    f.   Applied manufacturing overhead to production.

    g.   Completed work on products.

    h.   Sold finished goods on account.

LO3 **E3-6A.** **Job Order Cost Sheets** For each of the manufacturing transactions or activities indicated in Exercise E3-5A, briefly identify the detailed forms, records, or documents (if any) that would probably underlie each journal entry.

LO4 **E3-7A.** **Perpetual Inventories** The following summary data are from the job order cost sheets of Hampton Company:

	Dates			Total Costs Assigned	Total Production
Job	Started	Finished	Shipped	at April 30	Costs Added in May
1	4/10	4/20	5/9	$7,300	
2	4/18	4/30	5/20	5,400	
3	4/24	5/10	5/25	2,900	$5,700
4	4/28	5/20	6/3	3,600	4,800
5	5/15	6/10	6/20		2,600
6	5/22	6/18	6/28		3,800

Using the above data, compute (a) the finished goods inventory at May 1 and May 31, (b) the work in process inventory at May 1 and May 31, and (c) the cost of goods sold for May. Hampton began operations with Job 1.

LO4 **E3-8A.** **Finished Goods and Cost of Goods Sold** Before the completed production for June is recorded, the work in process inventory account for James Company appears as follows:

Work in Process Inventory	
Balance June 1.	16,000
Direct material	45,000
Direct labor.	32,000
Manufacturing overhead applied	34,000

Assume that completed production for June includes Jobs 107, 108, and 109 with total costs of $28,000, $59,000, and $25,000, respectively.

    a.   Determine the cost of unfinished jobs at June 30 and prepare a journal entry to record completed production.

    b.   Using general journal entries, record the sale of Job 107 for $40,000 on account.

E3-9A. **Preparing a Job Order Cost Sheet** Riverwood Accounting Company has the following account in its cost records:

LO4

Work in Process—Jones Audit			
Direct labor............	20,000	Services completed	44,000
Project overhead	28,000		

Riverwood applies overhead to projects at a predetermined rate based on direct labor costs. Assume that Riverwood uses a job order costing system and that Jones Audit is the only job in process at the end of the period. Complete the following cost sheet for services still in process for Jones Audit.

Job Order Cost Sheet—Jones Audit (Services in Process)	
Direct labor..............................	_____
Project overhead	_____
Total cost	_____

E3-10A. **Service Department Cost Allocation** Presented below are certain operating data for the four departments of Tally Manufacturing Company.

LO5

	Service		Production	
	1	**2**	**1**	**2**
Total manufacturing overhead costs either identifiable with or allocated to each department...............................	$60,000	$72,000	$90,000	$98,000
Square feet of factory floor space			40,000	80,000
Number of factory workers...................			50	10
Planned direct labor hours for the year			20,000	30,000

Allocate, to the two production departments, the costs of service departments 1 and 2, using factory floor space and number of workers, respectively, as bases.

What is the apparent overhead rate for each production department if planned direct labor hours are the overhead application base?

EXERCISES—SET B

E3-1B. **Calculate and Use Overhead Rate** Selected data for the consulting department of Kingman Consulting, Inc., follow:

LO3, 5

Estimated consulting overhead cost for the year................	$405,000
Estimated direct labor cost for the year (@ $9/hr.)...............	324,000
Actual consulting overhead cost for May......................	26,000
Actual direct labor cost for May (2,400 hrs.)	22,000

Assuming that direct labor cost is the basis for applying consulting overhead,

a. Calculate the predetermined overhead rate.
b. Prepare a journal entry that applies consulting overhead for May.
c. By what amount is consulting overhead over- or underapplied in May?

E3-2B. **Calculate and Use Overhead Rate** Using the data in Exercise E3-1B, but assuming that the basis for applying consulting overhead is direct labor hours, complete requirements (a) through (c).

LO3, 5

LO3 **E3-3B.** **Calculate and Use Manufacturing Overhead Rate** During the coming accounting year, Ester Manufacturing, Inc., anticipates the following costs, expenses, and operating data:

Direct material (15,000 lb.)	$45,000
Direct labor (@ $12/hr.).	96,000
Indirect material	7,000
Indirect labor	12,000
Sales commissions.	18,000
Factory administration	13,000
Nonfactory administrative expenses . . .	14,000
Other manufacturing overhead*	28,000

*Machine hours are 30,000 hours.

a. Calculate the predetermined manufacturing overhead rate for the coming year for each of the following application bases: (1) direct labor hours, (2) direct labor costs, and (3) machine hours.
b. For each item in requirement (a), determine the proper application of manufacturing overhead to Job 128, to which 9 direct labor hours, $100 of direct labor cost, and 32 machine hours have been charged.

LO4 **E3-4B.** **Applied vs. Actual Manufacturing Overhead** Sloan Manufacturing Corporation applies manufacturing overhead on the basis of 120% of direct labor cost. An analysis of the related accounts and job order cost sheets indicates that during the year total manufacturing overhead incurred was $210,000 and that at year-end Work in Process Inventory, Finished Goods Inventory, and Cost of Goods Sold included $30,000, $20,000, and $150,000, respectively, of direct labor incurred during the current year.

a. Determine the manufacturing overapplied overhead at year-end (assume it is significant).
b. Prepare a journal entry to record the disposition of the overapplied overhead.

LO3 **E3-5B.** **Flow of Product Costs Through Accounts** The following T accounts present a cost flow in which all or part of typical manufacturing transactions are indicated by parenthetical letters on the debit or credit side of each account.

Material Inventory		Wages Payable		Manufacturing Overhead	
(a)	(c)	(i)	(b)	(c)	(f)
	(e)		(d)	(d)	
				(e)	

Work in Process Inventory		Finished Goods Inventory		Cost of Goods Sold	
(c)	(g)			(h)	
(d)		(g)	(h)		
(f)					

For each parenthetical letter, present a general journal entry with explanation indicating the apparent transaction or procedure that has occurred (disregard amounts).

LO3 **E3-6B.** **Job Order Cost Sheets** For each of the manufacturing transactions or activities indicated by the parenthetical letters in Exercise E3-5B, briefly identify the detailed forms or documents (if any) that would probably underlie each journal entry.

LO4 **E3-7B.** **Perpetual Inventories** The following summary data are from the job order cost sheets of Castle Company:

	Dates			Total Assigned Costs at September 30	Total Production Costs Added in October
Job	Started	Finished	Shipped		
1	9/10	9/20	10/11	$9,000	
2	9/17	9/29	10/22	6,600	
3	9/25	10/11	10/27	3,500	$7,100
4	9/27	10/19	11/4	4,400	5,700
5	10/14	11/10	11/18		3,200
6	10/23	11/17	11/29		4,900

Using the data provided, compute (a) the finished goods inventory at October 1 and October 31, (b) the work in process inventory at October 1 and October 31, and (c) the cost of goods sold for October. Castle began operations with Job 1.

E3-8B. **Finished Goods and Cost of Goods Sold** Before the completed production for August is recorded, the work in process inventory account for Bayfield Company appears as follows:

LO4

Work in Process Inventory	
Balance, August 1	15,000
Direct material	33,000
Direct labor	20,000
Manufacturing overhead applied	20,000

Assume that completed production for August includes Jobs 317, 318, and 319 with total costs of $31,000, $18,000, and $22,000, respectively.

a. Determine the cost of unfinished jobs at August 31 and prepare a journal entry to record completed production.

b. Using general journal entries, record the sale of Job 317 for $45,000 on account.

E3-9B. **Job Order Cost Sheet** Everglade Accounting Company has the following account in its cost records:

LO4

Work in Process—Davis Audit			
Direct labor	48,000	Services completed	95,000
Project overhead	57,600		

Everglade applies overhead to projects at a predetermined rate based on direct labor costs. Assume that Everglade uses a job order costing system and that Davis Audit is the only job in process at the end of the period. Complete the following cost sheet for services still in process for Davis Audit.

Job Order Cost Sheet—Davis Audit (Services in Process)	
Direct labor	_____
Project overhead	_____
Total cost	_____

E3-10B. **Service Department Cost Allocation** Presented below are certain operating data for the four departments of Modern Manufacturing Company.

LO5

	Service		Production	
	1	2	1	2
Total overhead cost either identifiable with or to each department	$45,000	$60,000	$55,000	$116,000
Square feet of factory floor space			90,000	45,000
Number of factory workers			20	60
Planned direct labor hours for the year			25,000	32,000

Allocate, to the two production departments, the costs of service departments 1 and 2, using factory floor space and number of workers, respectively, as bases.

What is the apparent manufacturing overhead rate for each production department if planned direct labor hours are the overhead application base?

PROBLEMS—SET A

Note: *In both problem sets, assume perpetual inventory procedures, a single Manufacturing Overhead account, first-in, first-out (FIFO) costing of inventories, and that the Materials Inventory account is the control account for both direct material and indirect material.*

LO3, 5 **P3-1A.** **Determine and Use Overhead Rate** Cortez Consulting, Inc., expects the following costs and expenses during the coming year:

Direct labor (@ $9/hr.).	$162,000
Sales commissions.	37,000
Overhead	144,000

Required
a. Compute a predetermined overhead rate applied on the basis of direct labor hours.
b. Prepare a general journal entry to apply overhead during an interim period when 1,500 direct labor hours were worked.
c. What amount of overhead would be assigned to Job 466, to which $180 in direct labor had been charged?

LO3 **P3-2A.** **Determine and Use Overhead Rate** The following selected ledger accounts of Cameron Company are for February (the second month of its accounting year):

MATERIALS INVENTORY

Feb. 1 balance	31,500	February credits	113,000
February debits	104,000		

MANUFACTURING OVERHEAD

February debits	137,200	Feb. 1 balance	11,600
		February credits	136,350

WORK IN PROCESS INVENTORY

Feb. 1 balance	22,400	February credits	345,000
February debits:			
Direct material	95,000		
Direct labor	151,500		
Manufacturing overhead	136,350		

WAGES PAYABLE

February debits	193,500	Feb. 1 balance	45,000
		February credits	177,000

FINISHED GOODS INVENTORY

Feb. 1 balance	76,500	February credits	383,700
February debits	345,000		

Required
a. Determine the amount of indirect material requisitioned for production during February.
b. How much indirect labor cost was apparently incurred during February?
c. Calculate the manufacturing overhead rate based on direct labor cost.
d. Was manufacturing overhead for February under- or overapplied, and by what amount?
e. Was manufacturing overhead for the first two months of the year under- or overapplied, and by what amount?
f. What is the cost of production completed in February?
g. What is the cost of goods sold in February?

P3-3A. Job Cost Journal Entries Holiday Manufacturing had the following inventories at December 31, **LO3** 2015, the end of its fiscal year:

Materials inventory	$19,000
Work in process inventory	20,000
Finished goods inventory	13,000

During January 2016, the following transactions occurred:

1. Purchased materials on account, $126,000.
2. Requisitioned direct material of $110,000 and indirect material of $20,000.
3. Incurred wages payable, $61,000.
4. Assigned total wages payable, of which $11,000 was considered indirect labor.
5. Incurred other manufacturing overhead, $32,800. (Credit Accounts Payable.)
6. Applied manufacturing overhead on the basis of 110% of direct labor costs.
7. Determined completed production, $206,000. Use this information to determine the amount of WIP transferred to finished goods inventory.
8. Determined cost of goods sold, $203,000. Use this information to determine the reduction to finished goods inventory.

Required
a. Prepare general journal entries to record these transactions.
b. If the above transactions covered a full year's operations, prepare a journal entry to dispose of the overhead account balance. Assume that the balance is significant. Also assume that the following accounts contained the indicated amounts of manufacturing overhead applied during 2016:

Work in process inventory	$ 6,000
Finished goods	4,000
Cost of goods sold	45,000

P3-4A. Job Cost Journal Entries Prior to the beginning of 2016, Lowe Company estimated that it would in- **LO3, 4** cur $176,000 of manufacturing overhead cost during 2016, using 16,000 direct labor hours to produce the desired volume of goods. On January 1, 2016, beginning balances of Materials Inventory, Work in Process Inventory, and Finished Goods Inventory were $28,000, $-0-, and $43,000, respectively.

Required
Prepare general journal entries to record the following for 2016:

a. Purchased materials on account, $39,000.
b. Of the total dollar value of materials used, $31,000 represented direct material and $11,000 indirect material.
c. Determined total factory labor, $135,000 (15,000 hrs. @ $9/hr.).
d. Of the factory labor, 80% was direct and 20% indirect.
e. Applied manufacturing overhead based on direct labor hours to work in process.
f. Determined actual manufacturing overhead other than those items already recorded, $92,000. (Credit Accounts Payable.)
g. Ending inventories of work in process and finished goods were $32,000 and $57,000, respectively. Determine the cost of finished goods (credit WIP) and the cost of goods sold (credit FG inventory). Make separate entries.
h. Transferred the balance in Manufacturing Overhead to Cost of Goods Sold.

P3-5A. Job Cost Journal Entries and T Accounts Following are certain operating data for Durango **LO3, 4** Manufacturing Company for January 2016:

	Materials Inventory	Work in Process Inventory	Finished Goods Inventory
Beginning inventory	$57,000	$24,000	$75,000
Ending inventory	33,000	40,500	48,000

Total sales were $1,800,000, on which the company earned a 40% gross profit. Durango uses a predetermined manufacturing overhead rate of 120% of direct labor costs. Manufacturing overhead applied was $360,000. Exclusive of indirect material used, total manufacturing overhead incurred was $243,000; it was overapplied by $22,500.

Required

Compute the following items. (Set up T accounts for Materials Inventory, Work in Process Inventory, Finished Goods Inventory, and Manufacturing Overhead; fill in the known amounts; and then use the normal relationships among the various accounts to compute the unknown amounts.)

a.	Cost of goods sold.		*d.*	Direct material used.
b.	Cost of goods manufactured.		*e.*	Indirect material used.
c.	Direct labor incurred.		*f.*	Total materials purchased.

LO3, 4   P3-6A.   Job Cost Journal Entries and T Accounts Summarized data for the first month's operations of Dobson Welding Foundry during 2016 are presented below. A job order costing system is used.

1. Materials purchased on account, $58,000.
2. Amounts of materials requisitioned and foundry labor used:

Job	Materials	Foundry Labor
1	$ 4,400	$2,600
2	7,000	5,000
3	3,200	2,400
4	12,000	4,600
5	4,800	2,800
6	1,400	1,200
Indirect material	6,200	
Indirect labor		3,400

3. Foundry overhead is applied at the rate of 200% of direct labor costs.
4. Miscellaneous foundry overhead incurred:

Prepaid foundry insurance written off	$ 1,480
Property taxes on foundry building accrued	2,360
Foundry utilities payable accrued	5,280
Depreciation on foundry equipment.	7,440
Other costs incurred on account	10,320

5. Ending work in process consisted of Jobs 4 and 6.
6. Jobs 1 and 3 and one-half of Job 2 were sold on account for $20,000, $17,400, and $14,400, respectively.

Required

a. Open general ledger T accounts for Materials Inventory, Wages Payable, Foundry Overhead, Work in Process Inventory, Finished Goods Inventory, and Cost of Goods Sold. Also set up subsidiary T accounts as job order cost sheets for each job.

b. Prepare general journal entries to record the summarized transactions for the month, and post appropriate entries to any accounts listed in requirement (a). Key each entry parenthetically to the related number in the problem data.

c. Determine the balances of any accounts necessary and prepare schedules of jobs in ending work in process and jobs in ending finished goods to confirm that they agree with the related control accounts.

LO3, 4   P3-7A.   Complex Job Cost Journal Entries and Analysis During June 2016, its first month of operations, Weston Manufacturing Company completed the transactions listed below. Weston uses a job order costing system. Materials requisitions and the wages payable summary are analyzed on the 15th and the last day of each month, and charges for direct material and direct labor are entered directly on specific job order cost sheets. Manufacturing overhead at the rate of 140% of direct labor costs is recorded on individual job order cost sheets when a job is completed and at month-end for any job then in process. At month-end, entries to the general ledger accounts summarize materials requisitions, distribution of wages, payable costs, and the application of manufacturing overhead for the month. All other entries to general ledger accounts are made as they occur.

1. Purchased materials on account, $130,000.
2. Paid miscellaneous manufacturing overhead costs, $32,600.
3. An analysis of materials requisitions and the wages payable summary for June 1–15 indicates the following cost distribution:

Job	Materials	Factory Labor
1	$21,600	$36,800
2	10,400	16,000
3	4,400	10,800
Indirect material	7,600	
Indirect labor		35,400
	$44,000	$99,000

4. Jobs 1 and 2 were completed on June 15 and transferred to finished goods inventory on the next day. (Enter the appropriate manufacturing overhead amounts on the job order cost sheets, mark them completed, and make a general journal entry transferring the appropriate amount of cost to the Finished Goods Inventory account.)
5. Paid miscellaneous manufacturing overhead costs, $23,400.
6. Sold Job 1 on account, $185,600 (recognized its cost of sales in the general journal).
7. An analysis of materials requisitions and wages payable summary for June 16–30 indicates the following cost distribution:

Job	Materials	Factory Labor
3	$22,800	$16,800
4	18,000	32,400
5	7,800	13,000
6	3,000	4,600
Indirect material	6,800	
Indirect labor		29,400
	$58,400	$96,200

8. Jobs 3 and 4 were completed on June 30 and transferred to finished goods inventory on the same day. (See transaction 4.)
9. Sold Job 3 on account, $155,600 (recognized its cost of sales in the general journal).
10. Recorded the following additional manufacturing overhead:

Depreciation on factory building	$26,000
Depreciation on factory equipment	15,200
Expiration of prepaid factory insurance	4,200
Accrual of factory property taxes payable	7,000
	$52,400

11. Recorded monthly general journal entry for the costs of all materials used.
12. Recorded monthly general journal entry for the distribution of wages payable costs.
13. Recorded manufacturing overhead on the job order cost sheets for jobs in ending work in process and in the general journal for all manufacturing overhead applied during the month.

Required

a.   Set up the following general ledger T accounts: Materials Inventory, Wages Payable, Manufac-
     turing Overhead, Work in Process Inventory, Finished Goods Inventory, Cost of Goods Sold, and
     Sales.

b.   Set up T accounts for each of Jobs 1–6 as job order cost sheets.

c.   Noting the accounting procedures described in the first paragraph of the problem, do the
     following:

  i.   Record general journal entries for all transactions. Note that general journal entries are not
       required in transactions 3 and 7. Post only those portions of these entries affecting the gen-
       eral ledger accounts set up in requirement (a).

  ii. Enter the applicable amounts directly on the appropriate job order cost sheets for transac-
       tions 3, 4, 7, 8, and 13. Note parenthetically the nature of each amount entered.

d.   Present a brief analysis showing that the general ledger accounts for Work in Process Inventory
     and for Finished Goods Inventory agree with the related job order cost sheets.

e.   Explain in one sentence each what the balance of each general ledger account established in re-
     quirement (a) represents.

LO5, 6   **P3-8A.   Manufacturing Overhead Distribution Worksheet** The following are selected operating data for
the production and service departments of Bluestone Company for 2016.

	Departments			
	Service		Production	
	1	2	1	2
Overhead costs (identified by department)				
Indirect material	$48,400	$ 82,200	$ 25,440	$ 516,000
Indirect labor.	$97,200	$144,000	$ 32,584	$1,439,000
Square feet of building floor space used	4,800	7,200	12,000	24,000
Assessed value of equipment used	$21,000	$ 63,000	$126,000	$ 210,000
Cubic yards of factory space used			88,000	132,000
Machine hours			51,200	204,800
Direct labor.			$ 20,000	$ 400,000

Building depreciation of $96,000 is allocated on the basis of square feet of floor space. Personal prop-
erty taxes of $36,000 are allocated on the basis of assessed values of equipment used. Costs for service
departments 1 and 2 are allocated to production departments on the basis of cubic yards of factory space
and machine hours, respectively.

Required

a.   Prepare a 2016 overhead distribution worksheet for Bluestone Company similar to the one pre-
     pared for **Exhibit 3-16**.

b.   Compute the manufacturing overhead rates for production departments 1 and 2 using machine
     hours and direct labor costs, respectively, for allocation bases.

PROBLEMS—SET B

LO3, 5   **P3-1B.   Determine and Use Consulting Rate** Oxford Consulting, Inc., expects the following costs and expenses during the coming year:

Direct labor (@ $8/hr.).	$336,000
Sales commissions.	72,000
Overhead	378,000

Required

a.   Compute a predetermined overhead rate applied on the basis of direct labor hours.

b. Prepare a general journal entry to apply overhead during an interim period when 3,500 direct labor hours were worked.

c. What amount of overhead would be assigned to Job 325, to which $304 in direct labor had been charged?

P3-2B. Determine and Use Manufacturing Overhead Rate The following selected ledger accounts of the Lakewood Manufacturing Company are for May (the fifth month of its accounting year): **LO3**

Materials Inventory			
May 1 balance	40,000	May credits.	150,000
May debits	125,000		

Factory Overhead			
May debits	160,000	May 1 balance	14,000
		May credits.	144,000

Work in Process Inventory			
May 1 balance	28,000	May credits.	440,000
May debits:			
Direct material.	129,000		
Direct labor	180,000		
Manufacturing overhead. . .	144,000		

Factory Payroll Payable			
May debits	228,000	May 1 balance	50,000
		May credits.	196,000

Finished Goods Inventory			
May 1 balance	102,000	May credits.	510,000
May debits	440,000		

Required

a. Determine the amount of indirect material requisitioned for production during May.

b. How much indirect labor cost was apparently incurred during May?

c. Calculate the manufacturing overhead rate based on direct labor cost.

d. Was manufacturing overhead for May under- or overapplied, and by what amount?

e. Was manufacturing overhead for the first five months of the year under- or overapplied, and by what amount?

f. What is the cost of production completed in May?

g. What is the cost of goods sold in May?

P3-3B. Job Cost Journal Entries Dillon Manufacturing had the following inventories at December 31, 2015, the end of its fiscal year: **LO3**

Materials inventory	$15,000
Work in process inventory	17,000
Finished goods inventory	30,000

During January 2016, the following transactions occurred:

1. Purchased materials on account, $125,000.

2. Requisitioned total materials of $130,000, of which $8,000 was considered indirect material.

3. Incurred wages payable, $105,000.

4. Assigned total wages payable, of which $15,000 was considered indirect labor.

5. Incurred other manufacturing overhead, $57,000. (Credit Accounts Payable.)

6. Applied manufacturing overhead on the basis of 80% of direct labor costs.

7. Determined ending work in process, $14,000. Use this information to calculate the amount of WIP transferred to finished goods inventory (credit WIP).
8. Determined ending finished goods, $26,000. Use this information to calculate the cost of goods sold (credit FG inventory).

Required

a. Prepare general journal entries to record these transactions.
b. If the above transactions covered a full year's operations, prepare a journal entry to dispose of the overhead account balance. Assume that the balance is significant. Also assume that the following accounts contained the indicated amounts of manufacturing overhead applied during 2016:

Work in process inventory	$ 3,000
Finished goods inventory	6,000
Cost of goods sold	63,000

LO3, 4 **P3-4B.** **Job Cost Journal Entries** Prior to the beginning of 2016, Stapleton Company estimated that it would incur $153,000 of manufacturing overhead cost during 2016, using 17,000 direct labor hours to produce the desired volume of goods. On January 1, 2016, beginning balances of Materials Inventory, Work in Process Inventory, and Finished Goods Inventory were $48,000, $-0-, and $87,000, respectively.

Required

Prepare general journal entries to record the following for 2016:

a. Purchased materials on account, $316,000.
b. Of the total dollar value of materials used, $284,000 represented direct material and $35,000 indirect material.
c. Determined total factory labor, $189,000 (18,000 hrs. @ $10.50/hr.).
d. Of the factory labor, 15,800 were direct labor hours.
e. Applied manufacturing overhead based on direct labor hours to work in process.
f. Determined actual manufacturing overhead other than those items already recorded, $83,000. (Credit Accounts Payable.)
g. Ending inventories of work in process and finished goods were $57,000 and $71,800, respectively. Determine the cost of finished goods (credit WIP) and the cost of goods sold (credit FG inventory). Make separate entries.
h. Transferred the balance in Manufacturing Overhead to Cost of Goods Sold.

LO3, 4 **P3-5B.** **Job Cost Journal Entries and T Accounts** Following are certain operating data for Redwood Manufacturing Company for January 2016:

	Materials Inventory	Work in Process Inventory	Finished Goods Inventory
Beginning inventory	$40,000	$50,000	$80,000
Ending inventory	70,000	60,000	56,000

Total sales were $2,000,000, on which the company earned a 40% gross profit. Redwood uses a predetermined manufacturing overhead rate of 110% of direct labor costs. Manufacturing overhead applied was $396,000. Exclusive of indirect material used, total manufacturing overhead incurred was $300,000; it was underapplied by $24,000.

Required

Compute the following items. (Set up T accounts for Materials Inventory, Work in Process Inventory, Finished Goods Inventory, and Manufacturing Overhead; fill in the known amounts; and then use the normal relationships among the various accounts to compute the unknown amounts.)

a. Cost of goods sold.
b. Cost of goods manufactured.
c. Direct labor incurred.
d. Direct material used.
e. Indirect material used.
f. Total materials purchased.

P3-6B.   Job Cost Journal Entries and T Accounts Summarized data for the first month's operations of   **LO3, 4**
Slater Foundry during 2016 are presented below. A job order costing system is used.

1. Materials purchased on account, $88,000.
2. Amounts of materials requisitioned and foundry labor used:

Job	Materials	Foundry Labor
1	$ 4,600	$ 3,600
2	5,200	6,000
3	3,800	8,800
4	13,400	12,000
5	6,400	7,200
6	4,000	2,000
Indirect material	11,000	
Indirect labor		18,000

3. Foundry overhead is applied at the rate of 150% of direct labor costs.
4. Miscellaneous foundry overhead incurred:

Prepaid foundry insurance written off	$ 1,880
Property taxes on foundry building accrued	3,760
Foundry utilities payable accrued	4,400
Depreciation on foundry equipment.	8,400
Other costs incurred on account	14,640

5. Ending work in process consisted of Jobs 4 and 6. 6. Jobs 1 and 3 and one-half of Job 2 were sold
on account for $25,200, $31,600, and $18,920, respectively.

Required
a.   Open general ledger T accounts for Materials Inventory, Wages Payable, Foundry Overhead,
Work in Process Inventory, Finished Goods Inventory, and Cost of Goods Sold. Also set up subsidiary T accounts as job order cost sheets for each job.
b.   Prepare general journal entries to record the summarized transactions for the month, and post appropriate entries to any accounts listed in requirement (a). Key each entry parenthetically to the
related number in the problem data.
c.   Determine the balances of any accounts necessary and prepare schedules of jobs in ending work
in process and jobs in ending finished goods to confirm that they agree with the related control
accounts.

P3-7B.   Complex Job Cost Journal Entries and Analysis During June 2016, its first month of operations,   **LO3, 4**
Logan Manufacturing Company completed the transactions listed below. Logan uses a job order costing system. Materials requisitions and the wages payable summary are analyzed on the 15th and the
last day of each month, and charges for direct material and direct labor are entered directly on specific
job order cost sheets. Manufacturing overhead at the rate of 160% of direct labor costs is recorded on
individual job order cost sheets when a job is completed and at month-end for any job then in process.
At month-end, entries to the general ledger accounts summarize materials requisitions, distribution of
wages payable costs, and the application of manufacturing overhead for the month. All other entries
to general ledger accounts are made as they occur.

1. Purchased materials on account, $210,000.
2. Paid miscellaneous manufacturing overhead costs, $52,000.
3. An analysis of materials requisitions and the wages payable summary for June 1–15 indicates the
following cost distribution:

Job	Materials	Factory Labor
1	$34,000	$60,000
2	16,000	26,000
3	8,000	18,000
Indirect material	14,000	
Indirect labor		56,000
Total	$72,000	$160,000

4. Jobs 1 and 2 were completed on June 15 and transferred to finished goods inventory on the next day. (Enter the appropriate manufacturing overhead amounts on the job order cost sheets, mark them completed, and make a general journal entry transferring the appropriate amount of cost to the Finished Goods Inventory account.)
5. Paid miscellaneous manufacturing overhead costs, $38,000.
6. Sold Job 1 on account, $300,000 (recognized its cost of sales in the general journal).
7. An analysis of materials requisitions and wages payable summary for June 16–30 indicates the following cost distribution:

Job	Materials	Factory Labor
3	$36,000	$28,000
4	30,000	54,000
5	12,000	20,000
6	6,000	8,000
Indirect material	10,000	
Indirect labor		46,000
Total	$94,000	$156,000

8. Jobs 3 and 4 were completed on June 30 and transferred to finished goods inventory on the same day. (See transaction 5.)
9. Sold Job 3 on account, $250,000 (recognized its cost of sales in the general journal).
10. Recorded the following additional manufacturing overhead:

Depreciation on factory building	$42,000
Depreciation on factory equipment	24,000
Expiration of prepaid factory insurance	7,000
Payable.	13,000
	$86,000

11. Recorded monthly general journal entry for the costs of all materials used.
12. Recorded monthly general journal entry for the distribution of wages payable costs.
13. Recorded manufacturing overhead on the job order cost sheets for jobs in ending work in process and in the general journal for all manufacturing overhead applied during the month.
    a. Set up the following general ledger T accounts: Materials Inventory, Wages Payable, Manufacturing Overhead, Work in Process Inventory, Finished Goods Inventory, Cost of Goods Sold, and Sales.
    b. Set up T accounts for each of Jobs 1–6 as job order cost sheets.
    c. Noting the accounting procedures described in the first paragraph of the problem, do the following:
        1. Record general journal entries for all transactions. Note that general journal entries are not required in transactions 3 and 7. Post only those portions of these entries affecting the general ledger accounts set up in requirement (a).
        2. Enter the applicable amounts directly on the appropriate job order cost sheets for transactions 3, 4, 7, 8, and 13. Note parenthetically the nature of each amount entered.
    d. Present a brief analysis showing that the general ledger accounts for work in process inventory and for finished goods inventory agree with the related job order cost sheets.

e. Explain in one sentence each what the balance of each general ledger account established in requirement (a) represents.

P3-8B. Manufacturing Overhead Distribution Worksheet The following are selected operating data for the production and service departments of Danville Company for 2016.   **LO5, 6**

	Departments			
	Service		Production	
	1	**2**	**1**	**2**
Manufacturing overhead costs (identified by department)				
Factory supplies used	$12,800	$21,440	$ 67,840	$137,600
Indirect labor	$25,920	$38,400	$ 86,400	$384,000
Square feet of building floor space used	7,200	10,800	18,000	36,000
Assessed value of equipment used	$28,000	$84,000	$168,000	$280,000
Cubic yards of factory space used			132,000	198,000
Machine hours			51,200	204,800
Direct labor ($10 per hour)			$250,000	$500,000

Building depreciation of $51,200 is allocated on the basis of square feet of floor space. Personal property taxes of $19,200 are allocated on the basis of assessed values of equipment used. Costs for service departments 1 and 2 are allocated to production departments on the basis of cubic yards of factory space and machine hours, respectively.

Required

a. Prepare a 2016 manufacturing overhead distribution worksheet for Danville Company similar to the one prepared for **Exhibit 3-16**.

b. Compute the manufacturing overhead rates for production departments 1 and 2 using machine hours and direct labor hours, respectively, for allocation bases.

CERTIFIED MANAGEMENT ACCOUNTANT (CMA®) EXAM SAMPLE QUESTIONS

CMA3-1. Henry Manufacturing, which uses direct labor hours to apply overhead to its product line, undertook an extensive renovation and modernization program two years ago. Manufacturing processes were reengineered, considerable automated equipment was acquired, and 60% of the company's non-union factory workers were terminated.

Which of the following statements would apply to the situation at Henry?

I.   The company's factory overhead rate has likely increased.
II. The use of direct labor hours seems to be appropriate.
III. Henry will lack the ability to properly determine labor variances.
IV. Henry has likely reduced its ability to quickly cut costs in order to respond to economic downturns.

a. I, II, III, and IV.
b. I and IV only.
c. II and IV only.
d. I and III only.

CMA3-2. Using the following budget data for Valley Corporation, which produces only one product, calculate the company's predetermined manufacturing overhead application rate for variable overhead. *Hint:* The factory supervisor's salary is direct labor, since it is incurred regardless of production. SG&A expenses relate to the entire operations of Valley Corporation and not just related to manufacturing.

Units to be produced	11,000
Units to be sold	10,000
Indirect materials, varying with production	$ 1,000
Indirect labor, varying with production.	10,000
Factory supervisor's salary, incurred regardless of production.	20,000
Depreciation on factory building and equipment	30,000
Utilities to operate factory machines	12,000
Security lighting for factory	2,000
Selling, general and administrative (SG&A) expenses	5,000

    a. $2.09

    b. $2.30

    c. $4.73

    d. $5.00

CMA3-3. Baldwin Printing Company uses a job order costing system and applies overhead based on machine hours. A total of 150,000 machine hours have been budgeted for the year. During the year, an order for 1,000 units was completed and incurred the following.

Direct material costs.	$1,000
Direct labor costs	1,500
Actual overhead	1,980
Machine hours	450

The accountant calculated the inventory cost of this order to be $4.30 per unit. The annual budgeted overhead in dollars was

    a. $577,500.

    b. $600,000.

    c. $645,000.

    d. $660,000.

CMA3-4. Boston Furniture Company manufactures several steel products. It has three production departments, Fabricating, Assembly, and Finishing. The service departments include Maintenance, Material Handling, and Designing. Currently, the company does not allocate service department costs to the production departments. John Baker, who has recently joined the company as the new cost accountant, believes that service department rates should be developed and charged to the production departments for services requested. If the company adopts this new policy, the production department managers would be **least** likely to

    a.   request an excessive amount of service.

    b.   replace outdated and inefficient systems.

    c.   refrain from using necessary services.

    d.   be encouraged to control costs.

CMA3-5. John Sheng, cost accountant at Starlet Company, is developing departmental manufacturing overhead application rates for the company's tooling and fabricating departments. The budgeted overhead for each department and the data for one job are shown below.

	Departments	
	Tooling	**Fabricating**
Supplies	$ 850	$ 200
Supervisors' salaries	1,500	2,000
Indirect labor	1,200	4,880
Depreciation..	1,000	5,500
Repairs..	4,075	3,540
Total budgeted manufacturing overhead....................	$8,625	$16,120
Total direct labor hours	460	620
Direct labor hours on Job #231	12	3

Using the departmental overhead application rates, total overhead applied to Job #231 in the Tooling and Fabricating Departments will be

a. $225.
b. $303.
c. $537.
d. $671.

EXTENDING YOUR KNOWLEDGE

EYK3-1. Business Decision Case Elizabeth Flanigan and Associates is an engineering and design firm that specializes in developing plans for recycling plants for municipalities. The firm uses a job costing system to accumulate the cost associated with each design project. Flanigan employs three levels of employee: senior engineers, associate engineers, and clerical staff. The salary cost of the senior engineers and the associate engineers is assigned to each project as direct labor. The salary cost of the clerical staff is included in overhead, along with the cost of engineering supplies, automobile travel, and equipment depreciation. The cost of airline travel, motels, building permits, and fees from other consultants is charged to each project as direct material. Overhead is applied to projects using a predetermined overhead rate based on total engineering hours. The rate for 2014 is $5 per hour.

The six different salary levels for 2015 for the employees of Elizabeth Flanigan and Associates are listed below. The hourly rate is determined by dividing the yearly salary by 2,000 hours per year.

> **Senior engineer**
> Level 1: $44,000 per year ($22 per hour)
> Level 2: $36,000 per year ($18 per hour)
> **Associate engineer**
> Level 3: $30,000 per year ($15 per hour)
> Level 4: $24,000 per year ($12 per hour)
> **Clerical staff**
> Level 5: $16,000 per year ($8 per hour)
> Level 6: $12,000 per year ($6 per hour)

The billings that are sent to the municipalities for engineering services utilize cost-plus billing. Typically, the total costs accumulated for a project (direct material, direct labor, and overhead) are multiplied by 140% to determine the amount of the billing. The difference between the billed amount and the accumulated cost is the "plus" in cost plus.

During March 2015, Flanigan accumulated the following information related to Job 295 for Johnson Creek City:

Senior engineer hours	
Level 1	52
Level 2	84
Associate engineer hours	
Level 3	106
Level 4	44
Clerical hours	
Level 5	20
Level 6	66
Building permits	$1,500
Airline travel and motel	$865

Required

a. What amount should be billed to Johnson Creek City for March 2015?

b. How much profit was earned on Job 295 during March 2015?

EYK3-2. **Corporate Social Responsibility Problem** The CSR box in this chapter discusses CH2M Hill's efforts to offer summer programs at no cost introducing underrepresented groups to STEM education. The company's stated goal is twofold: to increase the pool of future engineering talent and to build better communities.

Some would look at these efforts as costly programs with no tangible financial benefit. There is certainly no guarantee that these children will work for CH2M Hill in the future, or even that they will choose careers in engineering. In fact, these efforts may end up supplying talent for CH2M Hill's competitors and driving up future engineering wages.

What do you think?

EYK3-3. **Ethics Case** Metal Creations, Inc., is a custom manufacturer that uses a job order costing system. Currently, Metal Creations has 35% excess capacity in its factory. Charlie Rollins, the president, has instituted a campaign to obtain new customers. Rollins has offered the salespeople a bonus equal to 25% of the gross profit on work for new customers. The average gross profit rate has been 30% of the contract price.

Steve Starling, the sales manager for Metal Creations, wants to submit a proposal to a new customer that undercuts the usual pricing structure by 30%. As a result, this job would have no gross profit using the regular job order costing system. Instead, Starling suggests that the overhead rate applied to this job should be only 40% of the normal overhead rate, resulting in a gross profit of 28%. Starling suggests that the controller should handle this contract herself, and that no one else in the organization should know about it, especially the other salespeople, because the creative approach to overhead application might create problems.

Required

Does taking an order at a significantly reduced price create an ethical problem? Does altering the accounting for a particular order create an ethical problem? Does asking the controller to handle the contract and keep the accounting confidential create an ethical problem?

ANSWERS TO SELF-STUDY QUESTIONS:

1. d, (p. 69)   2. c, (p. 73)   3. b, (p. 78)   4. b, (p. 79)   5. d, (pp. 84-85)

YOUR TURN! SOLUTIONS

Solution 3.1

Industry	Cost System
Chemicals	Process
Printing	Job order
Aircraft	Job order
Oil refining	Process
Paints	Process
Glass	Process
Furniture	Job order
Machinery	Job order

Solution 3.2

1. Manufacturing overhead cannot be traced directly to a particular product or job.
2. Manufacturing overhead consists of many unlike items.
3. Manufacturing actual overhead costs may not be known until after a period is over.

Solution 3.3

Estimated manufacturing overhead	$250,000
Divided by budgeted direct labor hours.	10,000
Predetermined overhead rate per direct labor hour.	$ 25
Actual direct labor hours	$ 9,000
Multiplied by predetermined overhead rate	× 25
Applied overhead	$225,000

Solution 3.4

1. Overhead cannot be traced directly to a particular product or job. Manufacturing overhead cost for one department might be significantly different from that of another department.
2. The activity basis in one department might be different from that of another. One department may be labor intensive and another department may be machine intensive.

DECISION TIME SOLUTION

Solution 3.1

c. Either *a* or *b*, depending on the significance of the amount.

4

Cost Accounting Systems: Process Costing

PAST

Chapter 3 introduced and explained job costing in more detail for both manufacturing and service industries. It also explained overhead allocation.

PRESENT

Chapter 4 introduces process costing and how it differs from job order costing. It illustrates equivalent units and the flow of costs through the inventory accounts, as well as introduces the product cost report.

FUTURE

Chapter 5 explores activity-based costing and its benefits relative to traditional plant-wide and departmental overhead allocation, and contrasts it with activity-based management.

LEARNING OBJECTIVES

1. **Compare** and **contrast** job order costing and process costing. *(p. 112)*

2. **Describe** the basic concepts of process costing. *(p. 114)*

3. **Explain** techniques for determining unit costs when process costing is used. *(p. 116)*

4. **Explain** the procedures used to prepare the product cost report using the weighted average method in a process costing system. *(p. 123)*

5. **Illustrate** the journal entries used with process costing. *(p. 125)*

6. Appendix 4A: **Explain** techniques for determining unit costs when the FIFO method for process costing is used. *(p. 130)*

7. Appendix 4A: **Explain** the procedures used to prepare the product cost report using the FIFO method in a process costing system. *(p. 136)*

8. Appendix 4A: **Illustrate** the journal entries used with FIFO process costing. *(p. 138)*

GENERAL MILLS INC.

General Mills Inc. is a Fortune 500 company based in Golden Valley, Minnesota. Consumers know General Mills best for its ready-to-eat cereal products, of which they consume 60 million servings per day. The quality of these cereal products can be traced back to Gold Medal flour in 1880, which today remains the number-one-selling brand of flour in the United States. General Mills' brand portfolio includes more than 100 leading U.S. brands and numerous category leaders around the world, with 2014 overall company sales reaching $17.9 billion. Some of the top-selling brands include Betty Crocker, Yoplait, Totinos, Pillsbury, Cheerios, Trix, and Lucky Charms. One unique manufacturing feature these brands share is that they are produced in mass quantities, with little to distinguish one cupful of cereal or yogurt from another.

Manufacturers like General Mills that produce massive quantities of inventory that are indistinguishable from one another rely on process costing to track inventory costs. The company had an inventory balance on May 31, 2015, of $1.5 billion, of which $486 million consisted of raw materials and work in process, and $1.3 billion consisted of finished goods. Rather than track the cost of each piece of cereal, General Mills tracks the total costs of inventory produced over a given period and divides these total costs by the pounds of inventory produced to obtain an average price per pound for each product. This costing system stands in stark contrast to industries such as custom cabinet manufacturing, in which costs are tallied on a job cost record for each unique custom cabinet rather than spreading them over multiple identical units of inventory.

This chapter examines how companies like General Mills utilize process costing in order to properly value their inventory. We focus on how the weighted average method of process costing provides useful information to managers and illustrates the journal entries required throughout the manufacturing process. We also introduce the concept of equivalent units and their application to process costing.

COST ACCOUNTING SYSTEMS: PROCESS COSTING					
Introduction to Process Costing	**Characteristics of Process Costing**	**Process Costing Steps**	**The Product Cost Report**	**Journal Entries Illustrated**	**Process Costing Using FIFO Method (Appendix 4A)**
• Job order costing review • Processing costing	• Manufacturing departments • Basic processing patterns	• Visualize physical flow of units • Calculate equivalent units • Determine per-unit costs • Calculate cost of goods manufactured • Calculate ending work in process inventory	• Illustration of the product cost report • Multiple production processes	• Material • Labor • Manufacturing overhead	• Process costing steps • The product cost report • Journal entries illustrated

INTRODUCTION TO PROCESS COSTING

LO1 **Compare** and **contrast** job order costing and process costing.

The early sections of this chapter explain and illustrate the concepts and procedures that are typical in a process costing system that involves only one processing department using the weighted average cost flow assumption. Appendix 4A illustrates the procedures and differences under the first-in, first-out (FIFO) cost flow assumption.

Job Order Costing Review

Prior chapters have introduced and discussed the concepts used in job order costing. Recall that job order costing accumulates costs for each specific job in a separate work in process inventory account dedicated to that unique job. **Exhibit 4-1** presents the typical flow of product costs in a job order costing system for Job 372. Direct material and direct labor are traced to each specific job, whereas indirect overhead costs are allocated to each job.

Exhibit 4-1	Product Cost Flows in a Job Order Costing System

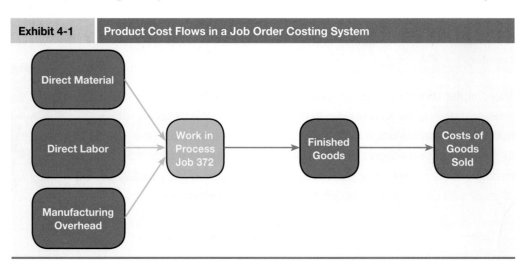

Although production costs are tracked separately for each job, companies also need to understand their total costs. Hence, costs for all of the individual jobs are accumulated in the work in process control account, which represents the overall cost summary of all jobs currently in production. For example, **Exhibit 4-2** lists four individual jobs that are currently in process. The work in process inventory control account represents the sum of all jobs that are currently in process. Overhead costs are accumulated and applied to the work in process inventory control account based on an annual predetermined overhead rate. Specifically, actual overhead costs, including indirect material and indirect labor, are accumulated in the manufacturing overhead account as debits, and the applied overhead is transferred to Work in Process Inventory with a credit. Perpetual inventory techniques are typically used to move product cost from Work in Process Inventory to Finished Goods Inventory and finally to Cost of Goods Sold, as illustrated in **Exhibit 4-2**.

Exhibit 4-2	Job Order Costing Summary (Accumulating Costs by Job)

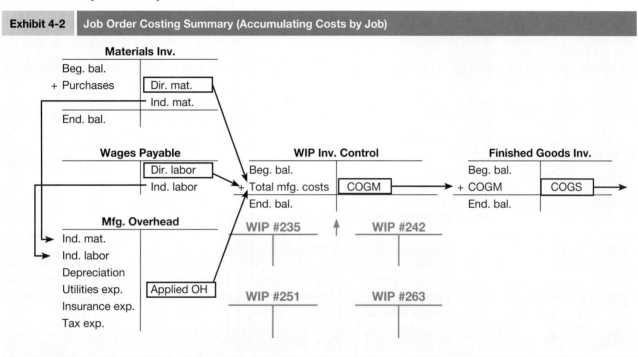

Job order costing is appropriate when products or services are characterized by customization to meet the customer's specifications. Job order costing can result when products are produced or jobs are undertaken to (1) fill specific customer orders or (2) produce a stock of products from which future orders can be filled.

Process Costing

Process costing, however, is used when large volumes of identical (homogeneous) products are manufactured in a continuous-flow operation, such as the production of fuels, chemicals, small appliances, building materials, and electricity. In process costing, product costs are accumulated by department, not by job or product. We note at the outset that although it is possible to use process costing in a service environment, it is not common. For example, a service agency that provides identical services to each customer could calculate an average cost per customer. However, most of the examples in this chapter focus on manufacturing companies because process costing is much more common in a manufacturing setting. We provide a detailed service example at the end of the chapter.

TAKEAWAY 4.1

Job order costing is used for unique products or orders, whereas process costing is used for uniform products.

CHARACTERISTICS OF PROCESS COSTING

LO2   **Describe** the basic concepts of process costing.

Exhibit 4-3 presents the typical flow of product cost in a **process costing system**. The following process costing characteristics are evident in **Exhibit 4-3**:

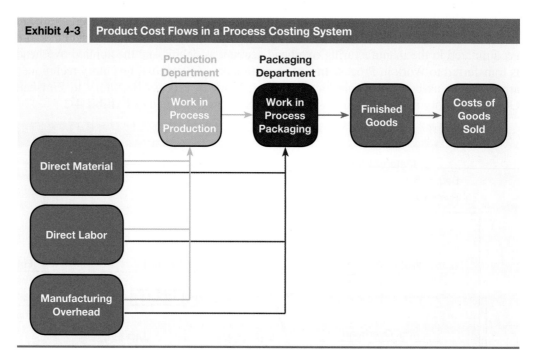

| Exhibit 4-3 | Product Cost Flows in a Process Costing System |

1. Each manufacturing department has a separate work in process inventory account. **Exhibit 4-3** assumes a company with two manufacturing departments: production and packaging. Costs are accumulated for each department in a separate work in process inventory account.

Hint: A process can be defined as a step in the manufacture of a product. In a process costing system, materials, labor, and overhead are charged to processing departments rather than to specific jobs.

2. **Exhibit 4-4** shows how the costs in this process flow through the accounts. Direct material, direct labor, and manufacturing overhead costs can be added to the work in process inventory account in each department. **Exhibit 4-4** shows all three elements of product cost being added to both work in process inventory accounts.

3. Products physically move through the process on a first-in, first-out (FIFO) basis. That is, the unfinished units in work in process are assumed to be completed first in the subsequent period before new units are started.

4. Under process costing, managers use a **product cost report** to accumulate costs by process or department. These costs are then allocated to specific units of product that pass through that process or department using either the weighted average or FIFO allocation method. In this chapter, we focus on the weighted average costing method, and Appendix 4A explains the FIFO costing method.

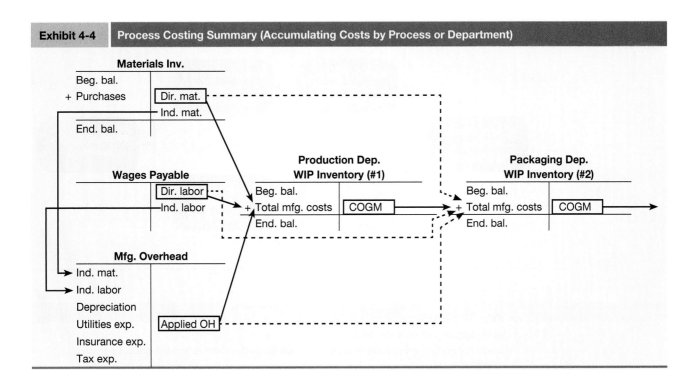

| Exhibit 4-4 | Process Costing Summary (Accumulating Costs by Process or Department) |

Manufacturing Departments

Typically, multiple manufacturing departments are identified when process costing is used. Products will flow through these departments at different stages of the manufacturing process. For example, a consumer product might be processed through three departments, machining, painting, and assembling. In any particular manufacturing plant, some products may go through many departments, and other products may go through only a few departments, depending on the nature of the work to be done. Regardless, the work in any department must be performed uniformly on all units, and the output of the department must be uniform in nature.

Basic Processing Patterns

There are two basic patterns for arranging the departments in a process costing setting: sequential and parallel processing. **Exhibit 4-5** presents a **sequential product processing** pattern, in which products follow a single path through the manufacturing process to finished goods inventory.

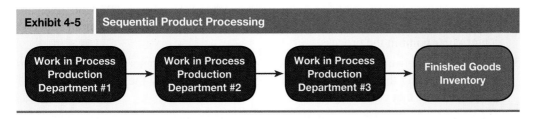

| Exhibit 4-5 | Sequential Product Processing |

Exhibit 4-6 presents a simple example of **parallel product processing**. Numerous variations of parallel processing are possible, but similar products may begin with the same raw materials or processing in one department and then follow slightly different processes to arrive in finished goods inventory.

Exhibit 4-6	Parallel Product Processing

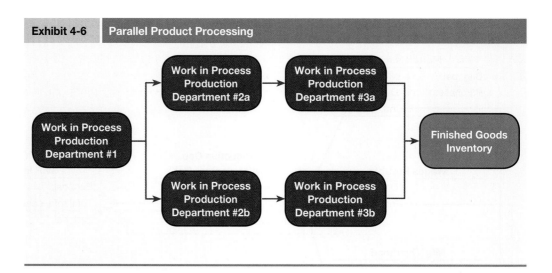

Each processing department has two essential features:
1. The activity performed in each department is performed uniformly on all products passing through it.
2. The output of each department is homogeneous.

PROCESS COSTING STEPS

LO3 **Explain** techniques for determining unit costs when process costing is used.

The techniques described in this chapter require the calculation of unit costs to facilitate the end-of-period transfer of product cost from one work in process inventory account to another, from the final work in process inventory account to the finished goods inventory account, and from the finished goods inventory account to the cost of goods sold account. In process costing, unit costs are usually calculated on a monthly basis. These unit costs can be compared to unit costs of prior accounting periods to determine when additional cost control measures are necessary.

Process costing requires five steps or calculations:

1. Visualize or chart the physical flow of the units through the system.

2. Determine the equivalent whole units of work completed (or **equivalent units** of production) during the period. This calculation is usually performed separately for materials and **conversion costs** (i.e., labor and overhead) because conversion costs are usually added uniformly throughout the process, whereas materials are often added at a particular point in the process.

3. Compute the per-unit cost of production for the period for materials and conversion costs by dividing the total costs incurred in each category by the equivalent units of production for that cost category.

4. Using the per-unit costs for material and conversion costs, compute the dollar value of the units completed and transferred (Cost of Goods Manufactured) to the next department.

5. Using the same per-unit costs, compute the dollar value of the unfinished units that remain in the department (these ending work in process units will usually be completed in the following period).

The objective of each step is the same for both the weighted average and FIFO methods of cost allocation. However, the execution of the steps is slightly different between the two methods. We discuss these steps in more detail for the weighted average method in the following sections. For illustration purposes, assume that the Big G division of General Mills uses process costing to account for its cereal production and that it has the results for January as illustrated in **Exhibit 4-7**.

Exhibit 4-7	Big G Process Costing Example	
Work in process, January 1:		
Direct materials	$	166,400
Direct labor		38,100
Manufacturing overhead		76,300
Total beginning work in process	$	280,800
Work done during January:		
Direct material (grain) added		$19,250,000
Direct labor incurred		3,210,000
Manufacturing overhead applied		9,540,000
Total costs incurred during January		$32,000,000
Units in process at January 1 (20% complete)		2,600 tons
Units started during January		58,500 tons
Units in process at January 31 (40% complete)		3,500 tons

Further, assume that all materials are added at the beginning of the process, whereas labor and manufacturing overhead costs are added evenly throughout the process. The T-account in **Exhibit 4-8** illustrates the purpose of process costing: to allocate actual costs incurred between units completed and transferred out, and partially completed units remaining in ending inventory.

Exhibit 4-8	The Objective: Allocate Costs between Ending Inventory and Those Transferred Out

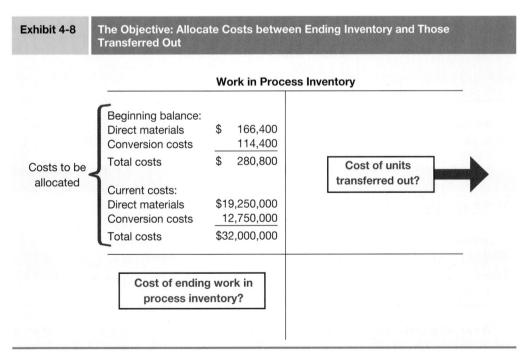

We know the costs associated with the beginning work in process inventory on January 1 ($280,800). We also know the costs incurred during the month of January for direct materials ($19,250,000), direct labor ($3,210,000), and manufacturing overhead ($9,540,000). For simplicity, because we assume both direct labor and manufacturing overhead costs are applied uniformly during the production process, we combine them and simply refer to them as "conversion costs." Because we started the period with partially completed inventory, during the period we will first finish the previously started units and then begin work on new units. We also end the period with partially completed units. We don't know how much of these costs should be applied to units transferred out at the end of the period and how much should remain with the partially complete ending inventory. Process costing helps us calculate an average cost per unit to apply to (1) the units completed and transferred out at the end of the period and (2) the units remaining in ending inventory.

Step 1: Visualize the Physical Flow of the Units

The starting point in process costing is to visualize how the units flow through the production process, as illustrated in **Exhibit 4-9**. In the General Mills Big G example, the quantity produced is measured in tons of cereal processed during the month of January. Sometimes it is useful to visualize how the units correspond to the dollars in the T-account in **Exhibit 4-8**.

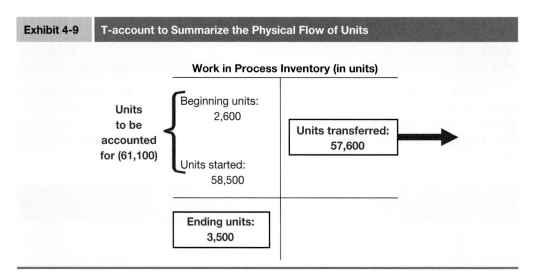

| Exhibit 4-9 | T-account to Summarize the Physical Flow of Units |

Work in Process Inventory (in units)

Units to be accounted for (61,100)
- Beginning units: 2,600
- Units started: 58,500

Units transferred: 57,600

Ending units: 3,500

Another way to visualize the flow of the cereal produced during January is by asking where the units come from and where they end up, as shown in **Exhibit 4-10**.

| Exhibit 4-10 | Step 1: Visualize the Physical Flow of the Units |

Where do the units come from?		Where do the units go?	
Beginning inventory	2,600	Complete/transferred....	57,600
Started	58,500	Ending inventory........	3,500
Total	61,100	Total	61,100

We assume that all of the beginning inventory is completed first. Of the 58,500 units started this month, 55,000 are complete by the end of the month, and 3,500 remain partially complete.

Step 2: Calculate the Equivalent Units

Introduction to Equivalent Units

The average cost per unit is calculated by dividing total costs by the total number of units produced. The work in process accounts described in **Exhibits 4-5** and **4-6** illustrate how total costs are accumulated and tracked through the system. Accountants are good at keeping track of costs. However, cost accountants face a major problem in allocating costs in continuous-flow manufacturing processes. At any given point in time, units of product are at various stages of completion. Hence, it is difficult to determine the number of units to use in the average cost per unit calculation:

Hint: Instead of tracking specific costs incurred to produce each unit of product as in job order costing, process costing accumulates costs by department and then calculates an average cost per unit to be assigned to all units of product produced during that period.

$$\text{Average cost per unit} = \frac{\text{Total costs incurred}}{\text{\# of equivalent units}} \quad \longleftarrow \quad \text{We know this.}$$
$$\longleftarrow \quad \text{We don't know this.}$$

The notion of equivalent units of production is a key concept in process costing. When units of product are produced in a continuous process, engineers and manufacturing supervisors must estimate the average percentage completion of units in a given department at the end of each period. Accountants use this information to estimate the number of equivalent *complete* units of product. For example, the following illustration shows eight glasses of water that are *half* full. How many *full* glasses of water is this equivalent to?

8 Glasses ½ Full = 4 Full Glasses

The eight half-full glasses are approximately equivalent to four full glasses. This example illustrates what accountants do each period in determining the average cost per unit in a given department.

To properly determine per-unit costs, we must first calculate equivalent units of production to be used in the denominator of the average cost per unit calculation. **Equivalent units** are the equivalent number of *whole units* completed during the period. In the previous illustration, the eight partially full glasses of water are equivalent to four full glasses (similar to four equivalent complete units of production). The calculation of equivalent units of production requires accountants to (1) track the *actual quantity* of products at each stage of production and (2) estimate the *average amount of work completed* on each unit of product in terms of conversion costs and direct material costs.

Engineers or production experts estimate the percentage of work completed in terms of conversion costs, on average. As illustrated in **Exhibit 4-11**, because the 2,600 tons of cereal on hand on January 1 is 20% complete (based on work completed during

December), Big G only has to complete the remaining 80% of the processing during the month of January. During January, Big G begins work on 55,000 tons of cereal that is both started and completed during the month of January. Finally, Big G begins work on an additional 3,500 tons of cereal that is not completed by the end of the month. Engineers determine that only 40% of the processing is complete on this batch of cereal by January 31.

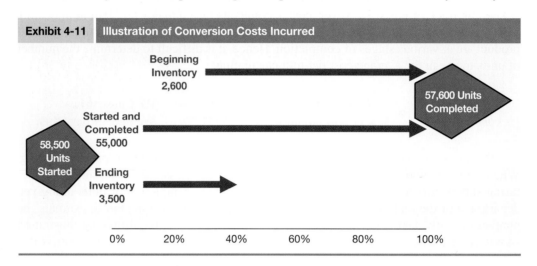

Exhibit 4-11	Illustration of Conversion Costs Incurred

Hint: The weighted average method is called a "rollback" method because the average includes all work done in the current period plus work done on beginning inventory in the prior period.

We assume that all direct material is added at the beginning of the process; therefore, the average amount of work completed on each unit of product related to direct materials is 100%.

Calculating equivalent units can be performed using either the weighted average or the FIFO cost flow assumption. We illustrate the **weighted average method** here and the FIFO method in **Appendix 4A**. A key difference between the two methods is that the weighted average method mixes inventory layers, whereas the **FIFO method** keeps inventory layers separate. To keep these layers separate, the FIFO method tracks costs incurred during December separate from those incurred during January, the weighted average method averages all costs incurred in the production of a batch of units, regardless of when those costs were incurred. Thus, the FIFO method asks "What costs were incurred during THIS PERIOD?" whereas the weighted average method simply asks "How much work is complete (regardless of when the work was done)?"

Equivalent Unit Calculation for Direct Materials—Weighted Average

Because materials are added at the beginning of the process, all units that have been started (61,100) are 100% complete with respect to materials. **Exhibit 4-12** illustrates the calculation of equivalent units in terms of direct materials based on the weighted average cost flow assumption.

Exhibit 4-12	Step 2: Calculate the Equivalent Units—Direct Materials

	Physical Units (tons)		Proportion Completed		Equivalent Units (tons)
Complete and transferred	57,600	×	100%	=	57,600
Ending inventory.	3,500	×	100%	=	3,500
Total	61,100				61,100

Equivalent Unit Calculation for Conversion Costs—Weighted Average

When considering conversion costs (direct labor and manufacturing overhead), it is often useful to visualize the amount of work done during the period on each unique set of inventory passing through the production process, as previously illustrated in **Exhibit 4-11**. Despite the fact that some of the units were started during December, the weighted average method simply asks what percentage of the work has been completed by the end of January, as illustrated in **Exhibit 4-13**.

Exhibit 4-13	Step 2: Calculate the Equivalent Units—Conversion Costs				
	Physical Units (tons)		Proportion Completed		Equivalent Units (tons)
Complete and transferred	57,600	×	100%	=	57,600
Ending inventory.	3,500	×	40%	=	1,400
Total	61,100				59,000

We can summarize the flow of the units worked on during the period and how the amount of work completed translates them into equivalent units, as illustrated in **Exhibit 4-14**.

Exhibit 4-14	Summary of Steps 1 and 2: Unit Flows and Equivalent Units Calculations						
				Step 2: Calculate the Equivalent Units			
Step 1: Visualize the Physical Flow of the Units				**Equivalent Units**			
Where do the units come from?		**Where do the units go?**		% Work Done?	Dir. Mat.	% Work Done?	Conv. Costs
Beg. Inv.	2,600 →	Compl./transf.	57,600	100%	57,600	100%	57,600
Started	58,500 →	End. Inv.	3,500	100%	3,500	40%	1,400
Total	61,100	Total	61,100		61,100		59,000

TAKEAWAY 4.3

An equivalent unit is the amount of work necessary to produce one complete physical unit of product. For example, doing 80% of the work on 200 units is equivalent to doing 100% of the work on 160 units.

YOUR TURN! 4.1

The solution is on page 157.

Assume all materials are added at the beginning of the production process, and conversion costs are added uniformly throughout the process. Beginning work in process is comprised of 100 units, which are 35% complete with respect to conversion costs. Also assume that 700 units are started and completed during the period, and ending work in process includes 90 units that are 75% complete with respect to conversion costs. Compute equivalent units of production for direct materials and conversion costs under the weighted average cost flow assumption. (*Hint:* For fractional units, round up.)

Step 3: Determine the Per-Unit Costs

The product cost report summarizes where the costs come from and where they go (i.e., where they are allocated). In order to calculate an average cost per unit of direct materials and conversion costs, we first need to summarize the total costs incurred for direct materials and conversion costs. These numbers were illustrated in the T-account in **Exhibit 4-8**. The top part of our product cost report simply asks where the costs come from and organizes them into categories: Direct Materials and Conversion Costs, as illustrated in **Exhibit 4-15**.

Exhibit 4-15	Product Cost Report: Where Do the Costs Come From?

Product Cost Report
General Mills Big G Division
January Production

Where do the costs come from?	Total	Direct Materials	Conversion Costs
Beginning inventory	$ 280,800	$ 166,400	$ 114,400
Current	32,000,000	19,250,000	12,750,000
Total costs to account for	$32,280,800	$19,416,400	$12,864,400

We then calculate the average cost per unit by dividing total costs in each category by total equivalent units in each category from Step 2. In other words, we divide total materials costs by total equivalent units of materials ($19,416,400/61,100 equivalent units) to get an average cost per unit of $317.78. Similarly, we divide total conversion costs by total equivalent units of conversion costs ($12,864,400/59,000 equivalent units) to get an average cost per unit of $218.04. **Exhibit 4-16** summarizes this calculation.

Exhibit 4-16	Step 3: Product Cost Report: Determine Per-Unit Costs

Product Cost Report
General Mills Big G Division
January Production

Where do the costs come from?	Total	Direct Materials	Conversion Costs
Beginning inventory	$ 280,800	$ 166,400	$ 114,400
Current	32,000,000	19,250,000	12,750,000
Total costs to account for	$32,280,800	$19,416,400	$12,864,400
÷ Total equivalent units		61,100	59,000
Average cost/unit		$ 317.7807	$ 218.0407

Note that the weighted average method includes *all* costs incurred on units worked on during the month, whereas the FIFO method only includes costs incurred during the *current* period. Hence, both the numerator (costs incurred) and the denominator (equivalent units) will differ between the weighted average and FIFO methods.

Step 4: Calculate the Cost of Goods Manufactured

At the end of each month and for each department, we calculate the cost of goods manufactured (illustrated in **Exhibit 4-17**), which is comprised of the cost of the goods that are completed and transferred to the finished goods inventory. Under the weighted average cost flow assumption, the Big G division's cost of goods manufactured during January consists of 57,600 equivalent units of materials and conversion costs (shown in **red** in **Exhibit 4-14**) multiplied by their respective per-unit costs computed in Step 2 (shown in **green** in **Exhibit 4-16**).

Exhibit 4-17	Step 4: Cost of Goods Manufactured Calculation		
Materials.	**[57,600 EU** × **$317.7807]**	18,304,168
Conversion costs	**[57,600 EU** × **$218.0407]**	12,559,143*
Total cost of goods manufactured.		$30,863,311

*Difference due to rounding

Step 5: Calculate the Ending Work in Process Inventory

Exhibit 4-18 illustrates the final step, which is to calculate the **cost of goods remaining** in ending work in process. Assuming all materials are added at the beginning and conversion costs are added evenly throughout the process, we multiply the equivalent units of materials and conversion costs in ending inventory (denoted in **red** in **Exhibit 4-14**) by their respective unit costs (shown in **green** in **Exhibit 4-16**) computed in Step 2, as shown in **Exhibit 4-18**.

Exhibit 4-18	Step 5: Calculate Cost of Ending Inventory		
Materials.	**[3,500 EU** × **$317.7807]**	1,112,232
Conversion costs	**[1,400 EU** × **$218.0407]**	305,257
Total cost of ending inventory		$1,417,489

	General Mills Tries to Make a Difference	CORPORATE SOCIAL RESPONSIBILITY

If you read the current popular media reports, you are likely to get the idea that the only stakeholders a corporation cares about are its shareholders. General Mills thinks differently. The goal of General Mills is to stand among the world's most socially responsible food companies. The company believes that being a good corporate citizen means considering all its stakeholders. To do this, General Mills seeks to create long-term economic, social, and environmental value.

General Mills recognizes that its customers depend on the company to provide healthy food choices. One example of what General Mills is doing in this area is an improvement in the health profile of 76% of its retail U.S. sales volume since 2005. To help the environment, General Mills has reduced its waste generation by 41% since 2005. General Mills' is also committed to sustainable sourcing, with a goal of 50% of its annual raw material purchases to be from sustainable sources by 2020. General Mills strives to create a culture of ethics with 95% of employees stating that General Mills leaders demonstrate a commitment to ethical business. Finally, General Mills commitment to community included over $151 million of donations to charitable causes in 2014 and over $1.5 billion since the General Mills Foundation was established in 1954.

Source: https://www.generalmills.com/en/Responsibility/Overview

THE PRODUCT COST REPORT

Using the Big G example, the product cost report illustrated in **Exhibit 4-19** summarizes all of the steps in the total cost allocation process from (1) visualizing the physical flow of the units, to (2) calculating equivalent units, to (3) calculating unit costs, to (4) calculating cost of goods manufactured, to (5) calculating ending inventory. Moreover, **Exhibit 4-19** also provides Big G's product cost report. Note that in this illustration, the equivalent units of production for materials and conversion costs (the numbers in **red**) are multiplied by the corresponding cost per unit figures for materials and conversion costs (the numbers in **green**) to calculate the cost allocation to cost of goods manufactured and ending inventory.

LO4 **Explain** the procedures used to prepare the product cost report using the weighted average method in a process costing system.

Exhibit 4-19	Summary of the Five Process Costing Steps

Flow of the Units and Equivalent Units Calculation

Step 1: Visualize the Physical Flow of the Units

Step 2: Calculate the Equivalent Units

Where do the units come from?		Where do the units go?			% Work Done?	Dir. Mat.	% Work Done?	Conv. Costs
Beg. inv.	2,600	Compl./transf..	57,600		100%	57,600	100%	57,600
Started	58,500	End. inv.	3,500		100%	3,500	40%	1,400
Total	61,100	Total	61,100			61,100		59,000

Product Cost Report
General Mills Big G Division
January Production

Step 3: Determine Per-Unit Costs

Where do the costs come from?	Total		Dir. Mat.	Conv. Costs
Beginning inventory	$ 280,800		$ 166,400	$ 114,400
Current	32,000,000		19,250,000	12,750,000
Total costs to account for	$32,280,800		$19,416,400	$12,864,400
÷ Total equivalent units			61,100	59,000
Average cost/equivalent unit			$317.7807	$218.0407

Where do the costs go?

Step 4: Calculate the Cost of Goods Manufactured

Complete/transferred:		
Materials.	$18,304,168	[57,600 × $317.7807]
Conversion costs	12,559,143*	[57,600 × $218.0407]
Cost of goods manuactured.	$30,863,311	

Step 5: Calculate the Cost of the Ending Inventory

Ending inventory:		
Materials.	$ 1,112,232	[3,500 × $317.7807]
Conversion costs	305,257	[1,400 × $218.0407]
Cost of ending inventory.	1,417,489	
Total costs allocated	$32,280,800	

*Difference due to rounding

Exhibit 4-20	Final Allocation of Costs to Ending Inventory and Cost of Goods Manufactured (and Transferred Out)

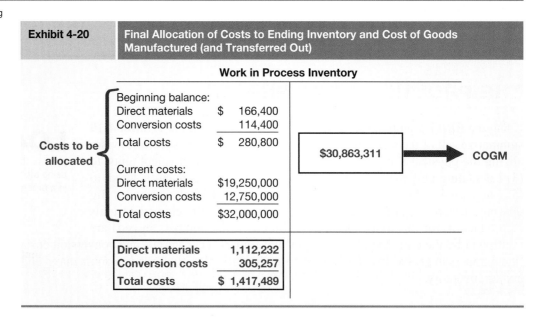

Work in Process Inventory

Beginning balance:		
Direct materials	$ 166,400	
Conversion costs	114,400	
Total costs	$ 280,800	
Current costs:		
Direct materials	$19,250,000	
Conversion costs	12,750,000	
Total costs	$32,000,000	

Costs to be allocated

$30,863,311 → COGM

Direct materials	1,112,232
Conversion costs	305,257
Total costs	$ 1,417,489

As a final check to see that we have performed all of the calculations correctly, the sum of the Cost of Goods Manufactured ($30,863,311) and the ending Working Process Inventory balance (1,417,489) should equal the total costs that we determined at the outset needed to be allocated (Beginning balance $280,800 + Current costs 32,000,000 = $32,280,800). Specifically, the T-account in **Exhibit 4-20** summarizes the process costing allocation of costs between costs transferred out and costs remaining in ending inventory.

Companies with Multiple Production Processes

At the outset of this chapter, we described situations in which a company produces its products through a long series of production processes. So far, we have illustrated process costing in a single department. When a company's production process involves a series of different departments, costs are accumulated by production process. The costs transferred out of one department are transferred into the next department. Hence, as units of product move from one department or process to the next, they carry the costs from all prior processes with them. From a practical perspective, the only thing that changes in the product costing process is that an extra column is added for transferred-in costs. For example, the $30,863,311 transferred out of the production process described in the previous section would become the transferred-in costs for the next department.

JOURNAL ENTRIES ILLUSTRATED

After computing these amounts, Big G would record the following journal entries related to January production. *These entries assume that materials are added at the beginning of the process, and that labor and overhead are added evenly over the month of January.*

LO5 Illustrate the journal entries used with process costing.

Material

During January, assume that Big G purchased $20,000,000 of grain on account. The following is a summary journal entry for the January purchases:

1	Materials inventory	20,000,000	
	Accounts payable		20,000,000
	To record January material purchases.		

The direct material requisitioned during January for the processing department is shown in the following entry:

2	Work in process	19,250,000	
	Materials inventory		19,250,000
	To record direct material used during January.		

Labor

During January, Big G accrued $3,210,000 of direct labor expense. The journal entry to record this payroll would be as follows:

3	Work in process	3,210,000	
	Wages payable		3,210,000
	To record the payroll for January.		

Manufacturing Overhead

Assume that Big G has recorded its manufacturing overhead costs (such as maintenance, depreciation, and utilities) in Manufacturing Overhead as incurred. Also assume that Big G applies manufacturing overhead costs to Work in Process using predetermined overhead rates. The following entry records the amount of applied manufacturing overhead for the processing department:

4	Work in process	9,540,000	
	Manufacturing overhead		9,540,000
	To apply manufacturing overhead to work in process		
	inventory.		

As a result of the journal entries recorded during the month, the Work in Process account contains the following balance as of the end of the month:

	Work in Process
Beginning balance	$ 280,800
Direct material	19,250,000
Direct labor.	3,210,000
Factory overhead	9,540,000
Balance before month-end adjustments	$32,280,800

At the end of the month, an additional journal entry is needed to transfer product costs from the processing department to Finished Goods (the amount of Cost of Goods Manufactured). The following entry records the Cost of Goods Manufactured:

5	Finished goods	30,863,311	
	Work in process		30,863,311
	To transfer the cost of completed product from work in		
	process inventory.		

YOUR TURN! 4.2

The solution is on page 157.

Assume the following cost information related to May production, and only one manufacturing department. What journal entries would be made to capture May production?

Direct material	$24,000
Direct labor.	32,400
Manufacturing overhead applied	48,600

SERVICE INDUSTRY IN FOCUS

SERVICE AND MERCHANDISING

Environmental Business Consultants, LLC (EBC) has a contract with Terrabean Coffee, a large retail coffee company with 5,000 shops across North America, to manage the company's waste disposal and recycling services. Under the contract with Terrabean, EBC is responsible for negotiating, monitoring, and servicing contracts with dozens of garbage and recycling collection companies in major cities throughout the United States and Canada. These contracts generally require the garbage and recycling collection companies to collect both garbage and recyclables on a daily basis from between 10 and 30 shops, 365 days per year. When collection is missed, invoices are questioned, service is changed, new shops are opened, or other issues arise, the shop managers call EBC for assistance.

EBC maintains a call center to receive these calls and coordinate the appropriate response. The call center employees record each call and refer the issue to the EBC manager responsible for that location for follow-up. Locations are assigned to one of five geographic regions: Northeast (includes major metropolitan areas in eastern Canada), Southeast, Midwest, Southwest, and Northwest (includes major metropolitan areas in western Canada). EBC uses process costing with a weighted average cost flow assumption to assign the call center cost to each geographic region on a per-call unit cost. Overhead is applied per labor hour worked. Thus, the percentage complete can be applied to both labor and overhead. Because some questions/complaints take more than a day or two to resolve, there are typically some "unfinished" calls at the end of each period.

For the fiscal year ended September 30, 2016, the EBC call center reported the following information regarding calls handled:

Work in process, October 1, 2015:	$350
Work done during fiscal year 2016:	
Direct labor incurred.	$262,500
Overhead applied.	245,000
Total costs incurred during fiscal year 2016	$507,500
Calls in process at October 1, 2015 (30% complete)	50 calls
Calls started and finished during fiscal year 2016	35,200 calls
Calls in process at September 30, 2016 (40% complete)	40 calls

Required

1. Determine the equivalent number of calls completed during fiscal year 2016.
2. Determine the per-unit cost of each call.
3. Determine the cost of the calls completed.
4. Determine the cost of ending work in process inventory at September 30, 2016.

Solution: Exhibit 4-21 shows the solution.

Exhibit 4-21	**Service Industry In Focus Solution**

Flow of the Units and Equivalent Units Calculation

Where do the units come from?		Where do the units go?		% Work Done?	Conv. Costs
Calls in process (10/1/2015) .	50	Calls complete	35,210	100%	**35,210**
Calls started and finished. . .	35,200	Calls in process (9/30/2016) . .	40	40%	16
Total	35,250	Total	35,250		35,226

Product Cost Report
Environmental Business Consultants, LLC
Fiscal 2016 Service Calls

Where do the costs come from?		Conv. Costs
Beginning WIP	$ 350	$ 350
Current period costs	507,500	507,500
Total costs to account for . .	$507,850	$507,850
÷ Total equivalent units		35,226
Average cost/equivalent unit (rounded)		**$14.4169**

Where do the costs go?		
Cost of calls completed . .	507,619*	[35,210 × $14.4169]
Cost of ending inventory. .	231	[16 × $14.4169]
Total costs allocated	$507,850	

*Difference due to rounding.

COMPREHENSIVE PROBLEM (INCLUDING TRANSFERRED-IN COSTS)

Kensington Corp. makes gourmet brownies. Brownies are produced in a three-stage process. In the Baking Department, the raw materials for the brownies are mixed, poured into large trays, and baked. In the Finishing Department, frosting is applied to the brownies and they are sliced while still in the baking trays. Finally, in the Packing Department, the brownies are divided into smaller packages containing 12 brownies per package and prepared for shipping. Kensington has tracked the following information for the Baking and Finishing Departments during October 2016:

	Baking	Finishing
Trays in beginning inventory	200	100
Trays started / transferred in	5,100	?
Trays in ending inventory	100	300
Total cost of brownies transferred out in October	$18,200	?

The beginning inventory in the Finishing Department included $350 of transferred-in costs from the Baking Department incurred during September, $25 of materials, and $80 of conversion costs. During October, the Finishing Department incurred $1,075 for materials and $4,170 for conversion costs. The Finishing Department's beginning inventory was estimated to be 60% complete, and the ending inventory was estimated to be 20% complete. The frosting (the only new material added in the Finishing Department) is added when the brownies are 25% through the production process.

One purpose of this comprehensive example is to illustrate a more realistic example of how costs flow through a process with multiple departments or processes. Therefore, because this problem focuses on the second of three departments (the Finishing Department), we must consider transferred-in costs in addition to the direct material costs and conversion costs incurred in the current department. Transferred-in costs merely represent the costs transferred from one department to the next and are therefore considered 100% complete as they are carried forward to the next department. In this problem, the costs incurred in the Baking Department stay with the trays of baked brownies as they come into the Finishing Department. The 100 trays in the beginning inventory (transferred in during September) carried $350 of costs from the Baking department, whereas the units transferred in during October carried $18,200 of costs from the Baking Department.

Required

1. Assuming Kensington uses the weighted average cost flow assumption, prepare the October product cost report for the Finishing Department. Be sure to include your equivalent units calculations.

2. Give the journal entry to transfer completed brownies from the Finishing Department to the Packing Department.

Solution To Comprehensive Problem

Before preparing the solution for the Finishing Department, it is important to first determine the number of trays transferred out of the Baking Department. The 5,200 trays transferred OUT of the Baking Department are the trays transferred IN to the Finishing Department. Obviously, Kensington would need to prepare a product cost report to determine the cost of the brownie trays transferred out. Because this problem focuses on the second department in the production process, the costs incurred to bake these 5,200 trays is simply given ($18,200). This number is used in the Finishing Department as the cost of trays transferred in.

1. We first illustrate the percentage complete and T-accounts (in units and dollars) that are helpful in preparing the product cost report. Note that each arrow in the timeline represents the conversion costs incurred in the Finishing Department during October for each inventory group: (1) the beginning inventory balance (BB), (2) the trays transferred in and finished during the period (Transferred-in/Finished), and (3) the trays transferred in and remaining in ending inventory (EB).

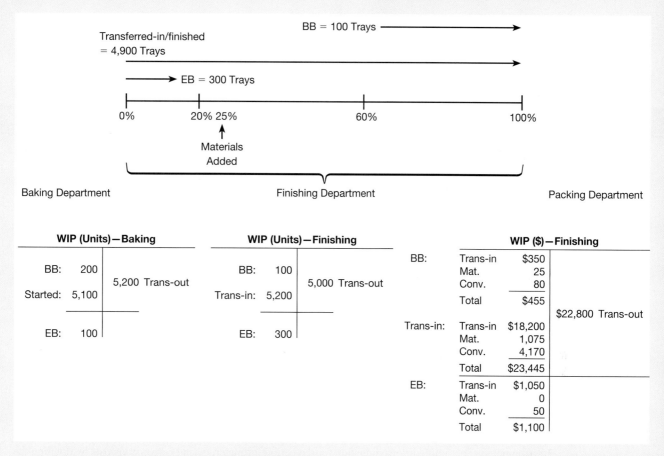

We then calculate equivalent units and prepare the product cost report.

		Finishing Department				Equivalent Units		
Where do the units come from?		**Where do the units go?**	**% Trans-in**	**Trans-in**	**% Work Done?**	**Dir. Mat.**	**% Work Done?**	**Conv. Costs**
Beg. inv.	100	Compl./transf.... 5,000	100%	5,000	100%	5,000	100%	5,000
Started	5,200	End. inv. 300	100%	300	0%	0	20%	60
Total	5,300	Total 5,300		5,300		5,000		5,060

Product Cost Report				
Where do the costs come from?		**Trans-in**	**Dir. Mat.**	**Conv. Costs**
Beg. inv.	$ 455	$ 350	$ 25	$ 80
Current	23,445	18,200	1,075	4,170
Total costs to account for ...	$23,900	$18,550	$ 1,100	$ 4,250
÷ Total equivalent units		5,300	5,000	5,060
Average cost/equiv. unit		$3.5000	$0.2200	$0.8399

Where do the costs go?				
Compl./transf.:				
Trans-in $17,500		[5,000 × $3.500]		
Direct materials 1,100			[5,000 × $0.2200]	
Conversion costs 4,200*				[5,000 × $0.8399]
COGM	$22,800			
End. inv.:				
Trans-in 1,050		[300 × $3.500]		
Direct materials .... —				
Conversion costs 50*				[60 × $0.8399]
Cost of ending inv........	1,100			
Total costs allocated	$23,900			

* Rounded to the nearest dollar.

2.

WIP—Packing Department	22,800	
WIP—Finishing Department		22,800

APPENDIX 4A: Process Costing Using FIFO Method

This appendix illustrates the use of process costing and the first-in, first-out method, or FIFO method, to assign product costs to the goods transferred out and to the ending work in process inventories. In this appendix, we will continue the Big G example introduced in the chapter.

PROCESS COSTING STEPS

LO6 **Explain** techniques for determining unit costs when the FIFO method for process costing is used.

In this chapter, we discussed process costing and the use of the weighted average cost allocation method to transfer product costs from one work in process inventory account to another, from the final work in process inventory account to the finished goods inventory account, and from the finished goods inventory account to the cost of goods sold account. In this appendix, we will accomplish the same task, but we will use the FIFO cost allocation method to assign and transfer product costs. The following steps are the same as those used for the weighted average method. However, the execution of these steps is slightly different.

Recall, process costing requires five steps or calculations:

1. Visualize or chart the physical flow of the units through the system.
2. Determine the equivalent whole units of work completed (or equivalent units of production) during the period. This calculation is usually performed separately for materials and conversion costs (i.e., labor and overhead) because conversion costs are usually added uniformly throughout the process, whereas materials are often added at a particular point in the process.
3. Compute the per-unit cost of production for the period for materials and conversion costs by dividing the total costs incurred in each category by the equivalent units of production for that cost category.
4. Using the per-unit costs for material and conversion costs, compute the dollar value of the units completed and transferred (Cost of Goods Manufactured) to the next department.
5. Using the same per-unit costs, compute the dollar value of the unfinished units that remain in the department (these ending work in process units will usually be completed in the following period).

We discuss these steps in more detail with respect to the FIFO cost allocation method in the following sections. Recall that the Big G division of General Mills uses process costing to account for its cereal production and that it had the results for January as illustrated in **Exhibit 4-1A**.

Exhibit 4-1A	Big G Process Costing Example
Work in process, January 1:	
Direct materials	$ 166,400
Direct labor.	38,100
Manufacturing overhead	76,300
Total beginning work in process	$ 280,800
Work done during January:	
Direct material (grain) added	$19,250,000
Direct labor incurred.	3,210,000
Manufacturing overhead applied	9,540,000
Total costs incurred during January.	$32,000,000
Units in process at January 1 (20% complete)	2,600 tons
Units started during January	58,500 tons
Units in process at January 31 (40% complete)	3,500 tons

Further, assume that all materials are added at the beginning of the process, whereas labor and manufacturing overhead costs are added evenly throughout the process. The T-account in **Exhibit 4-2A** illustrates the purpose of process costing, to allocate actual costs incurred between units completed and transferred out and partially completed units remaining in ending inventory:

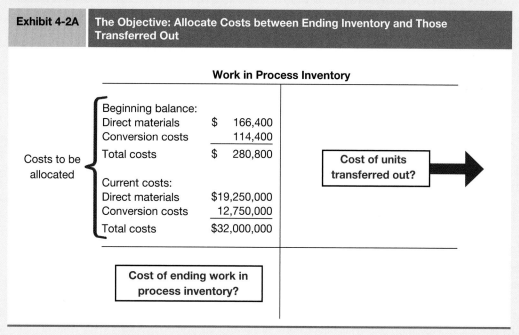

| Exhibit 4-2A | The Objective: Allocate Costs between Ending Inventory and Those Transferred Out |

We know the costs associated with the beginning work in process inventory on January 1 ($280,800). We also know the costs incurred during the month of January for direct materials ($19,250,000), direct labor ($3,210,000), and manufacturing overhead ($9,540,000). For simplicity, because we assume both direct labor and manufacturing overhead costs are applied uniformly during the production process, we combine them and simply refer to them as "conversion costs." Because we started the period with partially completed inventory, during the period we will finish the previously started units and also begin work on new units. We also end the period with partially completed units. We don't know how much of these costs should be applied to units transferred out at the end of the period and how much should remain with the partially complete ending inventory. Process costing helps us calculate an average cost per unit to apply to (1) the units completed and transferred out at the end of the period and (2) the units remaining in ending inventory.

Step 1: Visualize the Physical Flow of the Units

The starting point in process costing is to visualize how the units flow through the production process, as illustrated in **Exhibit 4-3A**. In the General Mills Big G example, the quantity produced is measured in tons of cereal processed during the month of January. Sometimes it is useful to visualize how the units correspond to the dollars in the T-account in **Exhibit 4-2A**.

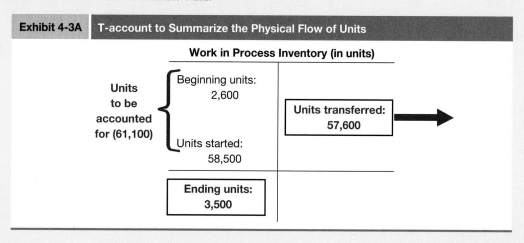

| Exhibit 4-3A | T-account to Summarize the Physical Flow of Units |

Another way to visualize the flow of the cereal produced during January is by asking where the units come from and where they end up, as shown in **Exhibit 4-4A**.

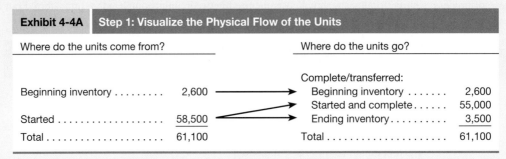

Exhibit 4-4A	Step 1: Visualize the Physical Flow of the Units	
Where do the units come from?	**Where do the units go?**	
	Complete/transferred:	
Beginning inventory 2,600	Beginning inventory 2,600	
	Started and complete 55,000	
Started 58,500	Ending inventory 3,500	
Total 61,100	Total 61,100	

We assume that all 2,600 units in beginning inventory are completed first. Then, of the 58,500 units started this month, 55,000 are complete by the end of the month, and 3,500 remain partially complete. Unlike the weighted average method, which mixes inventory layers (i.e., not distinguishing between work done in each period), the FIFO method keeps the beginning inventory separate from units started during the period and accounts for each inventory layer separately. Whereas the weighted average method does not distinguish between work done in different periods, the FIFO method does not mix costs incurred in different periods.

Step 2: Calculate the Equivalent Units

Introduction to Equivalent Units

Hint: Instead of tracking specific costs incurred to produce each unit of product as in job order costing, process costing accumulates costs by department and then calculates an average cost per unit to be assigned to all units of product produced during that period.

The average cost per unit is calculated by dividing total costs by the total number of units produced. The work in process accounts previously described in **Exhibits 4-5** and **4-6** illustrate how total costs are accumulated and tracked through the system. Accountants are good at keeping track of costs. However, cost accountants face a major problem in allocating costs in continuous-flow manufacturing processes. At any given point in time, units of product are at various stages of completion. Hence, it is difficult to determine the number of units to use in the average cost per unit calculation:

$$\text{Average cost per unit} = \frac{\text{Total costs incurred}}{\text{\# of equivalent units}} \qquad \begin{array}{l} \longleftarrow \text{ We know this.} \\ \longleftarrow \text{ We don't know this.} \end{array}$$

The notion of equivalent units of production is a key concept in process costing. When units of product are produced in a continuous process, engineers and manufacturing supervisors must estimate the average percentage completion of units in a given department at the end of each period. Accountants use this information to estimate the number of equivalent *complete* units of product. For example, the following illustration shows eight glasses of water that are *half* full. How many *full* glasses of water is this equivalent to?

The eight half-full glasses are approximately equivalent to four full glasses. This example illustrates what accountants do each period in determining the average cost per unit in a given department.

To properly determine per-unit costs, we must first calculate equivalent units of production to be used in the denominator of the average cost per unit calculation. **Equivalent units** are the equivalent number of *whole units* completed during the period. In the previous illustration, the eight partially full glasses of water are equivalent to four full glasses (similar to four equivalent complete units of production). The calculation of equivalent units of production requires accountants to (1) track the *actual quantity* of products at each stage of production and (2) estimate the *average amount of work completed* on each unit of product in terms of conversion costs and direct material costs.

Engineers or production experts estimate the percentage of work completed in terms of conversion costs, on average. As illustrated in **Exhibit 4-5A**, because the 2,600 tons of cereal on hand on January 1 is 20% complete (based on work completed during December), Big G only has to complete the remaining 80% of the processing during the month of January. During January, Big G begins work on 55,000 tons of cereal that is both started and completed during the month of January. Finally, Big G begins work on an additional 3,500 tons of cereal that is not completed by the end of the month. Engineers determine that only 40% of the processing is complete on this batch of cereal by January 31. We assume that all direct material is added at the beginning of the process; therefore, the average amount of work completed on each unit of product related to direct materials is 100%.

Exhibit 4-5A	Illustration of Conversion Costs Incurred

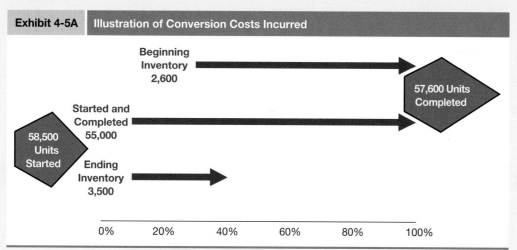

A key difference between the weighted average method and the FIFO method is that the weighted average mixes costs across inventory layers, whereas the FIFO method keeps costs incurred across inventory layers (i.e., incurred in different periods) separate. Whereas the weighted average method averages all costs incurred in the production of a batch of units, regardless of when those costs were incurred, the FIFO method keeps costs incurred during December separate from those incurred during January. Thus, the weighted average method asks "How much work is complete (regardless of when the work was done)?" whereas the FIFO method asks "What costs were incurred during THIS PERIOD?" A critical feature of the FIFO method is that because materials are added at the *beginning* of the process in this example, the beginning inventory units moved beyond the point of adding materials during the last period. Thus, NO materials are added THIS PERIOD. Because the beginning inventory was started last month, the materials for the beginning inventory were actually added during December. Thus, no new materials are added to these 2,600 units during January.

Hint: An item that is 20% complete at the beginning of the period means 80% of the work is done this period, not 20%.

Equivalent Unit Calculation for Direct Materials—FIFO

The materials for the units started and completed during the month and for the ending inventory are added during this period. **Exhibit 4-6A** illustrates the calculation of equivalent units based on the FIFO cost flow assumption. The units in each "layer" of inventory are multiplied by the percentage of materials added during the CURRENT period (January) to calculate the equivalent units of material added during THIS PERIOD, as shown in **Exhibit 4-6A**.

Exhibit 4-6A	Step 2: Calculate the Equivalent Units—Direct Materials

	Physical Units (tons)		Proportion Completed		Equivalent Units (tons)
Beginning inventory	2,600	×	0%	=	0
Started and finished during January	55,000	×	100%	=	55,000
Ending inventory.	3,500	×	100%	=	3,500
Total	61,100				58,500

Equivalent Unit Calculation for Conversion Costs—FIFO

When considering conversion costs (direct labor and manufacturing overhead), it is often useful to visualize the amount of work done during the period on each unique set of inventory passing through the production process, as previously illustrated in **Exhibit 4-5A**, which summarizes the work performed in the Big G division during the month of January. Because materials are added at the beginning of the period, the arrows only represent the amount of conversion costs applied to the process during the *current* period. We can then calculate the number of equivalent units with respect to conversion costs incurred during January, as illustrated in **Exhibit 4-7A**.

Exhibit 4-7A	Step 2: Calculate the Equivalent Units—Conversion Costs					
		Physical Units (tons)		Proportion Completed This Month		Equivalent Units (tons)
Beginning inventory		2,600	×	80%	=	2,080
Started and finished during January		55,000	×	100%	=	55,000
Ending inventory.		3,500	×	40%	=	1,400
Total		61,100				58,480

Again, we calculate equivalent units of production by multiplying the number of units in each "layer" of inventory by the percentage of conversion costs added during the current period.

We can then summarize the flow of the units worked on during the period and how the amount of work completed during the period translates them into equivalent units, as illustrated in **Exhibit 4-8A**.

Exhibit 4-8A	Summary of Steps 1 and 2: Unit Flows and Equivalent Units Calculations

Step 1: Visualize the Physical Flow of the Units

Step 2: Calculate the Equivalent Units

Where do the units come from?		Where do the units go?			% in Jan.?	Materials	% in Jan.?	Conv. Costs
		Complete/transferred:				Equivalent Units		
Beginning inventory . . .	2,600	Beginning inventory	2,600		0%	0	80%	2,080
		Started and completed	55,000		100%	55,000	100%	55,000
Started	58,500	Ending inventory.	3,500		100%	3,500	40%	1,400
Total	61,100	Total	61,100			58,500		58,480

An equivalent unit is the amount of work necessary to produce one complete physical unit of product. For example, doing 80% of the work on 200 units is equivalent to doing 100% of the work on 160 units.

YOUR TURN! 4.3

The solution is on page 157.

MBC

Assume all materials are added at the beginning of the production process, and conversion costs are added uniformly throughout the process. Beginning work in process is comprised of 100 units, which are 35% complete with respect to conversion costs. Also assume that 700 units are started and completed during the period, and ending work in process includes 90 units that are 75% complete with respect to conversion costs. Compute equivalent units of production for direct materials and conversion costs under the FIFO cost flow assumption. (*Hint:* For fractional units, round up.)

Step 3: Determine the Per-Unit Costs

The product cost report summarizes where the costs come from and where they go (i.e., where they are allocated). The FIFO method differs from the weighted average method in an important way. The FIFO method does not mix "layers" of costs incurred during different periods. The $280,800 of costs in beginning inventory at the start of the month were incurred during December. When we calculate the average cost per unit, we calculate the average cost per unit of costs incurred during the CURRENT PERIOD. Hence, the costs incurred last month to help the inventory to reach the 20% point stay with those beginning inventory units and are NOT

ALLOCATED across the units started during THIS PERIOD. In order to calculate an average cost per unit of materials and conversion costs incurred during THIS PERIOD, we first need to separate the current-period costs into their materials and conversion cost components. These numbers were illustrated in the T-account in **Exhibit 4-2A**. **Exhibit 4-9A** illustrates two important points. First, the beginning inventory costs incurred in the prior period are carried down and assigned to stay with the beginning inventory units. Second, only the costs incurred during the current period are allocated and used subsequently in the average cost per unit calculation.

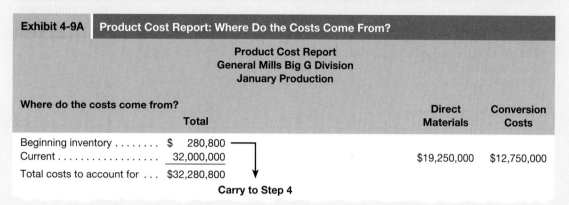

Exhibit 4-9A | **Product Cost Report: Where Do the Costs Come From?**

Product Cost Report
General Mills Big G Division
January Production

Where do the costs come from? Total		Direct Materials	Conversion Costs
Beginning inventory . . . . $ 280,800			
Current 32,000,000		$19,250,000	$12,750,000
Total costs to account for . . . $32,280,800			

Carry to Step 4

We then calculate the average cost per unit by dividing current-period costs in each category by total equivalent units in each category from Step 2. In other words, we divide current materials costs by total equivalent units of materials ($19,250,000 / 58,500 equivalent units) to get an average cost per unit of $329.06. Similarly, we divide current conversion costs by total equivalent units of conversion costs ($12,750,000 / 58,480 equivalent units) to get an average cost per unit of $218.02. **Exhibit 4-10A** summarizes this calculation.

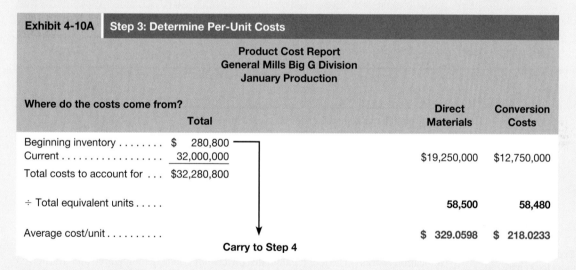

Exhibit 4-10A | **Step 3: Determine Per-Unit Costs**

Product Cost Report
General Mills Big G Division
January Production

Where do the costs come from? Total		Direct Materials	Conversion Costs
Beginning inventory . . . . $ 280,800			
Current 32,000,000		$19,250,000	$12,750,000
Total costs to account for . . . $32,280,800			
÷ Total equivalent units		58,500	58,480
Average cost/unit		$ 329.0598	$ 218.0233

Carry to Step 4

Note that under the FIFO cost flow assumption, the costs from the prior period associated with the beginning inventory stay with the beginning inventory and are not allocated to any other units. The costs incurred during the current period are allocated across all work incurred during the current period. Hence, under the FIFO cost flow assumption, the accountant keeps the "layers" of inventory separate. In the Big G example, note that the per-unit costs of materials and conversions costs only include costs incurred during January.

Step 4: Calculate the Cost of Goods Manufactured

At the end of each month and for each department, we calculate the cost of goods manufactured and transferred out (illustrated in **Exhibit 4-11A**). Under the FIFO cost flow assumption, the Big G division's product completed and transferred out during January consists of (1) the product in beginning work in process (2,080 equivalent tons) and (2) the product started and completed during the period (55,000 equivalent tons). Specifically, it is comprised of all costs to manufacture the beginning inventory (both this period and last period) and the cost of units started and finished this period. To determine the dollar cost value of the product transferred to finished goods (called Cost of Goods Manufactured), we multiply the equivalent units of materials and conversion costs transferred (shown in **red** in **Exhibit 4-8A**) by their respective per-unit costs computed in Step 2 (shown in **green** in **Exhibit 4-10A**) and add these costs to the cost value of the beginning work in process, as shown in **Exhibit 4-11A**.

Exhibit 4-11A	Step 4: Cost of Goods Manufactured Calculation	
		Carry from Step 3
Beginning inventory:		
Costs incurred in December..........................		$ 280,800
Conversion costs incurred in January	[2,080 EU × $218.0233]	453,488
Started and finished:		
Materials..	[55,000 EU × $329.0598]	18,098,291*
Conversion costs	[55,000 EU × $218.0233]	11,991,279*
Total cost of goods manufactured		$30,823,858

* Difference due to rounding.

Step 5: Calculate the Ending Work in Process Inventory

Exhibit 4-12A illustrates the final step, which is to calculate the cost of goods remaining in ending work in process inventory. Assuming all materials are added at the beginning and conversion costs are added evenly through the process, we multiply the equivalent units of materials and conversion costs in ending inventory (denoted in **red** in **Exhibit 4-8A**) by their respective unit costs (shown in **green** in **Exhibit 4-10A**) computed in Step 2, as follows:

Exhibit 4-12A	Step 5: Calculate Cost of Ending Inventory	
Materials..	[3,500 EU × $329.0598]	$ 1,151,709
Conversion costs	[1,400 EU × $218.0233]	305,233
Total cost of goods remaining in ending inventory		$ 1,456,942

Cost of goods manufactured and transferred out (**Exhibit 4-11A**)	$30,823,858
Cost of ending inventory (**Exhibit 4-12A**)........................	1,456,942
Total cost to account for (**Exhibit 4-10A**)........................	$32,280,800

THE PRODUCT COST REPORT

LO7 Explain the procedures used to prepare the product cost report using the FIFO method in a process costing system.

The product cost report in **Exhibit 4-13A** summarizes the last three steps in the cost allocation process. The report calculates the cost of goods manufactured and transferred out of work in process and into finished goods. The report also calculates the cost of the remaining ending balance in work in process. Using the Big G example, **Exhibit 4-13A** also summarizes all of the steps in the total cost allocation process from (1) visualizing the physical flow of the units, to (2) calculating equivalent units, to (3) calculating per-unit costs, to (4) calculating cost of goods manufactured, to (5) calculating ending inventory. Finally, **Exhibit 4-13A** provides Big G's product cost report. Note that in this illustration, the equivalent units of production for materials and conversion costs (the numbers in **red**) are multiplied by the corresponding cost per unit figures for materials and conversion costs (the numbers in **green**) to calculate the cost allocation amounts used to assign costs to cost of goods manufactured and ending inventory.

Exhibit 4-13A	Summary of the Five Process Costing Steps

Flow of the Units and Equivalent Units Calculation

Step 1: Visualize the Physical Flow of the Units

Step 2: Calculate the Equivalent Units

Where do the units come from?		Where do the units go?		% in Jan.?	Materials	% in Jan.?	Conversion Costs
						Equivalent Units	
		Complete/transferred:					
Beginning inventory	2,600 →	Beginning inventory	2,600	0%	0	80%	2,080
		Started and completed . .	55,000	100%	55,000	100%	55,000
Started	58,500 →	Ending inventory	3,500	100%	3,500	40%	1,400
Total	61,100	Total	61,100		58,500		58,480

Product Cost Report
General Mills Big G Division
January Production

Step 3: Determine Per-Unit Costs

Where do the costs come from?	Total		Direct Materials	Conversion Costs
Beginning inventory	$ 280,800			
Current	32,000,000		$19,250,000	$12,750,000
Total costs to account for	$32,280,800			
÷ Total equivalent units			58,500	58,480
Average cost/unit			**$329.0598**	**$218.0233**

Where do the costs go?

Step 4: Calculate the Cost of Goods Manufactured

Beginning inventory:			
Costs incurred in December	$ 280,800 ←		
Costs incurred in January	453,488	[0 × **$329.0598**] +	[2,080 × **$218.0233**]
Started and finished	30,089,570*	[55,000 × **$329.0598**] +	[55,000 × **$218.0233**]
Cost of goods manufactured	$30,823,858		

Step 5: Calculate the Cost of the Ending Inventory

Ending inventory:			
Materials	$ 1,151,709	[3,500 × **$329.0598**]	
Conversion costs	305,233		[1,400 × **$218.0233**]
Cost of ending inventory	1,456,942		
Total costs allocated	$32,280,800		

As a final check to see that we have performed all of the calculations correctly, the sum of Cost of Goods Manufactured ($30,823,858) and the ending work in process balance (1,456,942) should equal the total costs that we determined at the outset needed to be allocated (Beginning Balance $280,800 + Current Costs $32,000,000 = $32,280,800). Specifically, the T-account in **Exhibit 4-14A** summarizes the process costing allocation of costs between costs transferred out and costs remaining in ending inventory.

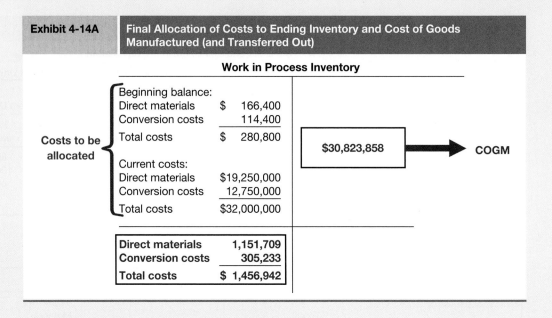

Exhibit 4-14A	Final Allocation of Costs to Ending Inventory and Cost of Goods Manufactured (and Transferred Out)

Work in Process Inventory

Costs to be allocated {

Beginning balance:
Direct materials $ 166,400
Conversion costs   114,400
Total costs $ 280,800

Current costs:
Direct materials $19,250,000
Conversion costs   12,750,000
Total costs $32,000,000

$30,823,858 → COGM

Direct materials	1,151,709
Conversion costs	305,233
Total costs	$ 1,456,942

Companies with Multiple Production Processes

At the outset of this chapter, we described situations in which a company produces its products through a long series of production processes. So far, we have illustrated process costing in a single department. When a company's production process involves a series of different departments, costs are accumulated by production process. The costs transferred out of one department are transferred into the next department. Hence, as units of product move from one department or process to the next, they carry the costs from all prior processes with them. From a practical perspective, the only thing that changes in the product costing process is that an extra column is added for transferred-in costs. For example, the $30,823,858 transferred out of the production process described in the previous section would become the **transferred-in costs** for the next department.

JOURNAL ENTRIES ILLUSTRATED

LO8   **Illustrate** the journal entries used with FIFO process costing.

After computing these amounts, Big G would record the following journal entries related to January production. *These entries assume that materials are added at the beginning of the process, and that labor and overhead are added evenly over the month of January.*

Material

During January, assume that Big G purchased $20,000,000 of grain on account. The following is a summary journal entry for the January purchases:

1	Materials inventory	20,000,000	
	Accounts payable		20,000,000
	To record January material purchases.		

The direct material requisitioned during January for the processing department is shown in the following entry:

2	Work in process	19,250,000	
	Materials inventory		19,250,000
	To record direct material used during January.		

Labor

During January, Big G accrued $3,210,000 of direct labor expense. The journal entry to record this payroll would be as follows:

3	Work in process	3,210,000	
	Wages payable		3,210,000
	To record the payroll for January.		

Manufacturing Overhead

Assume that Big G has recorded its manufacturing overhead costs (such as maintenance, depreciation, and utilities) in Manufacturing Overhead as incurred. Also assume that Big G applies manufacturing overhead costs to Work in Process using predetermined overhead rates. The following entry records the amount of applied manufacturing overhead for the processing department:

4	Work in process	9,540,000	
	Manufacturing overhead		9,540,000
	To apply manufacturing overhead to work in process inventory.		

As a result of the journal entries recorded during the month, the Work in Process account contains the following balance as of the end of the month:

	Work in Process
Beginning balance	$ 280,800
Direct material	19,250,000
Direct labor	3,210,000
Factory overhead	9,540,000
Balance before month-end adjustments	$32,280,800

At the end of the month, an additional journal entry is needed to transfer product costs from the processing department to Finished Goods (the amount of Cost of Goods Manufactured). The following entry records the Cost of Goods Manufactured:

5	Finished goods	30,823,858	
	Work in process		30,823,858
	To transfer the cost of completed product from work in process		
	inventory.		

Assume the following cost information for May production and only one manufacturing department. What journal entries would be made to capture May production?

Direct material	$24,000
Direct labor	32,400
Manufacturing overhead applied	48,600

YOUR TURN! 4.4

The solution is on page 157.

SUMMARY OF LEARNING OBJECTIVES

Compare and contrast job order costing and process costing. (p. 112)   **LO1**

■ Job order costing is used when production consists of a variety of different products or unique customer orders.

■ Process costing is used when production consists of a large volume of the same (homogeneous) product produced in a continual flow.

LO2 **Describe the basic concepts of process costing. (p. 114)**

■ There is a separate work in process account for each department under a process costing system, whereas there is only one work in process control account in a job order costing system.

■ In a process costing environment, products flow through multiple departments that are arranged in either a sequential pattern or a parallel pattern.

LO3 **Explain techniques for determining unit costs when process costing is used. (p. 116)**

■ Visualize or chart the physical flow of the units through the system.

■ Determine the equivalent whole units of work completed (or equivalent units of production) during the period. This calculation is usually performed separately for materials and conversion costs (i.e., labor and overhead) because conversion costs are usually added uniformly throughout the process, whereas materials are often added at a particular point in the process.

■ Compute the per-unit cost of production for the period for materials and conversion costs by dividing the total costs incurred in each category by the equivalent units of production for that cost category.

■ Using the per-unit costs for material and conversion costs, compute the dollar value of the units completed and transferred (cost of goods manufactured) to the next department.

■ Using the same per-unit costs, compute the dollar value of the unfinished units that remain in the department (these ending work in process units will usually be completed in the following period).

LO4 **Explain the procedures used to prepare the product cost report using the weighted average method in a process costing system. (p. 123)**

■ The product cost report and its supporting calculations include all of the five steps in the process costing procedure.

■ The weighted average method mixes inventory layers and asks the question "how much work has been completed?" in calculating equivalent units of production.

LO5 **Illustrate the journal entries used with process costing. (p. 125)**

■ At each stage of the manufacturing process, costs are added to the work in process account of the department where the work is completed. The journal entries are identical to those illustrated under a job order costing system.

■ Direct materials are added to the materials inventory account when they are purchased.

■ Materials used in the manufacturing process are transferred from the materials inventory account with a credit and debited to the appropriate work in process account.

■ Labor and overhead are recorded as debits to the appropriate work in process account.

LO6 **Appendix 4A: Explain techniques for determining unit costs when the FIFO method for process costing is used. (p. 130)**

■ The five process costing steps are the same under the FIFO method as under the weighted average method.

■ In assigning manufacturing costs, one must consider three batches (or layers) of product: units from beginning work in process, units started and finished during this period, and units remaining in the ending work in process. Instead of mixing the layers (as in the weighted average method), the FIFO method keeps these three layers of inventory separate.

■ The key difference between the weighted average and FIFO methods is that under the FIFO method, costs per equivalent unit are calculated by dividing current costs by current equivalent units; prior period costs and equivalent units are excluded from these calculations but are included in the total costs to be accounted for.

LO7 **Appendix 4A: Explain the procedures used to prepare the product cost report using the FIFO method in a process costing system. (p. 136)**

■ When work in process inventories exist at the beginning and the end of the accounting period, the measurement of work accomplished requires that partially finished units be converted to equivalent units for accounting purposes.

■ When materials are added at a different rate than conversion work is accomplished, equivalent units must be computed separately for material and conversion.

■ The product cost report and its supporting calculations include all of the five steps in the process costing procedure.

- The FIFO method keeps inventory layers separate and asks the question "how much work was completed during THIS PERIOD?" in calculating equivalent units of production.

Appendix 4A: Illustrate the journal entries used with FIFO process costing. (p. 138)   **LO8**

- At each stage of the manufacturing process, costs are added to the work in process account of the department where the work is completed. The journal entries are identical to those illustrated under a job order costing system.
- Direct materials are added to the materials inventory account when they are purchased.
- Materials used in the manufacturing process are transferred from the materials inventory account with a credit and debited to the appropriate work in process account.
- Labor and overhead are recorded as debits to the appropriate work in process account.

KEY TERMS

Conversion costs (p. 116)	Parallel product processing (p. 115)	Sequential product processing (p. 115)
Cost of goods remaining (p. 123)	Process costing (p. 113)	Transferred-in costs (p. 138)
Equivalent units (p. 116, 119, 132)	Process costing system (p. 114)	Weighted average method (p. 120)
FIFO method (p. 120)	Product cost report (p. 114)	

Assignments with the ⏱ logo in the margin are available in BusinessCourse.
See the Preface of the book for details.

SELF-STUDY QUESTIONS

(Answers to Self-Study Questions are at the end of this chapter.)

1. **Which of the following costs will not be part of product cost when using a process costing system?**   **LO2**
   a. Prior department cost
   b. Conversion cost
   c. Byproduct cost
   d. Material cost

2. **For which of the following will there be multiple accounts in the general ledger when using process costing?**   **LO2**
   a. Finished goods
   b. Work in process
   c. Materials
   d. Wages payable

3. **Which of the following will not influence the calculation of equivalent units when the FIFO cost flow assumption is used?**   **LO6**
   a. Units processed in prior departments.
   b. Ending inventory units
   c. Beginning inventory units
   d. Units sold

QUESTIONS

1. What are the important differences between job order and process costing systems?   **LO1**

2. How are all manufacturing costs for a series of processing departments accumulated into finished goods inventory?   **LO1, 2**

3. Why do unit cost computations in a manufacturing process require equivalent unit computations?   **LO2, 3**

4. Why do we say that process cost accounting is basically an averaging computation?   **LO3**

5. What is meant by the term *equivalent unit*?   **LO3**

6. What are conversion costs?   **LO3**

7. Why must we sometimes compute equivalent units separately for materials and for conversion costs?   **LO3**

8. Describe the three "layers" of inventory that are typically involved in a period's production under the FIFO accounting method. In what special situation are there only two layers?   **LO6, 7, 8**

9. Why is it true that in each department's work in process inventory account all beginning inventory and current-period costs must end up either being transferred out or in ending work in process inventory?   **LO3**

EXERCISES—SET A

LO3 **E4-1A.** **Equivalent Units Calculations—Weighted Average Method** Ferris Corporation makes a powdered rug shampoo in two sequential departments, Compounding and Drying. Materials are added at the beginning of the process in the Compounding Department. Conversion costs are added evenly throughout each process. Ferris uses the weighted average method of process costing. In the Compounding Department, beginning work in process was 4,000 pounds (70% processed), 37,000 pounds were started in process, 36,000 pounds transferred out, and ending work in process was 60% processed.

Calculate equivalent units for March 2016 for the Compounding Department.

LO3 **E4-2A.** **Equivalent Units Calculations—Weighted Average Method** The following are selected operating data for Jackson Company's Blending Department for April 2016. Tinting and packaging operations are carried out subsequently in other departments.

Beginning inventory	4,000 units, 60% complete
Started and completed.	70,000 units
Ending inventory.	6,000 units, 30% complete

Calculate the equivalent units completed using the weighted average method, assuming that the material is added at the beginning of the process and conversion costs are incurred evenly throughout.

LO3, 4 **E4-3A.** **Equivalent Units and Product Cost Report—Weighted Average Method** In its first month's operations (January 2016), Allred Company's Department 1 incurred charges of $120,000 for direct materials (10,000 units), $33,000 for direct labor, and $58,000 for manufacturing overhead. At month-end, 8,800 units had been finished and transferred out. The remaining units were finished with respect to material but only 25% complete with respect to conversion costs.

Assuming Allred uses the weighted average method and that materials are added at the beginning of the process and conversion costs occur evenly, compute the following:

a. The equivalent units of materials and conversion costs.
b. The cost per equivalent unit of materials and conversion costs.
c. The total cost assigned to the units transferred out.
d. The total cost assigned to the ending inventory.
e. Prove that your solutions to requirements (c) and (d) sum to the total costs to be accounted for.

LO3, 4 **E4-4A.** **Equivalent Units and Product Cost Report—Weighted Average Method** The following data (and annotations) are for the work in process account of the first of Crocker Company's four departments used in manufacturing its only product for October of 2016.

Work in Process—Department 1	
Beginning balance (2,000 units, 70% complete)	
Direct material.	$ 15,500
Conversion costs	9,600
Transferred to department 2: (20,000 units).	(a)
Direct material (21,000 units)	157,500
Direct labor.	145,200
Manufacturing overhead	48,300
Ending balance [____(b)____ units, 25% complete]	(c)

Assuming that Crocker uses the weighted average method and that materials are added at the beginning of the process and conversion costs are incurred evenly throughout, solve for the three missing numbers.

LO3, 4 **E4-5A.** **Equivalent Units and Product Cost Report—Weighted Average Method** The following data (and annotations) are for Sutter Company's processing department work in process account for the month of June 2016:

Beginning inventory (700 units, 40% complete)	
Direct naterial	$ 2,850
Conversion costs	7,930
Current period	
Direct material (5,000 units)	35,000
Direct labor	59,600
Manufacturing overhead applied	37,800

Sutter uses the weighted average method. Materials are added at the beginning of the process and conversion costs are incurred evenly throughout. Ending work in process is comprised of 900 units, 70% complete. Compute the following:

a. Equivalent units for materials and conversion.
b. Cost per equivalent unit for materials and conversion.
c. Total cost assigned to the units transferred out.

E4-6A. Equivalent Units Calculations—FIFO Method Ferris Corporation makes a powdered rug sham- **LO6** poo in two sequential departments, Compounding and Drying. Materials are added at the beginning of the process in the Compounding Department. Conversion costs are added evenly throughout each process. Ferris uses the FIFO method of process costing. In the Compounding Department, beginning work in process was 4,000 pounds (70% processed), 37,000 pounds were started in process, 36,000 pounds transferred out, and ending work in process was 60% processed.
Calculate equivalent units for March 2016 for the Compounding Department.

E4-7A. Equivalent Units Calculations—FIFO Method The following selected operating data are for **LO6** Jackson Company's Blending Department for the month of April 2016. Tinting and packaging operations are carried out subsequently in other departments.

Beginning inventory	4,000 units, 60% complete
Started and completed.	70,000 units
Ending inventory.	6,000 units, 30% complete

Calculate the equivalent units accomplished using the FIFO method, assuming that the material is added at the beginning of the process and conversion costs are incurred evenly throughout.

E4-8A. Equivalent Units and Product Cost Report—FIFO Method In its first month's operations **LO6, 7** (January 2016), Allred Company's Department 1 incurred charges of $120,000 for direct materials (10,000 units), $33,000 for direct labor, and $58,000 for manufacturing overhead. At month-end, 8,800 units had been finished and transferred out. The remaining units were finished with respect to material but only 25% complete with respect to conversion costs.
Assuming Allred uses the FIFO method and that materials are added at the beginning of the process and conversion costs occur evenly, compute the following:

a. The equivalent units for material and conversion.
b. The cost per equivalent unit for material and conversion.
c. The total cost assigned to the units transferred out.
d. The total cost assigned to the ending inventory.
e. Prove that your solutions to requirements (c) and (d) sum to the total costs to be accounted for.

E4-9A. Equivalent Units and Product Cost Report—FIFO Method The following data (and annotations) **LO6, 7** are for the work in process account of the first of Crocker Company's four departments used in manufacturing its only product October of 2016.

Work in Process—Department 1	
Beginning balance (2,000 units, 70% complete)	$ 25,100
Transferred to department 2: (20,000 units).	(a)
Direct material (21,000 units)	157,500
Direct labor.	145,200
Manufacturing overhead	48,300
Ending balance [____(b)____ units, 25% complete]	(c)

Assuming that Crocker uses the FIFO method and that materials are added at the beginning of the process and conversion costs are incurred evenly throughout, solve for the three missing numbers.

LO6, 7 **E4-10A. Equivalent Units and Product Cost Assignment—FIFO Method** The following data (and annotations) are related to the June 2016 charges appearing in the work in process account for Sutter Company's first processing department:

Beginning inventory (700 units, 40% complete)	
Direct material.	$ 5,780
Conversion costs	5,000
Current period	
Direct materials (5,000 units)	50,000
Direct labor.	59,600
Manufacturing overhead applied	22,800

Sutter uses the FIFO method. Direct materials are added at the beginning of the process and conversion costs are incurred evenly throughout. Ending work in process totals 900 units, 70% complete. Compute the following:

a. Equivalent units for direct materials and conversion costs.
b. Cost per equivalent unit for direct materials and conversion costs.
c. Total cost assigned to the units transferred out.

LO5 **E4-11A. Cost Flows Through Journal Entries** The Mixing Department performs a series of processes in which a fluid chemical is concentrated. Records indicate that the Mixing Department has been charged with $64,000 of direct labor costs. The manufacturing overhead rate is 150% of direct labor costs. Beginning work in process was $224,000, and ending work in process totaled $34,000. One-half of this period's completed products is sold on account at a price equal to 160% of its cost.

Prepare journal entries to record (1) various costs charged to the Mixing Department this period, (2) transfer of this period's completed product, and (3) sale of one-half of this period's production.

EXERCISES—SET B

LO3 **E4-1B. Equivalent Units Calculations—Weighted Average Method** Terrace Corporation makes an industrial cleaner in two sequential departments, Compounding and Drying. All material is added at the beginning of the process in the Compounding Department. Conversion costs are added evenly throughout each process. Terrace uses the weighted average method of process costing. In the Compounding Department, beginning work in process was 2,000 pounds (60% processed), 34,000 pounds were started, 32,000 pounds were transferred out, and ending work in process was 70% processed.

Calculate equivalent units for the Compounding Department for August 2016.

LO3 **E4-2B. Equivalent Units Calculations—Weighted Average Method** The following are selected operating data for Jackson Company's Blending Department for November 2016. Painting and packaging operations are carried out subsequently in other departments.

Beginning inventory	3,000 units, 70% complete
Started and completed.	60,000 units
Ending inventory.	5,000 units, 40% complete

Calculate the equivalent units finished for the month of November using the weighted average method, assuming that the material is added at the beginning of the process and conversion costs are incurred evenly throughout.

LO3, 4 **E4-3B. Equivalent Units and Product Cost Assignment—Weighted Average Method** In its first month of operations (May 2016), Allred Company's Department 1 incurred charges of $72,000 for direct materials (9,000 units), $38,700 for direct labor, and $13,500 for manufacturing overhead. At month-end, 8,500 units had been finished and transferred out. Those remaining were finished with respect to material but only 40% finished with respect to conversion.

Assuming Allred uses the weighted average method and that materials are added at the beginning of the process and conversion occurs evenly, compute the following:

a. The equivalent units for material and conversion.
b. The cost per equivalent unit for material and conversion.
c. The total cost assigned to the units transferred out.
d. The total cost assigned to the ending inventory.
e. Prove that your solutions to requirements (c) and (d) sum to the total costs to be accounted for.

E4-4B. **Equivalent Units and Product Cost Report—Weighted Average Method** The following data (and LO3, 4
annotations) for March 2016 are for the work in process account of the first of Olympus Company's four departments used in manufacturing its only product.

Work in Process—Department 1	
Beginning balance (3,000 units, 40% complete)	
Direct material.	$12,600
Conversion costs	5,600
Transferred to Department 2: (23,000 units)	(a)
Direct material (24,000 units)	96,000
Direct labor.	77,300
Manufacturing overhead	36,700
Ending balance [_____ (b) _____ units, 25% complete]	(c)

Assuming that Olympus uses the weighted average method, that materials are added at the beginning of the process and that conversion costs are incurred evenly throughout, solve for the three missing numbers.

E4-5B. **Equivalent Units and Product Cost Report—Weighted Average Method** The following data (and LO3, 4
annotations) are for Empire Company's processing department work in process account for the month of September 2016:

Beginning inventory (1,500 units, 70% complete)	
Direct material.	$21,950
Conversion costs	10,000
Current period	
Direct material (6,000 units)	50,000
Direct labor.	41,000
Manufacturing overhead applied	65,700

Empire uses the weighted average method. Materials are added at the beginning of the process and conversion costs are incurred evenly throughout. Ending work in process is comprised of 1,000 units, 60% complete. Compute the following:

a. Equivalent units for direct materials and conversion.
b. Cost per equivalent unit for direct materials and conversion.
c. Total cost assigned to the units transferred out.

E4-6B. **Equivalent Units Calculations—FIFO Method** Terrace Corporation makes an industrial cleaner in LO6
two sequential departments, Compounding and Drying. All material is added at the beginning of the process in the Compounding Department. Conversion costs are added evenly throughout each process. Terrace uses the FIFO method of process costing. In the Compounding Department, beginning work in process was 2,000 pounds (60% processed), 34,000 pounds were started, 32,000 pounds were transferred out, and ending work in process was 70% processed.

Calculate equivalent units for the Compounding Department for August 2016.

E4-7B. **Equivalent Units Calculations—FIFO Method** The following are selected operating data for LO6
Jackson Company's Blending Department for November 2016. Painting and packaging operations are carried out subsequently in other departments.

Beginning inventory	3,000 units, 70% complete
Started and completed.	60,000 units
Ending inventory.	5,000 units, 40% complete

Calculate the equivalent units finished for the month of November using the FIFO method, assuming that the material is added at the beginning of the process and conversion costs are incurred evenly throughout.

LO6, 7   **E4-8B.**   **Equivalent Units and Product Cost Report—FIFO Method** In its first month of operations (May of 2016), Allred Company's Department 1 incurred charges of $72,000 for direct material (9,000 units), $38,700 for direct labor, and $13,500 for manufacturing overhead. At month-end, 8,500 units had been finished and transferred out. Those units remaining were finished with respect to material but only 40% finished with respect to conversion.

Assuming Allred uses the FIFO method and that materials are added at the beginning of the process and conversion costs are incurred evenly throughout the period, compute the following:

a.   The equivalent units for materials and conversion costs.
b.   The cost per equivalent unit for materials and conversion costs.
c.   The total cost assigned to the units transferred out.
d.   The total cost assigned to the ending inventory.
e.   Prove that your solutions to requirements (c) and (d) sum to the total costs to be accounted for.

LO6, 7   **E4-9B.**   **Equivalent Units and Product Cost Report—FIFO Method** The following data (and annotations) for March 2016 are for the work in process account of the first of Olympus Company's four departments used in manufacturing its only product.

Work in Process—Department 1	
Beginning balance (3,000 units, 40% complete)	$18,200
Transferred to Department 2: (23,000 units)	(a)
Direct material (24,000 units)	96,000
Direct labor.	77,300
Manufacturing overhead	36,700
Ending balance [____(b)____ units, 25% complete]	(c)

Assuming that Olympus uses the FIFO method, that materials are added at the beginning of the process and that conversion costs are incurred evenly throughout, solve for the three missing numbers.

LO6, 7   **E4-10B.**   **Equivalent Units and Product Cost Report—FIFO Method** Following are the September 2016 charges (and certain annotations) appearing in the work in process account for Empire Company's processing department:

Beginning inventory (1,500 units, 70% complete)	
Direct material.	$21,950
Conversion costs	10,000
Current period	
Direct materials (6,000 units)	72,000
Direct labor	32,500
Manufacturing overhead applied	52,200

Empire uses the FIFO method. Materials are added at the beginning of the process and conversion costs are incurred evenly throughout. Ending work in process is comprised of 1,000 units, 60% complete. Compute the following:

a.   Equivalent units for direct materials and conversion.
b.   Cost per equivalent unit or units transferred in and conversion.
c.   Total cost assigned to the units transferred out.

LO5   **E4-11B.**   **Cost Flows Through Journal Entries** The Mixing Department performs a series of processes in which a fluid chemical is concentrated. Records indicate that the Mixing Department has been charged with $50,000 of direct labor costs. The manufacturing overhead rate is 170% of direct labor costs. Beginning work in process was $170,000, and ending work in process totaled $36,000. One-half of this period's completed products is sold on account at a price equal to 150% of its cost.

Prepare journal entries to record (1) various costs charged to the Mixing Department this period, (2) transfer of this period's completed product, and (3) sale of one-half of this period's production.

PROBLEMS—SET A

P4-1A. **Calculate Equivalent Units, Unit Costs, and Transferred Costs—Weighted Average Method**   **LO3, 4**
Godfrey Manufacturing, Inc., operates a plant that produces its own regionally-marketed Spicy Steak
Sauce. The sauce is produced in two processes, blending and bottling. In the Blending
Department, all materials are added at the start of the process, and labor and overhead are incurred
evenly throughout the process. Godfrey uses the weighted average method. The following data from
the Work in Process—Blending Department account for January 2016 is missing a few items:

Work in Process—Blending Department	
January 1 inventory (5,000 gallons, 60% processed)	
Direct material.	$ 12,000
Conversion costs	5,900
Transferred to Bottling Department (60,000 gallons).	——————
January charges:	
Direct material (61,000 gallons)	152,500
Direct labor.	73,600
Manufacturing overhead	48,800
January 31 inventory (_____ gallons, 70% processed)	——————

Required
Assuming Godfrey uses the weighted average method in process costing, calculate the following
amounts for the Blending Department:

a. Number of units in the January 31 inventory.
b. Equivalent units for materials and conversion costs.
c. January cost per equivalent unit for materials and conversion costs.
d. Cost of the units transferred to the Bottling Department.
e. Cost of the incomplete units in the January 31 inventory.

P4-2A. **Calculate Equivalent Units, Unit Costs, and Transferred Costs—Weighted Average**   **LO3, 4**
Method Arrow Company processes a food seasoning powder through its Compounding and
Packaging departments. In the Compounding Department, direct materials are added at the beginning of the process, and direct labor and manufacturing overhead are incurred evenly throughout the
process. Arrow uses the weighted average method. Costs in the Compounding Department can be
summarized as follows:

Inventory, August 1, 2016 (2,000 units, 40% complete)	
Direct material.	$ 980
Conversion costs	4,100
Current period (31,000 units started)	
Direct material.	33,050
Direct labor	62,560
Manufacturing overhead.	75,650
	$176,340

At August 31, 2016, 3,000 units were in process, 30% complete with respect to conversion costs.

Required
Calculate the following for the Compounding Department:

a. Equivalent units for materials and conversion costs during August.
b. Costs per equivalent unit for materials and conversion costs.
c. Total cost of units transferred to the Packaging Department.
d. Inventory cost at August 31, 2016.

P4-3A. **Product Cost Report—Weighted Average Method** Reston Manufacturing Corporation produces   **LO3, 4**
a cosmetic product in three consecutive processes. The costs of Department 1 for May 2016 were as
follows:

Cost of beginning inventory		
Direct material.		$ 9,800
Conversion costs		16,590
Costs added in Department 1:		
Direct material.	$295,400	
Direct labor	298,550	
Manufacturing overhead.	203,130	797,080

Department 1 handled the following units during May:

Units in process, May 1, 2016	2,000
Units started in Department 1	40,000
Units transferred to Department 2	39,000
Units in process, May 31, 2016	3,000

On average, the May 1 units were 30% complete. The May 31 units were 60% complete. Materials are added at the beginning of the process, and conversion costs occur evenly throughout the process in Department 1. Reston uses the weighted average method for process costing.

Required
Prepare the product cost report for Department 1 for May.

LO3, 4   **P4-4A.**   **Product Cost Report—Weighted Average Method** Morrow Manufacturing Company uses the weighted average method for process costing. Morrow produces processed food products that pass through three sequential departments. The costs for Department 1 for September 2016 were as follows:

Cost of beginning inventory:		
Material.		$ 11,850
Conversion		20,480
		$ 32,330
Costs added in Department 1 during September:		
Direct material.		$338,750
Direct labor		341,370
Manufacturing overhead.		245,990
		926,110
Department 2 handled the following units during September:		
Units in process, September 1.		2,000
Units started in Department 1.		48,000
Units transferred out to Department 2		46,000
Units in process, September 30.		4,000

On average, the September 1 units were 30% complete, and the September 30 units were 60% complete. Materials are added at the beginning of the process and conversion costs occur evenly throughout the process in Department 1.

Required
Prepare the product cost report for September for Department 1.

LO3, 4, 5   **P4-5A.**   **Two Departments, Journal Entries with Supporting Calculations—Weighted Average Method** (Note: This problem includes two departments. The second department may be beyond the scope of most classes. Instructors may choose to assign only the requirements related to Department 1.)

   Patterson Laboratories, Inc., produces one of its products in two successive departments. All materials are added at the beginning of the process in Department 1; no materials are used in Department 2. Conversion costs are incurred evenly in both departments. Patterson uses the weighted average method for process costing. January 1, 2016, inventory account balances are as follows:

Materials inventory	$30,000
Work in process—Department 1 (3,000 units, 30% complete)	
Direct materials	4,560
Conversion costs	10,640
Work in process—Department 2 (4,000 units, 40% complete)	48,100
Finished goods inventory (2,000 units @ $16)	32,000

During January, the following transactions occurred:

1. Purchased material on account, $90,000.
2. Placed $84,000 of material into process in Department 1. This $84,000 represents 24,000 units of materials.
3. Distributed total payroll costs: $108,000 of direct labor to Department 1, $62,700 of direct labor to Department 2, and $51,000 of indirect labor to Manufacturing Overhead.
4. Incurred other actual manufacturing overhead costs, $81,000. (Credit Other Accounts.)
5. Applied overhead to the two processing departments: $88,000 to Department 1 and $43,900 to Department 2.
6. Transferred 25,000 completed units from Department 1 to Department 2. The 2,000 units remaining in Department 1 were 20% completed with respect to conversion costs.
7. Transferred 26,000 completed units from Department 2 to finished goods inventory. The 3,000 units remaining in Department 2 were 75% completed with respect to conversion costs.
8. Sold 20,000 units on account at $27 per unit. Patterson uses FIFO inventory costing procedures for the finished goods inventory.

Required

a. Record the January transactions in general journal form for Department 1 and Department 2.
b. Prepare a product cost report (with its supporting calculations) for Department 1.
c. Prepare a product cost report (with its supporting calculations) for Department 2.
d. Determine the balances remaining in the Materials Inventory account, in each work in process account, and in the Finished Goods Inventory account.

P4-6A. **Calculate Equivalent Units, Unit Costs, and Transferred Costs—FIFO Method** Godfrey
Manufacturing, Inc., operates a plant that produces its own regionally marketed Spicy Steak Sauce.
The sauce is produced in two processes, blending and bottling. In the Blending Department, all ma-
terials are added at the start of the process, and labor and overhead are incurred evenly throughout
the process. Godfrey uses the FIFO method. The following data from the Work in Process—Blending
Department account for January 2016 is missing a few items:

LO6, 7

Work in Process—Blending Department	
January 1 inventory (5,000 gallons, 60% processed)	$17,900
Transferred to Bottling Department (60,000 gallons)	————
January charges:	
Direct material (61,000 gallons)	152,500
Direct labor	73,600
Manufacturing overhead	48,800
January 31 inventory (———— gallons, 70% processed)	————

Required

Assuming Godfrey uses the FIFO method in process costing, calculate the following amounts for the
Blending Department:

a. Number of units in the January 31 inventory.
b. Equivalent units for materials and conversion costs.
c. January cost per equivalent unit for materials and conversion costs.
d. Cost of the units transferred to the Bottling Department.
e. Cost of the incomplete units in the January 31 inventory

LO6, 7 **P4-7A.** **Calculate Equivalent Units, Unit Costs, and Transferred Costs—FIFO Method** Arrow Company processes a food seasoning powder through its Compounding and Packaging departments. In the Compounding Department, direct materials are added at the beginning of the process, and direct labor and manufacturing overhead are incurred evenly throughout the process. Arrow uses the FIFO method. August 2016 costs in the Compounding Department can be summarized as follows:

Inventory, August 1 (2,000 units, 40% complete)	$ 5,080
Direct material (31,000 units)	33,050
Direct labor	62,560
Manufacturing overhead	75,650
	$176,340

At August 31, 3,000 units were in process, 30% complete with respect to conversion costs.

Required
Calculate the following for the Compounding Department:

a. Equivalent units during August.
b. Costs per equivalent unit.
c. Total cost of units transferred to finished goods inventory.
d. Inventory cost at August 31.

LO7 **P4-8A.** **Product Cost Report—FIFO Method** Reston Manufacturing Corporation produces a cosmetic product in three consecutive processes. The costs of Department 1 for May 2016 were as follows:

Cost of beginning inventory		$606,390
Costs added in Department 1:		
Direct material	$80,400	
Direct labor	81,550	
Manufacturing overhead	55,130	217,080

Department 1 handled the following units during May:

Units in process, May 1	2,000
Units started in Department 1	40,000
Units transferred to Department 2	39,000
Units in process, May 31	3,000

On average, the May 1 units were 30% complete; the May 31 units were 60% complete. Materials are added at the beginning of the process and conversion costs occur evenly throughout the process in Department 1. Reston uses the FIFO method for process costing.

Required
Prepare the product cost report for Department 1 for May.

PROBLEMS—SET B

LO3, 4 **P4-1B.** **Calculate Equivalent Units, Unit Costs, and Transferred Costs—Weighted Average Method** Kipling Manufacturing, Inc., operates a plant that produces its own regionally-marketed Super Salad Dressing. The dressing is produced in two processes, blending and bottling. In the Blending Department, all materials are added at the beginning of the process, and labor and overhead are incurred evenly throughout the process. Kipling uses the weighted average method. The Work in Process—Blending Department account for January 2016 follows:

Work in Process—Blending Department	
January 1 inventory (4,000 gallons, 75% finished)	
Direct material.	$ 31,200
Conversion costs	8,800
Transferred to Bottling Department (70,000 gallons).	
January charges:	
Direct material (71,000 gallons)	568,000
Direct labor.	164,000
Manufacturing overhead.	186,000
January 31 inventory (_____ gallons, 60% processed)	

Required

Calculate the following amounts for the Blending Department:

a. Number of units in the January 31 inventory.
b. Equivalent units for materials cost and conversion costs.
c. January cost per equivalent unit for materials and conversion costs.
d. Cost of the units transferred to the Bottling Department.
e. Cost of the incomplete units in the January 31 inventory.

P4-2B. **Calculate Equivalent Units, Unit Costs, and Transferred Costs—Weighted Average** LO3, 4
Method Bradford Company processes a scouring powder through its Compounding Department and
Packaging Department. In the Compounding Department, direct materials are added at the beginning
of the process, and direct labor and manufacturing overhead are incurred evenly throughout the pro-
cess. Bradford uses the weighted average method. Costs charged to the Compounding Department in
October 2016 follow:

Inventory, October 1 (5,000 units, 25% complete)	
Direct material.	$ 2,400
Conversion costs	1,850
Current period (82,000 units started):	
Direct material.	171,550
Direct labor.	67,770
Manufacturing overhead.	71,470
	$315,040

At October 31, 7,000 units were in process, 40% completed.

Required

Calculate the following for the Compounding Department:

a. Equivalent units during October.
b. Costs per equivalent unit.
c. Total cost of units transferred to the Packaging Department.
d. Inventory cost at October 31.

P4-3B. **Product Cost Report—Weighted Average Method** Gomez Manufacturing Corporation produces a LO4
dandruff shampoo in three consecutive processes. The costs of Department 1 for June 2016 were as
follows:

Cost of beginning inventory		
Direct material.		$ 5,500
Conversion costs		12,740
Costs added in Department 1:		
Direct material.	$223,670	
Direct labor.	358,300	
Manufacturing overhead.	155,400	737,370

Department 1 handled the following units during June:

Units in process, June 1.	2,000
Units started in Department 1	45,000
Units transferred to Department 2	46,000
Units in process, June 30.	1,000

On average, the June 1 units were 40% complete; the June 30 units were 70% complete. Direct materials are added at the beginning of the process, and conversion costs occur evenly throughout the process in Department 1. Gomez uses the weighted average method for process costing.

Required
Prepare the product cost report for Department 1 for June.

LO3, 4 P4-4B. Equivalent Units and Product Cost Report—Weighted Average Method Summers Manufacturing Corporation produces chemical products using a continual process. Summers uses the weighted average method for process costing. All manufacturing is accomplished in one department. Materials are added at the beginning of the process while conversion costs are incurred evenly throughout the process.

The work in process inventory at the beginning of February 2016 consisted of 10,000 gallons that were 20% complete. The work in process at the end of February consisted of 15,000 gallons that were 40% complete. During February 195,000 gallons were transferred to finished goods.

The beginning inventory contained $90,000 of materials and $30,000 of conversion costs. Product costs incurred during February consisted of $2,010,000 of materials and $3,186,000 of conversion costs.

Required
Calculate equivalent units, cost per equivalent unit, and prepare the product cost report for Summers Manufacturing Corporation for the month of February.

LO3, 4, 5 P4-5B. Two Departments, Journal Entries with Supporting Calculations—Weighted Average Method (Note: This problem includes two departments. The second department may be beyond the scope of most classes. Instructors may choose to assign only the requirements related to Department 1.)

Parker Laboratories, Inc., produces one of its products in two successive departments. All materials are added at the beginning of the process in Department 1. No materials are used in Department 2. Conversion costs are incurred evenly in both departments. August 1, 2016, inventory account balances are as follows:

Materials inventory.	$15,000
Work in process—Department 1 (6,000 units, 25% finished)	
Direct materials.	11,500
Conversion costs	18,750
Work in process—Department 2 (4,000 units, 35% finished)	41,000
Finished goods inventory (4,000 units @ $12.50).	50,000

During August, the following transactions occurred:

1. Purchased material on account, $58,000.
2. Placed 16,000 units of material at $4 per unit into process in Department 1.
3. Distributed total payroll costs: $83,770 of direct labor to Department 1, $42,300 of direct labor to Department 2, and $19,100 of indirect labor to Manufacturing Overhead.
4. Incurred other actual manufacturing overhead costs, $21,200. (Credit Other Accounts.)
5. Applied overhead to the two processing departments: Department 1, $21,280, Department 2, $17,900.
6. Transferred 20,000 completed units from Department 1 to Department 2. The 2,000 units remaining in Department 1 were 30% completed with respect to conversion costs.
7. Transferred 15,000 completed units from Department 2 to Finished Goods Inventory. The 9,000 units remaining in Department 2 were 40% completed with respect to conversion costs.
8. Sold 13,000 units on account at $24 per unit. Parker uses weighted average inventory costing for finished goods inventory.

Required
a. Record the August transactions in general journal form for Department 1 and Department 2.

b. Prepare a product cost report (with its supporting calculations) for Department 1.

c. Prepare a product cost report (with its supporting calculations) for Department 2.

d. Determine the balances remaining in the Materials Inventory account, in each work in process account, and in the Finished Goods Inventory account.

P4-6B. Calculate Equivalent Units, Unit Costs, and Transferred Costs—FIFO Method Kipling Manufacturing, Inc., operates a plant that produces its own regionally-marketed Super Salad Dressing. The dressing is produced in two processes, blending and bottling. In the Blending Department, all materials are added at the beginning of the process, and labor and overhead are incurred evenly throughout the process. Kipling uses the FIFO method. The Work in Process—Blending Department account for January 2016 follows: **LO6, 7**

Work in Process—Blending Department	
January 1 inventory (4,000 gallons, 75% finished)	$ 40,000
Transferred to Bottling Department (70,000 gallons)	————
January charges:	
Direct material (71,000 gallons)	568,000
Direct labor	164,000
Manufacturing overhead	186,000
January 31 inventory (_____ gallons, 60% processed)	————

Required

Calculate the following amounts for the Blending Department:

a. Number of units in the January 31 inventory.

b. Equivalent units for materials cost and conversion costs.

c. January cost per equivalent unit for materials and conversion costs.

d. Cost of the units transferred to the Bottling Department.

e. Cost of the incomplete units in the January 31 inventory.

P4-7B. Calculate Equivalent Units, Unit Costs, and Transferred Costs—FIFO Method Bradford Company processes a scouring powder through its Compounding Department and Packaging Department. In the Compounding Department, direct materials are added at the beginning of the process, and direct labor and manufacturing overhead are incurred evenly throughout the process. Bradford uses the FIFO method. Costs charged to the Compounding Department in October 2016 follow: **LO6, 7**

Inventory, October 1 (5,000 units, 25% complete)	$ 4,250
Direct material (82,000 units)	245,550
Direct labor	31,770
Manufacturing overhead	33,470
	$315,040

At October 31, 7,000 units were in process, 40% completed.

Required

Calculate the following for the Compounding Department:

a. Equivalent units during October.

b. Costs per equivalent unit.

c. Total cost of units transferred to the Packaging Department.

d. Inventory cost at October 31.

P4-8B. Product Cost Report—FIFO Method Gomez Manufacturing Corporation produces a dandruff shampoo in three consecutive processes. The costs of Department 1 for June 2016 were as follows: **LO7**

Cost of beginning inventory		$ 18,240
Costs added in Department 1:		
Direct material	$219,670	
Direct labor	361,300	
Manufacturing overhead	156,400	737,370

Department 1 handled the following units during June:

Units in process, June 1.	2,000
Units started in Department 1	45,000
Units transferred to Department 2	46,000
Units in process, June 30.	1,000

On average, the June 1 units were 40% complete. The June 30 units were 70% complete. Materials are added at the beginning of the process and conversion costs occur evenly throughout the process in Department 1. Gomez uses the FIFO method for process costing.

Required
Prepare the product cost report for Department 1 for June.

CERTIFIED MANAGEMENT ACCOUNTANT (CMA®) EXAM SAMPLE QUESTIONS

CMA 4-1. During December, Krause Chemical Company had the following selected data concerning the manufacture of Xyzine, an industrial cleaner.

Production Flow	Physical Units	
Completed and transferred to the next department	100	
Add: Ending work-in-process inventory	10	(40% complete as to conversion)
Total units to account for	110	
Less: Beginning work-in-process inventory	20	(60% complete as to conversion)
Units started during December	90	

All material is added at the beginning of processing in this department, and conversion costs are added uniformly during the process. The beginning work-in-process inventory had $120 of raw material and $180 of conversion costs incurred. Material added during December was $540 and conversion costs of $1,484 were incurred. Krause uses the weighted-average process-costing method. The total raw material costs in the ending work-in-process inventory for December is

a. $120.
b. $72.
c. $60.
d. $36.

CMA 4-2. Mack Inc. uses a weighted-average process costing system. Direct materials and conversion costs are incurred evenly during the production process. During the month of October, the following costs were incurred.

Direct materials	$39,700
Conversion costs	70,000

The work-in-process inventory as of October 1 consisted of 5,000 units, valued at $4,300, that were 20% complete. During October, 27,000 units were transferred out. Inventory as of October 31 consisted of 3,000 units that were 50% complete. The weighted-average inventory cost per unit completed in October was

a. $3.51.
b. $3.88.
c. $3.99.
d. $4.00.

CMA 4-3. Colt Company uses a weighted-average process cost system to account for the cost of producing a chemical compound. As part of production, Material B is added when the goods are 80% complete. Beginning work-in-process inventory for the current month was 20,000 units, 90% complete. During the month, 70,000 units were started in process, and 65,000 units were completed. There were no lost or spoiled units. If the ending inventory was 60% complete, the total equivalent units for Material B for the month was

   a.   65,000 units.
   b.   70,000 units.
   c.   85,000 units.
   d.   90,000 units.

CMA 4-4. San Jose Inc. uses a weighted-average process costing system. All materials are introduced at the start of manufacturing, and conversion costs are incurred evenly throughout production. The company started 70,000 units during May and had the following work-in-process inventories at the beginning and end of the month.

May 1	30,000 units, 40% complete
May 31	24,000 units, 25% complete

Assuming no spoilage or defective units, the total equivalent units used to assign costs for May are

	Materials	Conversion Cost
a.	70,000	70,000.
b.	82,000	82,000.
c.	100,000	70,000.
d.	100,000	82,000.

CMA 4-5. During December, Krause Chemical Company had the following selected data concerning the manufacture of Xyzine, an industrial cleaner.

Production Flow	Physical Units	
Completed and transferred to the next department	100	
Add: Ending work-in-process inventory	10	(40% complete as to conversion)
Total units to account for	110	
Less: Beginning work-in-process inventory	20	(60% complete as to conversion)
Units started during December	90	

All material is added at the beginning of processing in this department, and conversion costs are added uniformly during the process. The beginning work-in-process inventory had $120 of raw material and $180 of conversion costs incurred. Material added during December was $540 and conversion costs of $1,484 were incurred. Krause uses the weighted-average process-costing method. The total conversion costs assigned to units transferred to the next department in December was

   a. $1,664.
   b. $1,600.
   c. $1,513.
   d. $1,484.

CMA 4-6. During December, Krause Chemical Company had the following selected data concerning the manufacture of Xyzine, an industrial cleaner.

Production Flow	Physical Units	
Completed and transferred to the next department	100	
Add: Ending work-in-process inventory	10	(40% complete as to conversion)
Total units to account for	110	
Less: Beginning work-in-process inventory	20	(60% complete as to conversion)
Units started during December	90	

All material is added at the beginning of processing in this department, and conversion costs are added uniformly during the process. The beginning work-in-process inventory had $120 of raw material and $180 of conversion costs incurred. Material added during December was $540 and conversion costs of $1,484 were incurred. Krause uses the first-in, first-out (FIFO) process-costing method. The equivalent units of production used to calculate conversion costs for December was

a. 110 units.
b. 104 units.
c. 100 units.
d. 92 units.

CMA 4-7. Jones Corporation uses a first-in, first-out (FIFO) process costing system. Jones has the following unit information for the month of August.

	Units
Beginning work-in-process inventory, 100% complete for materials, 75% complete for conversion cost.	10,000
Units completed and transferred out	90,000
Ending work-in-process inventory, 100% complete for materials, 60% complete for conversion costs.	8,000

The number of equivalent units of production for conversion costs for the month of August is

a. 87,300.
b. 88,000.
c. 92,300.
d. 92,700.

EXTENDING YOUR KNOWLEDGE

EYK4-1. Ethics Case Sweet Fragrances Company uses process costing to account for the manufacture of its perfume. The factory consists of three departments: blending, bottling, and packaging.

The production manager of the bottling department, Janine Post, has recommended that her department not be charged for new labels that are more elaborate and expensive than those used in previous years. The new labels were designed as a tie-in for the marketing and advertising campaigns. Post recommends that the costs of the labels be charged to advertising expense. This would result in slightly lower product costs charged to the bottling department than last year.

The company has instituted a bonus plan for all managers based on keeping costs within a range of previous years' costs.

Sam Block, the accounting manager, reviews all recommendations by all managers before they are presented to top management.

Required
What ethical considerations may arise from Janine Post's recommendation? What alternative recommendations might be made?

ANSWERS TO SELF-STUDY QUESTIONS:

1. c, (pp. 114–115) 2. b, (p. 115) 3. a, (p. 133)

YOUR TURN! SOLUTIONS

Solution 4.1

Remember that when using the weighted average method, the question is "what percentage of the work has been completed?"

Where do the units come from?		Where do the units go?		Equivalent Units			
				% Work Done?	Direct Materials	% Work Done?	Conversion Costs
Beginning inventory . . .	100	Complete/transferred . . .	800	100%	**800**	100%	**800**
Started	790	Ending inventory.	90	100%	**90**	75%	**68**
Total	890	Total	890		890		868

Solution 4.2

Work in process	24,000	
Materials inventory		24,000
Work in process	32,400	
Wages payable		32,400
Work in process	48,600	
Manufacturing overhead		48,600

Solution 4.3

Remember that when using the FIFO method, the question is "what percentage of the work was completed during THIS PERIOD?"

Where do the units come from?		Where do the units go?		Equivalent Units			
				% in Jan.?	Direct Materials	% in Jan.?	Conversion Costs
		Complete/transferred:					
Beginning inventory	100	Beginning inventory	100	0%	0	65%	65
		Started and completed . . .	700	100%	700	100%	700
Started	790	Ending inventory.	90	100%	90	75%	68
Total	890	Total	890		790		833

Solution 4.4

Work in process	24,000	
Materials inventory		24,000
Work in process	32,400	
Wages payable		32,400
Work in process	48,600	
Manufacturing overhead		48,600

5

Activity-Based Costing

LEARNING OBJECTIVES

1. **Explain** the changes in the modern production environment that have affected cost structures. *(p. 161)*

2. **Understand** the concept of activity-based costing (ABC) and how it is applied. *(p. 162)*

3. **Explain** the difference between traditional company-wide and departmental overhead methods and ABC. *(p. 165)*

4. **Describe** the implementation of an ABC system. *(p. 169)*

5. **Explain** customer profitability analysis based on ABC. *(p. 171)*

6. **Explain** the difference between ABC and activity-based management. *(p. 173)*

CALIFORNIA STATE BAR ASSOCIATION

Among its several responsibilities, the **California State Bar Association** regulates the professional conduct of the state's lawyers. The State Bar's discipline system is designed to protect the public, the courts, and the legal profession from lawyers who violate the state's ethical code of professional conduct, the Rules of Professional Conduct.

When a complaint is received from a member of the public regarding the conduct of one of its member lawyers, a complaint analyst determines whether the alleged conduct is in fact a violation of the Rules of Professional Conduct. If so, the complaint is referred to the Office of Investigation for investigation of the allegations. If the investigation concludes that probable misconduct occurred, the Office of Trials files formal charges and prosecutes the alleged attorney in the State Bar Court. The State Bar Court hears the charges and may recommend to the State Supreme Court to either suspend or disbar an attorney who is found to have violated the Rules of Professional Conduct or been convicted of serious crimes. If an allegation proceeds through the process to a formal trial, it can involve hundreds of hours of State Bar analysts', investigators', trial lawyers', judges' and other personnel's time, as well as significant expense.

The state's Business and Professions Code section 6086.10 authorizes the State Bar to recover a portion of the costs of pursuing action against disciplined lawyers. These costs include "charges determined by the State Bar to be 'reasonable costs' of investigation, hearing, and review." What constitutes "reasonable costs"?

To answer this question, the State Bar engaged an independent consulting firm to assist in the analysis. Over a two-week period, State Bar employees were asked to keep detailed track of the time that they spent performing various tasks related to disciplinary procedures. These and other data were then used to compute average times spent on the tasks by each employee type (analyst, investigator, trial lawyer, etc.). Multiplying these average times by the number of tasks performed for a particular type of complaint and the total number of complaints received in the period gave a measure of the work performed in each office. The total cost incurred by each office could then be divided by the amount of work performed to calculate the reasonable cost of an investigation of various types of complaints, hearings, and reviews. The result was a schedule of fees approved by the state legislature. For example, in 2013 a lawyer convicted of a violation of the Rules of Professional Conduct over the course of a multi-day trial would be assessed almost $16,000 in addition to other discipline.

The process used to determine the amount of "reasonable costs" is called activity-based costing (ABC). Each of the State Bar offices (Office of Investigation, Office of Trials, etc.) is a "cost pool" that is allocated to a "product" (a type of case) based on a "cost driver" (a task performed). Although ABC is traditionally used to determine the cost of products, it can have application in a service setting as well.

Understanding Indirect Costs Using ABC	Activity-Based Costing	Traditional Product Costing and ABC Compared	ABC Implementation Issues	ABC and Customer Profitability Analysis	Activity-Based Management
• Changing cost environment	• Purpose of ABC • ABC product costing model	• Applying overhead with activity-based costing • Limitations of ABC • Comparing traditional and activity-based costing	• Implementation of ABC • Implementation issues	• Customer profitability profile • ABC customer profitability analysis	• Activity-based management

UNDERSTANDING INDIRECT COSTS USING ACTIVITY-BASED COSTING

Effective management of costs is a hallmark of sound financial management, and indirect costs (commonly referred to as overhead) are the most challenging costs to measure and manage. Direct costs, including direct materials and direct labor, can be readily traced to a job, product, or other unit of work. Indirect costs, which are typically incurred for the benefit of several different products or cost objects, are not as easily traced to specific units or projects. Managing indirect costs is a major concern of managers because this broad category of costs has become increasingly more common over time.

Many companies that once thrived have failed, arguably, because they did not manage effectively a growing pool of indirect costs. You might say they failed because they did not fully understand their business or their business model. If a business's actual cost of producing and selling products is more than the revenues generated by those products, the business will not succeed in the long term.

It is well documented that for many years the **U.S. Postal Service (USPS)**, a service entity, has struggled with mounting losses while its competitors, **UPS** and **FedEx**, have thrived in a highly competitive marketplace. At a meeting of the President's Commission on the United States Postal Service (created to examine the problems of the USPS), the discussion focused on differences in the cost systems at the USPS and UPS. It was reported that the USPS cost system attributes only 58% of its operating costs to it various products, whereas UPS attributes 100% of its costs to its products. The UPS representative on the panel stated that UPS does not price any product below its full cost. With only 58% of its costs attributed to products, the USPS cannot know whether any of its products, individually, is making a profit.[1]

As global competition puts increasing pressure on companies to price products more competitively, cost management is increasingly important. Organizations and entities such as UPS, **Coca-Cola**, **IBM**, the **City of Indianapolis**, and **Toronto's Hospital for Sick Children** have benefited greatly from a type of cost system referred to as **activity-based costing (ABC)**. In this chapter we will define and discuss ABC systems, compare ABC with

---

[1] James A. Johnson and Harry J. Pearce, Co-chairs, "Minutes of Meeting of the President's Commission on the U.S. Postal Service," May 28, 2003, p3, http://www.ustreas.gov/offices/domestic-finance/usps/pdf/may_28_minutes.pdf

traditional costing systems, and demonstrate how ABC can be used to analyze customer profitability. Finally, we will introduce the notion of **activity-based management (ABM)**, which uses ABC information to better manage processes and activities within an organization.

Changing Cost Environment

As technology has advanced over the last century, there has been a fundamental shift in manufacturing organizations from labor-intensive to automated assembly processes. These changes have had a profound influence on the activities performed to meet customer needs and, consequently, the costs of producing goods and services.

LO1 **Explain** the changes in the modern production environment that have affected cost structures.

At the beginning of the twentieth century, products had long life cycles, production procedures were relatively straightforward, production was labor intensive, and only limited numbers of related products were produced in a single plant. It was said of the Model T Ford that "you could have any color you wanted, as long as it was black." The largest cost elements of most manufactured goods were the cost of raw materials and the wages paid to production employees. Manufacturing overhead was a relatively small portion of the overall cost of manufacturing products.

The twentieth century saw an accelerating shift from traditional labor-based activities to production procedures requiring large investments in automated equipment. In the past, production employees used equipment to assist them in performing their jobs. Now employees spend considerable time scheduling, setting up, maintaining, and moving materials to and from equipment. They spend relatively little time on actual production. The equipment does the work, and the employees keep it running efficiently. Increased complexity of production procedures and an increase in the variety of products produced in a single facility have also caused a shift toward more support personnel and fewer production employees. The result is a significant increase in manufacturing overhead as a percentage of total product cost. This change in the typical production cost structure over the past century is illustrated in **Exhibit 5-1**.

Exhibit 5-1	**Changing Cost Environment***

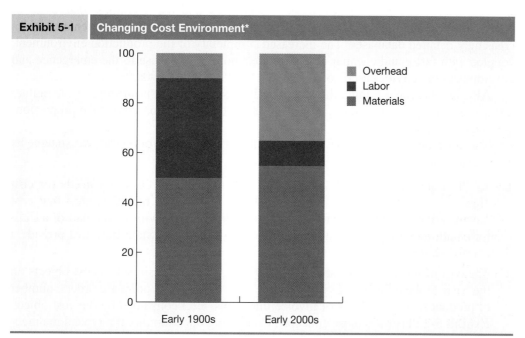

* "The Constraints Management Handbook," James F. Cox, III, Michael S. Spencer, CRC Press, 1997, p. 54.

In the "low-tech," labor-intensive manufacturing environment, factors related to direct labor were often the primary drivers of manufacturing overhead costs; however, in today's "high-tech" automated environment there are many other factors that drive manufacturing overhead costs, and the specific set of cost drivers differs from organization to organization.

Chapter 3 on product costing illustrates a simplified traditional system for allocating manufacturing overhead to products using a single, volume-based cost driver, such as direct labor hours. The following section introduces ABC, which recognizes the multiple activities that drive manufacturing overhead costs in today's production environment.

TAKEAWAY 5.1

Understanding overhead costs is becoming increasingly important in order to maintain a competitive edge in a given industry. This process can require a significant outflow of resources, but will likely result in higher-quality cost information, and thereby better pricing decisions.

ACTIVITY-BASED COSTING

LO2 **Understand** the concept of activity-based costing (ABC) and how it is applied.

The manufacturing overhead cost pool has been referred to as a "bucket" of common costs. The constant growth of costs classified as overhead has forced us to search for increasingly detailed methods to analyze these costs. If overhead costs are low in comparison with material and labor costs and if factories produce few products in large production runs, the use of a single overhead rate based on direct labor hours or machine hours may be adequate. However, as the amount of overhead costs grows, as manufacturing facilities produce a wider variety of products, and as competition intensifies, the inadequacies of a single overhead rate based on a single cost driver such as direct labor hours become evident.

Fortunately, advances in information technology and the declining costs of computerized information systems have facilitated the development and maintenance of increasingly detailed databases. The increased complexity of the production environment, coupled with faster and cheaper computing technology, gave rise to the emergence and development of activity-based costing during the 1980s and 1990s.

ABC involves determining the cost of **activities** (discrete tasks or steps in a manufacturing or service process) and tracing those costs to cost objects based on their proportionate usage of the activities.

The concepts underlying ABC can be summarized in the following two statements and illustrations:

1. As illustrated in **Exhibit 5-2**, activities performed to fill customer needs (or cost objects) consume resources (materials, labor, equipment, facilities, etc.) that cost money. For example, a client complaint regarding misbehavior on the part of a California attorney may require that a trial be conducted. The State Bar must provide a courtroom for the trial.

2. The cost of resources consumed by activities should be assigned to cost objects on the basis of the units of activity (machine hours, number of purchase orders, number of product returns, number of invoice line items, etc.) consumed by the cost object. **Exhibit 5-2** illustrates these concepts. Continuing our example, if a typical malpractice trial complaint takes eight hours to complete, the hourly cost of the courtroom should be assigned to the complaint. In addition to the court cost pool, other examples of State Bar cost pools include the costs associated with receiving and documenting customer complaints (intake), the costs associated with investigating the complaints

(investigation), and the costs associated with preparing and prosecuting the complaints (Office of Trials).

The cost object is typically a product or service provided to a customer. In our example, the cost object is the client's complaint—that is, we want to know what it costs to follow up on each client complaint so that we can recover the appropriate cost from the wayward attorney. Depending on the information needs of decision makers, as we will discuss later in this chapter, the cost object could be the customer.

To summarize, ABC is a system of analysis that identifies and measures the cost of key activities, and then traces these activity costs to products or other cost objects based on the quantity of activity consumed by the cost objects. ABC is based on the premise that activities drive costs and that costs should be assigned to products (or other cost objects) in proportion to the volume of activities they consume. Although activity cost analysis is most often associated with product costing, it offers many benefits for controlling and managing costs, as we will see later in this chapter. As the Accounting in Practice box, (page 164), explains, ABC was actually used first to improve cost management before it was used for product costing.

Exhibit 5-2	Activity-Based Costing Illustration

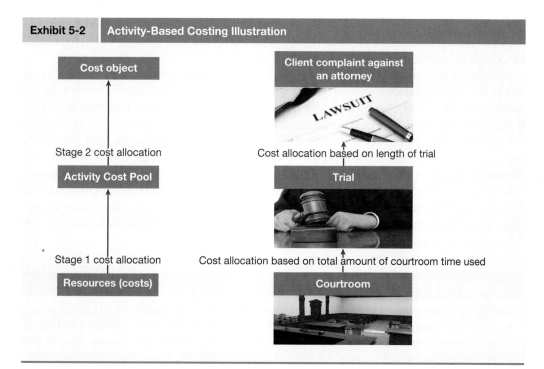

CORPORATE SOCIAL RESPONSIBILITY

Standards of Professionalism

The opening vignette of this chapter discusses how the California State Bar Association determines the reasonable costs of pursuing action against disciplined lawyers. Because of the extraordinary responsibility society places upon the attorneys within our democracy, it is critical that groups such as the California State Bar Association maintain the highest ethical standards for its members. Just how does the Association see this responsibility? The following is quoted from the California Attorney Guidelines of Civility and Professionalism:

> "As officers of the court with responsibilities to the administration of justice, attorneys have an obligation to be professional with clients, other parties and counsel, the courts and the public. This obligation includes civility, professional integrity, personal dignity, candor, diligence, respect, courtesy, and cooperation, all of which are essential to the fair administration of justice and conflict resolution."

ABC Product Costing Model

Traditional costing considers the cost of a product to be its direct costs for materials and labor plus some allocated portion of manufacturing overhead, using overhead rates typically based on direct labor or machine hours. ABC is based on the notion that companies incur costs because of the activities they conduct in pursuit of their goals and objectives. For example, various activities take place to produce a particular product, such as setting up, maintaining, or monitoring the machines to make the product, physically moving raw materials and work in process, and so forth. Each of these activities has a cost; therefore, the total cost of producing a product using ABC is the sum of the direct materials and direct labor costs of that product, plus the cost of other activities conducted to produce that product.

The left side of **Exhibit 5-2** illustrates the general two-stage ABC product cost model. The first stage includes the assignment of overhead resource costs, such as indirect labor, depreciation, and utilities, to activity cost pools for the key activities identified. Typical activity cost pools in a manufacturing environment include pools for machine setup, material movement, and engineering. The second stage assigns those activity cost pools to cost objects.

Remember that **Exhibit 5-2** is focused solely on overhead costs—the direct product or service costs, such as direct materials and direct labor, are directly assigned to cost objects and are excluded from the activity cost pools. Only indirect product costs (overhead) are assigned to products via activity cost pools.

Hint: If an increase in an activity does not cause a measurable increase in a particular cost, there is not a logical causal relationship.

Probably the most critical step in ABC is identifying **cost drivers**. The activity cost driver for a particular cost (or cost pool) is the characteristic selected for measuring the quantity of the activity for a particular period of time. In the example shown in **Exhibit 5-2**, if an activity cost pool is established for a trial, it is necessary to select some basis for measuring the quantity of trial activity associated with the costs in the pool. The quantity of trial activity could be measured by the number of trials held, the amount of time the courtroom is in use, the number of staff working in the courtroom, or some other measure. It is critical that the activity measure used has a logical causal relationship to the costs in the pool and that the quantity of the activity is highly correlated with the amount of cost in the pool. Statistical methods, such as regression analysis and correlation analysis, can be very useful in selecting activity cost drivers.

ACCOUNTING IN PRACTICE | **Development of ABC**

ABC came to the forefront in the 1980s and 1990s; however, it was beginning to evolve as early as the 1960s when finance and accounting staff at General Electric (GE) attempted to improve the usefulness of accounting information in controlling ever-increasing indirect costs. The GE staff noted that indirect costs were often the result of "upstream" decisions, such as engineering design and change orders, which were made long before the costs were actually incurred. Frequently, the engineering department was not informed of the consequences its actions had on the other parts of the organization.

The second phase of the development of ABC was accomplished by business consultants, professors, and manufacturing companies during the 1970s and early 1980s. By generating more accurate cost and profitability measures for the various products offered by companies, these consultants and professors hoped to improve product cost information used in pricing and product mix decisions. ABC has since been extended to assess customer profitability.

In the late 1980s and 1990s, ABC was being promoted by many of the leading consulting firms, and it almost became a fad, much as total quality management (TQM) and just-in-time (JIT) systems had before it. Consequently, many companies that jumped on the ABC bandwagon early in its life later determined that it was not for them. Most of the companies that abandoned ABC probably adopted it initially for the wrong reasons.

Knowledge of the historical development of ABC is important in order to clearly understand what ABC analysis was intended to accomplish, as well as what it was not intended to accomplish.

Once the budgeted cost in the activity pool and the budgeted activity cost driver have been determined, the cost per unit of activity is calculated as the total cost divided by the total amount of activity. This is the predetermined rate that will be used to apply costs to products or services during the period. For example, if total costs assigned to the trial activity pool in July were $100,000 and 100 hours of courtroom time were available in July, the cost per courtroom hour for the month would be $1,000. If during July a particular trial took eight hours of courtroom time, the total courtroom cost that would be assigned to the trial would be $8,000 ($1,000 × 8 hours).

TRADITIONAL PRODUCT COSTING AND ABC COMPARED

Recall that in Chapter 3, Fezzari Performance Bicycles applied overhead using a company-wide overhead rate of $17.00 per direct labor hour. This may seem to be a very low overhead rate until you remember that Fezzari is primarily assembling parts that have been manufactured by other suppliers. Fezzari's factory doesn't have large, expensive manufacturing equipment that you might associate with other types of manufacturers.

LO3 **Explain** the difference between traditional company-wide and departmental overhead methods and ABC.

We assumed that each hour of labor worked on a project caused $17.00 of overhead to be incurred. In that case, all overhead costs were associated with one factor, direct labor hours. As discussed at the beginning of this chapter, such an assumption is often not appropriate with modern methods of producing goods or services where manufacturing overhead is related to a diverse set of activities and cost drivers.

Where overhead costs or capacity measures vary significantly from one department to the next, a separate overhead rate may be calculated for each department. Chapter 3 introduced the concept of departmental overhead rates, where a separate overhead rate is predetermined for each producing department in a factory. In most multiproduct manufacturing environments, this approach represents a cost system improvement over using a single, company-wide overhead rate, and it reduces the likelihood of cost cross-subsidization, which occurs when one product is assigned too much cost as a result of another being assigned too little cost.

Assume that Fezzari has two production departments, Assembly and Packaging, and that these departments have overhead costs of $240,100 and $60,000, respectively. Assume, further, that Fezzari management determined that the Assembly Department overhead costs should be allocated to bicycles on the basis of direct labor hours and that the Packaging Department overhead costs should be allocated to bicycles on the basis of units produced. **Exhibit 5-3** shows that the resulting department predetermined overhead rates would be $10.00 per direct labor hour for the Assembly Department and $13.33 per unit for the Packaging Department.

Exhibit 5-3	Computing Department Overhead Rates		
Overhead costs per unit		**Assembly**	**Packaging**
Total department manufacturing overhead (direct department costs plus allocated costs). . . .		$240,100	$60,000
Quantity of overhead application base			
Direct Labor Hours		÷ 24,000	
Units Produced.			÷ 4.500
Department manufacturing overhead rates		$ 10.00 *per direct labor hour*	$13.33 *per unit*

Department overhead rates may improve product costing results for many organizations, and in fact may be satisfactory. However, this method does not attempt to reflect the actual activities used in producing the different products.

Applying Overhead with Activity-Based Costing

An even more precise method of measuring the cost of products than company-wide or departmental rates is the ABC method. As stated earlier, ABC typically involves two stages of cost allocation. The first stage is identifying and measuring the cost of activities used to produce the various products. The second stage is summing the cost of those activities to determine the ultimate cost of the products.

| ACCOUNTING IN PRACTICE | Benefits of ABC |

A 2009 study by Stratton, Desroches, Lawson, and Hatch of 348 manufacturing and service companies worldwide indicated that activity-based costing continues to provide strategic and operational benefits. Although the study showed that there has been a decline in ABC users since the 1990s, when it was first widely adopted, the following graphic from the study report supports the conclusion that users of ABC have a higher level of confidence than non-ABC users that their cost system provides more accurate cost measurements.

Comparisons of ABC to Non-ABC Users on Three Key Benefits

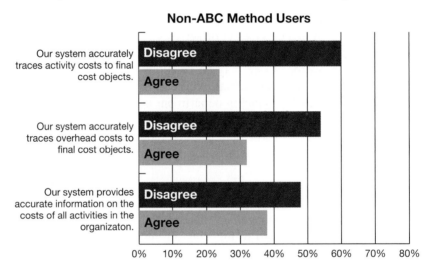

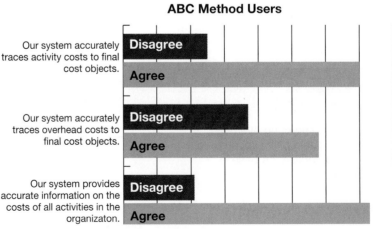

Source: W. O. Stratton, D. Desroches, R. A. Lawson, and T. Hatch. (2009). "Activity-Based Costing: Is It Still Relevant?" *Management Accounting Quarterly*, Vol.10, No. 3, pp. 31–40.

The overhead rates for each Fezzari department were determined in the last section as $10.00 and $13.33, respectively. The easiest way to assign these costs to products is by using one base and one rate for all products going through a given process (e.g., assembly). However, different products typically use different amounts of resources from a given process and using the same base and overhead rate for all may distort the cost for some or all products.

Overhead costs in the Assembly and Packaging Departments consisted of two types of costs: **production department costs** and support department costs. Production department overhead costs are costs that are incurred by the production department, such as indirect labor, indirect materials, depreciation on equipment, supervisory wages, and so forth. Support department costs are costs allocated from other departments (for the Fezzari example, the support departments include Design, Receiving/Inventory, and Building) that provide services to both Assembly and Packaging. Fezzari's accountant determined that the production department overhead costs in Assembly were driven primarily by labor hours, whereas support department overhead costs in Packaging were driven primarily by units produced. It was also determined that each component of design, receiving/inventory, and building represents a separate activity cost pool, and that these costs should be assigned to the products based on specific cost drivers rather than a single cost driver for the entire department.

Exhibit 5-4 presents a detailed analysis of overhead cost data for July's operations.

Exhibit 5-4	ABC Stage One: Assign Costs to Activities			
Overhead Activity	**Total Activity Cost**	**Activity Cost Driver (number of)**	**Quantity of Activity**	**Unit Activity Rates***
Production departmental overhead costs				
Assembly	$ 10,000	Direct labor hours.	24,000	$ 0.42
Packaging.	3,000	Units produced.	4,500	$ 0.67
Allocated support costs				
Receiving/Inventory	21,000	Units produced.	4,500	$ 4.67
Design.	20,000	Change orders	31,500	$ 0.63
Building.	246,100	Units produced.	4,500	$54.69
Total	$300,100			

* Rounded

Assume that Fezzari management wants to compare the use of a company-wide, departmental, and ABC overhead allocation method on the cost of two road bikes, the top-end T5 (from Chapter 3) and the entry-level Catania. The T5 is typically purchased by serious triathletes who are very particular about the setup and customization of their bikes, whereas the Catania is typically purchased by fitness newbies who know little about bike components and fit and are primarily driven by price in the selection of their bikes. For simplicity, assume that these are the only two bikes produced by Fezzari. The amounts of activity attributed to the T5 and Catania and the overhead cost per unit based on ABC costs are shown in **Exhibit 5-5**.

Exhibit 5-5	ABC Stage Two: Assign Activities to Cost Objects						
Bicycle Model				**T5**		**Catania**	
Activity	**Cost Driver**	**Cost per Unit of Activity**	**Quantity of Activity**	**Cost of Activity***	**Quantity of Activity**	**Cost of Activity***	
Assembly	Direct labor hours. . . .	$ 0.42	12,000	$ 5,000.00	12,000	$ 5,000.00	
Packaging	Units produced.	0.67	1,500	1,000.00	3,000	2,000.00	
Receiving/Inventory	Units produced.	4.67	1,500	7,000.00	3,000	14,000.00	
Design	Change orders	0.63	22,500	14,285.71	9,000	5,714.29	
Building	Units produced.	54.69	1,500	82,033.33	3,000	164,066.67	
Total overhead product cost				$109,319.04		$190,780.96	
Units produced.				1,500.00		3,000.00	
Overhead per unit of product*				$ 72.88		$ 63.59	

*Differences due to rounding.

Exhibit 5-6 summarizes the allocated overhead costs for Fezzari's two products using the three different overhead cost assignment methods.

Exhibit 5-6	Overhead Cost per Unit Using Various Overhead Methods		
		T5	**Catania**
Company-wide overhead rate*.		$136.00	$68.00
Departmental overhead rates**		93.33	53.33
ABC		72.88	63.59

*Direct labor hours per unit × $17.00 = (12,000/1,500) × $17 = $136 (T5); = (12,000/3,000) × $17 = $68 (Catania)

**(Direct labor hours per unit × $10) + $13.33 per unit = ((12,000/1,500) × $10) + $13.33 = $93.33 (T5);
  = ((12,000/3,000) × $10) + $13.33 = $53.33 (Catania)

ABC product costing reveals a different cost picture. Using either a company-wide overhead rate or departmental rates, the T5 bike is bearing more than its share of total overhead costs.

Using either of these methods could lead the company into pricing the T5 too high in the market. With a more accurate overhead cost of $72.88, rather than $93.33 or $136.00, the company clearly has the ability to compete on price with other companies in this market. In Fezzari's case, overhead is a relatively minor cost relative to the cost of the direct materials, as shown in Chapter 3. This is due to the fact that Fezzari is mainly an assembler of parts, rather than a manufacturer of those parts. However, in other industries, the effect of adopting ABC may be much more significant.

However, regardless of the differences among the various cost methods, inaccurate costing can affect management's assessment of product profitability and its decisions regarding which products to continue to produce and which products to discontinue. Flawed product costing information can cause management mistakenly to decide to keep products that are losing money, while deciding to discontinue products that are profitable. Using a company-wide or departmental overhead allocation method could have led Fezzari management to shift its emphasis from the high-end bike to the low-end bike market, a decision that could have been damaging to the company.

YOUR TURN! 5.1

The solution is on page 195.

Assume you are a controller for a manufacturing company that uses a traditional product costing system, but is looking to transition to ABC. The CEO has asked you why this would be a useful transition. What would you tell him regarding the benefits of activity-based costing?

Limitations of ABC Illustration

Several limitations of the Fezzari illustration should be mentioned. For the sake of simplicity, the example was limited to manufacturing cost considerations. A complete analysis would also require considerations of nonmanufacturing costs, such as marketing, distribution, and customer service, before a final determination of product profitability could be made. Finally, in calculating the activity cost per unit of activity, it is necessary to decide how to measure the total quantity of activity. For example, for Fezzari, the receiving/inventory cost per unit was calculated as $4.67 based on the actual quantity of 4,500 bicycles produced for the period. Alternatively, the receiving cost could have been calculated based on **practical capacity**, which is the maximum possible volume of activity, while allowing for normal downtime for repairs and maintenance. If the plant has a practical capacity to produce 5,000 bicycles per period, the cost per bike based on the practical capacity is $4.20 per purchase order. Using this overhead rate in costing products, only $18,900 would have been assigned to the two products, which required only 4,500 bicycles, and the remaining $2,100 for the 500 bicycles of excess (or idle) capacity not used would be written off as an operating expense of the period as underapplied overhead. Practical capacity is generally regarded as better than actual capacity for calculating activity costs because it does not hide the cost of idle capacity within product costs, and it gives a truer cost of the activities used to produce the product.

Comparing Traditional and Activity-Based Costing

Procedurally, ABC is not a new method for assigning costs to cost objectives. Traditional costing systems have used a two-stage allocation model (similar to the ABC model) to assign costs to cost pools (such as departments) and subsequently assign those cost pools to products using an allocation base. In most traditional costing systems, overhead is assigned to one or more cost pools based on departments and functional characteristics (such as labor-related, machine-related, and space-related costs) and then reassigned to products using a general allocation base such as direct labor hours or machine hours. ABC is different in that it divides the overall manufacturing processes into activities. ABC accumulates costs in cost pools for the major activities and then assigns the costs of these activities to products or other cost objectives that benefit from these activities. *Conceptually,* ABC is different because of the way it views the operations of the company; *procedurally,* it uses a methodology that has been around for a long time.

   The challenge in using ABC is specifying the model—that is, determining how many activity pools should be established for a given cost measurement purpose, which costs should be assigned to each activity pool, and the appropriate activity driver for each pool. Specifying the model also includes determining the resource cost drivers for assigning indirect resource costs to the various activity cost pools.

TAKEAWAY 5.2

It is important to note that although using traditional overhead costing or activity-based costing results in different per-unit overhead costs, the total amount of allocated overhead remains unchanged. Only the unit rates will change between the two methods.

ABC IMPLEMENTATION ISSUES

The distortion in product costs for Fezzari from using traditional cost systems based on company-wide or departmental rates, although hypothetical, is not uncommon. Studies have shown that distortions of this type occur regularly in traditional systems in which a significant variation exists in the volume and complexity of products and services produced. Traditional systems tend to over-cost high-volume, low-complexity products, and they tend to under-cost low-

LO4 ABC system.

Describe the implementation of an

volume, high-complexity products. These studies indicate that the typical amount of over-costing is up to 200% for high-volume products with low complexity and that the typical under-costing can be more than 1,000% for low-volume, highly complex products. In companies with a large number of different products, traditional costing can show that most products are profitable. After changing to ABC, however, these companies might find that 10 to 15% of the products are profitable while the remainder are unprofitable. Adopting ABC often leads to increased profits merely by changing the product mix to minimize the number of unprofitable products.[2]

Most companies initially do not abandon their traditional cost system and move to a system that uses ABC for management and financial reporting purposes because financial statements must withstand the scrutiny of auditors and tax authorities. This scrutiny typically implies more demands on the cost accounting system for consistency, objectivity, and uniformity than required when the system is used only for management purposes. In addition, ABC systems must be built facility by facility rather than being embedded in a software program that can be used by all facilities within the company.[3] Often, companies maintain traditional costing for external reporting purposes and ABC for pricing and other internal decision-making purposes.

Once an ABC system has been developed for a production facility, including an activities list (sometimes called an activities dictionary), identification of activity cost drivers, and calculation of cost per unit of driver activity, the activity costs of a current or proposed product can be readily determined. In ABC, as illustrated for Fezzari, manufacturing a product is viewed simply as the combination of activities selected to make it; therefore, the activity cost of a product or service is the sum of the costs of those activities. This approach to viewing a product enables management to evaluate the importance of each of the activities consumed in making a product. Possibly some activities can be eliminated or a lower-cost activity substituted for a more costly one without reducing the quality or performance of the product.

ACCOUNTING IN PRACTICE | **Results of ABC**

In the 1980s, the Coca-Cola Company used ABC to determine that it was less costly—and thus more profitable—to deliver soft drink concentrate to some fountain drink retailers (such as fast-food restaurants) in nonreturnable, disposable containers rather than in returnable stainless steel containers, which had been standard in the industry for many years.

Although an ABC system may be complex, it merely mirrors the complexity of an organization's design, manufacturing, and distribution systems. If a firm's products are diverse and its production and distribution procedures complex, the ABC system will also be complex; however, if its products are homogeneous and its production environment relatively simple, its ABC system should also be relatively simple. Even in highly complex manufacturing environments, ABC systems usually have no more than 10 to 20 cost pools. Many ABC experts in practice have observed that creating a large number of activity cost pools for a given costing application normally does not significantly improve cost accuracy above that of a smaller number of cost pools. As with any information system design, the costs of developing and maintaining the system must not exceed its benefits; hence, although adding more activity cost pools may result in some small amount of increased accuracy, it may be so small as not to be cost effective.

In addition to using ABC for product costing purposes, other important uses for ABC have also been found. One of the most useful applications for ABC discussed in the next section is in evaluating customer costs and distribution channel costs. Other applications

---

[2] Gary Cokins, Alan Stratton, and Jack Helbling, An ABC Manager's Primer (Montvale, NJ: Institute of Management Accountants, 1993).
[3] Robert S. Kaplan and Robin Cooper, *Cost and Effect* (Boston: Harvard Business School Press, 1998), p.105.

include costing administrative functions such as processing accounts receivable or accounts payable; costing the process of hiring and training employees; and costing such menial tasks as processing a letter or copying a document. As illustrated by the California State Bar illustration at the beginning of the chapter, any process, function, or activity performed in an organization, whether it is related to production, marketing and sales, finance and accounting, human resources, or even research and development, is a candidate for ABC analysis. In short, almost any cost objective that has more than an insignificant amount of indirect costs can be more effectively measured using ABC.

ABC AND CUSTOMER PROFITABILITY ANALYSIS

One of the most beneficial applications of activity-based costing is in the analysis of the profitability of customers. Companies that have a large number of diverse customers also usually have widely varied profits from serving those customers. Many companies never attempt to calculate the profit earned from individual customers. They merely assume that if they are selling products above their costs, and that overall the company is earning a profit, then each of the customers must be profitable. Unfortunately, the cost incurred to sell goods and services, and to provide services, to individual customers is not usually proportionate with the gross profits generated by those sales. Customers with high sales volume are not necessarily the most profitable. Profitability of individual customers depends on whether the gross profits from sales to those customers exceed the customer-specific costs of serving those customers. Some customers are simply more costly than others, and some may even be unprofitable, and the unprofitable customers are eating away at the total profits of the company. In an ideal world, only profitable customers would be retained, and unprofitable customers would be either converted to a profitable status or they would be dropped as customers.

LO5 Explain customer profitability analysis based on ABC.

Customer Profitability Profile

If a company knows the amount of profits (or losses) generated by each of its customers, a customer profitability profile can be prepared, as illustrated in the following section.

ABC Customer Profitability Analysis Illustrated

Let's assume that Pure Water Company is a "green" company located in the West that manufactures and sells all-natural compounds for purifying water distributed through large public water systems. Let's also assume that Ron James, the CEO and founder of Pure Water, personally developed the compounds using natural materials obtained from remote regions of the world. He knows that he has a product that is far superior to the traditional processes based on synthetic chemicals that have been used for generations to purify water. After five years in business, Pure Water has built a solid and growing customer base, but it has to invest significant time and expense servicing customers, especially those that have recently embraced its approach to water purification. Some customers require a lot of "hand-holding," with frequent visits and telephone calls, and they tend to purchase frequently in small amounts, often requiring repackaging. Other customers require little attention and support, and many of them purchase in large amounts once a year.

Although the company is making money, there is concern that profits could be higher if sales and other customer-related costs could be decreased. Ron James decided to ask Environmental Business Consultants (EBC; introduced in Chapter 1) to conduct a customer profitability analysis using activity-based costing. As a first step, EBC determined that there were five primary activities related to serving customers: visits of customers by sales representatives, remote contacts (phone, email, fax), processing and shipping of customer orders, repackaging, and billing and collection. After extensive analysis, including numerous

interviews and statistical analyses of activity and cost data, EBC determined the cost drivers
and cost per unit of activity for the five customer-related activities, shown in **Exhibit 5-7**.

Exhibit 5-7	Pure Water's Customer Service Activity Per-Unit Costs	
Activity	**Activity Cost Driver**	**Cost per Unit of Driver Activity**
Visits to customers	Visits......................	$800
Remote contacts	Number of contacts...........	75
Processing and Shipping	Customer orders	450
Repackaging	Number of requests...........	250
Billing and Collection	Invoices	90

After collecting activity driver data on each of these activities for Pure Water's major
customers, EBC prepared the customer activity cost and profitability analysis presented
in **Exhibit 5-8** for its five largest customers (in terms of sales dollars) in the order of
greatest to least profit for the most recent year.

Exhibit 5-8	Pure Water Customer Activity Cost and Profitability Analysis					
	Consolidated Water, Inc.	**West Coast Utilities**	**Seattle Water District**	**Manhattan Water Authority**	**Great Lakes Utility**	**Total**
Customer Activity Cost Analysis:						
Activity Cost Driver Data						
Visits to customers.............	1	1	3	5	4	
Remote contacts	3	2	5	7	8	
Processing and shipping	1	4	3	3	5	
Repackaging...................	0	0	0	2	3	
Billing and collection.............	1	4	3	3	5	
Customer Activity Cost						
Visits to customers.............	800	800	2,400	4,000	3,200	
Remote contacts	225	150	375	525	600	
Processing and shipping	450	1,800	1,350	1,350	2,250	
Repackaging...................	0	0	0	500	750	
Billing and collection.............	90	360	270	270	450	
Total Activity Cost..............	1,565	3,110	4,395	6,645	7,250	
Customer Profitability Analysis						
Customer sales.................	16,250	15,000	17,500	20,000	12,000	80,750
Less cost of goods sold	9,750	9,000	10,500	12,000	7,200	48,450
Gross profit on sales.............	6,500	6,000	7,000	8,000	4,800	32,300
Less activity costs	1,565	3,110	4,395	6,645	7,250	22,965
Customer profitability	4,935	2,890	2,605	1,355	(2,450)	9,335
Customer profitability ratio*	30.4%	19.3%	14.9%	6.8%	(20.4)%	11.6%

*Customer profitability ÷ Sales

Because Pure Water is selling only one product to all of its customers, and has the
same pricing policy for all customers, there is a constant 40% gross profit ratio across
all customers, and the combined net profitability of these customers is 11.6% of sales.
However, all customers are not equally profitable. The high level of support required by

Manhattan and Great Lakes resulted in a net customer loss from sales to Great Lakes and only a 6.8% customer profitability ratio for Manhattan.

Armed with the information in the customer activity cost and profitability analysis, Pure Water can take proactive steps to increase its overall profitability ratio. An obvious option would be to try to terminate its relationship with Great Lakes because the company is clearly losing money on that customer. If Great Lakes were terminated as a customer, and assuming that all of the activity costs associated with Great Lakes could be avoided by the termination, Pure Water's total sales would drop to $68,750 (or $80,750 minus $12,000), but its total profit would increase to $11,785 (or $9,335 plus $2,450), resulting in a profitability ratio on the remaining four customers of 17.1%.

A more proactive approach would be to work with Great Lakes and Manhattan, which have high support requirements, such as repackaging, frequent visits, and phone contacts, to try to lower the level of high-cost support activities without reducing sales to those customers. This could result in maintaining the current level of gross profit, but generating a significantly higher level of total net customer profitability.

Once a company has profitability data on each of its customers (or categories of customers), only then can it proceed to try to convert them to profitability, or seek to terminate the relationships with those customers. Just as we saw that ABC provided a model for producing more accurate product cost data, ABC is also a valuable tool for generating customer profitability data.

Two caveats should be considered when using activity cost data to manage customer profitability. First, there may be justifiable reasons (such as having a new customer that requires a high level of early-stage support, trying to penetrate a new geographic market, or existing relationships with other more profitable customers) for keeping customers that have lower profitability, or even customers that are not profitable. If so, these customers should be managed intensely to attempt to reduce the activities devoted to their support. Second, eliminating a customer may not immediately translate into an immediate reduction of activity costs. Some activity costs may not have a variable cost behavior pattern, and eliminating customers may merely create excess capacity in the short term.

TAKEAWAY 5.3

Increasing the volume of customers may not always be desirable. Customer profitability analysis helps management assess whether it is worthwhile to pursue increasing the company's customer base.

ACTIVITY-BASED MANAGEMENT

Activity-based costing has been highly touted as a technique for improving the measurement of the cost and profitability of products, customers, and other cost objectives. In the early development of ABC, it was discovered that a by-product of accurately measuring costs using ABC is that management invariably gains a much better understanding of the processes and activities that are used to create cost objects, such as products. Although ABC could be justified on the basis of its value as a tool in helping produce more accurate cost measurements for various cost objectives, its greatest potential value may be in its by-products. The access to ABC data enables managers to engage in **activity-based management (ABM),** defined as the identification and selection of activities to maximize the value of the activities while minimizing their cost from the perspective of the final consumer. In other words, ABM is concerned with how to efficiently and effectively manage activities and processes to provide value to the final consumer.

LO6 **Explain** the difference between ABC and activity-based management.

Defining processes and identifying key activities helps management better understand the business and evaluate whether activities being performed add value to the customer. ABM focuses managerial attention on what is most important among the activities performed to create value for customers.

A helpful analogy in understanding what ABC can do for a company is to compare a company's operations with a large retail store, such as a **Home Depot** store. In a Home Depot store there is a clearly marked price on each of the tens of thousands of individual items that customers may decide to purchase. Similarly, every activity that takes place in any organization has a cost that can be determined and that management can use to make a judgment about the activity's value. In an ideal world, a manager could walk through the business and evaluate the cost of every activity being performed—maybe thousands of different activities—and then decide which ones are worth the cost and which ones are not adding value. But because generating ABC data has a cost, management must decide which ABC data are likely to be useful and cost beneficial. Our discussion here is only an introduction to activity-based costing and some of its applications. As the following Accounting in Practice points out, over the past quarter of a century, ABC has matured well beyond merely accurately measuring costs of products and customers. More advanced ABC topics and methods are covered in advanced managerial accounting (or cost accounting) courses.

Hint: It is often not feasible to perform a cost analysis on every activity, so management must exercise judgment in choosing activities to track costs for.

ACCOUNTING IN PRACTICE | **Current Status of ABC**

One of the leading thinkers and authors on the topic of activity-based costing over the past 25 years has been Peter B. B. Turney. He recently traced the evolution of ABC within the context of a product life cycle, showing how ABC functionality has expanded since it was first introduced in the 1980s. Turney asserts that ABC is now in its fourth generation, where it has become "an integral part of business performance management solutions, including profitability management, performance measurement, financial management, sustainability, and human capital management." In its current state of development, a single ABC model can support a number of needs, including historical cost measurement, resource planning, performance measurement, and other analyses.

SERVICES INDUSTRY IN FOCUS

SERVICE AND MERCHANDISING

Customer Profitability Analysis

Environmental Business Consultants (EBC) serves three different sizes of clients (large, medium, and small). EBC's solid waste rate review projects are fairly standardized and routine; hence, the pricing is also standardized for all clients. Although the company is profitable overall, the CFO thinks the net margins should be higher. She is concerned that customer support costs are eating up some of the margin and has decided to do a customer profitability analysis based on the three different sizes of clients to see if some of the client groups may actually be less profitable than others. The following data for the most recent period have been collected to support the analysis:

Support Activity	Driver	Cost per Driver Unit
A. Scope change requests	Number of requests	$150
B. Visits to client	Number of visits	$200
C. Communication	Number of calls	$ 50

Customer Group	Activity A	Activity B	Activity C	Profit Before Support Costs
Large	36	72	180	$390,000
Medium	75	150	205	100,500
Small......................	21	42	80	52,000

Required

1. Calculate the customer profitability for each customer group, taking into account the support activity required for each customer group.

2. Comment on the usefulness of this type of analysis. What reasonable actions might the CEO take as a result of this analysis?

Solution

1. Activity A—Scope change requests

   Activity B—Visits to client

   Activity C—Communication

Activity	Large	Medium	Small
A (@ $150)	$ 5,400	$ 11,250	$ 3,150
B (@ $200)	14,400	30,000	8,400
C (@ $50)	9,000	10,250	4,000
Total support costs	$ 28,800	$ 51,500	$15,550
Profit before support costs	390,000	100,500	52,000
Customer profits.............................	$361,200	$ 49,000	$36,450
Ratio of support costs to profit before support costs:	7.4%	51.2%	29.9%

2. This analysis is beneficial to EBC because it shows that large clients consume the lowest amount in terms of support services required. Medium clients are a significantly larger consumer of activities for all three of the support activities. Calculating the ratio of total support costs to profit before support costs provides additional insight into the relative profitability of the client groups. All three client groups are profitable; however, this analysis provides useful information for improving profits by working with the medium and small client groups to control support activities and related costs and attempt to bring their support costs in line with the large client group.

SUMMARY OF LEARNING OBJECTIVES

Explain the changes in the modern production environment that have affected cost structures. (p. 161)   **LO1**

- Manufacturing organizations have shifted from labor-intensive to automated assembly processes.
- Activity-based costing recognizes that multiple activities drive manufacturing overhead costs in today's production environment.

Understand the concept of activity-based costing (ABC) and how it is applied. (p. 162)   **LO2**

- ABC involves determining the cost of activities and tracing those costs to cost objects based on their proportionate usage of the activities.
- ABC is based on the premise that activities drive costs and that costs should be assigned to products in proportion to the volume of activities they consume.

LO3 **Explain the difference between traditional company-wide and departmental overhead methods and ABC. (p. 165)**

- Company-wide and departmental overhead methods base overhead costs on one cost driver, whereas ABC allocates overhead based on a diverse set of activities and cost drivers.

- ABC divides the overall manufacturing processes into activities, accumulates costs in cost pools for the major activities, and then assigns the costs of these activities to products or other cost objectives that benefit from these activities.

- The challenge in using ABC is determining how many activity pools should be established for a given cost measurement purpose, which costs should be assigned to each activity pool, and the appropriate activity driver for each pool.

- A complete ABC analysis would require considerations of nonmanufacturing costs, such as marketing, distribution, and customer service, before a final determination of product profitability could be made.

- Practical capacity, the maximum possible volume of activity, is generally regarded as better than actual capacity for calculating activity costs because it does not hide the cost of idle capacity within product costs, and it gives a truer cost of the activities used to produce the product.

- Procedurally, ABC is not a new method for assigning costs to objects. Traditional costing systems have used a two-stage allocation model similar to ABC to assign costs to cost pools and subsequently assign those cost pools to products using an allocation base.

LO4 **Describe the implementation of an ABC system. (p. 169)**

- Most companies initially do not abandon their traditional cost system and move to a system that uses ABC for management and financial reporting purposes because financial statements must withstand the scrutiny of auditors and tax authorities.

- Often, companies maintain traditional costing for external reporting purposes and ABC for pricing and other internal decision-making purposes.

- Although an ABC system may be complex, it merely mirrors the complexity of an organization's design, manufacturing, and distribution systems. If a firm's products are diverse and its production and distribution procedures complex, the ABC system will also be complex; however, if its products are homogeneous and its production environment relatively simple, its ABC system should also be relatively simple.

- One of the most useful applications for ABC is evaluating customer costs and distribution channel costs.

LO5 **Explain customer profitability analysis based on ABC. (p. 171)**

- A customer profitability profile can be prepared if a company knows the amount of profits (or losses) generated by each of its customers.

- Even if the company is making a profit overall, individual customers may be sold to at a loss.

- If customers have low profitability, there may be justifiable reasons for keeping them, but they should be managed intensely to attempt to reduce the activities devoted to their support.

LO6 **Explain the difference between ABC and activity-based management. (p. 173)**

- The access to ABC data enables managers to engage in activity-based management (ABM), which is the identification and selection of activities to maximize the value of the activities while minimizing their cost from the perspective of the final consumer.

- ABM focuses managerial attention on what is most important among the activities performed to create value for customers.

KEY TERMS

Activities (p. 162)	Activity-based management (ABM) (p. 161, 173)	Practical capacity (p. 169)
Activity-based costing (ABC) (p. 160)	Cost drivers (p. 164)	Production department costs (p. 167)

Assignments with the logo in the margin are available in ᵐʸBusinessCourse.
See the Preface of the book for details.

SELF-STUDY QUESTIONS

(Answers to Self-Study Questions are at the end of this chapter.)

1. **Which of the following is not an element of ABC?**   LO2
   a. Tracing costs to cost objects
   b. Calculating a predetermined rate
   c. Identifying the cost drivers
   d. All are elements of ABC.

2. **ABC differs from traditional product costing in which of the following ways?**   LO4
   a. Overhead is allocated to products in ABC.
   b. Estimated costs are used.
   c. Diverse cost drivers are used.
   d. It is completely accurate.

3. **Which of the following is not a benefit of customer profitability analysis?**   LO5
   a. Identifies unprofitable customers
   b. Helps track cost spent on customers
   c. Helps managers identify actions to improve specific customer profitability
   d. Speeds up production process

QUESTIONS

1. Summarize the concepts underlying activity-based costing in two sentences.   LO2
2. What steps are required to implement the two-stage activity-based costing model?   LO2
3. Define activity cost pool, activity cost driver, and cost per unit of activity.   LO2
4. Name two possible activity cost drivers for each of the following activities: maintenance, materials movement, machine setup, inspection, materials purchases, and customer service.   LO2
5. What is the premise of activity-based costing for product costing purposes?   LO2
6. In what ways does ABC product costing differ from traditional product cost methods?   LO3
7. Explain why ABC often reveals that low-volume products are over-costed and high-volume products are under-costed.   LO4
8. How can ABC be used to improve customer profitability analysis?   LO5
9. Explain activity-based management and how it differs from activity-based costing.   LO6

EXERCISES—SET A

E5-1A. Activities and Cost Drivers For each of the following activities, select the most appropriate cost driver. Each cost driver may be used only once.   LO2

Activity	Cost Driver
1. Pay vendors	a. Number of different kinds of raw materials
2. Evaluate vendors	b. Number of classes offered
3. Inspect raw materials	c. Number of tables
4. Plan for purchases of raw materials	d. Number of employees
5. Packaging	e. Number of operating hours
6. Supervision	f. Number of units of raw materials received
7. Employee training	g. Number of moves
8. Clean tables	h. Number of vendors
9. Machine maintenance	i. Number of checks issued
10. Move in-process product from one work station to the next	j. Number of customer orders

E5-2A. Stage 1 ABC For Machine Shop: Assigning Costs to Activity As the chief engineer of a small fabrication shop, Brenda Tolliver refers to herself as a "jack-of-all-trades." When an order for a new product comes in, Brenda must do the following: LO2

1. Design the product to meet customer requirements.
2. Prepare a bill of materials (a list of materials required to produce the product).
3. Prepare an operations list (a sequential list of the steps involved in manufacturing the product).

Each time the foundry manufactures a batch of the product, Brenda must perform these activities:

1. Schedule the job.
2. Supervise the setup of machines that will work on the job.
3. Inspect the first unit produced to verify that it meets specifications.

Brenda supervises the production employees who perform the actual work on individual units of product. She is also responsible for employee training, ensuring that production facilities are in proper operating condition, and attending professional meetings. Brenda's estimates (in percent) of time spent on each of these activities last year are as follows:

Designing product	12%
Preparing bills of materials	5%
Preparing operations lists	12%
Scheduling jobs	15%
Supervising setups	5%
Inspecting first units	2%
Supervising production	20%
Training employees	18%
Maintaining facility	7%
Attending professional meetings	4%
	100%

Required

Assuming Brenda Tolliver's salary is $132,000 per year, determine the dollar amount of her salary assigned to unit-, batch-, product-, and facility-level activities. (You may need to review Chapter 2 before answering this question.)

LO2 **E5-3A.** **Two-Stage ABC for Manufacturing: Reassigning Costs to Cost Objectives** National Technology, LTD. has developed the following activity cost information for its manufacturing activities:

Activity	Activity Cost
Machine setup	$60.00 per batch
Movement	15.00 per batch
	0.10 per pound
Drilling	3.00 per hole
Welding	4.00 per inch
Shaping	25.00 per hour
Assembly	18.00 per hour
Inspection	2.00 per unit

Filling an order for a batch of 50 fireplace inserts that weighed 150 pounds each required the following:

- Three batch moves
- Two sets of inspections
- Drilling five holes in each unit
- Completing 80 inches of welds on each unit
- Thirty minutes of shaping for each unit
- One hour of assembly per unit

Required

Determine the activity cost of converting the raw materials into 50 fireplace inserts.

LO2 **E5-4A.** **Two-Stage ABC for Manufacturing** Assume Sherwin-Williams Company, a large paint manufacturer, has determined the following activity cost pools and cost driver levels for the latest period:

Activity Cost Pool	Activity Cost	Activity Cost Driver
Machine setup	$950,000	2,500 setup hours
Material handling	820,000	5,000 materials moves
Machine operation	200,000	20,000 machine hours

The following data are for the production of single batches of two products, Mirlite and Subdue:

	Mirlite	Subdue
Gallons produced.	50,000	30,000
Direct labor hours.	400	250
Machine hours	800	250
Direct labor cost.	$ 10,000	$ 7,500
Direct materials cost.	$350,000	$150,000
Setup hours	15	12
Material moves.	60	35

Required

Determine the batch and unit costs per gallon of Mirlite and Subdue using ABC.

E5-5A. **Customer Profitability Analysis** HyStandard Services, Inc. provides residential painting services for three home building companies, Alpine, Blue Ridge, and Pineola, and it uses a job costing system for determining the costs for completing each job. The job cost system does not capture any cost incurred by HyStandard for return touchups and refinishes after the homeowner occupies the home. HyStandard paints each house on a square footage contract price, which includes painting as well as all refinishes and touchups required after the homes are occupied. Each year, the company generates about one-third of its total revenues and gross profits from each of the three builders. The HyStandard owner has observed that the builders, however, require substantially different levels of support following the completion of jobs. The following data have been gathered:

LO5

SERVICE AND
MERCHANDISING

Support Activity	Driver	Cost per Driver Unit
Major refinishes	Hours on jobs	$60
Touchups	Number of visits	$100
Communication	Number of calls	$40

Builder	Major Refinishes	Touchups	Communication
Alpine	80	150	360
Blue Ridge	35	110	205
Pineola	42	115	190

Required

Assuming that each of the three customers produces gross profits of $100,000, calculate the profitability from each builder after taking into account the support activity required for each builder.

EXERCISES—SET B

E5-1B. **Developing List of Activities for Baggage Handling at an Airport** As part of a continuous improvement program, you have been asked to determine the activities involved in the baggage-handling process of a major airline at one of the airline's hubs. Prior to conducting observations and interviews, you decide that a list of possible activities would help you to better observe key activities and ask meaningful questions.

LO2

SERVICE AND
MERCHANDISING

Required

For incoming aircraft only, develop a sequential list of baggage-handling activities. Your list should contain between 8 and 10 activities.

E5-2B. **Stage 1 ABC at a College: Assigning Costs to Activities** An economics professor at Prince Town University devotes 50 percent of her time to teaching, 35 percent of her time to research and writing, and 15 percent of her time to service activities such as committee work and student advising. The professor teaches two semesters per year. During each semester, she teaches one section of an

LO2

SERVICE AND
MERCHANDISING

introductory economics course (with a maximum enrollment of 50 students) and one section of a graduate economics course (with a maximum enrollment of 30 students). Including course preparation, classroom instruction, and appointments with students, each course requires an equal amount of time. The economics professor is paid $135,000 per year.

Required
Determine the activity cost of instruction per student in both the introductory and the graduate economics courses.

LO2 **E5-3B.** **Stage 2 ABC for a Wholesale Company** Information is presented for the activity costs of Oxford Wholesale Company:

Activity Cost per Unit of Activity Driver	
Customer relations per month	$100.00 per customer
Selling.	0.06 per sales dollar
Accounting	5.00 per order
Warehousing	0.50 per unit shipped
Packing.	0.25 per unit shipped
Shipping	0.20 per pound shipped

The following information pertains to Oxford Wholesale Company's activities in Massachusetts for the month of March 2016:

Number of orders	235
Sales revenue	$122,200
Cost of goods sold	$68,940
Number of customers	25
Units shipped	4,700
Pounds shipped	70,500

Required
Determine the profitability of sales in Massachusetts for March 2016.

LO2 **E5-4B.** **Two-Stage ABC for Manufacturing** Detroit Foundry, a large manufacturer of heavy equipment components, has determined the following activity cost pools and cost driver levels for the year:

Activity Cost Pool	Activity Cost	Activity Cost Driver
Machine setup	$600,000	12,000 setup hours
Material handling	120,000	2,000 tons of materials
Machine operation	500,000	10,000 machine hours

The following data are for the production of single batches of two products, C23 Cams and U2 Shafts during the month of August:

	C23 Cams	U2 Shafts
Units produced.	500	300
Machine hours	4	5
Direct labor hours	200	400
Direct labor cost	$ 5,000	$10,000
Direct materials cost.	$30,000	$20,000
Tons of materials	13	8
Setup hours	3	7

Required
Determine the unit costs of C23 Cams and U2 Shafts using ABC.

LO2, 3 **E5-5B.** **Activity-Based Costing** Slack Corporation has the following predicted indirect costs and cost drivers for 2016 for the given activity cost pools:

	Fabrication Department	Finishing Department	Cost Driver
Maintenance.....................	$ 20,000	$10,000	Machine hours
Materials handling	30,000	15,000	Material moves
Machine setups	70,000	5,000	Machine setups
Inspections......................	—	25,000	Inspection hours
	$120,000	$55,000	

The following activity predictions were also made for the year:

	Fabrication Department	Finishing Department
Machine hours	10,000	5,000
Materials moves....................	3,000	1,500
Machine setups	700	50
Inspection hours....................	—	1,000

It is assumed that the cost per unit of activity for a given activity does not vary between departments.

Slack's president, Charles Slack, is trying to evaluate the company's product mix strategy regarding two of its five product models, ZX300 and SL500. The company has been using a company-wide overhead rate based on machine hours but is considering switching to either department rates or activity-based rates. The production manager has provided the following data for the production of a batch of 100 units for each of these models:

	ZX300	SL500
Direct materials cost.................	$12,000	$18,000
Direct labor cost....................	$5,000	$4,000
Machine hours (Fabrication)...........	500	700
Machine hours (Finishing).............	200	100
Materials moves....................	30	50
Machine setups	5	9
Inspection hours....................	30	60

Required

a. Determine the cost of one unit each of ZX300 and SL500, assuming a company-wide overhead rate is used based on total machine hours.

b. Determine the cost of one unit of ZX300 and SL500, assuming department overhead rates are used. Overhead is assigned based on machine hours in both departments.

c. Determine the cost of one unit of ZX300 and SL500, assuming activity-based overhead rates are used for maintenance, materials handling, machine setup, and inspection activities.

d. Comment on the results of these cost calculations.

PROBLEMS—SET A

P5-1A. Calculating Manufacturing Overhead Rates Glassman Company accumulated the following data for 2016: **LO3**

Milling Department manufacturing overhead...............	$344,000
Finishing Department manufacturing overhead.............	$120,000
Machine hours used	
Milling Department	10,000 hours
Finishing Department	2,000 hours
Labor hours used	
Milling Department	1,000 hours
Finishing Department	1,000 hours

Required

a. Calculate the company-wide manufacturing overhead rate using machine hours as the allocation base.

b. Calculate the company-wide manufacturing overhead rate using direct labor hours as the allocation base.

c. Calculate department overhead rates using machine hours in Milling and direct labor hours in Finishing as the allocation bases.

d. Calculate department overhead rates using direct labor hours in Milling and machine hours in Finishing as the allocation bases.

e. Which of these allocation systems seems to be more appropriate? Explain.

LO4   P5-2A.   Calculating Activity-Based Costing Overhead Rates Assume that manufacturing overhead for Glassman Company in the previous exercise consisted of the following activities and costs:

Setup (1,000 setup hours)	$144,000
Production scheduling (400 batches).	60,000
Production engineering (60 change orders).	120,000
Supervision (2,000 direct labor hours)	56,000
Machine maintenance (12,000 machine hours)	84,000
Total activity costs	$464,000

The following additional data were provided for Job 845:

Direct materials costs	$7,000
Direct labor cost (5 Milling direct labor hours;	
35 Finishing direct labor hours)	$1,000
Setup hours	5 hours
Production scheduling	1 batch
Machine hours used (25 Milling machine hours;	
5 Finishing machine hours).	30 hours
Production engineering	3 change orders

Required

a. Calculate the cost per unit of activity driver for each activity cost category.

b. Calculate the cost of Job 845 using ABC to assign the overhead costs.

c. Calculate the cost of Job 845 using the company-wide overhead rate based on machine hours calculated in the previous exercise.

d. Calculate the cost of Job 845 using a machine hour departmental overhead rate for the Milling Department and a direct labor hour overhead rate for the Finishing Department (see P5-1A).

LO3, 4   P5-3A.   Traditional Product Costing Versus Activity-Based Costing Assume that Panasonic Company has determined its estimated total manufacturing overhead cost for one of its plants to be $204,000, consisting of the following activity cost pools for the current month:

Activity Centers	Activity Costs	Cost Drivers	Activity Level
Assembly setups	$ 45,000	Setup hours	1,500
Materials handling	15,000	Number of moves.	300
Assembly	120,000	Assembly hours	12,000
Maintenance.	24,000	Maintenance hours.	1,200
Total	$204,000		

Total direct labor hours used during the month were 8,000. Panasonic produces many different electronic products, including the following two products produced during the current month:

	Model X301	Model Z205
Units produced.	1,000	1,000
Direct materials costs.	$15,000	$15,000
Direct labor costs.	$12,500	$12,500
Direct labor hours.	500	500
Setup hours	50	100
Materials moves.	25	50
Assembly hours	800	800
Maintenance hours.	10	40

Required

a. Calculate the total per-unit cost of each model using direct labor hours to assign manufacturing overhead to products.

b. Calculate the total per-unit cost of each model using activity-based costing to assign manufacturing overhead to products.

c. Comment on the accuracy of the two methods for determining product costs.

d. Discuss some of the strategic implications of your answers to the previous requirements.

P5-4A.   Customer Profitability Analysis Gonalong, Inc., has 10 customers that account for all of its $4,500,000 of net income. Its activity-based costing system is able to assign all costs, except for $650,000 of general administrative costs, to key activities incurred in connection with serving its customers. A customer profitability analysis based on activity costing produced the following customer profits and losses: **LO5**

Customer #1.	$ 346,000
#2	624,000
#3	(257,000)
#4	969,000
#5	1,040,000
#6	872,000
#7	628,000
#8	322,000
#9	(105,000)
#10	711,000
Total	$5,150,000

Required

Prepare a customer profitability profile graph. Sort the customers in order of profitability from most profitable to least profitable, then plot the cumulative profit with total profits along the y-axis and customers along the x-axis. What is the maximum amount of profit that Gonalong could achieve if they were to eliminate their unprofitable customers?

P5-5A.   Customer Profitability Analysis Refer to the previous exercise P5-4A for Gonalong, Inc.   **LO5**

Required

a. If Gonalong were to notify customers 3 and 9 that it will no longer be able to provide them services in the future, will that increase company profits by $362,000? Why or why not?

b. What is the primary benefit of preparing a customer profitability analysis?

P5-6A.   ABC—A Service Application Grand Haven is a senior living community that offers a full range of services including independent living, assisted living, and skilled nursing care. The assisted living division provides residential space, meals, and medical services (MS) to its residents. The current costing system adds the cost of all of these services (space, meals, and MS) and divides by total resident days to get a cost per resident day for each month. Recognizing that MS tends to vary significantly among the residents, Grand Haven's accountant recommended that an ABC system be designed to calculate more accurately the cost of MS provided to residents. She decided that residents should be classified into four categories (A, B, C, D) based on the level of services received, with group A representing the lowest level of service and D representing the highest level of service. Two cost drivers being considered for measuring MS costs are number of assistance calls and number of assistant contacts. A contact is registered each time an assistance professional provides medical services or aid to a resident. The accountant has gathered the following data for the most recent annual period: **LO2**

SERVICE AND MERCHANDISING

Resident Classification	Annual Resident Days	Annual Assistance Hours	Number of Assistance Contacts
A................	8,760	15,000	60,000
B................	6,570	20,000	52,000
C................	4,380	22,500	52,000
D................	2,190	32,500	52,000
	21,900	90,000	216,000

Other data:	
Total cost of medical services for the period	$2,500,000
Total cost of meals and residential space	$1,642,500

Required (Round Answers to the Nearest Dollar)

a. Determine the ABC cost of a resident day for each category of residents using assistance hours as the cost driver.

b. Determine the ABC cost of a resident day for each category of residents using assistance contacts as the cost driver.

c. Which cost driver do you think provides the more accurate measure of the cost per day for a Grand Haven resident?

LO2 **P5-7A. Two-Stage ABC for Manufacturing** Merlot Company has determined its activity cost pools and cost drivers to be the following:

Cost Pools	
Setup	$ 56,000
Material handling	12,800
Machine operation	240,000
Packing..	60,000
Total indirect manufacturing costs...........................	$368,800
Cost drivers	
Setups...	350
Material moves	640
Machine hours	20,000
Packing orders	1,200

One product made by Merlot, metal casements, used the following activities during the period to produce 500 units:

Setups	20
Material moves...	80
Machine hours	1,900
Packing orders	150

Required

a. Calculate the cost per unit of activity for each activity cost pool for Merlot Company.

b. Calculate the manufacturing overhead cost per metal casement manufactured during the period.

LO2 **P5-8A. Activity-Based Costing in a Service Organization** Red River Banking Company has ten automatic

teller machines (ATMs) spread throughout the city maintained by the ATM Department. You have been assigned the task of determining the cost of operating each machine. Management will use the information you develop, along with other information pertaining to the volume and type of transactions at each machine, to evaluate the desirability of continuing to operate each machine and/or changing security arrangements for a particular machine.

The ATM Department consists of a total of six employees: a supervisor, a head cashier, two associate cashiers, and two maintenance personnel. The associate cashiers make between two and four daily trips to each machine to collect and replenish cash and to replenish supplies, deposit tickets, and so forth. Each machine contains a small computer that automatically summarizes and reports transactions to the head cashier. The head cashier reconciles the activities of the two associate cashiers to the computerized reports. The supervisor, who does not handle cash, reviews the reconciliation. When an automatic teller's computer, a customer, or a cashier reports a problem, the two maintenance employees and one cashier are dispatched immediately. The cashier removes all cash and transaction records, and the maintenance employees repair the machine.

Maintenance employees spend all of their time on maintenance-related activities. The associate cashiers spend approximately 50 percent of their time on maintenance-related activities and 50 percent on daily trips. The head cashier's time is divided, with 75 percent directly related to daily trips to each machine and 25 percent related to supervising cashiers on maintenance calls. The supervisor devotes 20 percent of the time to daily trips to each machine and 80 percent to the equal supervision of each employee. Cost information for a recent month follows:

Salaries	
Supervisor.	$4,000
Head cashier.	3,000
Other ($1,800 each)	7,200
Lease and operating costs	
Cashiers' service vehicle	1,200
Maintenance service vehicle.	1,400
Office rent and utilities	2,300
Machine lease, space rent, and utilities ($1,500 each).	15,000
Total.	$34,100

Related monthly activity information for this month follows:

Machine	Routine Trips	Maintenance Hours
1.	30	5
2.	90	17
3.	60	15
4.	60	30
5.	120	15
6.	30	10
7.	90	25
8.	120	5
9.	60	20
10.	60	18
Total.	720	160

Additional information follows:

- The office is centrally located with about equal travel time to each machine.
- Maintenance hours include travel time.
- The cashiers' service vehicle is used exclusively for routine visits.
- The office space is divided equally between the supervisor and the head cashier.

Required
a. Determine the monthly operating costs of machines 7 and 8 when cost assignments are based on the number of machines.
b. Determine the activity cost of a routine trip and a maintenance hour for the month given. Round answers to the nearest cent.
c. Determine the operating costs assigned and reassigned to machines 7 and 8 when activity-based costing is used.
d. How can ABC cost information be used by Red River Banking Company to improve the overall management of monthly operating costs?

P5-9A. **Product Costing: Company-wide Overhead Versus ABC** LaMesa produces machine parts as a LO3, 4 contract provider for a large manufacturing company. LaMesa produces two particular parts, shafts and gears. The competition is keen among contract producers, and LaMesa's top management realizes how vulnerable its market is to cost-cutting competitors. Hence, having a very accurate understanding of costs is important to LaMesa's survival.

LaMesa's president, Jose Rodriguez, has observed that the company's current cost to produce shafts is $21.35, and the current cost to produce gears is $12.36. He indicated to the controller that he suspects some problems with the cost system because LaMesa is suddenly experiencing extraordinary competition on shafts, but it seems to have a virtual corner on the gears market. He is even considering dropping the shaft line and converting the company to a one-product manufacturer of gears. He asked the controller, Felix Bernhardt, to conduct a thorough cost study and to consider whether changes in the cost system are necessary. The controller collected the following data about the company's costs and various manufacturing activities for the most recent month:

	Shafts	Gears
Production units.	50,000	10,500
Selling price	$31.86	$24
Overhead per unit (based on direct labor hours)	$12.82	$6.10
Materials and direct labor cost per unit	$8.53	$6.26
Number of production runs	10	20
Number of purchasing and receiving orders processed	40	100
Number of machine hours	12,750	6,000
Number of direct labor hours.	25,000	2,500
Number of engineering hours.	5,000	5,000
Number of material moves.	50	40

The controller was able to summarize the company's total manufacturing overhead into the following pools:

Setup costs	$ 30,000
Machine cost	175,000
Purchasing and receiving costs	210,000
Engineering costs.	200,000
Materials handling costs	90,000
Total	$705,000

Required

a. Calculate LaMesa's current company-wide overhead rate based on direct labor hours.

b. Verify LaMesa's calculation of overhead cost per unit of $12.82 for shafts and $6.10 for gears.

c. Calculate the manufacturing overhead cost per unit for shafts and gears using activity-based costing, assuming each of the five cost pools represents a separate activity pool. Use the most appropriate activity driver for assigning activity costs to the two products.

d. Comment on LaMesa's current cost system and the reason the company is facing fierce competition for shafts but little competition for gears.

PROBLEMS—SET B

LO2, 3 **P5-1B.** **Activity-Based Costing and Conventional Costs Compared** Hickory Grill Company manufactures two types of cooking grills: the Gas Cooker and the Charcoal Smoker. The Cooker is a premium product sold in upscale outdoor shops; the Smoker is sold in major discount stores. Following is information pertaining to the manufacturing costs for the current month.

	Gas Cooker	Charcoal Smoker
Units.	1,000	5,000
Number of batches.	50	10
Number of batch moves.	80	20
Direct materials	$40,000	$100,000
Direct labor.	$20,000	$ 25,000

Manufacturing overhead follows:

Activity	Cost	Cost Driver
Materials acquisition and inspection	$30,800	Amount of direct materials cost
Materials movement.	16,200	Number of batch moves
Scheduling	36,000	Number of batches
	$83,000	

Required

a.   Determine the total and per-unit costs of manufacturing the Gas Cooker and Charcoal Smoker for the month, assuming all manufacturing overhead is assigned on the basis of direct labor dollars.

b.   Determine the total and per-unit costs of manufacturing the Gas Cooker and Charcoal Smoker for the month, assuming manufacturing overhead is assigned using activity-based costing.

P5-2B.   Activity-Based Costing Versus Conventional Costing Refer to the previous exercise in P5-1B for Hickory Grill.   **LO2, 3**

Required

a.   Comment on the differences between the solutions to requirements (a) and (b). Which is more accurate? What errors might managers make if all manufacturing overhead costs are assigned on the basis of direct labor dollars?

b.   Comment on the adequacy of the preceding data to meet management's needs.

P5-3B.   Traditional Product Costing Versus Activity-Based Costing High Country Outfitters, Inc., makes backpacks for large sporting goods chains that are sold under the customers' store brand names. The accounting department has identified the following overhead costs and cost drivers for next year: **LO2, 3**

Overhead Item	Expected Costs	Cost Driver	Maximum Quantity
Setup costs	$936,000	Number of setups.	7,200
Ordering costs	240,000	Number of orders	60,000
Maintenance.	1,200,000	Number of machine hours	80,000
Power	120,000	Number of kilowatt hours.	600,000

Total predicted direct labor hours for next year is 60,000. The following data are for two recently completed jobs:

	Job 201	Job 202
Cost of direct materials	$13,500	$15,000
Cost of direct labor.	$19,125	$71,250
Number of units completed	1,125	915
Number of direct labor hours	270	330
Number of setups.	18	22
Number of orders	24	45
Number of machine hours	540	450
Number of kilowatt hours.	270	360

Required

a.   Determine the unit cost for each job using a traditional company-wide overhead rate based on direct labor hours.

b.   Determine the unit cost for each job using ABC. (Round answers to two decimal places.)

c.   As the manager of High Country, is there additional information that you would want to help you evaluate the pricing and profitability of Jobs 201 and 202?

d.   Assuming the company has been using the method required in part *a*, how should management react to the findings in part *b*?

LO5 **P5-4B.** **Customer Profitability Analysis** Rogers Aeronautics, LTD, is a British aeronautics subcontract company that designs and manufactures electronic control systems for commercial airlines. The vast majority of all commercial aircraft are manufactured by Boeing in the U.S. and Airbus in Europe; however, there is a relatively small group of companies that manufacture narrow-body commercial jets. Assume for this exercise that Rogers does contract work for the two major manufacturers plus three companies in the second tier.

Because competition is intense in the industry, Rogers has always operated on a fairly thin 20% gross profit margin; hence, it is crucial that it manage non-manufacturing overhead costs effectively in order to achieve an acceptable net profit margin. With declining profit margins in recent years, Rogers Aeronautics' CEO, Len Rogers, has become concerned that the cost of obtaining contracts and maintaining relations with its five major customers may be getting out of hand. You have been hired to conduct a customer profitability analysis.

Rogers Aeronautics' non-manufacturing overhead consists of $2.5 million of general and administrative (G&A) expense, (including, among other expenses, the CEO's salary and bonus and the cost of operating the company's corporate jet) and selling and customer support expenses of $3 million (including 5% sales commissions and $1,050,000 of additional costs).

The accounting staff determined that the $1,050,000 of additional selling and customer support expenses related to the following four activity cost pools:

Activity	Activity Cost Driver	Cost per Unit of Activity
1. Sales visits	Number of visit days	$1,200
2. Product adjustments	Number of adjustments	1,500
3. Phone and email contacts	Number of calls/contacts	150
4. Promotion and entertainment events	Number of events	1,500

Financial and activity data on the five customers follows (Sales and Gross Profit data in millions):

Customer	Sales	Gross Profit	Quantity of Sales and Support Activity			
			Activity 1	Activity 2	Activity 3	Activity 4
#1	$17	$3.40	106	23	220	82
#2	$12	2.4	130	36	354	66
#3	$3	0.6	52	10	180	74
#4	$4	0.8	34	6	138	18
#5	$3	0.6	16	5	104	10
	$39	$7.80	338	80	996	250

In addition to the above, the sales staff used the corporate jet at a cost of $800 per hour for trips to customers as follows:

Customer #1.	24 hours
Customer #2.	36 hours
Customer #3.	5 hours
Customer #4.	0 hours
Customer #5.	6 hours

The total cost of operating the airplane is included in general and administrative expense; none is included in selling and customer support costs.

Required

a. Prepare a customer profitability analysis for Rogers Aeronautics that shows the gross profits less all expenses that can reasonably be assigned to the five customers.

b. Now assuming that the remaining general and administrative costs are assigned to the five customers based on relative sales dollars, calculate net profit for each customer.

c. Discuss the merits of the analysis in part *a* versus part *b*.

P5-5B. **Two-Stage ABC for Manufacturing with Variances** Montreat Manufacturing has developed the **LO2** following activity cost pool information for its 2016 manufacturing activities:

	Budgeted Activity Cost	Activity Cost Driver at Practical Capacity
Purchasing and materials handling	$675,000	900,000 kilograms
Setup	700,000	1,120 setups
Machine operations	954,000	12,000 hours
First unit inspection	50,000	1,000 batches
Packaging.	250,000	312,500 units

Actual 2016 production information is as follows:

	Standard Product A	Standard Product B	Specialty Products
Units	150,000	100,000	50,000
Batches	100	80	600
Setups*	300	160	900
Machine operations (hours)	6,000	3,000	2,000
Kilograms of raw materials.	400,000	300,000	200,000
Direct materials costs.	$900,000	$600,000	$820,000

*Some products require setups on two or more machines.

Required

a. Determine the unit cost of each product for Montreat Manufacturing.

b. Explain why the unit cost of the specialty products is so much higher than the unit cost of Standard Product A or Standard Product B.

P5-6B. **ABC Costing for a Service Organization** Fairfield Mortgage Company is a full-service residential **LO2** mortgage company in the Atlanta area that operates in a very competitive market. The CEO, Richard Sissom, is concerned about operating costs associated with processing mortgage applications and has decided to install an ABC costing system to help him get a handle on costs. Although labor hours seem to be the primary driver of the cost of processing a new mortgage, the labor cost for the different activities involved in processing new loans varies widely. The Accounting Department has provided the following data for the company's five major cost pools for 2016:

SERVICE AND MERCHANDISING

Activity Cost Pools		Activity Drivers	
Taking customer applications . . .	$ 300,000	Time—assistant managers.	12,000 hours
Conducting credit investigations .	450,000	Time—credit managers	16,500 hours
Underwriting.	525,000	Time—Underwriting Department . . .	10,000 hours
Preparing loan packages	200,000	Time—Processing Department	8,000 hours
Closing loans	600,000	Time—Legal Department hours	6,000 hours
	$2,075,000		52,500 hours

During 2016, the company processed and issued 5,000 new mortgages, two of which are summarized here with regard to activities used to process the mortgages:

	Loan 5066	Loan 5429
Application processing hours.	1.50	2.75
Credit investigating hours	4.00	3.00
Underwriting hours.	2.50	4.75
Processing hours	3.50	3.00
Legal processing hours	1.50	1.50
Total hours	13.00	15.00

Required

a.   Determine the cost per unit of activity for each activity cost pool.

b.   Determine the cost of processing loans 5066 and 5429.

c.   Determine the cost of preparing loans 5066 and 5429 assuming that an average cost per hour for all activities is used.

d.   Compare and discuss your answers to requirements (*b*) and (*c*).

LO3   **P5-7B.   Product Costing: Department Versus ABC for Overhead** Advertising Technologies, Inc. (ATI) specializes in providing both published and online advertising services for the business marketplace. The company monitors its costs based on the cost per column inch of published space printed in print advertising media and based on the cost per minute of telephone advertising time delivered on "The AD Line," a computer-based, online advertising service. ATI has one new competitor, Tel-a-Ad, in its local teleadvertising market; and with increased competition, ATI has seen a decline in sales of online advertising in recent years. ATI's president, Robert Beard, believes that predatory pricing by Tel-a-Ad has caused the problem. The following is a recent conversation between Robert and Jane Minnear, director of marketing for ATI.

Jane: I just received a call from one of our major customers concerning our advertising rates on "The AD Line" who said that a sales rep from another firm (it had to be Tel-a-Ad) had offered the same service at $1 per minute, which is $1.50 per minute less than our price.

Robert: It's costing about $1.27 per minute to produce that product. I don't see how they can afford to sell it so cheaply. I'm not convinced that we should meet the price. Perhaps the better strategy is to emphasize producing and selling more published ads, which we're more experienced with and where our margins are high and we have virtually no competition.

Jane: You may be right. Based on a recent survey of our customers, I think we can raise the price significantly for published advertising and still not lose business.

Robert: That sounds promising; however, before we make a major recommitment to publishing, let's explore other possible explanations. I want to know how our costs compare with our competitors. Maybe we could be more efficient and find a way to earn a good return on teleadvertising.

After this meeting, Robert and Jane requested an investigation of production costs and comparative efficiency of producing published versus online advertising services. The controller, Tim Gentry, indicated that ATI's efficiency was comparable to that of its competitors and prepared the following cost data:

	Published Advertising	Online Advertising
Estimated number of production units.	200,000	10,000,000
Selling price	$200	$2.50
Direct product costs.	$21,000,000	$5,000,000
Overhead allocation*	$9,800,000	$7,700,000
Overhead per unit.	$49	$0.77
Direct costs per unit.	$105	$0.50
Number of customers.	180,000	25,000
Number of salesperson days	32,000	5,500
Number of art and design hours	35,000	5,000
Number of creative services subcontract hours	100,000	25,000
Number of customer service calls	72,000	8,000

*Based on direct labor costs

Upon examining the data, Robert decided that he wanted to know more about the overhead costs because they were such a high proportion of total production costs. He was provided the following list of overhead costs and told that they were currently being assigned to products in proportion to direct labor costs.

Selling costs.	$7,500,000
Visual and audio design costs	3,000,000
Creative services costs	5,000,000
Customer service costs	2,000,000

Required

Using the data provided by the controller, prepare analyses to help Robert and Jane in making their decisions. (*Hint:* Prepare cost calculations for both product lines using ABC to see whether there is any significant difference in their unit costs). Should ATI switch from the fast-growing, online advertising market back into the well-established published advertising market? Does the charge of predatory pricing seem valid? Why are customers likely to be willing to pay a higher price to get published services? Do traditional costing and activity-based costing lead to the same conclusions?

P5-8B. **Unit-Level and Multiple-Level Cost Assignments** CarryAll Company produces briefcases from leather, fabric, and synthetic materials in a single production department. The basic product is a standard briefcase made from leather and lined with fabric. CarryAll has a good reputation in the market because the standard briefcase is a high-quality item that has been produced for many years.   **LO2**

Last year, the company decided to expand its product line and produce specialty briefcases for special orders. These briefcases differ from the standard in that they vary in size, contain both leather and synthetic materials, and are imprinted with the buyer's logo (the standard briefcase is simply imprinted with the CarryAll name in small letters). The decision to use some synthetic materials in the briefcase was made to hold down the materials cost. To reduce the labor costs per unit, most of the cutting and stitching on the specialty briefcases is done by automated machines, which are used to a much lesser degree in the production of the standard briefcases. Because of these changes in the design and production of the specialty briefcases, CarryAll management believed that they would cost less to produce than the standard briefcases. However, because they are specialty items, they were priced slightly higher; standards are priced at $30 and specialty briefcases at $32.

After reviewing last month's results of operations, CarryAll's president became concerned about the profitability of the two product lines because the standard briefcase showed a loss while the specialty briefcase showed a greater profit margin than expected. The president is wondering whether the company should drop the standard briefcase and focus entirely on specialty items. Units and cost data for last month's operations as reported to the president are as follows:

	Standard	Specialty
Units produced.	10,000	2,500
Direct materials		
Leather (1 sq. yd. × $15.00; ½ sq. yd. × $15.00)	$15.00	$ 7.50
Fabric (1 sq. yd. × $5.00; 1 sq. yd. × $5.00)	5.00	5.00
Synthetic.		5.00
Total Materials	20.00	17.50
Direct Labor (½ hr. × $12.00; ¼ hr. × $12.00).	6.00	3.00
Manufacturing Overhead (½ hr. × $8.98; ¼ hr. × $8.98).	4.49	2.25
Cost per unit.	$30.49	$22.75

Manufacturing overhead is applied on the basis of direct labor hours. The rate of $8.98 per direct labor hour was calculated by dividing the total overhead ($50,500) by the direct labor hours (5,625). As shown in the table, the cost of a standard briefcase is $0.49 higher than its $30 sales price; the specialty briefcase has a cost of only $22.75, for a gross profit per unit of $9.25. The problem with these costs is that they do not accurately reflect the activities involved in manufacturing each product. Determining the costs using ABC should provide better product costing data to help gauge the actual profitability of each product line.

The manufacturing overhead costs must be analyzed to determine the activities driving the costs. Assume that the following costs and cost drivers have been identified:

- The Purchasing Department's cost is $6,000. The major activity driving these costs is the number of purchase orders processed. During the month, the Purchasing Department prepared the following number of purchase orders for the materials indicated:

Leather	20
Fabric	30
Synthetic material.	50

- The cost of receiving and inspecting materials is $7,500. These costs are driven by the number of deliveries. During the month, the following number of deliveries were made:

Leather	30
Fabric	40
Synthetic material	80

- Production line setup cost is $10,000. Setup activities involve changing the machines to produce the different types of briefcases. Each setup for production of the standard briefcases requires one hour; each setup for specialty briefcases requires two hours. Standard briefcases are produced in batches of 200, and specialty briefcases are produced in batches of 25. During the last month, there were 50 setups for the standard item and 100 setups for the specialty item.
- The cost of inspecting finished goods is $8,000. All briefcases are inspected to ensure that quality standards are met. However, the final inspection of standard briefcases takes very little time because the employees identify and correct quality problems as they do the hand cutting and stitching. A survey of the personnel responsible for inspecting the final products showed that 150 hours were spent on standard briefcases and 250 hours on specialty briefcases during the month.
- Equipment-related costs are $6,000. Equipment-related costs include repairs, depreciation, and utilities. Management has determined that a logical basis for assigning these costs to products is machine hours. A standard briefcase requires 1/2 hour of machine time, and a specialty briefcase requires two hours. Thus, during the last month, 5,000 hours of machine time relate to the standard line and 5,000 hours relate to the specialty line.
- Plant-related costs are $13,000. These costs include property taxes, insurance, administration, and others. For the purpose of determining average unit costs, they are to be assigned to products using machine hours.

Required

a.   Using activity-based costing concepts, what overhead costs should be assigned to the two products?
b.   What is the unit cost of each product using activity-based costing concepts?
c.   Reevaluate the president's concern about the profitability of the two product lines.
d.   Discuss the merits of activity-based management as it relates to CarryAll's ABC cost system.

CERTIFIED MANAGEMENT ACCOUNTANT (CMA®) EXAM SAMPLE QUESTIONS

CMA5-1. A profitable company with five departments uses plantwide overhead rates for its highly diversified operation. The firm is studying a change to either allocating overhead by using departmental rates or using activity-based costing (ABC). Which one of these two methods will likely result in the use of a greater number of cost allocation bases and more accurate costing results?

	Greater Number of Allocation Bases	More Accurate Costing Results
a.	Departmental	Departmental
b.	Departmental	ABC
c.	ABC	Departmental
d.	ABC	ABC

CMA5-2. All of the following are likely to be used as a cost allocation base in activity-based costing **except** the

a.   number of different materials used to manufacture the product.
b.   units of materials used to manufacture the product.
c.   number of vendors supplying the materials used to manufacture the product.
d.   cost of materials used to manufacture the product.

CMA5-3. Pelder Products Company manufactures two types of engineering diagnostic equipment used in construction. The two products are based upon different technologies, x-ray and ultra-sound, but are manufactured in the same factory. Pelder has computed the manufacturing cost of the x-ray and ultra-sound products by adding together direct materials, direct labor, and overhead cost applied based on the number of direct labor hours. The factory has three overhead departments that support the single production line that makes both products. Budgeted overhead spending for the departments is as follows.

Department			
Engineering design	**Material handling**	**Setup**	**Total**
$6,000	$5,000	$3,000	$14,000

Pelder's budgeted manufacturing activities and costs for the period are as follows.

	Product	
Activity	**X-Ray**	**Ultra-Sound**
Units produced and sold	50	100
Direct materials used	$5,000	$ 8,000
Direct labor hours used	100	300
Direct labor cost	$4,000	$12,000
Number of parts used	400	600
Number of engineering changes	2	1
Number of product setups	8	7

The budgeted cost to manufacture one ultra-sound machine using the activity-based costing method is

a. $225.
b. $264.
c. $293.
d. $305.

CMA5-4. The Chocolate Baker specializes in chocolate baked goods. The firm has long assessed the profitability of a product line by comparing revenues to the cost of goods sold. However, Barry White, the firm's new accountant, wants to use an activity-based costing system that takes into consideration the cost of the delivery person. Listed below are activity and cost information relating to two of Chocolate Baker's major products.

	Muffins	Cheesecake
Revenue	$53,000	$46,000
Cost of goods sold	26,000	21,000
Delivery Activity		
Number of deliveries	150	85
Average length of delivery	10 Minutes	15 Minutes
Cost per hour for delivery	$20.00	$20.00

Using activity-based costing, which one of the following statements is correct?
a. The muffins are $2,000 more profitable.
b. The cheesecakes are $75 more profitable.
c. The muffins are $1,925 more profitable.
d. The muffins have a higher profitability as a percentage of sales and, therefore, are more advantageous.

CMA5-5. Atmel Inc. manufactures and sells two products. Data with regard to these products are given below.

	Product A	Product B
Units produced and sold	30,000	12,000
Machine hours required per unit	2	3
Receiving orders per product line	50	150
Production orders per product line	12	18
Production runs	8	12
Inspections.	20	30

Total budgeted machine hours are 100,000. The budgeted overhead costs are shown below.

Receiving costs	$ 450,000
Engineering costs.	300,000
Machine setup costs	25,000
Inspection costs.	200,000
Total budgeted overhead costs	$ 975,000

Using activity-based costing, the per unit overhead cost allocation of receiving costs for product A is

a. $3.75.
b. $10.75.
c. $19.50.
d. $28.13.

EXTENDING YOUR KNOWLEDGE

LO4

EYK5-1. **Business Decision Case** The Reserve Club is a traditional private golf and country club that has three different categories of memberships: golf, tennis & swimming, and social. Golf members have access to all amenities and programs in the Club, Tennis & Swimming members have access to all amenities and programs except use of the golf course, and Social members have access to only the social activities of the club, excluding golf, tennis, and swimming. All members have clubhouse privileges, including use of the bar and restaurant, which is operated by an outside contractor. During the past year, the average membership in each category, along with the number of club visits during the year, was

	Members	Visits
Golf.	260	9,360
Tennis & Swimming	50	1,500
Social	120	2,160

Some members of the Club have been complaining that heavy users of the Club are not bearing their share of the costs through their membership fees. Dess Rosmond, General Manager of the Reserve Club, agrees that monthly fees paid by the various member groups should be based on the annual average amount of cost-related activities provided by the club for the three groups, and he intends to set fees on that basis for the coming year. The annual direct costs of operating the golf course, tennis courts, and swimming pool have been calculated by the Club's controller as follows:

Golf course.	$900,000
Swimming pool.	50,000
Tennis courts	25,000

The operation of the bar and restaurant and all related costs, including depreciation on the bar and restaurant facilities, are excluded from this analysis. In addition to the above costs, the Club incurs general overhead costs in the following amounts for the most recent (and typical) year:

General Ledger Overhead Accounts	Amounts
Indirect labor for the Club management staff (the general manager, assistant general manager, membership manager, and club controller)......................	$250,000
Utilities (other than those directly related to golf, swimming and tennis)................	24,000
Website maintenance..	2,000
Postage	5,000
Computers and information systems maintenance	7,500
Clubhouse maintenance and depreciation.....................................	30,000
Liability insurance...	4,000
Security contract	12,000
	$334,500

Dess believes that the best way to assign most of the overhead costs to the three membership categories is with an activity-based system that recognizes four key activities that occur regularly in the club:

Recruiting and providing orientation for new members

Maintaining the membership roster and communicating with members

Planning, scheduling and managing Club events

Maintaining the financial records and reporting for the Club

Required

a. Identify and explain which overhead costs can reasonably be assigned to one or more of the four key activities, and suggest a basis for making the assignment.

b. Identify a cost driver for each activity cost pool that would seem to be suitable for assigning the activity cost pool to the three membership categories.

c. Suggest a method for assigning any overhead costs to the three membership categories that cannot reasonably be assigned to activity pools.

d. Comment on the suitability of ABC to this cost assignment situation.

ANSWERS TO SELF-STUDY QUESTIONS:

1. d, (pp. 164–165)   2. c, (p. 169)   3. d, (pp. 171–173)

YOUR TURN! SOLUTION

Solution 5.1

Your response might include the following major points:

1. An ABC costing system would help the company to more completely identify all of the activities that cause the company to incur the overhead cost in the first place.

2. An ABC costing system would provide for more accurate tracing of overhead costs to products because the overhead costs are more closely associated with the related activity (or cost driver).

3. Having a better understanding of the costs of each product will help management set production priorities, sales targets, and prices to maximize company profits.

6

Cost-Volume-Profit Relationships

PAST

Chapter 5 explored activity-based costing and its benefits relative to traditional company-wide and departmental overhead allocation, and contrasted it with activity-based management.

PRESENT

Chapter 6 utilizes our understanding of cost behavior to determine break-even and make planning and budgeting decisions.

FUTURE

Chapter 7 discusses the preparation of a variable income statement and reporting for segments of a business.

LEARNING OBJECTIVES

1. **Develop** an understanding of how specific types of costs change in response to volume changes. *(p. 198)*

2. **Define** the concept of *relevant range. (p. 201)*

3. **Outline** the approach to developing cost formulas. *(p. 202)*

4. **Present** a discussion of and a formula for calculating the break-even point. *(p. 207)*

5. **Define** *contribution margin* and *contribution margin ratio* and **present** alternate break-even formulas and examples of their application. *(p. 209)*

6. **Discuss** approaches to planning net income using cost-volume-profit analyses. *(p. 211)*

iTUNES

When your great-grandmother was growing up, if she wanted to listen to her favorite musician sing her latest smash hit over and over, she would purchase a vinyl record and play it on a small turntable in her bedroom or her parents' hi-fi stereo turntable in the living room. The only way to listen to music in the car was on the radio, with the choice of radio station usually controlled by her mom and dad. Your grandparents probably listened to 8-track cartridges (which consist of a continuous-loop magnetic tape) or compact cassettes through the car's entertainment system. However, by the time your parents were rebelling against their parents' musical preferences, vinyl record and cassette sales were in decline. For your parents, the compact disc (CD) was the medium of choice, and by the late 1980s other forms of recorded music began to disappear from music stores. The CD became the dominant form of recorded music sales.

Once again, the way the new generation acquires and listens to its favorite artists has changed with the rise of the Internet and electronic music files. The late 1990s and early 2000s witnessed a decline in the sales of music CDs due to the availability of MP3 file sharing over the Internet. This generation's teenagers and young adults can easily purchase and share their favorite music with friends over the Internet and, sometimes, download copies from easily accessible websites for free. Because the Internet provides easy opportunities for pirating, the music industry has been in a state of crisis.

Given the industry's struggles with the electronic dissemination of music, iTunes was launched by Apple in 2003. An Internet-based music retailing business, it was originally conceived as a "break-even" business intended to drive sales of Apple hardware, principally the iPod, which had been introduced in 2001. Apple's business strategy was to provide individual songs at "cost" that could be downloaded to the iPod as part of the customer's music library to be played on demand. Apple would make its profit on the sale of the iPod.

Many industry experts predicted that iTunes was doomed to fail from the start. Why would consumers pay even $0.99 per song when they could access songs for free on the Internet? Instead, during its first week, it witnessed the sale of more than 1 million songs and became the largest online music company in the world.[1] What happened? Consumers were drawn in by iTunes' simplicity and ease of use, and by the higher-quality downloads than were available from other Internet sites.

Now, just over 10 years later, iTunes is selling over 25 billion songs a month to its 800 million customers. And, due to the addition of the Mac App Store and the sale of Apple software through iTunes, it is no longer a "break-even" business, but a highly profitable one, generating by one estimate $2 billion per year, or a 15% operating margin.[2]

This chapter explores how cost-volume-profit analysis can help a company such as Apple to determine the number of songs that it would need to sell to break even on its new business, or help Fezzari to predict the number of bikes it must sell to achieve a particular profit level.

---

[1] https://www.apple.com/pr/library/2003/05/05iTunes-Music-Store-Sells-Over-One-Million-Songs-in-First-Week.html
[2] http://www.valuewalk.com/2013/03/apple-inc-aapl-itunes-store-from-break-even-to-15-margins/

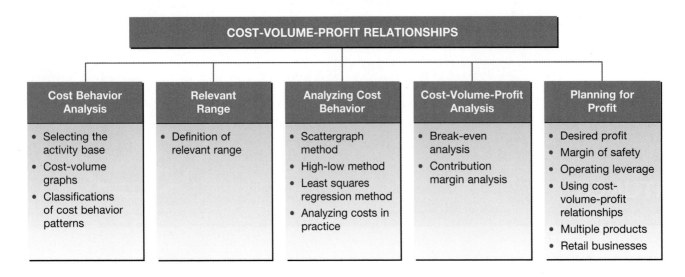

COST-VOLUME-PROFIT RELATIONSHIPS				
Cost Behavior Analysis	**Relevant Range**	**Analyzing Cost Behavior**	**Cost-Volume-Profit Analysis**	**Planning for Profit**
• Selecting the activity base • Cost-volume graphs • Classifications of cost behavior patterns	• Definition of relevant range	• Scattergraph method • High-low method • Least squares regression method • Analyzing costs in practice	• Break-even analysis • Contribution margin analysis	• Desired profit • Margin of safety • Operating leverage • Using cost-volume-profit relationships • Multiple products • Retail businesses

"We lose money on every sale—but make up the difference in volume."

ANONYMOUS

A.K.A. Cost-volume-profit analysis is often referred to in practice by its abbreviation, CVP, or break-even analysis.

Management must study a number of factors when planning the future course for an organization. One of the most important factors is the relationships among sales (revenue), costs (expenses), and profit (net income). **Cost-volume-profit (CVP) analysis** is used to study these relationships.

CVP analysis is appropriately used by for-profit organizations as well as not-for-profit (NFP) organizations. NFPs use the analysis with a target profit of zero. All of the relationships studied in the analysis are equally valid for both types of organizations.

COST BEHAVIOR ANALYSIS

LO1 **Develop** an understanding of how specific types of costs change in response to volume changes.

Cost behavior analysis is the study of how specific costs respond to changes in the volume of business activity. Each specific cost incurred by an organization may be affected differently by changes in the volume of business activity. Some costs will increase proportionately as volume increases, some costs will change disproportionately, and some costs will remain the same. Other factors besides volume can also cause changes in specific costs. For example, an increase in the assessment rate can increase property tax expense, whereas a decrease in electricity rates can lower total utility expense. These types of changes, however, are not typically caused by changes in business activity volume.

Selecting the Activity Basis

For meaningful managerial analysis, costs must be related to some measure of business activity. As we introduced in Chapter 3 and discussed further in Chapter 5, this measure of business activity is referred to as a cost driver. Cost drivers can include units of product, direct labor hours, machine hours, or percentage of capacity. A critical aspect is that the activity measure used must have a logical causal relation with costs, and the quantity of the activity must be highly correlated with the level of costs. Management must consider the objective of the analysis when selecting the most relevant and useful cost driver. For example, if iTunes managers want to analyze the cost of iTunes servers

for budgeting purposes, they might choose the number of song downloads as the business activity or cost driver. CVP analysis can often use several bases, depending on the objectives of the analysis.

To help demonstrate various cost behaviors, we'll return to the Fezzari example. Fezzari produces a carbon water bottle cage that can be used on both road and mountain bikes. In the first part of this chapter, we explore several examples related to the various costs associated with producing Fezzari's water bottle cages. We discuss various types of cost behaviors and graph those behaviors in cost-volume graphs. Later in the chapter, we further analyze those costs and how they relate to profits.

Cost-Volume Graphs

One of the most useful tools for analyzing the relationship between changes in cost and volume is the **cost-volume graph**. A cost-volume graph illustrates the relationship between costs and volume. These graphs typically plot total costs on the vertical axis and either volume or activity level on the horizontal axis. Recall from Chapter 2 that companies typically have both variable and fixed costs. **Exhibits 6-1** and **6-2** are examples of cost-volume graphs, plotting total cost on the *y*-axis and the number of water bottle cages on the *x*-axis. Keep in mind that the total cost line in **Exhibits 6-1** and **6-2** is comprised of both fixed and variable costs. Point A in **Exhibit 6-1** indicates that at a volume level of 5,000 units the associated cost is $7,500. Similarly, point B in **Exhibit 6-1** represents a cost of $22,500 for a volume level of 35,000 units.

Cost-volume graphs are particularly valuable when available cost-volume data are plotted on the same graph and other cost-volume relationships are estimated by fitting a line to the known points. In **Exhibit 6-1**, for example, we use three known data points (an increased number of known data points should be used to develop a more reliable graph). The known data points, represented by solid points, are as follows:

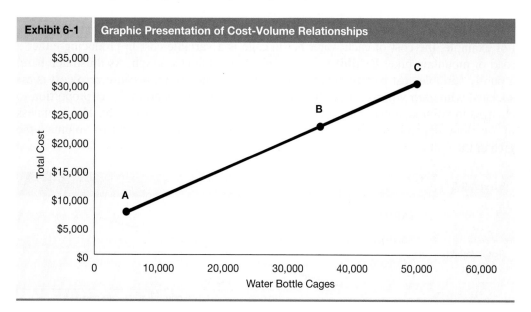

| Exhibit 6-1 | Graphic Presentation of Cost-Volume Relationships |

By connecting the known data points with a straight line, we can estimate the costs associated with other volume levels. For example, as illustrated in **Exhibit 6-2**, the open points indicate that for volumes of 22,500, 42,500, and 59,000 units, the related costs would be $16,250, $26,250, and $34,500, respectively. We discuss important limitations to using the cost-volume relationship to estimate costs later in the chapter.

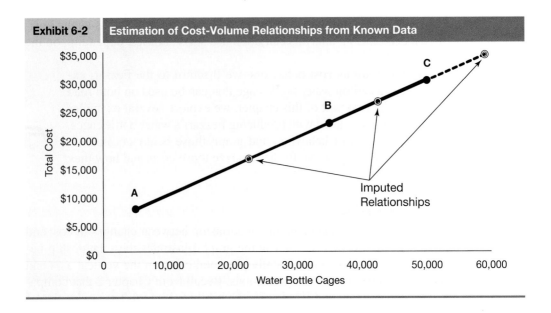

| Exhibit 6-2 | Estimation of Cost-Volume Relationships from Known Data |

Management often uses known data to estimate unknown data. More data typically will produce more reliable estimates. Having reliable estimates helps management predict profits or losses at various levels of activity.

Classifications of Cost Behavior Patterns

To better analyze cost behavior patterns, we typically classify costs (based on the definitions discussed in Chapter 2) as *variable, fixed,* or *mixed.*

Hint: The variable cost per unit is the slope of the line, commonly referred to as "rise over run."

Total variable costs change proportionately with changes in the volume of activity. For example, the cost of each water bottle cage is a variable cost in producing either a road or mountain bike. **Exhibit 6-3** is a typical variable cost graph. As illustrated here, a purely variable cost pattern always passes through the origin, because zero cost is associated with zero volume. Also, because variable costs respond in direct proportion to changes in volume, a variable cost line always slopes upward to the right. The steepness of the slope depends on the amount of cost associated with each unit of volume—the greater the unit cost, the steeper the slope.

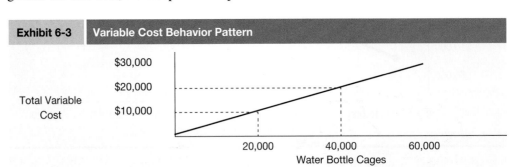

| Exhibit 6-3 | Variable Cost Behavior Pattern |

Fixed costs do not change when the volume of activity changes. Depreciation on manufacturing machinery is an example of a fixed cost.

Because fixed costs do not respond to changes in volume, they are represented by horizontal lines on a cost-volume graph. In **Exhibit 6-4**, fixed costs are $5,000 regardless of the volume level considered.

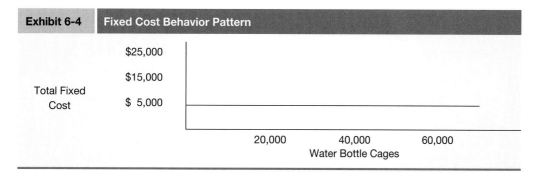

| Exhibit 6-4 | Fixed Cost Behavior Pattern |

Mixed costs—sometimes called *semi-variable costs*—can be described as having both fixed and variable components. Mixed costs respond to volume changes but less than proportionately. For example, assume that Fezzari has several sales associates who receive a fixed salary every month, but they also earn a commission based on their sales volume each month. Because sales associates' compensation is comprised of both a variable and a fixed component, compensation of sales associates would be considered a mixed cost

Hint: The fixed portion of a mixed service cost represents the basic charge for a service. The variable portion represents the charge for the use of the service.

A mixed cost is a single cost containing both a fixed and variable component. For analysis and planning purposes, mixed costs are typically broken down into their fixed and variable components. Total costs are then the sum of all of a company's fixed and variable costs over a period of time. As shown in **Exhibit 6-5**, total costs are comprised of both fixed and variable costs.

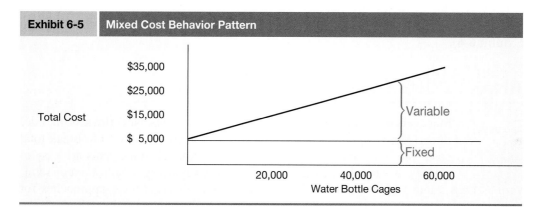

| Exhibit 6-5 | Mixed Cost Behavior Pattern |

RELEVANT RANGE

The cost behavior illustrations provided thus far are oversimplified because they portray linear cost behavior over the entire range of possible activity. Actually, plotting costs against volume may not always produce a single straight line. For example, certain costs may increase abruptly at intervals in a "step" pattern. Others may exhibit a curvilinear pattern when plotted over a wide range of activity. We present examples graphically of these cost patterns in **Exhibit 6-6**.

LO2 Define the concept of *relevant range.*

The **relevant range** is the range of activity over which the behavior of a cost behaves consistently. Clearly, an assumption of linear costs over the entire scale on either axis in these two cases causes some degree of error. The significance of this error is often minimized by the fact that many of the firm's decisions involve relatively small changes in volume. The actual cost pattern at extremely low or high volume levels is not relevant to the firm's decisions. The cost pattern only needs to be reasonably linear within this relevant range of activity. For example, **Exhibit 6-6** illustrates that the cost function approximates a straight line within the relevant range indicated, even though costs are clearly not linear outside this range.

Exhibit 6-6	Illustrations of Relevent Ranges

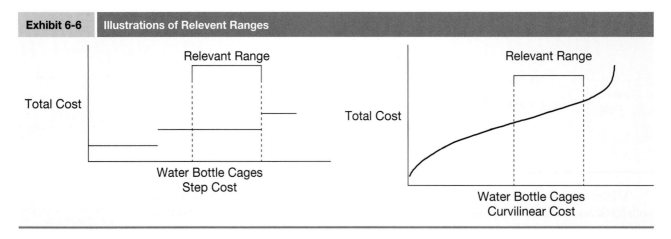

The cost-volume relationships for fixed cost, variable cost, and mixed cost typically remain the same for only one range of activity and for only one time period (frequently 1 year). Therefore fixed, variable, and mixed costs are assumed to have a consistent relationship in terms of volume within this relevant range during the given time period. The cost relationships, however, may change when moving to a different range of activity or a different time period. For example, a higher level of activity (above the current relevant range) could require a higher level of supervisory personnel, which would result in a higher level of fixed salary expense (as shown in the step cost graph in **Exhibit 6-6**). Alternatively, a higher direct material cost due to significantly higher demand for the direct material could lead to a different relationship (as shown in the curvilinear cost graph in **Exhibit 6-6**).

ANALYZING COST BEHAVIOR

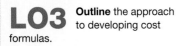

Outline the approach to developing cost formulas.

Managers often have detailed information about costs. Nevertheless, in order to perform CVP analysis to make better decisions, they need to break total costs into fixed and variable components. Although some costs are easy to classify as variable or fixed costs, it isn't always easy to split mixed (semi-variable) costs into variable and fixed components. We illustrate three approaches for better understanding the nature of a company's costs: (1) the scattergraph method, (2) the high-low method, and (3) the least squares regression method. We note at the outset that these methods differ both in their ease of application and in their accuracy. For example, the scattergraph method is fast and easy, but it isn't very accurate. On the other extreme, the least squares regression method may take a little more effort, but it is much more accurate. Managers need to weigh costs and benefits in determining which approach is most useful.

Scattergraph Method

For purposes of cost analysis, a mixed cost is divided into its fixed and variable components. We accomplish this by any one of several approaches that vary in their degree of sophistication. One simple method entails plotting the observed cost at several levels of volume on a graph. If cost behavior in actual situations were perfectly correlated, the observations (points) would form a straight line (see **Exhibit 6-1** for an example). More realistically, however, we expect only a discernible pattern.

Assume that Fezzari purchases its carbon water bottle cages from a company in Taiwan that produces similar products for companies around the world. **Exhibit 6-7** reports the supplier's manufacturing costs for various levels of production over the past eight months (sorted by production volume):

Cost	Water Bottle Cages
$27,000	44,000
$29,500	48,000
$30,000	51,000
$31,500	52,000
$32,500	54,000
$32,000	55,000
$36,000	63,000
$38,000	66,000

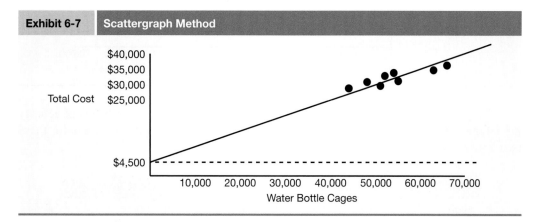

Exhibit 6-7   Scattergraph Method

After plotting the actual costs relative to volume over the past eight months, the individual performing the analysis would simply draw a line that places approximately half of the dots above and half below the line. The line in **Exhibit 6-7** has been subjectively determined to approximate the pattern of data points on this scattergraph. Extending this line to the vertical axis indicates a $4,500 fixed portion of total costs. To determine the approximate formula for the total cost line, we subtract this $4,500 fixed cost from the total $27,000 cost at 44,000 water bottle cages to find a total variable portion of $22,500. Therefore, the rate of variations is $22,500/44,000 cages, or $0.51, per water bottle cage. Hence, we could describe this mixed cost as $4,500 fixed cost plus $0.51 per water bottle cage of variable cost. We summarize the equation as follows:

Total cost = $4,500 + ($0.51 × water bottle cages)

Your manager asks you to interpret the semi-variable cost graph in **Exhibit 6-7** for your company. Briefly explain what is meant by each of the following points on the graph:
y-intercept   x-axis
Slope of the line   Any point along the line

YOUR TURN! 6.1

The solution is on page 239.

High-Low Method

When too few cost observations are available to plot a graph, or when the analyst wishes to avoid visually fitting lines to data, the high-low method can be used to approximate the position and slope of the cost line. This relatively simple method compares costs at the highest and lowest levels of activity for which representative cost data are available. The line is drawn between the highest- and lowest-volume data points, as shown in **Exhibit 6-8**. The variable cost per activity unit (here, per water bottle cage) is determined by dividing the difference in costs at these two levels by the difference in activity. The fixed element of cost is then isolated by multiplying the variable cost per unit by either the top or bottom level of activity and then subtracting the resulting product from the total cost at the selected activity level.

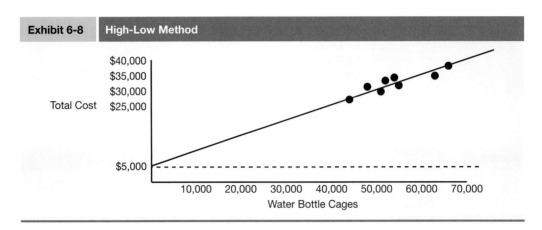

Exhibit 6-8	High-Low Method

Using the same data from our prior example, the lowest and highest levels of activity are 44,000 and 66,000 cages, respectively, and the following are the total costs for these two levels:

Level of Activity		**Total Cost**
High	66,000 Water bottle cages	$38,000
Low	44,000 Water bottle cages	$27,000
Difference	22,000 (increase)	$11,000 (increase)

Because an increase of 22,000 cages is associated with an $11,000 increase in total cost (remember that by definition only the variable portion of the cost could increase), the variable portion of the total mixed cost must be $11,000/22,000 water bottle cages, or $0.50 per water bottle cage. Subtracting the total variable portion from the total mixed cost at the high- and low-activity levels gives us the fixed portion of total cost as follows:

	Volume Levels	
	Low	**High**
Total mixed cost.	$27,000	$38,000
Less variable portions:		
$0.50 × 44,000 Water bottle cages	22,000	
$0.50 × 66,000 Water bottle cages		33,000
Fixed portion of total cost	$ 5,000	$ 5,000

The high-low analysis tells us that any volume level has $5,000 of fixed cost plus a variable portion of $0.50 per water bottle cage, which can be formulated as follows:

$$\text{Total cost} = \$5,000 + (\$0.50 \times \text{water bottle cages})$$

In other words, we can now easily compute the total cost for varying levels of production. However, if either the high or low value used in this method is not representative of the actual cost behavior (that is, the value is an outlier), the resulting cost formula is inexact.

Given the following levels of volume and cost, calculate the variable cost per unit and fixed cost within this relevant range using the high-low method:

YOUR TURN! 6.2

The solution is on page 239.

Cost	Volume	Cost	Volume
$15,000	5,000 units	$24,500	9,750 units
$13,000	4,000 units	$18,000	6,500 units
$19,300	7,150 units	$21,000	8,000 units

Least Squares Regression Method

We can obtain an even better approximation by fitting the line to the cost data points by the least squares regression method. The least squares regression method is a statistical tool that uses all of the data points to separate a mixed cost into its variable and fixed components. A regression line is fitted to the data points so that the distance from each point to the line is minimized for all points. **Exhibit 6-9** illustrates this concept using all data points.

Exhibit 6-9	Least Squares Regression

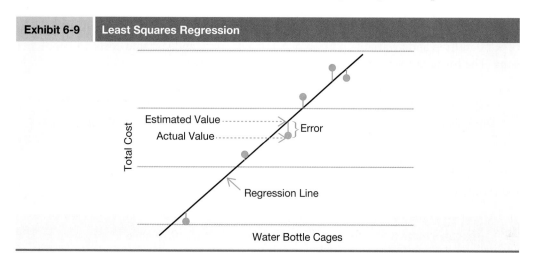

In **Exhibit 6-9**, the distances from the data points and the regression line are the regression errors—the amount by which the value estimated by the regression line differs from the actual data point.

The formulas that are used to compute the least squares regression are fairly complex and beyond the scope of this text. However, the computations can be easily made with a computer program. When the data points are entered into a Microsoft Excel spreadsheet and the least squares regression is executed, we get the following values for fixed cost and variable cost per unit:

Fixed cost:	**$6,083**
Variable cost per water bottle cage:	**$ 0.48**

The resulting linear equation would be written as:

Total cost = $6,083 + ($0.48 × water bottle cages)

Looking back, we can see how each method arrives at a somewhat different result:

Scattergraph equation:	**Total cost = $4,500 + ($0.51 × water bottle cages)**
High-low equation:	**Total cost = $5,000 + ($0.50 × water bottle cages)**
Least squares equation:	**Total cost = $6,083 + ($0.48 × water bottle cages)**

Although the scattergraph and high-low methods are the easiest to implement, they are also less accurate. They work well for quick estimates. However, with the availability of desktop computers and programs that can compute least squares regressions, and given the limitations of the scattergraph and high-low methods, managers generally prefer to use the least squares regression method to estimate the fixed and variable portions of a mixed cost.

Analyzing Costs in Practice

How might we use this understanding of cost behavior as business managers? The budget for a business, which is discussed in detail in **Chapter 9**, is a financial plan that reflects anticipated or planned amounts of such items as revenue, costs, cash balances, and net income. Underlying most aspects of budgeting is some assumed number of units or dollars of sales, as well as an analysis of the total cost incurred for that level of operation.

For an example, assume that iTunes management is preparing the budget for the next fiscal year. Because of uncertainty regarding the continued economic recovery from a recent recession, management wants to prepare a budget that will allow it to quickly determine expected costs if iTunes sales vary significantly from anticipated levels. Based on the previous year, total fixed costs are $2.0 billion, mixed costs have a fixed portion of $250 million and a variable portion of $0.05 per song, and variable costs are $0.35 per song. The formula for budgeting the total cost is as follows:

> **Total cost = Total fixed cost + (Variable cost per song × # of songs sold)**
>
> **Total cost = $2.25 billion fixed cost + ($0.40 Variable cost × # of songs sold)**

By using this formula, iTunes management can forecast costs at different levels of activity. **Exhibit 6-10** illustrates how each type of cost behavior pattern is considered in the formula.

Exhibit 6-10	iTunes Cost Factors Example							
Type of Cost	**Total Cost (in millions)**		**Total Fixed Cost (in millions)**		**Variable Cost per Song**		**Number of Songs (in millions)**	
Variable costs.......	$10,500	=	$ 0	+	$0.35	×	30,000	
Mixed costs:								
Variable portion....	1,500	=	$ 0	+	0.05	×	30,000	
Fixed portion......	250	=	$ 250	+	0	×	30,000	
Fixed costs.........	2,000	=	$2,000	+	0	×	30,000	
Total cost	$14,250	=	$2,250	+	$0.40	×	30,000	

Notice in **Exhibit 6-10** that by combining the various cost factors into the aggregate formula, iTunes management can determine expected costs not only at the 30-billion-song level but also at other levels simply by inserting the appropriate volume figure in the final formula. For example, total budgeted cost at 45 billion songs is $20.250 billion ($2.25 billion + [$0.40 × 45 billion songs]) and at 62 billion songs, total budgeted cost is $27.05 billion ($2.25 billion + [$0.40 × 62 billion songs]).

A word of caution is appropriate here. Because the cost formula relies so heavily on cost analysis, all of the limitations of cost analysis (assumed linearity, relevant ranges, and so on) apply. Also, categorizing many costs into fixed and variable components is often quite complex and inexact. All of these limitations to some degree affect the potential usefulness of managerial cost analysis. It is important to note that these models provide data that can be used to help managers make decisions. However, managers should not blindly follow the outputs from their models. Managers ultimately need to evaluate all relevant information to make sound decisions. In some cases, the simple analytical approach presented here is sufficient, but it cannot be followed blindly.

COST-VOLUME-PROFIT (CVP) ANALYSIS

Break-Even Analysis

Management frequently wants to know the sales level (in dollars) or the number of units that must be sold in order to cover its costs. The level at which total revenues equal total costs is called the **break-even point**. The break-even point can be expressed in dollars or in units sold. As an example, we illustrate several important calculations for one of Fezzari's medium-range road bikes, the Foré CR1, using the condensed income statement data shown in **Exhibit 6-11**.

LO4 **Present** a discussion of and a formula for calculating the break-even point.

Exhibit 6-11	Fezzari Foré CR1 Operating Income	
Sales (3,000 units @ $1,500)		$4,500,000
Costs:		
Variable cost (3,000 units @ $1,138)	$3,414,000	
Fixed cost	595,000	
Total cost		$4,009,000
Net operating income		$ 491,000

This information assumes that all mixed costs have been accurately divided into their fixed and variable components and combined with other fixed and variable costs. We now examine some of the uses of this information.

The Cost-Volume-Profit Chart

To prepare a cost-volume-profit (CVP) chart for the Foré CR1, we use the same basic graph employed previously to explain and portray cost behavior patterns. In **Exhibit 6-12** the vertical axis measures both total revenues and total costs. As in previous exhibits, volume is measured along the horizontal axis. In this Fezzari product line, the activity basis is the number of Foré CR1s manufactured and sold. Total revenues and total costs are measured in thousands of dollars along the vertical axis.

With zero revenue for zero units sold, the graph of total revenues always passes through the origin. We draw the total revenue line by connecting the origin with any other point that represents total revenue for some volume amount. For Fezzari's CR1, total revenue for 3,000 units is $4,500,000, point **A** in **Exhibit 6-12**. To construct the total revenue line, we simply draw a straight line from the origin to **A** and extend it beyond **A**.

We now construct the total cost line in the same manner. With fixed costs of $595,000, the total cost line must intersect the vertical axis at the fixed costs level, $595,000. To produce 3,000 bicycles, Fezzari incurs total costs of $4,009,000. Given this information, we can plot point **B** and draw the total cost line connecting the intersection of the fixed cost line and the vertical axis with **B** as shown in **Exhibit 6-12**. After constructing the total cost line, its intersection with the total revenue line marks the break-even point.

Extending the dashed horizontal and vertical lines from the break-even point, we find that Fezzari's break-even point can be described as either (1) 1,644 units of production or (2) $2,466,000 of total sales revenue. (We explain the calculation of these numbers next.) Note that all levels of sales below the break-even point indicate a loss, and levels of sales above the break-even point result in a profit. In other words, Fezzari earns a profit from its CR1 product line when the total revenue line is above the total cost line, and it incurs a loss when the reverse is true. **Exhibit 6-12** indicates the profit and loss areas. The amount of profit or loss at any volume level is determined by measuring the vertical distance between the total cost and total revenue lines. For example, the difference between points **A** and **B** indicates the profit of $491,000 for selling 3,000 CR1 road bikes.

Exhibit 6-12	**Fezzari Foré CR1 Cost-Volume-Profit Chart**

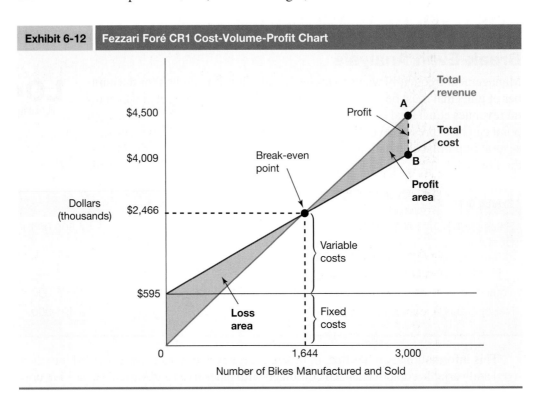

ACCOUNTING IN PRACTICE

Tesla Breaks Even!

On December 2, 2012, Tesla, the start-up electric car manufacturer, finally broke even! CEO Elon Musk announced that the company has stopped burning cash and reached the break-even point, a major milestone for any start-up. "Am happy to report that Tesla was narrowly cash flow positive last week. Continued improvement expected through year end," Musk tweeted. According to the *Wall Street Journal*, in November of 2012, Tesla told the Securities and Exchange Commission that it was producing 200 cars per week, "which is at the critical threshold needed for Tesla to generate positive operating cash flow," and expected to increase that to 400 cars per week in December.

The Basic Assumptions of Break-Even Analysis

In our construction of a break-even chart, we assumed linear relationships over a wide range of activity. This approach implies the following:

1. Total fixed cost and total variable cost per unit are constant over the entire range of analysis.

2. Selling price per unit remains the same regardless of the volume of sales.

3. When more than one product is involved and sales volume varies, each product's percentage of total sales (i.e., the sales mix) does not change.

Even though these assumptions somewhat limit the usefulness of break-even analysis, it is still a convenient method of measuring the effect of changes in sales, costs, volumes, and profits.

Break-Even Formula

The following formula reflects the basic relationship between the break-even point and costs; the break-even point is that point at which total revenue equals total cost:

> **Break-even sales = Total variable costs + Total fixed costs**

Break-even sales and total variable costs can be expressed as follows:

> **(Selling price per unit × Number of units) = (Variable cost per unit × Number of units) + Total fixed costs**

Using the data for Fezzari's Foré CR1 with this formula, we can calculate Fezzari's break-even point in units and sales dollars. First, we solve for Y, which represents the number of units at the break-even level. We can then multiply the number of break-even units by the sales price to determine break-even sales.

Break-even sales	**= Total variable costs + Total fixed costs**
$1,500 Y	= $1,138 Y + $595,000
$1,500 Y − $1,138 Y	= $595,000
$362 Y	= $595,000
Y	= **1,644 units (rounded)**
$1,500 × 1,644	= **$2,466,000**

Exhibit 6-13 illustrates the break-even calculation based on Fezzari's flexible budget using 1,644 units as the break-even level of activity. Obviously, "break-even" literally means net profit of exactly zero. Because it isn't practical to sell partial units, the break-even calculation will normally indicate how many full units must be sold to produce enough contribution margin to cover fixed costs. In this example, 1,644 CR1 road bikes sold allows the company to "break-even," with $128 left over, whereas selling 1,643 units would have resulted in a small loss. Hence, we round to the number of complete units that allows the company to just exceed the zero-profit threshold.

Exhibit 6-13	**Fezzari Foré CR1 Fezzari Break-Even Calculation**	
Sales (1,644 units @ $1,500)		$2,466,000
Variable cost (1,644 units @ $1,138)		1,870,872
Contribution margin		$ 595,128
Fixed cost		595,000
Net operating income		$ 128

Contribution Margin Analysis

Because total variable costs change proportionately with changes in total revenue, each time additional revenue is generated, additional variable costs are also generated. The difference between the revenue generated and the variable costs generated is called the **contribution margin**. The restructured **variable operating income statement** for Fezzari's CR1 shown in **Exhibit 6-14** illustrates the importance of contribution margin.

LO5 **Define** *contribution margin* and *contribution margin ratio* and **present** alternate break-even formulas and examples of their application.

Exhibit 6-14	Fezzari Foré CR1 Operating Income	
Sales (3,000 units @ $1,500)		$4,500,000
Variable cost (3,000 units @ $1,138)		3,414,000
Contribution margin		**$1,086,000**
Fixed cost		595,000
Net operating income		$ 491,000

When using the variable format for the income statement, we first deduct all variable costs from sales to calculate the contribution margin. We then deduct fixed costs from the contribution margin to calculate operating income. Thus, contribution margin can be viewed as a measure of what is left over after covering variable costs to go toward covering fixed costs and generating profits. At 3,000 units, the total contribution margin is $1,086,000. The contribution margin per unit is calculated as the selling price per unit minus the variable cost per unit. In the Fezzari CR1 example, the contribution margin per unit of $362 would be calculated as the selling price per unit of $1,500 minus the $1,138 variable cost per unit. The contribution margin per unit means that for each additional CR1 sold beyond the break-even point, $362 of additional contribution margin is generated to help produce additional profit.

Contribution Margin Ratio

Hint: The contribution margin is defined as the amount of sales revenue after variable expenses are deducted that is used to cover fixed costs and provide a profit. At the break-even point, the contribution margin equals fixed costs (i.e., profit is zero).

A related concept often used in break-even analysis is the **contribution margin ratio**, which is the ratio of the contribution margin to sales. The formula to calculate the contribution margin ratio can use either *total* amounts:

$$\text{Contribution margin ratio} = \frac{\text{Contribution margin}}{\text{Sales}}$$

or *per-unit* amounts:

$$\text{Contribution margin ratio} = \frac{\text{Unit contribution margin}}{\text{Unit sales price}}$$

In the Fezzari CR1 example:

$$\text{Contribution margin ratio} = \frac{\$1,086,000}{\$4,500,000} = 0.24 \text{ (rounded)}$$

or

$$\text{Contribution margin ratio} = \frac{\$362}{\$1,500} = 0.24 \text{ (rounded)}$$

The contribution margin ratio is easier to work with than the unit contribution margin if a company has more than one product line. The contribution margin ratio allows comparisons among product lines, which we illustrate later in the chapter.

Alternative Break-Even Formulas

Two alternative break-even formulas[3] can be directly derived from our previous break-even formula. To calculate the break-even point either in *units:*

$$\text{Break-even units} = \frac{\text{Total fixed cost}}{\text{Unit contribution margin}}$$

or in *sales dollars:*

$$\text{Break-even sales dollars} = \frac{\text{Total fixed cost}}{\text{Contribution margin ratio}}$$

In the Fezzari CR1 example, we can calculate the break-even point using these two formulas. Using the first formula (expressed in units):

$$\text{Break-even units} = \frac{\$595,000}{\$362} = 1,644 \text{ units}$$

Using the second formula (expressed in sales dollars):

$$\text{Break-even sales} = \frac{\$595,000}{0.24} = \$2,479,167^{\,4}$$

The results obtained from any of the break-even formulas can be verified by placing the amounts in an income statement format and verifying that net income equals zero.

TAKEAWAY 6.2

Break-even analysis is helpful to management because it helps determine the total sales volume or the selling price per unit that must be achieved in order to exactly cover total costs. If companies do not consider the break-even point, they may experience losses even though they were expecting profits.

PLANNING FOR PROFIT

Desired Profit

Target Profits without Taxes

With an understanding of the cost-volume-profit relationship, business managers can develop plans for desired levels of profit. Rather than making the

LO6 **Discuss** approaches to planning net income using cost-volume-profit analyses.

---

[3] These formulas can be derived from the general break-even formula provided previously:

Break-even sales = Total variable cost + Total fixed cost

(Selling price per unit × Number of units) = (Variable cost per unit × Number of units) + Total fixed costs

(Selling price per unit × Number of units) − (Variable cost per unit × Number of units) = Total fixed costs

(Selling price per unit − Variable cost per unit) × Number of units = Total fixed costs

(Contribution margin per unit) × Number of units = Total fixed costs

$$\text{Number of units} = \frac{\text{Total fixed costs}}{\text{Contribution margin per unit}}$$

The second formula can be derived simply by multiplying both sides of this equation by the selling price per unit.

[4] This solution differs from the sales revenue computed previously because the contribution margin used has been rounded to the nearest hundredth.

calculations for break-even, where profit is equal to zero, they use formulas that include a *desired profit*. These formulas are similar to the previous CVP break-even formula and take into consideration the additional desired net income (or profit):

Desired sales = Total variable costs + Total fixed costs + Desired net income [5]

A.K.A. The desired profit is also referred to as desired net income.

Recall that the definition of contribution margin is what is left over from sales, after covering variable costs, to cover fixed costs and generate profits. Using the contribution margin approach, we can then rearrange our CVP formula to solve for the level of units and sales to achieve our desired net income:

$$\textbf{Desired units} = \frac{\textbf{Total fixed costs} + \textbf{Desired net income}}{\textbf{Unit contribution margin}}$$

And

$$\textbf{Desired sales} = \frac{\textbf{Total fixed costs} + \textbf{Desired net income}}{\textbf{Contribution margin ratio}}$$

Assume that Fezzari wants to attain a net income of $1,000,000 before income tax on its CR1 line. Using these formulas, we can determine the level of output in sales dollars or units as follows:

Using the CVP equation:

$1,500 × Y	= $1,138Y + $595,000 + $1,000,000
$1,500Y − $1,138Y	= $1,595,000
$362Y	= $1,595,000
Y	= **4,406 units**
4,406 units × $1,500	= **$6,609,000**

Using the contribution margin approach:

$$\text{Desired units} = \frac{\$595,000 + \$1,000,000}{\$362}$$

$$= 4,406 \text{ units}$$

$$\text{Desired sales} = \frac{\$595,000 + \$1,000,000}{0.24}$$

$$= \$6,645,833^{7}$$

---

[5] Note that the desired net income in these formulas is pre-tax net income. When taxes are applicable, managers need to adjust the formulas to account for taxes in order to determine a desired after-tax net income.

[6] This calculation differs from the sales revenue computed using the first formula because the contribution margin used has been rounded to the nearest hundredth.

DECISION TIME

The solution is on
page 239.

A U.S. shoe retailer performed a CVP analysis and determined that at a level of $500,000 in sales, $350,000 in variable costs, and $200,000 in fixed costs would be incurred. Therefore, the company would have a loss of $50,000. If all else remains the same, what change or changes could the company make in order to break even or earn a profit?

   a. Increase selling price per unit

   b. Increase number of units sold

   c. Either or both of the above

Target Profits with Taxes

Fezzari's management might want to develop plans using net income (after tax) rather than net income before income taxes. In this case, net income (after tax) must be converted to net income before income tax so the formulas presented previously can be used:

$$\textbf{Net income before income tax} = \frac{\textbf{Net income}}{\textbf{1 – Income tax rate}}$$

Assume that Fezzari's management wants to attain an after-tax net income of $700,000 when the income tax rate is 30%. Net income before income tax can be calculated as follows:

$$\textbf{Net income before income tax} = \frac{\$700,000}{1 - 0.3} = \frac{\$700,000}{0.7} = \$1,000,000$$

A brief income statement verifies the calculations made in the preceding sections:

Sales (4,406 units × $1,500)	$6,609,000
Less: Variable cost (4,406 units × $1,138).	5,014,028
Contribution margin	$1,594,972
Less: Fixed cost	595,000
Net operating income.	$ 999,972
Income tax ($999,972 × 0.30)	299,992
Net income.	$ 699,980[8]

CVP Disclosure   ACCOUNTING IN PRACTICE

The Securities and Exchange Commission requires all publicly held companies to include a "management discussion and analysis (MD&A) of the results of operations" in quarterly and annual reports. This analysis may include cost-volume-profit data. For example, in its 2013 annual report, Yum! Brands, the parent company for restaurant chains such as Taco Bell, Kentucky Fried Chicken, and Pizza Hut, kicks off its MD&A section with a discussion of its focus on target profits, which is the result of careful CVP analysis on the part of management.

---

[7] Difference from target net income after tax of $700,000 due to rounding.

Margin of Safety

The **margin of safety** is the amount by which the actual sales level of a company exceeds the break-even sales level. It represents the company's "breathing room" in which it will remain profitable. If sales decrease by more than the margin of safety, then the company will incur an operating loss. The formula for calculating the margin of safety follows:

$$\text{Margin of safety} = \text{Actual sales} - \text{Break-even sales}$$

In the Fezzari CR1 example, **Exhibit 6-13** indicates that Fezzari needs sales of \$2,466,000 (i.e., 1,644 CR1s) to break even. Assume Fezzari achieves sales of \$3,000,000 in a given year. Its margin of safety for that year would be calculated as:

$$\text{Margin of safety} = \$3,000,000 - \$2,466,000 = \$534,000$$

In other words, Fezzari could decrease sales by up to \$534,000 and still achieve a profit.

Another way of looking at the "breathing room" beyond break-even sales is on a ratio (or percentage) basis, referred to as the margin-of-safety ratio. It is calculated as follows:

$$\text{Margin-of-safety ratio} = \frac{\text{Margin of safety}}{\text{Actual sales}}$$

For example, continuing the previous Fezzari example (and assuming sales of \$3,000,000), the margin-of-safety ratio would be calculated as:

$$\text{Margin-of-safety ratio} = \frac{\$534,000}{\$3,000,000} = 17.8\%$$

In other words, Fezzari could decrease CR1 sales by up to 17.8% and still achieve a profit.

Operating Leverage

Apple's iTunes division and Fezzari have relatively low fixed costs. On the other hand, other companies or industries are characterized by relatively high fixed costs, including utilities (e.g., Pacific Gas and Electric Co. and Florida Power & Light) and auto manufacturers (e.g., General Motors Company and Toyota Motor Corporation). One measure of a firm's relative level of fixed costs is **operating leverage**. Operating leverage is computed as follows:

$$\text{Operating leverage} = \frac{\text{Contribution margin}}{\text{Net operating income}}$$

Note that the difference between the numerator (contribution margin) and the denominator (net operating income) is the amount of fixed costs (look back at the variable income statement in **Exhibit 6-14** to confirm this). Thus, this ratio is really a measure of a company's operating cost structure, or its level of fixed costs (relative to variable costs). If two companies have the same level of sales and costs, but the cost structure (i.e., the mix between variable and fixed costs) is different, the company with relatively higher fixed costs will have the higher operating leverage. At one extreme, a company that has no fixed costs (i.e., all costs are variable) will have an operating leverage of 1.0

because its contribution margin and net operating income will be the same. **Exhibit 6-15** illustrates graphically a company with an operating leverage of 1.0. Note that because there are no fixed costs, as long as the per-unit sales price of the product is greater than the cost of the product, each sale generates an operating profit equal to the unit contribution margin.

Exhibit 6-15 **Structure with All Variable Costs**

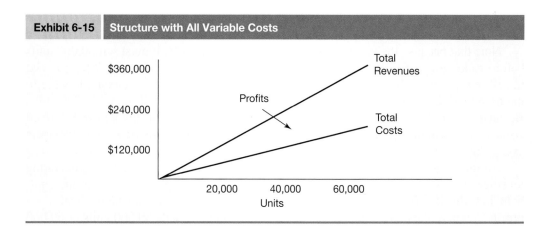

The company illustrated in **Exhibit 6-15** sells its products for $6 per unit, and the variable costs to produce a unit of product amount to $2 per unit. Thus, the contribution margin per unit is $4 ($6 – $2). Because the company has no fixed costs, when it sells its first unit of product to a customer, it will generate $4 of operating profit. Each additional unit of product sold will likewise result in additional operating profits of $4 per unit.

Because a world without fixed costs isn't reasonable, operating leverage is an important measure to help managers assess how their cost structure (their unique mix of variable and fixed costs) influences their break-even point. The higher a company's fixed costs, the more units it will need to sell in order to break even. Hence, a company struggling to break even would want to avoid fixed costs in order to lower its break-even point.

As a company's relative mix of costs shifts more toward fixed costs, its operating leverage increases, suggesting greater risk. **Exhibit 6-16** graphically illustrates a company with an operating leverage greater than 1.0 (i.e., with both fixed and variable costs). Assume the company has fixed costs of $120,000, variable costs of $2 per unit, and a selling price of $6 per unit.

Exhibit 6-16 **Structure with Fixed and Variable Costs**

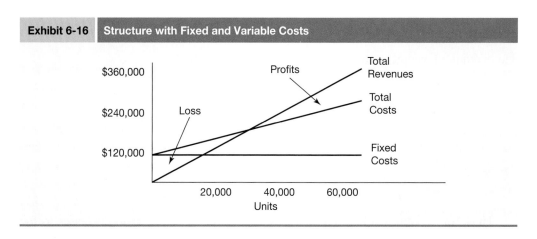

Break-even for this company would be computed as follows:

$$\textbf{Break-even units} = \frac{\textbf{Total fixed cost}}{\textbf{Unit contribution margin}}$$

$$\textbf{Break-even units} = \frac{\$120,000}{\$4\,/\,\textbf{unit}} = \textbf{30,000 units}$$

Note that because the company has $120,000 of fixed costs, it must sell 30,000 units before making a profit. What happens as a company's fixed costs increase? It will need to sell more units to break even. For example, if the company in this example were to increase its fixed costs to $160,000, its break-even point would shift up to 40,000 units. Because it would be harder for the company to break even with this higher level of fixed costs, its risk would increase. Operating leverage can be a useful metric to help managers assess the risk associated with their fixed costs.

An important thing to remember about operating leverage is that a firm's operating leverage changes with its level of output and sales. For example, assume that the company in **Exhibit 6-16** is operating at a level of sales above break-even where it achieves a profit. Compare the company's performance if the company sells 50,000 units or 60,000 units; its operating income would be calculated as follows:

	Sales Volume	
	50,000	60,000
Sales ($6/unit).	$300,000	$360,000
Less: Variable cost ($2/unit).	(100,000)	(120,000)
Contribution margin	200,000	240,000
Less: Fixed cost.	(120,000)	(120,000)
Net operating income.	$ 80,000	$120,000

Operating leverage at the 50,000 level of sales would be 2.5, computed as follows:

$$\textbf{Operating leverage} = \frac{\textbf{Contribution margin}}{\textbf{Net operating income}}$$

$$= \frac{\$200,000}{\$80,000}$$

$$= \textbf{2.5}$$

and operating leverage at the 60,000 level would change to 2.0:

$$\textbf{Operating leverage} = \frac{\textbf{Contribution margin}}{\textbf{Net operating income}}$$

$$= \frac{\$240,000}{\$120,000}$$

$$= \textbf{2.0}$$

Thus, for a given level of fixed costs, the operating leverage ratio decreases as the levels of output and sales increase. Another way of thinking about this concept is that for a given level of fixed costs, if the company can barely maintain a positive operating profit (i.e., it can barely cover its fixed costs), it is constantly operating under a high degree of uncertainty about whether or not it will be able to cover its fixed costs and turn a profit. Hence, its operating leverage would be high. To the extent that the company can comfortably sell more than the number of units required to break even (i.e., it has a high margin of safety), it has less risk of falling short and reporting a loss. Hence, for a given level of fixed costs, as output and sales increase, operating leverage (and the associated risk of reporting a loss) will decrease. The degree of operating leverage can be used to determine, at a given level of sales, how a percentage change in the level of sales will impact net operating profit:

% Increase in operating income = % Increase in sales × Operating leverage

Fezzari's CR1 example illustrates this concept. Assume that Fezzari's management anticipates a 20% increase in sales in the coming year. What should the resulting operating income be? From **Exhibit 6-17**, we can calculate Fezzari's operating leverage as follows:

$$\text{Operating leverage} = \frac{\textbf{Contribution margin}}{\textbf{Net operating income}}$$

$$\text{Operating leverage} = \frac{\$1,086,000}{\$491,000} = 2.2118 \text{ (rounded)}$$

If sales increase by 20%, operating income should be $708,200, calculated as follows:

% Increase in operating income = % Increase in sales × Operating leverage

$$44.236\% = 20\% \times 2.2118$$

$$\$708,200^* = \$491,000 \times (1 + 0.44236)$$

* Difference due to rounding.

Exhibit 6-17 proves this calculation.

Exhibit 6-17	Fezzari Foré CR1 Operating Income Comparison			
			Sales Increase	
Sales (3,000 units @ $1,500)	$4,500,000	20%		$5,400,000
Variable cost (3,000 units @ $1,138)	3,414,000	20%		$4,096,800
Contribution margin	$1,086,000			$1,303,200
Fixed cost	595,000			595,000
Net operating income	$ 491,000			$ 708,200

Note that operating leverage for the CR1 product line is not a constant, but is computed for each level of sales. For example, Fezzari's new operating leverage (following the 20% increase in sales) would be:

$$\text{Operating leverage} = \frac{\$1,303,200}{\$708,200} = 1.8402 \text{ (rounded)}$$

YOUR TURN! 6.3

The solution is on page 239.

Your supervisor is concerned about your company's degree of operating leverage. She explains that other companies in your industry have operating leverage averaging over 3.0. Your sales for the current year are $2,500,000, variable costs are $1,400,000, and fixed costs are $600,000. Should you be concerned?

CORPORATE SOCIAL RESPONSIBILITY

True Innovation

Anyone who pays monthly water bills for a home, condo, business, or anything else knows that water is becomingly increasingly scarce. Apple recognizes this, and has constructed manufacturing processes that reuse as much water as possible. When it comes to Apple's relationship with suppliers, the company does not simply criticize inefficient suppliers but rather works "with suppliers that don't meet our standards for water reuse" and "help them improve until they do."

Water use is not the only environmental impact Apple considers in its manufacturing processes; as highlighted on Apple's environmental responsibility web page, "We believe true innovation must consider everything." This all-inclusive approach to environmental consideration includes a partnership with the Conservation Fund to "protect and create the type of forests we use in our packaging," develop "a renewable micro-hydro project to power our data center in Prineville, Oregon," and construct "a solar farm in China to offset energy used by our offices and retail stores." While environmental impact is a necessary aspect of Apple's operations, the company has implemented processes that reduce the environmental impact and improve the company's relationship with its various stakeholders and with the general public.

Using Cost-Volume-Profit Relationships

Cost-volume-profit relationships can be used in a number of ways during planning and budgeting sessions to test possible courses of action. The following three independent situations, based on Fezzari's operating income presented in **Exhibit 6-11**, reveal ways that Fezzari might use cost-volume-profit relationships to make business decisions.

Situation 1

Assume that Fezzari's managers are considering reducing the average price of the CR1 (on a per-unit basis) from $1,500 to $1,300. *How would this change affect the break-even point in units?*

$$\text{Break-even units} = \frac{\text{Total fixed cost}}{\text{Unit contribution margin}}$$

$$= \frac{\$595,000}{(\$1,300 - \$1,138)}$$

$$= 3,673 \text{ units}$$

The $200 price decrease would cause the break-even point to increase from 1,644 units (previously calculated) to 3,673 units.

Situation 2

Assume that Fezzari's managers are considering an advertising campaign that would increase the CR1's fixed costs by $50,000 to $645,000 and allow a price increase from $1,500 to $1,600 per unit. *How would this change affect the break-even point in units* for the CR1 product line?

$$\text{Break-even units} = \frac{\text{Total fixed cost}}{\text{Unit contribution margin}}$$

$$= \frac{\$645,000}{(\$1,600 - \$1,138)}$$

$$= 1,396 \text{ units}$$

The $50,000 advertising campaign and the related $100 price increase would cause the CR1 break-even point to decrease from 1,644 units to 1,369 units.

Situation 3

Assume that Fezzari's managers are considering eliminating the sales commission program and increasing the sales force base salaries. This change would decrease the CR1 unit variable cost from $1,138 to $1,088 and would increase fixed costs from $595,000 to $695,000. Average unit sales price would remain at $1,500. If the company wants to achieve an after-tax net income for the CR1 product line of $700,000 and if the income tax rate is 30%, *what would the impact be on desired units sold of eliminating the sales commission program?*

$$\text{Desired units} = \frac{\text{Total fixed cost} + \text{Desired net income before income tax}}{\text{Unit contribution margin}}$$

With the current sales commissions program:

$$\text{Desired units} = \frac{\$595,000 + \dfrac{\$700,000}{(1 - 0.30)}}{\$1,500 - \$1,138} = 4,406 \text{ units}$$

Without the current sales commissions program:

$$\text{Desired units} = \frac{\$695,000 + \dfrac{\$700,000}{(1 - 0.30)}}{\$1,500 - \$1,088} = 4,114 \text{ units}$$

The elimination of the sales commission program would decrease the desired CR1 volume from 4,406 units to 4,114 units. As a result, Fezzari would be able to sell 292 fewer CR1s at the same price and still attain the same desired after-tax net income.

Break-Even Analysis and Multiple Products

As indicated previously, we must assume in break-even analysis that only one product is involved or that the product mix (the ratio of units of each product sold to the total units sold) is constant. Break-even sales can be computed for a sales mix of two or more products by calculating the weighted average unit contribution margin.

Assume that a company sells three units of product A for every unit of B (note that this information indicates that the sales mix is 75% A and 25% B) and has fixed costs of $88,000. Also assume the following relationships between selling price and variable costs:

	Product A	Product B
Unit selling price.	$14.00	$7.00
Less: Unit variable cost	8.00	3.00
Unit contribution margin.	$ 6.00	$4.00

The weighted average unit contribution margin can be calculated as follows:

Product A: $6.00 × 0.75 =	$4.50
Product B: $4.00 × 0.25 =	1.00
Weighted average unit contribution margin	$5.50

The break-even volume can then be calculated:

$$\text{Break-even units} = \frac{\text{Total fixed cost}}{\text{Unit contribution margin}}$$

$$= \frac{\$88,000}{\$5.50}$$

$$= 16,000 \text{ units}$$

The 16,000 units include units of A and units of B. The exact mix and related contribution margin are calculated as illustrated in **Exhibit 6-18**.

Exhibit 6-18	**Multiple Product Break-Even Analysis**			
Product	**Product Mix**	**Units Sold**	**Unit Contribution Margin**	**Total Contribution Margin**
A.	0.75	12,000	$6.00	$72,000
B.	0.25	4,000	$4.00	16,000
Total		16,000		$88,000

These concepts could be applied to any product mix or number of products.

TAKEAWAY 6.3

A change in the product mix will usually change the break-even point, because each product typically has a unique contribution margin.

Cost-Volume-Profit Analysis for Retail Businesses

SERVICE AND MERCHANDISING

Most retailing industries have developed relationships between product costs and retail price that need to be maintained in order to be profitable. Each segment of each industry has its own ideal relationship. For example, a men's clothing store would typically have a lower ratio of retail price to product cost than a custom tailor, whereas a downhill ski shop would typically have a higher ratio than a general sports retail store.

Many restaurants strive to have the price of their meals set at 2.5 times the cost of the food used in the meal. Portion control is a key element in applying this ratio. For each food item or ingredient to be included in one portion or meal, a standard quantity (weight or volume) must be established. This standard recipe can be used to determine the food cost of a meal. For example, if a restaurant serves 8 ounces of ingredient A (costing 35 cents per ounce) plus 2 ounces of ingredient B (costing 25 cents per ounce), this would yield a food cost of $3.30 per portion and a target price of $8.25 (based on the 2.5 rule).

Retail establishments also have varying staffing needs. The number of employees on duty will change, for example, depending on the time of day. For instance, assume Joe's Food Shack, located on a southern California beach, has one cook and one cashier working from 11:00 AM to 2:00 PM, two cooks and three cashiers working from 2:00 PM to 5:00 PM, and two cooks and two cashiers working from 5:00 PM to 9:00 PM. The number and type of employees on duty must be predetermined. Therefore, the cost to employ these servers and cooks is fixed over a given shift. They are typically paid the same amount regardless of how many meals are served. Customer tips (which are not an expense of the company) would vary, depending in part on the number of meals served.

These concepts should be incorporated in cost-volume-profit analysis for a restaurant. Assume Joe's Food Shack serves only three food choices: hamburgers, hot dogs, and nachos, with food costs per item of $5.00, $4.00, and $3.00, respectively. Because Joe's is the only establishment on the entire beach, Joe's can charge monopoly prices for its food items. Using the 2.5 ratio, the related prices are $12.50, $10.00, and $7.50, respectively. If 20% of the items sold are hamburgers, 50% are hot dogs, and 30% are nachos, then the average revenue per food item sold would be $9.75 and the average food cost would be $3.90, as illustrated in **Exhibit 6-19**.

Exhibit 6-19	Cost and Pricing Analysis for Joe's Food Shack				
Food Type	Proportion	Cost per Unit	Weighted Average Cost	Price per Unit	Weighted Average Price
Hamburger	20%	$5.00	$1.00	$12.50	$2.50
Hot dog	50%	4.00	2.00	10.00	5.00
Nachos	30%	3.00	0.90	7.50	2.25
Total			$3.90		$9.75

The weighted average unit contribution margin, therefore, is $9.75 − $3.90 = $5.85.

If the total fixed costs, including personnel, are $64,350 for a typical 30-day month when the restaurant is open every day for the scheduled hours, the break-even volume would be calculated as follows:

$$\frac{\$64,350}{\$5.85} = \textbf{11,000 food items per month}$$

Thus, this sales mix is comprised of 2,200 hamburgers (11,000 × 0.20), 5,500 hot dogs (11,000 × 0.50), and 3,300 nachos (11,000 × 0.30),

Management Perspective on Cost Analysis	ACCOUNTING IN PRACTICE

Managing costs is a prevailing concern for managers. The concepts introduced in this chapter underlie most efforts to analyze and project cost in a variety of decision situations. In practice, because projections of future costs are subject to many complicating factors, for most companies they are *estimates of probable costs* rather than precise determinations. Properly used—with full recognition of their limitations—cost behavior analyses can be highly useful to management.

SERVICE INDUSTRY IN FOCUS

Environmental Business Consultants (EBC) has two offices, one in northern California and one in southern California. EBC provides three basic services to its clients: rate reviews, contract procurement and negotiations, and operational studies. EBC management wants to determine how many projects of each service would need to be performed in 2015 to achieve a before-tax profit of $650,000. EBC managers have gathered the following information from 2013 for the analysis.

The proportion of projects done in each office was as follows:

	Northern California	Southern California
Rate reviews.................	30%	50%
Contract procurements	60%	30%
Operational studies	10%	20%

The average contribution margin for each project type was as follows:

	Northern California	Southern California
Rate reviews.................	$ 5,100	$24,124
Contract procurements	28,000	37,000
Operational studies	10,035	20,000

EBC has budgeted 2015 fixed expenses to be $2,251,159 and $644,341 in the northern and southern California offices, respectively.

Required

1. How many projects of each type must EBC perform in the northern California office if managers expect the office to generate $450,000 of the desired total income?

2. How many projects of each type must EBC perform in the southern California office if managers expect the office to generate $200,000 of the desired total income?

Solution

1. The weighted average contribution margin for the northern California office is:

$ 5,100 × 0.30 =	$ 1,530
$28,000 × 0.60 =	16,800
$10,035 × 0.10 =	1,004
Weighted average contribution margin	$19,334

The number of total projects needed is:

$$\textbf{Needed projects} = \frac{\$2,251,159 + \$450,000}{\$19,334}$$

$$= \textbf{140 projects (rounded)}$$

The number of projects by type is:

Rate reviews............	(140 × 0.30)	42
Contract procurements ...	(140 × 0.60)	84
Operational studies	(140 × 0.10)	14

2. The weighted average contribution margin for the southern California office is:

$24,124 × 0.50 =	$12,062
$37,000 × 0.30 =	11,100
$20,000 × 0.20 =	4,000
Weighted average contribution margin	$27,162

The number of total projects needed is:

$$\textbf{Needed projects} = \frac{\$644,341 + \$200,000}{\$27,162}$$

$$= \textbf{31 projects (rounded)}$$

The number of projects by type is:

Rate reviews............	(31 × 0.50)	16 (rounded)
Contract procurements ...	(31 × 0.30)	9 (rounded)
Operational studies	(31 × 0.20)	6 (rounded)

COMPREHENSIVE PROBLEM

Maricopa Corporation has developed the budget for its next year of operations. The budget included the following:

Sales of 100,000 units at $5	
Units sold will equal units produced	
Variable costs for 100,000 units:	
Direct material....................	$125,000
Direct labor......................	100,000
Variable overhead.................	30,000
Selling and administrative expense ...	45,000
Total fixed cost....................	120,000
Income tax rate of 30%	

Required

a. What is Maricopa's break-even point, in units and in dollars, for next year?

b. Demonstrate that the unit amount reconciles with the dollar amount.

c. What amount of sales revenue would Maricopa need to realize next year in order to generate a net income of $63,000 after tax?

d. Demonstrate the correctness of the calculations in requirement (c) by constructing an income statement.

Solution

a. Variable costs:

Direct material	$125,000
Direct labor.	100,000
Variable overhead.	30,000
Selling and administrative	45,000
Total variable cost at 100,000 units . . .	$300,000

$$\$300,000 \,/\, 100,000 \text{ units } = \$3 \text{ per unit}$$

$$\text{Unit contribution margin } = \$5 - \$3 = \$2$$

$$\text{Contribution margin ratio } = \frac{\$2}{\$5} = 0.4$$

$$\text{Break-even units} = \frac{\text{Total fixed cost}}{\text{Unit contribution margin}}$$
$$= \frac{\$120,000}{\$2}$$
$$= 60,000 \text{ units}$$

$$\text{Break-even sales} = \frac{\text{Total fixed cost}}{\text{Contribution margin ratio}}$$
$$= \frac{\$120,000}{0.4}$$
$$= \$300,000$$

b. 60,000 units $\times$ \$5 unit selling price = \$300,000

c.
$$\text{Desired sales} = \frac{\text{Total fixed cost} + \dfrac{\text{Net income}}{1 - \text{Income tax}}}{\text{Contribution margin ratio}}$$

$$= \frac{\$120,000 + \dfrac{\$63,000}{1 - 0.3}}{0.4}$$

$$= \$525,000$$

d.

Sales.	$525,000
Variable cost ([1 − 0.4] × $525,000) . . .	315,000
Contribution margin	$210,000
Fixed cost.	120,000
Net income before income tax.	$ 90,000
Income tax at 30%.	27,000
Net income.	$ 63,000

SUMMARY OF LEARNING OBJECTIVES

LO1 **Develop an understanding of how specific types of costs change in response to volume changes. (p. 198)**

- For meaningful managerial analysis, costs must be related to some measure of business activity or cost driver. A critical aspect is that the activity measure used must have a logical causal relation with costs, and the quantity of the activity must be highly correlated with the level of costs.

- One of the most useful tools for analyzing the relationship between changes in cost and volume is the *cost-volume graph.* Such graphs typically plot total costs on the vertical axis and either volume or activity level on the horizontal axis. Cost-volume graphs are particularly valuable when available cost-volume data are plotted on the same graph and other cost-volume relationships are estimated by fitting a line to the known points.

- The behavior of total cost in response to volume changes is divided into three basic categories within a relevant range:
  - ❏ Variable, which responds proportionately, with zero cost at zero volume
  - ❏ Fixed, which is constant
  - ❏ Mixed, which responds, but less than proportionately, due to the fixed component
- Total cost for most entities is best represented by the mixed cost pattern.

Define the concept of *relevant range.* (p. 201)   LO2

- We can assume linearity of cost because it is approximately true within the range of volume relevant to the analysis.
- The relevant range is the range of activity over which the behavior of a cost behaves consistently.
- Within the relevant range, *per-unit* costs behave as follows when volume is increased:
  - ❏ Variable costs remain constant.
  - ❏ Fixed costs decrease proportionately.
  - ❏ Variable plus fixed cost decreases, but not proportionately.

Outline the approach to developing cost formulas. (p. 202)   LO3

- In order to perform CVP analysis to make better decisions, total costs need to be broken into fixed and variable components. We illustrate three approaches for accomplishing this: (1) the scattergraph method, (2) the high-low method, and (3) the least squares regression method.
- The scattergraph method entails plotting the observed cost at several levels of volume on a graph, then drawing a line that places approximately half of the dots above and half below the line.
- The high-low method is relatively simple and compares costs at the highest and lowest levels of activity for which representative cost data are available. A line is then drawn between the highest- and lowest-volume data points.
- The least squares regression method is a statistical tool that uses all of the data points to separate a mixed cost into its variable and fixed components. A regression line is fitted to the data points so that the distance from each point to the line is minimized for all points.
- A general formula for planning total cost is as follows: Total cost = Total fixed cost + (Variable cost per unit $\times$ Number of units).

Present a discussion of and a formula for calculating the break-even point. (p. 207)   LO4

- The break-even point (where Revenues = Costs) can be derived by graph, formula, or contribution margin analysis.
- Assumptions underlying break-even analysis include the following:
  - ❏ Total fixed cost and per-unit variable cost are constant over the entire relevant range.
  - ❏ Selling price per unit remains the same regardless of the volume of sales.
  - ❏ When more than one product is involved and sales volume varies, each product's percentage of total sales (sales mix) does not change.

Define *contribution margin* and *contribution margin ratio* and present alternate break-even formulas   LO5
and examples of their application. (p. 209)

- Contribution margin = Revenue − Variable cost

- Contribution margin ratio = $\dfrac{\text{Contribution margin}}{\text{Sales}}$

  or

- Contribution margin ratio = $\dfrac{\text{Unit contribution margin}}{\text{Unit selling price}}$

■ Formulas used in break-even analysis include the following:

❏ $\text{Break-even units} = \dfrac{\text{Total fixed cost}}{\text{Unit contribution margin}}$

❏ $\text{Break-even sales} = \dfrac{\text{Total fixed cost}}{\text{Contribution margin ratio}}$

LO6 **Discuss approaches to planning net income using cost-volume-profit analyses. (p. 211)**

■ Formulas used in planning net income include the following:

❏ Desired sales = Total variable cost + Total fixed cost + Desired net income

❏ $\text{Desired units} = \dfrac{\text{Total fixed cost} + \text{Desired net income}}{\text{Unit contribution margin}}$

❏ $\text{Desired sales} = \dfrac{\text{Total fixed cost} + \text{Desired net income}}{\text{Contribution margin ratio}}$

■ Often management wants to develop plans using net income after tax instead of net income. The relationship between net income before income tax and net after-tax income is demonstrated by the following formula:

❏ $\text{Net income before income tax} = \dfrac{\text{Net after-tax income}}{1 - \text{Income tax rate}}$

■ Margin of safety = Actual sales − Break-even sales
■ One measure of a firm's relative level of fixed costs is operating leverage. Operating leverage is computed as follows:

❏ $\text{Operating leverage} = \dfrac{\text{Contribution margin}}{\text{Net operating income}}$

■ Break-even and net income planning computations involving multiple products incorporate the concept of weighted average unit contribution margin.

KEY TERMS

Break-even point (p. 207)	**Cost-volume-profit (CVP)** **analysis** (p. 198)	**Relevant range** (p. 201)
Contribution margin (p. 209)		**Total variable costs** (p. 200)
Contribution margin **ratio** (p. 210)	**Fixed costs** (p. 200)	**Variable operating income** **statement** (p. 209)
	Margin of safety (p. 214)	
Cost behavior analysis (p. 198)	**Mixed costs** (p. 201)	
Cost-volume graph (p. 199)	**Operating leverage** (p. 214)	

Assignments with the ⬤ logo in the margin are available in _{my}BusinessCourse.
See the Preface of the book for details.

SELF-STUDY QUESTIONS

(Answers to Self-Study Questions are at the end of this chapter.)

LO2 1. **When moving from the low end to the high end of a relevant range, straight-line depreciation expense per unit**
   a. Increases.
   b. Decreases.
   c. Remains the same.
   d. Changes unpredictably.

2. **In a typical cost formula**   **LO3**
   a. Fixed costs are per unit and variable costs are per unit.
   b. Fixed costs are per unit and variable costs are in total.
   c. Fixed costs are in total and variable costs are in total.
   d. Fixed costs are in total and variable costs are per unit.

3. **At the break-even point**   **LO4**
   a. Contribution margin = fixed costs.
   b. Variable costs = fixed costs.
   c. Sales = contribution margin.
   d. Contribution margin = 0.

4. **Contribution margin ratio is**   **LO5**
   a. Unit sales price/unit contribution margin.
   b. I/margin of safety.
   c. Total contribution margin/sales.
   d. Variable cost/fixed cost.

5. **Net income before income tax is**   **LO6**
   a. Net income/(1 – income tax rate).
   b. Income tax rate/net income.
   c. Net income + contribution margin.
   d. Net income/income tax rate.

QUESTIONS

1. Define the terms *cost behavior* and *relevant range*.   **LO1, 2**

2. Identify some common activity bases in terms of which the volume of a manufacturing operation might be   **LO1**
    stated. What general criterion might be used in choosing an activity base?

3. Name and define briefly the three most widely recognized cost behavior patterns.   **LO1**

4. Explain (a) how a mixed cost can be considered "partly fixed and partly variable," and (b) why a firm's   **LO1, 3**
    total cost is best represented by the mixed cost pattern.

5. Briefly describe the two most straightforward techniques for dividing a mixed cost into its fixed and vari-   **LO3**
    able components.

6. "Actual costs often behave in a nonlinear fashion. Therefore, assumptions of linearity invalidate most cost   **LO2**
    behavior analyses." Do you agree or disagree with this statement? Briefly defend your position.

7. Describe how fixed and variable costs per unit respond to volume increases.   **LO1, 3**

8. Present a formula based on units for planning total cost, and explain how mixed costs are incorporated into   **LO3**
    the formula.

9. Define and briefly explain three approaches to break-even analysis.   **LO4**

10. Patrick's Bakery Shop has fixed costs per month of $3,600, and variable costs are 55% of sales. What   **LO4**
    amount of monthly sales allows the shop to break even?

11. Quality Car Wash has fixed costs per month of $16,800, and variable costs are 20% of sales. The average   **LO4**
    amount collected per car washed during the past year has been $5. How many cars must be washed per
    month to break even?

12. You have graphed the cost-volume-profit relationships for a company on a break-even chart after being   **LO4**
    informed of certain assumptions. Explain how the lines on the chart would change if (a) fixed costs in-
    creased over the entire range of activity, (b) selling price per unit decreased, and (c) variable costs per unit
    increased.

13. Define *contribution margin*. Is it best expressed as a total amount or as a per-unit amount? In what way is   **LO5**
    the term descriptive of the concept it represents?

14. Explain the approach to break-even analysis that is used for a mix of two or more products.   **LO6**

15. Explain how break-even formulas can provide income-planning analyses.   **LO6**

16. In planning net income, how can (post tax) net income be incorporated into the planning formula?   **LO6**

EXERCISES—SET A

LO1

SERVICE AND
MERCHANDISING

E6-1A. Cost-Volume Graphs Set up a cost-volume graph. Volume should range from zero to 24,000 units (in 4,000-unit increments), and cost should range from zero to $24,000 (in $4,000 increments). Plot each of the following groups of cost data using different marks for each group. After completing the graph, indicate the type of cost behavior exhibited by each group.

Volume (applicable to each group)	Group A Costs	Group B Costs	Group C Costs
2,000	$ 6,600	$ 2,400	$8,000
6,000	9,800	7,000	8,000
10,000	13,000	12,000	8,000
20,000	21,000	24,000	8,000

LO3

SERVICE AND
MERCHANDISING

E6-2A. High-Low Method Apply the high-low method of cost analysis to the three cost data groups in E6-1A. What cost behavior patterns are apparent? Express each as a cost formula.

LO2, 3

MBC

E6-3A. Relevant Range and High-Low Method The following selected data relate to the major cost categories experienced by Shaw Company at varying levels of operating volumes. Assuming that all operating volumes are within the relevant range, calculate the appropriate costs in each column in which blanks appear.

	Total Cost (@ 3,000 units)	Total Cost (@ 4,000 units)	Variable Cost per Unit	Total Fixed Cost	Total Cost (@ 5,000 units)
Direct labor (variable)	$60,000	$80,000	_____	_____	_____
Factory supervision (semivariable). . .	50,000	65,000	_____	_____	_____
Factory depreciation (fixed)	30,000	30,000	_____	_____	_____

LO3

SERVICE AND
MERCHANDISING

MBC

E6-4A. Total Cost Formula Davis Company has analyzed its overhead costs and derived a general formula for their behavior: $60,000 + $14 per direct labor hour employed. The company expects to use 50,000 direct labor hours during the next accounting period. What overhead rate per direct labor hour should be applied to jobs worked during the period?

LO4

E6-5A. Break-Even Chart Set up a break-even chart similar to the one in **Exhibit 6-12** with proportional scales from zero to $72,000 (in $12,000 increments) on the vertical axis and from zero to 12,000 units of production (in 2,000-unit increments) on the horizontal axis. Prepare the break-even chart for Morton Company, assuming total fixed costs of $18,000 and unit selling price and unit variable cost for the company's one product of $6 and $4, respectively. Label the total revenue line and the total cost line. Indicate the break-even point in units and dollars.

LO6

MBC

E6-6A. Net Income Planning Nolden Company has charged a selling price of $20 per unit, incurred variable costs of $14 per unit, and total fixed costs of $90,000. What unit sales volume is necessary to earn the following related amounts of net income before income tax? (a) $18,000; (b) $27,000; or (c) equal to 20% of sales revenue.

LO4, 5, 6

MBC

E6-7A. Cost-Volume Profit Analysis Hailstorm Company sells a single product for $22 per unit. Variable costs are $14 per unit and fixed costs are $60,000 at an operating level of 7,000 to 12,000 units.
  a. What is Hailstorm Company's break-even point in units?
  b. How many units must be sold to earn $12,000 before income tax?
  c. How many units must be sold to earn $13,000 after income tax, assuming a 35% tax rate?

LO6

MBC

E6-8A. Break-Even with Multiple Products Warner Company has $228,000 of total fixed costs and sells products A and B with a product mix of 40% A and 60% B. Selling prices and variable costs for A and B result in contribution margins per unit of $10 and $6, respectively. Compute the break-even point.

LO1

MBC

E6-9A. Cost Patterns The graphs below represent approximations of cost behavior patterns. The horizontal axis of each graph represents units and the vertical axis represents dollars of total cost.

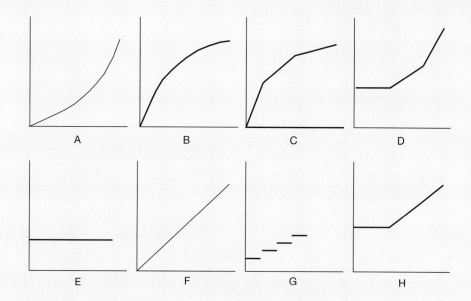

Select the graph that best matches each of the situations described below. Each graph may be selected more than once.

a. Straight-line depreciation of a factory building.

b. Utility bill for electricity that includes a fixed charge per month plus a constant usage rate per hour for hours in excess of 100.

c. Cost of microchip incorporated into a product.

d. Labor cost of machine operators who become more productive as they gain experience.

e. Water bill that includes a flat fee for the first 10,000 gallons used plus an increasing usage charge for each additional 10,000 gallons used.

f. Cost of factory supplies when increasing quantities bring cost discounts as each price break level is attained.

g. Salaries of quality inspectors when one additional inspector is hired for each 20,000 units produced.

h. Cost of an advertising campaign.

EXERCISES—SET B

E6-1B. **High-Low Method** The highest and lowest levels of activity for the Denton Company were 54,000 direct labor hours and 36,000 direct labor hours, respectively. If maintenance costs were $320,000 at the 54,000-hour level and $230,000 at the 36,000-hour level, what cost might we expect at an operating level of 40,000 direct labor hours?

LO3

SERVICE AND
MERCHANDISING

E6-2B. **High-Low Method** During the past year, Cutler, Inc., operated within the relevant range of its fixed costs. Monthly production volume during the year ranged from 40,000 to 60,000 units of product and corresponding total manufacturing costs ranged from $4.00 to $3.80 per unit. Determine the total cost behavior pattern experienced by Cutler, Inc.

LO3

E6-3B. **Relevant Range and High-Low Method** The following selected data relate to the major cost categories experienced by Sterling Company at varying levels of operating volumes. Assuming that all operating volumes are within the relevant range, calculate the appropriate costs in each column in which blanks appear:

LO2, 3

	Total Cost (@ 5,000 units)	Total Cost (@ 6,000 units)	Variable Cost per Unit	Total Fixed Cost	Total Cost (@ 7,000 units)
Direct labor (variable)	$60,000	$72,000	—	—	—
Factory supervision (semivariable). . .	20,000	22,000	—	—	—
Factory depreciation (fixed)	18,000	18,000	—	—	—

LO3   E6-4B.   **Cost Formula** The following amounts of various cost categories are experienced by Columbia Factories in producing and selling its only product:

Direct material	$8 per unit of product
Direct labor.	$10 per direct labor hour*
Manufacturing overhead	$12,000 + $4 per direct labor hour
Selling expenses	$14,000 + $3 per unit of product
Administrative.	$7,000 + $0.50 per unit of product

*Each unit of product requires one-half direct labor hour.

Combine the various cost factors into a general total cost formula for Columbia Factories and determine the total cost of producing and selling 20,000 units.

LO4   E6-5B.   **Break-Even Calculations** Compute the break-even point in units for each of the following independent situations:

	Unit Selling Price	Unit Variable Cost	Total Fixed Cost
a.	$10	$7	$ 90,000
b.	12	9	144,000
c.	5	3	54,000

Confirm each answer using contribution margin ratio analysis.

LO6   E6-6B.   **Net Income Planning** Holland Corporation earned an after-tax net income of $120,000 last year. Fixed costs were $600,000. The selling price per unit of its product was $120, of which $50 was a contribution to fixed cost and net income. The income tax rate was 40%.

  a.   How many units of product were sold last year?
  b.   What was the break-even point in units last year?
  c.   The company wishes to increase its after-tax net income by 20% this year. If selling prices and the income tax rate remain unchanged, how many units must be sold?

LO6   E6-7B.   **Cost-Volume-Profit Analysis** Gannon Company sells a single product for $15 per unit. Variable costs are $10 per unit and fixed costs are $90,000 at an operating level of 16,000 to 30,000 units.
  a.   What is Gannon Company's break-even point in units?
  b.   How many units must be sold to earn $20,000 before income tax?
  c.   How many units must be sold to earn $30,000 after income tax, assuming a 40% tax rate?

LO6   E6-8B.   **Multiple Product Break-Even Analysis** Wynn Company has $142,000 total fixed cost and sells products A and B with a product mix of 70% A and 30% B. Selling prices and variable costs for A and B result in contribution margins per unit of $8 and $5, respectively. Compute the break-even point.

LO1   E6-9B.   **Cost Patterns** The following graph depicts cost-volume relationships for Tallmadge Company:

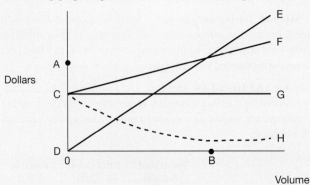

Choose a labeled point *or* line on the graph that *best* represents the behavior of each of the following items as operating volume is increased. Answers may be the same for more than one item. Answer each item independently.

a. Total sales revenue.
b. Total costs.
c. Total variable costs.
d. Total fixed costs.
e. Total mixed cost.
f. Break-even point.

PROBLEMS—SET A

P6-1A. Net Income Planning Selected operating data for Oakbrook Company in four independent situations are shown below.

LO4, 5

SERVICE AND
MERCHANDISING

	A	B	C	D
Sales.	$300,000	$ c.	$ e.	$260,000
Variable expense	$ a.	$91,000	$ f.	$ g.
Fixed expense	$ b.	$62,000	$43,200	$ 89,000
Net income before tax (loss).	$ 20,000	$15,000	$28,800	$ (11,000)
Units sold	30,000	d.		
Unit contribution margin.	$ 5.20	$ 7.00		
Contribution margin ratio			0.4	h.

Required
Fill in the blanks for each independent situation. Show your calculations.

P6-2A. Graphing Mixed Cost During a recent six-month period, Wade Corporation had the following monthly production volume and total monthly maintenance expense:

LO1, 2, 3

	Units Produced	Maintenance Expense
March	21,000	$140,000
April	15,000	112,000
May.	30,000	184,000
June	27,000	172,000
July.	35,000	208,000
August	25,000	160,000

Required
Assume that all volumes are in the relevant range.

a. Explain why the data indicate that the maintenance expense is neither a fixed nor a variable expense.
b. Construct a graph similar to the one in **Exhibit 6-7** and plot the maintenance expense data.
c. Fit a line (by sight) to the cost observation points and estimate the cost formula.
d. Confirm your answer in requirement (c) with high-low analysis.

P6-3A. Cost Formulas Shorewood Manufacturing produces a single product requiring the following direct material and direct labor:

LO2, 3, 6

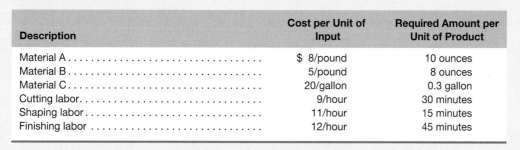

Description	Cost per Unit of Input	Required Amount per Unit of Product
Material A	$ 8/pound	10 ounces
Material B	5/pound	8 ounces
Material C	20/gallon	0.3 gallon
Cutting labor.	9/hour	30 minutes
Shaping labor	11/hour	15 minutes
Finishing labor	12/hour	45 minutes

Manufacturing overhead consists of indirect material, $0.60 per unit of product; indirect labor, $1,000 per month plus $0.70 per unit of product; factory maintenance, $14,000 per year plus $0.55 per unit of product; factory depreciation, $15,000 per year; and annual factory property taxes, $8,000. Selling and administrative expenses include the salaries of a sales manager, $30,000 per year; an office manager, $18,000 per year; and two salespersons, each of whom is paid a base salary of $11,000 per year and a commission of $3 per unit sold. Advertising and promotion of the product are done through a year-round media package program costing $1,000 per week.

Required

a. Analyze all cost and expense factors to determine a general formula (based on units of production) for total cost.

b. Assuming a relevant range of 10,000 to 20,000 units, what is the estimated unit cost for producing and selling 10,000 units? 20,000 units? Explain the variation in unit cost at the two levels of production.

c. If 15,000 units are produced and sold in a year, what selling price results in a net income before income tax of $60,000?

LO2, 3 **P6-4A.** **High-Low and Cost Formula** Harrison Company has accumulated the following total manufacturing overhead costs for two levels of activity (within the relevant range):

	Low	High
Activity (direct labor hours)...	80,000	120,000
Total manufacturing overhead......................................	$468,000	$604,000

The total overhead cost includes variable, fixed, and mixed costs. At 120,000 direct labor hours, the total cost breakdown is as follows:

Variable cost..	$264,000
Fixed cost..	160,000
Semi-mixed cost	180,000

Required

a. Using the high-low method of cost analysis, determine the variable portion of the semi-variable cost per direct labor hour. Determine the total fixed cost component of the mixed cost.

b. What should the total planned overhead cost be at 100,000 direct labor hours?

LO1, 2, 3 **P6-5A.** **Cost Formula** Princeton Manufacturing Company summarizes the following total cost data for the month of March. Princeton has a normal capacity per month of 25,000 units of product that sell for $40 each. For the foreseeable future, sales volume should equal normal capacity of production.

Direct material	$295,000
Direct labor..	165,000
Variable overhead..	85,000
Fixed overhead (Note 1)..	140,000
Selling expense (Note 2)..	80,000
Administrative expense (fixed)	56,000
	$821,000

Notes:

1. Beyond normal capacity, fixed overhead cost increases $6,350 for each 1,000 units *or fraction thereof until* a maximum capacity of 30,000 units is reached.

2. Selling expenses are a 5% sales commission plus shipping costs of $1.20 per unit.

Required

a. Using the information available, prepare a formula to estimate Princeton's total cost at various production volumes up to normal capacity.

b. Prove your answer in requirement (a) relative to the total cost figure for 25,000 units.

c. Calculate the planned total cost at 20,000 units, and explain why total cost did not decrease in proportion to the reduced volume.

d. If Princeton were operating at normal capacity and accepted an order for 500 more units, what would it have to charge for the order to earn a net income before income tax of $8 per unit on the new sale?

P6-6A.   Net Income Planning   Superior Corporation sells a single product for $60 per unit, of which $36 is contribution margin. Fixed costs total $72,000 and net income before income tax is $28,800.

LO4, 5, 6

SERVICE AND MERCHANDISING

MBC

Required
Determine the following (show key computations):

a. The present sales volume in dollars.
b. The break-even point in units.
c. The sales volume in units necessary to attain a net income before income tax of $39,600.
d. The sales volume in units necessary to attain a net income before income tax equal to 20% of sales revenue.
e. The sales volume in units necessary to attain an after-tax net income of $43,200 if the tax rate is 40%.

P6-7A.   Break-Even and Net Income Planning   The controller of Grafton Company is preparing data for a conference call concerning certain *independent* aspects of its operations.   LO4, 5, 6

Required
Prepare answers to the following questions for the controller:

a. Total fixed cost is $1,440,000 and a unit of product is sold for $12 in excess of its unit variable cost. What is the break-even in units?
b. The company will sell 60,000 units of product—each having a unit variable cost of $22—at a price that will enable the product to absorb $600,000 of fixed cost. What minimum unit sales price must be charged to break even?
c. Net income before income tax of $320,000 is desired after covering $1,200,000 of fixed costs. What minimum contribution margin ratio must be maintained if total sales revenue is to be $3,800,000?
d. Net income before income tax is 10% of sales revenue, the contribution margin ratio is 30%, and the break-even dollar sales is $640,000. What is the amount of total revenue?
e. Fixed costs total $1,000,000, the variable cost per unit is $30, and selling price per unit is $80. What dollar sales volume will generate an after-tax net income of $84,000 when the income tax rate is 40%?

P6-8A.   Break-Even and Net Income Planning   Paulson Company has recently leased facilities for the manufacture of a new product. Based on studies made by its accounting personnel, the following data are available: LO4, 5, 6
   Estimated annual sales: 40,000 units.

Estimated Costs	Amount	Unit Cost
Direct material	$ 696,000	$17.40
Direct labor	584,000	14.60
Manufacturing overhead	376,000	9.40
Administrative expenses	187,200	4.68
	$1,843,200	$46.08

Selling expenses are expected to be 10% of sales, and the selling price is $64 per unit. Ignore income tax in this problem.

Required
a. Compute a break-even point in dollars and in units. Assume that manufacturing overhead and administrative expenses are fixed but that other costs are variable.
b. What would net income before income tax be if 30,000 units were sold?
c. How many units must be sold to earn a net income before income tax of 10% of sales?

LO4, 5, 6 **P6-9A.** **Multiple Product Break-Even and Net Income Planning** Grand Company manufactures and sells the following three products:

	Economy	Standard	Deluxe
Unit sales	10,000	6,000	4,000
Unit sales price.	$48	$56	$68
Unit variable cost	$30	$32	$36

Required

Assume that total fixed cost is $339,000.

a. Compute the net income before income tax based on the sales volumes shown above.

b. Compute the break-even point in total dollars of revenue and in units for each product.

c. Prove your break-even calculations by computing the total contribution margin related to your answer in requirement (b).

PROBLEMS—SET B

LO4, 5 **P6-1B.** **Net Income Planning** Selected operating data for Verona Company in four independent situations are shown below.

	A	B	C	D
Sales.	$320,000	$ c.	$ e.	$280,000
Variable expense	$ a.	$48,000	$ f.	$ g.
Fixed expense	$ b.	$56,000	$240,000	$120,000
Net income before tax	$ 40,000	$16,000	$ 96,000	$ (8,000)
Units sold	7,000	d.		
Unit contribution margin.	$ 20	$ 9		
Contribution margin ratio			0.70	h.

Required

Fill in the blanks for each independent situation. Show your calculations.

LO1, 2, 3 **P6-2B.** **Graphing Mixed Cost** During the past operating year, Davenport Corporation had the following monthly volume of production and total monthly maintenance expense:

	Units Produced	Maintenance Expense		Units Produced	Maintenance Expense
January.	120,000	$22,400	July	124,000	$22,800
February	144,000	25,400	August	154,000	26,600
March	156,000	26,800	September	128,000	23,400
April	130,000	23,200	October	160,000	27,200
May.	140,000	25,000	November.	152,000	26,400
June	150,000	26,400	December.	156,000	26,800

Required

Assume that all volumes are in the relevant range.

a. Explain why the data indicate that the maintenance expense is neither a fixed nor a variable expense.

b. Construct a graph similar to the one in **Exhibit 6-7** and plot the maintenance expense data.

c. Fit a line (by sight) to the cost observation points, and estimate the cost formula.

d. Confirm your answer in requirement (c) with high-low analysis.

LO2, 3, 6 **P6-3B.** **Cost Formulas** Colonial Manufacturing produces a single product requiring the following direct material and direct labor:

Description	Cost per Unit of Input	Required Amount per Unit of Product
Material A.	$ 9/pound	24 ounces
Material B.	6/pound	12 ounces
Material C.	12/gallon	0.5 gallon
Cutting labor.	10/hour	45 minutes
Shaping labor.	12/hour	15 minutes
Finishing labor	11/hour	30 minutes

Manufacturing overhead consists of indirect materials, $0.80 per unit of product; indirect labor, $10,000 per year plus $1.20 per unit of product; factory maintenance, $1,000 per month plus $0.60 per unit of product; factory depreciation, $22,000 per year; and annual factory property taxes, $20,000. Selling and administrative expenses include the salaries of a sales manager, $30,000 per year, an office manager, $18,000 per year, and two salespersons, each of whom is paid a base salary of $12,000 per year and a commission of $4 per unit sold. Advertising and promotion of the product are done through a year-round media package program costing $600 per week.

Required
a. Analyze all cost and expense factors to determine a general formula (based on units of production) for total cost.
b. Assuming a relevant range of 20,000 to 40,000 units, what is the estimated unit cost for producing and selling 20,000 units? 40,000 units? Explain the variation in unit cost at the two levels of production
c. If 35,000 units are produced and sold in a year, what selling price results in a net income before taxes of $56,800?

P6-4B. High-Low and Cost Formula Adams Company has accumulated the following total manufacturing overhead costs for two levels of activity (within the relevant range): LO2, 3

	Low	High
Activity (direct labor hours).	30,000	50,000
Total manufacturing overhead	$270,000	$362,000

The total overhead cost includes variable, fixed, and mixed costs. At 50,000 direct labor hours, the total cost breakdown is as follows:

Variable cost.	$200,000
Fixed cost.	90,000
Semi-variable cost	72,000

Required
a. Using the high-low method of cost analysis, determine the variable portion of the mixed cost per direct labor hour. Determine the total fixed cost component of the mixed cost.
b. What should the total planned overhead cost be at 40,000 direct labor hours?

P6-5B. Cost Formula The following total cost data are for Phoenix Manufacturing Company, which has a normal capacity per period of 40,000 units of product that sell for $60 each. For the foreseeable future, sales volume should equal normal capacity of production. LO1, 2, 3

Direct material	$ 640,000
Direct labor.	400,000
Variable overhead.	200,000
Fixed overhead (Note 1).	216,000
Selling expense (Note 2).	280,000
Administrative expense (fixed)	88,000
	$1,824,000

Notes:

1. Beyond normal capacity, fixed overhead cost increases $6,240 for each 2,000 units *or fraction thereof* until a maximum capacity of 50,000 units is reached.
2. Selling expenses are a 10% sales commission plus shipping costs of $1 per unit.

Required

a. Using the information available, prepare a formula to estimate Phoenix's total cost at various production volumes up to normal capacity.
b. Prove your answer in requirement (a) against the above total cost figure at 40,000 units.
c. Calculate the planned total cost at 30,000 units, and explain why total cost did not decrease in proportion to the reduced volume.
d. If Phoenix were operating at normal capacity and accepted an order for 600 more units, what would it have to charge for the order to earn a net income before tax of $8 per unit on the new sale?

LO4, 5, 6 **P6-6B.** **Net Income Planning** Midvale Corporation sells a single product for $100 per unit, of which $40 is contribution margin. Total fixed cost is $120,000, and net income before income tax is $48,000.

Required

Determine the following (show key computations):

a. The present sales volume in dollars.
b. The break-even point in units.
c. The sales volume in units necessary to attain a net income before income tax of $60,000.
d. The sales volume in units necessary to attain a net income before income tax equal to 10% of sales revenue.
e. The sales volume in units necessary to attain a net income of $54,000 if the tax rate is 40%.

LO4, 5, 6 **P6-7B.** **Break-Even and Net Income Planning** The controller of Wright Company is preparing data for a conference concerning certain *independent* aspects of its operations.

Required

Prepare answers to the following questions for the controller:

a. Total fixed cost is $720,000, and a unit of product is sold for $10 in excess of its unit variable cost. What is the break-even unit volume?
b. The company will sell 30,000 units of product—each having a unit variable cost of $14—at a price that will enable the product to absorb $360,000 of fixed cost. What minimum unit sales price must be charged to break even?
c. Net income before income tax of $150,000 is desired after covering $410,000 of fixed cost. What minimum contribution margin ratio must be maintained if total sales revenue is to be $1,600,000?
d. Net income before income tax is 20% of sales revenue, the contribution margin ratio is 60%, and the break-even dollar sales is $200,000. What is the amount of total revenue?
e. Total fixed cost is $350,000, variable cost per unit is $26, and unit sales price is $50. What dollar sales volume will generate an after-tax net income of $60,000 when the income tax rate is 40%?

LO4, 5, 6 **P6-8B.** **Break-Even and Net Income Planning** Venice Company has recently leased facilities for the manufacture of a new product. Based on studies made by its accounting personnel, the following data are available:

Estimated annual sales	60,000 units

Estimated Costs	Amount	Unit Cost
Direct material	$ 666,000	$11.10
Direct labor	468,000	7.80
Manufacturing overhead	540,000	9.00
Administrative expenses	291,600	4.86
	$1,965,600	$32.76

Selling expenses are expected to be 10% of sales, and the selling price is $42 per unit. Ignore income tax in this problem.

Required

a. Compute a break-even point in dollars and in units. Assume that manufacturing overhead and administrative expenses are fixed but that other costs are variable.

b. What would net income before income tax be if 50,000 units were sold?

c. How many units must be sold to earn a net income before income tax of 10% of sales?

P6-9B. Multiple Product Break-Even and Net Income Planning Madison Company manufactures and sells the following three products:

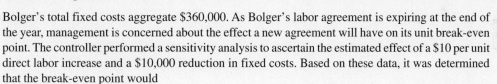

	Red	Blue	Green
Unit sales	20,000	30,000	50,000
Unit sales price	$30	$62	$18
Unit variable cost	$18	$38	$14

LO4, 5, 6

SERVICE AND
MERCHANDISING

Required

Assume that total fixed cost is $324,800.

a. Compute the net income before income tax based on the sales volumes shown above.

b. Compute the break-even point in total dollars of revenue and in specific unit sales volume for each product.

c. Prove your break-even calculations by computing the total contribution margin related to your answer in requirement (b).

CERTIFIED MANAGEMENT ACCOUNTANT (CMA®) EXAM SAMPLE QUESTIONS

CMA6-1. Bolger and Co. manufactures large gaskets for the turbine industry. Bolger's per unit sales price and variable costs for the current year are as follows.

Sales price per unit $300
Variable costs per unit   210

Bolger's total fixed costs aggregate $360,000. As Bolger's labor agreement is expiring at the end of the year, management is concerned about the effect a new agreement will have on its unit break-even point. The controller performed a sensitivity analysis to ascertain the estimated effect of a $10 per unit direct labor increase and a $10,000 reduction in fixed costs. Based on these data, it was determined that the break-even point would

a. decrease by 1,000 units.
b. decrease by 125 units.
c. increase by 375 units.
d. increase by 500 units.

CMA6-2. All of the following are assumptions of cost-volume-profit analysis **except**

a. total fixed costs do not change with a change in volume.
b. revenues change proportionately with volume.
c. variable costs per unit change proportionately with volume.
d. sales mix for multi-product situations do not vary with volume changes.

CMA6-3. Carson Inc. manufactures only one product and is preparing its budget for next year based on the following information.

Selling price per unit	$100
Variable costs per unit	75
Fixed costs	250,000
Effective tax rate	35%

If Carson wants to achieve a net income of $1.3 million next year, its sales must be

    a.   62,000 units.
    b.   70,200 units.
    c.   80,000 units.
    d.   90,000 units.

CMA6-4. Break-even quantity is defined as the volume of output at which revenues are equal to

    a.   marginal costs.
    b.   total costs.
    c.   variable costs.
    d.   fixed costs.

CMA6-5. Ticker Company sells two products. Product A provides a contribution margin of $3 per unit, and Product B provides a contribution margin of $4 per unit. If Ticker's sales mix shifts toward Product A, which one of the following statements is **correct**?

    a.   The total number of units necessary to break even will decrease.
    b.   The overall contribution margin ratio will increase.
    c.   Operating income will decrease if the total number of units sold remains constant.
    d.   The contribution margin ratios for Products A and B will change.

EXTENDING YOUR KNOWLEDGE

EYK4-1. **Business Decision Case** The following total cost data are for Ralston Manufacturing Company, which has a normal capacity per period of 400,000 units of product that sell for $18 each. For the foreseeable future, regular sales volume should continue at normal capacity of production.

Direct material	$1,720,000
Direct labor	1,120,000
Variable overhead	560,000
Fixed overhead (Note 1)	880,000
Selling expense (Note 2)	720,000
Administrative expense (fixed)	200,000
	$5,200,000

Notes:

1. Beyond normal capacity, fixed overhead cost increases $30,000 for each 20,000 units *or fraction thereof* until a maximum capacity of 640,000 units is reached.
2. Selling expenses are a 10% sales commission. Ralston pays only one-half of the regular sales commission rates on any sale of 20,000 or more units.

Ralston's sales manager has received a special order for 48,000 units from a large discount chain at a special price of $16 each, F.O.B. factory. The controller's office has furnished the following additional cost data related to the special order:

1. Changes in the product's construction will reduce direct material $1.80 per unit.
2. Special processing will add 25% to the per-unit direct labor costs.
3. Variable overhead will continue at the same proportion of direct labor costs.
4. Other costs should not be affected.

Required

    a.   Present an analysis supporting a decision to accept or reject the special order. Assume Ralston's regular sales are not affected by this special order.
    b.   What is the lowest unit sales price Ralston could receive and still make a before-tax profit of $39,600 on the special order?

EYK4-2. **Ethics Case** Gina DeMarc, a partner in a large CPA firm, has been approached by Bruce Jonas, a manager, with the following recommendation for incentive bonuses for staff members. Jonas recommends that the firm continue to pay each staff member a straight annual salary (which has been

traditionally the only payment made) plus a bonus based on the staff member's ability to achieve a 10% reduction in time spent on each client's work. The firm would also pay a 5% finder's fee for any new client the staff member brings into the firm.

Jonas believes this will motivate the staff to work more efficiently, to sell the firm to new clients, and to service more clients in any given time period. This should also generate more revenue for the firm.

Required
How would you advise Gina DeMarc? What ethical issues should she consider?

ANSWERS TO SELF-STUDY QUESTIONS:

1. b, (p. 202)   2. d, (p. 203)   3. a, (p. 208)   4. c, (p. 210)   5. a, (p. 213)

YOUR TURN! SOLUTIONS

Solution 6.1
y-intercept = Total fixed costs ($4,500)
Slope = Variable cost per unit
x-axis = Level of activity (water bottle cages produced)
Points on the line = Total costs at that level of output

Solution 6.2
Mixed cost: $2 per unit plus $5,000

$$\frac{\$24,500 - \$13,000}{9,750 - 4,000} = \$2 \text{ per unit}$$

$24,500 − ($2 × 9,750) = $5,000 fixed cost
Or
$13,000 − ($2 × 4,000) = $5,000 fixed cost

Solution 6.3

Sales.	$2,500,000
– Variable costs	(1,400,000)
Contribution margin	1,100,000
– Fixed costs	(600,000)
Operating income.	$ 500,000

Operating leverage = $1,100,000/$500,000 = 2.2
Depending on the industry, this may indicate a need for concern because the industry average is significantly higher.

DECISION TIME SOLUTION

Solution 6.1
c.   Either or both of the above.
If the retailer were to increase the average price of the shoes or quantity sold by 10% or more, it would break even or earn a profit.

7

Variable Costing: A Tool for Decision Making

PAST

Chapter 6 utilized our understanding of cost behavior to determine break-even and make planning and budgeting decisions.

PRESENT

Chapter 7 discusses the preparation of a variable income statement

FUTURE

Chapter 8 describes some of the tools and techniques that management can use in making strategic business decisions.

LEARNING OBJECTIVES

1. **Describe** the difference in the treatment of product costs between variable costing and absorption costing. *(p. 242)*

2. **Prepare** an income statement under both variable costing and absorption costing methods. *(p. 244)*

3. **Explain** why net income differs between absorption costing and variable costing. **Reconcile** the two different income amounts. *(p. 246)*

4. **Describe** the advantages and disadvantages of the variable costing method. *(p. 248)*

GENERAL MOTORS

General Motors (GM) designs, manufactures, and sells cars, trucks, and automobile parts worldwide. In North America, they are recognized by their Buick, Cadillac, Chevrolet, and GMC brands. Outside North America, in addition to these brands, they also manufacture and market vehicles under the Holden, Opel, and Vauxhall brands.

The global automotive industry is highly competitive and overall manufacturing capacity in the industry exceeds global demand. Many manufacturers have relatively high fixed labor costs as well as significant limitations on their ability to close facilities and reduce fixed costs. Automobile manufacturers typically respond to these relatively high fixed costs by attempting to sell more vehicles by adding vehicle enhancements, providing subsidized financing or leasing programs, offering marketing incentives, or reducing vehicle prices. In doing so, they are able to reduce the per-vehicle fixed manufacturing cost. However, manufacturers in lower-cost countries such as China and India have recently emerged as competitors in key emerging markets and announced their intention of exporting their products to the North American market as a bargain alternative to entry-level automobiles. These actions will limit GM's control over vehicle pricing, market share, and operating results, and present a significant risk to GM's ability to increase its per-vehicle prices.

In the year ending December 31, 2014, GM reported operating income of just over $1.5 billion.[1] This is a reduction of $3.6 billion from the prior fiscal year. GM reports the results of its operations in accordance with generally accepted accounting principles (GAAP). In accordance with GAAP, this means that the amount that GM reports for inventories on the balance sheet includes all production costs (materials, labor, and manufacturing overhead).

GM's reported inventories declined from $14.0 billion in 2013 to $13.6 billion in 2014, a decrease of approximately $400 million. As described more fully in this chapter, because a significant portion of GM's costs are fixed, this means that fixed manufacturing costs incurred in previous years (that had been recorded as part of inventories on the balance sheet) were expensed in 2014, reducing income from what it would have been had GM sold fewer vehicles! Say what? Read on…

---

[1] General Motors 10-K Report dated February 4, 2015.

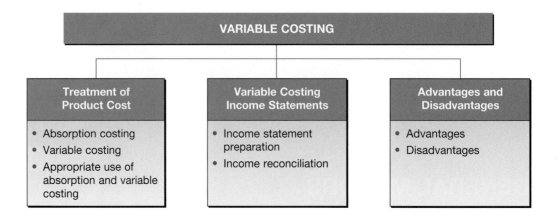

TREATMENT OF PRODUCT COSTS

LO1 **Describe** the difference in the treatment of product costs between variable costing and absorption costing.

A.K.A. Absorption costing is also referred to as *full costing* because it includes both variable and fixed components of product costs.

Absorption Costing

In **Chapter 2**, we define product costs as **all** manufacturing costs: direct material, direct labor, and variable and fixed manufacturing overhead. These costs are capitalized as inventory during the production period and recognized as expense (cost of goods sold) only when the related merchandise is sold. This method of attaching all manufacturing costs to the product is known as **absorption costing**. When using absorption costing, and production is greater than sales, a portion of the current period's fixed costs is attached to the inventory that is added to the balance sheet. As a result, a company can defer recognition of fixed costs as an expense by merely producing more inventory than it sells in a period. **Exhibit 7-1a** presents the absorption costing income statement for Fezzari.

Exhibit 7-1a	Absorption Costing Income Statement for Fezzari

FEZZARI PERFORMANCE BICYCLES Absorption Costing Income Statement For the Year Ended December 31, 2016		
Sales.		$4,500,000
Cost of goods sold (including fixed manufacturing costs). . . .		3,001,600
Gross profit on sales.		$1,498,400
Operating expenses:		
Selling expenses.	$400,000	
Administrative expenses.	340,000	740,000
Income from operations.		$ 758,400
Other income and expense:		
Interest expense.		5,000
Income before income tax		$ 753,400
Income tax expense.		263,690
Net income.		$ 489,710

A.K.A. Variable costing is also referred to as *direct costing.* The latter is a misnomer, however, because variable costs—not direct costs—are capitalized under direct costing.

Variable Costing

In contrast, for internal reporting purposes, some companies use **variable costing** to determine the cost of their manufactured products. Under variable costing, only *variable* manufacturing costs are capitalized as inventory. This includes direct material, direct labor, and the variable portion of manufacturing overhead. All fixed manufacturing overhead costs are expensed in the period incurred. These fixed manufacturing costs are treated as a period cost in the same manner as selling, general, and administrative expenses. As a result, under variable costing, costs of goods sold amounts do not include the fixed portion of manufacturing overhead. **Exhibit 7-1b** presents the variable costing income statement for Fezzari.

Exhibit 7-1b	Variable Costing Income Statement for Fezzari

FEZZARI PERFORMANCE BICYCLES
Variable Costing Income Statement
For the Year Ended December 31, 2016

Sales.		$4,500,000
Variable cost of goods sold	$2,776,500	
Variable selling expenses	300,000	
Variable non-factory administrative expenses	50,000	3,126,500
Contribution margin		$1,373,500
Fixed expenses:		
Fixed manufacturing costs	$ 225,100	
Fixed selling expenses	100,000	
Fixed non-factory administrative expenses	290,000	615,100
Income from operations		$ 758,400
Other income and expense:		
Interest expense		5,000
Income before income tax		$ 753,400
Income tax expense		263,690
Net income		$ 489,710

The only difference between absorption and variable costing is that when production exceeds sales, a portion of fixed manufacturing overhead is capitalized under absorption costing, whereas it is fully expensed under variable costing. **Exhibit 7-2** illustrates this difference.

Exhibit 7-2	Illustration of Absorption vs. Variable Costing

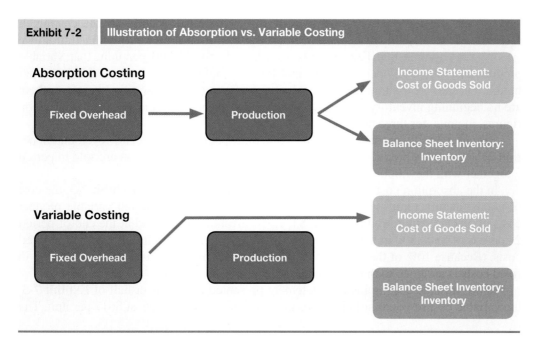

Appropriate Use of Absorption Costing and Variable Costing

In general, variable costing (carrying only variable costs in the inventory accounts) is considered a departure from generally accepted accounting standards. These standards require that published financial reports attested to by CPAs be prepared on an absorption costing basis. In these reports, all manufacturing costs should be attributed to products, and inventories of work in process and finished goods should contain their allocable shares of manufacturing costs, both fixed and variable. Likewise, the Internal Revenue Service has generally insisted on the use of absorption costing in determining net income for tax purposes, with some adjustments.

Although variable costing should not be used to prepare financial statements for external use, management may use variable costing statements for internal decision making. A principal benefit is that variable costing usually causes net income figures to move in the same direction as sales.

With absorption costing, net income may increase in periods when production volume exceeds sales (increasing inventory on the balance sheet) and decrease when sales volume exceeds production (decreasing inventory on the balance sheet). Why is this important to understand? This is important knowledge because it may be possible for managers to increase reported net income to meet analysts' expectations by increasing production of product during the last few weeks of a reporting period. Of course, this short-term "fix" could result in excess inventory levels that lead to obsolescence and inventory write-offs in subsequent periods.

TAKEAWAY 7.1

Variable costing cannot be used for external financial reporting.

VARIABLE COSTING INCOME STATEMENT

LO2 **Prepare** an income statement under both variable costing and absorption costing methods.

Income Statement Preparation

Exhibit 7-3 provides a comparison of partial income statements for Fezzari for three periods, using both absorption costing and variable costing. It clearly illustrates the effects just discussed. For this simple illustration, we assume that Fezzari sells each bicycle for $1,000 per unit, that variable product costs are $617 per unit, and that fixed manufacturing costs are $225,100 per period. Further, we assume that period 1 was the first year of operation (therefore, there are no beginning inventory balances). The exhibit also provides the sales and production figures, in units, for three periods.

Fezzari normally produces and sells 4,500 units per period. Note, however, that in period 2 the company produced an additional 500 units for inventory that are sold in period 3 together with the 4,000 units produced in period 3.

In the absorption costing statement presented in the top half of **Exhibit 7-3**, the cost of goods manufactured includes fixed product costs of $225,100 and variable product costs of $617 per unit produced. The $331,010 inventory presented at the end of period 2 consists of $308,500 in variable costs (500 units × $617 per unit) and $22,510 in fixed costs. (Because 10% of the units produced remains in inventory, 10% of the $225,100 in fixed costs is assigned to the inventory.)

In the variable costing income statement presented in the lower half of **Exhibit 7-3**, the variable cost of goods sold includes only variable product costs at $617 per unit. The

$308,500 inventory at the end of period 2 consists of only the $617 variable product cost times the 500 units in the inventory.

Exhibit 7-3	Absorption vs. Variable Costing Partial Income Statements

FEZZARI PERFORMANCE BICYCLES

	Period 1	Period 2	Period 3	Total
Beginning inventory (units).	—	—	500	—
Production (units).	4,500	5,000	4,000	13,500
Sales (units)	4,500	4,500	4,500	13,500
Ending inventory (units)	—	500	—	—

Variable cost: 500 units × $617 = $308,500
Fixed cost: 500 units × $225,100/5,000 units =   22,510
Total cost: $331,010

Absorption Costing Income Statement

		Period 1	Period 2	Period 3	Total
(1)	Sales.	$4,500,000	$4,500,000	$4,500,000	$13,500,000
(2)	Beginning inventory	—	—	331,010	—
(3)	Cost of goods manufactured	3,001,600	3,310,100	2,693,100	9,004,800
(4)	Less ending inventory.		331,010	—	—
(5)	Cost of goods sold [(2) + (3) − (4)]	$(3,001,600)	$(2,979,090)	$(3,024,110)	$ (9,004,800)
(6)	Gross profit on sales [(1) + (5)].	$1,498,400	$1,520,910	$1,475,890	$ 4,495,200

Variable cost: 500 units × $617 = $308,500
Fixed cost: 0
Total cost: $308,500

Variable Costing Income Statement

		Period 1	Period 2	Period 3	Total
(1)	Sales.	$4,500,000	$4,500,000	$4,500,000	$13,500,000
(2)	Beginning inventory	—	—	308,500	—
(3)	Variable cost of goods manufactured.	2,776,500	3,085,000	2,468,000	8,329,500
(4)	Less ending inventory.	—	308,500	—	—
(5)	Variable cost of goods sold [(2) + (3) − (4)]	$(2,776,500)	$(2,776,500)	$(2,776,500)	$ (8,329,500)
(6)	Contribution margin [(1) + (5)].	$1,723,500	$1,723,500	$1,723,500	$ 5,170,500
(7)	Fixed manufacturing costs.	(225,100)	(225,100)	(225,100)	(675,300)
(8)	Income from operations [(6) + (7)]	$1,498,400	$1,498,400	$1,498,400	$ 4,495,200

TAKEAWAY 7.2

Absorption costing and variable costing differ on only one item. Fixed manufacturing overhead is included in the cost of products under absorption costing but excluded from the cost of products under variable costing.

A total of $4,495,200 gross profit/income from operations is reported for the three periods under both methods. However, the variable costing method indicates the same income from operations figures in each period ($1,498,400), which are correlated with the constant sales volume over the three periods. On the other hand, under the absorption costing method, income from operations moves up and down with production (from $1,498,400 to $1,520,910 to $1,475,890). The reason, of course, is that the fixed costs are added to the inventory (and therefore not included in cost of goods sold) when production exceeds sales in period 2 and are released (through cost of goods sold) when the company sells more than it produces in period 3.

This chapter has introduced an internal reporting approach called variable costing, which allows management to more easily focus on the contribution of customers, products, product lines, business segments, and other business units to the overall profitability of the company. Another type of reporting has also gained in importance. That other type of reporting, called triple-bottom-line reporting, considers not just financial results, but also environmental and social results as well. GM is committed to acting in a socially responsible manner, behavior that earns high marks in a triple bottom line. As stated on GM's web site, "Through the lens of sustainability, we view industry challenges and change as new business opportunities that can drive additional value for our customers. We call this Customer-Driven Sustainability. From designing more fuel-efficient vehicles and deploying advanced-safety technologies to being the workplace of choice for employees and the neighbor of choice for communities, we make strategic decisions based on how the outcome of those decisions ultimately translates into value for our customers." An example of this behavior is illustrated by GM's greening of the General Motors Baltimore Operations complex. The LEED Silver building exceeds the voluntary U.S. Environmental Protection Agency's ENERGY STAR® Challenge for Industry, which requires a 10 percent reduction in energy intensity within 5 years. "We believe reducing our environmental footprint is good for the climate and good for our business," said Greg Martin, executive director of Global Public Policy. "Wherever we can, we are reducing our energy use, powering our plants with renewable energy and conserving resources."

Income Reconciliation

LO3 **Explain** why net income differs between absorption costing and variable costing. **Reconcile** the two different income amounts.

Once the relationship between variable costing and absorption costing is understood, it is possible to determine the differences between variable income and absorption income using a "short-cut" calculation without having to prepare separate financial statements. Remember that the only difference between variable income and absorption income is the treatment of the fixed costs of production—under absorption costing, some of these fixed production costs are included in inventory on the balance sheet, whereas they are all expensed under variable costing. So, if inventory increases by 500 units from one period to the next (as illustrated previously in **Exhibit 7-3**), each unit in inventory will have $45.02 ($22,510/500 units) of fixed manufacturing costs. Because all fixed manufacturing costs have been expensed under the variable costing approach, absorption income should be $22,510 more than variable income, as shown:

$45.02 fixed manufacturing cost per unit × 500 units added to inventory = $22,510

$1,520,910	−	$22,510	=	$1,498,400
(absorption income)		**(fixed manufacturing cost added to inventory)**		**(variable income)**

The impact of differences between production and sales under both absorption and variable costing is summarized in **Exhibit 7-4**.

Exhibit 7-4	Impact of Varying Levels of Production		
	Income Statement	**Balance Sheet**	**Explanation**
Production = Sales	No difference in reported income	No change in inventory values	Current period fixed costs expensed under both absorption and variable costing methods
Production > Sales	Absorption net income is greater than variable net income	Absorption balance sheet inventory increases by more than variable balance sheet inventory	Some current period fixed costs are added to inventory under absorption costing method, but all are expensed under variable costing method
Production < Sales	Absorption net income is less than variable net income	Absorption balance sheet inventory decreases by more than variable balance sheet inventory	Some prior period fixed costs that are in the beginning inventory balance under absorption costing method are expensed in the current period as cost of goods sold, but only current period fixed costs are expensed under variable costing method

---

Assume that Fezzari's reported absorption costing income was $1,600,000 in 2016. What would variable costing income be if Fezzari's inventory increased by 100 units during 2016 and fixed manufacturing cost was equal to $50 per unit?

YOUR TURN! 7.1

The solution is on page 260.

To highlight the effect of variable costing on inventories and income in the foregoing illustration, we consider only manufacturing costs. When detailed income statements are prepared under the variable costing method, fixed and variable costs of all types—including selling and administrative expenses—must be properly segregated. **Exhibit 7-5** presents an example of a detailed income statement prepared in accordance with the variable costing concept. As illustrated by the arrows in **Exhibit 7-5**, absorption net income changes with the level of production and variable net income changes with the level of sales. Because unit sales does not change over the three periods, reported variable net income does not change. The reason is that, as noted previously, fixed costs are not included in the inventory account on the balance sheet, but are expensed in the period that they are incurred under variable costing.

Contribution margin can be determined by deducting all variable expenses (cost of goods sold, selling, and administrative expenses) from sales. (This concept was previously introduced in Chapter 6.) All types of fixed expenses (manufacturing, selling, and administrative) are deducted to arrive at net income.

Exhibit 7-5	Absorption vs. Variable Costing Income Statements			

FEZZARI PERFORMANCE BICYCLES

	Period 1	Period 2	Period 3	Total
Beginning inventory (units)	—	—	500	—
Production (units)	4,500	5,000	4,000	13,500
Sales (units)	4,500	4,500	4,500	13,500
Ending inventory (units)	—	500	—	—

Absorption Costing Income Statement

		Period 1	Period 2	Period 3	Total
(1)	Sales	$ 4,500,000	$ 4,500,000	$ 4,500,000	$13,500,000
(2)	Beginning inventory	—	—	331,010	—
(3)	Cost of goods manufactured	3,001,600	3,310,100	2,693,100	9,004,800
(4)	Less ending inventory	—	331,010	—	—
(5)	Cost of goods sold [(2) + (3) − (4)]	$(3,001,600)	$(2,979,090)	$(3,024,110)	$ (9,004,800)
(6)	Gross profit on sales [(1) + (5)]	$ 1,498,400	$ 1,520,910	$ 1,475,890	$ 4,495,200
	Operating expenses:				
(7)	Selling expenses	(400,000)	(400,000)	(400,000)	(1,200,000)
(8)	Administrative expenses	(340,000)	(340,000)	(340,000)	(1,020,000)
(9)	Income from operations [(6) + (7) + (8)]	$ 758,400	$ 780,910	$ 735,890	$ 2,275,200

Variable Costing Income Statement

		Period 1	Period 2	Period 3	Total
(1)	Sales	$ 4,500,000	$ 4,500,000	$ 4,500,000	$13,500,000
(2)	Beginning inventory	—	—	308,500	—
(3)	Variable cost of goods manufactured	2,776,500	3,085,000	2,468,000	8,329,500
(4)	Less ending inventory	—	308,500	—	—
(5)	Variable cost of goods sold [(2) + (3) − (4)]	$(2,776,500)	$(2,776,500)	$(2,776,500)	$ (8,329,500)
(6)	Variable selling expenses	(300,000)	(300,000)	(300,000)	(900,000)
(7)	Variable administrative expenses	(50,000)	(50,000)	(50,000)	(150,000)
(8)	**Contribution margin** [(1) + (5) + (6) + (7)]	$ 1,373,500	$ 1,373,500	$ 1,373,500	$ 4,120,500
	Fixed expenses:				
(9)	Fixed manufacturing costs	(225,100)	(225,100)	(225,100)	(675,300)
(10)	Fixed selling expenses	(100,000)	(100,000)	(100,000)	(300,000)
(11)	Fixed administrative expenses	(290,000)	(290,000)	(290,000)	(870,000)
(12)	Income from operations [(8) + (9) + (10) + (11)]	$ 758,400	$ 758,400	$ 758,400	$ 2,275,200

ADVANTAGES AND DISADVANTAGES OF VARIABLE COSTING

The following advantages and disadvantages of using variable costing result from the fact that under variable costing no fixed overhead costs are assigned to inventory carrying values.

LO4 Describe the advantages and disadvantages of the variable costing methods.

Advantages

1. Variable costing assigns only variable costs to inventory. Reporting inventory values in this manner helps managers avoid making "death spiral" decisions.

2. Under variable costing, because all fixed costs are reported separately, managers are able to see how much fixed cost must be covered before a profit will be generated.

3. Reported net income tends to follow sales volume, eliminating the incentive to temporarily boost income by producing more product than can be sold in the short term.

4. Cost-volume-profit (CVP) relationships are more easily discerned from variable costing income statements than from conventional absorption costing statements. The cost information needed for CVP analysis (which was discussed in **Chapter 6**) is readily available from variable cost financial statements.

5. Variable costing statements make it easier to determine the contribution of customers, products, product lines, business segments, and other business units to the overall profitability of the company. This is typically obscured by the allocation of fixed costs under absorption costing.

Disadvantages

1. Accounting measures derived under variable costing are not in conformity with generally accepted accounting principles, nor are they acceptable for reporting purposes under the Internal Revenue Code.

2. Inventories (and therefore working capital and owners' equity) tend to be understated.

3. Carrying inventories at only their variable costs may lead to long-run pricing decisions that provide for recovery of variable cost only rather than total cost, which will not produce net income in the long run.

4. Variable costing generally requires that a "second set" of accounting records be kept, increasing the cost of the required accounting systems and possible confusion among managers.

Hint: A "death spiral" decision is one in which management eliminates a product or division that has a positive contribution margin, but shows a loss when other non-controllable costs are allocated to it. By eliminating the product or division, the positive contribution margin is lost so that other products or divisions now have to cover all of the fixed costs. This may cause another product or division to appear unprofitable, leading to additional decisions to eliminate products or divisions that have positive contribution margins.

SERVICES INDUSTRY IN FOCUS

Environmental Business Consultants (EBC) compensates all of its employees as salaried workers. Thus, EBC considers its labor cost as fixed—that is, EBC consultants are paid their full salary and benefits regardless of the number of consulting projects that they perform during a year. The only other fixed cost is the office lease expense. A partial trial balance for 2016 is provided below.

SERVICE AND MERCHANDISING

Description	Trial Balance Debit	Trial Balance Credit	Variable or Fixed	Direct Service or SGA
Sales.		4,146,000		
Reimbursable costs	431,000		V	D
Executive salaries.	844,500		F	D
Clerical salaries	217,500		F	D
Consultant salaries.	1,050,000		F	D
Employee benefits	145,500		F	D
Payroll taxes.	123,000		F	D
Employee bonuses.	126,000		V	SGA
Marketing expenses.	48,000		V	SGA
Employee continuing education expenses. . . .	27,000		V	SGA
Office lease expense	202,500		F	D
Office supplies expense.	64,500		V	D
Other general administrative expense	355,500		V	SGA

Assume that EBC's beginning absorption Work-in-Process Inventory is $223,000 and its ending absorption Work-in-Process (WIP) Inventory is $247,000. Further, assume that EBC's beginning variable WIP inventory is $5,400 and its ending variable WIP inventory is $6,000.

Required

a. Determine income from operations using

　　1. Absorption costing.

　　2. Variable costing.

b. Compare the income from operations derived under the two methods.

Solution

a. 1.

ENVIRONMENTAL BUSINESS CONSULTANTS, LLC Absorption Income Statement For the Year Ended December 31, 2016		
Gross sales.		$4,146,000
Less reimbursable costs		(431,000)
Net sales.		$3,715,000
Direct labor.		$2,380,500
General overhead:		
Office lease expense	$202,500	
Office supplies expense.	64,500	
Total general overhead.		267,000
Total service costs for the year		$2,647,500
Add: beginning work-in-process inventory		223,000
Total cost of work in process during the year		$2,870,500
Less: ending work-in-process inventory		(247,000)
Cost of services		2,623,500
Gross profit on sales.		$1,091,500
Operating expenses:		
Employee bonuses	$126,000	
Marketing expenses	48,000	
Employee continuing education expenses.	27,000	
Other general administrative expenses	355,500	
Total operating expenses.		556,500
Income from operations		$ 535,000

2.

ENVIRONMENTAL BUSINESS CONSULTANTS, LLC		
Variable Income Statement		
For the Year Ended December 31, 2016		
Gross sales.		$4,146,000
Less reimbursable costs		$ (431,000)
Net sales.		$3,715,000
Beginning variable WIP		$ 5,400
Variable costs		
Office supplies expense		64,500
Less ending variable WIP.		(6,000)
Variable cost of service		$ 63,900
Other variable expenses		
Employee bonuses.	$ 126,000	
Marketing expenses	48,000	
Employee continuing education expenses. . . .	27,000	
Other general administrative expenses	355,500	
Total other variable cost		556,500
Total variable costs		$ 620,400
Contribution margin		$3,094,600
Fixed costs		
Direct labor.	$2,380,500	
Office lease expense	202,500	
Total fixed costs.		2,583,000
Income from operations.		$ 511,600

b.

Absorption income from operations.		$535,000
Less:		
Increase in fixed costs in WIP inventory:		
Ending (247,000 − 6,000)	241,000	
Beginning (223,000 − 5,400)	217,600	
		(23,400)
Variable income from operations		$511,600

COMPREHENSIVE PROBLEM

Tuttle Manufacturing Company produces only one product, which sells for $50. Product costs at the normal level of manufacturing operations (10,000 units) are the following:

Direct material	$14 per unit
Direct labor.	$12 per unit
Variable overhead.	$ 4 per unit
Fixed overhead.	$49,500

Selling expenses (100% variable) are $3 per unit; administrative expenses (100% fixed) are $30,000. During the year, Tuttle produced 11,000 units and sold 9,000 units. Tuttle had no beginning inventory of product.

Required

a. Determine net income (ignoring income taxes) using
 1. Absorption costing.
 2. Variable costing.
b. Compare the total net income derived under the two methods.

Solution

a.

Absorption Costing		
Sales (9,000 units × $50).		$450,000
Cost of goods sold:		
Direct material (11,000 × $14)	$154,000	
Direct labor (11,000 × $12)	132,000	
Variable overhead (11,000 × $4)	44,000	
Fixed overhead.	49,500	
	379,500	
Less: Ending inventory [($379,500/11,000) × 2,000] . . .	69,000	
Cost of goods sold.		310,500
Gross profit.		$139,500
Selling expense (9,000 units × $3).	27,000	
Administrative expense	30,000	57,000
Net income.		$ 82,500

Variable Costing		
Sales (9,000 units × $50).		$450,000
Variable expenses:		
Direct material (11,000 × $14)	$154,000	
Direct labor (11,000 × $12)	132,000	
Variable overhead (11,000 × $4)	44,000	
	330,000	
Less: Ending inventory [($330,000/11,000) × 2,000] . . .	60,000	
Variable cost of goods sold		270,000
Variable selling expense (9,000 × $3)		27,000
Contribution margin		153,000
Fixed expenses:		
Fixed overhead.	49,500	
Administrative expense	30,000	79,500
Net income.		$ 73,500

b.

Comparison	
Absorption costing net income	$82,500
Variable costing net income	73,500
Difference (explained below)	$ 9,000

The amount of fixed overhead contained in the absorption costing ending inventory is $9,000 [($49,500/11,000) × 2,000].

The amount of fixed overhead contained in the variable costing ending inventory is 0. The different treatment of fixed overhead fully explains the difference.

SUMMARY OF LEARNING OBJECTIVES

Describe the difference in the treatment of product costs between variable costing and absorption costing. (p. 242)   **LO1**

- Absorption costing capitalizes all manufacturing costs as inventory during the production period and recognizes them as expense (cost of goods sold) only when the related merchandise is sold.
- Variable costing does not assign fixed manufacturing overhead as a product cost but expenses it in the period incurred.
- Accounting measures derived under variable costing are not in accord with generally accepted accounting principles, nor are they acceptable for tax reporting.

Prepare an income statement under both variable costing and absorption costing methods. (p. 244)   **LO2**

- For absorption costing, include the fixed costs and variable costs of manufacturing in the computation of cost of goods sold.
- For variable costing, only include the variable costs of manufacturing in the computation of cost of goods sold. Expense all fixed costs, including fixed manufacturing costs, in the period.

Explain why net income differs between absorption costing and variable costing. Reconcile the two different income amounts. (p. 246)   **LO3**

- The difference between absorption income and variable income will be the amount of fixed manufacturing costs either added to or subtracted from work-in-process inventory during the period.
- When production volume exceeds sales volume, absorption income will be greater than variable income.
- When production volume is less than sales volume, absorption income will be less than variable income.

Describe the advantages and disadvantages of the variable costing methods. (p. 248)   **LO4**

- The primary advantage of variable costing is that reported income follows changes in production volume, reducing the risk of "death spiral" decisions.
- Variable costing provides all of the information required for CVP analysis.
- The primary disadvantage of variable costing is that it is not acceptable for financial statement reporting or tax reporting.
- Because variable costing requires the maintenance of a "second set" of books, it is more costly.

KEY TERMS

Absorption costing (p. 242)   **Variable costing** (p. 242)
Contribution margin (p. 247)

Assignments with the ⊚ logo in the margin are available in BusinessCourse.
See the Preface of the book for details.

SELF-STUDY QUESTIONS

(Answers to Self-Study Questions are at the end of this chapter.)

LO1 1. **In determining inventory costs, which of the following cost elements is included when using absorption costing but excluded when using variable costing?**
   a. Selling costs
   b. Direct labor cost
   c. Non-factory administrative costs
   d. Fixed overhead

LO2 2. **If unit production exceeds unit sales during the period, absorption income will be**
   a. less than variable income.
   b. more than variable income.
   c. equal to variable income.

LO2 3. **If unit production is less than unit sales during the period, absorption income will be**
   a. less than variable income.
   b. more than variable income.
   c. equal to variable income.

LO2 4. **If unit production is equal to unit sales during the period, absorption income will be**
   a. less than variable income.
   b. more than variable income.
   c. equal to variable income.

LO1, 4 5. **True or false: Variable costing may be used by management in preparing audited financial statements.**
   a. True
   b. False

QUESTIONS

LO4 1. What is variable costing? List its advantages and disadvantages.

LO3 2. What generalizations can be made about the difference in income reported under variable and absorption costing?

LO3 3. When inventories are increasing, will absorption income be higher or lower than variable income?

LO1 4. Which method, absorption or variable costing, is used for internal management reporting purposes?

LO1 5. Which method, absorption or variable costing, is used for external reporting purposes in accordance with generally accepted accounting principles?

EXERCISES—SET A

LO2 **E7-1A.   Variable and Absorption Costing** During its first year, Walnut, Inc., showed an $18 per-unit profit under absorption costing but would have reported a total profit $16,000 less under variable costing. If production exceeded sales by 500 units and an average contribution margin of 62.5% was maintained, what is the apparent:
   a. Fixed cost per unit?
   b. Sales price per unit?
   c. Variable cost per unit?
   d. Unit sales volume if total profit under absorption costing was $198,000?

LO2 **E7-2A.   Variable and Absorption Costing** Chandler Company sells its product for $100 per unit. Variable manufacturing costs per unit are $40, and fixed manufacturing costs at the normal operating level of 12,000 units are $240,000. Variable selling expenses are $16 per unit sold. Fixed administrative expenses total $104,000. Chandler had no beginning inventory in 2016. During 2016, the company produced 12,000 units and sold 9,000. Would net income for Chandler Company in 2016 be higher if calculated using variable costing or using absorption costing? Calculate reported income using each method.

E7-3A. Variable and Absorption Costing—Service Company Lawn RX, Inc. prepares a variable costing income statement for internal management and an absorption costing income statement for its bank. Lawn RX provides a quarterly lawn care service that is sold for $150. The variable and fixed cost data are as follows:

Direct labor..	$ 100.00
Overhead:	
Variable cost per unit	$ 5.00
Fixed cost..	$100,000
Marketing, general, and administrative:	
Variable cost (per contract completed)	$ 6.00
Administrative expense (fixed) (per month)	$ 42,000

During 2016, 10,000 service contracts were signed and 9,500 service contracts were completed. Lawn RX had no service contracts at the beginning of the year.

Required
a. Calculate reported income for management.
b. Calculate reported income for the bank.
c. Reconcile the two income amounts.

EXERCISES—SET B

E7-1B. Variable and Absorption Costing During its first year, Concord, Inc., showed a $21 per-unit profit under absorption costing but would have reported a total profit $16,800 less under variable costing. If production exceeded sales by 700 units and an average contribution margin of 60% was maintained, what is the apparent:

a. Fixed cost per unit?
b. Sales price per unit?
c. Variable cost per unit?
d. Unit sales volume if total profit under absorption costing was $189,000?

E7-2B. Variable and Absorption Costing Grant Company sells its product for $50 per unit. Variable manufacturing costs per unit are $30, and fixed manufacturing costs at the normal operating level of 18,000 units are $90,000. Variable selling expenses are $4 per unit sold. Fixed administrative expenses total $155,000. Grant had 7,000 units at a per-unit cost of $35 in beginning inventory in 2016. During 2016, the company produced 18,000 units and sold 20,000. Would net income for Grant Company in 2016 be higher if calculated using variable costing or using absorption costing? Calculate reported income using each method.

E7-3B. Variable and Absorption Costing—Service Company Tech Helpers Company prepares a variable costing income statement for internal management and an absorption costing income statement for its bank. Tech Helpers provides a personal computer maintenance service that is sold for $100. The variable and fixed cost data are as follows:

Direct labor..	$ 25.00
Overhead:	
Variable cost per unit	$ 5.00
Fixed cost..	$240,000
Marketing, general, and administrative:	
Variable cost (per service contract completed)	$ 5.00
Fixed cost (per month)	$ 20,000

During 2015, 4,000 service contracts were started and 5,000 service contracts were completed. At the beginning of 2016, Tech Helpers had 1,000 service contracts in process at a per-unit cost of $90 in beginning work-in-process inventory.

Required

a. Calculate reported income for management.

b. Calculate reported income for the bank.

c. Reconcile the two income amounts.

PROBLEMS—SET A

LO2, 3   **P7-1A.** **Variable and Absorption Costing** Scott Manufacturing makes only one product with total unit manufacturing costs of $54, of which $36 is variable. No units were on hand at the beginning of 2015. During 2015 and 2016, the only product manufactured was sold for $84 per unit, and the cost structure did not change. Scott uses the first-in, first-out inventory method and has the following production and sales for 2015 and 2016:

	Units Manufactured	Units Sold
2015	120,000	90,000
2016	120,000	130,000

Required

a. Prepare gross profit computations for 2015 and 2016 using absorption costing.

b. Prepare gross profit computations for 2015 and 2016 using variable costing.

c. Explain how your answers illustrate the impact of differences between production and sales volumes on the gross profits reported each year under absorption and variable costing.

LO2   **P7-2A.** **Variable and Absorption Costing** Summarized data for 2016 (the first year of operations) for Gorman Products, Inc., are as follows:

Sales (75,000 units)	$3,000,000
Production costs (80,000 units):	
Direct material.	880,000
Direct labor	720,000
Manufacturing overhead:	
Variable.	544,000
Fixed	320,000
Operating expenses:	
Variable.	168,000
Fixed	240,000
Depreciation on equipment	60,000
Real estate taxes	18,000
Personal property taxes (on inventory and equipment)	28,800
Personnel department expenses	30,000

Required

a. Prepare an income statement based on full absorption costing.

b. Prepare an income statement based on variable costing.

c. Assume that you must decide quickly whether to accept a special one-time order for 1,000 units for $30 per unit. Which income statement presents the most relevant data? Determine the apparent profit or loss on the special order based solely on these data.

d. If the ending inventory is destroyed by fire, which costing approach would you use as a basis for filing an insurance claim for the fire loss? Why?

LO2   **P7-3A.** **Variable and Absorption Costing—Service Company** Jensen's Tailoring provides custom tailoring services. After the company's first year of operations, its owner prepared the following summarized data report for 2016:

Sales (500 completed jobs)	$100,000
Tailoring costs (550 jobs):	
Direct labor.......................................	47,000
Manufacturing overhead:	
Variable.......................................	12,000
Fixed...	9,000
Operating expenses:	
Variable.......................................	5,600
Fixed...	5,800

Required

a. Prepare an income statement based on full absorption costing.

b. Prepare an income statement based on variable costing.

c. Assume that you must decide quickly whether to accept a special one-time order to alter 50 band costumes for $150 per costume. Which income statement presents the most relevant data? Determine the apparent profit or loss on the special order based solely on these data.

PROBLEMS—SET B

P7-1B. Variable and Absorption Costing Frances Manufacturing makes a product with total unit manufacturing cost of $64, of which $36 is variable. No units were on hand at the beginning of 2015. During 2015 and 2016, the only product manufactured was sold for $96 per unit, and the cost structure did not change. Frances uses the first-in, first-out inventory method and has the following production and sales for 2015 and 2016:

LO2, 3

	Units Manufactured	Units Sold
2015	100,000	70,000
2016	100,000	120,000

Required

a. Prepare gross profit computations for 2015 and 2016 using absorption costing.

b. Prepare gross profit computations for 2015 and 2016 using variable costing.

c. Explain how your answers illustrate the impact of differences between production and sales volumes on the gross profits reported each year under absorption and variable costing.

P7-2B. Variable and Absorption Costing Summarized data for 2016 (the first year of operations) for Trenton Products, Inc., are as follows:

LO2

Sales (200,000 units)	$8,000,000
Production costs (210,000 units):	
Direct material.......................................	2,100,000
Direct labor...	1,680,000
Manufacturing overhead:	
Variable.......................................	1,260,000
Fixed...	1,050,000
Operating expenses:	
Variable.......................................	560,000
Fixed...	640,000

Required

a. Prepare an income statement based on full absorption costing.

b. Prepare an income statement based on variable costing.

c. Assume that you must decide quickly whether to accept a special one-time order for 1,000 units for $28 per unit. Which income statement presents the most relevant data? Determine the apparent profit or loss on the special order based solely on these data.

d. If the ending inventory is destroyed by fire, which costing approach would you use as a basis for filing an insurance claim for the fire loss? Why?

LO2

P7-3B. Variable And Absorption Costing—Service Company Rocky's Automotive specializes in performing automobile safety checks. After the company's first year of operations, its accountant prepared the following summarized data report for the safety checks for 2016:

Sales (7,000 safety checks)	$700,000
Production costs (7,010 safety checks):	
Direct labor	490,700
Shop overhead:	
Variable	112,160
Fixed	70,100
Operating expenses:	
Variable	21,030
Fixed	16,000

Required

a. Prepare an income statement based on full absorption costing.

b. Prepare an income statement based on variable costing.

c. Assume that you must decide quickly whether to accept a special one-time order for 20 safety checks on local police cars for $80 per safety check. Determine the apparent profit or loss on the special order based solely on these data.

CERTIFIED MANAGEMENT ACCOUNTANT (CMA®) EXAM SAMPLE QUESTIONS

CMA7-1. When comparing absorption costing with variable costing, the difference in operating income can be explained by the difference between the

a. units sold and the units produced, multiplied by the unit sales price.

b. ending inventory in units and the beginning inventory in units, multiplied by the budgeted fixed manufacturing cost per unit.

c. ending inventory in units and the beginning inventory in units, multiplied by the unit sales price.

d. units sold and the units produced, multiplied by the budgeted variable manufacturing cost per unit.

CMA7-2. Mill Corporation had the following unit costs for the recently concluded calendar year:

	Variable	Fixed
Manufacturing	$8.00	$3.00
Nonmanufacturing	$2.00	$5.50

Inventory for Mill's sole product totaled 6,000 units on January 1 and 5,200 units on December 31. When compared to variable costing income, Mill's absorption costing income is

a. $2,400 lower.

b. $2,400 higher.

c. $6,800 lower.

d. $6,800 higher.

CMA7-3. If a manufacturing company uses variable costing to cost inventories, which of the following costs are considered inventoriable costs?

a. Only raw material, direct labor, and variable manufacturing overhead costs.

b. Only raw material, direct labor, and variable and fixed manufacturing overhead costs

c.   Only raw material, direct labor, variable manufacturing overhead, and variable selling and administrative costs

d.   Only raw material and direct labor costs

CMA7-4. During the month of May, Robinson Corporation sold 1,000 units. The cost per unit for May was as follows:

	Cost Per Unit
Direct materials	$ 5.50
Direct labor	3.00
Variable manufacturing overhead	1.00
Fixed manufacturing overhead	1.50
Variable administrative costs	.50
Fixed administrative costs	3.50
Total	$15.00

May's income using absorption costing was $9,500. The income for May, if variable costing had been used, would have been $9,125. The number of units Robinson produced during May was

a.   750 units.

b.   925 units.

c.   1,075 units.

d.   1,250 units.

CMA7-5. Which one of the following is the **best** reason for using variable costing?

a.   Fixed factory overhead is more closely related to the capacity to produce than to the production of specific units.

b.   All costs are variable in the long term.

c.   Variable costing is acceptable for income tax reporting purposes.

d.   Variable costing usually results in higher operating income than if a company uses absorption costing.

EXTENDING YOUR KNOWLEDGE

EYK7-1.   Business Decision Case   Ben and Chris have been lifelong friends. They are engineer-minded and have always dreamed of starting a manufacturing company. They want to manufacture tires, but realize that this industry is heavily regulated and that achieving profitable operations will require skillful management. Despite the odds, they form Smooth Ride, Inc., and resolve to only stay in business if they report a positive net income after the company's first year of operations. At the end of 2016, its first year of operations, Smooth Ride reported the following summarized data:

Sales (105,000 tires)	$13,125,000
Production costs (120,000 tires):	
Direct material	4,750,000
Direct labor	3,675,000
Manufacturing overhead:	
Variable	2,300,000
Fixed	950,000
Operating expenses:	
Variable	1,050,000
Fixed	800,000
Depreciation on machinery	455,000
Property taxes	330,000
Personnel department expenses	140,000

Required

a. Prepare income statements based on full absorption costing and based on variable costing. Based on the reported incomes using these methods, did Smooth Ride exceed the expectations of Ben and Chris?

b. Smooth Ride follows generally accepted accounting standards. Which method, full absorption or variable costing, will the company use to report its net income?

ANSWERS TO SELF-STUDY QUESTIONS:

1. d, (pp. 242–243)   2. b, (p. 247)   3. a, (p. 247)   4. c, (p. 247)   5. b, (p. 249)

YOUR TURN! SOLUTION

Solution 7.1
$1,600,000 − (100 × $50) = $1,595,000

Relevant Costs and Short-Term Decision Making

PAST

Chapter 7 discussed the preparation of a variable income statement.

PRESENT

Chapter 8 describes some of the tools and techniques that management can use in making short-term business decisions.

FUTURE

Chapter 9 discusses the budgeting process, the components of the master budget, and the interrelationships of the individual budgets, and presents an illustration of a budget for a manufacturer and a service company.

LEARNING OBJECTIVES

1. **Describe** management's use of accounting information in the decision-making process. **Define** relevant costs and **describe** the use of differential analysis. *(p. 264)*

2. **Demonstrate** when to accept a special order. *(p. 269)*

3. **Demonstrate** when to make or buy needed parts. *(p. 271)*

4. **Demonstrate** when to drop an unprofitable product or segment. *(p. 272)*

5. **Demonstrate** when to sell a product or process it further. *(p. 273)*

6. **Demonstrate** how to determine which product to produce. *(p. 277)*

JOHN DEERE

What did you have for dinner last night? If it included fresh produce, grains, dairy, or meat from U.S. farms, there is a six in ten chance that it was planted, fertilized, irrigated, harvested, or fed with a John Deere product. As the global leader in the manufacture of agricultural equipment, John Deere's strategy is to be the equipment supplier of choice to the farmers who will help meet the worldwide growth in the demand for food.

John Deere didn't start out with the intent of becoming the world's largest manufacturer of agriculture and construction equipment. In 1837, John Deere, a blacksmith in Illinois, was simply looking for a way to help the local farmers plow their fields without frequently stopping to clean sticky prairie soil off of their wooden or cast-iron plows. A broken steel sawmill blade gave him the chance. He knew that the soil would easily slide off of a polished-steel plow, which he crafted from the sawmill blade. Five years later, he built 100 of the plows; in 1849, 2,136 plows; and in 1875, 50,000 plows.

In 1863, the company built the first Hawkeye Riding Cultivator, a farm implement adapted for riding. Twelve years later, the company developed the Gilpin Sulky Plow, which put the farmer on a seat. That plow would defeat 50 other plows in a field trial at the Paris Universal Exposition, winning first place. Before the end of the 19th century, steam tractors began to appear on the American farm, although John Deere did not begin manufacturing tractors until 1918.

One hundred and twenty-six years after John Deere made his first polished steel plow, the company he founded surpassed International Harvester to become the world's largest producer and seller of farm and industrial tractors and equipment. Today, the company's products and services include everything from small-engine lawn mowers for the home market to monster 9R tractors with up to 560-horsepower. How did this world-leading company grow out of a simple blacksmith shop? Along the way, the company's management faced many challenges and questions, including:

- Whether to introduce new products and product lines;
- Whether to produce or purchase new technology (e.g., steam tractors);
- Whether to drop products and product lines (e.g., bicycles and snowmobiles);
- How to deal with restricted production capacity during World War II; and,
- How to handle global expansion of manufacturing facilities and product sales.

In this chapter, we examine some of the decision tools and techniques that managers may use in answering these strategic questions.

RELEVANT COSTS AND SHORT-TERM DECISION MAKING

Management and the Decision-Making Process	The Special Order	Make/Buy Decisions	Dropping Unprofitable Segments	Sell or Process Further	Constrained Resources
• Who makes decisions? • Phases of decision making • Relevant costs and differential analysis	• Business situation • Analysis and recommendation • Additional decision factors	• Business situation • Analysis and recommendation • Additional decision factors	• Business situation • Analysis and recommendation • Additional decision factors	• Business situation • Analysis and recommendation • Joint products • Byproducts	• Business situation • Analysis and recommendation

The traditional measurement is not the right measurement; if it were, there would be no need for decisions.

PETER DRUCKER

A well-developed accounting system is a continuing source of operational information for management. The quality of information available to management will influence the success of the operating decisions based on that information. In this chapter, we consider the management decision-making process and some cost concepts that are used in managerial analyses.

There are many definitions of **management**. In the broad sense, anyone who directs the activities of others is a manager. For a manufacturing firm like John Deere, this includes shop supervisors, department heads, plant supervisors, division managers, and the company president. A large, complex firm may have many management levels.

MANAGEMENT AND THE DECISION-MAKING PROCESS

Who Makes Decisions?

LO1 Describe management's use of accounting information in the decision-making process. **Define** relevant costs and **describe** the use of differential analysis.

As **Exhibit 8-1** illustrates, upper-level management is responsible for establishing long-range goals and policies, including major financing, expansion into new markets (foreign and domestic), and acquisitions of or mergers with other firms. Middle-level management may deal with the strategies and tactics related to the automation of a department, the establishment of new product lines, and the direction of the marketing plan. Such matters as daily production quotas, compliance with planned costs, and other detailed operating concerns are the responsibility of lower-level management. To varying degrees, therefore, all levels of management are involved in decision making.

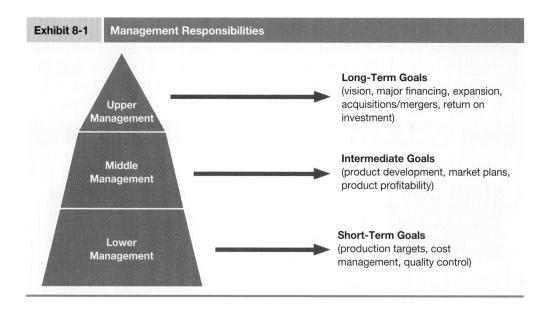

Exhibit 8-1   **Management Responsibilities**

Upper Management → **Long-Term Goals** (vision, major financing, expansion, acquisitions/mergers, return on investment)

Middle Management → **Intermediate Goals** (product development, market plans, product profitability)

Lower Management → **Short-Term Goals** (production targets, cost management, quality control)

One of the responsibilities of top management is the development of a strategic plan.

Decision making requires that a choice be made among alternatives. The business decision process is analogous to the play of a well-organized football team. Virtually all elements of decision making are present in football: the establishment of the objectives and goals that lead to winning; the development of organization, strategy, and tactics in a competitive environment; the creation of plays with the hope of achieving particular results; the period of execution; and, finally, the informal evaluation of performance on the field followed by a formal evaluation when game films are analyzed.

CORPORATE SOCIAL RESPONSIBILITY

This chapter discusses the concept of decision making. One of the decisions a company like John Deere must make is how many resources it should invest in items benefiting non-shareholder stakeholders, and whether these investments will benefit shareholders in the long run. John Deere has been making these types of decisions for well over a century. Some of the early decisions, noted on its web site, include:

- 1901—Deere implements voluntary workers' compensation program. This is 10 years before the first U.S. workers' compensation statutes.
- 1920—Deere designs and builds its own cloth-screen filtering system to clean exhaust from plow-grinding operations.
- 1936—First foundry equipped with air-pollution-controlled molding equipment.
- 1938—Product safety committee formed; warning decals placed on corn pickers; shielding for power take-offs introduced.
- 1940—Power take-off shields installed on tractors and made available in retrofit programs for tractors produced after 1932.
- 1947—Corporate industrial safety department established.
- 1949—First boiler equipped with a device to control fly-ash emission at Waterloo Tractor Works. Planter Works, Moline, Illinois, installs a wetcap to control cupola emissions.

These investments in its employees' welfare and in the environment appear to have been wise ones, as John Deere is still around more than a hundred years later, delivering billions of dollars of annual net income to its shareholders.

Phases of Decision Making

Decision making may be divided roughly into a planning phase, an execution phase, and an evaluation phase incorporating some form of remedial feedback. **Exhibit 8-2** illustrates the sequential nature of the elements of most decision processes.

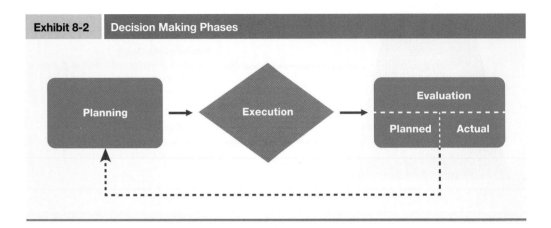

Exhibit 8-2 | **Decision Making Phases**

The **planning phase** begins with *goal identification,* the specification of objectives to be sought or accomplished. One of the most common business goals is the long-run optimization of net income, often expressed in terms of return on assets. Other goals include target growth rates in sales revenue or total assets, target market shares in various markets, or leadership in product research, innovation, and quality.

The next steps in planning are identifying feasible alternative courses of action for achieving desired goals and estimating their qualitative and quantitative effects on the specified goals. Because planning involves the future, data related to the alternative courses of action must be estimated and projected in an environment of uncertainty.

The **execution phase** begins with the actual moment of decision: management commits to a specific plan of action. Because of the complexity of modern business, some elaborate plans may need lead times of several years. Poor planning, or the absence of planning, may lead to operating crises that carry significant penalties for the firm in terms of extra costs, lost opportunities, and—in extreme cases— bankruptcy.

Once a decision has been made, the plan is implemented, which usually involves the acquisition and commitment of materials, labor, and long-lived assets such as machinery and buildings. Management is kept informed through periodic accounting reports on the acquisition and use of these facilities during the execution phase.

In the **evaluation phase**, steps are taken to control the outcome of a specific plan of action. Virtually every important aspect of business—costs, product quality, inventory levels, and sales revenue—must be reasonably well controlled if a firm is to operate successfully. Measuring performance is an essential element of control. Performance measurement must compare actual operations with planned operations to allow management to take remedial action when significant unfavorable variations exist. Managerial accounting data and reports play a key role in informing management about performance in various areas during the evaluation phase of decision making.

Decision processes do not, however, fall into three neatly divided phases. Changes in competition, technology, and customer demand must be considered. Furthermore, most management teams are engaged in all three decision-making phases at any given time. They may be planning decisions in one area, executing them in a second, and evaluating them in a third.

Feedback data are important for effective management. The generation of feedback data for management is one of the central purposes of managerial accounting.

RELEVANT COSTS AND DIFFERENTIAL ANALYSIS

Decision making involves choosing among different alternatives. In business, managers make decisions by evaluating the costs and benefits associated with each alternative. However, not all costs and benefits should be considered. Sound decision making is based on the widely accepted decision rule that only the aspects of a choice that differ among alternatives are relevant to a decision.

For example, imagine that you want to see an action movie in the theater. There are two theaters in your local community that are showing the movie. As a college student on a limited budget, you are careful with your money and want to choose the least-cost alternative, so you assemble the following information:

Cost/benefit	Theater #1	Theater #2
Ticket price.	$ 9.25	$ 9.25
Parking	$ 3.00	$ 4.00
Popcorn and drink	$10.00	$10.00
Concessions coupon	N/A	50% off
Gas for car	$0.10/mile	$0.10/mile
Car insurance (based on 10,000 miles per year)	$0.06/mile	$0.06/mile
Depreciation on car (based on 10,000 miles per year). . .	$0.30/mile	$0.30/mile
Distance to theater.	5 miles	10 miles

When you are deciding which theater to attend, the admission price is irrelevant if both theaters charge the same price. However, if the cost to park is $4 at one and $3 at the other, then the $1 differential parking cost is relevant to the choice. Likewise, if the popcorn and drink are $10 at both theaters, but you have a coupon for half off at one theater, the $5 savings is also relevant to the choice. If you plan to drive to the theater, the cost of the gas that would be consumed would be relevant if the theaters are different distances away, but the cost that you paid for your car (reflected in the annual depreciation cost) would not be because it was incurred in the past and is considered a **sunk cost**. Finally, the cost of insurance will be incurred regardless of which theater you choose, so it is not relevant to the decision. The decision process is simplified by concentrating only on the factors that are different between the alternatives the manager is evaluating. Thus, **relevant costs** in making a decision are defined as those that differ between alternatives.

In choosing between alternatives, managers must exercise care to avoid including irrelevant data that could lead to a poor decision. In the theater example, two categories of irrelevant costs were identified: costs that do not differ among the alternatives and sunk costs. Sunk costs are costs that have been incurred in the past and cannot be avoided regardless of the decision made.

Finally, managers should consider opportunity costs. Opportunity cost is the future benefit that is given up when a choice is made. In our theater example, assume that a third alternative is to stay home and study for an upcoming exam. A potential opportunity cost of choosing to go to the theater is the higher score that might result from the additional three hours of study.

ACCOUNTING IN PRACTICE   **Quantitative vs. Qualitative Factors in Decision Making**

Differential analysis considers revenues and expenses that differ among alternatives. However, it does not include qualitative factors, such as impact on labor force or customer base. Thus, the results of differential analysis are only one input into the decision-making process—successful managers must also consider qualitative factors.

Suppose that by 1860 John Deere had determined that he could use his blacksmith shop to produce and sell either plows or hayforks. His decision would have been in favor of the product promising the higher net income based on the estimated operating data shown in **Exhibit 8-3**.

Exhibit 8-3	John Deere Estimated Operating Data		
		Alternatives	
		Plows	**Hayforks**
Units that can be produced and sold.		14,000	20,000
Unit selling price.		$ 12.00	$ 7.00
Manufacturing costs:			
Variable (per unit)		$ 4.00	$ 2.00
Fixed (total).		$44,400	$44,400
Selling and administrative expenses:			
Variable (per unit)		$ 1.00	$ 1.00
Fixed (total).		$ 3,000	$ 3,000

We may compare the alternatives by preparing comparative income statements, as shown in **Exhibit 8-4**, from these data.

Exhibit 8-4	Product Choice Differential Analysis			
		Alternatives		
		Plows	**Hayforks**	**Difference**
Revenue				
(14,000 units @ $12)		$168,000		
(20,000 units @ $7)			$140,000	$28,000
Cost of goods sold (manufacturing costs):				
Variable (14,000 @ $4 per unit)		56,000		
(20,000 @ $2 per unit)			40,000	16,000
Fixed (total)		44,400	44,400	—
Selling and administrative expenses:				
Variable (@ $1.00 per unit)		14,000	20,000	(6,000)
Fixed (total)		3,000	3,000	—
Total expenses		$117,400	$107,400	$10,000
Net income		$ 50,600	$ 32,600	$18,000

This analysis shows an $18,000 increase in net income associated with plows as a result of a $28,000 increase in total revenue that is partially offset by a $10,000 net increase in cost of goods sold and variable selling and administrative expenses.

A simple differential analysis of the same situation is as follows, where consideration is limited to the revenue and expense factors that differ if plows are produced rather than hayforks:

Differential revenue:	
Revenue forgone on last 6,000 units [$7 × 6,000].	$(42,000)
Additional revenue from increased sales price [($12 − $7) × 14,000].	70,000
Net additional revenue	$ 28,000
Differential costs:	
Additional cost of goods sold [($4 − $2) × 14,000].	$ 28,000
Savings on last 6,000 units [$2 × 6,000]	(12,000)
Savings on variable selling and administrative expenses ($1.00 × 6,000) . .	(6,000)
Net differential income in favor of plows	$ 18,000

Note that the cost of John Deere's blacksmith shop would be considered a sunk cost, and not relevant to the choice between producing plows or hayforks.

Clearly, the differential approach indicates the same net advantage for plows as the income statements but it does so more concisely. In reality, a company's income statement is much more complex than that presented in Exhibit 8-4. Therefore, management uses the more efficient differential analysis in decision making.

A.K.A. A *differential cost*, also called an *incremental cost*, is any cost present in one alternative but absent in whole or part in another alternative.

Are fixed costs always irrelevant in differential analysis?

DECISION TIME 8.1

The solution is on page 295.

ILLUSTRATIONS OF DIFFERENTIAL ANALYSIS

The Special Order

Businesses occasionally receive special orders from purchasers who request a price concession. The prospective buyer may suggest a price or ask for a bid. Sometimes the buyer may request that the firm produce a special version of a product to be identified with the buyer's private brand. As long as no overriding qualitative considerations exist, management should evaluate such propositions and accept the special order if incremental revenues exceed incremental costs.

eLectures
MBC

LO2

Demonstrate when to accept a special order.

Business Situation

Assume that Fezzari Bicycles makes an entry-level mountain bike, the Lone Peak, which it sells to retail customers for $549. A bike share company has proposed that Fezzari supply 300 bikes for $400 per bike for a new bike share program in Salt Lake City, Utah. The bikes would carry the brand name of the bike share company. If Fezzari were to accept the order, a special machine attachment would be needed in production to differentiate the bike and affix the private brand logo. This attachment, which costs $1,500, would be discarded after the completion of this order. Also assume that Fezzari has unused production capacity, and thus anticipates no change in fixed capacity costs. The following unit cost data are available for the regular production of the Lone Peak bike:

Direct material	$233
Direct labor.	100
Variable manufacturing overhead.	20
Fixed manufacturing overhead (allocated)	47
Total cost per unit	$400

Analysis and Recommendation

At first glance, the proposal seems unprofitable because the unit cost figure is $400, which is exactly equal to the buyer's offered price, and an additional one-time cost of $1,500 must be incurred to process the order. However, the fixed overhead of $47 included in the $400 total unit cost is not relevant to the decision and should not be considered because Fezzari's total fixed costs will be incurred whether or not the special order is accepted. The differential cost and revenue analysis in **Exhibit 8-5** demonstrates that the special order should be accepted.

Exhibit 8-5	Special Order Differential Analysis			
Increase in sales revenue (300 units × $400)				$120,000
Increase in variable production costs:				
Direct material (300 units × $233)		(69,900)		
Direct labor (300 units × $100)		(30,000)		
Variable manufacturing overhead (300 units × $20)		(6,000)		
Total increase in production costs (300 units × $353). . .			(105,900)	
Cost of special attachment			(1,500)	
Total differential cost				(107,400)
Net advantage in accepting special order				$ 12,600

The differential costs of accepting the order consist of the variable production costs and the additional cost of the attachment needed to affix the private brand. Actually, with any price higher than $358 ($107,400 total differential costs ÷ 300 units), Fezzari would earn a profit on the order.

Note that excess production capacity is significant to the special order decision. Without sufficient excess capacity, the additional production would probably cause additional amounts of fixed costs to be incurred or the loss of productive capacity for Fezzari's normal bike production. In addition, Fezzari management would also want to consider the opportunity cost of utilizing the available production capacity for this special order, because accepting the order would limit Fezzari's ability to meet increased demand for a higher-margin bike. Also note that although the $1,500 special attachment in this example is a fixed cost, it is relevant to this decision because it differs between alternatives.

YOUR TURN! 8.1

The solution is on page 295.

Current sales are 50,000 units at $25 per unit. Production capacity is 80,000 units. Variable costs are $14 per unit. Fixed costs are $400,000. A special order for 10,000 units at $20 each is received. It will require the purchase of new equipment for $40,000. The equipment will have a salvage value of $5,000 at the end of the contract. Should the offer be accepted?

TAKEAWAY 8.3

The Special Order rule of thumb: ACCEPT the special order IF incremental revenues exceed incremental costs (assuming there are no qualitative factors deemed to outweigh the qualitative analysis).

Additional Decision Factors

Specific qualitative factors that should be considered here include ascertaining that (1) the special price does not constitute unfair price discrimination; (2) the special order does not negatively impact the actual or perceived quality of the retail bikes; and (3) the long-term price structure for the product is not adversely affected by the special order. Significant concern in any of these, or other areas, might be a basis for rejecting the special order despite the potential $12,600 profit.

Make or Buy?

Many manufacturing situations require the assembly of large numbers of specially designed components and subassemblies. Usually, the manufacturer must choose between making these components and subassemblies and buying them from outside suppliers. In each situation, management should evaluate the relative costs of the two choices and buy from outside if the differential cost of buying is less than the differential cost of making the components or subassemblies. Because making a component uses some portion of the firm's manufacturing capacity, we assume that no more attractive use of that capacity is available.

LO3 Demonstrate when to make or buy needed parts.

Business Situation

To illustrate the make-or-buy decision, we assume that John Deere manufactures a loader-backhoe with the following costs:

Manufactured Cab:	
Direct material	$3,000
Direct labor.	1,190
Variable manufacturing overhead.	750
Fixed manufacturing overhead.	650
Total cost	$5,590

Investigations by John Deere's purchasing department indicate that the loader-backhoe cab assembly can be purchased in sufficient quantities at a unit price of $5,031, an indicated savings of 10% per unit. At first glance, the opportunity to purchase seems attractive.

Analysis and Recommendation

A review of operations indicates that by purchasing the component, John Deere can reduce its variable costs of production, but the fixed overhead costs will remain. The fixed overhead costs related to equipment used to manufacture the cabs are an example of a sunk cost. The differential analysis in **Exhibit 8-6** indicates that by purchasing the cab, John Deere's overall costs would increase by $91 per unit. Thus, John Deere should continue to manufacture the cab.

Exhibit 8-6	Make or Buy Differential Analysis		

	Manufacture Cab	Purchase Cab	Increase (Decrease) in Cost if Cab Is Purchased
Cost per unit:			
Direct material	$3,000		$(3,000)
Direct labor.	1,190		(1,190)
Variable manufacturing overhead.	750		(750)
Fixed manufacturing overhead.	650	650	—
Purchase price of components		5,031	5,031
	$5,590	$5,681	$ 91

The following approach to this analysis confirms the more comprehensive one above:		
Cost to purchase cab.		$ 5,031
Less costs avoided by purchasing:		
Direct material.	$3,000	
Direct labor	1,190	
Variable manufacturing overhead	750	$ 4,940
Increase in acquisition cost by purchasing . . .		$ 91

Additional Decision Factors

These analyses assume that the manufacturing capacity released by the decision to purchase would not be used. However, should an opportunity arise to use this capacity to generate another product with more than $91 of contribution margin per unit, then the opportunity to purchase the components would be more attractive. However, qualitative factors, such as the effects on employee morale, product quality, and dependability of the supply chain, are also very important. Once a decision is reached based on the quantitative analyses, it should be weighed against these and other qualitative factors that may be important to management.

Dropping Unprofitable Segments

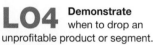

LO4 Demonstrate when to drop an unprofitable product or segment.

SERVICE AND MERCHANDISING

Occasionally, a company's financial reporting system provides its management with segment information that suggests that a particular division, department, office, product, or product line is losing money. In these situations, management should compare the direct segment cost saved to the revenue lost if the segment were to be dropped. The company should drop the segment if the cost saved is greater than the revenue lost.

Business Situation

Assume that EBC's segment financial statements show that the Water/Wastewater segment lost $5,298 for 2016. It would appear that dropping the segment would increase EBC's profit by $5,298, or almost 1% (see **Exhibit 8-7**).

Exhibit 8-7	Segment Income Statement		

ENVIRONMENTAL BUSINESS CONSULTANTS, LLC
Line of Business Statement
For the Year Ended December 31, 2016

	Solid Waste	Water/ Wastewater	Firm Total
Gross sales.	$3,676,000	$470,000	$ 4,146,000
Less reimbursable costs	(366,350)	(64,650)	(431,000)
Net sales.	$3,309,650	$405,350	$ 3,715,000
Cost of services	(2,238,787)	(384,713)	(2,623,500)
Gross profit on sales.	$1,070,863	$ 20,637	$ 1,091,500
Direct operating expenses	(166,065)	(25,935)	(192,000)
Line of business contribution	$ 904,798	$ (5,298)	$ 899,500
Common operating expenses			(364,500)
Interest revenue			7,500
Income before tax			$ 542,500

Assume that the Water/Wastewater cost of services includes an office lease expense of $38,625 that would continue even if the business line were discontinued. The rest of the Water/Wastewater cost of services and direct operating expenses are variable in nature and would be eliminated with the dropping of the segment.

Analysis and Recommendation

The differential analysis in **Exhibit 8-8** indicates that EBC's overall income would decrease, rather than increase, by discontinuing the Water/Wastewater.

Exhibit 8-8	Dropping Unprofitable Segment Differential Analysis		
Decrease in net revenue.			$(405,350)
Decrease in expenses:			
Variable cost of goods sold*.		$346,088	
Variable direct operating expenses		25,935	$ 372,023
Decrease in total contribution margin (and net income) from discontinuing Water/Wastewater.			$ (33,327)

*$384,713 − $38,625

Even though Water/Wastewater reports a $5,298 annual loss, it does generate a contribution margin of $33,327 toward the absorption of fixed costs and expenses. If Water/Wastewater is discontinued, there would be no contribution margin, although $38,625 of fixed cost would remain. This would result in a loss of $38,625, which is $33,327 worse than the current $5,298 loss. Thus, EBC should maintain its Water/Wastewater segment and look for ways to either increase revenue or decrease costs.

Additional Decision Factors

Management must often consider other factors in decisions of this type. Among these are (1) the potential termination of employees and subsequent effects on non-terminated employee morale, and (2) the possible effects on customer patronage (for example, customers of the Solid Waste line of business may go to other firms for all of their consulting services if Water/Wastewater's services are no longer available from the same source). On the other hand, EBC management might also begin to explore other potential services that might generate greater profits than the Water/Wastewater segment.

From a financial point of view, when should an unprofitable segment be dropped?	**DECISION TIME 8.2** The solution is on page 295.

TAKEAWAY 8.5

The Dropping an Unprofitable Segment rule of thumb: DROP the segment IF the direct cost savings is greater than the lost revenue (assuming there are no qualitative factors deemed to outweigh the qualitative analysis).

Sell or Process Further?

Firms sometimes face the decision of either selling products at one point in the production sequence or processing them further and selling them at a higher price. Examples are finished versus unfinished furniture, crude oil versus gasoline, and unassembled kits versus assembled units of product. In these process-further decision situations, management should compare the incremental revenue to the additional processing costs and process the products further if the incremental revenue exceeds the incremental processing costs.

LO5 Demonstrate when to sell a product or process it further.

Business Situation

Assume that Sunrise Landscape sells screened topsoil with the following values per yard:

Current sales price (per cubic yard)		$20.00
Costs:		
Direct material.	$5.00	
Direct labor	5.00	
Variable overhead.	1.00	
Fixed overhead*	2.50	13.50
Gross margin per unit.		$ 6.50

*Applied at 50% of direct labor costs.

Sunrise has excess productive capacity, which should remain available in the foreseeable future. Consequently, management believes that part of this excess capacity could be used to create a garden mix blended soil (topsoil that has been amended with compost and peat) and sell it at $30.00 per cubic yard to homeowners for their vegetable gardens and planting beds. A study carried out by the company's management indicates that the additional processing will add $5.00 to the direct material cost and $2.00 to the direct labor cost of each unit and that variable overhead will continue to be incurred at 20% of direct labor cost. See **Exhibit 8-9** for the specific steps involved.

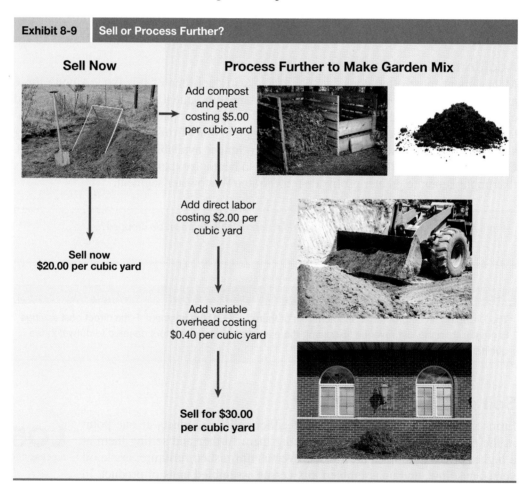

Exhibit 8-9 — Sell or Process Further?

Analysis and Recommendation

The differential analysis in **Exhibit 8-10** supports the proposal to process further:

Exhibit 8-10	Sell or Process Further Differential Analysis

		Per Cubic Yard
Differential revenue ($30.00 − $20.00)		$10.00
Differential cost:		
Direct material	$5.00	
Direct labor	2.00	
Variable manufacturing overhead (20% of direct labor)	0.40	
Fixed manufacturing overhead	—	
Total differential cost		7.40
Excess of differential revenue over differential cost		$ 2.60

The per-unit differential analyses indicate that Sunrise will earn an additional $2.60 per cubic yard for every yard of garden mix processed and sold.

> **TAKEAWAY 8.6**
>
> The Sell or Process Further rule of thumb: PROCESS further IF the differential revenues are greater than the differential costs after processing (assuming there are no qualitative factors deemed to outweigh the qualitative analysis).

Joint Products

Often, the processing of direct material results in two or more products of significant commercial value. Such products derived from a common input are **joint products**, and the related cost of the direct material is a joint product cost. An obvious example of a direct material whose processing results in joint products is crude oil, from which a variety of fuels, solvents, lubricants, and residual petrochemical pitches are derived. Cattle, from which the meat packer obtains many cuts and grades of meat, hides, and other products, are another example.

A.K.A. *Joint product costs* are manufacturing costs incurred in producing joint products up to the split-off point.

It is impossible to allocate a joint product cost among joint products in such a way that management can decide whether to continue production or what price to charge for a joint product. To decide to produce one joint product is to decide to produce all related joint products, even if some are discarded. Therefore, to make informed decisions about joint products, management must compare the total revenue generated by all joint products with their total production costs. The joint costs incurred to the point at which the joint products are separately identified are irrelevant with regard to decisions about whether to sell or process any of the joint products further.

The primary reason for allocating a joint product cost among two or more products is to assign cost to the ending inventories of joint products when determining periodic income. The most popular method of allocating joint product costs for inventory costing purposes is the relative sales value method. This approach uses arithmetic proportions. The total joint product cost is allocated to the various joint products in the proportions of their individual sales values to the total sales value of all joint products at the split-off point—that is, where physical separation takes place. For example, assume that 50,000 55-gallon barrels of crude oil costing $5,000,000 are processed into 800,000 gallons of fuel selling for $3.00 per gallon, 400,000 gallons of lubricants selling for $5.00 per gallon, and 1,000,000 gallons of petrochemical residues selling for $1.50 per gallon. The following calculations illustrate the joint product cost allocation using the relative sales value approach:

Joint Product	Quantity Produced (gallons)	Unit Sales Value	Product Sales Value	Proportion of Total Product Sales Value	Allocated Cost	Quantity Produced (gallons)	Cost per Unit
Fuel........	800,000	$3.00	$2,400,000	40.68%	$2,034,000	800,000	$2.54
Lubricants...	400,000	$5.00	2,000,000	33.90%	1,695,000	400,000	$4.24
Residues....	1,000,000	$1.50	1,500,000	25.42%	1,271,000	1,000,000	$1.27
			$5,900,000	100.00%	$5,000,000		

Note that the relative sales value approach results in assigned unit costs that are the same percentage of the selling price for each product. In our illustration, the cost per unit equals approximately 85% of the sales value per unit.

Exhibit 8-11 illustrates the allocation of the $5,000,000 joint product cost to the three joint products. Note also that each product may then incur additional manufacturing costs before it is completed and ready for sale. For example, in Exhibit 8-11, an additional $206,000 of costs are incurred after the split-off point to finish the production of the fuel. When added to the allocated joint costs, the total cost of the fuel is $2,240,000, or $2.80 per gallon.

Exhibit 8-11	Joint Product Costs

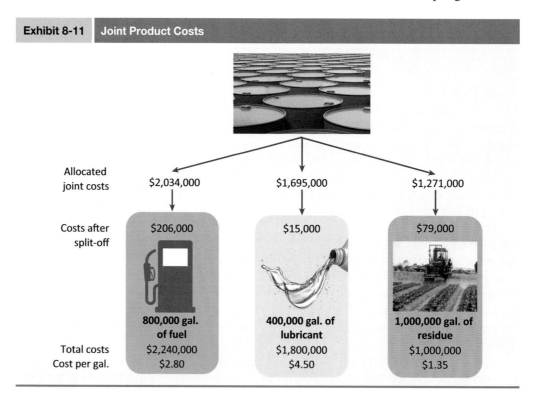

Byproducts

Byproducts have relatively little sales value compared with the other products derived from a particular process. Byproducts are considered incidental to the manufacture of the more important products. For example, the sawdust and shavings generated in a lumber mill or in a furniture manufacturer's cutting department are byproducts.

We may account for byproducts by assigning them a cost equal to their sales value less any disposal costs. This net amount is charged to an inventory account for the byproduct and credited to the work-in-process account that was charged with the original materials. For example, consider a furniture factory in which walnut boards are processed through a cutting and shaping department. In processing $40,000 worth of lumber, 800 bushels of sawdust and shavings are generated, which, after treatment costing $80, can be sold for $1 per bushel. The amount to be charged to the Sawdust and Shavings Inventory account would be $720 [(800 bushels × $1) − $80].

This procedure reduces the costs of the main products by the net amount recovered from byproducts.

Constrained Resources

Because most firms produce several products, management must continually examine operating data and decide which combination of products offers the greatest total long-term profit potential. The decisions related to product emphasis are seldom as simple as determining the most profitable product and confining production to that one product. For example, John Deere faces such operational constraints as limited demand for the most profitable products, the competitive necessity of offering a line of products with a variety of qualities and capacities, and, in seeking better utilization of existing capacity, the need to produce other, less profitable products.

LO6 **Demonstrate** how to determine which product to produce.

In a **constrained resource** analysis, an important and widely accepted generalization is that the firm optimizes its income when it maximizes the contribution margin earned per unit of constraining resource. The concept of constraining resource stems from the realization that as a firm increases its volume, some resource is eventually exhausted and thus constrains, or limits, the continued expansion of the firm. Which resources are constraining depends on the firm, the operating conditions, and even the products under consideration. Typical examples are key materials, labor skills, machine capacities, and factory floor space or storage space. Simply stated, management has optimized the firm's product mix when it maximizes the contribution margin earned on each unit of the particular resource that limits increased production.

A.K.A. Constrained resources are commonly referred to as *bottlenecks*.

Business Situation

To illustrate constrained resource decisions, assume that John Deere's Waterloo Works Tractor, Cab, and Assembly Operations in Waterloo, Illinois, produces three 6R Series row-crop tractors, the 6140R, the 6150R, and the 6170R. Also assume the operation's constraining resource is its factory machine capacity. John Deere operates at 90% capacity, and management wants to devote the unused capacity to one of the three products. The following data represent John Deere's current operations:

	Products		
	6140R	**6150R**	**6170R**
Per-unit data:			
Sales price	$130,000	$143,000	$150,000
Variable costs.	99,450	109,000	117,000
Contribution margin	$ 30,550	$ 34,000	$ 33,000
Fixed costs*	16,150	18,700	17,850
Net income.	$ 14,400	$ 15,300	$ 15,150
Machine hours required	38	44	42

*Allocated on basis of machine hours at $425 per hour.

Analysis and Recommendation

Intuition suggests that the extra capacity should be devoted either to the 6170R, which has the highest sales price, or to the 6150R, which has the highest per-unit contribution margin and net income. However, an analysis of the contribution margin of each product per unit of constraining resource (machine hour) reveals that the 6140R should receive the added capacity.

Note that fixed costs are allocated among products on the basis of machine hours—the constraining resource in our example. Furthermore, the unit allocations of fixed costs, noted previously, indicate that the 6170R requires 2 fewer machine hours than the 6150R and 4 more than the 6140R. The contribution per unit of machine capacity for each product is shown in **Exhibit 8-12**.

Exhibit 8-12	Constrained Resource Differential Analysis		
		Products	
	6140R	**6150R**	**6170R**
Contribution margin per unit	$30,550	$34,000	$33,000
Divided by machine hours required	38	44	42
Contribution margin per machine hour (the constraining resource).....................	$ 804	$ 773	$ 786

Use of the remaining capacity generates a greater contribution margin if devoted to the 6140R. As this example illustrates, in deciding how to utilize the constraining resource, management should use contribution margin per unit of constraining resource, rather than the relative sales prices, unit contribution margins, or even unit profit of various products.

YOUR TURN! 8.2

The solution is on page 295.

Product A requires 2 machine hours per unit, has a unit contribution margin of $15, and a contribution margin ratio of 60%. Product B requires 1 machine hour per unit, has a unit contribution margin of $12, and a contribution margin ratio of 40%. Which product should be emphasized if machine hours are limited?

TAKEAWAY 8.7

The Constrained Resource rule of thumb: MAXIMIZE the contribution margin per unit of scarce resource (assuming there are no qualitative factors deemed to outweigh the qualitative analysis).

SERVICE INDUSTRY IN FOCUS

SERVICE AND MERCHANDISING

Environmental Business Consultants, LLC (EBC) has been approached by Terrabean Coffee, a large retail coffee company with 5,000 shops across North America, to manage Terrabean Coffee's waste disposal and recycling services under a 3-year contract. It is unlikely that the contract would be extended beyond the initial 3-year term. Terrabean has asked EBC to provide these services at a discounted average hourly billing rate of $60 per hour.

In order to take on this major new contract, EBC would need to establish a call center to receive calls from the 5,000 shops and coordinate the appropriate response. The call center would be in a leased office space at a cost of $3,000 per month, including utilities. Additional capital, including office furniture, computers, and phones, would be purchased at a total cost of $35,000. The office furniture, computers, and phones are expected to have a value of $5,000 at the end of the contract and would not be of use to EBC in its regular business. The call center would be managed by a current EBC consultant that normally bills 1,800 hours per year at a rate of $125 per hour. An additional ten call center employees would be hired at an average hourly wage of $25, plus benefits equal to

50% of the hourly wage. Each employee would be expected to work 2,000 hours per year. EBC expects to bill Terrabean 20,000 hours per year for the call center under the contract.

Required

1. Determine whether EBC should accept this new contract offer from Terrabean. Calculate the differential net revenue or cost associated with the contract. (Hint: Don't forget that the call center manager is a current EBC employee and would not be available for any other work.)

2. What other factors should EBC management consider in making the decision?

Solution

1.

Solution	Service Industry in Focus	
Increase in annual revenue (20,000 hours × $60)		$1,200,000
Lost revenue from call center manager (1,800 × $125). . .		(225,000)
Total differential billing revenue		$ 975,000
Increase in costs:		
Direct labor (10 employees × 2,000 hours × $37.50) . . .	$750,000	
Office lease ($3,000 × 12 months).	36,000	
Other capital costs [($35,000 − 5,000)/3 years)]	10,000	
Total differential cost		$ 796,000
Net advantage in accepting contract offer.		$ 179,000

2. EBC management should consider the impact on the ten employees who will need to be hired for the call center. At the end of the contract term, these employees will need to be terminated unless other work can be found.

SUMMARY OF LEARNING OBJECTIVES

Describe management's use of accounting information in the decision-making process. Define relevant costs and describe the use of differential analysis. (p. 264)   LO1

■ Top management establishes long-range goals, middle management deals with intermediate goals, and lower management focuses on short-range goals.

■ Decision making, which is essentially choosing among alternatives, usually comprises three phases: planning, execution, and evaluation.

■ Relevant costs are those that differ between alternatives.

■ Differential analysis is the study of those amounts that are expected to differ among alternatives.

Demonstrate when to accept a special order. (p. 269)   LO2

■ Management should evaluate special order propositions and accept the special order if incremental revenues exceed incremental costs.

■ Management should also consider qualitative factors that could be the basis of rejecting a special order despite a net increase in revenues, such as unfair pricing, impact on quality, and long-term pricing impact.

Demonstrate when to make or buy needed parts. (p. 271)   LO3

■ Management should evaluate the relative costs of the two choices and buy from outside if the differential cost of buying is less than the differential cost of making the components or subassemblies.

■ Management should also consider qualitative factors such as the effects on employee morale, product quality, and dependability of the supply chain.

LO4 **Demonstrate when to drop an unprofitable product or segment. (p. 272)**

- Management should compare the direct segment cost saved to the revenue lost if the segment were to be dropped. The company should drop the segment if the cost saved is greater than the revenue lost.
- Management should also consider the potential termination of employees and subsequent effects on non-terminated employee morale, and the possible effects on customer patronage.

LO5 **Demonstrate when to sell a product or process it further. (p. 273)**

- Management should compare the incremental revenue to the additional processing costs and process the products further if the incremental revenue exceeds the incremental processing costs.
- The joint costs incurred to the point at which the joint products are separately identified are irrelevant with regard to decisions about whether to sell or process any of the joint products further.

LO6 **Demonstrate how to determine which product to produce. (p. 277)**

- Management should maximize the contribution margin earned on each unit of the particular resource that limits increased production.

KEY TERMS

Constrained resource (p. 277)	Execution phase (p. 266)	Planning phase (p. 266)
Decision making (p. 265)	Incremental cost (p. 269)	Relevant costs (p. 267)
Differential analysis (p. 268)	Joint product costs (p. 275)	Sunk cost (p. 267)
Differential cost (p. 269)	Joint products (p. 275)	
Evaluation phase (p. 266)	Management (p. 264)	

Assignments with the ⬤ logo in the margin are available in ᵐʸ BusinessCourse.
See the Preface of the book for details.

SELF-STUDY QUESTIONS

(Answers to Self-Study Questions are at the end of this chapter.)

LO1 1. **When using differential analysis to analyze two alternatives to the current operation, what factors should *not* be considered?**
   a. Direct material costs that are different
   b. Direct labor costs that exist for only one alternative
   c. Overhead costs that are the same for both alternatives
   d. Sales commissions that apply to only one alternative

LO2 2. **When considering a special order, management should accept the order if which of the following conditions is met?**
   a. Incremental costs are greater than incremental revenues.
   b. There is excess production capacity.
   c. Incremental costs are less than incremental revenues.
   d. Employees are willing to work overtime.

LO3 3. **When considering whether to continue to manufacture a part or buy it from an outside supplier, management should buy the part if the**
   a. incremental cost to buy is less than the incremental cost to manufacture the part.
   b. equipment used for making the part is fully depreciated.
   c. equipment used for making the part could be sold.
   d. incremental cost to buy is less than the total cost to manufacture the part.

LO4 4. **A business segment reports segment revenues of $1.2 million, segment costs of $1.0 million, and allocated corporate overhead costs of $300,000. If management were to drop the segment, overall corporate profits would**
   a. increase by $100,000.
   b. decrease by $100,000.
   c. increase by $200,000.
   d. decrease by $200,000.

5. True or false: Costs incurred to the split-off point in the manufacture of joint products are always relevant to the decision of whether to sell the joint products or process them further.   **LO5**
   a.   True
   b.   False

QUESTIONS

1. Identify three phases of decision making and briefly discuss the role of each phase in the decision process.   **LO1**
2. Although separate phases of decision making are identifiable, management is usually involved in all phases at the same time. Explain.   **LO1**
3. In the chapter we discuss quantitative methods to assist management in making business decisions. Discuss other common aspects of decision making that are not often subject to quantification.   **LO1**
4. Explain what is meant by the term *differential analysis*.   **LO1**
5. Explain how differential analysis can be applied to the following types of decisions: **LO2, 3, 4, 5, 6**
   a.   Accepting special orders
   b.   Making or buying product components
   c.   Dropping unprofitable segments of the firm
   d.   Selling or processing further
   e.   Product emphasis
6. Delton Company produces unassembled picture frames at the following average per-unit costs: direct material, $X; direct labor, $Y; and manufacturing overhead, $Z. Delton can assemble the frames at a unit cost of $2.50 and raise the selling price from $11 to $15. What is the apparent advantage or disadvantage of assembling the frames?   **LO5**
7. Explain the concept of *constraining resource*, and present a general rule for optimizing product mixes.   **LO6**
8. "In differential analysis, we can generally count on variable cost being relevant and fixed cost being irrelevant." Comment.   **LO1**
9. If both approaches to a decision lead to the same conclusion, why might differential analysis be considered superior to a comprehensive analysis that reflects all revenue and costs?   **LO1**

EXERCISES—SET A

E8-1A.   Dropping Unprofitable Department Thomas Corporation has four departments, all of which appear to be profitable except department 4. Operating data for 2016 are as follows: **LO4**

SERVICE AND MERCHANDISING

	Total	Departments 1–3	Department 4
Sales.	$950,000	$800,000	$150,000
Cost of sales.	634,000	520,000	114,000
Gross profit.	$316,000	$280,000	$ 36,000
Direct expenses	$144,000	$120,000	$ 24,000
Common expenses	123,000	105,000	18,000
Total expenses.	$267,000	$225,000	$ 42,000
Net income (Loss).	$ 49,000	$ 55,000	$ (6,000)

Required
a.   Calculate the gross profit percentage for departments 1–3 combined and for department 4.
b.   What effect would elimination of department 4 have had on total firm net income? (Ignore the effect of income tax.)

LO1 **E8-2A.** **Analyzing Operational Changes** Operating results for department B of Delta Company during 2016 are as follows:

Sales.	$540,000
Cost of goods sold.	378,000
Gross profit.	$162,000
Direct expenses	$120,000
Common expenses	66,000
Total expenses.	$186,000
Net loss	$ (24,000)

If department B could maintain the same physical volume of product sold while raising selling prices an average of 15% and making an additional advertising expenditure of $45,000, what would be the effect on the department's net income or net loss? (Ignore income tax in your calculations.)

LO1 **E8-3A.** **Analyzing Operational Changes** Suppose that department B in Exercise E8-2A could increase physical volume of product sold by 10% if it spent an additional $18,000 on advertising while leaving selling prices unchanged. What effect would this have on the department's net income or net loss? (Ignore income tax in your calculations.)

LO1 **E8-4A.** **Differential Analysis** In each of four independent cases, the amount of differential revenue or differential cost is as follows (parentheses indicate decreases):

	1	2	3	4
Increases (decreases) in:				
Revenue	$18,000	$-0-	?	?
Costs.	?	?	($12,000)	$-0-

For each case, determine the missing amount that would be necessary for the net differential amount to be

a. $10,000
b. ($6,000)

Indicate whether your answers reflect increases or decreases.

LO2 **E8-5A.** **Special Order** Carson Manufacturing, Inc., sells a single product for $36 per unit. At an operating level of 8,000 units, variable costs are $18 per unit and fixed costs $10 per unit.

Carson has been offered a price of $20 per unit on a special order of 2,000 units by Big Mart Discount Stores, which would use its own brand name on the item. If Carson accepts the order, material cost will be $3 less per unit than for regular production. However, special stamping equipment costing $4,000 would be needed to process the order; the equipment would then be discarded.

Assuming that volume remains within the relevant range, prepare an analysis of differential revenue and costs to determine whether Carson should accept the special order.

LO3 **E8-6A.** **Make or Buy** Eastside Company incurs a total cost of $120,000 in producing 10,000 units of a component needed in the assembly of its major product. The component can be purchased from an outside supplier for $11 per unit. A related cost study indicates that the total cost of the component includes fixed costs equal to 50% of the variable costs involved.

a. Should Eastside buy the component if it cannot otherwise use the released capacity? Present your answer in the form of differential analysis.
b. What would be your answer to requirement (a) if the released capacity could be used in a project that would generate $50,000 of contribution margin?

E8-7A. Sell or Process Further Jensen Manufacturing Company makes a partially completed assembly unit   **LO5**
that it sells for $36 per unit. Normally, 42,000 units are sold each year. Variable unit cost data on the
assembly are as follows:

Direct material	$10
Direct labor	8
Variable manufacturing overhead	4

The company is now using only 70% of its normal capacity; it could fully use its normal capacity by
processing the assembly further and selling it for $43 per unit. If the company does this, material and
labor costs will each increase by $2 per unit and variable overhead will go up by $1 per unit. Fixed
costs will increase from the current level of $160,000 to $220,000.

    Prepare an analysis showing whether Jensen should process the assemblies further.

E8-8A. Joint Cost Cheyenne, Inc. produces three products from a common input. The joint costs for a typi-   **LO5**
cal quarter follow:

Direct materials	$45,000
Direct labor	55,000
Overhead	60,000

The revenues from each product are as follows:

Product A	$75,000
Product B	$80,000
Product C	$30,000

Management is considering processing Product A beyond the split-off point, which would increase the
sales value of Product A to $116,000. However, to process Product A further means that the company
must rent some special equipment costing $17,500 per quarter. Additional materials and labor also
needed would cost $12,650 per quarter.

Required

a. What is the gross profit currently being earned by the three products for one quarter?
b. What is the effect on quarterly profits if the company decides to process Product A further?

E8-9A. Service Emphasis The following analysis of selected data is for each of the two services Gates Cor-   **LO6**
poration provides.

SERVICE AND
MERCHANDISING

	Service A	Service B
Per-service data at 10,000 services		
Sales price	$26	$22
Service costs:		
Variable	9	9
Fixed	6	4
Selling and administrative expenses:		
Variable	5	3
Fixed	3	1

In the Gates operation, labor capacity is the company's constraining resource. Each unit of A requires
3 hours of labor, and each unit of B requires 2 hours of labor. Assuming that all services can be sold
at a normal price, prepare an analysis showing which of the two services should be provided with any
unused productive capacity that Gates might have.

EXERCISES—SET B

LO4

SERVICE AND
MERCHANDISING

E8-1B. **Dropping Unprofitable Department** Penn Corporation has four departments, all of which appear to be profitable except department 4. Operating data for 2016 are as follows:

	Total	Departments 1-3	Department 4
Sales.	$1,052,000	$900,000	$152,000
Cost of sales.	654,000	540,000	114,000
Gross profit.	$ 398,000	$360,000	$ 38,000
Direct expenses	$ 177,000	$150,000	$ 27,000
Common expenses	140,000	120,000	20,000
Total expenses.	$ 317,000	$270,000	$ 47,000
Net income (loss)	$ 81,000	$ 90,000	$ (9,000)

 a. Calculate the gross profit percentage for departments 1–3 combined and for department 4.
 b. What effect would elimination of department 4 have had on total firm net income? (Ignore the effect of income tax.)

LO1

MBC

E8-2B. **Analyzing Operational Changes** Operating results for department B of Shaw Company during 2016 are as follows:

Sales.	$800,000
Cost of goods sold.	480,000
Gross profit.	$320,000
Direct expenses	$215,000
Common expenses	123,000
Total expenses.	$338,000
Net loss	$ (18,000)

If department B could maintain the same physical volume of product sold while raising selling prices an average of 10% and making an additional advertising expenditure of $50,000, what would be the effect on the department's net income or net loss? (Ignore income tax in your calculations.)

LO1

MBC

E8-3B. **Analyzing Operational Changes** Suppose that department B in Exercise E8-2B could increase physical volume of product sold by 10% if it spent an additional $40,000 on advertising while leaving selling prices unchanged. What effect would this have on the department's net income or net loss? (Ignore income tax in your calculations.)

LO1

MBC

E8-4B. **Differential Analysis** In each of four independent cases, the amount of differential revenue or differential cost is as follows (parentheses indicate decreases):

	1	2	3	4
Increases (decreases) in:				
Revenue	$36,000	$-0-	?	?
Costs.	?	?	$(20,000)	$-0-

For each case, determine the missing amount that would be necessary for the net differential amount to be
 a. $24,000
 b. ($16,000)

Indicate whether your answers reflect increases or decreases.

E8-5B. **Special Order** Northern Company regularly sells its only product for $34 per unit and has a 25% profit on each sale. The company has accepted a special order for a number of units, the production of which would use part of its unused capacity. The special order sales price is 50% of the normal price, and the profit margin is only 60% of the regular dollar profit. What, apparently, is

a. Northern's profit per unit on the special order?
b. Northern's variable cost per unit?
c. Northern's average fixed cost per unit on regular sales?

E8-6B. **Make or Buy** Harper Company incurs a total cost of $252,000 in producing 20,000 units of a component needed in the assembly of its major product. The component can be purchased from an outside supplier for $6 per unit. A related cost study indicates that the total cost of the component includes fixed costs equal to 80% of the variable costs involved.

a. Should Harper buy the component if it cannot otherwise use the released capacity? Present your answer in the form of differential analysis.
b. What would be your answer to requirement (a) if the released capacity could be used in a project that would generate $15,000 of contribution margin?

E8-7B. **Sell or Process Further** Turner Manufacturing Company makes a partially completed assembly unit that it sells for $50 per unit. Normally, 35,000 units are sold each year. Variable unit cost data on the assembly are as follows:

Direct material	$12
Direct labor.	7
Variable manufacturing overhead.	9

The company is now using only 75% of its normal capacity; it could fully use its normal capacity by processing the assembly further and selling it for $58 per unit. If the company does this, material and labor costs will each increase by $2 per unit and variable overhead will go up by $1 per unit. Fixed costs will increase from the current level of $125,000 to $165,000.

Prepare an analysis showing whether Turner should process the assemblies further.

E8-8B. **Service Emphasis** The following analysis of selected data is for each of the two services Rockville Corporation provides.

	Service G	Service H
Per-unit data @ 10,000 services		
Sales price	$29	$16
Service costs:		
Variable.	9	7
Fixed.	6	4
Selling and administrative expenses:		
Variable.	5	2
Fixed.	3	1

In Rockville's operation, labor capacity is the company's constraining resource. Each unit of G requires 3 hours of labor, and each unit of H requires 1 hour of labor. Assuming that all services can be sold at a normal price, prepare an analysis showing which of the two services should be provided with any unused productive capacity that Rockville might have.

PROBLEMS—SET A

P8-1A.   Analyze Operational Changes Richmond's is a retail store with eight departments, including a garden department that has been operating at a loss. The following condensed income statement gives the latest year's operating results:

	Garden Department	All Other Departments
Sales.	$336,000	$2,400,000
Cost of sales.	201,600	1,560,000
Gross profit.	$134,400	$ 840,000
Direct expenses	$108,000	$ 273,000
Common expenses	48,000	312,000
Total expenses.	$156,000	$ 585,000
Net income (Loss).	$ (21,600)	$ 255,000

Required

a.   Calculate the gross profit percentage for the garden department and for the other departments as a group.

b.   Suppose that if the garden department were discontinued, the space occupied could be rented to an outside firm for $18,000 per year, and the common expenses of the firm would be reduced by $4,500. What effect would this action have on Richmond's net income? (Ignore income tax in your calculations.)

c.   It is estimated that if an additional $6,000 were spent on advertising, prices in the garden center could be raised an average of 5% without a change in physical volume of products sold. What effect would this have on the operating results of the garden department? (Again, ignore income tax in your calculations.)

P8-2A.   Special Order Total cost data follow for Glendale Manufacturing Company, which has a normal capacity per period of 8,000 units of product that sell for $60 each. For the foreseeable future, regular sales volume should continue to equal normal capacity.

Direct material	$100,800
Direct labor.	62,400
Variable manufacturing overhead.	46,800
Fixed manufacturing overhead (Note 1).	38,400
Selling expense (Note 2).	35,200
Administrative expense (fixed)	15,000
	$298,600

Notes:

1. Beyond normal capacity, fixed overhead costs increase $1,800 for each 500 units *or fraction thereof* until a maximum capacity of 10,000 units is reached.

2. Selling expenses consist of a 6% sales commission and shipping costs of 80 cents per unit. Glendale pays only three-fourths of the regular sales commission on sales totaling 501 to 1,000 units and only two-thirds the regular commission on sales totaling 1,000 units or more.

     Glendale's sales manager has received a special order for 1,200 units from a large discount chain at a price of $36 each, F.O.B. factory. The controller's office has furnished the following additional cost data related to the special order:

1. Changes in the product's design will reduce direct material costs $1.50 per unit.

2. Special processing will add 20% to the per-unit direct labor costs.

3. Variable overhead will continue at the same proportion of direct labor costs.

4. Other costs should not be affected.

Required

a. Present an analysis supporting a decision to accept or reject the special order. (Round computations to the nearest cent.)

b. What is the lowest price Glendale could receive and still make a $3,600 profit before income taxes on the special order?

c. What general qualitative factors should Glendale consider?

P8-3A. Make or Buy Allen Corporation currently makes the nylon convertible top for its main product, a fiberglass boat designed especially for water skiing. The costs of producing the 1,500 tops needed each year follow:

LO3

Nylon fabric	$270,000
Aluminum tubing	96,000
Frame fittings	24,000
Direct labor.	162,000
Variable manufacturing overhead.	30,000
Fixed manufacturing overhead.	152,000

Dustin Company, a specialty fabricator of synthetic materials, can make the needed tops of comparable quality for $400 each, F.O.B. shipping point. Allen would furnish its own trademark insignia at a unit cost of $16. Transportation in would be $28 per unit, paid by Allen Corporation.

Allen's chief accountant has prepared a cost analysis that shows that only 20% of fixed overhead could be avoided if the tops are purchased. The tops have been made in a remote section of Allen's factory building, using equipment for which no alternate use is apparent in the foreseeable future.

Required

a. Prepare a differential analysis showing whether or not you would recommend that the convertible tops be purchased from Dustin Company.

b. Assuming that the production capacity released by purchasing the tops could be devoted to a subcontracting job for another company that netted a contribution margin of $41,600, what maximum purchase price could Allen Corporation pay for the tops?

c. Identify two important qualitative factors that Allen Corporation should consider in deciding whether to purchase the needed tops.

P8-4A. Dropping Unprofitable Division Based on the following analysis of last year's operations of Bingham, Inc., a financial vice president of the company believes that the firm's total net income could be increased by $200,000 if its engineering division were discontinued. (Amounts are given in thousands of dollars.)

LO4

SERVICE AND
MERCHANDISING

	Totals	All Other Divisions	Engineering Division
Sales.	$11,200	$8,000	$ 3,200
Cost of services:			
Variable.	(3,880)	(2,600)	(1,280)
Fixed	(2,120)	(1,400)	(720)
Gross profit.	$ 5,200	$4,000	$ 1,200
Operating expenses:			
Variable.	(3,000)	(2,000)	(1,000)
Fixed	(1,600)	(1,200)	(400)
Net income (loss)	$ 600	$ 800	$ (200)

Required

Provide answers for each of the following independent situations:

a. Assuming that total fixed costs and expenses would not be affected by discontinuing the engineering division, prepare an analysis showing why you agree or disagree with the vice president.

b. Assume that discontinuance of the engineering division will enable the company to avoid 20% of the fixed portion of cost of services and 25% of the fixed operating expenses allocated to the engineering division. Calculate the resulting effect on net income.

c.   Assume that in addition to the cost avoidance in requirement (b), the capacity released by discontinuance of the engineering division can be used to provide 6,000 new services that would have a variable cost per service of $36 and would require additional fixed costs totaling $68,000. At what unit price must the new service be sold if Bingham is to increase its total net income by $120,000?

LO5   P8-5A.   Joint Cost   The Sun-Kissed Company manufactures two skin-care lotions, Soft Skin and Silken Skin, out of a joint process. The joint (common) costs incurred are $420,000 for a standard production run that generates 180,000 gallons of Soft Skin and 120,000 gallons of Silken Skin. Additional processing costs beyond the split-off point are $1.40 per gallon for Soft Skin and $0.90 per gallon for Silken Skin. Soft Skin sells for $2.40 per gallon while Silken Skin sells for $3.90 per gallon.

The Best Eastern Hotel chain has asked the Sun-Kissed Company to supply it with 240,000 gallons of Silken Skin at a price of $3.65 per gallon. Best Eastern plans to have the Silken Skin bottled in 1.5-ounce personal-use containers that are supplied in each of its hotel rooms as part of the complimentary personal products for guest use.

If Sun-Kissed accepts the order, it will save $0.05 per gallon in packaging of Silken Skin. There is sufficient excess capacity in Sun-Kissed's production system to handle just one more production run in order to have sufficient Silken Skin for this special order. However, the nature of the joint process always results in 180,000 gallons of Soft Skin and 120,000 gallons of Silken Skin. Also, the market for Soft Skin is saturated; hence, any additional sales of Soft Skin would take place at a price of $1.60 per gallon.

Required
a.   What is the profit normally earned on one production run of Soft Skin and Silken Skin?
b.   What is the incremental effect on overall income if the Sun-Kissed Company accepts the special order for Silken Skin?

LO6   P8-6A.   Product Emphasis   Lowell Corporation manufactures both a deluxe and a standard model of a household food blender. Because of limited demand, for several years production has been at 80% of estimated capacity, which is thought to be limited by the number of machine hours available. At current operation levels, a profit analysis for each product line shows the following data:

	Per-Unit Data			
	Deluxe		**Standard**	
Sales price		$216		$84
Production costs:				
Direct material.	$89		$12	
Direct labor	36		23	
Variable manufacturing overhead.	15		11	
Fixed manufacturing overhead*	25	$165	10	$56
Variable operating expenses		18		10
Fixed operating expenses		8		5
Total cost		$191		$71
Operating income.		$ 25		$13

* Assigned on the basis of machine hours at normal capacity.

Management wants to utilize the company's current excess capacity by increasing production.

Required
a.   What general decision guideline applies in this situation?
b.   Assuming that sufficient units of either product can be sold at current prices to use existing capacity fully and that total fixed cost will not be affected, prepare an analysis showing which product line should be emphasized if net income for the firm is the decision basis.

PROBLEMS—SET B

P8-1B.   **Analyze Operational Changes**   The management of Manchester's Department Store is concerned about the operation of its sporting goods department, which has not been very successful. The following condensed income statement gives the latest year's results:

LO1

SERVICE AND
MERCHANDISING

	Sporting Goods Department	All Other Departments
Sales....................	$480,000	$2,400,000
Cost of goods sold...........	360,000	1,560,000
Gross profit.................	$120,000	$ 840,000
Direct expenses.............	$ 67,500	$ 336,000
Indirect expenses............	48,000	240,000
Total expenses..............	$115,500	$ 576,000
Net income.................	$ 4,500	$ 264,000

Required

a.   Calculate the gross profit percentage for the sporting goods department and for the other departments as a group.

b.   It is estimated that if an additional $10,500 were spent on promotion of sporting goods, average prices can be raised 5% without affecting physical volume of goods sold. What effect would this have on the operating results of the sporting goods department? (Ignore the effect of income tax.)

c.   Alternatively, it is estimated that physical volume of goods sold could be increased 8% if an additional $15,000 were spent on promotion of sporting goods and prices were not increased. Assuming that operating expenses remain the same, what effect would this have on the operating results of the sporting goods department? (Ignore the effect of income tax.)

P8-2B.   **Special Order**   Total cost data follow for Greenfield Manufacturing Company, which has a normal capacity per period of 20,000 units of product that sell for $54 each. For the foreseeable future, regular sales volume should continue to equal normal capacity.

LO2

Direct material	$266,800
Direct labor..	200,000
Variable manufacturing overhead....................................	152,000
Fixed manufacturing overhead (Note 1)...............................	118,800
Selling expense (Note 2)..	129,600
Administrative expense (fixed)	50,000
	$917,200

Notes:

1.   Beyond normal capacity, fixed overhead costs increase $4,500 for each 1,000 units *or fraction thereof* until a maximum capacity of 24,000 units is reached.

2.   Selling expenses consist of a 10% sales commission and shipping costs of $1 per unit. Greenfield pays only one-half of the regular sales commission rates on sales amounting to $3,000 or more.

Greenfield's sales manager has received a special order for 2,500 units from a large discount chain at a price of $44 each, F.O.B. factory. The controller's office has furnished the following additional cost data related to the special order:

1.   Changes in the product's design will reduce direct material costs by $4 per unit.

2.   Special processing will add 10% to the per-unit direct labor costs.

3.   Variable overhead will continue at the same proportion of direct labor costs.

4.   Other costs should not be affected.

Required

a.   Present an analysis supporting a decision to accept or reject the special order.
b.   What is the lowest price Greenfield could receive and still make a profit of $5,000 before income taxes on the special order?
c.   What general qualitative factors should Greenfield consider?

LO3   P8-3B.   Make or Buy   Walsh Corporation currently makes the nylon mooring cover for its main product, a fiberglass boat designed for tournament bass fishing. The costs of producing the 2,000 covers needed each year follow:

Nylon fabric	$320,000
Wood battens.	64,000
Brass fittings.	32,000
Direct labor.	128,000
Variable manufacturing overhead.	96,000
Fixed manufacturing overhead.	160,000

Calvin Company, a specialty fabricator of synthetic materials, can make the needed covers of comparable quality for $320 each, F.O.B. shipping point. Walsh would furnish its own trademark insignia at a unit cost of $20. Transportation in would be $16 per unit, paid by Walsh Corporation.

Walsh's chief accountant has prepared a cost analysis that shows that only 30% of fixed overhead could be avoided if the covers are purchased. The covers have been made in a remote section of Walsh's factory building, using equipment for which no alternate use is apparent in the foreseeable future.

Required

a.   Prepare a differential analysis showing whether or not you would recommend that the mooring covers be purchased from Calvin Company.
b.   Assuming that the production capacity released by purchasing the covers could be devoted to a subcontracting job for another company that netted a contribution margin of $64,000, what maximum purchase price could Walsh pay for the covers?
c.   Identify two important qualitative factors that Walsh Corporation should consider in deciding whether to purchase the needed covers.

LO4   P8-4B.   Dropping Unprofitable Division   Based on the following analysis of last year's operations of Groves, Inc., a financial vice president of the company believes that the firm's total net income could be increased by $160,000 if its design division were discontinued. (Amounts are given in thousands of dollars.)

	Totals	All Other Divisions	Design Division
Sales.	$18,800	$14,400	$4,400
Cost of services:			
Variable.	(7,600)	(5,600)	(2,000)
Fixed.	(4,800)	(4,000)	(800)
Gross profit	$ 6,400	$ 4,800	$1,600
Operating expenses:			
Variable.	(3,360)	(2,000)	(1,360)
Fixed.	(1,600)	(1,200)	(400)
Net income (loss)	$ 1,440	$ 1,600	$ (160)

Required

Provide answers for each of the following independent situations:

a.   Assuming that total fixed costs and expenses would not be affected by discontinuing the design division, prepare an analysis showing why you agree or disagree with the vice president.
b.   Assume that discontinuance of the design division will enable the company to avoid 30% of the fixed portion of cost of services and 40% of the fixed operating expenses allocated to the design division. Calculate the resulting effect on net income.

c. Assume that in addition to the cost avoidance in requirement (b), the capacity released by discontinuance of the design division can be used to provide 6,000 new services that would have a variable cost per service of $60 and would require additional fixed costs totaling $68,000. At what unit price must the new service be sold if Groves is to increase its total net income by $180,000?

P8-5B. **Product Emphasis** McDermott Corporation manufactures both automatic and manual residential   **LO6**
water treatment units. Because of limited demand, for several years production has been at 90% of estimated capacity, which is thought to be limited by the number of machine hours available. At current operation levels, a profit analysis for each product line shows the following:

	Per-Unit Data			
	Automatic		**Manual**	
Sales price		$800		$416
Production costs:				
Direct material.	$144		$80	
Direct labor	128		64	
Variable manufacturing overhead.	64		32	
Fixed manufacturing overhead*	144	$480	72	$248
Variable operating expenses		80		16
Fixed operating expenses		144		96
Total cost		$704		$360
Operating income.		$ 96		$ 56

*Assigned on the basis of machine hours at normal capacity.

Management wants to utilize the company's current excess capacity by increasing production.

Required

a. What general decision guideline applies in this situation?
b. Assuming that sufficient units of either product can be sold at current prices to use existing capacity fully and that total fixed cost will not be affected, prepare an analysis showing which product line should be emphasized if net income for the firm is the decision basis.

CERTIFIED MANAGEMENT ACCOUNTANT (CMA®) EXAM SAMPLE QUESTIONS

CMA 8-1. Tucariz Company processes Duo into two joint products, Big and Mini. Duo is purchased in 1,000-gallon drums for $2,000. Processing costs are $3,000 to process the 1,000 gallons of Duo into 800 gallons of Big and 200 gallons of Mini. The selling price is $9 per gallon for Big and $4 per gallon for Mini. If the sales value at split-off method is used to allocate joint costs to the final products, the per-gallon cost (rounded to the nearest cent) of producing Big is

a. $5.63 per gallon.
b. $5.00 per gallon.
c. $4.50 per gallon.
d. $3.38 per gallon.

CMA 8-2. Current business segment operations for Whitman, a mass retailer, are presented below.

	Merchandise	**Automotive**	**Restaurant**	**Total**
Sales.	$500,000	$400,000	$100,000	$1,000,000
Variable costs.	300,000	200,000	70,000	570,000
Fixed costs.	100,000	100,000	50,000	250,000
Operating income (loss) . . .	$100,000	$100,000	$ (20,000)	$ 180,000

Management is contemplating the discontinuance of the Restaurant segment because "it is losing money." If this segment is discontinued, $30,000 of its fixed costs will be eliminated. In addition,

Merchandise and Automotive sales will decrease 5% from their current levels. What will Whitman's total contribution margin be if the Restaurant segment is discontinued?

a. $160,000
b. $220,000
c. $367,650
d. $380,000

CMA 8-3. Johnson Company manufactures a variety of shoes, and has received a special one-time-only order directly from a wholesaler. Johnson has sufficient idle capacity to accept the special order to manufacture 15,000 pairs of sneakers at a price of $7.50 per pair. Johnson's normal selling price is $11.50 per pair of sneakers. Variable manufacturing costs are $5.00 per pair and fixed manufacturing costs are $3.00 a pair. Johnson's variable selling expense for its normal line of sneakers is $1.00 per pair. What would the effect on Johnson's operating income be if the company accepted the special order?

a. Decrease by $60,000
b. Increase by $22,500
c. Increase by $37,500
d. Increase by $52,500

CMA 8-4. The loss of a key customer has temporarily caused Bedford Machining to have some excess manufacturing capacity. Bedford is considering the acceptance of a special order, one that involves Bedford's most popular product. Consider the following types of costs.

I. Variable costs of the product
II. Fixed costs of the product
III. Direct fixed costs associated with the order
IV. Opportunity cost of the temporarily idle capacity

Which one of the following combinations of cost types should be considered in the special order acceptance decision?

a. I and II
b. I and IV
c. II and III
d. I, III, and IV

CMA 8-5. Refrigerator Company manufactures ice-makers for installation in refrigerators. The costs per unit, for 20,000 units of ice-makers, are as follows.

Direct materials	$ 7
Direct labor	12
Variable overhead	5
Fixed overhead	10
Total costs	$34

Cool Compartments Inc. has offered to sell 20,000 ice-makers to Refrigerator Company for $28 per unit. If Refrigerator accepts Cool Compartments' offer, the facilities used to manufacture ice-makers could be used to produce water filtration units. Revenues from the sale of water filtration units are estimated at $80,000, with variable costs amounting to 60% of sales. In addition, $6 per unit of the fixed overhead associated with the manufacture of ice-makers could be eliminated.

For Refrigerator Company to determine the **most** appropriate action to take in this situation, the total relevant costs of make vs. buy, respectively, are

a. $600,000 vs. $560,000.
b. $648,000 vs. $528,000.
c. $600,000 vs. $528,000.
d. $680,000 vs. $440,000.

EKY8-1. **Business Decision Case** Marvin Corporation manufactures both an automatic and a manual household dehumidifier. Because of limited demand, for several years production has been at 80% of estimated capacity, which is thought to be limited by the number of machine hours available. At current operation levels, a profit analysis for each product line shows the following:

	Per-unit Data			
	Automatic		**Manual**	
Sales price		$350		$150
Production costs:				
Direct material.	$65		$32	
Direct labor	35		25	
Variable manufacturing overhead.	68		16	
Fixed manufacturing overhead.	50	$218	18	$ 91
Variable operating expenses		52		21
Fixed operating expenses		30		13
Total cost		$300		$125
Operating income.		$ 50		$ 25

Management wants to make use of the company's current excess capacity by increasing production. Each unit of the automatic model requires 2.5 machine hours; the manual model requires 1 machine hour per unit.

Required

Present answers for the following questions in each independent situation:

a. Assume that sufficient units of either product can be sold at current prices to utilize existing capacity fully and that fixed costs will not be affected.
   1. To which product should the excess capacity be devoted if the decision basis is maximization of contribution margin per unit of product?
   2. Prepare an analysis showing which product line should be emphasized if the firm's net income is the decision basis.
   3. What general decision guideline applies in this situation?

b. Suppose the excess capacity represents 10,000 machine hours, which can be used to make 4,000 automatic units or 10,000 manual units or any proportionate combination. The only market available for these extra units is a foreign market in which the sales prices must be reduced by 20% and in which no more than 6,000 units of either model can be sold. All costs will remain the same except that the sales commission of 10% (included in the variable operating expenses) will be avoided. Prepare an analysis showing which product should be emphasized and the effect on the firm's net income.

c. Assume that the excess capacity can be used as indicated in requirement (b) and that the firm's market research department believes that the production available from using the excess capacity exclusively on either model can be sold in the domestic market at regular prices if a promotion campaign costing $225,000 is undertaken for the automatic model or $235,000 for the manual model. Prepare an analysis indicating for which product the campaign should be undertaken.

EKY8-2. **Business Decision Case** Hall Manufacturing Corporation makes a new high-tech adhesive in a single process that blends and bottles die product, which currently sells for $20 per gallon. Market demand for the product seems good, but management is not satisfied with the product's seemingly low profit margin and has sought your advice.

Because of its concern, management has allocated a $60,000 fund for a program of product promotion or cost reduction, or both. Members of the firm's controller's office and marketing staff have identified the following three possible plans:

1. Plan A: Devote all funds to product promotion, which allows all costs and the sales volume to remain the same, but permits a sales price increase of $3.50 per gallon.
2. Plan B: Spend $32,000 on product promotion and $28,000 on cost reduction techniques, which maintains sales volume, permits a price increase of $2 per gallon, and reduces conversion costs by 10% per gallon.
3. Plan C: Devote all funds to cost reduction efforts. Sales volume and price do not change. For each gallon produced, however, direct material cost decreases 10%, and conversion cost decreases 20%.

The controller's office also provides you with the following operating data for a typical period (all materials are added initially; conversion costs occur evenly throughout the process; the weighted average method is used for process costing):

Beginning work in process (2,500 gallons, 60% processed)	$ 32,250
Units started in process (34,000 gallons)	
Ending work in process (3,500 gallons, 60% processed)	
Costs charged to the department:	
Direct material	275,400
Direct labor.	186,390
Manufacturing overhead	156,330
	$650,370

Required
Using the data from this representative production period, analyze the apparent relative benefits derived from each plan and make a recommendation supported by relevant calculations. Assume that sales for each period will equal units completed in that period. *Hint:* You will need to prepare a Production Report, Cost per Equivalent Unit Report, and Production Cost Report to analyze the three plans. These reports were discussed in Chapter 4.

EKY8-3.   **Ethics Case** Swan Sports manufactures golfing equipment. Traditionally, the company has been busy all year but has noticed that over the past few years business has fallen off in October and November. If new business does not come in this year, the company will have to lay off some long-time employees for those 2 months. Rob Patell, a sales representative, received an order from Better Equipment Co., a competitor. Better Equipment cannot meet a customer's rush order on time and is willing to subcontract the work to Swan Sports on the condition that the Better Equipment Co. name—not Swan Sports' name—appear on all products. The order is at a price substantially below Swan Sports' usual selling price. The only way this order can be produced is to use lower-quality materials than Swan Sports normally uses in its own products.

Rob Patell has recommended to his supervisor that this order be accepted and that lower-quality materials be used. Patell's reasoning includes the following points:

a.   It is clearly a one-time order.
b.   Swan Sports' name will not appear on it.
c.   Workers will not have to be laid off during October and November.

A differential analysis shows that Swan Sports will lose $1,000 on the order.

Required
What should the sales supervisor consider before making a decision?

EKY8-4.   **Corporate Social Responsibility** The "Corporate Social Responsibility" box in this chapter highlights some early citizenship milestones of John Deere. Go to John Deere's web site and search under the "Our Company" tab for "Citizenship." Under the citizenship page find the link to learning about John Deere's citizenship milestones. Select a more recent time period and read about some of the reported moments that became milestones. Can you think of a good business purpose for these reported achievements, or are they simply things that make John Deere a good corporate citizen?

ANSWERS TO SELF-STUDY QUESTIONS:

1. c, (p. 267)   2. c, (p. 270)   3. a, (pp. 271–272)   4. d, (pp. 272–273)   5. b, (p. 275)

YOUR TURN! SOLUTIONS

Solution 8.1
Yes.

Differential revenue.	$200,000
Differential cost (10,000 × $14) + ($40,000 − $5,000)	175,000
Net increase in profit	$ 25,000

Solution 8.2
Product B. ($12/1 hour is greater than $15/2 hours)

DECISION TIME SOLUTIONS

Solution 8.1
No. Fixed costs that differ among alternatives are relevant.

Solution 8.2
The segment should be dropped if the company will avoid more in fixed costs than it loses in contribution margin.

9 Planning and Budgeting

LEARNING OBJECTIVES

1. **Describe** the planning process, including strategic planning and operational planning. *(p. 298)*

2. **Discuss** the budgeting process and **summarize** its advantages. **Define** the key elements of effective budgeting. *(p. 301)*

3. **Define** the components of a master budget and **illustrate** the interrelationships of the individual budgets that comprise the master budget. *(p. 305)*

4. **Prepare** individual budgets for a manufacturing and a service company, including the cash budget. *(p. 306)*

5. **Prepare** budgeted financial statements. *(p. 315)*

MONSANTO

MONSANTO

Monsanto manufactures agricultural products for farmers throughout the world. The company's products include 21 types of conventional and biotech vegetable seeds and herbicides, including Roundup®, to enable farmers to produce more from their land while conserving water and energy. Monsanto's seeds include corn, soybean, cotton, wheat, canola, sorghum, and sugar cane seeds. In some cases, Monsanto uses genetic modification to bring beneficial traits, such as drought tolerance or the ability to ward off pests, to the resulting plant. Its herbicides are used on both farms for agricultural purposes and in industrial and large non-farm areas such as parks, golf courses, and zoos.

Monsanto's business is highly seasonal, with approximately three-fourths of its seed sales occurring during the second and third quarters of its fiscal year, which ends August 31. The seasonality corresponds to the North American purchasing and growing patterns. The season for several of Monsanto's herbicide products is even shorter—about 2 months long. The capital investment required to produce all required product during the 2-month sales period would be substantial—instead, Monsanto must project product demand, produce the product well in advance, and store or ship the products to its distributors, wholesalers, and retailers before the growing season begins each year.

Its business is also influenced by weather. With climate shifts becoming more volatile, planting time may vary by several weeks in a specific location. The combination of seasonality and weather, together with normal economic variability, makes Monsanto's business very challenging to forecast. Because Monsanto must produce its products well in advance of the season, even a small error in forecasting demand for its products can result in either (1) significant inventory left at the end of the season or (2) lost sales due to product shortages.

Historically, sales forecasts were developed by corporate headquarters 6 to 9 months prior to the actual sales period. The manufacturing of finished goods was largely driven by the production of the active ingredients, which were produced year-round. Thus, product was shipped ahead of actual demand because of limited storage capabilities at Monsanto's production facilities. If demand were affected by weather or some other market effect, more product might have been shipped to a particular site than was needed and not enough product might have been shipped to another site. Inaccurate forecasts required costly redistribution of product to match supply with demand.

More recently, Monsanto has attempted to address the uncertainties regarding demand for its products by employing local sales employees to develop more frequent (as often as weekly) forecasts of the local market demand. These forecasts are aggregated into weekly demand forecasts that are used to develop production and distribution plans. Nevertheless, demand uncertainty will always be an issue for Monsanto's management, making the budgeting process a challenge to manage!

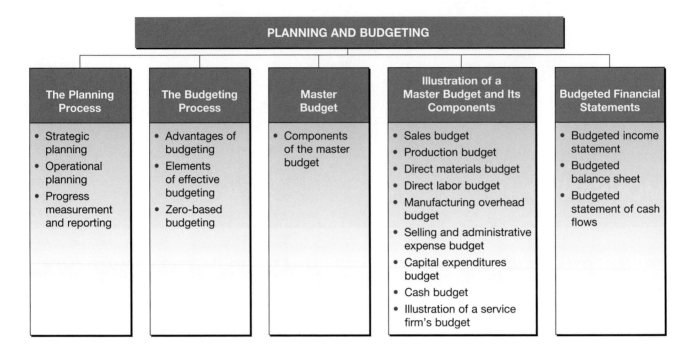

Prediction is very difficult, especially about the future.

NIELS BOHR

Your ability to live within your means over the long term and meet your financial obligations from paycheck to paycheck depends in large part on your ability to accurately identify your income and manage your expenses. If you consistently overestimate your income or underestimate your expenses, you may find yourself getting deeper and deeper into debt. Without a financial plan, or budget, you run the risk of financial hardship or ruin.

Likewise, to be successful, every business needs to produce products or provide services at competitive costs for a growing customer base to ensure that reasonable profits are made to continue to grow the business. Management has a basic responsibility to plan, control, and measure performance and to make decisions. To carry out these responsibilities, management must develop plans and budgets, determine actual operating results, compare actual results to planned results, evaluate differences, and take corrective action to improve operations. This chapter focuses on managerial planning and budgeting.

THE PLANNING PROCESS

LO1 **Describe** the planning process, including strategic planning and operational planning.

All types of organizations—service organizations, merchandising firms, manufacturing companies, government agencies, and not-for-profit entities—can benefit from formalized planning. A formal planning process usually includes strategic planning and operational planning.

A **planning horizon** is the future time span, usually expressed in years, for which a particular plan is developed. Different types of plans have different planning horizons. Typically, longer planning horizons are associated with higher-level planning (such as strategic planning), whereas shorter planning horizons are associated with lower-level planning (such as annual operational planning.) **Exhibit 9-1** is an example of a formal planning process. As illustrated, the planning process begins with the definition of a vision or mission statement. This statement defines what the company is and provides a focus for its strategy and operational planning. The best vision statements are succinct and clear. Monsanto states that it is a sustainable agriculture company that supports farmers, enabling them to produce more from their land while conserving the world's natural resources, such as water and energy.

Exhibit 9-1	Planning Process

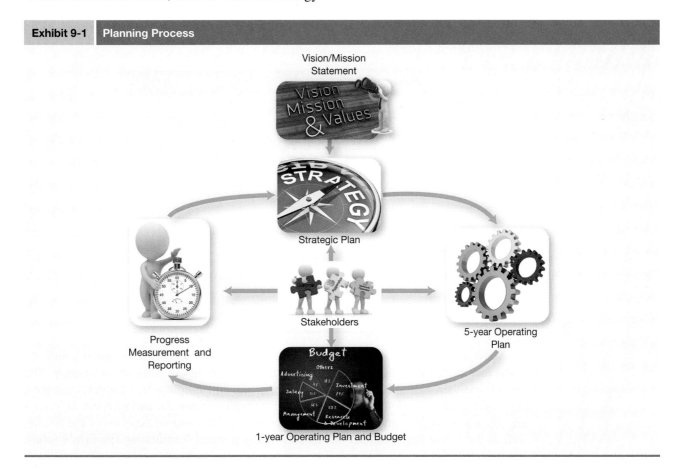

Strategic Planning

Strategic planning is a formal process that addresses and documents the overall mission and long-term goals of the organization based on the vision statement. Management must evaluate and decide what directions the organization should go in the future. Issues to be decided include what basic lines of business to pursue, which geographic markets to establish, what organization structure to develop, where to locate facilities, which means of sales and distribution to use, and how aggressively the organization should grow. For example, Monsanto's strategic plan is to provide healthy and nutritious food for a world population that is growing faster than food production. In keeping with this strategy, Monsanto's management sold its animal agricultural products business (its dairy business) in 2008 to focus on seeds and improving crop productivity.

General Motors Strategic Plans	ACCOUNTING IN PRACTICE

The 2014 **General Motors** annual report included a letter to stockholders from Chief Executive Officer Mary T. Barra highlighting the goal for GM to become the most valued automotive company. It included the following strategic initiatives:

1. Introduce a new mid-sized truck
2. Restore Cadillac to a position of leadership in the global luxury segment
3. Rebuild the Opel brand
4. Expand in China, Brazil and other developing markets
5. Expand ability to offer customers financing and leasing

Management must accumulate and analyze a great deal of information to create an appropriate strategic plan incorporating these decisions. Many companies use a technique such as a **strengths, weaknesses, opportunities, and threats (SWOT) analysis** to begin this accumulation and analysis process. **Exhibit 9-2** illustrates this process in the form of a 2×2 matrix.

Exhibit 9-2	SWOT Matrix	
	Helpful	Harmful
Internal	Strengths	Weaknesses
External	Opportunities	Threats

Management uses SWOT analysis to analyze and document those internal and external factors that both help and harm the company's ability to achieve its strategy. The SWOT analysis will specifically address management, employees, products, services, physical facilities, customers, competitors, distribution channels, and systems. It is very important to recognize and document the current strengths and weaknesses of the firm as well as the future opportunities and threats facing it when formulating the firm's future strategic directions.

Management takes the information accumulated during the SWOT analysis, makes assumptions about the economy and the future competitive environment, and formulates management strategies for the entity. A 5- or 10-year planning horizon is typical. These strategies are documented in the strategic plan, which is typically updated and revised annually for changing conditions. Frequently, elements of a SWOT analysis can be seen in the Management's Discussion and Analysis section of a public company's Form 10-K filing with the Securities and Exchange Commission.

YOUR TURN! 9.1

The solution is on page 337.

Assume you are performing a SWOT analysis for the retail company **Target** and have been assigned to focus on threats to its business. List some threats that could impact the company in coming years.

Operational Planning

Management also prepares operating plans consistent with the strategic plan. **Operational planning** is the process of developing specific goals and objectives for the entity as a whole and its individual departments, formulating an operating plan to accomplish the goals and objectives, and preparing written documentation of the goals and objectives as well as the operating plan. Firms frequently develop a long-term operating plan that covers a 3- to 5-year planning horizon as well as an annual operating plan that covers a 1-year planning horizon. The annual operating plan is typically more detailed than the long-term operating plan.

The annual operating plan projects some of the current operations as they exist and provides for changes in others to reflect management's desires for improvements in the operations. The annual operating plan reflects the strategies, goals, objectives, and action plan documented in the strategic plan and the long-term operating plan. Further, the annual operating plan is usually not in a format that enables management to determine whether the plans are economically feasible. Management tests the economic feasibility of the annual operating plan through the development of the annual operating budget.

For example, Monsanto's 2014 Annual Report[1] identifies plans to improve its vegetable seeds business, in part through strategic acquisitions and continued investment in seeds, genomics, and biotechnology.

Progress Measurement and Reporting

No planning process is complete without an accounting of the progress achieved in pursuing the plans made. A periodic accounting is helpful in measuring progress, holding individuals accountable for aspects of the plan that are within their area of responsibility, and evaluating whether changes need to be made to future plans based on changes in the internal or external environment in which the company operates. This accounting takes many forms, including internal management reports and external reports to owners, creditors, and other stakeholders. For example, Monsanto's external reports include quarterly earnings releases, numerous Securities and Exchange Commission reports, and a corporate sustainability report. Each of these reports highlights different results of Monsanto's operations.

Monsanto's Employee Volunteer Program—Monsantogether	CORPORATE SOCIAL RESPONSIBILITY

This chapter discusses the importance of budgeting to a company's financial performance. A recent *Forbes* article discusses the importance of budgeting for corporate social responsibility success.* The article discusses how doing good through employee volunteering programs leads to the company doing well through increased employee engagement, employee retention, and employee recruitment.

Monsanto appears to agree with what the article author writes. As noted on Monsanto's web site, "Monsanto employees are fighting rural hunger as part of a coordinated volunteer effort in areas where Monsanto employees live and work across the United States. . . . [in two events] 965 Monsanto employees worked more than 3,800 volunteer hours at 96 food bank or food drive locations. The effort is part of an employee volunteer program called Monsantogether, which is focused on enriching the communities where Monsanto employees live and work. Both individual employees and groups of employees can earn money through Monsantogether for qualified non-profit organizations where they volunteer, simply as a result of volunteering a minimum of 20 hours. In 2012, Monsanto awarded more than $225,000 in grants to non-profit organizations based on nearly 50,000 employee volunteer hours. Of that amount, $15,000 was directed toward food banks and food pantries across the U.S. to help address local community needs. The Fighting Rural Hunger volunteer events are part of Monsanto's larger effort to eradicate hunger in rural America through partnerships and philanthropy."

*Ryan Scott, "'Tis the Season to Budget for CSR Success," *Forbes*, November 19, 2012.

THE BUDGETING PROCESS

A **budget** is a detailed plan for the acquisition and use of financial resources during a specific period of time.

Budgeting is the process of developing a formal, written operating plan that presents management's planned actions in financial terms. Budgeting should reflect the conclusions reached in the strategic plan and the operating plan. Two budgets usually result from the budgeting process: the annual operating budget and the capital expenditures budget. We present and discuss the

LO2 Discuss the budgeting process and **summarize** its advantages. **Define** the key elements of effective budgeting.

A.K.A. The annual operating budget is also called the **master budget**.

---

[1] http://www.monsanto.com/investors/documents/annual%20report/2014/2014_monsanto_annualreport.pdf, page 29.

annual operating budget in this chapter and the capital expenditures budget in Chapter 12. **Exhibit 9-1** presents the sequence for preparing the various types of plans and budgets.

All types of entities can derive benefits from the budgeting process. Although the basic concepts of budgeting apply to all types of entities, the precise budget form will vary among those entities. Budgeting typically incorporates many accounting concepts discussed in previous chapters. In fact, some components of the annual operating budget have familiar accounting formats.

TAKEAWAY 9.1

In practice, budgeting rarely turns out to be 100% accurate. However, it is still an important process because it forces management and other involved parties to consider all aspects of a company and how managerial decisions impact company performance.

Advantages of Budgeting

The use of budgets to manage and control a firm's activities is known as **budgetary control.** Budgetary control involves the steps taken by management to ensure that the goals and objectives established during the planning stage are attained, and to ensure that all segments of the firm operate in a manner consistent with organizational policies. Used properly, a budget can sharpen management's focus, ensure that operating activities will help achieve management's overall strategy, and be useful in evaluating performance.

The annual planning and budgeting process forces management to step back from the daily operations of the entity, examine current operations, decide what improvements are necessary, and formulate plans and budgets that implement the established goals and objectives for the entity. The annual operating budget represents a specific plan for accomplishing these goals and objectives.

A budget can be used to control operations. When a business is large enough to be divided into departments, management needs to ensure that the operation of each department is consistent with the overall plans for the entity as a whole. The budget provides guidance for the departmental managers so their decisions will be consistent with decisions in other departments. For example, the budget provides guidance so the purchasing department buys quantities of material consistent with the factory's budget of units to be manufactured; that budget, in turn, is consistent with the sales department's budget of units to be sold.

TAKEAWAY 9.2

Assume management budgets sales of 10,000 units and has only 1,000 currently on hand. In this scenario, management would not budget production at 2,000 units because that would only leave 3,000 available for sale (1,000 on hand + 2,000 produced). Failure to budget for sufficient production to make 10,000 units available for sale would be considered a lack of consistency among departmental budgets.

Budgets serve as guides and targets to managers when they make decisions and as one basis for performance evaluation. Performance evaluations could be based on comparison of actual results to prior-period results. However, comparison to prior-period results fails to take into account the changes and improvements that have been incorporated into the budget. As a result, the budget is frequently the basis for evaluating performance. Because the budget is used as a basis for evaluating performance, it can also be a motivating factor for individual managers. Assuming that the budget is realistic, it provides a target that each manager will try to attain.

DECISION TIME 9.1

The solution is on page 337.

What are the advantages of budgeting?

Elements of Effective Budgeting

Even though specific budgeting procedures vary widely among business firms, all entities engaged in comprehensive budgeting should consider the following elements of effective budgeting.

Identifying a **budget director** is vital to effective budgeting. Budget director may be a full-time or part-time position, depending on the size and complexity of the business. The budget director must be well organized and a good communicator, since he or she is responsible for organizing the budgeting process, communicating with the people involved in budgeting, and monitoring the process to ensure that it proceeds on a timely basis.

The **budget committee** generally consists of representatives from all major areas of the firm, such as sales, manufacturing, purchasing, and accounting, and is usually headed by the budget director. The primary functions of the budget committee are to provide central guidance to the budget preparation process, ensure that all departments participate in the process, and evaluate the proposed budget segments for reasonableness.

The task of developing the detailed amounts for the budget is usually not done by the budget director or the budget committee. **Participative budgeting** requires that detailed budget amounts be formulated "from the bottom up." That is, all departments should participate in the development and refinement of the budget amounts so they will be accepted by the departments as reasonable standards of performance. The participants in this process are illustrated in **Exhibit 9-3**.

Exhibit 9-3	Participants in a Participative Budgeting Process

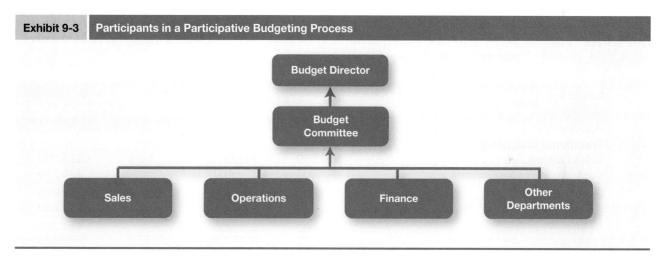

There are advantages to participative budgeting:

1. Individuals at all levels are part of a team.
2. The person in direct contact with the activity is in the best position to make the estimates.
3. A person has ownership of and is therefore more motivated to work at fulfilling a budget that he or she has helped establish.

The **budget period,** the future time span for which the budget is prepared, varies according to the nature of the specific activity involved. Most companies, however, prepare annual operating budgets, which are segmented into quarterly or monthly budgets. Short-term operating budgets covering a month or a quarter may be useful benchmarks as one element of performance evaluations, enabling management to compare budgeted amounts to actual results and initiate corrective action as required.

The capital expenditures budget usually covers a multiyear period, often 3 to 5 years. This longer budget period is necessary because of the long time period required to construct or acquire long-term assets of a unique nature.

A.K.A. Continuous **budgets** are also known as **perpetual** or **rolling budgets**.

Many businesses use **continuous budgeting** techniques for the operating budget. As each monthly or quarterly budget period passes, the oldest month or quarter is removed from the budget and another month or quarter is added to extend the budget to a full year in the future. With this approach, regardless of the time of the year, the budget always covers 12 months or four quarters.

Zero-Base Budgeting

Traditional budgeting procedures typically use an incremental approach to the development of the annual operating budget. For example, the level of each expense for the prior year is used as the starting point for determining the budgeted level for the next year. The person preparing the budget then either adds to or subtracts from the amount in the previous budget. During the budget process, only the increase or decrease is justified to the managers reviewing the proposed budget drafts. The prior year base amount is assumed to be reasonable. For example, the simple traditional budget example in **Exhibit 9-4** shows a budget based on a 10% increase from the current year.

Many organizations—manufacturing companies, merchandising firms, service organizations, governmental agencies, and not-for-profit entities—have experienced increases in their annual operating budgets that they deem to be unacceptable. Some of these organizations have decided to use zero-base budgeting techniques to address this problem. **Zero-base budgeting** requires budget preparers to start at a zero level for every item in the budget and justify every dollar, not just the increases or decreases. In effect, the budget is prepared "from the ground up" as if the entity had just been formed. The simple zero-base budget example in **Exhibit 9-4** shows that the budget is created without reference to the previous year's budgets.

Exhibit 9-4	Traditional Budgeting vs. Zero-Base Budgeting				
		Prior Year	**Current Year**	**Adjustment**	**Budget Year**
Traditional Budgeting					
Sales revenue..........................		$10,000	$12,000	10%	$13,200
Cost of goods sold.....................		$ 7,000	$ 8,400	10%	$ 9,240
Gross profit...........................		$ 3,000	$ 3,600		$ 3,960
Sales, general, & administrative expenses...		$ 2,000	$ 2,400	10%	$ 2,640
Operating income......................		$ 1,000	$ 1,200		$ 1,320
Zero-base Budgeting					
Sales revenue..........................		$ —	$ —	$13,200	$13,200
Cost of goods sold.....................		$ —	$ —	$ 9,240	$ 9,240
Gross profit...........................		$ —	$ —	$ 3,960	$ 3,960
Sales, general, & administrative expenses...		$ —	$ —	$ 2,640	$ 2,640
Operating income......................		$ —	$ —	$ 1,320	$ 1,320

Organizations that have adopted zero-base budgeting use a variety of specific procedures. A common approach is to segment the budget into "decision packages" in which the preparer ranks all of the activities according to their relative importance for each activity. The preparer might note the consequences of not performing the activity, possible alternative activities, and whether there is an external mandate to perform the activity. This approach enables various levels of management to eliminate low-ranking activities until a desired budget level is reached.

Note that zero-base budgeting is a time-consuming and costly process. As a result, many entities that employ the technique usually do not apply it to all portions of the operating budget each year. Some use zero-base budgeting every year but apply the technique to only selected segments of the budget so that all segments will be subjected to the technique once during each 5-year period. Others apply the technique to all segments periodically (such as every third year). As a result, traditional budgeting techniques might be used to prepare budgets for years 1 and 2, with zero-base budgeting used to prepare the budget for year 3.

Zero-base budgeting requires that a manager:

1. Determine goals, operations, and costs for all activities under his or her jurisdiction.
2. Determine alternative means of conducting the activity.
3. Evaluate the implications of changes in the level of each activity.
4. Establish workload.
5. Rank activities in order of importance.

THE FRAMEWORK OF THE MASTER BUDGET

Master budget is the name given to the comprehensive annual operating budget. The master budget combines and integrates all of the individual, detailed operating budgets for all of the firm's various activities for the year. All amounts in the master budget are usually based on the expected level of operations. The exact structure of the master budget varies according to whether the firm's operations are manufacturing, merchandising, service, or government oriented. In this chapter, we illustrate budgeting and a master budget for Fezzari, the small bicycle manufacturer introduced in Chapter 1. The following budgets constitute Fezzari's master budget:

LO3 **Define** the components of a master budget and **illustrate** the interrelationships of the individual budgets that comprise the master budget.

1. Sales budget
2. Production budget
3. Direct material budget
4. Direct labor budget
5. Manufacturing overhead budget
6. Selling and administrative expense budget
7. Capital expenditures budget
8. Cash budget
9. Budgeted income statement
10. Budgeted balance sheet
11. Budgeted statement of cash flows

Fezzari's master budget includes budgets that are interdependent and must be prepared in a specific sequence. **Exhibit 9-5** presents Fezzari's master budget and the data flows that are necessary between the individual budgets during their preparation.

The sales budget is prepared first. It is based on the sales forecast and typically includes both sales dollars and quantities. As the sales budget feeds into each of the succeeding budgets, the quality of the sales forecast determines the success of the remaining process. Then the production budget is prepared to identify the number of units of each product to be manufactured. Then the direct material budget, the direct labor budget, and the manufacturing overhead budget determine the levels of product cost to be incurred based on the units to be manufactured. The selling and administrative expense budget determines the level of selling and general administrative expense necessary to support the sales budget.

A.K.A. Budgets may be called **pro forma statements**. They are forecasted financial statements instead of actual financial statements.

The cash budget receives input from the budgets established previously as well as the capital expenditures budget and the budgeted income statement. In turn, the cash budget provides inputs to the budgeted balance sheet and the budgeted statement of cash flows. The budgeted balance sheet also receives input from the budgeted income statement and the capital expenditures budget and supplies input to the budgeted income statement. We illustrate these interrelationships in the following example.

Exhibit 9-5	Budgets and Data Flows in Fezzari's Master Budget

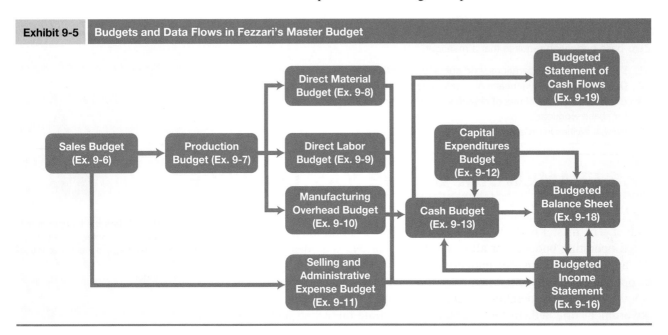

ILLUSTRATION OF A MASTER BUDGET AND ITS COMPONENTS

Sales Budget

LO4 **Prepare** individual budgets for a manufacturing and a service company, including the cash budget.

The **sales budget** provides the basis for all subsequent budgets. Anticipated unit sales volume is based on the **sales forecast**. The sales forecast is the sales department's best estimate of what sales will be for the company and the industry in which it operates. Factors that are evaluated in preparing the sales forecast include prior company sales levels, future pricing policies, market research studies, general economic conditions, specific economic indicators, advertising and promotion plans, and anticipated activities of the competition. Over-estimating sales volume can lead to large unwanted inventories, which in turn result in extra storage costs and possibly sales price reductions when liquidating the excess inventory. Underestimating sales can lead to loss of sales revenue and customer ill will stemming from unfilled orders.

Assume that Fezzari managers are preparing their budget for the upcoming fiscal year. As we have discussed in earlier chapters, Fezzari sells two types of bikes, road and mountain, with several different models of each type. For purposes of this illustration, we will assume that the budget is prepared at the bike-type level, although in reality the budget would be prepared at the model level. Further, assume that Fezzari's management anticipates a 20% growth in sales in the next year.

The estimated unit sales volume of each product is multiplied by planned average unit sales prices to estimate total sales revenue. We present an example of a sales budget in **Exhibit 9-6**. To simplify the presentation of the cash budget, assume all Fezzari's sales are on a cash basis; therefore Fezzari carries no accounts receivable balances. We will demonstrate a sales budget for a service firm with credit sales later in the chapter.

Exhibit 9-6	Sales Budget Illustration

FEZZARI PERFORMANCE BICYCLES
Sales Budget
For the Year Ended December 31, 2016

	Forecast Unit Sales Volume	Average Unit Sales Price	Budgeted Total Sales
Road bicycles.	2,160	$1,250	$2,700,000
Mountain bicycles	3,240	$1,000	3,240,000
Total bicycles	5,400		$5,940,000
Other bicycle accessories			297,000
Total sales revenue			$6,237,000

Production Budget

The **production budget** reflects the quantity of each product to be produced during the budget period. Scheduled production should specifically provide for anticipated sales and desired ending inventories and, of course, consider the beginning inventories of each product. Assume that Fezzari wants to increase its inventory of road bikes from 8 to 12 units and its inventory of mountain bikes from 14 to 18 units. Fezzari's production budget appears in **Exhibit 9-7**. Note that the desired change in inventory of each product is accomplished by scheduling the appropriate production volumes. Because bicycle accessories are not manufactured by Fezzari, but simply purchased from vendors for resale, they are not included in the production budget.

Hint: Companies that do not use the just-in-time inventory method often determine required inventory levels based on a percentage of unit sales.

Like Fezzari, many manufacturing companies use the just-in-time approach for finished goods inventory to reduce their inventory carrying costs. When the **just-in-time inventory** approach is used, finished goods are not produced until they are needed for shipment to customers. As a result, the planned ending inventory of finished goods is zero or nearly zero.

Exhibit 9-7	Production Budget Illustration

FEZZARI PERFORMANCE BICYCLES
Production Budget
For the Year Ended December 31, 2016

	Units of Finished Product	
	Road Bikes	Mountain Bikes
Forecast unit sales	2,160	3,240
Desired ending finished goods inventories	12	18
Quantities to be available	2,172	3,258
Less: beginning finished goods inventories	8	14
Total production to be scheduled	2,164	3,244

This approach is practical only for companies that can forecast their sales very accurately, that do not have highly seasonal demand, and that have highly reliable suppliers of the materials and components needed to manufacture the finished goods. Many companies prefer to maintain a **safety stock** of finished goods inventory so they minimize the risk of running out of stock. Safety stock is defined as a quantity of inventory maintained

Hint: Running out of an item of inventory not only results in the loss of a current sale, but could also cause the loss of future sales due to negative publicity.

to supply unexpected demand or to provide stock when manufacturing is slowed through delays in receipt of materials and components from suppliers.

Direct Material Budget

The quantities of material to be purchased to meet scheduled production and desired ending materials inventory requirements are presented in the **direct material budget**. Any beginning material inventory must be considered in estimating purchases for the budget period. Because Fezzari assembles its bikes only after receiving a customer order, it does not maintain a large inventory of direct materials. The quantities to be acquired are multiplied by the anticipated unit prices to calculate the total dollar amounts of material purchases. In the direct material budget illustrated in **Exhibit 9-8**, we assume that Fezzari uses only two direct materials, a frame and a build kit containing all of the other components, in producing road and mountain bikes. Further, Fezzari targets to have sufficient frames and build kits in ending inventory for 6 road bikes and 10 mountain bikes.

Exhibit 9-8	Direct Materials Budget Illustration		
FEZZARI PERFORMANCE BICYCLES **Direct Materials Budget** **For the Year Ended December 31, 2016**			
	Frame	**Build Kit**	**Total**
Direct material required:			
Road bicycles.	2,164	2,164	
Desired ending material inventory	6	6	
Total units of material to be available.	2,170	2,170	
Less: beginning material inventory.	8	8	
Total units of material to be purchased	2,162	2,162	
Average unit purchase price.	$ 325	$ 275	
Total road bike material purchases	$ 702,650	$ 594,550	$1,297,200
Direct material required:			
Mountain bicycles	3,244	3,244	
Desired ending material inventory	10	10	
Total units of material to be available.	3,254	3,254	
Less: beginning material inventory.	14	14	
Total units of material to be purchased	3,240	3,240	
Average unit purchase price.	$ 350	$ 290	
Total mountain bike material purchases	$1,134,000	$ 939,600	$2,073,600
Total material purchases	$1,836,650	$1,534,150	$3,370,800
Add: beginning accounts payable balance . . .			50,000
Less: ending accounts payable balance			(75,000)
Cash budgeted for material purchases			$3,345,800

The just-in-time inventory philosophy may also apply to the materials inventory of manufacturing firms. Under this philosophy, materials and components needed to manufacture finished products would not be received from the suppliers until immediately before they are needed for manufacturing. As a result, the material inventory would be zero or nearly zero. Many firms prefer to carry safety stocks of materials and components to ensure that the manufacturing facility is not slowed or stopped by a supplier missing a scheduled delivery.

The direct materials budget in **Exhibit 9-8** shows the total purchases that are budgeted for 2016. However, because Fezzari purchases these materials on credit from its suppliers, the dollar amount of purchases may not equal the cash that will be expended for materials during 2016. Thus, in preparing the cash budget, an adjustment must be made for the change in the accounts payable balance during the year. **Exhibit 9-8** illustrates how the cash expended for direct materials might be calculated, assuming that the balance in accounts payable was expected to increase from $50,000 to $75,000 in 2016.

The increase in the accounts payable balance of $25,000 over the year means that Fezzari will spend $25,000 less than the total material purchases in cash.

Direct Labor Budget

The **direct labor budget** presents the number of direct labor hours necessary for the production volume planned for the budget period. These hours are multiplied by the applicable hourly labor rates to determine the total dollar amounts of direct labor costs to be budgeted. In the direct labor budget for Fezzari in **Exhibit 9-9**, we have assumed that both road and mountain bikes require the following average hours in the assembly and quality control and packaging departments:

	Assembly Hours	Quality Control and Packaging Hours
Road bikes.	5.5	2.0
Mountain bikes.	7.0	2.0

Exhibit 9-9	Direct Labor Budget Illustration

FEZZARI PERFORMANCE BICYCLES
Direct Labor Budget
For the Year Ended December 31, 2016

	Assembly Department	Quality Control and Packaging Department	Total
Direct labor			
Road Bicycles (average 5.5 hours assembly, 2 hours packaging)	11,902[1]	4,328[2]	
Mountain Bicycles (average 7 hours assembly, 2 hours packaging)	22,708[3]	6,488[4]	
Total direct labor hours	34,610	10,816	45,426
Hourly rate for direct labor	$ 25	$ 20	
Total direct labor cost	$865,250	$216,320	$1,081,570

[1] (2,164 bikes $\times$ 5.5 hours)

[2] (2,164 bikes $\times$ 2 hours)

[3] (3,244 bikes $\times$ 7 hours)

[4] (3,244 bikes $\times$ 2 hours)

Manufacturing Overhead Budget

Recall from earlier chapters that manufacturing overhead comprises all manufacturing costs that are not direct material or direct labor. Examples of manufacturing overhead are indirect material, indirect labor, supervisory salaries, utilities, depreciation, maintenance,

Hint: Manufacturing overhead is any cost incurred within the factory that is not direct in nature. Hence, factory costs – direct costs = indirect costs.

property taxes, and insurance. Because of the variety of cost factors, manufacturing overhead includes both variable and fixed cost elements.

The **manufacturing overhead budget** for Fezzari's Assembly and Packaging departments is shown in **Exhibit 9-10**. Note that the format separates variable and fixed overhead cost elements and presents budgeted overhead costs for the 45,426 direct labor hours expected to be incurred.

Management would determine the budgeted variable costs based on purchase agreements with its vendors (indirect material), labor agreements with its employees (indirect labor), and contracted rates for other services (utilities). Management would determine the budgeted fixed costs based on lease agreements, insurance contracts, local government tax notices, and current levels of equipment. These amounts would not be expected to vary from year to year. Usually, lease agreements are multiyear agreements with fixed rates for each year of the agreement and insurance coverage is adjusted only as manufacturing facilities are expanded. To simplify the presentation of the cash budget, assume that all overhead expenses, except depreciation, are paid in the month they are incurred.

Exhibit 9-10	Manufacturing Overhead Budget Illustration

FEZZARI PERFORMANCE BICYCLES
Manufacturing Overhead Budget
For the Year Ended December 31, 2016

	Variable Cost Per Direct Labor Hour	Total Costs at 45,426 Direct Labor Hours
Variable manufacturing costs		
Indirect material	$0.08	$ 3,634
Indirect labor.	$0.78	$ 35,432
Factory utilities	$0.86	$ 39,066
Other.	$0.36	$ 16,353
Total variable manufacturing overhead.	$2.08	$ 94,485
Fixed manufacturing costs		
Lease expense		$100,000
Insurance		68,000
Property taxes		12,000
Depreciation		45,100
Total fixed manufacturing overhead		225,100
Total manufacturing overhead		$319,585
Less: depreciation		(45,100)
Cash budgeted for manufacturing overhead		$274,485
Direct labor hours.		45,426
Budgeted predetermined manufacturing overhead rate (rounded) . . .		*$ 7.0353

* ($319,585/45,426)

As we discussed in **Chapter 3**, the predetermined overhead rate is determined by dividing the total budgeted manufacturing overhead by the budgeted activity level, or direct labor hours in this example. For the year ended December 31, 2016, the total cost formula for overhead at the planned operating volume of 45,426 direct labor hours (DLH) would be as follows:

Total manufacturing overhead cost = $2.08 × DLH + $225,100

Selling and Administrative Expense Budget

The **selling and administrative expense budget** will consist of variable and fixed expenses. The variable selling expenses will typically vary with dollars of sales. To simplify the presentation of the cash budget, assume that selling and administrative expenses, except depreciation, are paid in the month incurred. **Exhibit 9-11** presents Fezzari's selling and administrative expense budget.

Exhibit 9-11	Selling and Administrative Expenses Budget Illustration

FEZZARI PERFORMANCE BICYCLES
Selling and Administrative Expenses Budget
For the Year Ended December 31, 2016

	Percentage of Sales	Total Cost
Selling expenses		
Variable costs:		
Sales commissions	2%	$124,740
Shipping expense	3%	187,110
Fixed costs:		
Advertising expense		120,000
Administrative expenses:		
Fixed costs:		
Executive salaries expense		200,000
Other administrative expenses		
Legal costs		30,000
Accounting costs		95,000
Depreciation		5,000
General liability insurance		15,000
Total selling and administrative expenses		$776,850
Less: depreciation		(5,000)
Cash budgeted for selling and administrative expenses		$771,850

Capital Expenditures Budget

Expenditures for property, plant, and equipment are among a firm's most important transactions. The type of analysis that is undertaken to determine whether a particular item should be acquired is known as capital budgeting and is discussed in detail in Chapter 12. The **capital expenditures budget** lists long-term assets that are planned to be acquired over a multiyear period. **Exhibit 9-12** presents an illustration for Fezzari. We will assume that it is abstracted from the complete capital expenditures budget.

Exhibit 9-12	Capital Expenditures Budget Illustration

FEZZARI PERFORMANCE BICYCLES
Capital Expenditures Budget
For the Year Ended December 31, 2016

	1st Quarter	2nd Quarter	3rd Quarter	4th Quarter	Total
Assembly equipment	$25,000		$25,000		$50,000
Packaging equipment		$10,000			$10,000
Administrative computers				$5,000	$ 5,000
Total	$25,000	$10,000	$25,000	$5,000	$65,000

The capital expenditures budget has an impact on many other budgets. The plant and equipment available at any point in time determine the productive capacity of the firm. Further, depreciation expense in both the overhead budgets and the selling and administrative expense budget is affected by the capital expenditures budget, as are the cash expenditures in the cash budget and the property, plant, and equipment assets on the balance sheet.

Cash Budget

The **cash budget** presents the projected cash flows during the budget period. The budgeted cash flows are separated into two groups, *cash receipts* (inflows of cash) and *cash disbursements* (outflows of cash). *Cash receipts* include cash sales, collections of accounts receivable, sale of investments and unneeded assets, and proceeds from borrowings and stock sales. *Cash disbursements* include payments for manufacturing costs (direct material, direct labor, and manufacturing overhead), payments for selling and administrative expenses, interest expense, capital expenditures (land, buildings, and equipment), income tax payments, and cash dividends.

ACCOUNTING IN PRACTICE	**Financing Cash Flows**
	In practice, the cash budget often includes a separate section for financing activities. This section would provide details of borrowings and repayments, including interest payments.

Much of the information needed to prepare the cash budget is available in the previously prepared budgets. However, because of characteristic time lags between transactions and their related effects on cash, cash budgeting often requires the analysis of other data as well. For example, sales precede collections from customers, purchases precede payments on account, depreciation is not a cash outflow, and prepayments call for cash outlays before the related expenses are recognized. **Exhibit 9-13** shows the cash budget for Fezzari. For simplicity, the cash budget assumes that all sales are made in cash and that all expenses, with the exception of depreciation and direct materials, are paid in cash. We demonstrate the determination of cash from sales when sales are made on account in the following section.

Exhibit 9-13	Cash Budget Illustration

FEZZARI PERFORMANCE BICYCLES
Cash Budget
For the Year Ended December 31, 2016

	Amount	Source
Cash receipts:		
Sales	$6,237,000	Exhibit 9-6
Cash disbursements:		
Direct materials	(3,345,800)	Exhibit 9-8
Direct labor	(1,081,570)	Exhibit 9-9
Manufacturing overhead	(274,485)	Exhibit 9-10 (excluding depreciation)
Selling and administrative costs	(771,850)	Exhibit 9-11
Capital expenditures	(65,000)	Exhibit 9-12
Interest	(5,000)	Financing budget (not shown)
Income taxes	(240,250)	Exhibit 9-16
Net change in cash	$453,045	
Beginning cash	550,631	
Ending cash	$1,003,676	

What are some examples of noncash expenses excluded from a cash budget?

YOUR TURN! 9.2

The solution is on page 337.

SERVICE AND MERCHANDISING

Illustration of a Service Firm's Budgets

Assume that Environmental Business Consultants (EBC) has collected the following actual data for February and March 2016 and developed the following forecasted data for the quarter ended June 30, 2016:

1. Actual sales for February and March 2016, were the following:

	Actual Credit Sales
February	$310,000
March	290,000

2. Forecast sales for the quarter ended June 30, 2016, are as follows:

	Forecast Credit Sales
April	$400,000
May	350,000
June	380,000

3. The collection of cash from credit sales during the quarter ended June 30, 2016, will follow the same pattern as the previous quarter:

   a. In the month of sale, 10% is collected.

   b. In the month following sale, 50% is collected.

   c. In the second month following sale, 38% is collected. The remaining 2% of accounts receivable are written off as uncollectible.

   Based on the information in items 1–3, the cash collections can be computed as follows:

Month of Credit Sale	Cash Collections from Customers			
	April	May	June	Quarter Total
February	$117,800			
March	$145,000	$110,200		
April	$ 40,000	$200,000	$152,000	
May		$ 35,000	$175,000	
June			$ 38,000	
Month total	$302,800	$345,200	$365,000	$1,013,000

4. Forecast cash disbursements for the quarter ended June 30, 2016, are as follows:

	Forecast Cash Disbursements		
	April	May	June
Labor	$195,000	$195,000	$195,000
Office lease.	$ 16,875	$ 16,875	$ 16,875
Office supplies	$ 2,000	$ 5,000	$ 3,000
Selling and administrative expenses	31,000	32,000	62,000
Interest expense (on existing debt)	$ 417	$ 417	$ 417
Cash distributions to owners	—	—	100,000

The increase in the selling and administrative expense in June is due to the anticipated payment of employee mid-year bonuses.

5. EBC has a policy of maintaining a cash balance of $500,000. All borrowings and re-payments are made at the end of the month and the short-term loan carries an annual interest rate of 6%.

The cash budget for EBC is shown in **Exhibit 9-14**. A three-column format is used so the cash flow of each month of the quarter can be analyzed separately. The starting point in preparing this cash budget is a beginning cash balance for April of $400,000. The cash receipts and cash disbursements for April are then added to the budget. Note that interest is assumed to be paid in the period in which it is incurred. The preliminary ending cash balance of $457,508 is then calculated.

Remember that EBC has a policy of maintaining a cash balance of $500,000. As shown in **Exhibit 9-14**, EBC starts and ends the month of April with a cash balance below this target. To meet its target by the end of April, EBC could budget to borrow $42,492 ($500,000 – $457,508) on a short-term basis. In May, EBC would have sufficient cash to repay this short-term borrowing.

The budgeted ending cash balance for April becomes the budgeted beginning cash balance for May. The procedure described earlier is then repeated for May.

Exhibit 9-14	Service Firm Cash Budget Illustration		
ENVIRONMENTAL BUSINESS CONSULTANTS **Cash Budget** **For the Quarter Ended June 30, 2016**			
	April	**May**	**June**
Beginning cash balance.....................	$400,000	$500,000	$553,204
Cash receipts			
Collections from customers	302,800	345,200	365,000
Cash available	$702,800	$845,200	$918,204
Cash disbursements			
Labor..................................	$195,000	$195,000	$195,000
Office lease............................	16,875	16,875	16,875
Office supplies	2,000	5,000	3,000
Selling and administrative costs..............	31,000	32,000	62,000
Interest (on existing debt)..................	417	629*	417
Cash distributions to owners	—	—	100,000
Total disbursements.......................	$245,292	$249,504	$377,292
Preliminary ending cash balance	$457,508	$595,696	$540,912
Target cash balance.......................	$500,000	$500,000	$500,000
Required short-term borrowing (repayment)	42,492	(42,492)	—
Final ending cash balance	$500,000	$553,204	$540,912

```
* Interest on existing debt.................................... $417
  Interest on $42,492 short-term borrowing ($42,492 × (6.0%/12)).....  212
     Total interest......................................... $629
```

The budgeted ending cash balance for May then becomes the budgeted beginning cash balance for June and the process is repeated again. One additional cash disbursement appears in June: the $100,000 quarterly cash distribution to the owners.

Budgeted Financial Statements

Budgeted Income Statement

The development of the master budget is completed with the preparation of the budgeted financial statements: the budgeted income statement, the budgeted balance sheet, and the budgeted statement of cash flows. The **budgeted income statement** is usually prepared first. In addition to the budgets that were previously prepared, supplemental schedules and worksheets may be needed to prepare the budgeted income statement. Returning to the Fezzari example, one of these supplementary schedules is the schedule of estimated product cost per unit, which is presented in **Exhibit 9-15**. We then use the estimated cost per unit to calculate our budgeted cost of goods sold, which is included in our budgeted income statement (**Exhibit 9-16**).

LO5 **Prepare** budgeted financial statements.

Exhibit 9-15	Estimated Product Cost per Unit Illustration

FEZZARI PERFORMANCE BICYCLES
Estimated Product Cost per Unit
For the Year Ended December 31, 2016

			Cost			
	Quantity		Road Bicycle	Mountain Bicycle	Road Bicycle	Mountain Bicycle
Direct material						
Frame	1.0	×	$325.00	$350.00	= $325.00	$350.00
Build kit.	1.0	×	275.00	290.00	= 275.00	290.00

	Cost per unit		Quantity			
Direct labor:						
Assembly	$ 25.00	×	5.5	7.0	= 137.50	175.00
QC and packaging	$ 20.00	×	2.0	2.0	= 40.00	40.00
Manufacturing overhead:						
Combined.	$7.0353*	×	7.5	9.0	= 52.76	63.32
Product cost per unit					$830.26	$918.32

* $319,585/45,426 DLH =$7.0353 (rounded) (see Exhibit 9-10)

Exhibit 9-16	Budgeted Income Statement Illustration

FEZZARI PERFORMANCE BICYCLES
Budgeted Income Statement
For the Year Ended December 31, 2016

Sales (from Exhibit 9-6)	$6,237,000
Less: cost of goods sold	
Road bicycles: 2,160 units × $830.26 (from Exhibit 9-15).	1,793,372*
Mountain bicycles: 3,240 units × $918.32 (from Exhibit 9-15)	2,975,349*
Gross profit.	$1,468,279
Less: selling and administrative expense (from Exhibit 9-11)	776,850
Income from operations.	$ 691,429
Less: interest expense (from financing budget not shown)	5,000
Income before income taxes	$ 686,429
Less: Income taxes (separate schedule not shown)	240,250
Net income.	$ 446,179

*Difference due to rounding

Budgeted Balance Sheet

The preparation of the **budgeted balance sheet** usually follows the preparation of the budgeted income statement. It is important to note that the budgeted balance sheet is based on the ending balance sheet from the prior year adjusted for budgeted changes. **Exhibit 9-17** presents Fezzari's beginning balance sheet as of December 31, 2015.

Exhibit 9-17	Actual Balance Sheet

FEZZARI PERFORMANCE BICYCLES
Balance Sheet
As of December 31, 2015

Assets		
Current assets:		
Cash		$550,631
Inventories		33,252
Total current assets		$583,883
Plant assets:		
Equipment	$135,300	
Less: accumulated depreciation	(45,100)	90,200
Total assets		$674,083
Liabilities		
Current liabilities		
Accounts payable		50,000
Long-term liabilities:		
Long-term borrowing		83,333
Total liabilities		$133,333
Stockholders' Equity		
Common stock ($1 par value; 10,000 shares authorized and issued) . . .	$10,000	
Paid in capital—excess of par-common stock	90,000	
Total paid-in capital		$100,000
Retained earnings		440,750
Total stockholders' equity		$540,750
Total liabilities and stockholders' equity		$674,083

Exhibit 9-18 presents the budgeted balance sheet for December 31, 2016. This balance sheet reflects the changes in the asset, liability, and equity accounts that result from the budgeted activity for the year. For 2016, Fezzari management has assumed that there will be no additional borrowings or stock sales.

Exhibit 9-18	Budgeted Balance Sheet Illustration

FEZZARI PERFORMANCE BICYCLES
Budgeted Balance Sheet
As of December 31, 2016

Assets
Current assets:

Cash..		$1,003,676	a
Inventories			
Direct materials..	$ 10,000		b
Finished goods..	26,493	36,493	c
Total current assets		$1,040,169	
Plant assets:			
Equipment..	$200,300		d
Less: accumulated depreciation............................	(95,200)	105,100	e
Total assets		$1,145,269	
Liabilities			
Current liabilities			
Accounts payable......................................		75,000	
Long-term liabilities:			
Long-term borrowing		83,333	f
Total liabilities......................................		$ 158,333	
Stockholders' Equity			
Common stock ($1 par value; 10,000 shares authorized and issued)...	$ 10,000		f
Paid in capital—excess of par-common stock	90,000		f
Total paid-in capital		$ 100,000	
Retained earnings		886,936	g
Total stockholders' equity		$ 986,936	
Total liabilities and stockholders' equity		$1,145,269	

[a] Beginning cash balance from Exhibit 9-17 plus net cash increase from Exhibit 9-13.

[b] (6 road bike units × [$325 + $275]) + (10 mountain bike units × [$350 + $290]) = $10,000

[c] (12 road bike units × $830.26) + (18 units mountain bike units × $918.32) = $26,494. Difference due to rounding.

[d] Beginning equipment ($135,300) plus budgeted capital purchases from Exhibit 9-12 ($65,000).

[e] Beginning accumulated depreciation ($45,100) plus current year depreciation from Exhibit 9-10 ($45,100) and Exhibit 9-11 ($5,000).

[f] No change.

[g] Beginning retained earnings ($440,750) plus net income from Exhibit 9-16 ($446,179). Difference due to rounding.

Budgeted Statement of Cash Flows

The **budgeted statement of cash flows** follows directly from the cash budget. The dollar amounts will be the same, but the grouping and sequence will usually be different. **Exhibit 9-19** presents Fezzari's budgeted statement of cash flows. Note that this statement groups the cash flows into three sections: cash flows from operating activities, cash flows from investing activities, and cash flows from financing activities.

Exhibit 9-19	Budgeted Statement of Cash Flows Illustration

FEZZARI PERFORMANCE BICYCLES
Budgeted Statement of Cash Flows—Direct Method
For the Period Ended December 31, 2016

Cash flows from operating activities

Cash receipts from customers	$6,237,000	
Cash payments for inventory	(4,701,855)	
Cash paid for selling and administrative expenses	(771,850)	
Cash paid for interest	(5,000)	
Income tax payment	(240,250)	
Net cash provided by operating activities		$ 518,045
Cash flows from investing activities		
Capital expenditures	(65,000)	
Net cash used by investing activities		(65,000)
Cash flows from financing activities		
Net cash provided by financing activities		—
Net increase (decrease) in cash		$ 453,045
Beginning cash balance		550,631
Ending cash balance		$1,003,676

SERVICES INDUSTRY IN FOCUS

SERVICE AND MERCHANDISING

Refer to the Environmental Business Consultants (EBC) illustration on page 314 in the chapter. Assume that local governments (EBC's target market) are experiencing a sharp reduction in the collection of tax revenues due to a recession in the general economy. EBC anticipates that this will impact the timeliness of payments made by its clients *beginning in April* as shown below:

　　a. In the month of sale, 10% is collected.

　　b. In the month following sale, 30% is collected.

　　c. In the second month following sale, 30% is collected.

　　d. In the third month following sale, 20% is collected. The remaining 10% of accounts receivable will be written off as uncollectible.

Note that payments related to the February and March sales that have yet to be collected will be impacted by the recession also. For example, 10% of the February sales were collected in February, 50% were collected in March, but only 30% will be collected in April (not 38%) and the remaining 10% will be written off. Further, 10% of the March sales were collected in March, but only 30% will be collected in April (not 50%), 30% will be collected in May, and 20% will be collected in June. Assume that all other forecasted data remain the same.

Assume that because of the recession, EBC has temporarily eliminated its policy of maintaining a cash balance of $500,000.

Required

1. Re-compute the forecasted cash collections for the quarter ended June 30, 2016.

2. Prepare a new cash budget reflecting these new cash collections.

Solution

1.

Month of Credit Sale	Cash Collections from Customers			
	April	May	June	Quarter Total
February	$ 93,000			
March	$ 87,000	$ 87,000	$ 58,000	
April	$ 40,000	$120,000	$120,000	
May		$ 35,000	$105,000	
June			$ 38,000	
Month total	$220,000	$242,000	$321,000	$783,000

2.

ENVIRONMENTAL BUSINESS CONSULTANTS Cash Budget For the Quarter Ended June 30, 2016			
	April	May	June
Beginning cash balance	$400,000	$374,708	$367,416
Cash receipts			
Collections from customers	220,000	242,000	321,000
Cash available	$620,000	$616,708	$688,416
Cash disbursements			
Labor	$195,000	$195,000	$195,000
Office lease	16,875	16,875	16,875
Office supplies	2,000	5,000	3,000
Selling and administrative expenses	31,000	32,000	62,000
Interest expense (on existing debt)	417	417	417
Cash distributions to owners	—	—	100,000
Total disbursements	$245,292	$249,292	$377,292
Ending cash balance	$374,708	$367,416	$311,124

COMPREHENSIVE PROBLEM

The sales department of Jackson Manufacturing, Inc. has completed the following sales forecast for the months of January through March 20X5 for its only two products: 40,000 units of X1 to be sold at $110 each and 20,000 units of X2 to be sold at $85 each. The desired unit inventories at March 31, 20X5, are 10% of the next quarter's unit sales forecast, which are 50,000 units of X1 and 25,000 units of X2. The January 1, 20X5, unit inventories were 7,000 units of X1 and 1,500 units of X2.

Each unit of X1 requires 4 pounds of material R and 2 pounds of material S for its manufacture; X2 requires 2 pounds of R and 3 pounds of S. The purchase cost of R is $10 per pound and of S is $5 per pound. Materials on hand at January 1, 20X5, were 20,000 pounds of R and 8,000 pounds of S. Desired inventories at March 31, 20X5, are 15,000 pounds of R and 6,000 pounds of S.

Each unit of X1 requires 0.5 hour of direct labor in the factory; each unit of X2 requires 1.0 hour of direct labor. The average hourly rate for direct labor is $12 per hour. Estimated manufacturing overhead cost is $8 per direct labor hour plus $100,000 per month. Selling and administrative expenses are estimated to be 10% of sales revenue plus $200,000 per month.

Cash sales in December 20X4 were $250,000 and credit sales were $2,000,000. Cash sales for the first quarter are estimated to be $200,000 per month. It is forecast that 40% of the credit sales for the quarter ended March 31, 20X5, will occur in January, 30% in February, and 30% in March. Of credit sales (December through March), 40% will be collected as cash in the month of sale and 50% will be collected in the following month. The remainder will be uncollectible.

The January 1, 20X5, cash balance was $60,000. The minimum acceptable cash balance at the end of each month is $50,000. Short-term borrowings are made in multiples of $10,000 with interest charged at the rate of 1% per month. The first interest payment is made the month following the borrowing. Cash disbursements (excluding interest on short-term borrowings) are estimated as follows:

	January	February	March
Manufacturing costs.	$1,200,000	$1,100,000	$1,000,000
Selling and administrative expenses	$ 380,000	$ 400,000	$ 340,000
Interest expense.	$ 100,000	$ 100,000	$ 100,000
Income tax payment.	—	—	200,000
Capital expenditures	100,000	340,000	60,000
Cash dividends.	400,000	—	—

Required

a. Prepare the sales budget for the quarter ended March 31, 20X5.

b. Prepare the production budget for the quarter ended March 31, 20X5.

c. Prepare the direct material budget for the quarter ended March 31, 20X5.

d. Prepare the direct labor budget for the quarter ended March 31, 20X5.

e. Prepare the overhead budget for the quarter ended March 31, 20X5.

f. Prepare a schedule of estimated product cost per unit for the quarter ended March 31, 20X5.

g. Prepare a schedule of cash collected from customers for the quarter ended March 31, 20X5.

h. Prepare the cash budget for the quarter ended March 31, 20X5.

SOLUTION TO COMPREHENSIVE PROBLEM

a.

JACKSON MANUFACTURING, INC.
Sales Budget
For the Quarter Ended March 31, 20X5

Product	Forecasted Unit Sales Volume	Planned Unit Sales Price	Budgeted Total Sales
X1	40,000	$110.00	$4,400,000
X2	20,000	$ 85.00	1,700,000
Total sales revenue.			$6,100,000

b.

JACKSON MANUFACTURING, INC.
Production Budget
For the Quarter Ended March 31, 20X5

	Units of Finished Product	
	X1	X2
Forecast unit sales	40,000	20,000
Desired ending inventories:		
10% × 50,000.	5,000	
10% × 25,000.		2,500
Quantities to be available.	45,000	22,500
Less: Beginning inventories	7,000	1,500
Total production to be scheduled	38,000	21,000

c.

JACKSON MANUFACTURING, INC.
Direct Material Budget
For the Quarter Ended March 31, 20X5

	Material R	Material S
Direct material required:		
Product X1: 38,000 × 4	152,000	
38,000 × 2		76,000
Product X2: 21,000 × 2	42,000	
21,000 × 3		63,000
Desired ending material inventories	15,000	6,000
Total pounds of material to be available	209,000	145,000
Less: Beginning material inventories	20,000	8,000
Total pounds of material to be purchased	189,000	137,000
Unit purchase price	$ 10.00	$ 5.00
Total material purchases	$1,890,000	$685,000

d.

JACKSON MANUFACTURING, INC.
Direct Labor Budget
For the Quarter Ended March 31, 20X5

Direct labor hours required for production:	
Product X1: 38,000 × 0.5 hours	19,000
Product X2: 21,000 × 1.0 hours	21,000
Total direct labor hours required	40,000
Hourly rate for direct labor	$ 12.00
Total direct labor cost	$480,000

e.

JACKSON MANUFACTURING, INC.
Overhead Budget
For the Quarter Ended March 31, 20X5

Total direct labor hours	40,000
Variable manufacturing overhead rate	$ 8.00
Variable manufacturing overhead cost	$320,000
Fixed manufacturing overhead cost ($100,000 × 3 months)	$300,000
Total manufacturing overhead cost	$620,000

f.

JACKSON MANUFACTURING, INC.
Schedule of Estimated Product Cost Per Unit
For the Quarter Ended March 31, 20X5

	Quantity		Cost	Product X1	Product X2
	Product X1	Product X2			
Direct material:					
Material R	4	2	$10.00	$40.00	$20.00
Material S	2	3	$ 5.00	$10.00	$15.00
Direct labor	0.5	1	$12.00	$ 6.00	$12.00
Manufacturing overhead	0.5	1	*$15.50	$ 7.75	$15.50
Product cost per unit				$63.75	$62.50

*$620,000/40,000 = $15.50 per direct labor hour

g.

JACKSON MANUFACTURING, INC. Schedule of Cash Collected From Customers For the Quarter Ended March 31, 20X5	January	February	March
Cash sales	$ 200,000	$ 200,000	$ 200,000
Credit sales			
December: $2,000,000 × 50%	1,000,000		
January: $2,200,000* × 40%	880,000		
$2,200,000* × 50%		1,100,000	
February: $1,650,000** × 40%		660,000	
$1,650,000** × 50%			825,000
March: $1,650,000** × 40%			660,000
	$1,880,000	$1,760,000	$1,485,000
Total cash collected	$2,080,000	$1,960,000	$1,685,000

*($6,100,000 total sales − $600,000 cash sales) × 40% = $2,200,000

**($6,100,000 total sales − $600,000 cash sales) × 30% = $1,650,000

h.

JACKSON MANUFACTURING, INC. Cash Budget For the Quarter Ended March 31, 20X5	January	February	March
Beginning cash balance.	$ 60,000	$ 50,000	$ 69,100
Cash receipts:			
Cash sales.	200,000	200,000	200,000
Collections from credit customers	1,880,000	1,760,000	1,485,000
Short-term borrowing	90,000	—	—
Cash available.	$2,230,000	$2,010,000	$1,754,100
Cash disbursements:			
Manufacturing costs	$1,200,000	$1,100,000	$1,000,000
Selling and administrative expenses.	380,000	400,000	340,000
Interest expense*.	100,000	100,900	100,900
Income tax payments	—	—	200,000
Capital expenditures	100,000	340,000	60,000
Cash dividends	400,000	—	—
Total disbursements.	$2,180,000	$1,940,900	$1,700,900
Ending cash balance	$ 50,000	$ 69,100	$ 53,200

* For February and March: $100,000 + ($90,000 × 1%) = $100,900

SUMMARY OF LEARNING OBJECTIVES

LO1 **Describe the planning process, including strategic planning and operational planning. (p. 298)**
- Strategic planning is a formal process that addresses and documents the mission and long-term goals of the organization. SWOT analysis is used to develop and analyze the data needed for this type of planning.
- Operational planning is the development of specific goals and objectives for the entity as a whole and its individual departments, the formulation of a plan of attack to accomplish the goals and objectives, and the written documentation of the goals and objectives and the plan of attack.

LO2 **Discuss the budgeting process and summarize its advantages. Define the key elements of effective budgeting. (p. 301)**

- Budgeting is the process of developing a formal, written operational plan that presents management's planned actions in financial terms.

- Two budgets result from the budgeting process: the annual operating budget that covers a 1-year budget period and the capital expenditures budget that covers a multiple-year budget period.
- Budgets represent a plan for accomplishing goals and objectives. They provide operational guidance to the department managers so they make decisions that are consistent with decisions made in other departments.
- Because the budget is used as a basis for evaluating performance, it serves as a target for individual managers.
- A budget director should be identified to organize the budgeting process, communicate with people involved in budgeting, and monitor the budgeting process.
- A budget committee, consisting of representatives from all major areas of the company, should provide general guidance to the budgeting process and evaluate proposed budget segments for reasonableness.
- Participative budgeting requires that all departments participate in the development and refinement of the budget amounts so that departmental managers will accept the budget as a reasonable standard of performance.
- The future time span, for which the budget is prepared, known as the budget period, varies according to the activity involved.
- The use of budgets to manage and control a firm's activities is known as budgetary control.
- Zero-base budgeting requires budget preparers to start at a zero level for every item in the budget and justify every dollar, not just the increases or decreases.

Define the components of the master budget and illustrate the interrelationships of the individual budgets that comprise the master budget. (p. 305)   **LO3**

- The master budget for a manufacturing firm consists of at least the following individual budgets:
    Sales budget
    Production budget
    Direct material budget
    Direct labor budget
    Manufacturing overhead budget
    Selling and administrative expense budget
    Capital expenditures budget
    Cash budget
    Budgeted income statement
    Budgeted balance sheet
    Budgeted statement of cash flows
- The individual budgets must be prepared in a specific sequence, beginning with the sales budget, to properly reflect the interrelationships among the individual budgets.

Prepare individual budgets for a manufacturing and a service company, including the cash budget. (p. 306)   **LO4**

- The sales budget is based on the sales forecast.
- The production budget determines the number of units of each product that should be manufactured during the budget period.
- The direct material budget displays the amount of each direct material item that should be purchased to supply the budgeted production.
- The direct labor budget presents the amount of direct labor, by department, that is required to accomplish the budgeted production.
- The manufacturing overhead budget determines, for each factory department, the amount of variable overhead and the amount of fixed overhead needed to complete the budgeted production.
- The selling and administrative expense budget accumulates the variable and fixed selling and administrative expenses for the entity. Some of the expenses may vary with sales; others may vary with production.
- The capital expenditures budget presents the planned expenditures for property, plant, and equipment over an extended budget period, possibly 5 years.
- The cash budget, usually segmented by month, presents all of the cash receipts and cash disbursements planned for the budget period.

- Much of the information needed to prepare the cash budget comes from previously prepared budgets. However, additional schedules and worksheets are usually needed to place required information in proper form.
- Cash collected from customers from prior credit sales needs careful analysis to take into account timing, cash discounts, and uncollectible accounts.

LO5 **Prepare budgeted financial statements. (p. 315)**

- The budgeted income statement is prepared for the budget period.
- The budgeted balance sheet is prepared as of the ending date of the budget period.
- The budgeted statement of cash flows is prepared for the budget period, based primarily on data from the cash budget.

KEY TERMS

Budget (p. 301)	Cash budget (p. 312)	Production budget (p. 307)
Budgetary control (p. 302)	Continuous budgeting (p. 304)	Safety stock (p. 307)
Budget committee (p. 303)	Direct labor budget (p. 309)	Sales budget (p. 306)
Budget director (p. 303)	Direct material budget (p. 308)	Sales forecast (p. 306)
Budget period (p. 303)	Just-in-time inventory (p. 307)	Selling and administrative expense budget (p. 311)
Budgeted balance sheet (p. 316)	Manufacturing overhead budget (p. 310)	Strategic planning (p. 299)
Budgeted income statement (p. 315)	Master budget (p. 305)	Strengths, weaknesses, opportunities, and threats (SWOT) analysis (p. 300)
Budgeted statement of cash flows (p. 317)	Operational planning (p. 300)	
	Participative budgeting (p. 303)	
Budgeting (p. 301)	Planning horizon (p. 298)	Zero-base budgeting (p. 304)
Capital expenditures budget (p. 311)		

Assignments with the ⬤ logo in the margin are available in BusinessCourse.
See the Preface of the book for details.

SELF-STUDY QUESTIONS

(Answers to Self-Study Questions are at the end of this chapter.)

LO2 1. **If a company uses participative budgeting, which group should prepare the initial set of budget dollar amounts?**
   - *a.* Budget committee
   - *b.* Operating department managers
   - *c.* Top management
   - *d.* Accounting department

LO4 2. **Which of the following budgets will typically have the longest budget period?**
   - *a.* Capital expenditures budget
   - *b.* Cash budget
   - *c.* Sales budget
   - *d.* Budgeted income statement

LO3 3. **Which of the following budgets should be prepared before all of the others listed below?**
   - *a.* Cash budget
   - *b.* Direct materials budget
   - *c.* Manufacturing overhead budget
   - *d.* Production budget

LO4 4. **If the beginning inventory of a company that manufactures only one product is 5,000 units, the sales forecast is 34,000 units sold, and the desired ending inventory is 6,000 units, how many units should be produced?**
   - *a.* 35,000
   - *b.* 33,000
   - *c.* 40,000
   - *d.* 39,000

5. Smith Company started business on September 1. Smith had credit sales of $200,000 in September and $300,000 in October. The pattern for collection of cash from customers is expected to be 40% in the month of sale (subject to a 2% cash discount), 50% in the month following the month of sale, and 7% in the second month following the month of sale, with 3% uncollectible. How much cash did Smith Company receive from customers on account during October? **LO4**

    a. $120,000   *c.* $217,600

    b. $117,600   *d.* $220,000

QUESTIONS

1. What is a planning horizon? How will it differ between strategic planning and operational planning? **LO1**
2. Describe strategic planning. **LO1**
3. Describe operational planning. **LO1**
4. Define budgeting. **LO2**
5. List and briefly explain four advantages of budgeting. **LO2**
6. Describe the budget committee. **LO2**
7. Why is participative budgeting important to the success of the budgeting process? **LO2**
8. What is meant by continuous budgeting? **LO2**
9. What is the master budget? List, in the order of preparation, the various budgets that the master budget for a small manufacturing company might comprise. **LO3**
10. Why do most firms prepare the sales budget first? **LO3**
11. Beginning finished goods inventory is 10,000 units, anticipated sales volume is 60,000 units, and the desired ending finished goods inventory is 12,000 units. What number of units should be produced? **LO4**
12. Three pounds of material R (costing $5 per pound) and 4 pounds of material S (costing $7 per pound) are required to make one unit of product T. If management plans to increase the inventory of material R by 500 pounds and reduce the inventory of material S by 800 pounds during a period when 3,000 units of product T are to be produced, what are the budgeted purchase costs of material R and material S? **LO4**
13. Carroll Manufacturing Company has two labor operations in its factory: machining and assembly. Workers in the machining department are paid $14 per hour; workers in the assembly department are paid $12 per hour. During January, 10,000 units of product A and 20,000 units of product B are to be manufactured. Each unit of A requires 1 hour of machining and 2 hours of assembly; each unit of B requires 3 hours of machining and 1 hour of assembly. What is the total direct labor budget for January? **LO4**
14. Johnson Manufacturing Company has budgeted 30,000 direct labor hours for March. The budgeted cost formula for monthly manufacturing overhead is $4 per direct labor hour plus $65,000. What is the manufacturing overhead budget for March? **LO4**
15. A company collects cash from its credit sales in the following pattern: 30% in the month of sale, 50% in the month following the month of sale, and 20% in the second month following the month of sale. What percentage of which months' credit sales will be collected during October? **LO4**
16. What are the three major groupings of cash flows in the budgeted statement of cash flows? **LO4**

EXERCISES—SET A

E9-1A. Budgeting Inventories For each independent situation below, determine the amounts indicated by the question marks: **LO4**

	A	B	C	D
Beginning inventory	10,000	?	7,000	?
Produced	40,000	27,000	?	60,000
Available	?	?	26,000	64,000
Sold	45,000	28,000	?	?
Ending inventory	?	10,000	6,000	2,000

LO4 **E9-2A.** **Budget Preparation** Collins Company is preparing its master budget for April. Use the given estimates to determine the amounts necessary for each of the following requirements. (Estimates may be related to more than one requirement.)

a. What should total sales revenue be if territories A and B estimate sales of 10,000 and 12,000 units, respectively, and the unit selling price is $40?

b. If the beginning finished goods inventory is an estimated 2,000 units and the desired ending inventory is 3,000 units, how many units should be produced?

c. What dollar amount of material should be purchased at $4 per pound if each unit of product requires 3 pounds and beginning and ending materials inventories should be 5,000 and 4,000 pounds, respectively?

d. How much direct labor cost should be incurred if each unit produced requires 1.5 hours at an hourly rate of $13?

e. How much manufacturing overhead should be incurred if fixed manufacturing overhead is $50,000 and variable manufacturing overhead is $2.50 per direct labor hour?

LO4 **E9-3A.** **Budget Preparation** Westport Company is preparing its master budget for May. Use the estimates provided to determine the amounts necessary for each of the following requirements. (Estimates may be related to more than one requirement.)

a. What should total sales revenue be if territories E and W estimate sales of 50,000 and 100,000 units, respectively, and the unit selling price is $27?

b. If the beginning finished goods inventory is an estimated 7,000 units and the desired ending inventory is 6,000 units, how many units should be produced?

c. What dollar amount of material should be purchased at $2 per pound if each unit of product requires 2.5 pounds and beginning and ending materials inventories should be 13,500 and 12,000 pounds, respectively?

d. How much direct labor cost should be incurred if each unit produced requires 0.5 hours at an hourly rate of $11?

e. How much manufacturing overhead should be incurred if fixed manufacturing overhead is $45,000 and variable manufacturing overhead is $1.30 per direct labor hour?

LO4 **E9-4A.** **Budgeting Cash Collections** Spencer Consulting, which invoices its clients on terms 2/10, n/30, had credit sales for May and June of $70,000 and $80,000, respectively. Analysis of Spencer's operations indicates that the pattern of customers' payments on account is as follows (percentages are of total monthly credit sales):

	Receiving Discount	Beyond Discount Period	Totals
In month of sale	50%	20%	70%
In month following sale.	15%	10%	25%
Uncollectible accounts, returns, and allowances.			5%
			$100%

Determine the estimated cash collected on customers' accounts in June.

LO4 **E9-5A.** **Budgeting Cash Flow** The following various elements relate to Whitfield, Inc.'s cash budget for April of the current year. For each item, determine the amount of cash that Whitfield should receive or pay in April.

a. At $28 each, unit sales are 5,000 and 6,000 for March and April, respectively. Total sales are typically 40% for cash and 60% on credit; 30% of credit sales are collected in the month of sale, with the balance collected in the following month. Uncollectible accounts are negligible.

b. Merchandise purchases were $45,000 and $78,000 for March and April, respectively. Typically, 20% of total purchases are paid for in the month of purchase with a 5% cash discount. The balance of purchases is paid for (without discount) in the following month.

c. Fixed administrative expenses, which total $11,000 per month, are paid in the month incurred. Variable administrative expenses amount to 20% of total monthly sales revenue, one-half of which is paid in the month incurred, with the balance paid in the following month.

d. A store asset originally costing $8,000, on which $6,000 depreciation has been taken, is sold for cash at a loss of $400.

E9-6A. **Prepare Cash Budget For 3 Months** Brewster Corporation expects the following cash receipts and disbursements during the first quarter of 2016 (receipts exclude new borrowings and disbursements exclude interest payments on borrowings since January 1, 2016): LO4

	January	February	March
Cash receipts	$260,000	$280,000	$250,000
Cash disbursements	240,000	320,000	260,000

The expected cash balance at January 1, 2016, is $42,000. Brewster wants to maintain a cash balance at the end of each month of at least $40,000. Short-term borrowings at 1% interest per month will be used to accomplish this, if necessary. Borrowings (in multiples of $1,000) will be made at the beginning of the month in which they are needed, with interest for that month paid at the end of the month. Prepare a cash budget for the quarter ended March 31, 2016.

E9-7A. **Prepare Cash Budget From Budgeted Transactions** Prepare a cash budget for the month ended May 31, 2016. Campton Company anticipates a cash balance of $84,000 on May 1, 2016. The following budgeted transactions for May 2016 present data related to anticipated cash receipts and cash disbursements: LO4

1. For May, budgeted cash sales are $60,000 and budgeted credit sales are $500,000. (Credit sales for April were $450,000.) In the month of sale, 40% of credit sales are collected, with the balance collected in the month following sale.
2. Budgeted merchandise purchases for May are $280,000. (Merchandise purchases in April were $240,000.) In the month of purchase, 70% of merchandise purchases are paid for, and the balance is paid for in the following month.
3. Budgeted cash disbursements for salaries and operating expenses for May total $165,000.
4. During May, $25,000 of principal repayment and $4,000 of interest payment are due to the bank.
5. A $20,000 income tax deposit is due to the federal government during May.
6. A new delivery truck will be purchased during May for $6,000 cash and an $8,000 note payable. Depreciation for May will be $500.

Prepare a cash budget for Campton Company for the month of May 2016.

EXERCISES—SET B

E9-1B. **Budgeting Inventories** For each independent situation below, determine the amounts indicated by the question marks. LO4

Number of Units	A	B	C	D
Beginning inventory	9,000	?	6,000	?
Produced	15,000	27,000	?	75,000
Available	?	?	46,000	85,000
Sold	18,000	28,000	?	?
Ending inventory	?	3,000	8,000	11,000

E9-2B. **Budget Preparation** Reeves Company is preparing its master budget for July. Use the given estimates to determine the amounts necessary for each of the following requirements. (Estimates may be related to more than one requirement.) LO4

a. What should total sales revenue be if territories A and B estimate sales of 8,000 and 20,000 units, respectively, and the unit selling price is $50?
b. If the beginning finished goods inventory is an estimated 1,500 units and the desired ending inventory is 2,500 units, how many units should be produced?

c. What dollar amount of material should be purchased at $3 per pound if each unit of product requires 2 pounds and beginning and ending materials inventories should be 4,000 and 3,000 pounds, respectively?

d. How much direct labor cost should be incurred if each unit produced requires 1.5 hours at an hourly rate of $14?

e. How much manufacturing overhead should be incurred if fixed manufacturing overhead is $60,000 and variable manufacturing overhead is $1.50 per direct labor hour?

LO4   E9-3B.   Budget Preparation Tuttle Company is preparing its master budget for November. Use the estimates provided to determine the necessary amounts for each of the following requirements. (Estimates may be related to more than one requirement.)

a. What should total sales revenue be if territories N and S estimate sales of 40,000 and 80,000 units, respectively and the unit selling price is $18?

b. If the beginning finished goods inventory is an estimated 6,000 units and the desired ending inventory is 5,000 units, how many units should be produced?

c. What dollar amount of material should be purchased at $2 per pound if each unit of product requires 3 pounds and beginning and ending materials inventories should be 12,000 and 10,000 pounds, respectively?

d. How much direct labor cost should be incurred if each unit produced requires 0.5 hours at an hourly rate of $10?

e. How much manufacturing overhead should be incurred if fixed manufacturing overhead is $32,000 and variable manufacturing overhead is $1 per direct labor hour?

LO4   E9-4B.   Budgeting Cash Collections Lowell Consulting, which sells on terms 2/10, n/30, had credit sales for March and April of $60,000 and $50,000, respectively. Analysis of Lowell's operations indicates that the pattern of customers' payments on account is as follows (percentages are of total monthly credit sales):

	Receiving Discount	Beyond Discount Period	Totals
In month of sale	40%	20%	60%
In month following sale.	15%	20%	35%
Uncollectible accounts, returns, and allowances.			5%
			100%

Determine the estimated cash collected on customers' accounts in April.

LO4   E9-5B.   Budgeting Cash Flow The following various elements relate to Murphy, Inc.'s cash budget for October of the current year. For each item, determine the amount of cash that Murphy should receive or pay in October.

a. At $24 each, unit sales are 10,000 and 12,000 for September and October, respectively. Total sales are typically 30% for cash and 70% on credit; 40% of credit sales are collected in the month of sale, with the balance collected in the following month. Uncollectible accounts are negligible.

b. Merchandise purchases were $43,000 and $76,000 for September and October, respectively. Typically, 20% of total purchases are paid for in the month of purchase with a 5% cash discount. The balance of purchases is paid for (without discount) in the following month.

c. Fixed administrative expenses, which total $15,000 per month, are paid in the month incurred. Variable administrative expenses amount to 20% of total monthly sales revenue, 65% of which is paid in the month incurred, with the balance paid in the following month.

d. Fixed selling expenses, which total $4,200 per month, are paid in the month incurred. Variable selling expenses, which are 5% of total sales revenue, are paid in the month following their incurrence.

LO4   E9-6B.   Prepare Cash Budget For 3 Months Windsor Corporation expects the following cash receipts and disbursements during the first quarter of 2016 (receipts exclude new borrowings and disbursements exclude interest payments on borrowings since January 1, 2016):

	January	February	March
Cash receipts	$430,000	$440,000	$400,000
Cash disbursements	390,000	520,000	420,000

The expected cash balance at January 1, 2016, is $75,000. Windsor wants to maintain a cash balance at the end of each month of at least $60,000. Short-term borrowings at 1% interest per month will be used to accomplish this, if necessary. Borrowings (in multiples of $1,000) will be made at the beginning of the month in which they are needed, with interest for that month paid at the end of the month.

Prepare a cash budget for the quarter ended March 31, 2016.

E9-7B. **Prepare Cash Budget From Budgeted Transactions** McCall Company anticipates a cash balance of $100,000 on July 1, 2016. The following budgeted transactions for July 2016 present data related to anticipated cash receipts and cash disbursements:

LO4

SERVICE AND
MERCHANDISING

1. For July, budgeted cash sales are $72,000 and budgeted credit sales are $600,000. (Credit sales for June were $550,000.) In the month of sale, 40% of credit sales are collected, with the balance collected in the month following sale.
2. Budgeted merchandise purchases for July are $340,000. (Merchandise purchases in June were $290,000.) In the month of purchase, 70% of merchandise purchases are paid for, and the balance is paid for in the following month.
3. Budgeted cash disbursements for salaries and operating expenses for July total $200,000.
4. During July, $30,000 of principal repayment and $5,000 of interest payment are due to the bank.
5. A $25,000 income tax deposit is due to the federal government during July.
6. A new delivery truck will be purchased during July for $7,000 cash and a $10,000 note payable. Depreciation for July will be $600.

Prepare a cash budget for McCall Company for the month of July 2016.

PROBLEMS—SET A

P9-1A. **Budgeting Cash** Whitney's, Inc., sells on terms of 5% discount for "cash and carry" or 2/10, n/30 and estimates its total sales for the second calendar quarter of next year as follows: April, $300,000; May, $240,000; and June, $360,000. An analysis of operations indicates the following customer collection patterns:

LO4

	Portions of Total Sales
In month of sale:	
Cash at time of sale	25%
On account, during discount period.	15%
On account, after discount period	10%
In month following sale:	
On account, during discount period.	20%
On account, after discount period	10%
In second month following sale:	
On account, after discount period	15%
Average portion uncollectible.	5%
	100%

Prepare an estimate of the cash to be collected from customers during June.

P9-2A. **Preparation of Individual Budgets** During the first calendar quarter of 2016, Clinton Corporation is planning to manufacture a new product and introduce it in two regions. Market research indicates that sales will be 6,000 units in the urban region at a unit price of $53 and 5,000 units in the rural region at $48 each. Because the sales manager expects the product to catch on, he has asked for production sufficient to generate a 4,000-unit ending inventory. The production manager has furnished the following estimates related to manufacturing costs and operating expenses:

LO4

	Variable (per unit)	Fixed (total)
Manufacturing costs:		
Direct material:		
A (4 lb. @ $3.15/lb.)	$12.60	—
B (2 lb. @ $4.65/lb.)	9.30	—
Direct labor (0.5 hr. per unit)	7.50	—
Manufacturing overhead:		
Depreciation	—	$ 7,650
Factory supplies	0.90	4,500
Supervisory salaries	—	28,800
Other	0.75	22,950
Operating expenses:		
Selling:		
Advertising	—	22,500
Sales salaries and commissions*	1.50	15,000
Other*	0.90	3,000
Administrative:		
Office salaries	—	2,700
Supplies	0.15	1,050
Other	0.08	1,950

*Varies per unit sold, not per unit produced.

Required

a. Assuming that the desired ending inventories of materials A and B are 4,000 and 6,000 pounds, respectively, and that work-in-process inventories are immaterial, prepare budgets for the calendar quarter in which the new product will be introduced for each of the following operating factors:
  1. Total sales
  2. Production
  3. Material purchases cost
  4. Direct labor costs
  5. Manufacturing overhead costs
  6. Selling and administrative expenses

b. Using data generated in requirement (a), prepare a budgeted income statement for the calendar quarter. Assume an overall effective income tax rate of 30%.

LO4 **P9-3A.** **Monthly Cash Budget** Grove, Inc. is a wholesaler for its only product, deluxe wireless electric drills, which sell for $90 each and cost Grove $54 each. On December 1, 2016, Grove's management requested a cash budget for December. The following selected account balances at November 30, 2016, were gathered by the accounting department:

Cash	$ 135,000
Marketable securities (at cost)	210,000
Accounts receivable (all trade)	1,710,000
Inventories (15,000 units)	810,000
Operating expenses payable	140,400
Accounts payable (all merchandise)	583,200
Note payable (due 12/31/2016)	393,000

Actual sales for the months of October and November were 20,000 and 30,000 units, respectively. Projected unit sales for December and January are 50,000 and 40,000, respectively. Experience indicates that 50% of sales should be collected in the month of sale, 30% in the month following sale, and the balance in the second month following sale. Uncollectible accounts, returns, and allowances are negligible.

Planned purchases should provide ending inventories equal to 30% of next month's unit sales volume. Approximately 70% of the purchases are paid for in the month of purchase and the balance in the following month.

Monthly operating expenses are budgeted at $8.10 per unit sold plus a fixed amount of $189,000 including depreciation of $81,000. Except for depreciation, 60% of operating expenses are paid in the month incurred and the balance in the following month. Interest expense is included in operating expenses.

Special anticipated year-end transactions include the following:

1. Declaration of a $22,500 cash dividend to be paid 2 weeks after the December 20 date of record.
2. Sale of one-half of the marketable securities held on November 30; a gain of $21,000 is anticipated.
3. Pay off the note payable due December 31, 2016.
4. Trade-in of an old computer originally costing $675,000 and now having accumulated depreciation of $540,000 at a gain of $157,500 on a new computer costing $1,350,000. Sufficient cash will be paid at the time of trade-in so that only 50% of the total price will have to be financed.
5. Grove's treasurer has a policy of maintaining a minimum month-end cash balance of $135,000 but wants to raise this to $225,000 at December 31. She has a standing arrangement with the bank to borrow any amount up to a limit of $450,000.

Required
Prepare a cash budget for Grove, Inc., for December 2016.

P9-4A. **Budgeting Production and Purchases and Just-In-Time Materials Inventory** Hancock Manufacturing, Inc. is preparing budgets for the third quarter of 2016. Hancock produces only one product in its factory. This product requires 5 pounds of material B, 2 pounds of material G, and a component, K, that is purchased from another manufacturer. Hancock operates on a just-in-time basis for material B. As a result, Hancock maintains no inventory of material B. On July 1, 2016, the inventory of material G is expected to be 2,000 pounds and the inventory of component K is expected to be 500 units. Hancock wants the inventories of G and K at September 30, 2016, to be 20% less than the inventories at July 1, 2016. The inventory of finished products at June 30, 2016, is expected to be 1,000 units; the desired inventory at September 30, 2016, is 3,000 units to allow a buildup for heavy sales in the fourth quarter. The sales forecast for the third quarter is 12,000 units at $300 each. Budgeted purchase costs are $10 per pound for B, $7 per pound for G, and $40 per component for K.

LO5

Required
a. Prepare the production budget for Hancock Manufacturing, Inc., for the third quarter of 2016.
b. Prepare the direct material budget for Hancock Manufacturing, Inc., for the third quarter of 2016.

P9-5A. **Prepare and Evaluate Budgeted Income Statement** Fairfield Stores, a retailer in a shopping mall, prepared the following income statement for its operations for the month just ended:

LO4

SERVICE AND
MERCHANDISING

FAIRFIELD STORES Income Statement for the Month Ended April 30, 2016		
Sales.		$500,000
Cost of goods sold.		240,000
Gross profit.		$260,000
Operating expenses:		
Sales commissions expense	$25,000	
Advertising expense	60,000	
Lease expense	20,000	
Depreciation expense.	10,000	
Salaries expense.	30,000	
Other operating expenses	15,000	160,000
Income before income taxes		$100,000
Income tax expense.		30,000
Net income.		$ 70,000

Sales commissions were 5% of sales. Income taxes were 30% of income before income taxes. Both should continue at the same rate for the remainder of the year.

Fairfield Stores is preparing the budget for the month of May 2016. If no basic changes are made, Fairfield management expects that the income statement would be virtually identical to the one for April. However, Fairfield's management has decided to make some changes in the operations. The plans include the following:

1. Increase advertising expense by 40%.
2. Decrease all selling prices by 10%.
3. Increase the number of units sold by 25% as a result of the first two changes.

Required

a. Prepare a budgeted income statement for the month of May 2016. (Round all amounts on the income statement to the nearest dollar.)

b. Should Fairfield's management make the planned changes?

PROBLEMS—SET B

LO4   P9-1B.   Budgeting Cash Judson, Inc., sells on terms of 5% discount for "cash and carry" or 2/10, n/30 and estimates its total sales for the second calendar quarter of next year as follows: July, $225,000; August, $150,000; and September, $180,000. An analysis of operations indicates the following customer collection patterns:

	Portions of Total Sales
In month of sale:	
Cash at time of sale	30%
On account, during discount period.	20%
On account, after discount period	10%
In month following sale:	
On account, during discount period.	20%
On account, after discount period	10%
In second month following sale:	
On account, after discount period	7%
Average portion uncollectible.	3%
	100%

Required

Prepare an estimate of the cash to be collected from customers during September.

LO4   P9-2B.   Preparation of Individual Budgets During the first calendar quarter of 2016, Williams Corporation is planning to manufacture a new product and introduce it in two regions. Market research indicates that sales will be 8,000 units in the urban region at a unit price of $65 and 6,000 units in the rural region at $55 each. Because the sales manager expects the product to catch on, she has asked for production sufficient to generate a 4,000-unit ending inventory. The production manager has furnished the following estimates related to manufacturing costs and operating expenses:

	Variable (per unit)	Fixed (total)
Manufacturing costs:		
Direct material:		
A (2 lb. @ $2.50/lb.).	$ 5	—
B (5 lb. @ $1.40/lb.).	7	—
Direct labor (2 hrs. per unit)	10	—
Manufacturing overhead:		
Depreciation	—	$22,500
Factory supplies	0.55	2,500
Supervisory salaries	—	16,250
Other.	0.65	9,200
Operating expenses:		
Selling:		
Advertising	—	12,500
Sales salaries and commissions*	1.25	20,000
Other*	0.50	4,200
Administrative:		
Office salaries	—	15,000
Supplies	0.40	1,200
Other.	0.25	5,000

*Varies per unit sold, not per unit produced.

Required

a. Assuming that the desired ending inventories of materials A and B are 4,000 and 20,000 pounds, respectively, and that work-in-process inventories are immaterial, prepare budgets for the calendar quarter in which the new product will be introduced for each of the following operating factors:
  1. Total sales
  2. Production
  3. Material purchases cost
  4. Direct labor costs
  5. Manufacturing overhead costs
  6. Selling and administrative expenses

b. Using data generated in requirement (a), prepare a budgeted income statement for the calendar quarter. Assume an overall effective income tax rate of 35%. (Round income statement amounts to nearest dollar.)

P9-3B. Monthly Cash Budget Sutter, Inc. is a wholesaler for its only product, deluxe wireless rechargeable electric shavers, which sell for $70 each and cost Sutter $48 each. On June 1, 2016, Sutter's management requested a cash budget for June. The following selected account balances at May 31, 2016, were gathered by the accounting department:

LO4

Cash..	$ 56,000
Marketable securities (at cost).................................	160,000
Accounts receivable (all trade)................................	2,170,000
Inventories (12,000 units).....................................	576,000
Operating expenses payable....................................	196,800
Accounts payable (all merchandise)............................	902,400
Note payable...	600,000

Actual sales for April and May were 30,000 and 50,000 units, respectively. Projected unit sales for June and July are 40,000 and 20,000, respectively. Experience indicates that 50% of sales should be collected in the month of sale, 30% in the month following sale, and the balance in the second month following sale. Uncollectible accounts, returns, and allowances are negligible.

Planned purchases should provide ending inventories equal to 30% of next month's unit sales volume. Approximately 60% of the purchases are paid for in the month of purchase and the balance in the following month.

Monthly operating expenses are budgeted at $9.60 per unit sold plus a fixed amount of $288,000 including depreciation of $112,000. Except for depreciation, 70% of operating expenses are paid in the month incurred and the balance in the following month. Interest expense is included in operating expenses.

Special anticipated June transactions include the following:

1. Declaration of a $60,000 cash dividend to be paid 2 weeks after the June 20 date of record.
2. Sale of all but $40,000 of the marketable securities held on May 31; a gain of $18,000 is anticipated.
3. Payment of $50,000 installment on the note payable.
4. Trade-in of an old company plane originally costing $300,000 and now having accumulated depreciation of $200,000 at a gain of $160,000 on a new plane costing $2,000,000. Sufficient cash will be paid at the time of trade-in so that only 50% of the total price will have to be financed.
5. Sutter's treasurer has a policy of maintaining a minimum month-end cash balance of $40,000 and has a standing arrangement with the bank to borrow any amount up to a limit of $400,000.

Required
Prepare a cash budget for Sutter, Inc., for June 2016.

P9-4B. Budgeting Production and Purchases and Just-In-Time Materials Inventory Central Manufacturing, Inc. is preparing budgets for the second quarter of 2016. Central produces only one product in its factory. This product requires 4 pounds of material C, 3 pounds of material H, and a component, M, that is purchased from another manufacturer. Central operates on a just-in-time basis for material C. As a result, Central maintains no inventory of material C. On April 1, 2016, the inventory of material H is expected to be 3,000 pounds and the inventory of component M is expected to be 600 units. Central wants the inventories of H and M at June 30, 2016, to be 20% less than the inventories at April 1, 2016. The inventory of finished products at March 31, 2016, is expected to be 2,000 units; the desired inventory at June 30, 2016, is 4,000 units to allow a buildup for heavy sales

LO4

in the third quarter. The sales forecast for the second quarter is 14,000 units at $200 each. Budgeted purchase costs are $5 per pound for C, $6 per pound for H, and $50 per component for M.

Required

a. Prepare the production budget for the second quarter of 2016.

b. Prepare the direct material budget for the second quarter of 2016.

P9-5B. **Prepare and Evaluate Budgeted Income Statement** Medford Stores, a retailer in a shopping mall, prepared the following income statement for its operations for the month just ended:

MEDFORD STORES Income Statement for the Month Ended April 30, 2016		
Sales.		$700,000
Cost of goods sold.		330,000
Gross profit.		$370,000
Operating expenses:		
Sales commissions expense	$35,000	
Advertising expense.	90,000	
Lease expense	50,000	
Depreciation expense.	20,000	
Salaries expense.	40,000	
Other operating expenses	25,000	260,000
Income before income taxes		$110,000
Income tax expense.		33,000
Net income.		$ 77,000

Sales commissions were 5% of sales. Income taxes were 30% of income before income taxes. Both should continue at the same rate for the remainder of the year.

Medford Stores is preparing the budget for the month of May 2016. If no basic changes are made, Medford's management expects that the income statement would be virtually identical to the one for April. However, Medford's management has decided to make some changes in the operations. The plans include the following:

1. Increase advertising expense by 30%.
2. Decrease all selling prices by 10%.
3. Increase the number of units sold by 20% as a result of the first two changes.

Required

a. Prepare a budgeted income statement for the month of May 2016. (Round all amounts on the income statement to the nearest dollar.)

b. Should Medford's management make the planned changes?

CERTIFIED MANAGEMENT ACCOUNTANT (CMA®) EXAM SAMPLE QUESTIONS

CMA9-1. All of the following are advantages of the use of budgets in a management control system, *except* that budgets

   a. force management planning.

   b. provide performance criteria.

   c. promote communication and coordination within the organization.

   d. limit unauthorized expenditures.

CMA9-2. Which one of the following items would most likely cause the planning and budgeting system to fail?

   a. Lack of historical financial data

   b. Lack of input from several levels of management

   c. Lack of top management support

   d. Lack of adherence to rigid budgets during the year

CMA9-3. Which one of the following statements concerning approaches for the budget development process is **correct**?

    a.   The authoritative approach to budgeting discourages strict adherence to strategic organizational goals.

    b.   To prevent ambiguity, once departmental budgeted goals have been developed, they should remain fixed even if the sales forecast upon which they are based proves to be wrong in the middle of the fiscal year.

    c.   With the information technology available, the role of budgets as an organizational communication device has declined.

    d.   Because department managers have the most detailed knowledge about organizational operations, they should use this information as the building blocks of the operating budget.

CMA9-4. What would be the correct chronological order of preparation for the following budgets?

    I.   Cost of goods sold budget.

    II.   Production budget.

    III.   Purchases budget.

    IV.   Administrative budget.

    a.   I, II, III, IV.

    b.   III, II, IV, I.

    c.   IV, II, III, I.

    d.   II, III, I, IV.

CMA9-5. Hannon Retailing Company prices its products by adding 30% to its cost. Hannon anticipates sales of $715,000 in July, $728,000 in August, and $624,000 in September. Hannon's policy is to have on hand enough inventory at the end of the month to cover 25% of the next month's sales. What will be the cost of the inventory that Hannon should budget for purchase in August?

    a. $509,600

    b. $540,000

    c. $560,000

    d. $680,000

EXTENDING YOUR KNOWLEDGE

EYK9-1.   **Business Decision Case** The sales department of Donovan Manufacturing, Inc. has completed the   **LO4** following sales forecast for the months of January through March 2016 for its only two products: 50,000 units of J to be sold at $90 each and 30,000 units of K to be sold at $70 each. The desired unit inventories at March 31, 2016, are 10% of the next quarter's unit sales forecast, which are 60,000 units of J and 30,000 units of K. The January 1, 2016, unit inventories were 5,000 units of J and 2,000 units of K.

    Each unit of J requires 3 pounds of material A and 2 pounds of material B for its manufacture; K requires 2 pounds of A and 4 pounds of B. The purchase cost of A is $9 per pound and the purchase cost of B is $5 per pound. Materials A and B on hand at January 1, 2016, were 19,000 pounds of A and 7,000 pounds of B. Desired inventories at March 31, 2016, are 14,000 pounds of A and 8,000 pounds of B.

    Each unit of J requires 0.5 hour of direct labor in the factory; each unit of K requires 1.0 hour of direct labor. The average hourly rate for direct labor is $12 per hour. Estimated manufacturing overhead cost is $6 per direct labor hour plus $90,000 per month. Selling and administrative expenses are estimated to be 10% of sales revenue plus $180,000 per month.

Cash sales for the first quarter are estimated to be $300,000 per month. It is forecast that 30% of the credit sales for the quarter ended March 31, 2016, will occur in January, 30% in February, and 40% in March. Of credit sales (December through March), 40% will be collected as cash in the month of sale and 55% will be collected in the following month. The remainder will be uncollectible. Cash collected in January 2016 from December 2015 sales will be $1,050,000.

The January 1, 2016, cash balance was $70,000. The minimum acceptable cash balance at the end of each month is $60,000. Short-term borrowings (6-month term) are made in multiples of $10,000. Interest is charged at the rate of 1% per month on short-term borrowings. The first interest payment is made the month following the borrowing. Cash disbursements (excluding interest on short-term borrowings) are estimated as follows:

	January	February	March
Manufacturing costs.	$1,500,000	$1,300,000	$1,400,000
Selling and administrative expenses	390,000	410,000	400,000
Interest expense.	90,000	90,000	90,000
Income tax payment.	0	0	210,000
Capital expenditures	124,000	110,000	50,000
Cash dividends.	300,000	0	0

Required

a. Prepare the sales budget for the quarter ended March 31, 2016.
b. Prepare the production budget for the quarter ended March 31, 2016.
c. Prepare the direct material budget for the quarter ended March 31, 2016.
d. Prepare the direct labor budget for the quarter ended March 31, 2016.
e. Prepare the manufacturing overhead budget for the quarter ended March 31, 2016.
f. Prepare the selling and administrative expense budget for the quarter ended March 31, 2016.
g. Prepare a schedule of cash collected from customers for the quarter ended March 31, 2016.
h. Prepare the cash budget for the quarter ended March 31, 2016.

LO3

SERVICE AND
MERCHANDISING

EYK9-2.   **Ethics Case** Steve Waller is the corporate accounting manager for Giant Video Stores. As part of the budgeting process for the entire corporation, he has asked the manager of each video store to prepare a store master budget.

The manager of one of the largest stores, Jeff Miller, decides to understate the sales budget and overstate all the budgets related to expenses. Jeff believes this is a more conservative approach than using the estimated numbers he honestly believes will be achieved for the year. He also thinks that the corporate office will look more favorably on his store's actual achievements when they are subsequently compared to this budget.

Jeff has asked Lisa Dorton, his assistant manager, to review the budget before it is submitted. Lisa is aware of the real estimates that Jeff made.

Required

What is the impact of Jeff Miller's budget for the corporation? What ethical issues face Lisa Dorton?

ANSWERS TO SELF-STUDY QUESTIONS:

1. b, (pp. 303–304)   2. a, (pp. 311–312)   3. d, (pp. 305–306)   4. a, (pp. 307–308)   5. c, (p. 313)

DECISION TIME SOLUTION

Solution 9.1

1. It requires management to give priority to planning.
2. It provides a way of formalizing a plan.
3. It provides a benchmark for evaluation.
4. It serves as a motivating factor.
5. It coordinates the entire organization.

YOUR TURN! SOLUTIONS

Solution 9.1

Threats might include the emergence of online retailers such as Amazon.com, increased minimum wages, intense competition from Walmart and other similar retailers, and an economic slowdown in the United States.

Solution 9.2

Depreciation, depletion, amortization, and uncollectible accounts expense

10

Standard Costing and Variance Analysis

LEARNING OBJECTIVES

1. **Define** standard costs and **describe** their use in standard cost accounting. *(p. 340)*

2. **Develop** an overall understanding of the determination of standard costs for direct material, direct labor, and variable overhead. *(p. 342)*

3. **Understand** and **calculate** direct materials variances. *(p. 346)*

4. **Understand** and **calculate** direct labor variances. *(p. 350)*

5. **Understand** and **calculate** variable overhead variances. *(p. 353)*

6. **Present** and **illustrate** the use of standard costs in financial statements. *(p. 355)*

7. Appendix 10A: **Present** journal entries associated with standard costs. *(p. 357)*

BOEING

Boeing is the world's largest aerospace company and a leading manufacturer of commercial jetliners and defense, space, and security systems. Its products include commercial and military aircraft, satellites, weapons, electronic and defense systems, launch systems, and advanced information and communication systems. Approximately 75% of the world's fleet of commercial jetliners in service, almost 12,000 jets, were made by Boeing (including those made by McDonnell Douglas, which merged with Boeing in 1997). The main commercial jetliner products include the familiar 737, 747, 767, and 777 families of airplanes. New jetliner products under development include the 787 Dreamliner and the 747-8.

The 787 Dreamliner is a new, super-efficient airplane that incorporates advanced composite materials, systems, and an engine that was expected to improve fuel efficiency by 20% over existing small twin-aisle airplanes and reduce maintenance and replacement costs. Boeing's approach to the design and manufacture of the 787 involved significant outsourcing that was intended to reduce the 787's development time from 6 to 4 years and development cost from $10 billion to $6 billion. The customers' travel experience was to be improved also, because the composite material used would allow for increased humidity and pressure and would enable the 787 to fly nonstop between any pair of cities without layovers. Because of these promised improvements, the 787 became the fastest-selling plane in aviation history. The actual results have been not what Boeing executives expected when the development of the 787 began. The first of the 787s was to have been delivered in 2008. Due to a host of management problems, including outsourcing of major components and systems, lack of on-site support for outsourced components, delegation of detailed engineering and procurement to subcontractors, inadequate communication and oversight of foreign suppliers, and other management failures, the first 787 wasn't delivered until 2011. Subsequent operational problems included brake problems, fuel leaks, a cracked windshield, a couple of electrical fires, and an emergency landing followed by the grounding of all 787s that had been delivered. As of early 2013, less than 10% of the planes sold had been delivered.

For products as complex as the 787 aircraft, manufacturers often use a standard costing system. Standard costs are developed for all direct materials, direct labor, and overhead associated with the product. Actual results can then be compared to the established standard costs to identify where there are significant variances and take appropriate action to improve performance. In its 2013 Annual Report, Boeing reports that the first three flight-test 787s could not be sold due to an inordinate amount of rework and extensive modifications. Boeing included the costs of those three planes in its research and development expense. In effect, Boeing wrote off 100% of the cost of three planes, representing a multibillion-dollar variance!

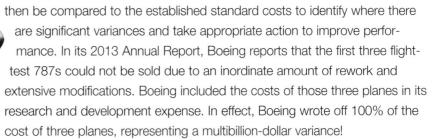

STANDARD COSTING AND VARIANCE ANALYSIS						
Standard Costs	**Determining Standard Costs**	**Direct Materials Variances**	**Direct Labor Variances**	**Variable Overhead Variances**	**Financial Statements**	**Cost Variance Journal Entries (Appendix 10A)**
• Definition • Uses	• Direct material standards • Direct labor standards • Variable overhead standards • Total standard costs	• Cost variances • Materials price variance • Materials efficiency variance • Fezzari direct materials variances	• Labor rate variance • Labor efficiency variance • Fezzari direct labor variances	• Spending variances • Efficiency variances • Fezzari variable overhead variances	• Standard costs in financial statements	• Raw materials variances • Direct labor variances • Variable overhead variances

STANDARD COSTS

LO1 **Define** standard costs and **describe** their use in standard cost accounting.

Managers follow a cycle of planning (budgeting) before each accounting period and then following up with performance evaluation after the period ends. An important tool that managers use in both the pre-planning phase and in the post-evaluation phase is standard costing. Standard costing consists of setting targets, benchmarks, or goals for performance. In other words, managers define standards or expectations of what they consider to be efficient quantities, costs, and rates they expect to achieve in the production process. After setting these objectives at the beginning of the period (during the budgeting phase), they use them to evaluate performance after the period ends. Specifically, in order to budget expected costs for a period, managers determine how much they "should" spend to produce products or services. Thus, **standard costs** are the costs that should be incurred under normal, efficient operating conditions to produce specific products or to perform specific services. Standards should be attainable through efficient efforts by the typical worker at a task. A complex process, involving engineering specifications, time and motion studies, estimates of supply and demand, and analyses of historical trends, is used to develop standard costs. Standard costs are usually stated per unit of product or service and are useful for a number of purposes, including preparing flexible budgets and master budgets, establishing selling prices, and preparing performance reports.

Standard costs are budgeted costs, the costs that should be incurred during the upcoming year. Obviously, managers use past performance to set standards, but these standards are not intended to simply be a description of past performance, but are intended to be their best projection of *future* performance. In other words, managers want to spend their time looking through the windshield to see where they are going rather than looking at the rearview mirror. Nevertheless, the past is often the best way to project the firm's trajectory for the future. Reasonably attainable levels of efficiency and productivity are used to establish standard costs, so they can serve as a motivating factor and a standard of performance. Typically, standard costs are revised no more frequently than once each year.

Standard costs are usually established prior to the beginning of each year as part of the budgeting process. They should not be updated during the year unless there are major, unexpected changes in vendor costs, wage rates, technology, or product design. One of the important uses of standard costs is to compare them to actual costs to identify significant differences. This comparison process will be most meaningful when the standards used represent the level of efficiency and productivity that was planned during the budgeting process.

Uses of Standard Cost Accounting

Many companies, especially manufacturing firms, adopt **standard cost accounting** for product costs. Although we focus on manufacturing firms in this chapter, it is important to note that standard costing concepts also apply in service companies. The concepts discussed in this chapter relative to labor and overhead apply equally in service and manufacturing environments. When this approach is taken in a manufacturing setting, all inventory accounts—material, work in process, and finished goods—and the cost of goods sold account are stated in terms of standard or predetermined costs rather than actual costs incurred. Specifically, standard costs are used for direct material, direct labor, variable overhead, and fixed overhead. (Fixed overhead standard costs and variances are beyond the scope of this textbook. We will limit our discussion to variable production costs.)

Standard cost accounting can be used with either job order costing or process costing. When standard cost accounting is used, standard costs are carried in the inventory accounts and the cost of goods sold account and the differences between the standard costs and actual costs are recorded as **variances**. Essentially, variances are the deviations from the company's predetermined standards. Thus, variances serve as an important evaluation tool to help managers assess how realistic their budgeted costs determined at the beginning of the period were. Moreover, they allow managers to pinpoint areas for improvement in future periods. **Exhibit 10-1** illustrates how standard costs are set at the beginning of the period. Managers rely on many sources to determine the costs they "should" incur under efficient operating conditions by consulting with engineers regarding historical and projected production rates, past purchase contracts for materials, historical labor rates, and so forth. These standard costs become the basis for the current-period budget. At the end of the period, managers compare the actual costs to the previously defined standard costs to evaluate performance and to help them identify areas for improvement.

Exhibit 10-1	Comparing Standard Cost Budgets to Actual Results

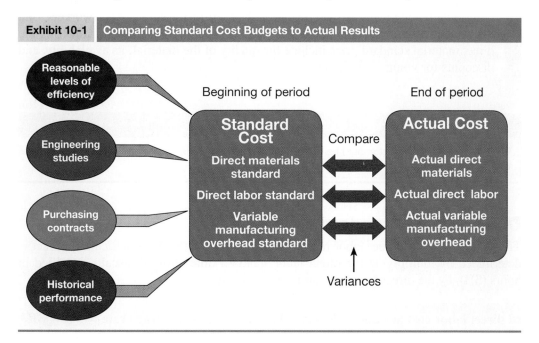

DETERMINING STANDARD COSTS

LO2 **Develop** an overall understanding of the determination of standard costs for direct material, direct labor, and variable overhead.

The development of standard costs per unit of product for all variable inputs requires the use of six components: (1) direct material standard price, (2) direct material standard quantity, (3) direct labor standard rate, (4) direct labor standard time allowed, (5) standard variable overhead rate, and (6) variable overhead standard capacity. The cost-related components are developed and updated as part of the budgeting process, and quantity and capacity standards are usually developed as part of the product design and engineering process. We describe the six standard costing components in the following sections.

Direct Material Standards

Hint: The product of direct material standard price and direct material standard quantity is part of a static budget.

The standard direct material cost to produce a unit of a particular finished product is determined by multiplying the direct material standard quantity (SQ) per unit by the direct material standard price (SP) per unit:

> **Standard direct material cost per unit = Standard quantity × Standard price = SQ × SP**

To illustrate this calculation, consider the fact that each of Boeing's 787 jetliners requires seat-back tray tables. Assume that the standard quantity of seat-back tray tables per 787 is 232. Moreover, assume that Boeing has a supplier that produces the tray tables and that the standard purchase price per tray table is $50. Given this information, the standard direct material cost to provide seat-back tray tables for a Boeing 787 would be calculated as follows:

Standard tray table cost per 787 airplane	=	SQ × SP
	=	232 tables per 787 × $50 per table
	=	$11,600 per 787

A number of factors affect the direct material standard quantity, including material quality, engineering specifications, the skill of the direct labor workers, and the capabilities of the equipment used to process the material. Factors affecting the direct material standard price include the quality of the material, its availability, and discounts for volume purchases.

ACCOUNTING IN PRACTICE **Standard Cost of Material**

The standard material cost should be the expected cost of material including delivery costs and net of any discounts.

Direct Labor Standards

The standard cost of direct labor required to produce one unit of a particular product is determined by multiplying the direct labor standard time allowed, usually specified in hours (SH), by the direct labor standard wage rate (SR):

> **Standard direct labor cost per unit = Standard hours × Standard wage rate = SH × SR**

Continuing the Boeing illustration, assume that the standard amount of direct labor needed to install the seat-back tray tables is 8 hours per 787 and that the standard hourly wage rate for direct labor is $30. The resulting standard direct labor cost per 787 is $240:

Standard direct labor cost per 787	=	SH × SR
	=	8 Direct labor hours per 787 × $30 per direct labor hour
	=	$240 per 787

The direct labor standard wage rate represents the expected weighted average of labor rates for all levels of workers who undertake direct labor tasks on the product. The rates for the various levels of workers are set by the company or prescribed by labor contract. Direct labor standard times are based primarily on prior employee performance and current time and motion studies. Moreover, these wage rates include all compensation components guaranteed to employees (such as health insurance, payroll taxes, retirement plans, etc.).

Standard Cost of Labor   ACCOUNTING IN PRACTICE

The direct labor standard time should include an allowance for breaks, personal needs, cleanup, and so on.

Variable Overhead Standards

The standard cost of variable overhead needed to manufacture one unit of a particular product is determined by multiplying the variable overhead standard capacity (SC), by the standard (or predetermined) variable overhead application rate (SR):

$$\text{Standard variable overhead cost per unit} = \text{Variable overhead standard capacity} \times \text{Variable overhead application rate} = \text{SC} \times \text{SR}$$

Traditionally we separate overhead costs into fixed and variable components. This is necessary because fixed costs hold constant within all production levels within our relevant range. Only the variable component fluctuates in response to changes in volume. Therefore our variable overhead application rate (SR) is the variable portion of the predetermined overhead application rate that was explained in the discussion of job order costing in **Chapter 3**. Recall that the basis for determining the rate can be direct labor hours, direct labor dollars, machine hours, or some other overhead application base. The basis selected should be the best common measure of variable overhead capacity utilized during production.

The variable overhead standard capacity (SC) should be stated in the same terms as the rate (SR). For instance, if the basis for the variable overhead application rate is direct labor hours, then the variable overhead standard capacity allowed will be the number of direct labor hours expected to produce one unit. This will also typically be the same application base used to apply the overhead application rate to production.

In the Boeing illustration, assume that Boeing allocates variable overhead based on direct labor hours and that the standard variable overhead application rate (SR) is calculated to be $50 per direct labor hour and that the variable overhead standard capacity (SC) for installing the seat-back tray tables is 8 direct labor hours per 787 (i.e., the same as the direct labor standard time or SH allowed). The resulting standard variable overhead cost per 787 associated with the tray installation is calculated as follows:

Standard variable overhead cost per 787 =	SC × SR
=	8 Direct labor hours per 787 × $50 per direct labor hour
=	$400 per 787

A.K.A. The *standard variable overhead rate* is also known as the *predetermined variable overhead rate*.

The standard variable overhead rate is based on the expected level of operations. Because a wide variety of cost items is included in variable overhead, many different factors affect the rate. The variable overhead standard capacity is influenced by such factors as prior employee performance, prior machine performance, and current time and motion studies.

TAKEAWAY 10.1

It is good practice for management to understand and utilize standard costs and variances. Establishing standards helps managers track their expectations against actual results for a period. This information can then guide management to a better understanding of costs and the factors that cause cost fluctuations.

Total Standard Costs

Exhibit 10-2 summarizes the relationships described so far. Most firms that use standard costs prepare a summary of the standard product costs for each product that they produce.

Exhibit 10-2	**Standard Cost Summary**
Standard direct material cost per unit . . . . . . =	SQ × SP
Standard direct labor cost per unit . . . . =	SH × SR
Standard variable overhead cost per unit . . . =	SC × SR

Where: SQ = Standard Quantity
SP = Standard Price
SH = Standard Hours
SR = Standard Rate
SC = Standard Capacity

Based on the preceding concepts, Boeing's standard cost summary for seat-back tray tables in a 787 would appear as in **Exhibit 10-3**.

Exhibit 10-3	**Standard Cost Summary**	
BOEING 787 **Seat-Back Tray Tables**		
Direct material	(232 tables × $50 per table) =	$11,600
Direct labor.	(8 DLH × $30 per DLH) =	240
Variable overhead.	(8 DLH × $50 per DLH) =	400
Total standard product cost per 787		$12,240

Where: DLH = Direct Labor Hours

Standard costs are also used in determining product cost variances. The remaining sections of this chapter deal with the calculation and use of product cost variances.

Use of Standard Costs in Setting Selling Prices	**ACCOUNTING IN PRACTICE**

Standard costs of products are an important consideration in setting selling prices, but are certainly not the only, or even the most important, consideration. Prices of competitors' products and prices of substitute products must also be considered when determining product selling prices.

COST VARIANCES

Standard costs are extremely helpful in budgeting prior to the start of a fiscal period. Moreover, they can also be very useful in evaluating performance at the end of a period. Even in well-managed companies with carefully established and currently maintained cost standards, actual costs will differ from standard costs. The differences, often called *variances*, should be analyzed for indications of their cause so that appropriate action may be taken to prevent them in future periods.

We first provide an overview of each type of variance and then illustrate the calculation of these variances based on the production data for an important Fezzari product. Suppose that during June 2016, Fezzari Bicycles produced 100 Fore CR2 road bikes for which it incurred the following actual costs (assume no beginning or ending work in process inventories):

Direct material:	
Frame	$33,600
Build kit.	31,500
Direct labor:	
Assembly	15,000
Quality control and packaging	5,000
Variable overhead.	1,525
Total actual variable production costs	$86,625

Exhibit 10-4 compares the actual costs with standard costs to produce 100 bikes, and calculates the differences, or variances, for each cost category. We multiply the standard costs by the actual quantity of 100 bikes produced in June. Note that both favorable and unfavorable variances exist and that the overall net variance of $7,315 is unfavorable. To initiate remedial action, management must analyze the variance for each manufacturing cost element to determine the underlying causal factors related to prices paid, quantities used, and productive capacity used.

Exhibit 10-4	Comparison of Standard and Actual Costs			
	FEZZARI PERFORMANCE BICYCLES **Variance Analysis** **June 30, 2016**			
	Actual Costs	**Standard Costs**	**Total Flexible Budget Variances**	
Direct material	$65,100	$60,000	$5,100	Unfavorable*
Direct labor.	20,000	17,750	2,250	Unfavorable
Variable overhead.	1,525	1,560	(35)	Favorable
	$86,625	$79,310	$7,315	Unfavorable

*The total material variance calculated in the next section is not equal to the difference between the total standard costs and total actual costs because the amount purchased is different from the amount used in production. See the chapter discussion for a detailed explanation.

Direct Materials Variances

LO3 Understand and calculate direct materials variances.

We begin our discussion with direct materials variances. Direct materials variances are often slightly more complicated than the other variable manufacturing cost variances simply because the quantity of materials purchased often differs from the quantity used in production during the period. To aid in (1) understanding how variances work, (2) remembering how they are calculated, and (3) visualizing each type of variance, we present each type of variable manufacturing cost variance using a simple "fork diagram." **Exhibit 10-5** provides a simple diagram for materials (assuming the quantity purchased is equal to the quantity used in production).

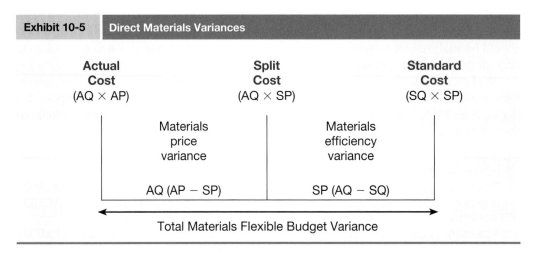

Exhibit 10-5	Direct Materials Variances

Variance analysis simply compares actual costs with standard costs. We place the actual materials cost on the left. How much did we spend to purchase materials? Actual materials purchased equals the actual quantity (AQ) purchased times the actual price per unit (AP). We place the standard cost of materials allowed for this level of production on the far right of the diagram. How much should we have spent on raw materials at this level of production? As explained previously, standard materials cost equals the standard quantity allowed (SQ) for this level of output times the standard price per unit (SP). The total difference between actual and standard costs (as explained in more detail in **Chapter 11**) is called the total materials flexible budget variance. However, there are two reasons we may spend more or less than our standards would indicate. First, we may pay too much or too little when we purchase the materials. Second, we may not use the materials efficiently in the production process. Hence, it is useful to split the total materials flexible budget variance into its two main components: (1) the **materials price variance** and (2) the **materials efficiency variance**. In order to facilitate this analysis, we place a new number in the middle of the diagram (the split cost), which takes the actual quantity purchased (AQ) from the far left of the diagram and multiplies it by the standard price (SP) from the far right of the diagram. This number represents the standard price we should have spent to buy the actual quantity purchased (AQ × SP).

We calculate the materials price variance by subtracting the standard price we should have paid for the actual quantity purchased from our actual purchase price:

$$\text{Materials price variance} = (AQ \times AP) - (AQ \times SP)$$

Using simple algebra, we can factor out the common element in each number (AQ) and rewrite the materials price variance as follows:

$$\text{Materials price variance} = AQ (AP - SP)$$

Written this way, we see that the *cause* of this variance is the difference between the actual price paid to purchase materials compared to the standard price management had budgeted at the beginning of the period. If the actual price exceeds the standard price (i.e., we paid too much), the materials price variance will appear as a positive number. Thus, positive price variance is "unfavorable" because it would indicate that we paid too much per unit when we purchased the materials. On the other hand, if the materials price variance is a negative number (i.e., we paid less than our standards had predicted), the variance is "favorable."

We calculate the materials efficiency variance by subtracting the standard materials cost (SQ × SP) from what we should have paid for the actual quantity purchased according to our standards (AQ × SP):

$$\textbf{Materials efficiency variance} = (\textbf{AQ} \times \textbf{SP}) - (\textbf{SQ} \times \textbf{SP})$$

Again, we can use basic algebra to factor out the common element (SP) to rewrite the materials efficiency variance to better illustrate what causes the variance:

$$\textbf{Materials efficiency variance} = \textbf{SP} \, (\textbf{AQ} - \textbf{SQ})$$

When expressed this way, it is clear that, holding the standard price constant, what *causes* the variance is the quantity used. If we do not use the materials efficiently in production, we may spend too much or too little. Similar to what we observe for the materials price variance, if the actual quantity exceeds the standard quantity (i.e., we used too much of the material in producing products during this period), the materials efficiency variance will appear as a positive number, suggesting that we did not use our materials efficiently (thus the variance will be "unfavorable"). On the other hand, if we use less than our budgeted standards would dictate (i.e., the materials efficiency variance is negative), we conclude that we used less than we expected (and we would label this negative number as a "favorable" materials efficiency variance).

When the quantity of materials purchased is exactly equal to the quantity used in production, this simple diagram indicates that the total materials flexible budget variance is equal to the sum of the materials price variance and the materials efficiency variance. However, it is common in practice that companies purchase more or less than they actually use in production. To account for these common differences, **Exhibit 10-6** illustrates how we modify the "fork diagram" for materials to better differentiate between these two quantities because the materials price variance is based on the quantity of materials *purchased*, whereas the materials efficiency variance depends on the amount of materials *used* in the production process. In other words, the split cost number (AQ × SP), the actual quantity at the standard price, must actually be shown twice because the price variance is based on the quantity *purchased*, whereas the efficiency variance is calculated using the actual quantity *used* in the production process. It is easy to make mistakes in calculating variances if you don't pay close attention to which quantity you are referring to! The version of the materials "fork diagram" in **Exhibit 10-6** can help you to avoid these careless errors. We illustrate these calculations next.

| Managing Variances | ACCOUNTING IN PRACTICE |

Managers may trade off one variance for another. For example, a manager may decide to use a pre-cut material rather than a bulk material. This usually will result in higher cost (unfavorable price variance) and lower quantities (favorable quantity variance) than budgeted.

Exhibit 10-6	Direct Materials Variances

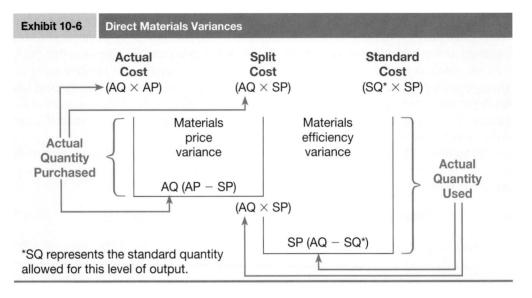

*SQ represents the standard quantity allowed for this level of output.

Fezzari's Direct Materials Variances

We first calculate the materials price variance for frames. Fezzari actually **purchased** 105 frames at a price of $320 per frame and **used** 101 in production during the month. Assume that the standard price is $325 per frame.

The calculations in **Exhibit 10-7** indicate a favorable price variance for frames of $525. This is calculated as the difference between the actual and budgeted price for frames ($320 − $325) multiplied by the number of frames purchased (105). The variance is favorable because Fezzari spent $5 less per frame than anticipated in the budget. However, these calculations also indicate an unfavorable efficiency variance of $325. This is calculated as the budgeted price per frame ($325) multiplied by the difference between the actual number of frames used and the budgeted number of frames used (101 − 100). Fezzari used one more frame than anticipated for this level of production because one bike was damaged beyond repair during production.

Exhibit 10-7	Direct Materials Variances—Frames

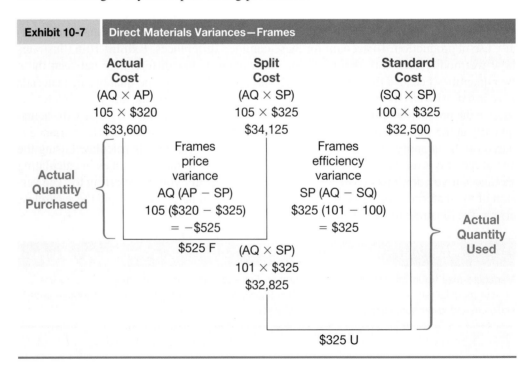

Next, we use the same process to calculate the materials price variance for build kits. Fezzari actually ***purchased*** 105 build kits at a price of $300 per build kit and ***used*** 101 in production during the month. Assume that the standard price is $275 per build kit.

Exhibit 10-8	Direct Materials Variances—Build Kits

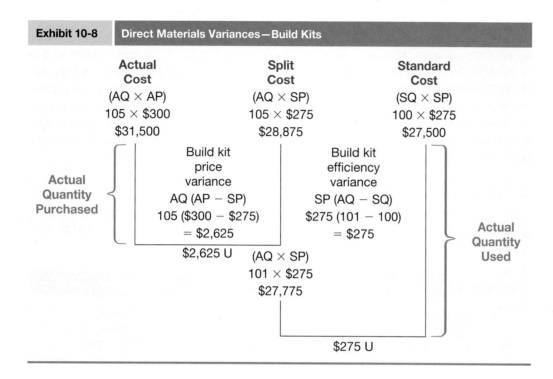

The calculations in **Exhibit 10-8** indicate an unfavorable price variance for build kits of $2,625 (105 build kits × $25 per build kit) because Fezzari spent $25 more per build kit than anticipated in the budget. These calculations also indicate an unfavorable efficiency variance of $275 ($275 × 1 extra build kit). Fezzari used one more build kit than would normally be anticipated for this level of production because one bike was damaged beyond repair during production.

The net materials price variance of $2,100 ($2,625 U − $525 F) is unfavorable because the actual price for build kits was $25 per unit greater than the standard price (even though the price of frames was actually $5 per unit lower than anticipated). Note that for the materials price variance, the quantity represents the number of units purchased, not the number of units manufactured.

The net materials efficiency variance of $600 ($325 U + $275 U) is unfavorable because the actual quantity is greater than the standard quantity (because one frame and one build kit were damaged beyond repair, Fezzari used materials for 101 bikes to only produce 100 usable bikes). Note that for the materials efficiency variance, the quantity represents the number of units issued into production, not the number of units purchased.

A company purchased and used 90,000 feet of material at $2.90 per foot to make 22,000 units of a finished product. The per-unit standard for material is 4 feet @ $3.00 = $12.00. What were the materials price variance and the materials efficiency variance?

YOUR TURN! 10.1

The solution is on page 372.

Exhibit 10-4 indicates that the total flexible budget variance for direct materials is $5,100 U. However, the sum of the materials price and efficiency variances is only $2,700 U:

Materials price variance	$2,100 U
Materials efficiency variance	600 U
Sum of material variances	$2,700 U

The sum of the material variances does not agree with the total flexible budget variance because the quantities of frames and build kits purchased do not equal the amounts used in production. Although the sums of individual variances always add up to the total flexible budget variance for labor and variable overhead variances, this relationship only holds for materials if the quantity purchased equals the quantity used in production during the period.

The unfavorable price variance may have been caused by increases in supplier prices, improper purchasing, or other factors. The unfavorable efficiency variance may have been caused by inefficient workers, inferior-quality material, or other factors.

Direct Labor Variances

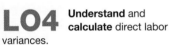

LO4 **Understand** and **calculate** direct labor variances.

After learning how to work with materials variances, labor variances are really easy! In order to visualize direct labor variances, we use a similar "fork diagram," as illustrated in **Exhibit 10-9**.

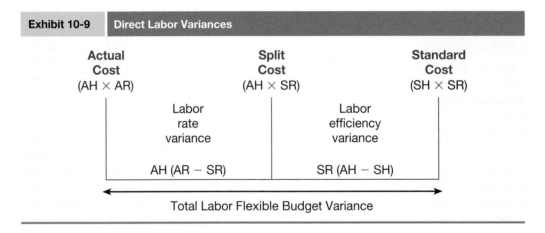

Exhibit 10-9	Direct Labor Variances

Similar to materials variances, we place the actual direct labor cost on the left. How much did we pay our labor force? Actual labor costs equal the actual number of hours worked (AH) times the actual wage rate (AR). We place the standard direct labor cost on the far right of the diagram. How much should we have paid our employees to produce this level of output? As explained previously, standard labor costs equal the standard number of hours to produce this many units (SH) times the standard hourly wage rate (SR). The total difference between actual and standard costs (as explained in more detail in Chapter 11) is called the total labor flexible budget variance. However, there are two reasons we may spend more or less than our standards would indicate. First, we may pay our employees too much or too little relative to what we expected when we prepared our budget at the beginning of the period. Second, we may not use our workforce efficiently in producing inventory. Similar to what we observed for materials, it is useful to split the total labor flexible budget variance into its two main components: (1) the **labor rate variance** and (2) the **labor efficiency variance**. In order to facilitate this analysis, we place a split cost number in the middle of the diagram, which takes the actual hours worked (AH) from the far left of the diagram and multiplies it by the standard wage rate (SR) from the far right of the diagram. This number represents the standard amount we should have spent to pay our workforce (AH × SR) to produce this level of output.

We calculate the labor rate variance by subtracting the standard price we should have paid our employees for the actual level of production from our actual labor costs:

$$\textbf{Labor rate variance} = (\textbf{AH} \times \textbf{AR}) - (\textbf{AH} \times \textbf{SR})$$

Using simple algebra, we can factor out the common element in each number (AH) and rewrite the labor rate variance as follows:

$$\textbf{Labor rate variance} = \textbf{AH (AR} - \textbf{SR)}$$

Written this way, we see that the *cause* of this variance is the difference between the actual wage rate as compared with the standard wage rate management had forecasted at the beginning of the period. If the actual rate exceeds the standard rate (i.e., we paid employees more than expected), the labor rate variance will appear as a positive number. Thus, a positive price variance is "unfavorable" because we paid more than we had budgeted. On the other hand, if the labor rate variance is a negative number (i.e., we paid less than our standards had predicted), the variance is "favorable."

We calculate the labor efficiency variance by subtracting the standard labor cost (SH × SR) from what we should have paid for the actual hours worked according to our standards (AH × SR):

$$\textbf{Labor efficiency variance} = (\textbf{AH} \times \textbf{SR}) - (\textbf{SH} \times \textbf{SR})$$

Again, we can use basic algebra to factor out the common element (SR) to rewrite the labor efficiency variance to better illustrate what causes the variance:

$$\textbf{Labor efficiency variance} = \textbf{SR (AH} - \textbf{SH)}$$

When expressed this way, it is clear that holding the standard wage rate constant, what *causes* the variance is the number of hours used. If we do not use our employees efficiently in production, we may spend too much or too little. If the actual number of hours worked exceeds the standard number of hours (i.e., we used too many employee hours), the labor efficiency variance will appear as a positive number, suggesting that we did not use our labor force efficiently (thus the variance will be "unfavorable"). On the other hand, if we use fewer hours than our standards would have predicted (i.e., the labor efficiency variance is negative), we conclude that we were able to use our workers less than we expected (and we would label this negative number as a "favorable" labor efficiency variance).

Fezzari's Direct Labor Variances

We illustrate the calculation of direct labor variances using the Fezzari data presented previously. Specifically, we use the data for the assembly department. Assembly personnel actually worked 750 hours during June at an average rate of $20 per hour. However, the standard number of hours to produce 100 CR2 bikes is 550 hours and the standard wage rate in this department is $25 per hour. Using this information, we can calculate assembly labor variances as illustrated in **Exhibit 10-10**. These calculations indicate a favorable rate variance in the assembly department of $3,750, calculated as 750 hours multiplied by the $5-per-hour difference between the actual and standard rate. The variance is favorable because Fezzari paid an average of $5 less per hour than anticipated in the budget. However, these calculations also indicate an unfavorable efficiency variance of $5,000 ($25 standard rate × 200 extra hours) because Fezzari's assembly crew worked 200 hours more than anticipated for this level of production.

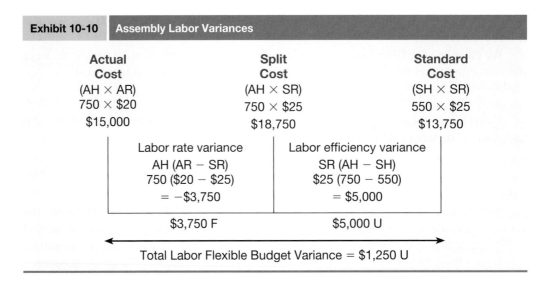

Exhibit 10-10 | **Assembly Labor Variances**

Actual Cost (AH × AR) 750 × $20 $15,000		Split Cost (AH × SR) 750 × $25 $18,750		Standard Cost (SH × SR) 550 × $25 $13,750

Labor rate variance
AH (AR − SR)
750 ($20 − $25)
= −$3,750

Labor efficiency variance
SR (AH − SH)
$25 (750 − 550)
= $5,000

$3,750 F $5,000 U

Total Labor Flexible Budget Variance = $1,250 U

Next, **Exhibit 10-11** calculates the labor variances for the quality control (QC) and packaging department. Employees in this department actually worked 250 hours during June at an average rate of $20 per hour. Assume that the standard number of hours at this production level is 200 and the standard wage rate is exactly $20 per hour.

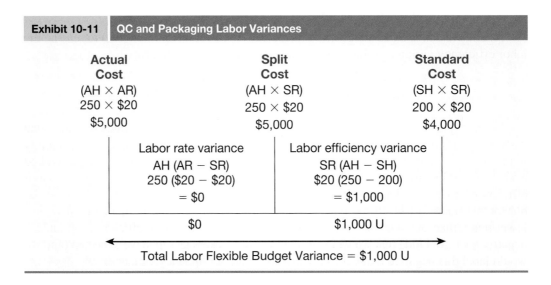

Exhibit 10-11 | **QC and Packaging Labor Variances**

Actual Cost (AH × AR) 250 × $20 $5,000		Split Cost (AH × SR) 250 × $20 $5,000		Standard Cost (SH × SR) 200 × $20 $4,000

Labor rate variance
AH (AR − SR)
250 ($20 − $20)
= $0

Labor efficiency variance
SR (AH − SH)
$20 (250 − 200)
= $1,000

$0 $1,000 U

Total Labor Flexible Budget Variance = $1,000 U

Because the actual wage rate coincides perfectly with the standard wage rate, there is no labor rate variance. However, these calculations indicate an unfavorable efficiency variance of $1,000 ($20 standard rate × 50 extra hours) because Fezzari's QC and packaging employees worked 50 hours more than anticipated for this level of production.

YOUR TURN! 10.2

The solution is on page 372.

Actual hours worked were 35,000 at a rate of $7.50 per hour to make 22,000 units of a finished product. The per-unit standard for labor is 1.5 hours @ $7.00 = $10.50. What were the labor rate variance and the labor efficiency variance?

Combining the results for the assembly and the QC and packaging departments, we calculate the following total variances:

Labor rate variance	$3,750 F
Labor efficiency variance	6,000 U
Total flexible budget variance for labor	$2,250 U

Notice that the sum of the labor rate and efficiency variances equals the total flexible budget variance for labor in **Exhibit 10-4**.

Variable Overhead Variances

Variable overhead variances are virtually identical to labor variances. Therefore we can visualize variable overhead variances using the **Exhibit 10-12** "fork diagram" that is very similar to the direct labor diagram. As explained previously, overhead may be applied to product cost based on any application base that represents the "cost driver." Therefore the standard cost of variable overhead needed to manufacture one unit of a particular product, shown on the far right of the diagram, is determined by multiplying the variable overhead standard capacity (SC) of that "cost driver" by the standard (or predetermined) variable overhead application rate (SR). Note that variable overhead items are recorded as "actual" debits to the manufacturing overhead account as they occur. There is no "rate" applied to these actual amounts. The "actual" amount spent, shown on the far left of the diagram, is simply the sum of all indirect variable items (such as indirect materials, indirect labor, etc.). For simplicity, assume that a company uses direct labor hours as that cost driver in developing a predetermined variable overhead application rate.

LO5 Understand and calculate variable overhead variances.

Exhibit 10-12	**Variable Overhead Variances**

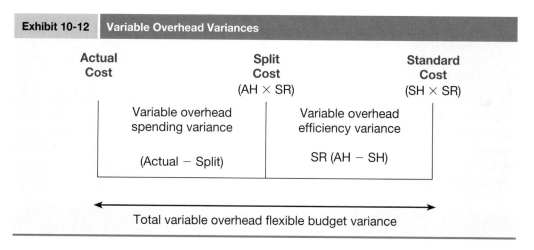

In this diagram, the predetermined variable overhead application rate (i.e., the standard rate, SR) is based on direct labor hours. The variable overhead spending variance (i.e., the rate variance) determines whether that predetermined overhead application rate is higher or lower than the standard rate determined by managers in the budgeting process. Similarly, variable overhead efficiency variance is attributable to the use of that overhead application base or "driver." In this diagram, we list the number of direct labor hours as the "cause" of the efficiency variance. Obviously, if some other application base were used to calculate the predetermined overhead application rate, such as machine hours, direct labor dollars, or quality inspections, the efficiency variance would be based on that factor. For example, if we had used the number of inspections as our variable overhead application base, the formula for the variable overhead efficiency variance would be SR (AI − SI), where "AI" would represent the actual number of quality inspections and "SI" would represent the standard number of quality inspections for that production run.

FEZZARI'S VARIABLE OVERHEAD VARIANCES

Fezzari's variable overhead variances result from paying more or less than planned for items that comprise variable overhead (the **variable overhead spending variance**) and from using more or less than the standard amount of capacity (the **variable overhead efficiency variance**).

ACCOUNTING IN PRACTICE	**Standard Capacity**

The standard capacity allowed for variable overhead and fixed overhead will be stated in terms of a common measure of plant capacity, such as direct labor hours or machine hours. A different measure may be used for variable overhead and fixed overhead.

Assume that Fezzari incurs actual variable overhead during the month of June of $1,525, comprised of the following items:

Indirect material	$ 55
Indirect labor	550
Factory utilities	645
Other.	275
Total	$1,525

These items would be recorded as debits to the manufacturing overhead account as incurred:

Manufacturing overhead	1,525	
Raw materials inventory		55
Wages payable		550
Utilities payable		645
Other payables (or cash)		275

Also assume that during its budgeting process for the year, Fezzari decided to allocate variable overhead based on estimated labor hours in the QC and packaging department and that the predetermined overhead application rate is $7.80 per hour. Therefore, the variable overhead variances for Fezzari are computed and recorded as shown in **Exhibit 10-13**. The calculations are similar to those for material and labor, which, like variable overhead, are variable product cost components.

Exhibit 10-13	Variable Overhead Variances

Actual Cost	**Split Cost** (AH × SR) 250 × $7.80	**Standard Cost** (SH × SR) 200 × $7.80
$1,525	$1,950	$1,560

Variable overhead spending variance	Variable overhead efficiency variance
(Actual − Split) $1,525 − $1,950 = −$425	SR (AH − SH) $7.80 (250 − 200) = $390
$425 F	$390 U

Total variable overhead flexible budget variance = $35 F

The actual variable overhead costs are less than would be projected, based on the actual number of hours worked in this department multiplied by the predetermined (standard) variable overhead application rate. Therefore, the variable overhead spending variance is $425 favorable. The variable overhead efficiency variance is $390 unfavorable simply because employees in the QC and packaging department worked 50 hours more than was anticipated for this level of projection.

The total variable overhead variance would be as follows:

Variable overhead spending variance	$425 F
Variable overhead efficiency variance	390 U
Total variable overhead variance	$ 35 F

Notice that the total variable overhead variance agrees with the amount in **Exhibit 10-4**.

Actual variable overhead was $63,000. Actual hours were 35,000 to make 22,000 finished products. The per-unit standard for variable overhead is 1.5 hours @ $2.00, or $3.00. What were the variable overhead spending variance and the variable overhead efficiency variance?

YOUR TURN! 10.3

The solution is on page 372.

The following is a list of cost variances a company experienced during the first year of its operations. List reasons why these variances could have occurred.

Materials price variance	$4,500 Unfavorable
Materials usage variance	$6,700 Unfavorable
Labor rate variance	$12,000 Favorable
Labor efficiency variance	$9,600 Unfavorable

DECISION TIME 10.1

The solution is on page 372.

STANDARD COSTS IN FINANCIAL STATEMENTS

When the standard costs and related variances for direct material, direct labor, and variable overhead are recorded as previously illustrated, the work in process account is debited for each in amounts representing standard quantities and standard prices. All variances—favorable and unfavorable—are carried in separate accounts with appropriate titles. Fezzari records completed production for June in the following entry (assume no beginning or ending work in process inventories):

LO6 Present and **Illustrate** the use of standard costs in financial statements.

Finished goods inventory (at standard cost)	79,310	
Work in process inventory (at standard cost)		79,310
To record completion of June's production of 100 units at a standard variable unit cost of $793.10 ($60,000 material, $17,750 labor, and $1,560 variable overhead).		

As each month's production is sold, the related amounts of standard costs are transferred from Finished Goods Inventory to Cost of Goods Sold.

Standard costs and related variances are usually reported in financial reports intended only for management's use. **Exhibit 10-14** contains a partial income statement that illustrates how variances might appear on interim financial statements for Fezzari's internal use (amounts are assumed).

Exhibit 10-14	Summary

FEZZARI PERFORMANCE BICYCLES
Partial Income Statement
For the Month Ended June 30, 2016

Sales.	$375,000
Cost of goods sold at standard cost	250,000
Gross profit at standard cost	$125,000
Less: Net unfavorable cost variance	6,500
Gross profit.	$118,500

The total net variance could be broken down into sub-variances or detailed in a schedule of variances accompanying the financial statements.

At year-end, firms commonly close the variance accounts by transferring their balances to Cost of Goods Sold. In effect, this transfer converts Cost of Goods Sold from standard costs to actual costs. If large variances exist at year-end and there is evidence that the standards may not apply, a firm may be justified in allocating all or part of the variances to Work in Process Inventory, Finished Goods Inventory, and Cost of Goods Sold.

SERVICES INDUSTRY IN FOCUS

SERVICE AND MERCHANDISING

Environmental Business Consultants, Inc. (EBC) has hired several new staff members in the last year and has invested considerable effort in training these new employees in the EBC approach to conducting rate review projects. Due to the unique market in which EBC operates, there are not commercial training conferences or online training materials available to provide the necessary training. Therefore, the training is done primarily on the job by EBC managers, resulting in extra hours over what is typically incurred in completing this type of project. EBC management is interested in estimating the cost of this on-the-job training in terms of "lost billings," that is, the billing value of the extra hours incurred by both managers and staff as compared with normal budgeted hours. This is equivalent to the labor efficiency variance.

Assume that for the year just ended, EBC completed 25 rate review projects. The following table shows the normal hourly budget for managers and staff on a rate review project. EBC managers billed a total of 1,200 hours and staff billed a total of 3,500 hours on rate review projects during the year. For the year, managers were billed at a standard rate of $200 per hour and staff were billed at a standard rate of $120 per hour.

	Managers	Staff
Budgeted hours per rate review project.	40	120

Required:
Determine the total labor efficiency variance for both managers and staff for the year.

Solution

Labor Efficiency Variance—Managers	
Split Cost	**Standard Cost**
(AH × SR)	(SH × SR)
1,200 × $200.00	1,000 × $200.00
$240,000	$200,000

Labor efficiency variance
SR (AH − SH)
$200.00 (1,200 − 1,000)
= $40,000

$40,000 U

Labor Efficiency Variance—Staff	
Split Cost	**Standard Cost**
(AH × SR)	(SH × SR)
3,500 × $120.00	3,000 × $120.00
$420,000	$360,000

Labor efficiency variance
SR (AH − SH)
$120.00 (3,500 − 3,000)
= $60,000

$60,000 U

Total Efficiency Variance = $40,000 U + $60,000 U = $100,000 U

APPENDIX 10A: Cost Variance Journal Entries Illustrated

This appendix illustrates the journal entries used in a standard costing system to record materials, labor, and variable overhead variances based on the Fezzari example used throughout the chapter.

LO7 **Present** journal entries associated with standard costs.

JOURNAL ENTRIES ILLUSTRATED

The materials price variance is recorded in the accounting system at the time materials are purchased. Although the amount paid to suppliers is always the "actual" invoice price, we enter materials into the raw materials inventory account at the standard price:

Raw materials inventory	(AQ × SP)	
Materials price variance	U	or **F**
Accounts payable (or cash)		(AQ × AP)

Thus, the credit to Accounts Payable (or Cash) is for the actual amount (AQ × AP), whereas the debit to Raw Materials Inventory is for the standard price to purchase the actual quantity acquired (AQ × SP). We record the difference as the raw materials price variance to allow the manager of the purchasing department to explain the variance at the end of the fiscal period. Note that the materials price variance can either be a debit or a credit. Unfavorable variances (U) are bad news. Hence, they are recorded with a debit (similar to an expense or a loss). On the other hand, favorable variances (F) are good news and are recorded with a credit (similar to a revenue or a gain).

The materials efficiency variance is recorded in the accounting records when raw materials are used in production:

Work in process inventory	(SQ × SP)	
Materials efficiency variance	U	or **F**
Raw materials inventory		(AQ × SP)

We note that when raw materials were purchased, they were recorded at the actual quantity purchased times the standard price per unit. When we use materials in the production process, we take them out of Raw Materials Inventory as the actual quantity used times the standard price per unit (AQ × SP). However, we enter materials into Work in Process Inventory completely at standard (SQ × SP). We record the difference as the materials efficiency variance to allow the production manager to explain the variance at the end of the fiscal period. We again note that the materials efficiency variance can either be a debit or a credit. Unfavorable variances (U) are bad news. Hence, they are recorded with a debit (similar to an expense or a loss). On the other hand, favorable variances (F) are good news and are recorded with a credit (similar to a revenue or a gain).

Fezzari's journal entry to record material purchases and the price variance for CR2 road bikes would be as follows (see Exhibits 10-7 and 10-8):

Raw materials inventory	63,000	
Materials price variance	2,100	
Accounts payable (or cash)		65,100

Moreover, Fezzari's journal entry to record the materials that are used in production for CR2s would be as follows:

Work in process inventory	60,000	
Materials efficiency variance	600	
Raw materials inventory		60,600

The purchasing department's manager can best explain the higher-than-expected prices paid for materials and the production manager would be responsible for explaining the unfavorable materials efficiency variance.

YOUR TURN! 10.4

The solution is on pages 372–373.

> Truck Company purchased and used 55,000 pounds of material at $5.30 per pound to produce 11,000 units of a finished product. The per-unit standard for material established by management was 4 pounds @ $5.10 = $20.40. What were the materials price and efficiency variances, and what journal entry would management make to record these variances?

We only record one entry in the accounting records relative to direct labor. As employees work directly on our products (or in providing services), we increase Work in Process Inventory and show either a decrease to cash or an increased liability, as follows:

Work in process inventory	(SH × SR)	
Labor rate variance	U	or F
Labor efficiency variance	U	or F
Wages payable (or cash)		(AH × AR)

Obviously, our employees won't continue working for us if we don't pay them for their services. Moreover, they are not likely to be happy if we tell them, "We're sorry, but your wage rates are higher than our budget anticipated, so we're only going to pay you the standard wage rate." We have to pay our employees whatever wage rate we contracted with them when we hired them (or when they received their last raise). Hence, the credit to Wages Payable (or Cash) must be for the amount the employees actually earned (AH × AR). However, as explained previously, under a standard costing approach, we record manufacturing costs in Work in Process Inventory completely at standard (SH × SR). Thus, the difference between actual and standard costs can be explained by both the labor rate variance and the labor efficiency variance. As explained previously, positive variances are deemed to be "unfavorable" (U) and are recorded with debits, whereas negative variances are deemed to be "favorable" (F) and are recorded with a credit.

The following journal entry records these costs and variances (see Exhibits 10-10 and 10-11):

Work in process inventory	17,750	
Labor efficiency variance	6,000	
Labor rate variance		3,750
Wages payable (or cash)		20,000

The journal entry charges Work in Process Inventory with standard direct labor costs, records the unfavorable labor efficiency variance as a debit and the favorable labor rate variance as a credit, and records the liability for direct labor (or cash) at the amount owed, which is determined using actual hours worked and actual rates paid.

The unfavorable labor efficiency variance might be charged to the production supervisor, who presumably oversees the production teams. The favorable labor rate variance resulted from assigning lower-paid employees to perform the assembly. Other reasons for a favorable labor rate variance include using less overtime or paying decreased labor rates.

> Car Company used 23,000 actual direct labor hours at a rate of $3.00 per hour to make 15,000 units of a finished product. The per-unit standard for labor is 2 hours @ 3.50 = $7.00. What were the labor rate and efficiency variances, and what journal entry would management make to record these variances?

YOUR TURN! 10.5

The solution is on page 373.

Similar to direct labor, we only record one entry in the accounting records relative to the application of variable overhead to units produced. In this example, because we use direct labor hours as the application base in our predetermined variable overhead rate, it would be driven by the actual number of direct labor hours. As employees work directly on our products (or in providing services), we apply more variable overhead to Work in Process Inventory and a corresponding decrease to Manufacturing Overhead, as follows:

Work in process inventory	(SC × SR)	
Variable overhead spending variance	U	or **F**
Variable overhead efficiency variance	U	or **F**
Manufacturing overhead		(AC × AR)

The interpretations of the variable overhead variances are identical to those for the labor variances.

For Fezzari, the general journal entry to record variable overhead costs and variances is as follows (see Exhibit 10-13):

Work in process inventory	1,560	
Variable overhead efficiency variance	390	
Variable overhead spending variance		425
Manufacturing overhead		1,525

This journal entry assumes that no overhead is applied to Work in Process Inventory until the end of the accounting period. When this entry is recorded at period end, all of the efficiency and spending variances are recorded simultaneously. In this example, the "applied overhead" for the entire period is actually $1,950 (250 actual hours worked × 7.80 predetermined overhead rate). If overhead were applied to Work in Process during the period as jobs were completed, the applied overhead for each job would be analogous to smaller pieces of the middle number in the fork diagram (i.e., the credit to Manufacturing Overhead) and a portion of the variable overhead efficiency variance would be recorded with each portion of the overhead applied. The entire variable overhead spending variance would be recorded at the end of the period as the over- or under-applied overhead amount written off to Cost of Goods sold.

This journal entry charges Work in Process Inventory with standard variable overhead costs, and records the unfavorable variable overhead efficiency variance as a debit and the favorable variable overhead spending variance as a credit.

COMPREHENSIVE PROBLEM

Crenshaw Manufacturing, Inc. planned to produce 25,000 units of its only product during the year. The standard cost data for this product are as follows:

	Per Unit
Direct material (3 lbs. @ $2 per lb.)...	$ 6
Direct labor (0.5 hr. @ $8 per hr.)..	4
Variable overhead (0.5 hr. @ $4 per hr.).....................................	2
Total standard cost per unit..	$12

The actual level of production was 24,000 units, with the following actual total costs incurred:

	Total Cost
Direct material (74,000 lbs. @ $1.80)	$133,200
Direct labor (13,000 hrs. @ $8.10)	105,300
Variable overhead.	50,200
Total actual cost.	$288,700

Required

a. Calculate the variances for material, labor, and variable overhead.

b. Is the difference between total actual cost and total standard cost equal to the sum of all the variances? Why?

Solution to Comprehensive Problem

a.

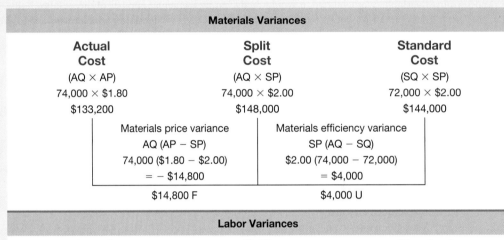

Materials Variances

Actual Cost	Split Cost	Standard Cost
(AQ × AP)	(AQ × SP)	(SQ × SP)
74,000 × $1.80	74,000 × $2.00	72,000 × $2.00
$133,200	$148,000	$144,000

Materials price variance	Materials efficiency variance
AQ (AP − SP)	SP (AQ − SQ)
74,000 ($1.80 − $2.00)	$2.00 (74,000 − 72,000)
= − $14,800	= $4,000
$14,800 F	$4,000 U

Labor Variances

Actual Cost	Split Cost	Standard Cost
(AH × AR)	(AH × SR)	(SH × SR)
13,000 × $8.10	13,000 × $8.00	12,000 × $8.00
$105,300	$104,000	$96,000

Labor rate variance	Labor efficiency variance
AH (AR − SR)	SR (AH − SH)
13,000 ($8.10 − $8.00)	$8.00 (13,000 − 12,000)
= $1,300	= $8,000
$1,300 U	$8,000 U

Variable Overhead Variances

Actual Cost	Split Cost	Standard Cost
	(AH × SR)	(SH × SR)
(AH × AR)	(13,000 × $4.00)	(12,000 × $4.00)
$50,200	$52,000	$48,000

Variable overhead spending variance	Variable overhead efficiency variance
(Actual − Split)	SR (AH − SH)
($50,200 − $52,000)	$4.00 (13,000 −12,000)
= −$1,800	= $4,000
$1,800 F	$4,000 U

b.

Total actual cost.	$288,700
Total standard cost ($12 X 24,000)	288,000
Total variance	$700 U
Material price variance.	$ 14,800 F
Material quantity variance	4,000 U
Labor rate variance.	1,300 U
Labor efficiency variance	8,000 U
Variable overhead spending variance	1,800 F
Variable overhead efficiency variance	4,000 U
Sum of all variances	$ 700 U

In this example, the difference between total actual cost and total standard cost is equal to the sum of all variances. However, this is only true because, in this example, the amount of direct materials *purchased* is equal to the direct materials *used* in production. If this were not the case, the materials price variance plus the materials efficiency variance would not be equal to the total flexible budget variance for materials. Hence, in a broader sense, it is also true that if the amount of direct materials *purchased* had not been equal to the direct materials *used* in production, the difference between total actual costs and total standard costs would not have been equal to the sum of all of the variances. This is a key concept to remember.

SUMMARY OF LEARNING OBJECTIVES

Define standard costs and their use in standard cost accounting. (p. 340)   LO1

- Standard costs represent the costs per unit that should be incurred during the upcoming year. They are established as part of the budgeting process.
- When standard cost accounting is used, all inventory accounts—material, work in process, and finished goods—and the cost of goods sold account are stated in terms of standard costs. Actual costs are accumulated separately.

Develop an overall understanding of the determination of standard costs for direct material, direct labor, and variable overhead. (p. 342)   LO2

- Six components are required to develop standard variable product costs:
  - Direct material standard price
  - Direct material standard quantity
  - Direct labor standard rate
  - Direct labor standard time allowed
  - Standard variable overhead rate
  - Variable overhead standard capacity
- The standard direct material cost to produce a unit of a particular finished product is determined by multiplying the direct material standard quantity per unit by the direct material standard price per unit.
- The standard cost of direct labor required to produce one unit of a particular product is determined by multiplying the direct labor standard time allowed, usually specified in hours, by the direct labor standard wage rate.
- The standard cost of variable overhead needed to manufacture one unit of a particular product is determined by multiplying the variable overhead standard capacity by the standard (or predetermined) variable overhead application rate.
- A standard cost summary is usually prepared for each product that is manufactured. Standard costs are extremely helpful in budgeting prior to the start of a fiscal period. Moreover, they can also be very useful in evaluating performance at the end of a period.

Understand and calculate direct materials variances. (p. 346)   LO3

- We calculate the materials price variance by subtracting the standard price we should have paid for the actual quantity purchased from our actual purchase price.
- We calculate the materials efficiency variance by subtracting the standard materials cost from what we should have paid according to our standards for the actual quantity purchased.
- Each variance can be either favorable or unfavorable.

LO4 **Understand and calculate direct labor variances. (p. 350)**

- We calculate the labor rate variance by subtracting the standard price we should have paid our employees for the actual level of production from our actual labor costs.
- We calculate the labor efficiency variance by subtracting the standard labor cost from what we should have paid according to our standards for the actual hours worked.
- Each variance can be either favorable or unfavorable.

LO5 **Understand and calculate variable overhead variances. (p. 353)**

- The variable overhead "rate" variance (i.e., the spending variance) determines whether the predetermined overhead application rate is higher or lower than the standard rate determined by managers in the budgeting process.
- Similarly, variable overhead efficiency variance is attributable to the use of that overhead application base or "driver."
- Each variance can be either favorable or unfavorable.

LO6 **Present and illustrate the use of standard costs in financial statements. (p. 355)**

- When the standard costs and related variances for direct material, direct labor, and variable overhead are recorded, the work in process account is debited for each in amounts representing standard quantities and standard prices.
- All variances—favorable and unfavorable—are carried in separate accounts with appropriate titles.
- Standard costs are typically used in financial statements for internal use only by management.
- At year-end, firms commonly close the variance accounts by transferring their balances to Cost of Goods Sold.
- If large variances exist at year-end and there is evidence that the standards may not apply, a firm may be justified in allocating all or part of the variances to Work in Process Inventory, Finished Goods Inventory, and Cost of Goods Sold.

LO7 **Appendix 10A: Present journal entries associated with standard costs. (p. 357)**

- Illustration of journal entries related to raw materials
- Illustration of journal entries related to direct labor
- Illustration of journal entries related to variable overhead

KEY TERMS

Labor efficiency variance (p. 350)	Materials price variance (p. 346)	Variable overhead efficiency variance (p. 354)
Labor rate variance (p. 350)	Standard cost accounting (p. 341)	Variable overhead spending variance (p. 354)
Materials efficiency variance (p. 346)	Standard costs (p. 340)	Variances (p. 341)

Assignments with the logo in the margin are available in ⁱᵐʸ BusinessCourse.
See the Preface of the book for details.

SELF-STUDY QUESTIONS

(Answers to Self-Study Questions are at the end of this chapter.)

LO1 1. **When a standard costing system is used, which of the following accounts will be reported at standard costs?**

    a. Accounts payable   *c.* Work in process inventory

    b. Wages payable   *d.* Accounts receivable

LO2 2. **In what terms are standard variable overhead application rates (SR) usually stated?**

    a. Per dollar   *c.* Per unit of product

    b. Per direct labor hour   *d.* Per month

3. The formula [(Actual Price − Standard Price) × Actual Quantity] can be used to calculate which **LO3** cost variance?
   a. Variable overhead volume
   b. Labor efficiency
   c. Materials efficiency
   d. Materials price

4. Which variance considers production capacity not used? **LO5**
   a. Variable overhead efficiency
   b. Labor efficiency
   c. Variable overhead spending
   d. Materials efficiency

5. The gross profit on the interim income statement of a firm using standard costs is computed as: **LO6**
   a. Sales less cost of goods sold at standard
   b. Sales less cost of goods sold at standard plus net unfavorable variances
   c. Sales less cost of goods sold at standard less net unfavorable variances
   d. Sales less cost of goods sold at actual

QUESTIONS

1. What is the difference between budgeted costs and standard costs? **LO1**
2. Define standard costs and describe how they are developed. **LO2**
3. When should standard costs be established and how often should such standards be changed? **LO1**
4. "Standard costs can be set too high or too low for motivational purposes." Comment. **LO1**
5. What is standard cost accounting? **LO2**
6. A finished product requires 2 pounds of a material costing $6 per pound. What is the standard cost of direct material per unit of product? **LO2**
7. A finished product requires 20 minutes of direct labor to complete each unit. Factory workers are paid $12 per hour. What is the standard cost of direct labor per unit of product? **LO2**
8. Assume that the variable overhead rate for the product described in Question 7 is $9 per hour. What is the standard cost of variable overhead per unit of product? **LO2**
9. Name and briefly describe the two direct material variances. **LO3**
10. Garcia Company used 6,300 pounds of direct material costing $7.80 per pound for a batch of products that should have consumed 6,000 pounds costing $8 per pound. What are the material variances? **LO3**
11. Name and briefly describe the two direct labor variances. **LO4**
12. Wong Lee used 1,200 direct labor hours at an average wage rate of $8.70 to manufacture products that should have used 1,300 direct labor hours at an average wage rate of $8.50 per hour. What are the labor variances? **LO4**
13. "Total actual cost exactly equals total standard cost, so everything must be okay." Comment. **LO1**
14. The variable overhead rate is $5 per direct labor hour; 31,000 direct labor hours were used to produce 7,500 units of product. The standard is 4 direct labor hours per unit. Actual, variable overhead cost was $153,000. Determine the variable overhead variances. **LO5**
15. Who in the firm might be responsible for each of the following variances? **LO7**
   a. Materials price and efficiency variances
   b. Labor rate and efficiency variances
   c. Variable overhead spending and efficiency variances
16. Briefly explain how standard cost variances are reported on financial statements. **LO6**

EXERCISES—SET A

E10-1A. Standard Product Costs Deerfield Company manufactures product M in its factory. Production of **LO2** M requires 2 pounds of material P, costing $4 per pound and 0.5 hour of direct labor costing, $10 per hour. The variable overhead rate is $8 per direct labor hour, and the fixed overhead rate is $12 per direct labor hour. What is the standard product cost for product M?

E10-2A. Material and Labor Variances The following actual and standard cost data for direct material and **LO3, 4** direct labor relate to the production of 2,000 units of a product:

	Actual costs	Standard costs
Direct material	3,900 lb. @ $5.30	4,000 lb. @ $5.10
Direct labor.	6,200 hrs. @ $8.40	6,000 hrs. @ $8.70

Determine the following variances:

a. Materials price
c. Labor rate
b. Materials efficiency
d. Labor efficiency

LO5

E10-3A. Variable Overhead Variances Morgan Tax Company considers 6,000 direct labor hours or 300 tax returns its normal monthly capacity. Its standard variable overhead rate is $5 per direct labor hour. During the current month, $25,400 of variable overhead cost was incurred in working 5,600 direct labor hours to prepare 270 tax returns. Determine the following variances, and indicate whether each is favorable or unfavorable:

a. Variable overhead spending
b. Variable overhead efficiency

LO3, 4, 5

E10-4A. Material, Labor, and Variable Overhead Variances The following summarized manufacturing data relate to Thomas Corporation's April operations, during which 2,000 finished units of product were produced. Normal monthly capacity is 1,100 direct labor hours.

	Standard Unit Costs	Total Actual Costs
Direct material:		
Standard (2 lb. @ $9/lb.)	$18	
Actual (4,200 lb. @ $10.20/lb.)		$42,840
Direct labor:		
Standard (0.5 hr. @ $24/hr.)	12	
Actual (950 hrs. @ $23.40/hr.).		22,230
Variable overhead:		
Standard (0.5 hr. @ $6/hr.)	3	
Actual		6,450
Total	$33	$71,520

Determine the materials price and efficiency variances, labor rate and efficiency variances, and variable overhead spending and efficiency variances.

LO3, 4, 5

E10-5A. Working With Variances From the following data, determine the total actual costs incurred for direct material, direct labor, and variable overhead.

	Standard Costs	Variances
Direct material	$120,000	
Price variance.		$3,000 U
Quantity variance		4,000 F
Direct labor.	100,000	
Rate variance		1,400 U
Efficiency variance		1,800 U
Variable overhead.	44,000	
Spending variance		1,000 F
Efficiency variance		600 U

EXERCISES—SET B

LO2

E10-1B. Standard Product Costs Harrison Company manufactures product Q in its factory. Production of Q requires 3 pounds of material T, costing $7 per pound and 2 hours of direct labor, costing $10 per hour. The variable overhead rate is $6 per direct labor hour, and the fixed overhead rate is $9 per direct labor hour. What is the standard product cost for product Q?

E10-2B. Material and Labor Variances The following actual and standard cost data for direct material and   **LO3, 4**
direct labor relate to the production of 2,000 units of a product:

	Actual Costs	Standard Costs
Direct material	4,200 lb. @ $4.90	4,000 lb. @ $5.20
Direct labor.	5,700 hrs. @ $9.30	6,000 hrs. @ $9.50

Determine the following variances:

a. Materials price   c. Labor rate
b. Materials efficiency   d. Labor efficiency

E10-3B. Variable Overhead Variances Marshfield Tax Company considers 8,000 direct labor hours or 400   **LO5**
tax returns its normal monthly capacity. Its standard variable overhead rate is $4 per direct labor hour.
During the current month, $31,500 of variable overhead cost was incurred in working 7,500 direct
labor hours to produce 360 units of product. Determine the following variances, and indicate whether
each is favorable or unfavorable:

a. Variable overhead spending
b. Variable overhead efficiency

E10-4B. Material, Labor, and Variable Overhead Variances The following summarized manufacturing   **LO3, 4, 5**
data relate to Brown Corporation's May operations, during which 2,000 finished units of product
were produced. Normal monthly capacity is 1,100 direct labor hours.

	Standard Unit Costs	Total Actual Costs
Direct material:		
Standard (3 lb. @ $2.00/lb.)	$ 6	
Actual (6,400 lb. @ $2.20/lb.)		$14,080
Direct labor:		
Standard (0.5 hr. @ $14/hr.)	7	
Actual (950 hrs. @ $13.70/hr.).		13,015
Variable overhead:		
Standard (0.5 hr. @ $4/hr.)	2	
Actual		4,300
Total	$15	$31,395

Determine the materials price and efficiency variances, labor rate and efficiency variances, and variable
overhead spending and efficiency variances.

E10-5B. Working With Variances From the following data, determine the total actual costs incurred for di-   **LO3, 4, 5**
rect material, direct labor, and variable overhead.

	Standard Costs	Variances
Direct material	$55,000	
Price variance.		$1,200 U
Quantity variance		2,200 F
Direct labor.	46,000	
Rate variance		500 U
Efficiency variance		800 U
Variable overhead.	18,000	
Spending variance		400 F
Efficiency variance		700 U

PROBLEMS—SET A

LO3, 4, 5

P10-1A. Calculate Variances The following summary data relate to the operations of Dobson Company for April, during which 9,000 finished units were produced. Normal monthly capacity was 20,000 direct labor hours.

	Standard Unit Costs	Total Actual Costs
Direct material:		
Standard (4 lb. @ $2.20/lb.)	$ 8.80	
Actual (38,000 lb. @ $2.00/lb.)		$ 76,000
Direct labor:		
Standard (2 hrs. @ $11.00/hr.)	22.00	
Actual (18,500 hrs. @ $11.30/hr.)		209,050
Variable overhead:		
Standard (2 hrs. @ $3.00/hr.)	6.00	
Actual		54,900
Total	$36.80	$339,950

Required

Determine the following variances and indicate whether each is favorable or unfavorable:

a. Materials price and efficiency variances
b. Labor rate and efficiency variances
c. Variable overhead spending and efficiency variances

LO3, 4, 5, 6,7

P10-2A. Variances, Entries, and Income Statement A summary of Glendale Company's manufacturing variance report for May 2016 follows:

	Total Standard Costs (9,200 units)	Total Actual Costs (9,200 units)	Variances
Direct material	$ 38,640	$ 42,630	$3,990 U
Direct labor.	193,200	193,120	80 F
Variable overhead.	23,460	23,230	230 F
Fixed overhead.	9,660	9,660	
	$264,960	$268,640	$3,680 U

Standard material cost per unit of product is 0.5 pounds at $8.40 per pound, and standard direct labor cost is 1.5 hours at $14.00 per hour. The total actual materials cost represents 4,900 pounds purchased at $8.70 per pound. Total actual labor cost represents 14,200 hours at $13.60 per hour. According to standards, variable overhead rate is applied at $1.70 per direct labor hour (based on a normal capacity of 15,000 direct labor hours or 10,000 units of product). Assume that all fixed overhead is applied to work in progress inventory.

Required

a. Calculate variances for materials price and efficiency, labor rate and efficiency, and variable overhead spending and efficiency.
b. Prepare general journal entries to record standard costs, actual costs, and related variances for material, labor, and overhead.
c. Prepare journal entries to record the transfer of all completed units to Finished Goods Inventory and the subsequent sale of 8,400 units on account at $54 each (assume no beginning finished goods inventory).
d. Prepare a partial income statement (through gross profit on sales) showing gross profit based on standard costs, the incorporation of variances, and gross profit based on actual costs.

P10-3A. Variances and Journal Entries Jacobs Company manufactures a single product and uses a standard   LO3, 4, 5, 7
costing system. The nature of its product dictates that it be sold in the period it is produced. Thus, no
ending work in process or finished goods inventories remain at the end of the period. However, raw
materials can be stored and are purchased in bulk when prices are favorable. Per-unit standard product
costs are material, $8 (4 pounds); labor, $6 (0.5 hour); and variable overhead, $4 (based on direct
labor hours). Budgeted fixed overhead is $54,000.

Jacobs accounts for all inventories and cost of goods sold at standard cost and records each variance
in a separate account. The following data relate to May 2016 when 17,700 finished units were produced.

Required

a. Assume Jacobs purchased 69,000 pounds of raw materials on account at $2.20 per pound and
used 67,000 pounds in May's production, prepare a journal entry to record the purchase of raw
materials and a separate journal entry to record the use of raw materials in production. Record
these entries using standard costs and include the appropriate materials variances.

b. Assuming employees worked 8,900 direct labor hours at an average hourly rate of $11.70, pre-
pare a journal entry to record actual costs, standard costs, and any labor variances.

c. Assuming Jacobs' actual and applied variable overhead was $74,200 and that budgeted and ac-
tual fixed overhead incurred was $54,000, prepare a journal entry to record actual and standard
overhead costs and any overhead variances.

P10-4A. Variances, Total Overhead Variances, and Variance Reconciliation Milton Company planned to   LO3, 4, 5
produce 21,000 units of its only product during the year. Milton established the following standard
cost data for this product prior to the beginning of the year:

	Per Unit
Direct material (3 lbs. @ $5.00 per lb.)	$15.00
Direct labor (2 hrs. @ $17.50 per hr.)	35.00
Variable overhead (2 hrs. @ $6 per hr.)	12.00
Total standard cost per unit	$62.00

Total budgeted fixed overhead is $400,000.

Assume that Milton (1) actually produced 22,000 units, (2) used 68,000 pounds of direct materials in
production, (3) and incurred the following actual total costs:

	Total Cost
Direct materials purchased (70,000 lbs. @ 4.80)	$ 336,000
Direct labor (43,000 hrs. @ $18.00)	774,000
Variable overhead.	262,320
Fixed overhead.	400,000
Total actual costs	$1,772,320

Required

a. Calculate the variances for materials, labor, and variable overhead.

b. Does the difference between total actual costs and total standard costs equal the sum of all of the
variances? Explain.

PROBLEMS—SET B

LO3, 4, 5   **P10-1B. Calculate Variances** The following summary data relate to the operations of Randolph Company for July, during which 4,500 finished units were produced:

	Standard Total Unit Costs	Total Actual Costs
Direct material:		
Standard (0.6 lb. @ $9.00/lb.)	$ 5.40	
Actual (3,000 lb. @ $9.40/lb.)		$ 28.200
Direct labor:		
Standard (0.8 hr. @ $12.80/hr.)	10.24	
Actual (3,800 hrs. @ $12.50/hr.)		47,500
Variable overhead:		
Standard (0.8 hr. @ $7.50/hr.)	6.00	
Actual		30,100
Total	$21.64	$105,800

Required

Determine the following variances and indicate whether each is favorable or unfavorable:

a.   Materials price variance and efficiency variance
b.   Labor rate variance and efficiency variance
c.   Variable overhead spending variance and efficiency variance

LO3, 4, 5, 6 ,7   **P10-2B. Variances, Entries, and Income Statement** A summary of Blake Company's manufacturing variance report for June 2016 follows.

	Total Standard Costs (7,600 units)	Total Actual Costs (7,600 units)	Variances
Direct material	$ 66,880	$ 65,100	$1,780 F
Direct labor.	77,520	82,800	5,280 U
Variable overhead.	34,200	33,000	1,200 F
Fixed overhead.	102,600	102,600	
	$281,200	$283,500	$2,300 U

Standard material cost per unit of product is 4 pounds at $2.20 per pound, and standard direct labor cost is 0.75 hours at $13.60 per hour. Total actual material cost represents 31,000 pounds purchased at $2.10 per pound. Total actual labor cost represents 6,000 hours at $13.80 per hour. According to standards, variable overhead rate is applied at $6 per direct labor hour (based on a normal capacity of 6,000 direct labor hours or 8,000 units of product). Assume that all fixed overhead is applied to work in progress inventory.

Required

a.   Calculate variances for materials price and efficiency, labor rate and efficiency, and variable overhead spending and efficiency.
b.   Prepare general journal entries to record standard costs, actual costs, and related variances for material, labor, and overhead.
c.   Prepare journal entries to record the transfer of all completed units to Finished Goods Inventory and the subsequent sale of 6,400 units on account at $60 each (assume no beginning finished goods inventory).
d.   Prepare a partial income statement (through gross profit on sales) showing gross profit based on standard costs, the incorporation of variances, and gross profit based on actual costs.

LO3, 4, 5, 7   **P10-3B. Variances and Journal Entries** Kent Company manufactures a single product and uses a standard costing system. The nature of its product dictates that it be sold in the period it is produced. Thus, no ending work in process or finished goods inventories remain at the end of the period. However, raw materials can be stored and are purchased in bulk when prices are favorable. Per-unit, standard product costs are material, $6 (0.5 pound); labor, $15 (1.5 hours); and variable overhead, $3 (based on direct labor hours). Budgeted fixed overhead is $96,000.

Kent Company accounts for all inventories and cost of goods sold at standard cost and records each variance in a separate account. The following data relate to June, 2016 when 7,800 finished units were produced.

Required

a. Assume Kent purchased 4,500 pounds of raw materials on account at $11.60 per pound and used 4,200 pounds in June's production, prepare a journal entry to record the purchase of raw materials and a separate journal entry to record the use of raw materials in production. Record these entries using standard costs and include the appropriate materials variances.

b. Assuming Kent's employees worked 12,000 direct labor hours at an average hourly rate of $10.50, prepare a journal entry to record actual costs, standard costs, and any labor variances.

c. Assuming Kent's actual and applied variable overhead was $23,100 and that budgeted and actual fixed overhead incurred was $96,000, prepare a journal entry to record actual and standard overhead costs and any overhead variances.

P10-4B. Variances, Total Overhead Variances, and Variance Reconciliation Sanchez Company planned to produce 10,000 units of its only product during the year. Sanchez established the following standard cost data for this product prior to the beginning of the year: **LO3, 4, 5**

	Per Unit
Direct material (2 lb. @ $7.50 per lb.)	$15.00
Direct labor (1.5 hrs. @ $13.50 per hr.).	20.25
Variable overhead (1.5 hrs. @ $6 per hr.)	9.00
Total standard cost per unit.	$44.25

Total budgeted fixed overhead is $144,000.

Assume that Sanchez (1) actually produced 9,000 units, (2) used 17,000 pounds of direct materials in production, (3) and incurred the following actual total costs:

	Total Cost
Direct materials purchased (19,000 lb. @ 7.80)	$148,200
Direct labor (14,000 hrs. @ $13.35)	186,900
Variable overhead.	80,250
Fixed overhead.	144,000
Total actual costs	$559,350

Required

a. Calculate the variances for materials, labor, and variable overhead.

b. Does the difference between total actual costs and total standard costs equal the sum of all of the variances? Explain.

CERTIFIED MANAGEMENT ACCOUNTANT (CMA®) EXAM SAMPLE QUESTIONS

CMA10-1. Which one of the following statements is correct concerning a flexible budget cost formula? Variable costs are stated

a. per unit and fixed costs are stated in total.

b. in total and fixed costs are stated per unit.

c. in total and fixed costs are stated in total.

d. per unit and fixed costs are stated per unit.

CMA10-2. Of the following pairs of variances found in a flexible budget report, which pair is most likely to be related?

 a. Materials price variance and variable overhead efficiency variance.
 b. Labor rate variance and variable overhead efficiency variance.
 c. Material usage variance and labor efficiency variance.
 d. Labor efficiency variance and fixed overhead volume variance.

CMA10-3. Lee manufacturing uses a standard cost system with overhead applied based on direct labor hours. The manufacturing budget for the production of 5,000 units for the month of June included 10,000 hours of direct labor at $15 per hour, $150,000. During June, 4,500 units were produced, using 9,600 direct labor hours, incurring $39,360 of variable overhead, and showing a variable overhead efficiency variance of $2,400 unfavorable. The standard variable overhead rate per direct labor hour was

 a. $3.85.
 b. $4.00.
 c. $4.10.
 d. $6.00.

CMA10-4. Marten Company has a cost-benefit policy to investigate any variance that is greater than $1,000 or 10% of budget, whichever is larger. Actual results for the previous month indicate the following.

	Budget	Actual
Raw material.	$100,000	$89,000
Direct labor.	50,000	54,000

The company should investigate

 a. neither the material variance nor the labor variance.
 b. the material variance only.
 c. the labor variance only.
 d. both the material variance and the labor variance.

CMA10-5. Frisco Company recently purchased 108,000 units of raw material for $583,200. Three units of raw materials are budgeted for use in each finished good manufactured, with the raw material standard set at $16.50 for each completed product. Frisco manufactured 32,700 finished units during the period just ended and used 99,200 units of raw material. If management is concerned about the timely reporting of variances in an effort to improve cost control and bottom-line performance, the materials purchase price variance should be reported as

 a. $6,050 unfavorable.
 b. $9,920 favorable.
 c. $10,800 unfavorable.
 d. $10,800 favorable.

EXTENDING YOUR KNOWLEDGE

EYK10-1. Business Decision Case Porter Corporation has just hired Bill Harlow as its new controller. Although Harlow has had little formal accounting training, he professes to be highly experienced, having learned accounting "the hard way" in the field. At the end of his first month's work, Harlow prepared the following performance report:

PORTER CORPORATION
Performance Report
for the Month of June, 2015

	Total Actual Costs	Total Budgeted Costs	Variances
Direct material	$216,630	$237,600	$20,970 F
Direct labor.	119,340	132,000	12,660 F
Variable overhead.	63,000	66,000	3,000 F
Fixed overhead.	184,000	184,000	
	$582,970	$619,600	$36,630 F

In his presentation at Porter's month-end management meeting, Harlow indicated that things were going "fantastically." "The figures indicate," he said, "that the firm is beating its budget in all cost categories." This good news made everyone at the meeting happy and furthered Harlow's acceptance as a member of the management team.

After the management meeting, Susan Jones, Porter's general manager, asked you, as an independent consultant, to review Harlow's report. Jones' concern stemmed from the fact that Porter has never operated as favorably as Harlow's report seems to imply, and she cannot explain the apparent significant improvement.

While reviewing Harlow's report, you are provided the following cost and operating data for June: Porter has a monthly normal capacity of 11,000 direct labor hours or 8,800 units of product. Standard costs per unit for its only product are direct material, 3 pounds at $9 per pound; direct labor, 1.25 hours at $12 per hour; and variable overhead rate per direct labor hour of $6. During June, Porter produced 8,000 units of product, using 24,900 pounds of material costing $8.70 each, 10,200 direct labor hours at an average rate of $11.70 each, and incurred variable overhead costs of $63,000 and fixed overhead costs of $184,000.

After reviewing Porter's June cost data, you tell Harlow that his cost report contains a classic budgeting error, and you explain how he can remedy it. In response to your suggestion, Harlow revises his report as follows:

	Total Actual Costs	Total Budgeted Costs	Variances
Direct material	$216,630	$216,000	$ 630 U
Direct labor.	119,340	120,000	660 F
Variable overhead.	63,000	60,000	3,000 U
Fixed overhead.	184,000	184,000	
	$582,970	$580,000	$2,970 U

Harlow's revised report is accompanied by remarks expressing regret at the oversight in the original report.

Required

In your role as consultant,

a. Verify that Harlow's actual cost figures are correct.
b. Identify and explain the classic budgeting error that Harlow apparently incorporated into his original cost report.
c. Explain why Harlow's revised figures could be considered deficient.
d. Further analyze Harlow's revised variances, isolating underlying potential causal factors. How do your analyses indicate bases for concern to management?

EYK10-2.   Ethics Case Custom Furniture, manufacturer of handmade furniture, uses standard cost accounting for the company. Standards are developed annually based on input from production workers and supervisors.

The supervisor of the table department has approached several employees that work for him and suggested that the employees overestimate the amount of material (by 20%) and labor (by 30%) involved in producing certain new tables. He states that it is better to overestimate than underestimate costs as the product has never been manufactured in quantity before and it is uncertain what the actual materials and labor will be. In addition, he states that this would result in any variances being favorable to the department.

The employees are not sure what estimates they should discuss with the accounting department. The accounting department wants accurate input that it will adjust for uncertainty.

Required

How would you advise the employees? What ethical issues are involved?

ANSWERS TO SELF-STUDY QUESTIONS:

1. c, (p. 341)   2. b, (p. 343)   3. d, (p. 346)   4. a, (p. 353)   5. c, (pp. 355–356)

DECISION TIME SOLUTION

Solution 10.1

- An unfavorable materials price variance suggests that personnel in the purchasing department paid more for materials than the company's standard costs would normally allow.
- An unfavorable materials efficiency variance would mean that assembly workers used more material (or parts) in production than standards would normally allow.
- A favorable labor rate variance suggests that human resource personnel were able to hire production workers at wage rates below what standards would normally allow.
- An unfavorable labor efficiency variance would indicate that workers spent more time to produce the actual number of outputs than standards would normally allow.

YOUR TURN! SOLUTIONS

Solution 10.1
Materials price variance: AQ (AP − SP) = 90,000 ($2.90 − $3.00) = $9,000 F
Materials efficiency variance: SP (AQ − SQ) = $3.00 [90,000 − (4 × 22,000)] = $6,000 U

Solution 10.2
Labor rate variance: AH (AR − SR) = 35,000 × ($7.50 − $7.00) = $17,500 U
Labor efficiency variance: SR (AH − SH) = $7.00 [35,000 − (1.5 × 22,000)] = $14,000 U

Solution 10.3
Variable overhead spending variance: Actual VOH − (AQ × AR) = $63,000 − (35,000 × $2.00) = $7,000 F
Variable overhead efficiency variance: SR (AH − SH) = $2.00 [35,000 − (1.5 × 22,000)] = $4,000 U

Solution 10.4
Materials price variance: AQ (AP − SP) = 55,000 ($5.30 − $5.10) = $11,000 U
Materials efficiency variance: SP (AQ − SQ) = $5.10 [55,000 − (4 × 11,000)] = $56,100 U

Raw Materials Inventory	280,500	
Materials Price Variance	11,000	
Accounts Payable (or Cash)		291,500

Work in Process Inventory	224,400	
Materials Efficiency Variance	56,100	
Raw Materials Inventory		280,500

Solution 10.5

Labor rate variance: AH (AR − SR) = 23,000 ($3.00 − $3.50) = $11,500 F
Labor efficiency variance: SR (AH − SH) = $3.50 [23,000 − (2 × 15,000)] = $24,500 F

Work in Process Inventory	105,000	
Labor Rate Variance		11,500
Labor Efficiency Variance		24,500
Wages Payable		69,000

11

Flexible Budgets, Segment Reporting, and Performance Analysis

PAST

Chapter 10 defined standard costs and standard cost variances: direct material, direct labor, and variable overhead variances.

PRESENT

Chapter 11 introduces flexible budgets and performance evaluation of business segments. In addition, it explores both performance and variance analysis.

FUTURE

Chapter 12 introduces capital budgeting and illustrates how capital budgeting is used to make capital investment decisions.

LEARNING OBJECTIVES

1. **Describe** a static budget, **illustrate** its use, and **present** an example of a static budget performance report. *(p. 376)*

2. **Introduce** the flexible budget and **present** an example of a flexible budget performance report. **Explain** how flexible budgeting helps in variance analysis. *(p. 377)*

3. **Present** an overview of reporting operations for segments of a business. *(p. 383)*

4. **Construct** a segmented contribution margin income statement. **Identify** the difference between traceable and common fixed costs. *(p. 386)*

5. **Compute** return on investment, return on sales, return on assets, and residual income for business segments. **Discuss** the importance of each indicator in assessing a company's performance. *(p. 393)*

6. Appendix 11A: **Determine** the proper transfer price to maximize company profit with and without excess productive capacity. *(p. 400)*

MICROSOFT CORPORATION

When was the last time you fired up and used your computer? Chances are the software you used was produced by Microsoft Corporation. Microsoft commands a dominating presence in the software industry, boasting a 95% market share in the productivity software market, 75% share in the operating system market, and approximately 75% share in the server software market.[1] As the global leader in software production and one of the world's most valuable companies, Microsoft's strategy (as reported in its fiscal year ended June 30, 2014, 10-K) is to provide powerful, flexible, secure, and easy-to-use solutions that work across a variety of devices. With successful operations in over 100 countries, Microsoft's strategy yields strong results.

Microsoft was founded by Bill Gates and Paul Allen on April 4, 1975, to develop and sell BASIC interpreters for the Altair 8800. These childhood friends shared a passion for computer programming, and were instrumental figures in the company's explosive growth. The name Microsoft was selected as a combination of "microcomputer" and "software," and within 2 years the company formed its first international office, ASCII Microsoft, in Japan. Microsoft entered the operating software business in 1980, with its MS-DOS product driving its growth. Microsoft has since produced the Windows operating systems and Microsoft Office, and expanded into phones, personal computers, and tablets.

While the company has grown significantly since its founding, it has maintained an edge in the software industry through the careful application of managerial accounting concepts. In budgeting sales and production needs for future periods, Microsoft is never 100% accurate in its forecasts, as sales frequently grow more slowly or quickly than expected. To accommodate the fluctuation in sales, the company can find a meaningful method of comparing actual results to budgeted results, with the number of units produced remaining the same for both. In a previous chapter, we presented and discussed the components of the master budget. In this chapter, we will examine flexible budgeting, and the advantages of using flexible budgeting over static budgeting. In addition, we will introduce segment reporting and performance analysis, and explain performance measures that are helpful in assessing the health of a company.

Performance analysis is essential in the management process of any entity. Budgetary control involves the steps taken by management to ensure that the goals and objectives established during the planning stage are attained, and

to ensure that all segments of the firm operate in a manner consistent with organizational policies. Budgets should serve as guides or targets for managers when they make decisions because the budget is usually the basis for performance evaluation. Segment reporting allows managers to compare and assess the performance of individual segments or employees across the company by evaluating segments' key performance indicators, such as return on investment, return on sales, return on assets, and residual income. Another and more comprehensive tool used to assess performance is the balanced scorecard, which includes both financial and nonfinancial measures of performance.

---

[1] http://www.forbes.com/sites/greatspeculations/2013/01/09/an-overview-why-microsofts-worth-42/

FLEXIBLE BUDGETS, SEGMENT REPORTING, AND PERFORMANCE ANALYSIS					
Static Budgets	**Flexible Budgets**	**Internal Reporting of Segment Operations**	**Performance Reporting**	**Performance Analysis**	**Transfer Pricing (Appendix 11A)**
• Definition • Uses	• Flexible budgets in a manufacturing environment • Variance analysis of flexible budget differences • Flexible budgets in a service environment	• Decentralized organizations • Segment reporting • Types of business segments	• Departmental operations • Contribution margin income statement • Segment performance evaluation • Service company segment reporting illustration	• Return on investment • Return on sales • Asset utilization • Residual income • Balanced scorecard	• Domestic transfer pricing • International transfer pricing

It is critically important that management have a means of measuring and evaluating the performance of employees, departments, segments, and the overall company to ensure that all are working toward the achievement of the company's strategic vision. In this chapter, we discuss several tools available to assist managers in evaluating performance: flexible budgets, segment reporting, and performance analysis and reporting.

STATIC BUDGETS

LO1 **Describe** a static budget, **illustrate** its use, and **present** an example of a static budget performance report.

A.K.A. Static budgets are also called *nonmoving* or *stationary budgets*.

The master budget is made up of budgets known as static budgets. A **static budget** is a financial plan developed for a fixed level of operating activity, typically the expected or most likely level. The static budget is the budgeted amount used to calculate the standard costs that we discussed in Chapter 10. If actual results are compared to a static budget, the variances that result are of little use to management, because the budget is often based on a different level of activity than the actual operations. The following example illustrates this point.

Exhibit 11-1 presents a simple static budget for Fezzari's Foré CR1 product line for the 2016 fiscal year. Although Fezzari's management has a target production of 5,000 Foré CR1 road bikes during the year, it anticipates that this may be an aggressive projection.

Exhibit 11-1	Static Budget Illustration

FEZZARI FORÉ CR1 PRODUCT LINE
Static Budget for Product Costs
For the Year Ended December 31, 2016

Budgeted units of production	5,000
Budgeted costs:	
Direct material	$2,500,000
Direct labor	285,000
Manufacturing overhead	525,000
Total	$3,310,000

Exhibit 11-2 presents a static budget performance report for the CR1 product line for 2016. The static budget performance report compares the *actual* costs to produce 4,800 units with the *budgeted* costs to produce 5,000 units. The performance report accurately reveals that actual units of CR1 production were 200 less than management had budgeted. In a performance report comparing actual costs to budgeted costs, "F" indicates a favorable variance and "U" identifies an unfavorable variance.

Exhibit 11-2	Static Budget Performance Report Illustration

FEZZARI FORÉ CR1 PRODUCT LINE
Static Budget Performance Report
For the Year Ended December 31, 2016

Budgeted units of production		5,000	
Actual units of production		4,800	
Units of production variance		200	U

	Actual Cost Incurred for 4,800 Units	Budget Based on 5,000 Units	Cost Variances	
Direct material	$2,486,400	$2,500,000	$(13,600)	F
Direct labor.	302,400	285,000	17,400	U
Manufacturing overhead	490,000	525,000	(35,000)	F
Total	$3,278,800	$3,310,000	$(31,200)	F

U = Unfavorable
F = Favorable

The static budget performance report, however, provides misleading cost variances. For example, the direct material variance is $13,600 favorable (i.e., the actual cost is less than budgeted cost). This comparison is misleading because the actual cost to produce 4,800 units is being compared to the budgeted cost to produce 5,000 units, not 4,800 units. Moreover, although the total variance is $31,200 favorable, the actual cost per unit is about $683 per unit ($3,278,800/4,800 CR1s), and the budgeted cost per CR1 is only $662 ($3,310,000/5,000 CR1s). Hence, although the cost per unit is actually higher than the budgeted cost per unit, the total static budget variance appears to be favorable simply because the company produced 200 fewer CR1s than it anticipated.

FLEXIBLE BUDGETS

A **flexible budget** is a financial plan in the form of a cost formula or a multiple-column presentation that makes cost projections for various activity levels within a relevant range.

LO2 Introduce the flexible budget and **present** an example of a flexible budget performance report. **Explain** how flexible budgeting helps in variance analysis.

Flexible Budgets in a Manufacturing Environment

Exhibit 11-3 presents a 2016 flexible budget for Fezzari's Foré CR1 product line. The first two columns show the CR1 budgeted per-unit variable costs and budgeted total fixed costs of production. The last three columns present the budget for different levels of production. The middle column is the budget for 5,000 units of production that would be comparable to the static budget in **Exhibit 11-1**. Knowing the per-unit variable costs and the fixed costs of production allows Fezzari management to prepare a budget for any level of production within the relevant range.

Exhibit 11-3	Flexible Budget for Fezzari Foré CR1

FEZZARI FORÉ CR1 PRODUCT LINE
Flexible Product Costs Budget
For the Year Ended December 31, 2016

	1		2		
	Variable Cost per Unit	Total Fixed Cost	4,500 Units	5,000 Units	5,500 Units
Variable costs					
Direct material	$500.00		$2,250,000	$2,500,000	$2,750,000
Direct labor.	57.00		256,500	285,000	313,500
Variable overhead. . . .	60.00		270,000	300,000	330,000
	$617.00		$2,776,500	$3,085,000	$3,393,500
Fixed costs					
Fixed overhead.		$225,000	$ 225,000	$ 225,000	$ 225,000
Total			$3,001,500	$3,310,000	$3,618,500

Exhibit 11-3 demonstrates a number of the characteristics about flexible budgets. First, the flexible budget usually divides costs and expenses into two groups: variable and fixed. Second, the flexible budget typically presents the variable costs and expenses on a per-unit basis and the fixed costs and expenses in total. Third, in using a columnar format, all of the columns are based on levels of activity within the relevant range. It is important to remember that the flexible budget formula is valid only for the range of activity for which it is formulated.

ACCOUNTING IN PRACTICE	Relevant Range

To illustrate the concept of relevant range, assume that XYZ Company has one manufacturing building in which it manufactures toys. As long as no more than 10,000 toys are produced, the fixed costs associated with this building belong to one relevant range, 0–10,000 toys. If more than 10,000 toys are produced, XYZ will need an additional building, thus incurring additional fixed costs. The costs will be in a new relevant range.

A flexible budget, prepared with columns representing different projected levels of activity, provides managers with targets for various activity levels. Hence, during the period, a flexible budget can help managers assess the reasonableness of the firm's performance as the period progresses. However, one of the most important uses of the flexible budget comes not during, but *after* the end of the period. The flexible budget formula also allows managers to compare actual costs to budgeted costs based on the actual production level achieved. Specifically, the flexible budget performance report compares actual costs at the actual level of activity to the budgeted costs at the actual level of activity.

Exhibit 11-4 presents Fezzari's 2016 flexible budget performance report for the Foré CR1 product line. This performance report allows managers to evaluate how the company's actual performance compares to budgeted performance (based on the actual level of production) for different products. Specifically, the flexible budget performance report compares actual performance in column A to budgeted performance in column B with a flexible budget (rate or price) variance, as discussed in Chapter 10, for each component of product cost (direct materials, direct labor, variable overhead, and fixed overhead). Further, it compares the flexible budget in column A (based on 4,800 actual units) to the static budget in column C (based on 5,000 budgeted units). These differences are the efficiency variances, as discussed in Chapter 10.

Exhibit 11-4	Flexible Budget Performance Report Illustration

FEZZARI FORÉ CR1 PRODUCT LINE
Flexible Budget Performance Report
For the Year Ended December 31, 2016

Budgeted units of production . . .	5,000	
Actual units of production	4,800	
Units of production variance	200	U

	A Actual Costs Incurred for 4,800 Units	B Flexible Budget Based on 4,800 Units	(A-B) Price or Rate Variances	C Static Budget Based on 5,000 Units	(B-C) Efficiency Variances
Variable costs:					
Direct material.	$2,486,400	$2,400,000	$86,400 U	$2,500,000	$(100,000) F
Direct labor	302,400	273,600	28,800 U	285,000	(11,400) F
Variable overhead	268,800	288,000	(19,200) F	300,000	(12,000) F
	$3,057,600	$2,961,600	$96,000 U	$3,085,000	$(123,400) F
Fixed costs:					
Fixed overhead	$ 221,200	$ 225,000	$ (3,800) F	$ 225,000	$ —
Total	$3,278,800	$3,186,600	$92,200 U	$3,310,000	$(123,400) F

U = Unfavorable

F = Favorable

In essence, the flexible budget performance report compares "what we actually spent" to "what we should have spent" for the final production level. The flexible performance report is prepared by simply using the flexible budget formula to budget what the company "should have spent" based on the actual level of production (i.e., inserting the actual number of CR1 units produced, 4,800, into the flexible product costs budget).

A comparison of cost variances in the static budget performance report (**Exhibit 11-2**) and the flexible budget performance report (**Exhibit 11-4**) reveals a very different result. The static budget performance report indicates a total favorable cost variance of $31,200, whereas the flexible budget performance report reveals a total unfavorable rate or price variance of $92,200 and a total favorable efficiency variance of $123,400. As explained previously, one reason the budget projections in **Exhibit 11-2** do not provide an accurate depiction of budgeted costs is that the static budget is based on the projected production level (5,000 CR1s) when actual production fell short (4,800 CR1s). Thus, part of the difference in the two comparisons is related to the volume differential (i.e., actual production came up 200 units short of the static budget production level). Clearly, the variances from the flexible budget performance report provide a more complete explanation because they are based on a comparison of what the costs actually were to what the costs should have been at the actual level of activity.

As discussed in Chapter 10, management can delve further into the causes for the overall flexible budget variance (columns A and B) by breaking each component of the variance down into individual price/rate variances. For example, to explain the $86,400 unfavorable price variance for direct materials, price variances could be calculated for *each* direct material used in producing a Foré CR1.

Similarly, labor rate variances would be computed to explain the overall $28,800 unfavorable labor rate variance and the overall $19,200 favorable variable overhead variance.

Management by Exception

Performance reports should incorporate the management-by-exception concept. Variances outside acceptable ranges should be identified so management attention can be directed to those exceptional items.

Flexible Budgets in a Service Environment

SERVICE AND MERCHANDISING

Flexible budgets can be used in a service company just like in a manufacturing firm. For example, Old Rosebud is a 400-acre farm on the outskirts of the Kentucky Bluegrass region that specializes in boarding broodmares and their foals. An economic downturn in the thoroughbred industry has led to a decline in breeding activities. As a consequence, the demand for thoroughbred boarding has decreased, making the boarding business extremely competitive. To meet the competition, in 2016 Old Rosebud planned to entertain clients, advertise, and absorb expenses formerly borne by clients (for example, the company would pay for both veterinary and blacksmith's fees).

Exhibit 11-5 presents the variances between Old Rosebud's actual operating results in 2016 and amounts budgeted for the year. Its budget—like those of most service organizations—was a static budget (i.e., it forecast an expected level of activity). Old Rosebud expected to log 21,900 boarding days, and it budgeted boarding rates at $25 per day per mare.

The variable expenses per mare per day were budgeted as follows:

Feed	$5.00
Veterinary fees	$3.00
Blacksmith fees	$0.30
Supplies	$0.40

All other budgeted expenses were either semi-fixed or fixed.

The static budget in **Exhibit 11-5** can be used to explain only two factors: sales and fixed expenses. As sales volume problems arose during the year, Old Rosebud decided not to replace a farm worker who quit in March. It also developed a new farm brochure and entertained more potential clients. These strategies generated the fixed-expense variances—that is, the differences between the budgeted and actual line item amounts in the income statement.

No sound conclusions can be drawn about either the effect of price changes on the decrease in net income or the expense variances. When sales volume declines, sales revenue and variable expenses may be expected to decrease proportionately. However, the rate of Old Rosebud's decline in the number of boarding days (13%) differs from the rate of decrease in sales revenue (31%) and the rate of decrease in variable expenses (7%).

A plausible interpretation of the variances in **Exhibit 11-5** is that the large variance in net income is caused by a decrease in sales volume. This interpretation follows from the large unfavorable sales revenue variance and the generally favorable expense variances.

Indeed, at first glance, it appears as though expenses are well under control. All variable-expense variances are favorable, and the total of the two unfavorable fixed-expense variances is insignificant in relation to the total sales-revenue variance. The unfavorable advertising and entertainment variances may be interpreted as having prevented the unfavorable net income variance from being even greater. More business might have been lost had Old Rosebud not overspent its budgeted amounts for those items.

Because sales are down and expenses are well under control, this analysis suggests an obvious but faulty remedy: Do more advertising and entertaining.

Exhibit 11-5	Static Budget Illustration—Service

OLD ROSEBUD
Static Budget Income Statement
Year Ended December 31, 2016

	Actual	Static Budget	Variance
Number of mares	52	60	(8) U
Number of boarding days	18,980	21,900	(2,920) U
Sales.	$379,600	$547,500	$(167,900) U
Less variable expenses:			
Feed	104,390	109,500	(5,110) F
Veterinary fees	58,838	65,700	(6,862) F
Blacksmith fees	6,074	6,570	(496) F
Supplies	7,402	8,760	(1,358) F
Total variable expenses	$176,704	$190,530	(13,826) F
Contribution margin	$202,896	$356,970	$(154,074) U
Less fixed expenses:			
Depreciation	$ 45,000	$ 45,000	$ —
Insurance	11,000	11,000	—
Utilities	12,000	14,000	(2,000) F
Repairs and maintenance.	10,000	11,000	(1,000) F
Labor.	88,000	96,000	(8,000) F
Advertisement.	11,000	8,000	3,000 U
Entertainment	8,000	5,000	3,000 U
Total fixed expenses	$185,000	$190,000	$ (5,000) F
Net income.	$ 17,896	$166,970	$(149,074) U

U = Unfavorable
F = Favorable

Exhibit 11-6 compares Old Rosebud's actual operating results with those in a flexible budget for 2016. The flexible budget takes the same budgeted per-unit amounts for sales and variable expenses and applies them to the actual number of boarding days achieved in 2016. Because, by definition, fixed expenses don't vary with volume, they're the same as in the static budget. A budget constructed in this way removes the distortion in the sales-revenue and variable-expense variances of a static budget.

Two surprises are immediately apparent. First, when the unfavorable sales-revenue variance of $167,900 is separated into the unfavorable sales-price ($94,900) and unfavorable sales-volume ($73,000) variances, it becomes clear that the sales-price variance is larger. Further investigation of the sales-price variance revealed that Old Rosebud lost a major client in 2016. Moreover, because of fierce competition, the farm reduced its boarding charges well below $25 per day per mare as the year progressed. As a result, the average boarding rate declined for the year.

The second surprise in **Exhibit 11-6** is that expense control was far worse than analysis of the static budget variance had indicated. All variable-expense variances, except supplies, were unfavorable. The unfavorable feed variance of $9,490 alone accounted for nearly 82% of the net unfavorable variable-expense variances of $11,578. The large feed variance was explained by the drought that hit Kentucky and most of the rest of the nation in 2016. In addition, several recent studies had indicated that copper feed supplements may be necessary to minimize skeletal bone disease in young horses. Old Rosebud incorporated the supplement at an increased cost and continued to feed first-class hay despite the drought.

Exhibit 11-6	Flexible Budget Illustration—Service

OLD ROSEBUD
Flexible Budget Income Statement
Year Ended December 31, 2016

Budgeted number of boarding days . . . 21,900
Actual number of boarding days 18,980

	Budget (per mare per day)	Actual	Flexible Budget	Variance
Number of mares		52	52	0
Number of boarding days		18,980	18,980	0
Sales.	$25.00	$379,600	$474,500	$ (94,900) U
Less variable expenses:				
Feed	5.00	104,390	94,900	9,490 U
Veterinary fees	3.00	58,838	56,940	1,898 U
Blacksmith fees	0.30	6,074	5,694	380 U
Supplies	0.40	7,402	7,592	(190) F
Total variable expenses	$ 8.70	$176,704	$165,126	$ 11,578 U
Contribution margin	$16.30	$202,896	$309,374	$(106,478) U
Less fixed expenses:				
Depreciation		$ 45,000	$ 45,000	$ —
Insurance		11,000	11,000	—
Utilities		12,000	14,000	(2,000) F
Repairs and maintenance.		10,000	11,000	(1,000) F
Labor.		88,000	96,000	(8,000) F
Advertisement.		11,000	8,000	3,000 U
Entertainment		8,000	5,000	3,000 U
Total fixed expenses		$185,000	$190,000	(5,000) F
Net income.		$ 17,896	$119,374	$(101,478) U

U = Unfavorable
F = Favorable

Accurate information about what causes the differences between actual and expected results is a precondition for corrective action. Variance analysis can lead to an accurate analysis. In contrast, a static budget can focus only on sales and fixed expenses that differ from budgeted figures, and not realizing this may lead to faulty analysis of the results. Flexible budget variances aren't misleading because they incorporate actual levels of activity if different from those expected.

For Old Rosebud, the main problem is price—not volume. Had the farm been able to maintain its boarding rates but not the number of boarding days, its actual net income would have been:

Sales revenue.	$474,500
Less total variable expenses	(176,704)
Less total fixed expenses.	(185,000)
Net income.	$112,796

This amount is six times greater than the net income of $17,896 actually achieved. The farm needs to develop a strategy that restores boarding rates more than it needs to replace the eight horses it lost.[2]

Managers prepare static budgets based on the expected or budgeted level of operating activity. They then use a flexible budget based on the actual level of production to evaluate differences between actual and expected results.

Microsoft's Corporate Citizenship "Budget"	CORPORATE SOCIAL RESPONSIBILITY

The opening vignette discussed the importance of budgeting to Microsoft's operations, in particular financial measures such as sales. The process of budgeting as discussed in this chapter is applicable to far more than just financial results. Microsoft uses budgets to track revenues and expenses that are eventually communicated to interested parties in its annual financial report. In addition, Microsoft sets goals and tracks these goals with budgeting techniques outlined in this chapter for its annual Citizenship Report. In this report Microsoft highlights its performance in such areas as Ethical Business Conduct and Governance, People, Serving Communities, Human Rights, Responsible Sourcing, and Environmental Sustainability. The report can be found at and downloaded from Microsoft's website under the Corporate Citizenship section at the following link: https://www.microsoft.com/about/corporatecitizenship/en-us/

INTERNAL REPORTING OF SEGMENT OPERATIONS

Decentralized Organizations

As businesses grow, management of the organization becomes more and more difficult. Most large businesses are decentralized, meaning that the authority to make decisions is spread throughout the business.

LO3 **Present** an overview of reporting operations for segments of a business.

Although decentralization occurs almost out of necessity as businesses grow, there are significant advantages to involving lower-level management in the decision-making process of the business:

1. Delegation of day-to-day operational decisions frees up upper management to focus on strategy and business development.

2. Involvement of lower-level management in running the business provides excellent on-the-job training for those who will eventually become the upper management of the business.

3. Empowering lower-level managers may increase their job satisfaction and motivation to work hard.

4. Because lower-level managers are more familiar with the day-to-day operation of the business, they are more likely to identify and react more quickly to trends in the marketplace.

On the other hand, decentralization can lead to less desirable consequences:

1. Lower-level managers may not be privy to the larger business strategy.

---

[2] SOURCE: Adapted from Hans Sprohge and John Talbott, "New Applications for Variance Analysis," *Journal of Accountancy*, April 1989, pp. 137, 138, 140, 141. Reprinted with permission from the *Journal of Public Accountancy*, copyright © 1989 by the American Institute of Certified Public Accountants, Inc. Opinions of the authors are their own and do not necessarily reflect the policies of the AICPA.

2. Decisions made by lower-level managers may not be consistent with and supportive of goals and objectives of other departments or divisions within the business.

3. Largely autonomous departments or divisions may lead to "silos" within the business, resulting in important operating information or innovative ideas not being shared with other departments or divisions, to the detriment of the business overall.

Segment Reporting

Many business entities are very complex, with diverse divisions and departments in multiple locations. Managers of this type of entity often find it useful to divide the entity into segments to enhance managerial planning and control. Segments usually are based on organizational units (divisions or departments) or areas of economic activity (geographic regions or product lines). Many large companies have found that segmentation by organizational unit is the approach that proves most useful. It is important that the managerial accounting systems and procedures that develop information for planning and control decisions be structured to reflect the segmentation.

Internal reporting of segment operations deals primarily with the measurement of operating performance. As a result, segmented reports usually take the format of a contribution margin income statement. These statements may provide information to answer the following types of questions:

1. What amount does each segment contribute to the sales and operating income of the entity as a whole?

2. How do revenues and expenses for each segment compare to planned or budgeted amounts?

3. What is the rate of profitability of each segment? Should any segment be expanded, reduced, or eliminated?

4. Which areas need corrective action, and what should be done?

5. Where should promotional efforts be directed?

Types of Business Segments

With delegated authority comes accountability. In a decentralized organization, segment managers must demonstrate that the results of their decisions support and are congruent with the overall business strategy of the organization. Portions of a business for which a manager has been given a measure of authority and accountability are often referred to as **responsibility centers**. Depending on the authority delegated, these responsibility centers may be described as cost centers, profit centers, and investment centers. An example of these responsibility centers may be seen in PACCAR, a heavy-duty truck manufacturer.

PACCAR is a Fortune 200 company that designs, manufactures, and distributes trucks and related aftermarket parts that are sold worldwide under the Kenworth, Peterbilt, and DAF nameplates. It ranked as the third-largest manufacturer of medium- and heavy-duty trucks in the world in 2012.

The company has its headquarters in Bellevue, Washington. It began in 1905 as Seattle Car Manufacturing Company, at which time it produced railway and logging equipment. Over time, it expanded through acquisitions of commercial truck manufacturers and parts suppliers. As it grew and became more complex, management organized various business segments or responsibility centers. As described in the following discussion, some of PACCAR's responsibility centers might be considered cost centers, profit centers, or investment centers.

Access the most recent 10-K filing of PACCAR at edgar.sec.gov. What operating segments does PACCAR report (search for the term "segment" under Item 1 of the 10-K filing)?

YOUR TURN! 11.1

The solution is on page 420.

The manager of a **cost center** is responsible for the costs and expenses of only that segment of the business. He or she has no responsibility for revenue generation. An example of a PACCAR cost center is its Technical Centers, which provide research, development, and testing for new products. The output of these Technical Centers is a service to other PACCAR divisions or segments that is not sold to consumers outside the company. As a result, no revenue is generated directly by these centers.

The manager of a **profit center** is responsible for revenue generation as well as for cost and expense control. An example of a PACCAR profit center is its PACCAR Parts business, which operates a network of parts distribution centers that offer aftermarket support to its truck dealerships and customers throughout the world. PACCAR evaluates the performance of PACCAR Parts on its operating profit or segment contribution margin.

The manager of an **investment center** is responsible for the use of capital (productive assets), along with revenues and costs. The manager is typically evaluated on a measure of return on assets or return on investment. An example of a PACCAR investment center is its PACCAR Mexico (KENMEX) division, which manufactures trucks for Mexico and exports to other countries in a 590,000-square-foot facility.

Managerial reports that measure the operating performance of a business entity and its segments reflect whether the segments are investment, profit, or cost centers. Return on investment, revenue, expenses, and profits are reported for investment centers; revenue, expenses, and profits are reported for profit centers; and only expenses are reported for cost centers. **Exhibit 11-7** illustrates the relationship among the different reporting segments.

Exhibit 11-7 | **Reporting Segments**

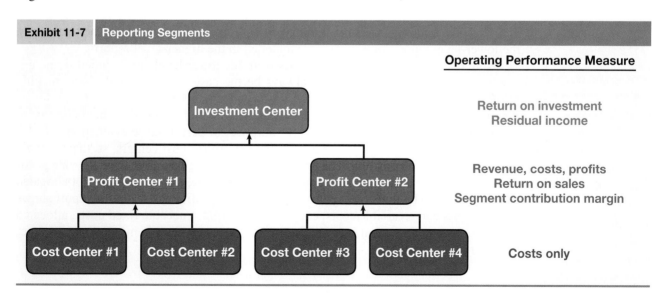

Operating Performance Measure

Investment Center — Return on investment / Residual income

Profit Center #1   Profit Center #2 — Revenue, costs, profits / Return on sales / Segment contribution margin

Cost Center #1   Cost Center #2   Cost Center #3   Cost Center #4 — Costs only

In June 2013, the Securities and Exchange Commission (SEC) charged PACCAR for various accounting deficiencies that obscured the company's financial reporting to investors and regulators from 2008 through 2012. Among the charges was that PACCAR failed to report the operating results of its aftermarket parts business separately from its truck sales business as required under segment reporting requirements. These requirements are intended to allow investors to gain the same insight into the company's operations as its executives.

How significant was this violation of generally accepted accounting principles (GAAP)? In its 2009 annual report, PACCAR reported $68 million in income before taxes for its truck segment. However, had it followed GAAP, it would have reported a $474 million loss in the truck segment and a $542 million profit in its parts segment.

The SEC and PACCAR agreed to a settlement under which, without admitting or denying the charges, PACCAR agreed to the entry of a permanent injunction and the payment of a $225,000 penalty. Michael S. Dicke, associate regional director of the SEC's San Francisco Regional Office said, "Companies must continually and diligently monitor their internal accounting systems to ensure that the information they are providing investors is accurate and consistent with relevant accounting guidance. The deficient controls and procedures at PACCAR caused inconsistencies in its financial reporting and kept investors and regulators from seeing the company through the eyes of management."
http://www.sec.gov/News/PressRelease/Detail/PressRelease/1365171575142#.VATK9_IdV8E

TAKEAWAY 7.2

Managers divide complex businesses into segments to enhance planning and control and provide for performance accountability.

PERFORMANCE REPORTING

LO4 **Construct** a segmented contribution margin income statement. **Identify** the difference between traceable and common fixed costs.

Hint: Direct expenses do not need to be allocated.

Performance reports are usually constructed periodically for each investment, profit, and cost center. They contain different levels of detail for different levels of managerial responsibility. Whereas top managers need highly summarized information, lower-level managers require more detailed, specialized reports.

Exhibit 11-8 presents multilevel performance reports for three successively higher levels of management. The arrows show how the totals from the lower-level reports flow to and are included in the higher-level reports.

Note that in this illustration, all costs from the lower level are included in the upper level. In practice, this may not always be the case—for proper decision-making purposes, only those costs that are directly traceable (see Chapter 2 for a discussion of direct versus indirect costs) to each department should be assigned to that department. Common costs would not be assigned for purposes of performance evaluation.

Also note that the reports in Panels B and C are for cost centers, so these reports only contain cost information. The manager of machining operations and the vice president of operations do not have responsibility for revenue, so revenues are not allocated to their reports. The divisions shown in Panel A are profit centers, so the report shows revenues, traceable variable costs, contribution margin, traceable fixed costs, allocated segment costs, and segment contribution margin in a contribution margin income statement format.

Exhibit 11-8	Segment Performance Reports

Panel A: First-Level Segment Report of Metal Works

METAL WORKS INC.
For the Month of August 20X1
Profit Center

| | Divisions | | Total |
	Kitchen Cutlery	Hand Tools	Total Company
Sales	$180,000	$340,000	$520,000
Less variable costs..........................	117,300	248,000	365,300
Contribution margin	$ 62,700	$ 92,000	$154,700
Less traceable fixed costs	39,600*	60,000	99,600
Plant margin................................	$ 23,100	$ 32,000	$ 55,100
Allocated division costs	8,000	9,000	17,000
Division margin.............................	$ 15,100	$ 23,000	$ 38,100
Common and unallocated company overhead ...			22,500
Net income.................................			$ 15,600

* $39,600 = Fixed manufacturing overhead ($9,600) + Common and unallocated plant overhead ($30,000) from Panel B.

Panel B: Second-Level Segment Report of the Kitchen Cutlery Division

Plant Operations—Kitchen Cutlery
For the Month of August 20X1
Cost Center

| | Departments | | | Total Kitchen Cutlery |
	Machining	Fabricating	Assembly	Total Kitchen Cutlery
Variable costs:				
Direct material..........................	$16,000	$ 25,545	$ 1,295	$ 42,840
Direct labor............................	18,000	28,739	20,720	67,459
Variable manufacturing overhead...........	1,200	1,916	3,885	7,001
Total variable costs......................	$35,200	$ 56,200	$ 25,900	$117,300
Fixed manufacturing overhead...............	3,000	5,400	1,200	9,600
Total department costs	$38,200	$ 61,600	$ 27,100	$126,900
Common and unallocated plant overhead.......				30,000
Total costs				$156,900

Panel C: Third-Level Segment Report of the Kitchen Cutlery Machining Department

Machining Department—Kitchen Cutlery
For the Month of August 20X1
Cost Center

Variable costs:	
Direct material..	$ 16,000
Direct labor...	18,000
Variable manufacturing overhead...........................	1,200
Total variable costs.......................................	$ 35,200
Fixed manufacturing overhead..............................	3,000
Total department costs	$ 38,200

Departmental Operations

Departmentalization is a common and logical type of segmentation for many firms. In many companies, departments are classified by processes performed. In the previous example, the Kitchen Cutlery division is composed of three segments, or departments: machining, fabricating, and assembly. These departments represent the primary processes performed in making the knives, forks, and spoons that comprise a set of kitchen cutlery.

In other companies, departments might be classified by products sold. The very term *department store* signifies a type of merchandising by product (men's clothing, women's clothing, home furnishings, etc.). Grocery stores are also commonly departmentalized by product groups such as meat, produce, groceries, bakery, and delicatessen. Sometimes departments are classified by type of customer. For example, home improvement centers selling such products as floor coverings, lighting fixtures, and heating and air-conditioning units may separate commercial sales operations from residential sales operations.

The methods of accounting and reporting departmental operating activities depend on the performance measures used and the degree of analysis desired by management. Some firms may desire to identify only contribution margin by department. Others may adopt a more detailed performance measure, such as contribution margin less those fixed costs directly incurred by the department (segment or department income).

Contribution Margin Income Statement

The main reason for analyzing segment contribution margin is that it permits management to review pricing policies and supplier costs. Comparisons can be made among segments to determine areas with high segment contribution margin and areas that may need major promotional efforts. For example, in the Metal Works, Inc. example in **Exhibit 11-8**, the segment report permits a comparison of the Cutlery and Hand Tools divisions (or segments) of the company. Comparisons can also be made with contribution margin achieved in previous periods or with statistics for other firms selling similar products. (These statistics may be obtained from trade association publications and credit agencies.[3]) A very low segment contribution margin may signal a need to investigate purchasing policies or to revise prices.

To obtain contribution margin figures by segment or department, a firm customarily creates a contribution margin income statement. A contribution margin income statement allows managers to identify those costs that are controllable by the segment and for which the segment manager should be held accountable. The use of a contribution margin income statement requires management to segregate those costs that are attributable to the segment from those costs that are attributable to other segments. As shown in Panel A of **Exhibit 11-8**, the attributable costs must be further classified as variable and fixed costs (both traceable to the department and common). Recall that in a contribution margin income statement, cost of goods sold consists of only variable manufacturing costs, all variable costs (both production and selling and administrative) are deducted from sales revenue to compute the contribution margin, and all fixed costs are deducted from contribution margin to compute the division margin. Note that in creating a segment contribution margin income statement, only fixed costs that are traceable to the segment are deducted to arrive at the segment contribution margin.

Segment Performance Evaluation

Department managers should be held responsible only for costs and expenses that they control. Therefore in segment reporting, costs are commonly classified and reported as trace-

---

[3] For example, the Risk Management Association publishes the RMA Annual Statement Studies, which is a source of comparative data drawn from the financial statements of the small- and medium-sized business customers of RMA's member institutions.

able (controlled by the segment) or common (not controlled by the segment). **Traceable expenses** are those operating expenses or costs traceable to and incurred for the benefit of a single department and thus ordinarily controllable by the department. **Common expenses** are those operating expenses or costs incurred for the benefit of multiple departments and thus neither traceable to nor controllable by a specific department. In Panel A of **Exhibit 11-8**, $22,500 of company expenses is determined to be common and unallocated to the Kitchen Cutlery and Hand Tools divisions.

Frequently, costs are considered controllable at one level of management but not at other levels. For example, the vice president of marketing for Metal Works, Inc. may be responsible for decisions related to advertising. Even though the cost of advertising is incurred at the division level (Kitchen Cutlery and Hand Tools), the manager of these divisions should not be held responsible for that expense if the vice president of marketing makes all the decisions relative to that cost or expense. These costs would be included in the common and unallocated company overhead costs shown in Panel A of **Exhibit 11-8**.

TAKEAWAY 11.3

Segment managers should be held responsible for traceable expenses but not common expenses.

SERVICE COMPANY SEGMENT REPORTING ILLUSTRATION

Let's review an example of segment reporting with Environmental Business Consultants (EBC). EBC, which has two offices in northern and southern California, was introduced to you in earlier chapters. Within EBC, each office is considered a department—the word *department* is used interchangeably with *office* in the following discussion.

SERVICE AND MERCHANDISING

Office Margin

EBC maintains its accounting records to produce absorption income statements in accordance with GAAP as required by its bank. However, assume that EBC's management desires a better measure of operating performance. It is then faced with the problem of assigning or *allocating* operating expenses to the offices. If managers desire a measure of office margin, it is necessary to trace the operating expenses to the offices.

Some expenses may be readily identified with the operation of particular offices, but others cannot be. To identify expenses with offices, it is helpful to classify them into traceable and common expenses. For example, payroll expense related to personnel who work exclusively in one office is a traceable expense of that office. Payroll expense related to administrative personnel whose work benefits all offices is a common expense of the offices. EBC also has several common expenses, incurred for the benefit of both offices. Some examples are marketing expenses, some administrative salaries, and a variety of other administrative expenses. These expenses must be fairly assigned, where traceable, to the offices if the measure of office net income is to be meaningful. Note that some general administrative costs such as executive salaries, general accounting expenses, and general legal expenses should not be allocated for purposes of evaluating an office's performance because the office manager has no control over those items.

Assume that EBC management classifies its operating costs as variable or fixed as follows:

Variable Expenses	Amount
Employee bonuses.	$126,000
Marketing expenses.	48,000
Office supplies expense.	64,500
Other general administrative expenses	70,000
Total variable operating expenses	$308,500

Fixed Expenses	Amount
Executive salaries.	$ 844,500
Clerical salaries	217,500
Consultant salaries.	1,050,000
Employee benefits	145,500
Payroll taxes.	123,000
Employee continuing education expenses.	27,000
Office lease expense	202,500
Other general administrative expenses	285,500
Total fixed operating expenses	$2,895,500

In preparing an office income statement, EBC might analyze and assign these expenses as described in the following subsections.

Employee Bonuses

All EBC employees are eligible for bonuses based on the profits earned during the year. Because each employee is assigned to an office, the bonuses for each office can be directly determined from payroll records, which show $96,178 for northern California and $29,822 for southern California.

Marketing Expenses

Of EBC's $48,000 marketing expenses, $28,000 was spent on proposal preparation in northern California, $11,000 on proposal preparation in southern California, $4,000 on attendance at industry trade shows that benefit both markets, and $5,000 on general professional journal advertisements directed at both markets. The latter two amounts are not assigned to the offices because they are considered common expenses, as shown in **Exhibit 11-9**.

Exhibit 11-9	Marketing Expenses Allocation		
	Northern California	Southern California	Firm Total
Proposal preparation	$28,000*	$11,000*	$39,000
Trade shows.			4,000
Advertising			5,000
			$48,000

* Directly identified

Office Supplies Expenses

Office supplies are purchased by each office as needed, so they are easily traceable to each office. EBC records show that $51,600 and $12,900 of office supplies were purchased by the northern and southern California offices, respectively, during the year.

Other General Administrative Expenses

Other general administrative expenses include the salaries and benefits for the office manager and bookkeeper and other costs associated with billings, collections, and customer inquiries. These costs, both the variable and fixed portions, are considered common costs and are not assigned to the individual offices.

Salaries and Related Benefits

Executive, clerical, and consultant salaries and related employee benefits and taxes are traceable to the office in which the employee works. EBC payroll records show that the total salaries, benefits, and taxes for each office are $1,876,200 and $504,300 for the northern and southern California offices, respectively.

Employee Continuing Education Expenses

All professional consultants are required to complete 40 hours of continuing education (CE) credits each year. As with salaries and related benefits, these costs can be determined directly for each office. The firm's time records show CE expenses of $20,828 for northern California consultants and $6,172 for southern California consultants.

Office Lease Expense

Each of the EBC offices negotiates and pays for its own office space. EBC records show that $154,500 in lease expense was paid by the northern California office and $48,000 was paid by the southern California office.

TAKEAWAY 11.4

Some costs are not large enough to justify being allocated individually. These costs are pooled and allocated together.

Exhibit 11-10 presents a summary of the operating expenses, showing the traceable variable and traceable fixed expenses of each department and common expenses for the firm.

Exhibit 11-10	Operating Expense Assignment			
	Northern California	Southern California	Common	Firm Total
Variable costs				
Employee bonuses	$ 96,178	$ 29,822		$ 126,000
Marketing expenses	28,000	11,000	9,000	48,000
Office supplies expense	51,600	12,900		64,500
Other general administrative expenses			70,000	70,000
Total variable costs	$ 175,778	$ 53,722	$ 79,000	$ 308,500
Fixed costs				
Salaries and benefits	$1,876,200	$504,300		$2,380,500
Employee continuing education expenses	20,828	6,172		27,000
Office lease expense	154,500	48,000		202,500
Other general administrative expenses			$285,500	285,500
Total fixed costs	$2,051,528	$558,472	$285,500	$2,895,500
Total costs	$2,227,306	$612,194	$364,500	$3,204,000

ACCOUNTING IN PRACTICE

Expense Allocation for Federal Government Grants and Contracts

Organizations, such as universities, that do business with the federal government under grants and contracts must use federal-government-specified allocation methods. The guidelines, known as OMB Circular A-87, establish the principles and standards for determining allowable costs for federal awards carried out through grants, cost reimbursement contracts, and other agreements with state and local governments. Allowable costs must meet certain criteria, including being necessary and reasonable, legally incurred under state or local law, consistent with federal policies and regulations, consistently applied, and adequately documented.

This departmental expense distribution is used to prepare the variable income statement for EBC shown in **Exhibit 11-11**, which extends the departmental operating results through office margin. Note that in this presentation, traceable variable costs are deducted to compute office contribution margin, from which traceable fixed costs are subtracted to compute office margin. Common expenses are not allocated to the individual offices.

Exhibit 11-11   Office Margin Statement

ENVIRONMENTAL BUSINESS CONSULTANTS, LLC
Office Margin Statement
For the Year Ended December 31, 2016

	Northern California	Southern California	Firm Total
Gross sales.	$2,900,000	$1,246,000	$4,146,000
Less reimbursable costs	(344,800)	(86,200)	(431,000)
Net sales.	2,555,200	1,159,800	3,715,000
Traceable variable costs	(175,778)	(53,722)	(229,500)
Office contribution margin	2,379,422	1,106,078	3,485,500
Traceable fixed costs	(2,051,528)	(558,472)	(2,610,000)
Office margin	$ 327,894	$ 547,606	875,500
Common expenses			(364,500)
Operating income.			511,000
Interest revenue			7,500
Income before tax			$ 518,500

Operating statements that extend departmental results to operating or net income measures are often criticized on the grounds that the indirect or common expenses are not controllable at the departmental level and therefore should not be assigned to departments when measuring performance. An additional criticism is that the bases for assignment of common expenses are frequently arbitrary.

In the EBC example, the other general administrative costs, although necessary expenses for the firm overall, are not controllable by the individual office managers. Thus, they should not be allocated to the offices at all. To allocate these costs on some arbitrary basis could lead management to draw incorrect conclusions and make poor business decisions.

YOUR TURN! 11.2

The solution is on
page 420.

Departmental revenue is $600,000 for Company X, and departmental operating income is $350,000. Traceable expenses for this department are as follows:

Direct labor	$25,000
Other traceable costs	$40,000
Direct materials	$30,000

Compute common expenses for this department.

PERFORMANCE ANALYSIS

The contribution margin income statement that was discussed in the previous section may be used to evaluate the performance of a profit center. This section addresses evaluation of investment centers.

LO5 Compute return on investment, return on sales, return on assets, and residual income for business segments. **Discuss** the importance of each indicator in assessing a company's performance.

Managers use a number of methods for evaluating the performance of investment centers. We explore several performance evaluation methods and discuss their relative strengths and weaknesses. To illustrate these different performance methods, we compare hypothetical data for Fezzari's mountain bike and road bike divisions. **Exhibit 11-12** indicates that the mountain bike division earned $2.5 million during 2016, and the road bike division earned $1.7 million. It also shows that the mountain bike division's investment in operating assets is $18.3 million, and the road bike division's investment is $11 million. We use this information to demonstrate the relative pros and cons of the various performance methods.

Exhibit 11-12 Performance Analysis

FEZZARI PERFORMANCE BICYCLES
Division Performance
For the Year Ended December 31, 2016

	Divisions	
(in thousands)	Mountain	Road
Sales	$14,400	$ 7,900
Expenses	(11,900)	(6,200)
Operating income	$ 2,500	$ 1,700
Asset investment	$18,300	$11,000

We note that one might be tempted to simply compare the operating income numbers of the two divisions and conclude that the mountain bike division is outperforming the road bike division because it has a higher operating income for the period. However, some of the other performance metrics we discuss here may provide different insights.

Return on Investment

One of the problems with simply comparing the net income figures of the two divisions is that they differ in size. One way to "level the playing field" of two divisions of different sizes is to compare the divisions on a relative basis based on a ratio.

One ratio that is useful in comparing the profitability of two divisions is the **return on investment** (ROI) ratio, which is calculated as the operating income number divided by the investment in operating assets:

$$ROI = \frac{\text{Operating income}}{\text{Operating asset investment}}$$

ROI examines the division's operating income as a percentage of the asset base used to generate that income.

Given the information in **Exhibit 11-12**, Fezzari's mountain bike division has an ROI of 13.7% ($2,500/$18,300), and the road bike division has an ROI of 15.5% ($1,700/$11,000). Therefore, the ROI ratio indicates that the road bike division earns a higher rate of return on its investment in assets than the mountain bike division earns on its investment. Thus, Fezzari's division ROI measures indicate that the mountain bike division generates 13.7 cents of profit for every dollar invested in assets, and the road bike division earns 15.5 cents of profit on every dollar invested in its asset base. Therefore, the ROI ratio provides evidence that the road bike division is more profitable on a relative basis, given its investment in assets.

In the 1920s, the DuPont brothers recognized that ROI could be further divided into two ratios, return on sales and asset utilization (or asset turnover), which provided managers additional levers to improve the overall ROI. This has come to be referred to as the **DuPont formula**. The formula for ROI can be expressed as:

$$ROI = \text{Return on sales (ROS)} \times \text{Asset utilization} = \frac{\text{Operating income}}{\text{Sales}} \times \frac{\text{Sales}}{\text{Investment}}$$

Exhibit 11-13 summarizes the calculation of ROI based on the DuPont formula for Fezzari's mountain and road bike divisions. The calculations of Fezzari's return on sales and asset utilization are discussed in the following sections.

Exhibit 11-13	ROI Analysis

FEZZARI PERFORMANCE BICYCLES
DuPont ROI Analysis
For the Year Ended December 31, 2016

	ROS	×	Asset Utilization	=	ROI
Mountain	17.4%	×	78.7%	=	13.7%
Road	21.5%	×	71.8%	=	15.5%*

* Difference due to rounding.

Return on Sales

The **return on sales** (ROS) ratio (the first component of the DuPont ROI formula) is useful in comparing the profitability of two divisions, which is simply calculated as the operating income number divided by sales:

$$ROS = \frac{\text{Operating income}}{\text{Sales}}$$

As shown in **Exhibit 11-13**, Fezzari's mountain bike division has an ROS of 17.4% ($2,500/$14,400), whereas the road bike division has an ROS of 21.5% ($1,700/$7,900). Thus, even though the road bike division has a lower net income than the mountain bike division, it is higher as a percentage of sales. One way of interpreting the ROS ratio is the number of pennies left over from each dollar of sales after covering all costs. Thus, Fezzari's division ROS measures indicate that although the mountain bike division may have a greater operating income number, it does not manage expenses as efficiently as the road bike division, because only 17.4 cents of every sales dollar is left over after covering operating costs, whereas the road bike division generates 21.5 cents of operating income for every sales dollar generated. At least based on this profitability measure, the road bike division is actually relatively more profitable.

Asset Utilization

The **asset utilization** ratio (the second component of the DuPont ROI formula) is used to compare the efficiency with which the divisions are using their operating assets to generate sales. It is calculated as sales divided by the investment in operating assets:

$$\text{Asset utilization} = \frac{\text{Sales}}{\text{Investment}}$$

As shown in **Exhibit 11-13**, Fezzari's mountain bike division has an asset utilization ratio of 78.7% ($14,400/$18,300), and the road bike division has an ROS of 71.8% ($7,900/$11,000). This means that the mountain bike division generates 78.7 cents in sales for every dollar of operating assets, whereas the road bike division generates only 71.8 cents in sales for every dollar of operating assets. The mountain bike division uses its operating assets more efficiently.

Interestingly, the DuPont analysis indicates that the road bike division has higher core profitability but the mountain bike division uses its assets more efficiently. Nevertheless, the result of multiplying the ROS ratio by the asset turnover ratio is that the road bike division has a higher ROI.

Residual Income

Another method for comparing two subsidiary companies or operating divisions is based on **residual income**. Similar to ROI, residual income takes the size of the division into account. However, unlike ROI, residual income is not a ratio; it is defined as the income that is left over after the company or division earns some minimum return on investment. Residual income is based on the idea that owners or investors expect a company to provide a reasonable rate of return on their investment. Investors could invest their money in other types of investments, so they likely have some minimum rate of return (called a hurdle rate) they would like to earn on their investment in the company. Another way of looking at residual income is to calculate the amount of extra income after a division earns a minimum ROI. The formula for residual income is:

Residual income = Net operating income − (Average operating assets × Minimum ROI)

One of many variations of residual income is Economic Value Added (EVA®), which has been trademarked by the consulting firm Stern, Stewart & Co. EVA makes certain adjustments to the calculation of net operating income (e.g., goodwill amortization and other non-cash expenses are added back) and uses the firm's weighted cost of capital as the minimum required return. A detailed discussion of EVA® will be left to a more advanced managerial or finance textbook.

Exhibit 11-14 first assumes that managers or owners expect each division to earn a hurdle rate of 5%. Given the mountain bike division's investment in assets of $18.3 million and the company's desired ROI of $915,000 ($18.3 million × 0.05), it has residual income of $1.59 million. Similarly, the road bike division has a desired ROI of $550,000 ($11.0 million × 0.05) and residual income of $1.15 million. Thus, we would conclude that the mountain bike division generates more residual income than the road bike division.

Exhibit 11-14	Residual Income Analysis		

FEZZARI PERFORMANCE BICYCLES
Residual Income Analysis
For the Year Ended December 31, 2016

		Divisions	
(in thousands)		Mountain	Road
Net income...		$2,500	$1,700
Required return (5% rate).............................		(915)	(550)
Residual income.....................................		$1,585	$1,150
Net income...		$2,500	$1,700
Required return (12% rate)............................		(2,196)	(1,320)
Residual income.....................................		$ 304	$ 380

On the other hand, what if managers or owners expect each division to earn a hurdle rate of 12%? Given the mountain bike division's investment in assets of $18.3 million and the company's desired ROI of $2.20 million ($18.3 million × 0.12), it has residual income of $304,000. Similarly, the road bike division has a desired ROI of $1.32 million ($11.0 million × 0.12) and residual income of $380,000. Thus, we would conclude that the road bike division's $380,000 of residual income exceeds the mountain bike division's $304,000 of residual income.

How is it possible that the mountain bike division has higher residual income if the required ROI is 5% and the road bike division has a higher residual income when the desired ROI is 12%? The answer is in the size of the asset base. When interest rates are low, it is relatively inexpensive to borrow money to buy assets. However, when interest rates are high, it becomes more costly to borrow money to buy assets. Hence, when the required ROI is low, larger divisions are favored, but when the desired ROI is high, smaller divisions have an advantage.

Balanced Scorecard

One drawback to the performance measures discussed so far is that they focus solely on financial measures. Over time, managers have become more aware of the fact that there are also many *nonfinancial* measures that influence both performance and other major corporate decisions. Thus, in recent years, many companies have begun evaluating performance using the balanced scorecard.[4] The **balanced scorecard** seeks to provide a "balanced view" of company performance by evaluating a company's subunits based on both financial and nonfinancial measures in each of the following areas:

1. Financial performance
2. Customer satisfaction
3. Internal business processes
4. Learning and growth

---

[4] The balanced scorecard originated in the 1990s with Robert Kaplan and David Norton at the Harvard Business School ("Using the Balanced Scorecard as a Strategic Management System," *Harvard Business Review,* January–February 1996, p. 76).

Obviously, financial performance remains perhaps the most important area of focus for most managers, because if a business isn't profitable and if it doesn't generate positive cash flows, it won't survive for long. Examples of financial measures include ratios and other financial statement measures. However, the long-term health of a company depends largely on its ability to attract and retain customers. Hence, the second focus area relates to customer satisfaction. Customer-related performance measures include such factors as the number of customer complaints. A well-run company seeks to achieve the highest level of efficiency. In their quest to maximize financial goals and maintain customer satisfaction, companies constantly seek to improve internal operations to achieve highly efficient processes. Evaluation of internal processes can measure factors such as throughput time and the number of quality inspection failures. Finally, effective organizations recognize that their greatest asset doesn't appear on the balance sheet. A company's employees bring perhaps the greatest value in determining the organization's continued success. Attracting and developing the best people is a constant struggle for any organization and is directly associated with an organization's capacity to grow and improve. Thus, the learning and growth aspect of a business can measure factors such as training and employee development efforts.

Exhibit 11-15 illustrates how Fezzari might evaluate itself based on the objectives it has defined in each of the four areas of focus.

Assume that you are the managing partner of a small CPA firm. You have decided to evaluate the firm's performance using a balanced scorecard. Identify at least one measure that you might use in each of the four areas of the balanced scorecard: financial performance, customer satisfaction, internal business processes, and learning and growth.	**DECISION TIME 11.1** The solution is on page 420.

TAKEAWAY 11.5

Managers use a variety of measures to evaluate the performance of investment centers, including return on investment, return on sales, asset utilization, residual income, and a balanced scorecard.

Exhibit 11-15	Balanced Scorecard Illustration

FEZZARI PERFORMANCE BICYCLES
Balanced Scorecard
For the Year Ended December 31, 2016

	Objectives	Measures	Targets	Initiatives
Financial	Maximize returns	ROI	14%	
	Profitable growth	Revenue growth	6%	
	Manage operating costs	Operating costs/customer	$1,000	
Customer	Industry-leading customer loyalty	Customer satisfaction survey	90%	Customer loyalty program
Internal Processes	Business growth			
	-Use alliances and joint ventures	% of customers serviced through alliances	10%	
	Customer service excellence			
	-Educate customers	% education plans executed	90%	
	-Effective customer service	Problem resolution cycle time	6 hrs.	Customer service software integration
Learning & Growth	Leading employee satisfaction	Employee satisfaction rating	3 on 5-point scale	Performance compensation link

SERVICE INDUSTRY IN FOCUS

In addition to evaluating its operations by office as shown earlier, EBC also wishes to evaluate the performance of its two lines of business, Solid Waste and Water/Wastewater (Water/WW). EBC management has prepared the following line of business income statement:

ENVIRONMENTAL BUSINESS CONSULTANTS, LLC
Line of Business Statement
For the Year Ended December 31, 2016

	Solid Waste	Water/WW	Firm Total
Gross sales	$3,676,000	$470,000	$ 4,146,000
Less reimbursable costs	(366,350)	(64,650)	$ (431,000)
Net sales	$3,309,650	$405,350	$ 3,715,000
Cost of services	(2,256,787)	(390,713)	$(2,647,500)
Gross profit on sales	$1,052,863	$ 14,637	$ 1,067,500
Operating expenses			(556,500)
Operating income			$ 511,000
Interest revenue			7,500
Income before tax			$ 518,500

EBC accountants have provided the following analysis of the cost of services, all of which are considered traceable:

Cost of Services

	Solid Waste			Water/WW			
	Variable	Fixed	Total	Variable	Fixed	Total	Firm Total
	$51,600	$2,205,187	$2,256,787	$12,900	$377,813	$390,713	$2,647,500

In addition, EBC has accumulated the following information regarding the operating expenses. Variable costs are shown in red; fixed costs are shown in black.

Operating Expenses Allocation

	Solid Waste			Water/WW			
	Traceable	Common	Total	Traceable	Common	Total	Firm Total
Employee bonuses	$109,722	$ —	$109,722	$16,278	$ —	$16,278	$126,000
Proposal preparation	31,400	—	31,400	7,600	—	7,600	39,000
Trade shows	—	3,000	3,000	—	1,000	1,000	4,000
Advertising	—	4,000	4,000	—	1,000	1,000	5,000
Employee CE expenses	24,943	—	24,943	2,057	—	2,057	27,000
Other general admin. expenses	—	306,849	306,849	—	48,651	48,651	355,500
	$166,065	$313,849	$479,914	$25,935	$50,651	$76,586	$556,500

Required

1. Prepare a line of business contribution margin statement for EBC (similar to **Exhibit 11-11**) that extends the line of business operating results through line of business contribution to common expenses.

2. Comment on the operating results for each line of business. What should EBC management do with regard to the Water/WW business based on these results?

Solution

1.

Solution 1	Service Industry in Focus		

ENVIRONMENTAL BUSINESS CONSULTANTS, LLC
Line of Business Statement
For the Year Ended December 31, 2016

	Solid Waste	Water/WW	Firm Total
Gross sales.	$3,676,000	$470,000	$4,146,000
Less reimbursable costs	(366,350)	(64,650)	(431,000)
Net sales.	$3,309,650	$405,350	$3,715,000
Traceable variable costs	(192,722)*	(36,778)*	(229,500)
Contribution margin	$3,116,928	$368,572	$3,485,500
Traceable fixed costs.	(2,230,130)**	(379,870)**	(2,610,000)
Line of business contribution.	$ 886,798	$ (11,298)	$ 875,500
Common operating expenses			(364,500)
Interest revenue			7,500
Income before tax			$ 518,500

*Solid Waste: $51,600 + $109,722 + $31,400 = $192,722
  Water/WW: $12,900 + $16,278 + $7,600 = $36,778

**Solid Waste: $2,205,187 + $24,943 = $2,230,130
  Water/WW: $377,813 + $2,057 = $379,870

2. The Water/WW line of business has a net loss at the line of business contribution level. It is not covering its own traceable operating costs, let alone contributing to the firm's common operating expenses. EBC management has several possible courses of action to consider:

   a. Determine whether revenues can be increased through higher fees for the service provided. An increase of just over 2.4% (11,298/470,000) would eliminate the loss.

   b. Carefully review the classification of expenses as cost of service and traceable operating expenses. Even a minor misclassification of an expense could make a difference in the reported results.

   c. Consider whether some of the Water/WW traceable expenses could be reduced or eliminated. For example, given these results, perhaps Water/WW employees should not be receiving bonuses.

   d. Consider whether the Water/WW line of business should be spun off or eliminated. This is a major decision with significant implications for EBC and its owners and employees. It may be that the Water/WW line of business provides cross-selling opportunities for the Solid Waste line of business that would have a greater impact on income before tax if eliminated.

APPENDIX 11A: Transfer Pricing

eLectures

MBC

DOMESTIC TRANSFER PRICING

LO6   **Determine** the proper transfer price to maximize company profit with and without excess productive capacity.

Management of a large, complex company usually divides the business into a number of segments. A segment is a logical portion of a business, such as a division or department. When a segment is established as a profit center, the segment's manager is responsible for revenue generation as well as cost and expense control. If the profit center receives products or services from another profit center within the same business or provides products or services to another profit center within the same business, the two profit center managers must agree on a transfer price for the product or service. The **transfer price** is the price that the selling profit center will charge the buying profit center for the product or service provided.

Objectives for Transfer Pricing

Two objectives should be met when establishing transfer prices. First, the transfer price of the product or service transferred should allow both the selling and buying divisions to make a reasonable gross profit. Second, the contribution margin of the entire business should be maximized.

Reasonable Gross Profit

Assume that John Deere Waterloo Works has two operating divisions, the Drivetrain Operations division and the Tractor, Cab, and Assembly Operations division. Top management has decided that the Drivetrain Operations division should sell a particular component to the Tractor, Cab, and Assembly Operations division, which will incorporate the component into the 6170R tractor that it manufactures and sells for $150,000 per unit. The per-unit product costs incurred in this process are the following:

	Drivetrain Operations Division	Tractor, Cab, and Assembly Operations Division
Direct material	$6,250	$62,250
Direct labor	1,500	27,750
Variable overhead	1,000	17,000
Fixed overhead	1,250	17,850
Transfer price of component	?	

A negotiated transfer price below market price can be justified. Expenses may be less when intercompany sales are made, or volume may be large enough to justify quantity discounts.

BUSINESS SITUATION 1: Assume that the transfer price is established as $10,000, the total absorption product cost of the component in the Drivetrain Operations division ($6,250 + $1,500 + $1,000 + $1,250 = $10,000). The resulting gross profit per unit for the two divisions would be calculated as follows:

	Drivetrain Operations Division	Tractor, Cab, and Assembly Operations Division
Revenue:		
Transfer price	$10,000	
Sales price		$150,000
Cost:		
Transfer price		$10,000
Direct material	$6,250	62,250
Direct labor	1,500	27,750
Variable overhead	1,000	17,000
Fixed overhead	1,250	17,850
	10,000	$134,850
Gross profit per unit	$ —	$ 15,150

BUSINESS SITUATION 2: Assume that the transfer price is established as $12,000, the price that the Drivetrain Operations division would receive from an outside customer and the cost that the Tractor, Cab, and Assembly Operations division would incur from an outside supplier. The resulting gross profit per unit for the two divisions would be calculated as follows:

	Drivetrain Operations Division	Tractor, Cab, and Assembly Operations Division
Revenue:		
Transfer price	$12,000	
Sales price		$150,000
Cost:		
Transfer price		$12,000
Direct material.	$6,250	62,250
Direct labor	1,500	27,750
Variable overhead	1,000	17,000
Fixed overhead	1,250	17,850
	10,000	$136,850
Gross profit per unit	$ 2,000	$ 13,150

In situation 1, the Tractor, Cab, and Assembly Operations division generates a 10.1% gross profit ($15,150/$150,000 = 0.101), and the Drivetrain Operations division generates no gross profit. In situation 2, the Drivetrain Operations division generates a gross profit of $2,000 and the Tractor, Cab, and Assembly division generates a gross profit of $13,150. Situation 1 illustrates a full absorption product cost transfer price, and situation 2 illustrates a market price transfer price. In both situations, total John Deere gross profit per 6170R is $15,150.

Situation 2 meets the first objective—the transfer price of the product or service transferred should allow both the selling and buying divisions to make a reasonable gross profit. In general, a transfer price based on market price, not absorption product cost, will satisfy the objective of reasonable gross profits for both the selling and buying profit centers or divisions.

Maximize Contribution Margin

The second objective—that the contribution margin of the entire business should be maximized—can be met by identifying a proper minimum transfer price and allowing the manager of the buying profit center to decide whether to buy from the selling profit center or from an outside supplier. As shown in **Exhibit 11A-1**, assume the Drivetrain Operations division of John Deere is currently manufacturing and selling only component A to outside customers for $7,500 per unit.

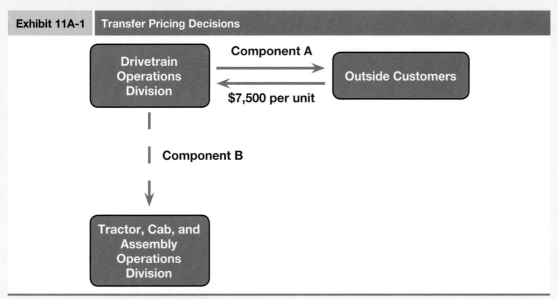

Exhibit 11A-1 **Transfer Pricing Decisions**

The Tractor, Cab, and Assembly Operations division has proposed that the Drivetrain Operations division begin manufacturing and selling 2,000 units of component B per year to the Tractor, Cab, and Assembly Operations division. The formula for the minimum transfer price for component B is the following:

Product B minimum transfer price	=	Variable cost of product B, per unit	+	Contribution margin lost from not selling product A, per unit of product B

Next we will apply these objectives of transfer pricing to two situations, one in which the supplier does not have any excess capacity and one in which the supplier does have excess capacity.

No Excess Capacity

Assume the Drivetrain Operations division has no excess manufacturing capacity. Therefore, if the Drivetrain Operations division produces component B for the Tractor, Cab, and Assembly Operations division, the Drivetrain Operations division will have to reduce its production and sale of component A to outside customers. Assume that 5,000 fewer units of component A will have to be produced and sold to allow the manufacture of 2,000 units of component B.

The minimum transfer price that the Drivetrain Operations division is willing to accept is one that maintains the contribution margin of the Drivetrain Operations division at its current level. The formula given earlier will generate a transfer price that would allow this to happen. Assume that the variable cost per unit of component A is $5,000, and its selling price is $7,500. The variable cost per unit of component B is $8,750. The total contribution margin that would be given up on 5,000 units of component A is $12,500,000 (5,000 units × [$7,500 − $5,000]). Using the formula, the minimum transfer price for component B is $15,000 ($8,750 + [$12,500,000/2,000 units of B]) (see **Exhibit 11A-2**).

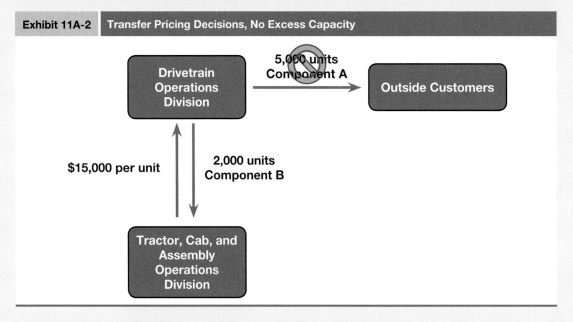

Exhibit 11A-2   **Transfer Pricing Decisions, No Excess Capacity**

The switch from the production and sale of 5,000 units of component A to 2,000 units of component B would not affect total fixed costs, would create new variable costs of $8,750 per unit, and would eliminate $12,500,000 of contribution margin. The $15,000 transfer price would reimburse the Drivetrain Operations division for the additional variable costs and the lost contribution margin. As a result, the Drivetrain Operations division would generate exactly the same contribution margin whether it produced and sold component A or component B.

TAKEAWAY 11.2

Total gross profit for the firm is unaffected by the transfer price; all transfer prices yield the same total gross profit.

With the transfer price set at $15,000, the Tractor, Cab, and Assembly Operations division is in a position to make a decision that will maximize its contribution margin and the contribution margin of the entire business. Assume that the Tractor, Cab, and Assembly Operations division adds $107,000 of variable cost in addition to the costs of the Drivetrain Operations division and then sells the end product for $150,000. If the Tractor, Cab, and Assembly Operations division can only buy component B from an outside supplier for a price greater than $15,000, then it will choose to buy component B from the Drivetrain Operations division. However, if the product division can buy component B from an outside supplier for a price less than $15,000, then it will choose to buy the component from the outside supplier (see **Exhibit 11A-3**). In either case, the contribution margin of the company as a whole has been maximized.

Exhibit 11A-3	Transfer Pricing Decisions, No Excess Capacity

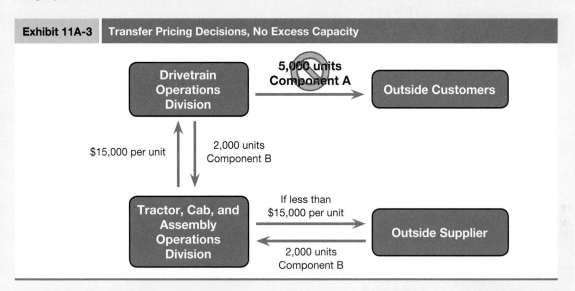

To illustrate, let us assume two situations:
(1) the outside supplier's price is $16,000; and,
(2) the outside supplier's price is $14,000.

BUSINESS SITUATION 1:   **Exhibit 11A-4** shows the calculation of the contribution margin for the first situation. If the Tractor, Cab, and Assembly Operations division purchases component B from the Drivetrain Operations division at a per-unit transfer price of $15,000, the Drivetrain Operations division would earn a contribution margin of $12,500,000 and the Tractor, Cab, and Assembly Operations division would earn a contribution margin of $56,000,000 on the sale of the 6170R to its customers, for a total contribution margin of $68,500,000.

Exhibit 11A-4	Transfer Pricing Decisions, No Excess Capacity

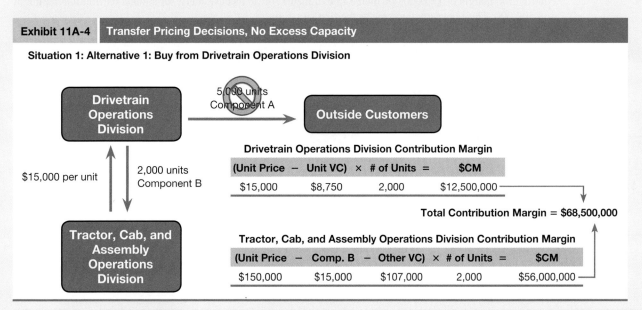

Situation 1: Alternative 1: Buy from Drivetrain Operations Division

However, **Exhibit 11A-5** shows the calculation of the contribution margin if the Tractor, Cab, and Assembly Operations division purchases component B from outside suppliers at a price of $16,000 per unit. This would allow the Drivetrain Operations division to continue to sell component A to its outside customers at a contribution margin of $12,500,000. The Tractor, Cab, and Assembly Operations division would earn a contribution margin of $54,000,000 on the sale of the 6170R, for a total contribution margin of $66,500,000.

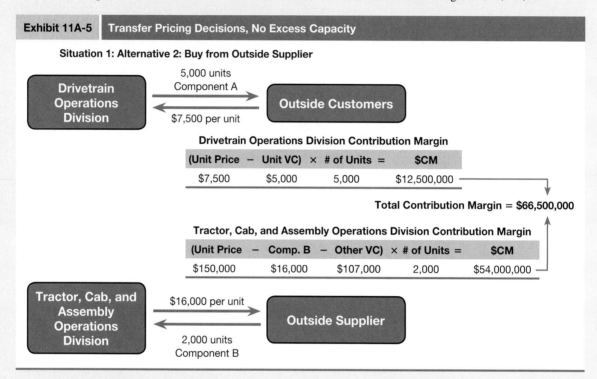

Exhibit 11A-5	Transfer Pricing Decisions, No Excess Capacity

Situation 1: Alternative 2: Buy from Outside Supplier

Drivetrain Operations Division → 5,000 units Component A → **Outside Customers**
← $7,500 per unit

Drivetrain Operations Division Contribution Margin

(Unit Price	− Unit VC)	× # of Units =	$CM
$7,500	$5,000	5,000	$12,500,000

Total Contribution Margin = $66,500,000

Tractor, Cab, and Assembly Operations Division Contribution Margin

(Unit Price	− Comp. B	− Other VC)	× # of Units =	$CM
$150,000	$16,000	$107,000	2,000	$54,000,000

Tractor, Cab, and Assembly Operations Division → $16,000 per unit → **Outside Supplier**
← 2,000 units Component B

A careful study of **Exhibits 11A-4** and **11A-5** shows that John Deere will earn $2,000,000 more in contribution margin by purchasing component B from the Drivetrain Operations division.

BUSINESS SITUATION 2:   **Exhibit 11A-6** shows the calculation of the contribution margin for the second situation. If the Tractor, Cab, and Assembly Operations division purchases component B from the Drivetrain Operations division at a per-unit transfer price of $15,000, the Drivetrain Operations division would earn a contribution margin of $12,500,000 and the Tractor, Cab, and Assembly Operations division would earn a contribution margin of $56,000,000 on the sale of the 6170R to its customers, for a total contribution margin of $68,500,000. This is exactly the same as the first situation.

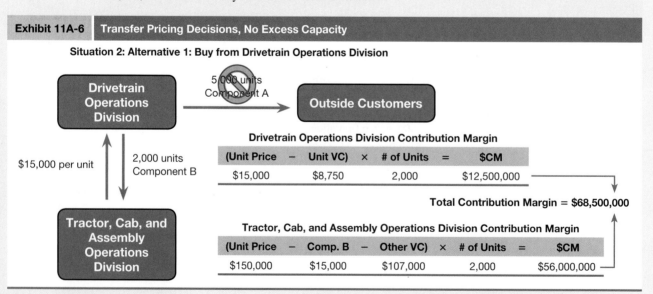

Exhibit 11A-6	Transfer Pricing Decisions, No Excess Capacity

Situation 2: Alternative 1: Buy from Drivetrain Operations Division

Drivetrain Operations Division → 5,000 units Component A → **Outside Customers**

$15,000 per unit   2,000 units Component B

Drivetrain Operations Division Contribution Margin

(Unit Price	− Unit VC)	× # of Units	=	$CM
$15,000	$8,750	2,000		$12,500,000

Total Contribution Margin = $68,500,000

Tractor, Cab, and Assembly Operations Division

Tractor, Cab, and Assembly Operations Division Contribution Margin

(Unit Price	− Comp. B	− Other VC)	× # of Units	=	$CM
$150,000	$15,000	$107,000	2,000		$56,000,000

However, **Exhibit 11A-7** shows the calculation of the contribution margin if the Tractor, Cab, and Assembly Operations division purchases component B from outside suppliers at a price of $14,000 per unit. This would allow the Drivetrain Operations division to continue to sell component A to its outside customers at a contribution margin of $12,500,000. The Tractor, Cab, and Assembly Operations division would earn a contribution margin of $58,000,000 on the sale of the 6170R, for a total contribution margin of $70,500,000.

Exhibit 11A-7	Transfer Pricing Decisions, No Excess Capacity

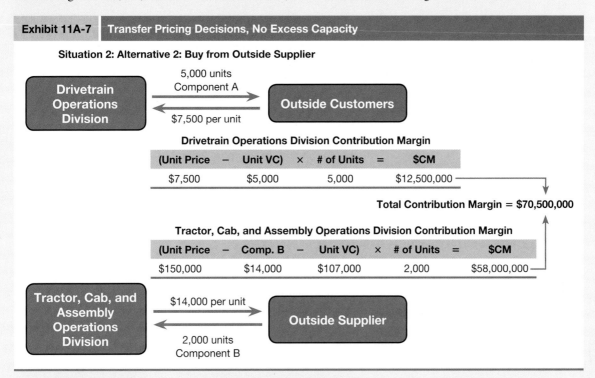

Situation 2: Alternative 2: Buy from Outside Supplier

Drivetrain Operations Division Contribution Margin

(Unit Price	−	Unit VC)	×	# of Units	=	$CM
$7,500		$5,000		5,000		$12,500,000

Total Contribution Margin = $70,500,000

Tractor, Cab, and Assembly Operations Division Contribution Margin

(Unit Price	−	Comp. B	−	Unit VC)	×	# of Units	=	$CM
$150,000		$14,000		$107,000		2,000		$58,000,000

A comparison of **Exhibits 11A-6** and **11A-7** shows that John Deere will earn $2,000,000 more in contribution margin by purchasing component B from the outside supplier.

Excess Capacity

In the John Deere example, we assumed that the Drivetrain Operations division had no excess manufacturing capacity. If we now assume that the Drivetrain Operations division has sufficient capacity to produce and sell the 2,000 units of component B without reducing the production and sale of component A, we will determine a different minimum transfer price. Applying the previous formula for the minimum transfer price, we determine that the minimum transfer price is $8,750 ($8,750 + [$0/2,000]) (see **Exhibit 11A-8**).

Exhibit 11A-8	Transfer Pricing Decisions, Excess Capacity

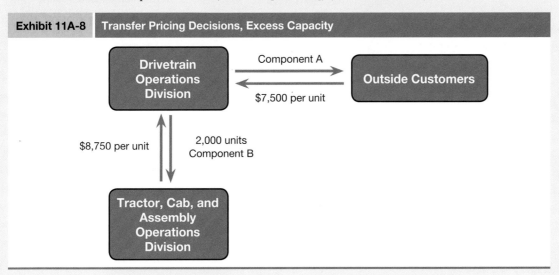

In this case, the production and sale of 2,000 units of component B would not affect total fixed costs, would create new variable costs of $8,750 per unit, and would eliminate no contribution margin from the production and sale of component A. The $8,750 transfer price would reimburse the Drivetrain Operations division for the additional variable costs. As a result, the Drivetrain Operations division would generate exactly the same contribution margin whether or not it produced and sold product B.

Negotiated Transfer Prices

The formula that determines minimum transfer price results in a transfer price that is frequently different from the market value of the product or service being transferred. If the minimum transfer price is greater than the market price, then the buying profit center will buy the product or service from an outside supplier and there will be no need for a transfer price.

If the minimum transfer price is less than the market price, however, then the buying profit center will buy the product or service from the other profit center in the same company. The exact transfer price will be negotiated by the two profit centers. The resulting amount will be greater than or equal to the minimum transfer price and less than or equal to the market price. Any negotiated transfer price within this range will result in the same total contribution margin for the firm. In the John Deere example, with a minimum transfer price of $8,750 and a market price of $15,000, any transfer price from $8,750 to $15,000 results in a contribution margin of $12,500,000 for John Deere.

INTERNATIONAL TRANSFER PRICING

Transfer pricing becomes more complex if one of the segments is in a different country than the other. When products or services are being transferred between segments in different countries, the two objectives stated earlier still apply. However, there also are additional objectives that may conflict with the two previously mentioned. The additional objectives include minimization of international income taxes and tariffs and conformance with international trade agreements. These topics are beyond the scope of this introduction to transfer pricing. Intermediate cost accounting textbooks generally provide a more in-depth coverage of these topics related to international transfer pricing.

COMPREHENSIVE PROBLEM

LT Roofing Company sells roofing products through two departments, composite and steel. Operating information for 2016 is as follows:

	Composite Department	Steel Department
Inventory, January 1, 2016.	$ 90,000	$ 39,000
Inventory, December 31, 2016.	75,000	45,000
Net sales.	1,170,000	720,000
Purchases.	726,000	543,000
Purchases returns	42,000	12,000
Purchases discounts	24,000	6,000
Transportation in	27,000	21,000
Traceable department expenses	162,000	84,000

Common operating expenses of the firm were $180,000.

Required

a. Prepare a department income statement showing department contribution to common expenses and net income of the firm. Assume an overall effective income tax rate of 30%. LT uses a periodic inventory system.

b. Calculate the gross profit percentage for each department.

c. If the common expenses were allocated 55% to the composite department and 45% to the steel department, what would the net income be for each department?

Solution

LT ROOFING COMPANY
Department Income Statement
For the Year Ended December 31, 2016

a.

	Composite Department	Steel Department	Total
Net sales.	$1,170,000	$720,000	$1,890,000
Cost of goods sold:			
Inventory, January 1, 2016	90,000	39,000	129,000
Purchases.	726,000	543,000	1,269,000
Less: Purchases returns	(42,000)	(12,000)	(54,000)
Purchases discounts.	(24,000)	(6,000)	(30,000)
Transportation in.	27,000	21,000	48,000
Cost of goods available for sale	$ 777,000	$585,000	$1,362,000
Inventory, December 31, 2016	75,000	45,000	120,000
Cost of goods sold	$ 702,000	$540,000	$1,242,000
Gross profit.	$ 468,000	$180,000	$ 648,000
Traceable department expenses	162,000	84,000	246,000
Department margin	$ 306,000	$ 96,000	$ 402,000
Common expenses			180,000
Income before tax			$ 222,000
Income tax expense (30% × $222,000).			66,600
Net income.			$ 155,400

b. Gross profit percentages:
Composite dept.: $468,000/$1,170,000 = 40%
Steel dept.: $180,000/$720,000 = 25%

c.

	Composite Department	Steel Department	Total
Department margin	$ 306,000	$ 96,000	$ 402,000
Common expenses*	99,000	81,000	180,000
Income before tax	$ 207,000	$ 15,000	$ 222,000
Income tax expense (30% × $207,000 and 30% × $15,000)	62,100	4,500	66,600
Net income	$ 144,900	$ 10,500	$ 155,400

* 55% × $180,000 = $99,000
45% × $180,000 = $81,000

SUMMARY OF LEARNING OBJECTIVES

Describe a static budget, illustrate its use, and present an example of a static budget performance report. (p. 376)

LO1

- A static budget is a financial plan developed for a fixed level of operating activity, typically the expected or most likely level.
- If actual results are compared to a static budget, the variances that result are of little use to management, because the budget is often based on a different level of activity than the actual operations.

LO2 **Introduce the flexible budget and present an example of a flexible budget performance report. Explain how flexible budgeting helps in variance analysis. (p. 377)**

- A flexible budget is a financial plan that makes cost projections for various activity levels within a relevant range.
- A flexible budget usually divides costs and expenses into variable and fixed costs.
- A flexible budget performance report compares actual costs to budgeted costs based on the actual production level achieved.

LO3 **Present an overview of reporting operations for segments of a business. (p. 383)**

- Business segments may consist of organizational units (departments or divisions) or areas of economic activity (product lines or markets).
- A business segment may be an investment center (where management is responsible for the efficient use of capital as well as revenues and expenses), a profit center (where management is responsible for both revenues and expenses), or a cost center (where management is responsible for expenses only).
- Internal reporting of segment operations deals primarily with the measurement of operating performance.
- Accounting and reporting by business segment are indispensable to management and very important to external groups such as investors and creditors.

LO4 **Construct a segmented contribution margin income statement. Identify the difference between traceable and common fixed costs. (p. 386)**

- Total amounts from lower-level reports flow to and are included in higher-level reports.
- A performance report is usually prepared for each accounting period for each profit center and each cost center.
- Expenses incurred by, or for the benefit of, one business segment are called traceable expenses. Expenses incurred for more than one business segment are called common expenses.
- Reporting for segments of a firm is typically extended to contribution to common expenses. Only traceable expenses are deducted.

LO5 **Compute return on investment, return on sales, return on assets, and residual income for business segments. Discuss the importance of each indicator in assessing a company's performance. (p. 393)**

- Return on investment is operating income as a percentage of the asset base used to generate that income. It illustrates the amount of profit generated for every dollar invested in the company's asset base.
- The DuPont formula recognizes that ROI can be further divided into two ratios, return on sales and asset utilization.
- Return on sales is operating income as a percentage of sales revenue. It may be interpreted as the number of pennies left over from each dollar of sales after covering all costs.
- Asset utilization is sales divided by the investment in operating assets. It is a measure of a company's efficiency in utilizing its operating assets. It represents the amount of sales per dollar of operating asset.
- Residual income is the income that is left over after the company or division earns some minimum return on investment.
- The balanced scorecard seeks to provide a "balanced view" of company performance by evaluating a company's subunits based on both financial and nonfinancial measures, including financial performance, customer satisfaction, internal business processes, and learning and growth.

LO6 **Determine the proper transfer price to maximize company profit with and without excess productive capacity. (p. 400)**

- The transfer price of the product or service transferred should allow both the selling and buying divisions to make a reasonable gross profit.
- The negotiated transfer price should maximize the contribution margin of the entire business.
- A transfer price based on market price will satisfy the objective of reasonable gross profits for both the selling and buying profit centers or divisions.

KEY TERMS

Asset utilization (p. 395)	Investment center (p. 385)	Return on sales (p. 394)
Balanced scorecard (p. 396)	Performance reports (p. 386)	Static budget (p. 376)
Common expenses (p. 389)	Profit center (p. 385)	Traceable expenses (p. 389)
Cost center (p. 385)	Residual income (p. 395)	Transfer price (p. 400)
DuPont formula (p. 394)	Responsibility centers (p. 384)	
Flexible budget (p. 377)	Return on investment (p. 393)	

Assignments with the 🔵 logo in the margin are available in BusinessCourse.
See the Preface of the book for details.

SELF-STUDY QUESTIONS

(Answers to Self-Study Questions are at the end of this chapter.)

1. The manager of which of the following segments of a business is responsible for revenue generation as well as for cost and expense control?   **LO3**
   a. Cost center
   b. Accounting department
   c. Profit center
   d. Assembly line

2. Which of the following is not considered in determining contribution to common expenses?   **LO4**
   a. Income taxes   c. Traceable expenses
   b. Cost of goods sold   d. Net sales

3. In performance reporting (budgeted cost compared to actual cost), which performance report must be prepared first?   **LO4**
   a. Division, consisting of five departments
   b. Region, consisting of three divisions
   c. Department, consisting of four cost centers
   d. Company, consisting of two regions

4. Which of the following is the correct formula for return on sales?   **LO5**
   a. Income/Investment
   b. Investment/Income
   c. Income/Revenue
   d. Revenue/Investment

5. During the past twelve months, the Aaron Corporation had a net income of $50,000. What is the amount of the investment if the return on investment is 20%?   **LO5**
   a. $100,000
   b. $200,000
   c. $250,000
   d. $500,000

QUESTIONS

1. Give examples of segments of business firms segmented by (a) organizational unit and (b) economic activity.   **LO3**
2. Distinguish between a profit center and a cost center.   **LO3**
3. Explain the difference between a static budget and a flexible budget.   **LO1, 2**
4. Explain what is meant by a static budget variance and a flexible budget variance.   **LO1, 2**
5. Distinguish between traceable expenses and common expenses. Which are more likely to be controllable at the department level?   **LO4**
6. If a firm wishes to compare the performance of two divisions, why might divisional operating income be a poor basis for comparison?   **LO5**

LO4   **7.** Suggest an allocation basis for each of the following traceable expenses of a departmentalized firm that uses a net income measure to determine the profitability of departments:

    a. Janitorial expense
    b. Plant manager's salary
    c. Utilities (heat, light, and air conditioning)
    d. Property taxes

LO4   **8.** What is meant by departmental contribution to common expenses? What advantages does this measure have over net income in measuring departmental performance?

LO2   **9.** "The higher the management level receiving reports, the more detailed the reports should be." Comment.

LO4   **10.** Department B of the local Top Value Store shows a contribution to common expenses of $22,000 and a net loss of $9,000 (before taxes). The firm believes that discontinuing department B will not affect sales, gross profit, or traceable expenses of other departments. If total common expenses remain unchanged, what effect will discontinuing department B have on the income before taxes of the Top Value Store?

LO4   **11.** Department 2 of Kapp Company has a gross profit of $100,000, representing 40% of net departmental sales. Traceable departmental expenses are $75,000. Management believes that an increase of $6,500 in advertising, coupled with a 5% average increase in sales prices, will permit the physical volume of products sold to remain the same next period but will improve the department's contribution to common expenses. If management's expectations are correct, what will be the effect on this contribution?

LO4   **12.** Department A of Racine Company has a gross profit of $140,000, representing 35% of net departmental sales. Management believes that an increase of $36,000 in advertising will increase volume of product sold by 20%. Other traceable departmental expenses are $64,000. What effect will this decision have on department A's contribution to common expenses?

LO6   **13.** What is the maximum amount that one division should pay to another division of the same company for a component needed in manufacturing its product?

LO5   **14.** What is the primary purpose of the balanced scorecard?

LO5   **15.** What are the four key performance measures in the balanced scorecard?

EXERCISES—SET A

LO1, 2   **E11-1A. Static and Flexible Budgets** Graham Corporation used the following data to evaluate its current operating system. The company sells items for $10 each and used a budgeted selling price of $10 per unit.

	Actual	Budgeted
Units sold	495,000 units	500,000 units
Variable costs.	$1,250,000	$1,500,000
Fixed costs.	$925,000	$900,000

    a. Prepare the actual income statement, flexible budget, and static budget.
    b. What is the static-budget variance of revenues?
    c. What is the flexible budget variance for variable costs?
    d. What is the flexible budget variance for fixed costs?

LO2   **E11-2A. Using Flexible Budgets** The following summary data are from a performance report for Sterling Company for May, during which 9,600 units were produced. The budget reflects the company's normal capacity of 10,000 units.

	Budget (10,000 Units)	Actual Costs (9,600 Units)	Variances
Direct material	$140,000	$136,800	$3,200 F
Direct labor.................................	280,000	277,200	2,800 F
Variable overhead...........................	96,000	98,400	2,400 U
Fixed overhead.............................	72,000	72,400	400 U
Total	$588,000	$584,800	$3,200 F

a. What is the general implication of the performance report? Why might Sterling question the significance of the report?

b. Revise the performance report using flexible budgeting, and comment on the general implication of the revised report.

E11-3A. Assigning Traceable Fixed Expenses Selected data for Miller Company, which operates three departments, follow: **LO4**

	Department A	Department B	Department C
Inventory....................................	$ 80,000	$288,000	$112,000
Equipment (average cost)..................	720,000	432,000	288,000
Payroll......................................	405,000	360,000	135,000
Square feet of floor space	18,000	9,000	3,000

During the year, the company's fixed expenses included the following:

Depreciation on equipment	$80,000
Real estate taxes	24,000
Personal property taxes (on inventory and equipment).........................	38,400
Personnel department expenses	40,000

Assume that the property tax rate is the same for both inventory and equipment. Using the most causally related bases, prepare a schedule assigning the fixed expenses to the three departments. *Hint:* Not all fixed expenses are traceable to the three departments. One of these fixed costs should be considered a common cost and not traceable to the departments.

E11-4A. Return on Investment and Residual Income Johnson Company has two sources of funds: long-term debt and equity capital. Johnson Company has profit centers in the following locations with the following net incomes and total assets: **LO5**

SERVICE AND MERCHANDISING

	Net Income	Assets
Las Vegas...	$ 960,000	$ 4,000,000
Dallas	$1,200,000	$ 8,000,000
Tampa	$2,040,000	$12,000,000

a. Calculate ROI for each profit center and rank them from highest to lowest based on ROI.

b. Calculate residual income for each profit center based on a desired ROI of 5% and rank them from highest to lowest based on residual income.

EXERCISES—SET B

E11-1B. Using Flexible Budgets The following summary data are from a performance report for Hyland Company for June, during which 9,600 units were produced. The budget reflects the company's normal capacity of 10,000 units.   **LO2**

	Budget (10,000 Units)	Actual Costs (9,600 Units)	Variances
Direct material	$105,000	$102,600	$2,400 F
Direct labor	210,000	207,900	2,100 F
Variable overhead	72,000	73,800	1,800 U
Fixed overhead	54,000	54,300	300 U
Total	$441,000	$438,600	$2,400 F

a. What is the general implication of the performance report? Why might Hyland question the significance of the report?

b. Revise the performance report using flexible budgeting and comment on the general implication of the revised report.

LO4 **E11-2B. Assigning Traceable Fixed Expenses** Selected data for Colony Company, which operates three departments, follow:

	Department A	Department B	Department C
Inventory	$ 40,000	$144,000	$ 56,000
Equipment (average cost)	360,000	216,000	144,000
Payroll	607,500	540,000	202,500
Square feet of floor space	27,000	13,500	4,500

During the year, the company's fixed expenses included the following:

Depreciation on equipment	$60,000
Real estate taxes	18,000
Personal property taxes (on inventory and equipment)	28,800
Personnel department expenses	30,000

Assume that the property tax rate is the same for both inventory and equipment. Using the most causally related bases, prepare a schedule assigning the fixed expenses to the three departments. *Hint:* Not all fixed expenses are traceable to the three departments. One of these fixed costs should be considered a common cost and not traceable to the departments.

LO5 **E11-3B. Return on Investment and Residual Income** The Emergency Medical Services Company has two divisions that operate independently of one another. The financial data for the year 20X5 reported the following results:

	North	South
Sales	$3,000,000	$2,500,000
Operating income	750,000	550,000
Taxable income	650,000	375,000
Investment	6,000,000	5,000,000

The company's desired rate of return is 10%. Income is defined as operating income.

a. What are the respective return-on-investment ratios for the North and South divisions?

b. What are the respective residual incomes for the North and South divisions?

c. Which division has the better return on investment and which division has the better residual income figure, respectively?

LO5 **E11-4B. Evaluating Investment Centers** Terry Enterprises, Inc. has two divisions—the Foods division and the Clothes division. Historically, Terry has used the division's ROI as the performance measure for the bonus determinations. Terry Foods division has gross total assets of $1,000,000, accumulated depreciation of $350,000, current liabilities of $250,000, and sales of $2,000,000. Foods' operating income is $200,000. Terry Clothes division has gross total assets of $5,000,000, accumulated depreciation of $2,100,000, current liabilities of $1,500,000, and sales of $8,000,000. Clothes' operating income is $750,000.

Required

Use the DuPont formula to compute ROI for each division and for Terry Enterprises as a whole. Use operating income and gross total assets as the measures of income and investment. *Hint:* Calculate the ROI for Terry Enterprises (as a whole), to three decimal places.

PROBLEMS—SET A

P11-1A. Flexible Budget Application   The polishing department of Taylor Manufacturing Company operated during April 2016 with the following manufacturing overhead cost budget based on 5,000 hours of monthly productive capacity:

 LO2

TAYLOR MANUFACTURING COMPANY Polishing Department Overhead Budget (5,000 Hours) for the Month of April 2016		
Variable costs:		
Factory supplies	$100,000	
Indirect labor	152,000	
Utilities (usage charge)	68,000	
Patent royalties on secret process	296,000	
Total variable overhead		$ 616,000
Fixed costs:		
Supervisory salaries	$160,000	
Depreciation on factory equipment	144,000	
Factory taxes	48,000	
Factory insurance	32,000	
Utilities (base charge)	80,000	
Total fixed overhead		$ 464,000
Total manufacturing overhead		$1,080,000

The polishing department was operated for 4,600 hours during April and incurred the following manufacturing overhead costs:

Factory supplies	$ 97,520
Indirect labor	136,160
Utilities (usage factor)	82,800
Utilities (base factor)	96,000
Patent royalties	280,416
Supervisory salaries	168,000
Depreciation on factory equipment	144,000
Factory taxes	56,000
Factory insurance	32,000
Total manufacturing overhead incurred	$1,092,896

Required

Using a flexible budgeting approach, prepare a performance report for the polishing department for April 2016, comparing actual overhead costs with budgeted overhead costs for 4,600 hours. Separate overhead costs into variable and fixed components and show the amounts of any variances between actual and budgeted amounts.

LO4   **P11-2A. Departmental Income Statement** Elgin Flooring Company sells floor coverings through two departments, carpeting and hard covering (tile and linoleum). Operating information for 2016 appears below.

	Carpeting Department	Hard Covering Department
Inventory, January 1, 2016.	$ 60,000	$ 26,000
Inventory, December 31, 2016.	50,000	30,000
Net sales.	780,000	480,000
Purchases.	484,000	362,000
Purchases returns	28,000	8,000
Purchases discounts	16,000	4,000
Transportation in	18,000	14,000
Traceable departmental expenses.	108,000	56,000

Common operating expenses of the firm were $120,000.

Required

a.   Prepare a departmental income statement showing departmental contribution to common expenses and net income of the firm. Assume an overall effective income tax rate of 35%. Elgin uses a periodic inventory system.

b.   Calculate the gross profit percentage for each department.

c.   If the common expenses were allocated 60% to the carpeting department and 40% to the hard covering department, what would the net income be for each department?

LO4   **P11-3A. Departmental Income Statement** The following information was obtained from the ledger of Woodfield Candies, Inc., at the end of 2016:

WOODFIELD CANDIES, INC, Trial Balance December 31, 2016		
	Debit	**Credit**
Cash.	$ 42,000	
Accounts receivable (net).	156,000	
Inventory, December 31, 2016.	180,000	
Equipment and fixtures (net)	540,000	
Accounts payable.		$ 108,000
Common stock.		450,000
Retained earnings		180,000
Revenue—department X		840,000
Revenue—department Y		360,000
Cost of goods sold—department X	420,000	
Cost of goods sold—department Y	216,000	
Sales salaries expense.	192,000	
Advertising expense.	42,000	
Insurance expense.	24,000	
Uncollectible accounts expense	9,000	
Occupancy expense.	36,000	
Office and other administrative expense	81,000	
	$1,938,000	$1,938,000

Woodfield analyzes its operating expenses at the end of each period in order to prepare an income statement that will exhibit departmental contribution to common expenses. From payroll records, advertising copy, and other records, the following tabulation was obtained:

	Traceable Expense		Common Expense
	Dept. X	Dept. Y	
Sales salaries expense.	$147,000	$45,000	
Advertising expense.	18,000	6,000	$18,000
Insurance expense.	15,000	9,000	
Uncollectible accounts expense	6,000	3,000	
Occupancy expense.			36,000
Office and other administrative expense.	12,000	9,000	60,000

Required

Prepare a departmental income statement for Woodfield Candies, Inc., showing departmental contribution to common expenses, assuming an overall income tax rate of 35%.

P11-4A. Departmental Contribution to Common Expenses Certain operating information is shown below for Palmer Department Store:

LO4

SERVICE AND MERCHANDISING

	Department A	Department B	All Other Departments
Sales.	$600,000	$900,000	$2,100,000
Traceable expenses	105,000	165,000	600,000
Common expenses	90,000	120,000	300,000
Gross profit percentage	30%	40%	50%

The managers are disappointed with the operating results of department A. They do not believe that competition will permit raising prices; however, they believe that spending $21,000 more for promoting this department's products will increase the physical volume of products sold by 20%.

An alternative is to discontinue department A and use the space to expand department B. It is believed that department B's physical volume of products sold can thus be increased 37.5%. Special sales personnel are needed, however, and department B's traceable expenses would increase by $90,000. Neither alternative would appreciably affect the total common departmental expense.

Required

a. Calculate the contribution now being made to common expenses by department A, by department B, and by the combination of other departments.

b. Which of the two alternatives should management choose: increase promotional outlays for department A or discontinue department A and expand department B? Support your answer with calculations.

PROBLEMS—SET B

P11-1B. Flexible Budget Application The cutting department of Liberty Manufacturing Company operated during September 2016 with the following manufacturing overhead cost budget based on 6,000 hours of monthly productive capacity:

LO2

MBC

LIBERTY MANUFACTURING COMPANY
Cutting Department
Overhead Budget (6,000 Hours)
for the Month of September 2016

Variable costs:		
Factory supplies	$ 48,000	
Indirect labor.	72,000	
Utilities (usage charge)	36,000	
Patent royalties on secret process	144,000	
Total variable overhead.		$300,000
Fixed costs:		
Supervisory salaries	$ 96,000	
Depreciation on factory equipment	140,000	
Factory taxes	40,000	
Factory insurance	24,000	
Utilities (base charge)	32,000	
Total fixed overhead		$332,000
Total manufacturing overhead		$632,000

The cutting department was operated for 5,500 hours during September and incurred the following manufacturing overhead costs:

Factory supplies	$ 40,400
Indirect labor	67,200
Utilities (usage factor).	38,100
Utilities (base factor).	32,000
Patent royalties.	134,000
Supervisory salaries	96,000
Depreciation on factory equipment	140,000
Factory taxes	43,400
Factory insurance.	27,000
Total manufacturing overhead incurred	$618,100

Required

Using a flexible budgeting approach, prepare a performance report for the cutting department for September 2016, comparing actual overhead costs with budgeted overhead costs for 5,500 hours. Separate overhead costs into variable and fixed components and show the amounts of any variances between actual and budgeted amounts.

LO4 **P11-2B. Departmental Income Statement** Perkins Appliance & Furniture Company has two departments, appliances and furniture. Operating information for 2016 appears below.

	Appliance Department	Furniture Department
Inventory, January 1, 2016.	$ 120,000	$ 90,000
Inventory, December 31, 2016.	75,600	48,000
Net sales.	1,120,000	760,000
Purchases.	640,000	480,000
Purchases discounts	8,000	6,000
Transportation in	18,000	16,000
Traceable departmental expenses.	199,600	82,000

Common operating expenses of the firm were $180,000.

Required

a. Prepare a departmental income statement showing departmental contribution to common expenses and net income of the firm. Assume an overall effective income tax rate of 40%. Perkins uses a periodic inventory system.

b. Calculate the gross profit percentage for each department.

c. If the common expenses were allocated 70% to the appliance department and 30% to the furniture department, what would the net income be for each department?

P11-3B. Departmental Income Statement The following information was obtained from the ledger of Stillwell Emporium, Inc., at the end of 2016:

LO4

STILLWELL EMPORIUM, INC. Trial Balance December 31, 2016		
	Debit	Credit
Cash.	$ 18,000	
Accounts receivable (net).	70,000	
Inventory, December 31, 2016.	45,000	
Equipment and fixtures (net)	97,000	
Accounts payable.		$ 34,000
Common stock.		120,000
Retained earnings		30,000
Sales—department a		360,000
Sales—department b		140,000
Cost of goods sold—department a	216,000	
Cost of goods sold—department b	70,000	
Sales salaries expense.	74,000	
Advertising expense.	31,000	
Insurance expense (on merchandise).	10,000	
Uncollectible accounts expense	3,000	
Occupancy expense.	16,000	
Office and other administrative expense	34,000	
	$684,000	$684,000

Stillwell analyzes its operating expenses at the end of each period in order to prepare an income statement that will exhibit departmental contribution to common expenses. From payroll records, advertising copy, and other records, the following tabulation was obtained:

	Traceable Expense		Common Expense
	Dept. A	Dept. B	
Sales salaries expense.	$48,000	$20,000	$ 6,000
Advertising expense.	15,000	6,000	10,000
Insurance expense.	8,000	2,000	
Occupancy expense.			16,000
Uncollectible accounts expense	2,000	1,000	
Office and other administrative expense	17,000	9,000	8,000

Required

Prepare a departmental income statement for Stillwell Emporium, Inc., showing departmental contribution to common expenses, assuming an overall income tax rate of 30%.

P11-4B. Departmental Contribution to Common Expenses Certain operating information is shown below for Harris Department Store:

LO4

	Department R	Department S	All Other Departments
Sales.	$320,000	$480,000	$1,120,000
Traceable expenses.	56,000	88,000	320,000
Common expenses	48,000	64,000	160,000
Gross profit percentage.	30%	40%	50%

The managers are disappointed with the operating results of department R. They do not believe that competition will permit raising prices; however, they believe that spending $10,000 more for promoting this department's products will increase the physical volume of products sold by 20%.

An alternative is to discontinue department R and use the space to expand department S. It is believed that department S's physical volume of products sold can thus be increased 35%. Special sales personnel are needed, however, and department S's traceable expenses would increase by $48,000. Neither alternative would appreciably affect the total common departmental expense.

Required

a.   Calculate the contribution now being made to common expenses by department R, by department S, and by the combination of other departments.

b.   Which of the two alternatives should management choose: increase promotional outlays for department R, or discontinue department R and expand department S? Support your answer with calculations.

CERTIFIED MANAGEMENT ACCOUNTANT (CMA®) EXAM SAMPLE QUESTIONS

CMA11-1.   Rainbow Inc. recently appointed Margaret Joyce as vice president of finance and asked her to design a new budgeting system. Joyce has changed to a monthly budgeting system by dividing the company's annual budget by twelve. Joyce then prepared monthly budgets for each department and asked the managers to submit monthly reports comparing actual to budget. A sample monthly report for Department A is shown below.

RAINBOW INC. Monthly Report for Department A			
	Actual	**Budget**	**Variance**
Units	1,000	900	100F
Variable production costs			
Direct material.	$ 2,800	$ 2,700	$ 100U
Direct labor	4,800	4,500	300U
Variable factory overhead.	4,250	4,050	200U
Fixed costs			
Depreciation	3,000	2,700	300U
Taxes	1,000	900	100U
Insurance	1,500	1,350	150U
Administration	1,100	990	110U
Marketing	1,000	900	100U
Total costs	$19,450	$18,090	$1,360U

This monthly budget has been imposed from the top and will create behavior problems. All of the following are causes of such problems **except**

a.   the use of a flexible budget rather than a fixed budget.

b.   top management authoritarian attitude toward the budget process.

c.   the inclusion of non-controllable costs such as depreciation.

d.   the lack of consideration for factors such as seasonality.

CMA11-2.   When compared to static budgets, flexible budgets

a.   offer managers a more realistic comparison of budget and actual fixed cost items under their control.

b.   provide a better understanding of the capacity variances during the period being evaluated.

c.   encourage managers to use less fixed costs items and more variable cost items that are under their control.

d.   offer managers a more realistic comparison of budget and actual revenue and cost items under their control.

CMA11-3. Arkin Co.'s controller has prepared a flexible budget for the year just ended, adjusting the original static budget for the unexpected large increase in the volume of sales. Arkin's costs are mostly variable. The controller is pleased to note that both actual revenues and actual costs approximated amounts shown on the flexible budget. If actual revenues and actual costs are compared with amounts shown on the original (static) budget, what variances would arise?

a. Both revenue variances and cost variances would be favorable.
b. Revenue variances would be favorable and cost variances would be unfavorable.
c. Revenue variances would be unfavorable and cost variances would be favorable.
d. Both revenue variances and cost variances would be unfavorable.

CMA11-4. Of the following pairs of variances found in a flexible budget report, which pair is **most likely** to be related?

a. Material price variance and variable overhead efficiency variance.
b. Labor rate variance and variable overhead efficiency variance.
c. Material usage variance and labor efficiency variance.
d. Labor efficiency variance and fixed overhead volume variance.

CMA11-5. Sara Bellows, manager of the telecommunication sales team, has the following department budget.

Billings—long distance.	$350,000
Billings—phone card	75,000
Billings—toll free.	265,000

Her responsibility center is **best** described as a

a. cost center.
b. revenue center.
c. profit center.
d. investment center.

EXTENDING YOUR KNOWLEDGE

EYK11-1. **Business Decision Case** The monthly sales volume of Shugart Corporation varies from 7,000 units to 9,800 units over the course of a year. Management is currently studying anticipated selling expenses along with the related cash resources that will be needed. Which type of budget (flexible or static) (1) should be used by Shugart in planning, and (2) will provide Shugart the best feedback in performance reports for comparing planned expenditures with actual amounts? When Shugart's CEO asks you why it is advantageous to use a flexible budget instead of a static budget, what is one example you could give him?

EYK11-2. **Ethics Case** CJ Corporation manufactures steel rebar for use in construction. The accounting staff is currently preparing next year's budget. Bob Johnson is new to the firm and is interested in learning how this process occurs. He has lunch with the sales manager and the production manager to discuss further the planning process. Over the course of lunch, Bob discovers that the sales manager adjusts sales projections between a flexible amount and a static amount based on which will reflect the lowest variance from actual results. The production manager does the same for cost estimates. Both managers' year-end bonus is determined based on how low of a variance is achieved. When Bob asks about why they adjust their projections between flexible and static budgets, the response is simply that everyone around here does it.

Required
a. What do the sales and production managers hope to accomplish by their methods?
b. How might this backfire and work against them?
c. Are the actions of the sales and production managers unethical?

ANSWERS TO SELF-STUDY QUESTIONS

1. c, (p. 385)   2. a, (p. 389)   3. c, (pp. 386–387)   4. c, (p. 394)   5. c, (p. 394)

YOUR TURN! SOLUTIONS

Solution 11.1
PACCAR Parts segment, Trucks segment, and Financial Services segment.

Solution 11.2

Revenue	$600,000
Traceable departmental expenses:	
Direct materials.	$30,000
Direct labor	25,000
Other traceable expenses.	40,000
Department contribution	$505,000
Common expenses.	**155,000**
Departmental operating income.	$350,000

DECISION TIME SOLUTION

Solution 11.1

A CPA firm's balanced scorecard might include some of the following measures:

Financial Performance
Segment margin by practice area (tax, audit, consulting)
Average collection period by practice area
Revenue by partner

Customer Satisfaction
Summary of customer satisfaction survey results
Percentage of repeat customers
Average number of years completing customer tax returns

Internal Business Processes
Ratio of new sales to billings for the period
Ratio of chargeable hours to total available hours by staff level
Ratio of billable hours to hours (actually) charged

Learning and Growth
Average number of annual continuing education hours
Partner-to-staff ratio
Average number of community service hours per staff

12

Capital Budgeting

LEARNING OBJECTIVES

WASTE MANAGEMENT

If you have ever thrown away trash in the United States, there is a greater than 50% chance that either Waste Management (WM) or its chief competitor, Republic Services, Inc., handled the garbage collection. WM is the largest environmental solutions provider in North America, serving more than 20 million customers in the United States and Canada. The company has reason to boast, as it has the largest network of recycling facilities, transfer stations, and landfills in the industry. The network includes 367 collection operations, 355 transfer stations, 273 active landfill disposal sites, 16 waste-to-energy plants, 134 recycling plants, 111 beneficial-use landfill projects, and 6 independent power production plants. It also boasts the largest trucking fleet in the United States. How did WM grow to dominance in this industry?

WM was formed in 1968 and began aggressively purchasing many of the smaller garbage collection companies across the United States. The company went public in 1971 and within a year had made 133 acquisitions, with over $82 million in revenue. In the 1980s, WM continued its aggressive expansion and acquired Service Corporation of America to become the largest waste hauler in the country. Current company projections include managing more than 20 million tons every year by 2020, up from the more than 12 million tons the company handled in 2012.

Behind every capital expenditure at WM is a team dedicated to evaluating new opportunities. With explosive growth and seemingly continuous capital expenditure opportunities, it is no surprise that the company would dedicate a full team to expansion. The current facilities that WM operates require additional capital outlays to upgrade or replace old equipment and buildings and close and maintain old landfills. In addition, expenditures are needed for new equipment and buildings to accommodate the company's growth strategy. When analyzing capital expenditures, the Waste Management team calculates the company's cost of capital to determine whether a proposed project can generate value for shareholders. If the cost of capital cannot be achieved through the cash flows generated by the newly acquired capital, the company rejects the project.

For example, in the early 2000s, a joint-powers authority that included four jurisdictions in northern California issued a request for proposal for garbage and recycling collection services. WM (including its predecessor company) had been providing these services for many decades. When the proposals were received and evaluated, WM's proposal was the most expensive. WM representatives reported that the proposed amount was the amount required to meet the cost of capital threshold established by the corporate office. As a result, the new contract was offered to one of WM's competitors.

```
┌─────────────────────────────────────────────────────────────────────────────────┐
│                          CAPITAL BUDGETING                                        │
└─────────────────────────────────────────────────────────────────────────────────┘
```

The Elements of Capital Budgeting	Performing Net Present Value Calculations	Net Present Value Analysis	Time Value of Money Calculations (Appendix 12A)
• Capital budgeting phases • Capital expenditure analysis	• Single-sum cash flows • Annuity flows	• Basic steps • Illustration of NPV analysis • Liquidation proceeds • Excess PV index	• Using a financial calculator • Using an electronic spreadsheet

Required Rates of Return and the Time Value of Money	Measurements of Investments and Returns	Other Capital Budgeting Analyses
• Cost of capital • Time value of money	• Cash flows • After-tax cash flows • Depreciation tax shield • Cash flow illustration • Summary	• Cash payback analysis • Average rate of return analysis

Planning long-term investments in productive assets is known as **capital budgeting**. The term reflects the fact that for most firms the total cost of all attractive investment opportunities exceeds the available investment capital. Thus, management must ration, or budget, investment capital among competing investment proposals. In deciding which new long-term assets to acquire, management must seek investments that promise to optimize return on the funds employed.

Capital budgeting is most valuable for organizations in which managers are responsible for the long-term profitability of their area of concern and are therefore encouraged to develop new products and more efficient production processes. Firms often make their most capable employees responsible for capital budgeting decisions, because such decisions determine how large sums of money are invested and commit the firm for extended future periods. Furthermore, investment decision errors are often difficult and costly to remedy or abandon.

Managers as well as accountants should be familiar with the special analytical techniques that evaluate the relative attractiveness of alternative uses of available capital. In this chapter, we first discuss the nature and procedures of capital budgeting, how required investment earning rates are determined, the time value of money, and the effect of income taxes on capital expenditure decisions. We conclude by illustrating three approaches to capital expenditure analysis: the net present value method, the cash payback method, and the average rate of return method.

ELEMENTS OF CAPITAL BUDGETING

LO1 Introduce and illustrate the elements of capital budgeting.

Capital Budgeting Phases

Capital budgeting has three phases:

1. Identify potential investments,
2. Select investments to be undertaken, and
3. Monitor the selected investments.

Many firms have a capital budgeting calendar calling for consideration of capital expenditure proposals at regular intervals, for example, every 6 months or every year. Proposals are usually examined with respect to (1) compliance with capital budget policies and procedures; (2) aspects of operational urgency, such as the need to replace critical equipment; (3) established criteria for minimum return on capital investments; and, (4) consistency with the firm's operating policies and long-term goals. Proposals for relatively small cash outlays may require the approval of low-level management only, whereas major proposals are subject to approval at high management levels, perhaps including the board of directors. These major proposals and the decisions based on them profoundly affect a firm's long-term success.

Once approved, capital expenditures should be monitored to ensure that amounts and purposes are consistent with the original proposal. At appropriate intervals, the actual rates of return earned on important expenditures should be compared with projected rates. These periodic reviews encourage those responsible to formulate thorough and realistic proposals, and often provide an incentive for improving overall capital budgeting procedures.

Hint: Inventory and other current asset purchases are not capital expenditures, even though they are commonly referred to as working "capital."

Capital Expenditure Analysis

The scope of capital expenditures varies widely, ranging from the routine replacement of production equipment to the construction of entire manufacturing complexes. Whatever their size, most capital expenditure projects have the three stages shown in **Exhibit 12-1**.

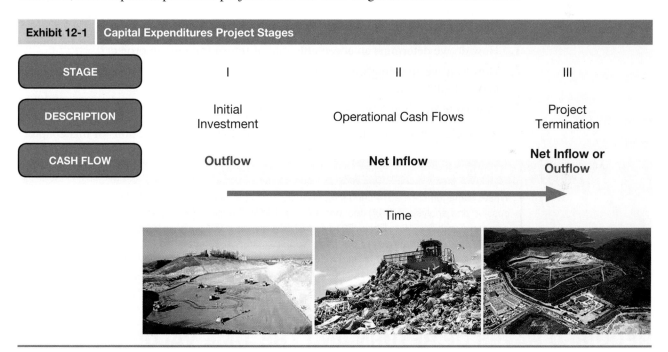

Exhibit 12-1	Capital Expenditures Project Stages

STAGE	I	II	III
DESCRIPTION	Initial Investment	Operational Cash Flows	Project Termination
CASH FLOW	Outflow	Net Inflow	Net Inflow or Outflow

Time

Initial investment (stage I) consists of a net cash outlay for a project or an asset. Net operational cash flows during the life of the project (stage II) may result from either an excess of periodic cash revenues over related cash expenditures or a periodic saving in some cash expenditure. Finally, the termination of a project (stage III) often results in some amount of liquidation proceeds from the sale of the project capital or could result in some cash outlay for the removal of the project or restoration of the property to its former condition.

For example, the development of a new WM municipal waste landfill (stage I) requires millions of dollars for the purchase of the property, performance of the necessary environmental studies, obtainment of land use approvals and permits, and the development of appropriate access roads, gatehouse and vehicle scales, administrative buildings, security fencing, and environmental protection systems.

Over the life of the landfill (stage II), WM will collect cash fees from users of the landfill and expend cash for the compacting and covering of the trash and the monitoring, collection, and treatment of liquids and methane gas created by the decomposing waste.

Finally, once the landfill reaches its permitted capacity, WM must close the landfill (stage III), applying a final cap on the waste, and then monitor, collect, and treat the liquids and methane gas created by the decomposing waste for a period of 30 to 40 years.

The attractiveness of a particular investment is determined in large part by the quantitative relationship between the cash investment in stage I and the net cash receipts expected in stages II and III. In its simplest form, this relationship is usually expressed as a ratio known as the **rate of return**:

$$\text{Rate of return} = \frac{\text{Returns}}{\text{Investment}}$$

All other things being equal, the higher the expected rate of return, the more attractive the investment opportunity. Proposed investments can be ranked according to their expected rates of return, and capital outlays can be allocated among the most attractive investments. Capital expenditure analysis consists of judging the attractiveness of income-producing or cost-saving opportunities in relation to required investments. The results of this analysis are among the most important input data in capital budgeting decisions.

Three questions are of considerable concern in capital budgeting:

1. How do we determine an acceptable rate of return for a given project?

2. How can we meaningfully compare investments made now with returns to be received in the future?

3. In what terms should investments and returns be measured?

These challenging problems are considered in the following sections of this chapter.

ACCOUNTING IN PRACTICE | **Capital Budgeting in Growing a Company**

Waste Management's 2014 annual report includes the following on page 67 of the management discussion and analysis (MD&A) section: "We used $1,271 million during 2013 for capital expenditures, compared with $1,510 million in 2012 and $1,324 million in 2011. The increase in capital expenditures in 2012 and 2011 is a result of our increased spending on compressed natural gas vehicles, related fueling infrastructure, and information technology infrastructure and growth initiatives, as well as our taking advantage of the bonus depreciation legislation."

REQUIRED RATES OF RETURN AND THE TIME VALUE OF MONEY

The mix of capital sources (i.e., available cash or proceeds from new debt or equity) that a company uses will depend on market conditions as well as the philosophies of the members of the board of directors and the management team.

LO2 Discuss required rates of return and the time value of money.

Cost of Capital

In determining an acceptable rate of return for a given project, we must consider not only the initial capital outlay, but also all of the costs associated with the acquisition of that capital. The parties providing the funds expect to be reasonably compensated for their use. When the money is borrowed from a bank or through a bond issuance, the interest paid by the firm is a cost of using the funds. When stockholder funds are used, we assume that some combination of dividend payments and increase in the value of the capital stock compensates stockholders for furnishing the investment capital. The cost to the firm of acquiring the funds used in capital investment projects—typically expressed as an annual percentage rate—is called the **cost of capital**.

A firm may acquire capital by issuing preferred or common stock, using retained earnings, borrowing, or some combination of these. Consequently, the overall cost of capital for a given project should reflect the cost rates of the several sources of funds in proportion to the amounts obtained from each source. This is called the **weighted average cost of capital**, or **WACC**.

Assume that a particular company had acquired capital through all four sources and in the proportions and with the cost of capital rates as shown here:

Hint: Because the earnings retained by the firm might otherwise have been distributed to the common shareholders in the form of dividends, firms often use the same cost of capital for retained earnings as is used for common stock.

Source of Capital	Percentage of Total	×	Cost of Capital Rate	=	Weighted Average Cost of Capital Component
Debt	40%	×	8%	=	3.2%
Preferred stock	10%	×	9%	=	0.9%
Common stock	20%	×	12%	=	2.4%
Retained earnings	30%	×	12%	=	3.6%
Weighted average cost of capital . . .					10.1%

Multiplying the percentage of each capital source by its cost of capital rate provides weighted cost factors whose sum is the weighted average cost of capital. This percentage (in this case, 10.1%) can then be used to compare the attractiveness of proposed investments.

TAKEAWAY 12.1

The cost of capital is calculated based on all sources of financing, including both debt financing and equity financing.

Logically, for a capital investment to be considered favorably by a firm, its expected rate of return must be at least as high as the cost of capital. Therefore, the cost of capital represents a minimum required rate of return, or **hurdle rate**. In other words, a firm whose cost of capital is 10% will ordinarily want to invest only in an asset or project whose expected rate of return is more than 10%. An investment whose return is less than the cost of capital would be economically detrimental, although firms sometimes disregard their cost of capital if qualitative considerations override the quantitative aspects of the decision. Qualitative considerations might include the desire to achieve certain environmental goals, the desire to maintain research leadership in the industry, and the need to maintain full employment of the work force during a business slowdown.

Some firms consider only investments whose rates of return are at least a certain number of percentage points higher than the cost of capital. This **buffer margin** acts as a safety factor, because proposals that project estimated cash inflows and outflows years into the future have a significant amount of uncertainty regarding the amount and timing of those cash flows. Of course, in an environment of limited resources, even proposals whose expected rate of return is higher than the hurdle rate may be rejected if other investment opportunities offer still higher returns.

YOUR TURN! 12.1

The solution is on page 464.

The following sources of financing, their proportions, and their cost of capital rates are for a merchandising company. Calculate and interpret the WACC for this company.

	Percentage of Total	Cost of Capital Rate
Bank loan	45%	12%
Equity capital	55%	9%

Time Value of Money

We have seen that in determining the desirability of a proposed capital investment, management compares the amount of investment required at the beginning of a project with its expected returns—typically a series of returns extending several years into the future. This comparison, which is so important in capital budgeting decisions, cannot be made properly using the absolute amounts of the future returns because money has a time value. The **time value of money** means that the right to receive an amount of money today is worth more than the right to receive the same amount at some future date, because a current receipt can be invested to earn interest over the intervening period. Thus, if 10% annual interest can be obtained on investments, $100 received today is equal in value to $110 received 1 year from now. One year from now, today's $100 has a future value of $110; conversely, the present value of a $110 receipt expected 1 year from today is $100.

The difference between present and future values is a function of interest rates and time periods. The higher the interest rate or longer the time period involved, the higher the amount by which a future value is reduced, or discounted, in deriving its present value. For example, **Exhibit 12-2** shows just how significant the time value of money can be at various interest rates and time periods. As the table indicates, 5 years from now $100 has a present value of $78, $62, or $50 if the applicable interest rates are 5%, 10%, and 15%, respectively. Note also that the higher the time period or the interest rate, the larger the difference between the future value of $100 and its present value. Comparing a current investment with its future returns without discounting the returns to their present value would substantially overstate the economic significance of the returns. We must therefore recognize the time value of money in capital budgeting procedures.

Exhibit 12-2	Time Value of Money		
Present Value of $100 **(Rounded to Nearest Dollar)**			
		Rate	
Years	**5%**	**10%**	**15%**
1	$95	$91	$87
2	91	83	76
3	86	75	66
4	82	68	57
5	78	62	50
10	61	39	25
20	38	15	6
30	23	6	2
40	14	2	0
50	9	1	0

Techniques for discounting future cash flows to their present values apply to both cash receipts and cash outlays. In other words, the current value of the right to receive—or the current value of the obligation to pay—a sum in the future is its present value computed at an appropriate interest rate. We maximize our economic position by arranging to receive amounts as early as possible and postponing amounts to be paid as long as possible. These generalizations will be apparent in the capital budgeting illustrations later in the chapter.

TAKEAWAY 12.2

Discounted cash flows (DCFs) focus on cash receipts and cash payments, not on net income as computed on an accrual basis.

PERFORMING NET PRESENT VALUE CALCULATIONS

Present value tables simplify our work considerably in computing present values. These tables provide factors for combinations of time periods and interest rates that may be multiplied by a stream of cash flows or a one-time future cash flow to determine its present value. In this chapter we demonstrate how to do these calculations using factors from present value tables. These tables can be found in Appendix A of the text, along with a more detailed discussion of time value of money concepts. In Appendix 12A we demonstrate how to use a financial calculator and an Excel spreadsheet to perform those same calculations.

LO3 **Demonstrate** the use of present value factors to perform time value of money calculations.

Throughout the chapter, the following abbreviations, related to time value of money calculations, are used:

> PV = present value at time 0
> FV = future value at time N
> i = interest at which the amount compounds each period
> N = number of periods (time)
> PMT = periodic cash flow (payment)

Single-Sum Cash Flows

Let us first consider how to compute the present value of a single-sum cash flow. This calculation will be used to determine the present value of sporadic cash flows when the returns expected on an investment, or the expenditures it requires, are unequal amounts or are expected at irregular intervals during or at the end of the life of the investment.

To illustrate, we assume that an investment project promises a return of $2,000 at the end of 2 years and another $1,000 at the end of 5 years. The desired rate of return is 10% per year. **Exhibit 12-3** illustrates the cash flows on a timeline.

Exhibit 12-3	Calculating the Present Vsalue of a Lump Sum

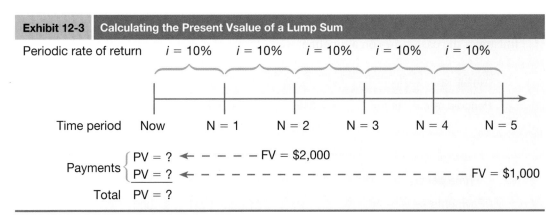

Using factors from Table III, Present Value of $1, from Appendix A, we calculate the present value of each cash flow separately using the following process.

First, calculate the present value of the $2,000 cash flow. The formula for calculating the present value of a future sum is as follows:

> **Present value (PV) = Future value (FV) × PV table factor***
>
> PV = $2,000 × 0.82645
> PV = $1,652.90

*Because the $2,000 cash flow occurs at the end of Year 2, we use the factor associated with a 10% rate of return and 2 years (0.82645; see Table III in Appendix A).

This value may be interpreted as the amount that, if invested today in an account paying 10% interest, would allow for the withdrawal of $2,000 at the end of 2 years. This can be proved as follows: $1,652.90 invested today would earn $165.29 in interest in the first year, for a total value of $1,818.19 ($1,652.90 + $165.29). This balance would earn $181.82 in interest in the second year, for a total value of $2,000.01 ($1,818.19 + $181.82).

Next, calculate the present value of the $1,000 cash flow:

> **PV = FV × PV table factor***
>
> PV = $1,000 × 0.62092
> PV = $620.92

*Because the $1,000 cash flow occurs at the end of Year 5, we use the factor from a present value table for a single amount associated with a 10% rate of return and 5 years (0.62092; see Table III in Appendix A).

This value may be interpreted as the amount that, if invested today in an account paying 10% interest, would allow for the withdrawal of $1,000 at the end of 5 years.

The total present value of the combined flows is $2,273.82 ($1,652.90 + $620.92). That is, $2,273.82 invested today in an account paying 10% interest would allow withdrawal of $2,000 at the end of 2 years and $1,000 at the end of 5 years.

YOUR TURN! 12.2

The solution is on page 464.

An investment project promises a return of $2,000 at the end of 3 years and $4,000 at the end of 4 years. If the company's cost of capital is 12%, what is the total present value of these cash flows?

Annuity Flows

Let us next consider how to compute the present value of an annuity. An **annuity** is cash flows that are the same each period over two or more equal periods.

To illustrate, we assume that a project has expected cash inflows of $1,000 at the end of each of the next three periods, and 8% is the appropriate cost of capital. **Exhibit 12-4** illustrates the cash flows on a timeline.

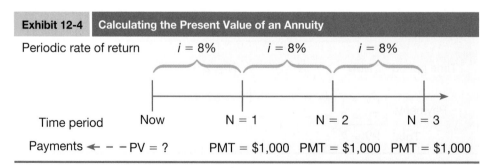

| Exhibit 12-4 | Calculating the Present Value of an Annuity |

Using factors from Table IV, Present Value of an Ordinary Annuity of $1 per Period, from Appendix A, we calculate the present value of these cash flows using the following formula:

> **PV = PMT × PV table factor***
>
> PV = $1,000 × 2.57710
> PV = $2,577.10

*Because the $1,000 cash flow occurs at the end of each year for 3 years, we use the factor associated with an 8% rate of return and 3 years (2.57710; see Table IV in Appendix A).

This value may be interpreted as the amount that, if invested today in an account paying 8% interest annually, would allow for the withdrawal of $1,000 at the end of each year for the next 3 years. This can be proved as follows: $2,577.10 invested today would earn $206.17 ($2,577.10 × 0.08) in interest in the first year, for a total value of $2,783.27 ($2,577.10 + $206.17). A withdrawal of $1,000 would leave a balance of $1,783.27. This balance would earn $142.66 ($1,783.27 × 0.08) in interest in the second year, for a total value of $1,925.93 ($1,783.27 + $142.66). A second withdrawal of $1,000 would leave a balance of $925.93. This balance would earn $74.07 ($925.93 × 0.08) in interest in the third year, for a total value of $1,000 ($925.93 + $74.07), allowing for a third and final withdrawal of $1,000.

Both illustrations assume that all cash flows occur at the end of the periods. This assumption is somewhat simplistic, because cash receipts or cost savings from most industrial investments occur in a steady stream throughout the operating periods. Nevertheless, businesses assume end-of-period cash flows for ease of use. These calculations will understate the present values of flows that are gradual throughout the period, because the present values of cash flows early in the period are higher than similar inflows or outlays at the end of the period. The difference, however, is normally not material.

An investment project promises a return of $5,000 at the end of each of the next 7 years. If the company's cost of capital is 6%, what is the total present value of these cash flows?

YOUR TURN! 12.3

The solution is on page 464.

MEASUREMENT OF INVESTMENTS AND RETURNS

Cash Flows

When present value analysis is used to make investment decisions, investments and returns must be stated in the form of cash flows. Present value determinations are basically interest calculations, and therefore only money amounts—cash flows—are properly used in interest calculations. Furthermore, only the *incremental* cash flows that will occur if the project is accepted should be considered in the analysis.

LO4 Explain and illustrate the determination of after-tax cash flows.

Typically, financial data available in the accounts are not stated in terms of cash flows because accrual-basis accounting is used. Amounts compiled on the accrual basis must be restated in terms of the appropriate cash flows for capital budgeting purposes. For example, apportioning the cost of an asset over its life through depreciation accounting is an important feature of accrual accounting. When present value analysis is used, the cost of an asset is treated as a cash outlay when the asset is paid for. In measuring future returns related to the asset, depreciation expense does not represent a cash outlay. However, depreciation expense affects cash flows indirectly by reducing cash outlays for income tax payments.

Likewise, earnings from projects should reflect the cash inflows rather than the revenue amounts computed using accrual accounting. The timing of the cash collections is important, too, because the essence of present value analysis is that cash received can be reinvested.

After-Tax Cash Flows

Both federal and state income taxes are important to investment decisions; for some companies, the combined federal and state income tax rate may approach 40%. Generally, income taxes reduce the economic significance of taxable receipts and deductible expenditures.

Exhibit 12-5	Tax Impact on Cash Flows		
		Inflow	**Outflow**
Pre-tax amount.		$40,000	$(15,000)
Income tax rate		40%	40%
Tax benefit/(expense)		(16,000)	6,000
After-tax amount		24,000	(9,000)

As illustrated in **Exhibit 12-5**, assuming a 40% tax rate, a $40,000 before-tax gain (cash inflow) would increase taxable income by $40,000 and income taxes by $16,000 (40% × $40,000), resulting in a $24,000 after-tax cash inflow. A $15,000 before-tax expense would reduce taxable income by $15,000 and income taxes by $6,000 (40% × $15,000), resulting in a $9,000 after-tax cash outflow. In general terms, the formulas for determining after-tax cash flows are as follows:

After-tax cash inflow = Pre-tax cash inflow × (1 − tax rate)

After-tax cash outflow = Pre-tax cash outflow × (1 − tax rate)

After-tax cash flows are more relevant than before-tax cash flows because they represent the amounts available to retire debt, finance expansions, or pay dividends. For this reason, investment decision analyses must be formulated in terms of after-tax cash flows.

Depreciation Tax Shield

Depreciation deductions *shield* revenues from taxation and thus reduce the taxes a company must pay. Depreciation creates a tax savings. **Exhibit 12-6** illustrates how to compute the amount of tax savings created by depreciation.

Exhibit 12-6	Tax Impact of Depreciation	
		Inflow
Pre-tax amount.		$30,000
Income tax rate		40%
Tax benefit/(expense).		12,000

To understand this effect, assume that a company had taxable revenues of $30,000 and no expenses. Assuming a 40% tax rate, this company would owe $12,000 in tax ($30,000 × 40%). Now, assume that the company had one deductible expense: depreciation in the amount of $30,000. In this case, the company would owe no taxes, because it can deduct the depreciation expense from its taxable revenue ($30,000 − $30,000 = $0 taxable income). Thus, the depreciation saved the company from having to pay $12,000 in tax. The formula for determining the tax shield is as follows:

After-tax depreciation tax shield = Depreciation expense × Tax rate

Illustration of After-Tax Cash Flows

Thinking in terms of after-tax cash flows represents a significant departure from the accrual-based accounting for revenue and expenses. However, remember that the pre-tax cash flows are available to us in the cash flow statement. We can use our understanding of the cash flow statement to determine the after-tax cash flows needed for capital budgeting and other time value of money analyses.

To explore the relationship between the traditional income statement and the related after-tax cash flows, let's revisit Fezzari's 2016 income statement from Chapter 9. **Exhibit 12-7** shows Fezzari's income statement in column A. Column B identifies the related cash flows from Fezzari's cash flow statement. An understanding of **Exhibit 12-7** will provide a basis for understanding the comprehensive illustration of capital budgeting later in the chapter.

Column A in **Exhibit 12-7** is the traditional income statement, showing that revenue minus operating expenses and income taxes results in a net income of $446,179. For simplicity, we assume that revenue and cash expenses involve no significant accruals and that depreciation is the same on both the books and the tax return. Ordinarily, net income does not represent after-tax cash flows because depreciation expense—a noncash expense—is deducted to derive net income. As indicated in column A of **Exhibit 12-7**, to convert the $446,179 net income to after-tax cash flow, we must add back the depreciation of $45,100, resulting in $491,279 of after-tax cash flow.

Exhibit 12-7	Illustration of Determining After-Tax Cash Flows

Fezzari Performance Bicycles
For the Period Ended December 31, 2016

	A	B	C
	Traditional Income Statement	Income Statement Cash Inflows (Outflows)	Individual After-Tax Cash Inflow (Outflow) Effects
Sales.	$6,237,000	$6,237,000	$ 4,054,050
Less: Cost of goods sold (excluding depreciation) . . .	4,723,621	(4,723,621)	$(3,070,354)
Less: Depreciation expense.	45,100		15,785
Gross profit.	$1,468,279		
Less: Selling and administrative expense	776,850	(776,850)	$ (504,952)
Income from operations.	$ 691,429		
Less: Interest expense.	5,000	(5,000)	$ (3,250)
Income before income taxes	$ 686,429		
Less: Income taxes	240,250	(240,250)	
Net income.	$ 446,179		
Add back depreciation expense.	45,100		
After-tax cash flow.	$ 491,279	$ 491,279	$ 491,279

Column B of **Exhibit 12-7** confirms the $491,279 amount of after-tax cash flow determined in column A. This is accomplished by simply listing the amounts in column A that constitute cash inflows (revenue of $6,237,000) and cash outflows (cash expenses of

$4,723,621, $776,850, and $5,000 and income tax payments of $240,250). Depreciation is excluded because it does not represent a cash payment.

Column C in **Exhibit 12-7** illustrates the determination of the individual amounts of after-tax cash flows for each item on the income statement. We use this approach in the comprehensive illustration of capital budgeting appearing later in the chapter. Amounts in column C are determined as follows (again, a 35% income tax rate is assumed).

Receipt of $6,237,000 cash revenue
Receipt of $6,237,000 cash revenue would, by itself, increase taxable income by $6,237,000, adding $2,182,950 ($6,237,000 × 35%) to income taxes. The $4,054,050 after-tax cash inflow is the difference between the $6,237,000 cash revenue received and the related $2,182,950 increase in income taxes (a cash outflow). Applying the previous formula for an after-tax inflow results in the same amount:

After-tax cash inflow = Pre-tax cash inflow × (1 − Tax rate)

OR

$4,054,050 = $6,237,000 × (1 − 0.35)

Payment of $4,723,621 in cash operating expenses
Payment of $4,723,621 in cash operating expenses represents a deductible cash outflow that reduces taxable income by $4,723,621 and thus reduces income taxes by $1,653,267 ($4,723,621 × 35%). The $3,070,354 net cash outflow is the difference between the $4,723,621 actually paid out for expenses and the $1,653,267 of income tax payments avoided by virtue of the tax deductibility of the expenses. Applying the previous formula for an after-tax outflow results in the same amount:

After-tax cash outflow = Pre-tax cash outflow × (1 − Tax rate)

OR

$3,070,354 = $4,723,621 × (1 − 0.35)

Notice that *avoiding a cash outflow* has the same effect on net cash flows as a cash inflow. In other words, total net cash inflows can be increased by adding to cash inflows or by avoiding cash outflows.

Recording $45,100 of depreciation expense
Although depreciation expense is tax deductible, no related cash expenditure occurs during the period. The $45,100 deduction reduces taxable income by $45,100 and income taxes by $15,785 ($45,100 × 35%). Depreciation expense and similar noncash expense deductions are often referred to as *tax shields* because they shield an equal amount of income from whatever income tax rate is applicable.

Payment of $776,850 in cash selling and administrative expenses
Payment of $776,850 in cash selling and administrative expenses represents a deductible cash outflow that reduces taxable income by $776,850 and thus reduces income taxes by $271,898 ($776,850 × 35%). The $504,952 net cash outflow is the difference between the $776,850 actually paid out for expenses and the $271,898 of income tax payments avoided by virtue of the tax deductibility of the expenses. Applying the previous formula for an after-tax outflow results in the same amount:

After-tax cash outflow = Pre-tax cash outflow × (1 − Tax rate)

OR

$504,952* = $776,850 × (1 − 0.35)

Hint: The depreciation amount that provides a tax shield is the depreciation deduction on the tax return. Tax depreciation deductions are governed by tax regulations, not by generally accepted accounting principles. Often the periodic tax depreciation will differ from depreciation expense on the income statement (in Exhibit 12-7 we assume that the amounts are equal). When identifying the depreciation tax shield in capital budgeting analysis, then, it is important to use the depreciation amount from the tax return.

* Difference due to rounding.

Payment of $5,000 in cash interest expense

Payment of $5,000 in cash interest expense represents a deductible cash outflow that reduces taxable income by $5,000 and thus reduces income taxes by $1,750 ($5,000 × 35%). The $3,250 net cash outflow is the difference between the $5,000 actually paid out for interest expense and the $1,750 of income tax payments avoided by virtue of the tax deductibility of the expense. Applying the previous formula for an after-tax outflow results in the same amount:

$$\textbf{After-tax cash outflow = Pre-tax cash outflow} \times \textbf{(1 − Tax rate)}$$

OR

$$\textbf{\$3,250 = \$5,000} \times \textbf{(1 − 0.35)}$$

Combining the after-tax cash flow effect of each individual amount in column C again confirms that net cash inflows total $491,279.

Summary of Concerns Underlying Capital Budgeting

1. The typical investment pattern involves a present investment of funds resulting in anticipated returns, often extending years into the future.

2. The basic question in capital budgeting is whether present investments are justified by related future returns.

3. Because money has a time value, returns that occur in the future must be discounted to their present values for a proper comparison with present investments.

4. To use discounting (interest) calculations properly, we must state amounts in capital budgeting analyses in terms of cash flows.

5. Because income tax rates are substantial, capital budgeting analyses should be formulated in terms of after-tax cash flows.

Thus far in the chapter, we have presented a number of important aspects of capital budgeting as background for the review of several approaches to capital expenditure analysis. These background materials have focused on the analytical concept known as net present value. Accountants generally concede that the net present value approach is conceptually and analytically superior to the other two approaches that we will also illustrate: cash payback and average rate of return.

NET PRESENT VALUE ANALYSIS

Basic Steps

The basic approach to the **net present value method** is shown in **Exhibit 12-8**. Each step described here and used in the example that follows is color coded to correspond to the exhibit. Referring to the items in the exhibit, the steps in the net present value approach are to:

LO5 Describe the net present value method of capital expenditure analysis.

Step 1: Determine the amount of the **investment outlay** required in terms of incremental after-tax cash flows.

Step 2: Estimate the amounts and timing of **future operating receipts or cost savings** in terms of incremental after-tax cash flows.

Step 3: Estimate any **incremental after-tax liquidation proceeds** to be received on termination of the project.

Step 4: Discount all future cash flows to their **present value** at an appropriate interest rate, usually the minimum desired rate of return on capital.

Step 5: Subtract the investment outlay from the total present value of future cash flows to determine **net present value.** If net present value is zero or positive (returns equal or exceed investment), then the project's rate of return equals or exceeds the minimum desired rate and should be accepted. Negative net present values indicate that the project's return is less than desired, and the project should be rejected.

ACCOUNTING IN PRACTICE

Undertaking Negative-NPV Projects

There are reasons companies may follow through with a capital investment even though it has a projected negative NPV. Reasons for this include projects that support other projects, hope that the investment will return more than originally expected, response to competition, and response to government regulations. These and other qualitative factors should be considered by management.

Exhibit 12-8	Net Present Value Method Approach

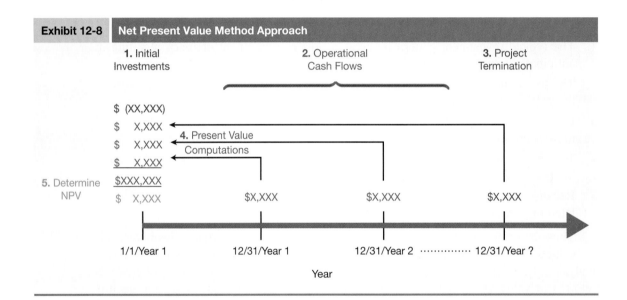

Illustration of Net Present Value Analysis

To illustrate net present value analysis, assume that Fezzari owns its bicycle assembly facility. The building is 30 years old, and its heating, ventilating, and air-conditioning (HVAC) systems are functioning, but significantly out of date. A local HVAC contractor has told Fezzari management that new HVAC technology could significantly reduce Fezzari's monthly utility bill. The HVAC contractor has offered to replace the current HVAC system with a new, state-of-the-art system for an installed price of $150,000. The new system has an expected useful life of 20 years, at which point it will be worthless, but it will save an estimated $22,500 per year in cash utilities expenses during its useful life. Fezzari management has a minimum desired return of 10% on any capital project. Fezzari's tax rate is 35%.

To evaluate the local contractor's proposal, management decides to use a net present value analysis.

Recall that depreciation is based on the depreciation deduction from the tax return. Based on a half-year convention (one-half of the first year's depreciation is recognized in the year of acquisition and disposition), the annual depreciation (rounded to the nearest dollar) would be computed as follows:

Year	Capitalized Cost	Depreciation Rate	Annual Depreciation*
1	$150,000	3.750%	$ 5,625
2	150,000	7.219	10,829
3	150,000	6.677	10,016
4	150,000	6.177	9,266
5	150,000	5.713	8,570
6	150,000	5.285	7,928
7	150,000	4.888	7,332
8	150,000	4.522	6,783
9	150,000	4.462	6,693
10	150,000	4.461	6,692
11	150,000	4.462	6,693
12	150,000	4.461	6,692
13	150,000	4.462	6,693
14	150,000	4.461	6,692
15	150,000	4.462	6,693
16	150,000	4.461	6,692
17	150,000	4.462	6,693
18	150,000	4.461	6,692
19	150,000	4.462	6,693
20	150,000	4.461	6,692
21	150,000	2.231	3,347

*Tax return depreciation, 150% declining balance, half-year convention.

Exhibit 12-9 presents a net present value analysis of the HVAC system as an investment project. Note that the format (including the color coding) follows the analysis outlined in **Exhibit 12-8**: Future returns are stated in terms of after-tax cash flows; then the present values of future cash flows are determined and compared with the investment. The computations shown in **Exhibit 12-9** are explained in the following subsections.

Step 1: Initial investment
The initial investment of $150,000 occurs at the beginning of Year 1, which we identify as Year 0. It is shown in **Exhibit 12-9** as a negative number, signifying that it represents an outflow of cash.

Step 2: Annual cash flows (expense savings)
Cash savings or expense reductions have the same effects as cash revenue, income, or gains. Thus, these amounts are shown as positive amounts, signifying that they represent an inflow of cash. They also have the same consequence of increasing income taxes. In our example, saving $22,500 in cash expenses each year raises taxable income by $22,500, which leads to an increase in taxes of $7,875 ($22,500 × 35%). Thus, the annual after-tax cash flow is $14,625—the $22,500 savings less the $7,875 tax increase.

Annual depreciation tax shield: The depreciation deduction on the tax return shields an equal amount of income from taxes. The avoided taxes are equal to the depreciation deduction multiplied by the applicable tax rate. In our illustration, the annual tax savings from the depreciation tax shield are as follows:

Exhibit 12-9 Illustration of Net Present Value Analysis: After-Tax Cash Flows (Rounded to Nearest Dollar)

	Present Value	Year 0	Year 1	Year 2	Year 3	Year 4	Year 5	Year 6	Year 7	Year 8	Year 9	......	Year 19	Year 20	Year 21
							Projected After-Tax Cash Flows								
Initial investment	$(150,000)	$(150,000)													
Annual cash exp. savings			$22,500	$22,500	$22,500	$22,500	$22,500	$22,500	$22,500	$22,500	$22,500		$22,500	$22,500	
Less income tax @ 35%			7,875	7,875	7,875	7,875	7,875	7,875	7,875	7,875	7,875		7,875	7,875	—
After-tax exp. savings	$124,511		$14,625	$14,625	$14,625	$14,625	$14,625	$14,625	$14,625	$14,625	$14,625		$14,625	$14,625	$ —
Tax savings from depr. tax shield:															
Year1	$ 1,790		$ 1,969												
Year2	3,132			$ 3,790											
Year3	2,634				$ 3,506										
Year4	2,215					$ 3,243									
Year5	1,863						$ 3,000								
Year6	1,566							$ 2,775							
Year7	1,317								$ 2,566						
Year8	1,107									$ 2,374					
Year9	994										$ 2,343				
Year10	903														
Year11	821														
Year12	746														
Year13	679														
Year14	617														
Year15	561														
Year16	510														
Year17	464														
Year18	421														
Year19	383												$ 2,343		
Year20	348													$ 2,342	
Year21	158														$1,171
Ttl. PV of future cash flows	$147,740		$16,594	$18,415	$18,131	$17,868	$17,625	$17,400	$17,191	$16,999	$16,968		$16,968	$16,967	$1,171
Net present value	$ (2,260)														

Year	Annual Depreciation*	Tax Rate	Tax Shield
1	$ 5,625	35%	$1,969
2	10,829	35	3,790
3	10,016	35	3,506
4	9,266	35	3,243
5	8,570	35	3,000
6	7,928	35	2,775
7	7,332	35	2,566
8	6,783	35	2,374
9	6,693	35	2,343
10	6,692	35	2,342
11	6,693	35	2,343
12	6,692	35	2,342
13	6,693	35	2,343
14	6,692	35	2,342
15	6,693	35	2,343
16	6,692	35	2,342
17	6,693	35	2,343
18	6,692	35	2,342
19	6,693	35	2,343
20	6,692	35	2,342
21	3,347	35	1,171

*Tax return depreciation, 150% declining balance, half-year convention

Step 3: Project termination

For purposes of this illustration, we have assumed that the HVAC system will be worthless at the end of its 20-year life. Thus, there will be no additional incremental cash flow at the end of the project. When the system is replaced, any cost of removing the old system will be added to the cost of the installation of a new HVAC system as part of the initial investment in the new system.

Step 4: Present value calculations

The present value column in **Exhibit 12-9** shows the results of the calculations of the present values of the cash flows discussed earlier. Proper consideration of the required investment involves neither an income tax nor a present value calculation. Fezzari's $150,000 investment itself is not tax deductible; the related depreciation deductions are tax deductible, and are, of course, incorporated into our previous analysis. Because the investment expenditure is immediate, no discounting for present value is required. Thus, $150,000 represents the after-tax present value of the required investment outflow.

The $14,625 saved each year for 20 years can be treated as an annuity. The present value of an annuity of $14,625 for 20 years at 10% is $124,511 (PV = $14,625 × 8.51356).

Because the tax shield amounts differ from year to year based on the tax depreciation deduction, the present value of each year's amount must be computed separately. These amounts are computed using the PV factors as shown below:

Year	Depreciation	PV Factor*	PV
1	$1,969	0.90909	$1,790
2	3,790	0.82645	3,132
3	3,506	0.75131	2,634
4	3,243	0.68301	2,215
5	3,000	0.62092	1,863
6	2,775	0.56447	1,566
7	2,566	0.51316	1,317
8	2,374	0.46651	1,107
9	2,343	0.42410	994
10	2,342	0.38554	903
11	2,343	0.35049	821
12	2,342	0.31863	746
13	2,343	0.28966	679
14	2,342	0.26333	617
15	2,343	0.23939	561
16	2,342	0.21763	510
17	2,343	0.19784	464
18	2,342	0.17986	421
19	2,343	0.16351	383
20	2,342	0.14864	348

* Present value of a single sum payment, over 20 periods, at a 10% discount factor. See Table III in Appendix A.

These amounts are summed to arrive at the total present value of the future cash flows, or $147,740.

Step 5: Net present value calculation

The net present value is calculated by subtracting the initial investment from the total present value of the future cash flows. With its annual savings of cash expense and tax savings from the depreciation tax shield, the $150,000 investment results in future cash flows with a total present value of $147,740 and therefore a net present value of $(2,260). This negative return on the capital invested, adjusted for the time value of money, means that the project will return less than the 10% return sought by Fezzari management.

On the basis of the net present value analysis alone, it would appear that Fezzari management should reject the proposal. However, rather than reject it outright, this analysis may provide a basis for negotiating a better price for the HVAC system, or looking for modifications to the system's features that might result in a lower initial price. For example, Fezzari could pay as much as $147,740 for the system and still attain the desired 10% rate of return. Management may also wish to take a closer look at the anticipated utility savings—for example, the analysis did not include any anticipated increases in the utility costs over the 20-year life of the HVAC system. If utility costs are expected to increase in the future, it may make the anticipated savings even more significant.

**DECISION TIME
12.1**

The solution is on page 464.

Mining Equipment Manufacturer is considering the purchase of a new building. The building would require an initial outlay of $350,000. It would be depreciated using the straight-line method over 20 years, with a $15,000 salvage value. The building would generate cash inflows of $47,200/year; the company's income tax rate is 30% and WACC is 8%. Calculate the NPV of this project and decide whether the investment should be undertaken.

Liquidation Proceeds

The amount realized when an asset is liquidated contributes to the relative attractiveness of an investment in capital equipment. Liquidation proceeds on long-lived assets are sometimes disregarded because their occurrence is so far in the future that the amounts are difficult to predict, and their present values tend to be small. When useful lives are short, however, liquidation proceeds may be a deciding factor in the analysis. In our illustration, the HVAC system has a 20-year life with no salvage value. However, assume that as a sales promotion, the manufacturer of the HVAC system guaranteed to buy back the system for $20,000 after 20 years. For tax purposes, salvage value may be ignored in computing depreciation, so the machine is fully depreciated over the 20 years to a zero book value. The HVAC's sale for $20,000, then, creates a $20,000 gain on the tax return ($20,000 sales price − $0 tax book value). The $20,000 gain increases income taxes by $7,000, which is deducted from the sales price of $20,000 to produce a net after-tax cash flow of $13,000 in Year 20. The present value of $13,000 for 20 years at 10% is $1,932.32 ($13,000 × 0.14864; see Table III in Appendix A).

Note that if an asset is sold before the end of its tax depreciation period, a loss may be generated for tax purposes. The loss operates as a tax shield because it shields an equal amount of income from taxes. The tax savings is added to the cash proceeds to determine the net after-tax cash flow.

YOUR TURN! 12.4

The solution is on page 464.

If a machine with a book value of $10,000 is sold for $7,500 cash, what is the after-tax cash flow from the sale? The income tax rate is 35%.

TAKEAWAY 12.3

Remember that all transactions that relate to an investment, including depreciation and gains or losses on liquidation, are included in an NPV analysis. Although depreciation and gains or losses do not directly impact cash flows, they do have an indirect effect through changing the taxes a company must pay.

Excess Present Value Index

Alternative capital expenditure proposals may be compared in terms of their **excess present value index**, defined as follows:

$$\text{Excess present value index} = \frac{\text{Total present value of future cash flows}}{\text{Initial investment}}$$

For the investment presented in **Exhibit 12-9**, the excess present value index would be

$$\frac{\$147,740}{\$150,000} = 0.985$$

The higher the ratio of return on investment, the more attractive is the proposal. A ratio below 1.00 means that the project returns less than the target rate of return, and a ratio above 1.00 means that the project return exceeds the target rate of return. Although the excess present value index may be a convenient measure for ranking various proposals, it does not reflect the amount of the investment. Two proposals, requiring initial cash investments of $5,000 and $5,000,000, respectively, could have identical excess present value indexes but could hardly be considered equal investment opportunities.

OTHER CAPITAL BUDGETING ANALYSES

LO6 Present the cash payback and average rate of return methods of capital expenditure analysis.

Cash Payback Analysis

The **cash payback method** is a form of capital expenditure analysis that evaluates investment proposals in terms of the **cash payback period**. The cash payback period is the time in years that it takes net future after-tax cash inflows to equal the original investment.

Assume that Fezzari received a competing proposal for its new HVAC system. Management is considering purchasing either system A or system B, for which the following data are given:

System	Investment Required	Annual Net After-Tax Cash Inflows	Useful Life
A...........................	$150,000	$17,250	20 years
B...........................	115,000	15,000	15 years

For this illustration, we have assumed that the systems will be depreciated on a straight-line basis for tax purposes, making the annual net cash inflows equal over time. The cash payback period is computed as follows:

$$\frac{\text{Original investment}}{\text{Annual net cash inflows}} = \text{Cash payback in years}$$

Thus, for the two systems, we obtain:

$$\text{System A: } \frac{\$150,000}{\$17,250} = 8.70\text{-year cash payback}$$

$$\text{System B: } \frac{\$115,000}{\$15,000} = 7.67\text{-year cash payback}$$

This analysis shows that system A will pay back its required investment in 8.7 years, and system B will take 7.67 years. Because the decision rule in cash payback analysis states that the shorter the payback period, the better, system B would be considered the better investment.

If annual net cash inflows are not equal, the cash payback period is computed by summing the annual cash inflows until the cumulative amount equals the initial investment. For example, refer back to **Exhibit 12-9**. The investment is expected to generate annual net after-tax cash inflows for 9 years, as follows:

Year	Annual After-Tax Cash Inflows	Cumulative Cash Payback	Amount Required to Reach $150,000
1......................	$16,594	$ 16,594	$133,406
2......................	18,415	35,009	114,991
3......................	18,131	53,140	96,860
4......................	17,868	71,008	78,992
5......................	17,625	88,633	61,367
6......................	17,400	106,033	43,967
7......................	17,191	123,224	26,776
8......................	16,999	140,223	9,777
9......................	16,968	157,191	

As shown in the amount required to reach $150,000 column, the original investment in the HVAC system will be recovered in cash partway through Year 9. The portion of the year required may be computed by dividing the remaining amount needed by the next year's inflow ($9,777/$16,968 = 0.576). The cash payback period, then, is 8.576 years.

Concern for the payback of investments is quite natural because the shorter a project's payback period, the more quickly the funds invested in that project are recovered and available for other investments. In high-risk investments, the payback period indicates how soon a firm is "bailed out" of an investment should projected cash inflows prove inaccurate.

TAKEAWAY 12.4

The cash payback period is important to new companies that are short on cash. A project with a short payback period and a low rate of return might be preferable to another project with a longer payback period and higher rate of return. The company may need a fast recovery of cash.

The cash payback method is considered less sophisticated than net present value analysis. A primary limitation of cash payback analysis is that the relative profitability of various investments is not specifically considered. Note, for example, that in the previous illustration, system B has the better (shorter) cash payback period. However, its useful life, which is ignored in cash payback analysis, indicates that system B will stop generating cash inflows about 7 years beyond payback. In contrast, although system A has a longer payback period, it will generate future cash inflows for over 11 years beyond payback and therefore promises to be more profitable.

Regardless of its failure to consider profitability, cash payback analysis is widely used, probably because of its relative simplicity. It can be useful in conjunction with other analyses or as a preliminary screening device for investment projects under consideration.

Average Rate of Return Analysis

The **average rate of return method** uses accrual accounting information in its calculation, not cash flows. This approach addresses the future impact on the income statement.

This measure is calculated as follows:

$$\textbf{Average rate of return} = \frac{\textbf{Average annual net income from investment}}{\textbf{Average investment}}$$

Note that the focus here is not on after-tax cash flows but on traditional accounting net income.

Assume that system A described earlier requires an initial investment of $150,000, provides $17,250 annual cash inflows from operations, and has a useful life of 20 years. Assuming no salvage value, the accounting annual straight-line depreciation on system A would be ($150,000/20), or $7,500. With an income tax rate of 35%, the average annual net income from the investment would be $6,337, computed as follows:

Cash inflow from operations	$17,250
Depreciation expense	7,500
Pre-tax income from investment	$ 9,750
Income tax expense	3,413
Net income from investment	$ 6,337

If the annual net incomes from investment are unequal, we would compute the average annual net income from investment by (1) summing the annual net incomes and (2) dividing by the number of years.

We may calculate average investment simply by adding the beginning and ending investments and dividing by 2. The ending investment is the expected salvage value. In our illustration, system A has no salvage value, so the ending investment is zero. Average investment is therefore $75,000 [($150,000 + $0)/2].

The average rate of return on system A is

$$\frac{\$6,337}{\$75,000} = 8.45\%$$

The decision rule for average rate of return analyses states that the higher the return, the more attractive the investment.

U.S. Business Capital Expenditures

What are U.S businesses doing to keep up with their foreign rivals? According to a PwC January 2015 Manufacturing Barometer report, plans for new investments of capital rose in the fourth quarter of 2014. Forty-three percent of the respondents anticipated increased outlays during the next 12 months.

Source: http://www.pwc.com/en_US/us/industrial-manufacturing/assets/pwc-manufacturing-barometer-q4-2014.pdf

According to the U.S. Census Bureau's 2013 Annual Capital Expenditures Survey, U.S. businesses are increasing their capital expenditures. After declining in 2009 due to the U.S. recession, capital spending by U.S. nonfarm businesses increased 1.4% from 2009 to 2010 and 10.8% (or $120 billion) from 2010 to 2011. Capital spending between 2002 and 2011 in U.S. mining was up 252% (or $107.0 billion), transportation and warehousing were up 53.3% (or 25.1 billion), utilities were up 49.7% (or $32.5 billion), health care and social assistance were up 40.2% (or 23.9 billion), and manufacturing was up 23% or ($36.1 billion).

Source: http://www.census.gov/econ/aces/report/2013/csr_summary_of_findings.html

---

As an approach to capital expenditure analysis, the average rate of return method is often defended as being most easily understood by management personnel who are accustomed to thinking in accounting terms and concepts. It has two major limitations, however. First, the calculations rely heavily on accounting computations of net income and depreciation, and are thus subject to arbitrary choices, such as the selection of a depreciation method. Second, average rate of return calculations do not consider the time value of money. Future cash flows are treated the same as current cash flows. Our discussion of net present value analysis illustrates the often substantial differences between future values and related present values discounted by even moderate interest rates.

As an example of how deceptive the average annual income figures used in average rate of return computations can be, consider three investment proposals, each of which requires a $40,000 initial investment (with a zero salvage value) and promises the annual cash inflows shown in **Exhibit 12-10**. Note that cash flows are concentrated in Year 1 in proposal A, are uniform in proposal B, and are concentrated in Year 5 in proposal C. Because average rate of return calculations fail to consider the timing of cash flows from operations, these three proposals would have identical 10% average rates of return and therefore would be considered equally attractive. Such an implication is hardly defensible in view of the substantial differences in the relative net present values of the operating cash flows. In our illustration, the difference between the present values of A and C is $12,968, an amount equal to 41% of the present value of C.

Exhibit 12-10	Present Value Comparison of Equal Annual Average Incomes		
		Proposals	
Annual Net Cash Inflows	**A**	**B**	**C**
Year 1	$46,000	$10,000	$ 1,000
2	1,000	10,000	1,000
3	1,000	10,000	1,000
4	1,000	10,000	1,000
5	1,000	10,000	46,000
Aggregate net cash inflows	$50,000	$50,000	$50,000
Average annual net cash inflows ($50,000/5).	$10,000	$10,000	$10,000
Less depreciation ($40,000/5)	8,000	8,000	8,000
Average annual net income	$ 2,000	$ 2,000	$ 2,000
Average rate of return on investment. . . . . $2,000/[($40,000 + $0)/2].	10%	10%	10%
Present value of net cash inflows at 10%	$44,700	$37,908	$31,732

In practice, NPV projects often involve the use of sensitivity analysis. Sensitivity analysis provides a method of assessing the amount of risk involved in a proposed project. Sensitivity analysis also involves calculating the impact of variations on different quantifiable components of a project, helping management identify potential pitfalls. Management may also use sensitivity analysis to identify components (such as the discount rate or yearly cash inflows) of a plan that, when changed even slightly, will most impact the outcome of a project.

Capital Budgeting: A Complex Subject

Because it incorporates aspects of such fields as economics, finance, business management, and accounting, the subject of capital budgeting is too complex to treat comprehensively in an introductory accounting book. In this chapter, we have simply provided some insight into problem-solving techniques in capital budgeting by stating decision rules in their simplest form, showing the relevance of present value concepts and after-tax cash flows, and creating an awareness of the potentials and limitations of several widely used approaches to capital expenditure analysis. The illustrations have highlighted key relationships. The rudiments presented here should serve as a basis for further study in finance and economics courses.

SERVICE INDUSTRY IN FOCUS

Environmental Business Consultants (EBC) is deciding whether to purchase an office building. EBC has found a three-story Class A office building in San Jose, California, with a purchase price of $2,000,000. Only two stories are needed to operate, and as such EBC can lease out the lower story, which consists of 3,000 square feet of floor space. The average full-service market lease rate for Class A office buildings in San Jose is $40 per square foot per year. In order to prepare the lower floor for lease, EBC will need to spend $250,000 on leasehold improvements. The building will be useful for 30 years and will be depreciated on a straight-line basis. EBC's income tax rate is 35% and its cost of capital is 10%.

SERVICE AND MERCHANDISING

The following table summarizes the cash flows from purchasing the building and leasing out the lower floor:

Initial outflows:	
Building purchase.	$(2,000,000)
Leasehold improvements	(250,000)
Total initial outflows	$(2,250,000)

Annual cash flows:	
Lease revenue*	$ 120,000
Total annual inflows	$ 120,000

Annual depreciation expense**	$ 75,000
Building useful life (years).	30
Income tax rate	35%
Cost of capital	10%

* 3,000 sq. ft. × $40/sq. ft. per year
** $2,250,000/30 years

Required

Perform a capital expenditure analysis to decide whether EBC should purchase the building, analyzing the net present value as well as payback period and average rate of return.

Solution

Net present value analysis:		
Annual after-tax revenues	$120,000 × (1 − 35%)	$ 78,000
Tax shield from depreciation	$75,000 × 35%	26,250
Annual net cash inflows	$78,000 + $26,250	$ 104,250
Present value of the annual cash inflows	($104,250 × 9.42691)	$ 982,756
Net present value		
Initial outflows.		$(2,250,000)
PV of future cash flows.		982,756
NPV.		$(1,267,244)

Cash payback analysis:		
Initial cash outflow	$2,250,000	
Divided by the annual net cash inflows . . .	$104,250	
Payback period	21.58 years	

Average rate of return analysis:		
Annual revenues.		$ 120,000
Annual expenses		75,000
Average annual net income		45,000
Income tax @ 35%		15,750
Average after-tax net income.		29,250
Initial investment.		2,250,000
Ending investment		0
Average investment	($2,250,000 + $0)/2	$ 1,125,000
Average rate of return	$29,250/$1,125,000	2.60%

Based on the negative NPV, the long cash payback period and the small average rate of return, EBC should *not* purchase the building for $2,000,000.

APPENDIX 12A: Time Value of Money Calculations

Using a Financial Calculator

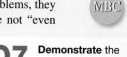

Although present value tables can provide a handy method to solve some time value of money problems, they are not suitable for many real-world situations. For example, many real-world interest rates are not "even integers" like those appearing in Table I through Table IV of Appendix A, nor are many problems limited to the number of time periods appearing in the tables. Although it is still possible to solve these problems with the provided formulas, a financial calculator provides a quicker solution. Financial calculators can be distinguished from other calculators by the presence of dedicated keys for present and future values, along with keys for the number of periods, interest rates, and annuity payments.

LO7 **Demonstrate** the use of a financial calculator and an electronic spreadsheet to perform time value of money calculations.

There exist many brands of financial calculators; however, all of them work in much the same way. We demonstrate the calculation of time value of money problems using a Hewlett-Packard 10BII financial calculator, as illustrated in **Exhibit 12A-1**. (It is usually necessary to do some preliminary setup on a financial calculator before performing time value of money calculations. For example, the HP 10BII calculator has a default setting of monthly compounding; this may need to be changed if the problem calls for a different number of compounding periods, such as annual. In addition, the calculator assumes interest payments occur at the end of each period; this will need to be changed if the problem requires beginning-of-period payments. See your calculator manual to determine how to make these setting changes.)

Exhibit 12A-1	Hewlett-Packard 10BII Financial Calculator

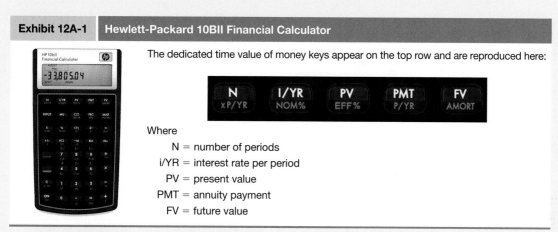

The dedicated time value of money keys appear on the top row and are reproduced here:

Where

- N = number of periods
- i/YR = interest rate per period
- PV = present value
- PMT = annuity payment
- FV = future value

To solve a time value of money problem using a financial calculator, input the known values and then press the key of the unknown value. **Exhibit 12A-2** illustrates the time value of money calculations from the NPV analysis example related to Fezzari's proposed new HVAC system presented earlier in the chapter in **Exhibit 12-9**. Panel 1 of **Exhibit 12A-2** demonstrates the present value of the project's expense savings of $14,625 (PMT = $14,625). Panels 2 and 3 present the present values of the depreciation tax shield amounts for Years 1 and 2 (FV Year 1 = $1,969; FV Year 2 = $3,790). These numbers are shown as positive numbers, indicating cash inflows or cash savings. Solving for the present value of these cash flows yields the present value in today's dollars. Financial calculators require cash outflows and inflows to be of opposite signs. If we were to enter PMT and FV as negative numbers, PV would be displayed as a positive number. Calculator solutions can be slightly different from the solutions using either the tables or the formulas due to rounding of the future value and present value multipliers.

Exhibit 12A-2	Time Value of Money Calculations Using a Financial Calculator

(1) Present value of after-tax expense savings of $14,625, over 20 years, discounted at 10%.*

Enter		Display		
20	N	N	=	20
10	i/YR	i/YR	=	10
14,625	PMT	PMT	=	14,625
0	FV	FV	=	0
Press	PV	PV	=	(124,511)

(2) Present value of Year 1 depreciation tax shield, discounted at 10%.*

Enter		Display		
1	N	N	=	1
10	i/YR	i/YR	=	10
0	PMT	PMT	=	0
1,969	FV	FV	=	1,969
Press	PV	PV	=	(1,790)

(3) Present value of Year 2 depreciation tax shield, discounted at 10%.*

Enter		Display		
2	N	N	=	2
10	i/YR	i/YR	=	10
0	PMT	PMT	=	0
3,790	FV	FV	=	3,790
Press	PV	PV	=	(3,132)

* Be sure to "clear all" and preset your compounding to annual.

Using an Electronic Spreadsheet

In addition to present value tables and financial calculators, another way to solve time value of money problems is with an electronic spreadsheet such as Excel. Excel has several built-in functions that allow calculation of time value of money problems. Depending on the version of Excel, these functions are accessed differently. Within Excel 2013, select Financial within the Formulas tab and then select PV from the drop-down menu. The following examples show how to use Excel to solve the same problems we previously solved using a financial calculator.

Example 1

Find the present value of 20 cash inflows of $14,625 at a 10% discount rate. Use the PV function and enter the values as follows:

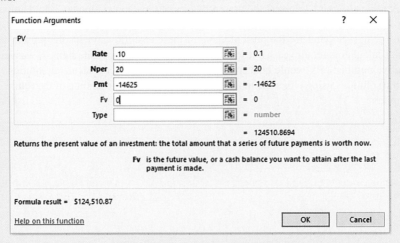

Example 2

Find the present value of a $1,969 depreciation tax shield for 1 year at a 10% discount rate. Use the PV function and enter the values as follows:

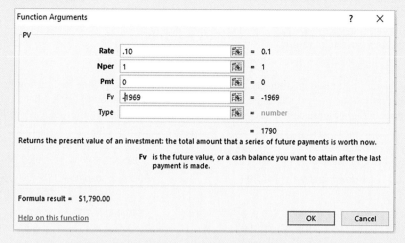

Example 3

Find the present value of a $3,790 depreciation tax shield for 2 years at a 10% discount rate. Use the PV function and enter the values as follows:

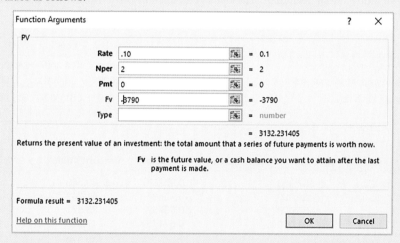

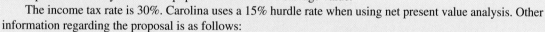

COMPREHENSIVE PROBLEM

Carolina Company is evaluating a possible $150,000 investment in equipment that would increase cash flows from operations for 4 years. The equipment will have no salvage value.

The income tax rate is 30%. Carolina uses a 15% hurdle rate when using net present value analysis. Other information regarding the proposal is as follows:

	Year 1	Year 2	Year 3	Year 4
Cash inflow from operations (pre-tax)	$60,000	$87,000	$42,000	$40,000
Depreciation on tax return	50,000	67,000	22,000	11,000
Depreciation in financial statements	37,500	37,500	37,500	37,500
Net income from investment	15,750	34,650	3,150	1,750
PV Factor @ 15%	0.86957	0.75614	0.65752	0.57175

Required

a. What are the annual net after-tax cash inflows from this proposal?

b. Compute the net present value and indicate whether it is positive or negative (round amounts to nearest dollar).

c. Compute the cash payback period.

d. Compute the average rate of return.

Solution

a. We may compute the individual after-tax cash effects by multiplying (1) the cash inflow from operations by 70% (that is, 1 – Income tax rate) and (2) the tax return depreciation by 30% (that is, the income tax rate). Combining the individual after-tax cash effects gives the annual net after-tax cash inflows:

Year 1:	$60,000 × 70% = $42,000	Year 3:	$42,000 × 70% = $29,400
	50,000 × 30% = 15,000		22,000 × 30% = 6,600
	After-tax cash flow $57,000		After-tax cash flow $36,000

Year 2:	$87,000 × 70% = $60,900	Year 4:	$40,000 × 70% = $28,000
	67,000 × 30% = 20,100		11,000 × 30% = 3,300
	After-tax cash flow $81,000		After-tax cash flow $31,300

Alternatively, we may compute the net after-tax cash inflows by subtracting the cash income tax payments from the cash inflows from operations. The annual cash income tax payments are 30% of the cash inflow from operations less the tax return depreciation.

	Year 1	Year 2	Year 3	Year 4
Cash inflow from operations	$60,000	$87,000	$42,000	$40,000
Cash payment for income taxes	3,000	6,000	6,000	8,700
After-tax cash flows	$57,000	$81,000	$36,000	$31,300

b.

Year	Annual Net After-Tax Cash Inflows	PV Factor	Present Value
1	$57,000	0.86957	$ 49,565
2	81,000	0.75614	61,247
3	36,000	0.65752	23,671
4	31,300	0.57175	17,896
	Total present value.		152,379
	Investment required in equipment		150,000
	Net positive present value		$ 2,379

c. The cash payback period is 2 1/3 years, computed as follows:

Year	Annual Net After-Tax Cash Inflows	Cumulative Cash Payback	
1	$57,000	$ 57,000	
2	81,000	138,000	
3	36,000	150,000	(requires 1/3 of $36,000 to reach $150,000)
4	31,300		

d.

Annual net income from investment:	Year 1	$15,750
	Year 2	34,650
	Year 3	3,150
	Year 4	1,750
	Total	$55,300

Average annual net income from investment: $55,300/4 = $13,825
Average investment: ($150,000 + $0)/2 = $75,000
Average rate of return: $13,825/$75,000 = 18.4%

SUMMARY OF LEARNING OBJECTIVES

Introduce and illustrate the elements of capital budgeting. (p. 424)　　　　　LO1

■　Capital budgeting is the planning of long-lived asset investments. Capital expenditure analysis basically examines how well prospective future returns justify related current investments.

■　Most capital expenditures have three stages: (1) initial investment, (2) operational cash flows, and (3) project termination.

Discuss required rates of return and the time value of money. (p. 426)　　　　　LO2

■　Cost of capital is a measure of the firm's cost for investment capital; it usually represents the minimum acceptable return for investment opportunities.

■　The time value of money concept recognizes that the further into the future cash flows occur, the less current economic worth they have.

■　The difference between present and future values is a function of interest rates and time periods.

Demonstrate the use of present value factors to perform time value of money calculations. (p. 429)　　　　　LO3

■　Present value factor tables enable us to compute the present values of future cash flows at appropriate interest rates.

■　The present value calculations used most frequently in capital budgeting are those for future single-sum flows and end-of-period annuity flows.

■　The present value of a single sum calculation is used to determine the present value of sporadic cash flows when the returns expected on an investment, or the expenditures it requires, are unequal amounts or are expected at irregular intervals during or at the end of the life of the investment. The formula for the present value of a single sum is PV = FV × PV table factor.

■　The present value of an annuity is used to determine the present value of cash flows that are the same each period over two or more equal periods. The formula for the present value of an annuity is PV = PMT × PV table factor.

Explain and illustrate the determination of after-tax cash flows. (p. 431)　　　　　LO4

■　After-tax cash flows probably represent the most relevant measure of the prospective returns of proposed investments.

■　We convert cash flows from revenues and expenses into after-tax amounts by multiplying them by (1 − Income tax rate).

■　Depreciation deductions shield revenues from taxation, referred to as a tax shield. We convert depreciation deductions into their after-tax cash flow effect by multiplying the deduction by the applicable income tax rate.

Describe the net present value method of capital expenditure analysis. (p. 435)　　　　　LO5

■　Net present value analysis compares the present value of net future cash flow returns with the investment. Projects having zero or positive net present value are acceptable.

■　Alternative investment proposals may be compared in terms of their excess present value index; the higher the index, the more attractive is the proposal.

LO6 **Present the cash payback and average rate of return methods of capital expenditure analysis. (p. 442)**

- Cash payback analysis measures the time in years necessary for the net future after-tax cash flows to equal the original investment. In this type of analysis, the shorter the payback period, the more attractive is the investment.
- Average rate of return analysis compares the annual average net income with the average investment. The higher this ratio is, the more attractive is the investment.
- Cash payback analysis fails to consider the relative profitability of alternative projects. Average rate of return analysis fails to consider the time value of money.

LO7 **Demonstrate the use of a financial calculator and an electronic spreadsheet to perform time value of money calculations. (p. 447)**

- Financial calculators and spreadsheet programs also enable us to compute the present values of future cash flows at appropriate interest rates.

KEY TERMS

Annuity (p. 430)	Cash payback period (p. 442)	Net present value method (p. 435)
Average rate of return method (p. 443)	Cost of capital (p. 427)	
	Excess present value index (p. 441)	Rate of return (p. 426)
Buffer margin (p. 427)		Time value of money (p. 428)
Capital budgeting (p. 424)	Hurdle rate (p. 427)	Weighted average cost of capital, or WACC (p. 427)
Cash payback method (p. 442)		

Assignments with the ⬤ logo in the margin are available in BusinessCourse.
See the Preface of the book for details.

SELF-STUDY QUESTIONS

(Answers to Self-Study Questions are at the end of this chapter.)

LO2 1. **A firm's cost of acquiring the funds for capital investment projects is known as the**
   a. Payback period.
   b. Rate of return.
   c. Cost of capital.
   d. Time value of money.

LO2 2. **All other things remaining the same, when the interest rate used to discount future values increases, present values**
   a. Decrease.
   b. Increase in proportion to the interest rate increase.
   c. Remain the same.
   d. Increase but not in proportion to the interest rate increase.

LO4 3. **Although depreciation is a noncash expense, it does have an indirect effect on cash flows because it shelters an equal amount of income from income taxes. This feature is known as a**
   a. Buffer margin.
   b. Cash payback.
   c. Depreciation flow.
   d. Tax shield.

LO5 4. **Blaine Company is considering four investment proposals, each requiring the same amount of initial cash investment. The excess present value index for each proposal is listed below. Using the index as a selection criterion, identify the index of the most attractive proposal.**
   a. 90
   b. 100
   c. 110
   d. 115

LO6 5. **The primary limitation of the cash payback method is that it**
   a. Uses before-tax cash flows.
   b. Identifies the length of time it will take to recover the investment outlay in cash.
   c. Ignores the profitability of one investment project as compared to another.
   d. Involves a more sophisticated analysis than the net present value method.

QUESTIONS

1. What is capital budgeting? **LO1**
2. List three reasons why capital budgeting decisions are often important. **LO1**
3. What are the three stages typical of most investments in plant and equipment? **LO1**
4. Briefly describe the concept of weighted average cost of capital. **LO2**
5. In what sense does the cost of capital limit a firm's investment considerations? **LO2**
6. A company plans to accumulate 75% of its needed investment capital by issuing bonds having a capital **LO2** cost percentage of 12%; the balance will be raised by issuing stock having a capital cost percentage of 16%. What would be the weighted average cost of capital for the total amount of capital?
7. Briefly describe the concept of the time value of money. **LO2**
8. You have the right to receive $30,000 at the end of each of the next four years, and money is worth 8%. **LO3, 7** Using the PV tables, your financial calculator, or Excel, compute the present value of this annuity.
9. A rich uncle allows you to stipulate which of two ways you receive your inheritance: **LO3, 7**
    a. $850,000 one year after his death or
    b. $250,000 on his death and $200,000 each year at the end of the first, second, and third years following his death. If money is worth 10%, what is the relative advantage of the more attractive alternative?
10. You can settle a debt with either a single payment now of $30,000 or with payments of $8,000 at the end **LO3, 7** of each of the next five years. If money is worth 10%, what is the relative advantage of the most attractive alternative? If money is worth 12%, would your answer change? Why?
11. Explain how to convert before-tax cash operating expenses and depreciation deductions into after-tax **LO4** amounts.
12. What is meant by the term *depreciation tax shield*? **LO4**
13. What amounts are compared in net present value analysis? State the related decision rule. **LO3, 5**
14. What is an excess present value index? **LO5**
15. Define cash payback period, state the related decision rule, and specify an important limitation of this **LO6** analysis.
16. Define average rate of return, state the related decision rule, and specify an important limitation of this **LO6** analysis.

EXERCISES—SET A

E12-1A. Weighted Average Cost of Capital Gardner, Inc., plans to finance its expansion by raising the **LO2** needed investment capital from the following sources in the indicated proportions and respective capital cost rates:

	Capital Cost	
Source	Proportion	Rate
Bonds	40%	13%
Preferred stock	20	9
Common stock	30	12
Retained earnings	10	9
	100%	

Calculate the weighted average cost of capital.

E12-2A. Present Value Computations Assuming that money is worth 10%, compute the present value of **LO3**

1. $7,000 received 15 years from today.
2. The right to inherit $1,000,000 14 years from now.
3. The right to receive $1,000 at the end of each of the next six years.
4. The obligation to pay $3,000 at the end of each of the next 10 years.
5. The right to receive $5,000 at the end of the 7th, 8th, 9th, and 10th years from today.

LO4 **E12-3A. After-Tax Cash Flows** For each of the following independent situations, compute the net after-tax cash flow amount by subtracting cash outlays for operating expenses and income taxes from cash revenue. The cash outlay for income taxes is determined by applying the income tax rate to the cash revenue received less the cash and noncash (depreciation) expenses.

SERVICE AND MERCHANDISING

	A	B	C
Cash revenue received......................................	$90,000	$450,000	$220,000
Cash operating expenses paid...........................	54,000	315,000	145,000
Depreciation on tax return	12,000	30,000	20,000
Income tax rate	40%	30%	20%

LO4 **E12-4A. After-Tax Cash Flows** Using the data in E12-3A, (a) calculate the individual after-tax cash flow effect of each relevant item in each independent situation, and (b) sum the individual after-tax cash flows in each situation to determine the overall net after-tax cash flow.

SERVICE AND MERCHANDISING

LO4 **E12-5A. Depreciation Tax Shields** Lincoln Company has purchased equipment for $200,000. After it is fully depreciated, the equipment will have no salvage value. Lincoln may select either of the following depreciation schedules for tax purposes:

Year	Option 1 Depreciation	Option 2 Depreciation
1..	$40,000	$20,000
2..	64,000	40,000
3..	38,400	40,000
4..	23,040	40,000
5..	23,040	40,000
6..	11,520	20,000

Assuming a 40% tax rate and a 12% desired annual return, compute the total present value of the tax savings provided by these alternative depreciation tax shields. Which depreciation schedule would be more attractive to Lincoln?

LO5 **E12-6A. Net Present Value Analysis** Anderson Company must evaluate two capital expenditure proposals. Anderson's hurdle rate is 12%. Data for the two proposals follow.

	Proposal X	Proposal Y
Required investment	$120,000	$120,000
Annual after-tax cash inflows....................................	24,000	
After-tax cash inflows at the end of years 3, 6, 9, and 12		72,000
Life of project...	12 years	12 years

Using net present value analysis, which proposal is the more attractive? If Anderson has sufficient funds available, should both proposals be accepted?

LO6 **E12-7A. Cash Payback** Refer to the data in E12-6A. What is the cash payback period for Proposal X? For Proposal Y?

LO6 **E12-8A. Average Rate of Return** Lakeland Company is considering the purchase of equipment for $150,000. The equipment will expand the Company's production and increase revenue by $40,000 per year. Annual cash operating expenses will increase by $10,000. The equipment's useful life is 10 years with no salvage value. Lakeland uses straight-line depreciation. The income tax rate is 35%. What is the average rate of return on the investment?

EXERCISES—SET B

LO2 **E12-1B. Weighted Average Cost of Capital** Austin, Inc. plans to finance its expansion by raising the needed investment capital from the following sources in the indicated proportions and respective capital cost rates.

Source	Proportion	Capital Cost Rate
Bonds.	45%	10%
Preferred stock.	10	8
Common stock.	25	14
Retained earnings	20	12
	100%	

Calculate the weighted average cost of capital.

E12-2B. Present Value Computations Assuming that money is worth 10%, compute the present value of **LO3**

1. $6,000 received 15 years from today.
2. The right to inherit $2,000,000 14 years from now.
3. The right to receive $2,000 at the end of each of the next six years.
4. The obligation to pay $1,000 at the end of each of the next 10 years.
5. The right to receive $10,000 at the end of the 7th, 8th, 9th, and 10th years from today.

E12-3B. After-Tax Cash Flows For each of the following independent situations, compute the net after-tax **LO4** cash flow amount by subtracting cash outlays for operating expenses and income taxes from cash revenue. The cash outlay for income taxes is determined by applying the income tax rate to the cash revenue received less the cash and noncash (depreciation) expenses.

	A	B	C
Cash revenue received.	$80,000	$400,000	$200,000
Cash operating expenses paid.	45,000	260,000	120,000
Depreciation on tax return	10,000	25,000	15,000
Income tax rate	30%	40%	20%

E12-4B. After-Tax Cash Flows Using the data in E12-3B, (a) calculate the individual after-tax cash flow **LO4** effect of each relevant item in each independent situation, and (b) sum the individual after-tax cash flows in each situation to determine the overall net after-tax cash flow.

E12-5B. Depreciation Tax Shields Mendota Company has purchased equipment for $100,000. After it is **LO4** fully depreciated, the equipment will have no salvage value. Mendota may select either of the following depreciation schedules for tax purposes:

Year	Option 1 Depreciation	Option 2 Depreciation
1.	$20,000	$10,000
2.	32,000	20,000
3.	19,200	20,000
4.	11,520	20,000
5.	11,520	20,000
6.	5,760	10,000

Assuming a 40% tax rate and a 12% desired annual return, compute the total present value of the tax savings provided by these alternative depreciation tax shields. Which depreciation schedule would be more attractive to Mendota?

E12-6B. Net Present Value Analysis Hermson Company must evaluate two capital expenditure proposals. **LO5** Hermson's hurdle rate is 12%. Data for the two proposals follow.

	Proposal X	Proposal Y
Required investment	$140,000	$140,000
Annual after-tax cash inflows.	33,000	
After-tax cash inflows at the end of years 3, 6, 9, and 12		99,000
Life of project.	12 years	12 years

Using net present value analysis, which proposal do you find to be the more attractive? If Hermson has sufficient funds available, should both proposals be accepted?

LO6 **E12-7B. Cash Payback** Refer to the data in E12-6B. What is the cash payback period for proposal X? for proposal Y?

LO6 **E12-8B. Average Rate of Return** Clancy Company is considering the purchase of equipment for $100,000. The equipment will expand the company's production and increase revenue by $30,000 per year. Annual cash operating expenses will increase by $8,000. The equipment's useful life is 10 years with no salvage value. Clancy uses straight-line depreciation. The income tax rate is 35%. What is the average rate of return on the investment?

PROBLEMS—SET A

LO4 **P12-1A. After-Tax Cash Flows** Below is a list of aspects of various capital expenditure proposals that the capital budgeting team of Anchor, Inc., has incorporated into its net present value analyses during the past year. Unless otherwise noted, the items listed are unrelated to each other. All situations assume a 40% income tax rate and an 11% minimum desired rate of return.

1. Pre-tax savings of $4,000 in cash expenses will occur in each of the next three years.
2. A machine is purchased now for $37,000 cash.
3. A long-haul tractor costing $27,000 will be depreciated $9,000, $12,000, $4,050, and $1,950, respectively, on the tax return over four years.
4. Equipment costing $200,000 will be depreciated over five years on the tax return in the following amounts: $25,000; $50,000; $50,000; $50,000; and $25,000.
5. Pre-tax savings of $8,800 in cash expenses will occur in each of the next six years.
6. Pre-tax savings of $7,000 in cash expenses will occur in the first, third, and fifth years from now.
7. The tractor described in aspect 3 will be sold after four years for $5,000 cash.
8. The equipment described in aspect 4 will be sold after four years for $20,000 cash.

Required
Set up an answer form with the two column headings as shown below. Answer each investment aspect separately. Prepare your calculations on a separate paper and key them to each item. The answer to investment aspect 1 is presented as an example.

Investment Aspect 1	A After-tax Cash Flow Effect(s) Inflows (Outflows)	B Year(s) of Cash Flow
	$2,400	1, 2, 3
Calculations:		
1. Pre-tax cash savings		$4,000
Less income tax at 40%......................		1,600
After-tax cash inflow.........................		$2,400

a. Calculate and record in column A the related after-tax cash flow effect(s). Place parentheses around outflows.
b. Indicate in column B the timing of each cash flow shown in column A. Use 0 to indicate immediately and 1, 2, 3, 4, and so on for each year involved.

LO5 **P12-2A. Net Present Value Analysis** Champion Company is considering a contract that would require an expansion of its food processing capabilities. The contract covers five years. To provide the required products, Champion would have to purchase additional equipment for $64,000. Champion estimates the contract will provide annual net cash inflows (before taxes) of $26,000. For tax purposes, the equipment will be depreciated as follows:

Year 1...	$ 8,000
Year 2...	16,000
Year 3...	16,000
Year 4...	16,000
Year 5...	8,000

Although salvage value is ignored in the tax depreciation calculations, Champion estimates the equipment will be sold for $8,000 after five years.

Required

Assuming a 35% income tax rate and a 10% hurdle rate, compute the net present value of this contract proposal. Using net present value analysis, should Champion accept the contract? (Round amounts to the nearest dollar.)

P12-3A. Net Present Value, Cash Payback, and Average Rate of Return Methods Western Company is evaluating a possible $42,000 investment in special tools that would increase cash flows from operations for four years. The tools will have no salvage value. The income tax rate is 40%. Western uses a 12% hurdle rate when using present value analysis. Other information regarding the proposal is as follows: **LO5, 6**

	Year 1	Year 2	Year 3	Year 4
Cash inflow from operations (pre-tax)	$15,000	$20,000	$16,500	$12,000
Depreciation on tax return	14,000	18,500	6,500	3,000
Depreciation in financial statements	10,500	10,500	10,500	10,500
Net income from investment	2,700	5,700	3,600	900

Required

a.   What are the annual net after-tax cash inflows from this proposal?
b.   Compute the net present value and indicate whether it is positive or negative (round amounts to nearest dollar).
c.   Compute the excess present value index.
d.   Compute the cash payback period.
e.   Compute the average rate of return.

P12-4A. Excess Present Value Index and Average Rate of Return Highpoint Company is evaluating five different capital expenditure proposals. The company's hurdle rate for net present value analyses is 12%. A 10% salvage value is expected from each of the investments. Information on the five proposals is as follows: **LO5, 6**

Proposal	Required Investment	Present Value at 12% of After-tax Cash Flows	Average Annual Net Income from Investment
A.....................................	$270,000	$310,030	$37,400
B.....................................	200,000	236,780	26,000
C.....................................	160,000	173,040	19,200
D.....................................	180,000	216,300	27,600
E.....................................	128,000	136,990	14,960

Required

a.   Compute the excess present value index for each of the five proposals.
b.   Compute the average rate of return for each of the five proposals.
c.   Assume that Highpoint will commit no more than $500,000 to new capital expenditure proposals. Using the excess present value index, which proposals would be accepted? Using the average rate of return, which proposals would be accepted?

P12-5A. Cash Payback, Average Rate of Return, and Net Present Value Methods Landover Amusement Park is considering the construction of a new facility to house a curved, multistory movie screen. The facility will cost $400,000 and be useful for 10 years, with no salvage value. The facility will be   **LO5, 6**

SERVICE AND MERCHANDISING

depreciated on a straight-line basis over 10 years on both the books and the tax return. The following annual results are expected if the facility is constructed:

Increase in annual cash revenue		$200,000
Increase in expenses:		
Cash operating expenses.	$80,000	
Depreciation	40,000	120,000
Pretax income		$ 80,000
Income tax expense (40%).		32,000
Net income.		$ 48,000

Landover uses a 12% hurdle rate when analyzing capital expenditure proposals using net present value.

Required
a. What are the annual net cash flows (net inflows) from this project?
b. Compute the cash payback period.
c. Compute the average rate of return.
d. Compute the net present value and indicate whether it is positive or negative.
e. Assume that Landover decides to use a 10% hurdle rate when using net present value analysis. Compute the net present value using a 10% hurdle rate and indicate whether it is positive or negative.

LO2, 5   **P12-6A.** **Weighted Average Cost of Capital and Net Present Value Analysis** Tate Company is considering a proposal to acquire new equipment for its manufacturing division. The equipment will cost $192,000, be useful for four years, and have a $12,000 salvage value. Tate expects annual savings in cash operating expenses (before taxes) of $68,000. For tax purposes, the annual depreciation deduction will be $64,000, $86,000, $28,000, and $14,000, respectively, for the four years (the salvage value is ignored on the tax return). The income tax rate is 40%.

Tate establishes a hurdle rate for a net present value analysis at the company's weighted average cost of capital plus 1 percentage point. Tate's capital is provided in the following proportions: debt, 60%; common stock, 20%; and retained earnings, 20%. The cost rates for these capital sources are debt, 10%; common stock, 12%; and retained earnings, 13%.

Required
a. Compute Tate's (1) weighted average cost of capital and (2) hurdle rate.
b. Using Tate's hurdle rate, compute the net present value of this capital expenditure proposal. Under net present value analysis, should Tate accept the proposal? (Round amounts to the nearest dollar.)

PROBLEMS—SET B

LO4   **P12-1B.** **After-Tax Cash Flows** Below is a list of aspects of various capital expenditure proposals that the capital budgeting team of Modern Systems, Inc., has incorporated into its net present value analyses during the past year. Unless otherwise noted, the items listed are unrelated to each other. All situations assume a 30% income tax rate and a 10% minimum desired rate of return.

1. Pre-tax savings of $5,000 in cash expenses will occur in each of the next three years.
2. A machine is purchased now for $82,000.
3. Special tools costing $45,000 will be depreciated $9,000, $18,000, and $18,000, respectively, on the tax return over a three-year life.
4. A patent purchased for $330,000 will be amortized on a straight-line basis over 15 years on the tax return. No salvage value is expected.
5. Pre-tax savings of $8,000 in cash expenses will occur in each of the next seven years.
6. Pre-tax savings of $5,500 in cash expenses will occur in the first, fourth, and seventh years from now.
7. The special tools described in aspect 3 will be sold after three years for $10,000 cash.
8. A truck with a tax book value of $7,200 after two years will be sold at that time for $4,600.

Required

Set up an answer form with the four column headings as shown below. Answer each investment aspect separately. Prepare your calculations on a separate paper and key them to each item. The answer to investment aspect 1 is presented as an example.

Investment Aspect 1	A After-tax Cash Flow Effect(s) Inflows (Outflows)	B Year(s) of Cash Flow
	$3,500	1, 2, 3
Calculations:		
1. Pre-tax cash savings		$5,000
Less income tax at 30%.		1,500
After-tax cash inflow.		$3,500

a.   Calculate and record in column A the related after-tax cash flow effect(s). Place parentheses around outflows.

b.   Indicate in column B the timing of each cash flow shown in column A. Use 0 to indicate immediately and 1, 2, 3, 4, and so on for each year involved.

P12-2B. Net Present Value Analysis You have an opportunity to invest in a concession at a world exposition. **LO5**
To use the building and exhibits more fully, the venture is expected to cover a six-year period consisting of a preliminary year, the two years of formal exposition, and a three-year period of reduced operation as a regional exposition.

The terms of the concession agreement specify the following:

1.   At inception, a $60,000 deposit is paid to Global Expo, Inc., the promoting organization. This amount is returned in full at the end of the six years if the operator maintains the concession in order and keeps it open during scheduled hours. The deposit is not tax deductible, nor is its return subject to income taxes.

2.   The operator must install certain fixtures that will cost $240,000. The fixtures become the property of Global Expo, Inc., at the end of the six years.

After careful investigation and consultation with local experts, you conclude that the following schedule reflects the estimated pre-tax income of the concession (amounts in thousands of dollars):

	Year 1	Year 2	Year 3	Year 4	Year 5	Year 6
Sales (all cash)	$150	$435	$488	$300	$240	$180
Operating expenses:						
Cash	$ 75	$228	$279	$170	$140	$106
Tax depreciation.	48	77	46	28	28	13
Total expenses	$123	$305	$325	$198	$168	$119
Pre-tax income.	$ 27	$130	$163	$102	$ 72	$ 61

Required

Assuming an income tax rate of 40% and a desired annual return of 9%, what is the net present value of this investment opportunity? What is the maximum amount that could be invested and still earning a 9% annual return? (Round amounts to the nearest dollar.)

P12-3B. Cash Payback, Average Rate of Return, and Net Present Value Methods At a cash cost of **LO5, 6**
$330,000, Monona, Inc., can acquire equipment that will save $100,000 in annual cash operating expenses. No salvage value is expected at the end of its five-year useful life. Assume the machine will be depreciated over five years on a straight-line basis on both the books and the tax return. The income tax rate is 30% and Monona has a 10% hurdle rate when using a net present value analysis.

Required

a.   What are the annual after-tax cash savings in operating expenses?

b.   What are the annual tax savings from the depreciation tax shield?

    c.   Compute the cash payback period.

    d.   Compute the average rate of return.

    e.   Compute the net present value and indicate whether it is positive or negative (round amounts to nearest dollar).

    f.   Compute the excess present value index.

LO5, 6

P12-4B. Excess Present Value Index and Average Rate of Return Swanson Corporation is evaluating five different capital expenditure proposals. The company's hurdle rate for net present value analysis is 12%. A 15% salvage value is expected from each of the investments. Information on the five proposals is as follows:

Proposal	Required Investment	Net Present Value	Average Annual Net Income from Investment
A..	$ 50,000	$ 8,996	$ 9,100
B..	80,000	5,812	12,000
C..	110,000	27,034	18,300
D..	150,000	7,544	21,500
E..	72,000	15,822	13,960

Required

a.   Compute the excess present value index for each of the five proposals.

b.   Compute the average rate of return for each of the five proposals.

c.   Assume that Swanson will commit no more than $200,000 to new capital expenditure proposals. Using the excess present value index, which proposals would be accepted? Using the average rate of return, which proposals would be accepted?

LO5, 6

P12-5B. Cash Payback, Average Rate of Return, and Net Present Value Methods Lyle Company is considering whether to enter into a franchise agreement that would give the company exclusive distribution rights in a three-state region to a quality line of leisure spas. The franchise agreement will extend eight years and cost $600,000. There is no salvage value. The franchise cost will be amortized on a straight-line basis over eight years on both the books and the tax return. The following annual results are expected if the franchise is acquired:

Increase in annual cash revenue		$230,000
Increase in expenses:		
Cash operating expenses.......................................	$95,000	
Amortization	75,000	170,000
Pretax income		$ 60,000
Income tax expense (35%).		21,000
Net income..		$ 39,000

Lyle uses a 12% hurdle rate when analyzing capital expenditure proposals using net present value.

Required

a.   What are the annual net cash flows (net inflows) from this proposal?

b.   Compute the cash payback period.

c.   Compute the average rate of return.

d.   Compute the net present value and indicate whether it is positive or negative.

e.   Assume that Lyle decides to use a 10% hurdle rate when using net present value analysis. Compute the net present value using a 10% hurdle rate and indicate whether it is positive or negative.

LO2, 5

P12-6B. Weighted Average Cost of Capital and Net Present Value Analysis Manchester Company is considering a proposal to purchase special equipment at a cost of $640,000. The equipment will be useful for five years and has an expected $60,000 salvage value. Manchester expects annual savings in cash operating expenses (before taxes) of $230,000. For tax purposes, the annual depreciation deduction will be as follows (salvage value is ignored on the tax return):

Year 1	$ 80,000
Year 2	160,000
Year 3	160,000
Year 4	160,000
Year 5	80,000

The income tax rate is 40%.

Manchester establishes a hurdle rate for a net present value analysis at the company's weighted average cost of capital plus 2 percentage points. Manchester's capital is provided in the following proportions: debt, 70%; common stock, 20%; and retained earnings, 10%. The cost rates for these capital sources are debt, 8%; common stock, 12%; and retained earnings, 10%.

Required
a. Compute Manchester's (1) weighted average cost of capital and (2) hurdle rate.
b. Using Manchester's hurdle rate, compute the net present value of this capital expenditure proposal. Under net present value analysis, should Manchester accept the proposal?

CERTIFIED MANAGEMENT ACCOUNTANT (CMA®) EXAM SAMPLE QUESTIONS

CMA12-1. An accountant for Stability Inc. must calculate the weighted average cost of capital of the corporation using the following information.

		Interest Rate
Accounts payable	$35,000,000	0
Long-term debt	10,000,000	8%
Common stock	10,000,000	15%
Retained earnings	5,000,000	18%

What is the weighted average cost of capital of Stability?
a. 6.88%
b. 8.00%
c. 10.25%
d. 12.80%

CMA12-2. Kielly Machines Inc. is planning an expansion program estimated to cost $100 million. Kielly is going to raise funds according to its target capital structure shown below.

Debt	0.30
Preferred stock	0.24
Equity	0.46

Kielly had net income available to common shareholders of $184 million last year of which 75% was paid out in dividends. The company has a marginal tax rate of 40%.

Additional data:
- The before-tax cost of debt is estimated to be 11%.
- The market yield of preferred stock is estimated to be 12%.
- The after-tax cost of common stock is estimated to be 16%.

What is Kielly's weighted average cost of capital?

a.   12.22%

b.   13.00%

c.   13.54%

d.   14.00%

CMA12-3. Which one of the following items is **least** likely to directly impact an equipment replacement capital expenditure decision?

a.   The net present value of the equipment that is being replaced.

b.   The depreciation rate that will be used for tax purposes on the new asset.

c.   The amount of additional accounts receivable that will be generated from increased production and sales.

d.   The sales value of the asset that is being replaced.

CMA12-4. Wilcox Corporation won a settlement in a lawsuit and was offered four different payment alternatives by the defendant's insurance company. A review of interest rates indicates that 8% is appropriate for analyzing this situation. Ignoring any tax considerations, which one of the following four alternatives should the controller recommend to Wilcox management?

a. $135,000 now

b. $40,000 per year at the end of each of the next four years

c. $5,000 now and $20,000 per year at the end of each of the next ten years

d. $5,000 now and $5,000 per year at the end of each of the next nine years, plus a lump-sum payment of $200,000 at the end of the tenth year

CMA12-5. The following schedule reflects the incremental costs and revenues for a capital project. The company uses straight-line depreciation. The interest expense reflects an allocation of interest on the amount of this investment, based on the company's weighted average cost of capital.

Revenues		$650,000
Direct costs	$270,000	
Variable overhead.	50,000	
Fixed overhead.	20,000	
Depreciation.	70,000	
General & administrative	40,000	
Interest expense.	8,000	
Total costs		458,000
Net profit before taxes		$192,000

The annual cash flow from this investment, before tax considerations, would be

a. $192,000.   c. $262,000.

b. $200,000.   d. $270,000.

EXTENDING YOUR KNOWLEDGE

EYK12-1. **Business Decision Case** New Haven Corporation recently identified an investment opportunity involving the purchase of a patent that will permit the company to modify its line of CD recorders. The patent's purchase price is $720,000 and the legal protection it provides will last for five more years; there is no salvage value. However, after preparing the capital expenditure analysis below, New Haven's treasurer has recommended to the company's capital budgeting committee that the investment be rejected. Brad Decker, chairperson of the capital budgeting committee, finds it difficult to accept the treasurer's analysis because he "feels intuitively" that the investment is attractive. For this reason, he has retained you to review the treasurer's analysis and recommendation. You are provided with the following data and summary of the treasurer's analysis:

1.   Required investment: $720,000 cash for the patent to be amortized on a straight-line basis, five-year useful life, with a zero salvage value.

2. Projected cash revenue and operating expenses:

Year	Cash Revenue	Cash Expenses
1	$ 620,000	$240,000
2	560,000	200,000
3	400,000	170,000
4	250,000	80,000
5	200,000	50,000
	$2,030,000	$740,000

3. Source of capital: New Haven plans to raise 10% of the needed capital by issuing bonds, 30% by issuing stock, and the balance from retained earnings. For these sources, the capital cost rates are 8%, 9%, and 10%, respectively. New Haven has a policy of seeking a return equal to the weighted average cost of capital plus 2.5 percentage points as a "buffer margin" for the uncertainties involved.

4. Income taxes: New Haven has an overall income tax rate of 30%.

5. Treasurer's analysis:

Average cost of capital		
(8% + 9% + 10%)/3 = 9%		
Total cash revenue.		$2,030,000
Total cash expenses.	$740,000	
Total amortization.	720,000	
Total operating expenses.		1,460,000
Projected net income over five years.		$ 570,000
Average annual income		$ 114,000
Present value of future returns.		$ 443,420
Required investment		720,000
Negative net present value.		$ (276,580)

Recommendation: Reject investment because of insufficient net present value.

Required

a. Review the treasurer's analysis, identifying any questionable aspects and briefly comment on the apparent effect of each such item on the treasurer's analysis.

b. Prepare your own analysis of the investment, including a calculation of the proper cost of capital and hurdle rates, a net present value analysis of the project, and a brief recommendation to Decker regarding the investment (round amounts to nearest dollar).

c. Because of his concern for the uncertainties of the CD recorder business, Decker also has asked you to provide analyses supporting whether or not your recommendation would change

  1. If estimates of projected cash revenue were reduced by 10%.

  2. If the "buffer margin" were tripled from 2.5% to 7.5%.

EYK12-2. Ethics Case Sandy Williams is the manager of General Company's cutting department, which employs 70 people. The cutting department desperately needs new equipment to increase productivity and thus avoid the layoff of 25 people. This department is one of four departments being considered for new equipment. The budget committee has announced that only one department's capital request will be approved this year.

Williams works up the cost savings from the new machinery and contacts suppliers to learn the equipment's estimated cost. Williams knows that General Company uses the payback method to evaluate capital projects. The estimated costs for the equipment are extremely high, particularly with all the safety shields recommended by the manufacturer. If one of these recommended safety features, electronic safety sensors not on the current equipment, were left off, the cost would be $200,000 less and the payback period would decrease by three years. If only minimum electronic safety sensors required by the union contract were included, the cost would be $70,000 less and the payback period would decrease by one year.

Required

What are the ethical considerations Sandy Williams faces as she prepares the equipment proposal?

ANSWERS TO SELF-STUDY QUESTIONS:

1. c, (p. 427)   2. a, (p. 428)   3. d, (p. 432)   4. d, (p. 431)   5. c, (p. 443)

YOUR TURN! SOLUTIONS

Solution 12.1

Bank loan	45% × 12% =	5.40%
Equity capital	55% × 9% =	4.95%
Weighted average cost of capital		10.35%

Solution 12.2

N = 3; i/YR = 12; FV = $2,000; PV = $2,000 × .71178, so PV = $1,423.56.
N = 4; i/YR = 12; FV = $4,000; PV = $4,000 × .63552, so PV = $2,542.08.
Total PV = $3,965.64.

Solution 12.3

N = 7; i/YR = 6; PMT = $5,000; PV = $5,000 × 5.58238, so PV = $27,911.90.

Solution 12.4

Book value	$10,000
Cash selling price	7,500
Loss on sale	$ 2,500
Income tax rate	× 35%
Tax saving	$ 875
Plus: Cash selling price	7,500
After-tax cash flow	$ 8,375

DECISION TIME SOLUTIONS

Solution 12.1

Depreciation tax shield:
    [($350,000 − $15,000)/20 years] × 0.30 = $5,025

After-tax cash inflow:
    [$47,200 × (1 − 0.30)] = $33,040

Total cash inflow:
    ($5,025 + $33,040) = $38,065

Present value of cash flows:
    N = 20; i/YR = 8; PMT = 38,065; PV = $38,065 × 9.81815, so PV = $373,727.87.

NPV:
    ($350,000) + $373,727.87 = $23,727.87

Because the NPV is positive, the company should purchase the building.

13

Statement of Cash Flows

PAST

Chapter 12 introduced capital budgeting and illustrated how capital budgeting is used to make capital investment decisions.

PRESENT

In this chapter we turn our attention to the statement of cash flows.

FUTURE

Chapter 14 completes our study of managerial accounting by looking at the analysis and interpretation of financial statements.

LEARNING OBJECTIVES

1. **Discuss** the content and format of the statement of cash flows. *(p. 468)*

2. **Explain** the preparation of a statement of cash flows using the indirect method. *(p. 474)*

3. **Define** several ratios used to analyze the statement of cash flows and **explain** their use. *(p. 482)*

4. Appendix 13A: **Explain** the preparation of a statement of cash flows using the direct method. *(p. 487)*.

HOME DEPOT: A Company with a Vision

Home Depot is the largest home improvement retailer in the United States. Founded in 1978 in Atlanta, Georgia, the company now operates over 2,200 stores in the United States, Canada, and Mexico. The company's founders had a vision that led to the company's tremendous growth:

> "We founded [The Home Depot] with a special vision—to create a company that would keep alive the values that were important to us. Values like respect among all people, excellent customer service and giving back to communities and society."
>
> —Arthur Blank, co-founder, Home Depot

It takes a lot of cash to build and operate over 2,200 stores, especially when the average Home Depot store is over 105,000 square feet. In fiscal year 2014 Home Depot spent over $1.4 billion on capital expenditures. This represents the fifth year in a row that the company expended over $1 billion dollars in capital expenditures.

How can a financial statement user determine where a company obtained the cash to fund such growth? In this chapter we examine the statement of cash flows and learn how a company discloses both the sources and uses of its cash. Understanding the content, format, and construction of the statement of cash flows enables a financial statement user to assess just how a company like Home Depot was able to finance its capital expenditures for new store growth.

STATEMENT OF CASH FLOWS

Classification of Cash Flows	Preparing the Statement of Cash Flows	Analyzing Cash Flows
• Cash and cash equivalents • Operating activities • Investing activities • Financing activities	• Indirect method • Direct method (Appendix 13A)	• Free cash flow • Operating-cash-flow-to-current-liabilities • Operating-cash-flow-to-capital-expenditures ratio

CASH AND CASH EQUIVALENTS

eLectures
MBC

LO1 **Discuss** the content and format of the statement of cash flows.

Do you maintain a checkbook in which you record the checks you write and the bank deposits you make? If so, you are keeping a record of your cash flows—the checks you write are your cash outflows and the bank deposits you make are your cash inflows. Businesses also experience cash inflows and outflows; but, they do more than just record their cash flows because GAAP requires that businesses prepare an entirely separate financial statement explaining where their cash flow came from and how it was used.

The statement of cash flows complements the balance sheet and the income statement. While a balance sheet reports a company's financial position as of a point in time, usually the end of a fiscal period, the statement of cash flows explains the change in one component of a company's financial position—its cash—from one balance sheet date to the next. The income statement, on the other hand, reveals the results of a company's operating activities for the period, and these operating activities are a major source and use of the cash reported in a company's statement of cash flows.

In the eyes of most creditors, investors, and managers, cash is a business's most important asset. Without cash, a business would be unable to pay its employees, its lenders, its suppliers, its service providers, or its shareholders. In short, cash is the only asset that a business can't operate without.

The dilemma for most managers, however, is knowing exactly how much cash to keep on hand. Although managers know that they need to keep some cash on hand in a checking account and/or petty cash fund to pay their immediate bills, they also know that cash is the lowest return generating asset that a business has. Keeping too much cash on hand means that a business is not maximizing the value of its assets. For this reason, most managers spend considerable time assessing their cash needs—an activity called **cash management**. Because the science of cash management is inexact, managers have derived ways to help them minimize the amount of cash that they need to keep on hand while also maximizing the return on a business's assets. One such method is to invest any excess cash in alternative investments that are readily convertible back into cash and earn a higher rate of return than cash, but which do not place the invested cash at risk of loss. These alternative investments are known as cash equivalents.

Cash equivalents are short-term, highly liquid investments that are (1) easily convertible into cash and (2) close enough to maturity so that their market value is relatively insensitive to interest rate changes (generally, investments with maturities of three months or less). U.S. Treasury bills, certificates of deposit (CDs), commercial paper (short-term notes issued by corporations), and money market funds are examples of cash equivalents. Because firms may differ as to exactly which investments they consider to be cash equivalents, GAAP requires that each firm disclose in the notes to the financial statements the company's policy regarding which investments are treated as cash equivalents.

When preparing a statement of cash flows, the cash and cash equivalents are added together and treated as a single amount. This is done because the purchase and sale of investments in cash equivalents are considered to be part of a firm's overall cash management strategy rather than a source or use of cash. As financial statement users evaluate a firm's cash flows, it should not matter whether the cash is on hand, deposited in a bank account, or invested in cash equivalents. Transfers back and forth between a firm's Cash account and its investments in cash equivalents, consequently, are not treated as cash inflows or outflows in the statement of cash flows.

When discussing the statement of cash flows, accountants often just use the word *cash* rather than the term *cash and cash equivalents*. We follow that practice in this chapter.

Definition of Cash Equivalents	ACCOUNTING IN PRACTICE

There are some differences between firms regarding which investments of cash are considered to be cash equivalents. For example, **PepsiCo, Inc.**, the beverage and snack food company, states in the notes to its financial statements that "Cash equivalents are investments with original maturities of three months or less." **International Game Technology**, a manufacturer of gaming machines and proprietory gaming software systems, on the other hand, notes that "In addition to cash deposits at major banks, cash and equivalents include other marketable securities with original maturities of 90 days or less, primarily in U.S. Treasury-backed money market funds." The commonality among all firms, however, is that cash equivalents represent a temporary investment of excess cash in risk-free investments until such time as the cash is needed to support a business's operations.

ACTIVITY CLASSIFICATIONS IN THE STATEMENT OF CASH FLOWS

A statement of cash flows classifies a company's cash receipts and cash payments into three major business activity categories: operating activities, investing activities, and financing activities. Grouping cash flows into these categories identifies the effect on cash of each of the major business activities of a firm. The combined effects on cash from all three categories explain the net change in cash for the period. The net change in cash is then reconciled with the beginning and ending balances of cash from the balance sheet. **Exhibit 13-1** illustrates the basic format for a statement of cash flows.

Exhibit 13-1	Format for the Statement of Cash Flows

SAMPLE COMPANY
Statement of Cash Flows
For Year Ended December 31, 2016

Cash Flow from Operating Activities		
(Details of cash flow from operating activities)...............	$###	
Cash provided (used) by operating activities...............		$###
Cash Flow from Investing Activities		
(Details of investing cash inflows and outflows)...............	###	
Cash provided (used) by investing activities...............		###
Cash Flow from Financing Activities		
(Details of financing cash inflows and outflows)...............	###	
Cash provided (used) by financing activities...............		###
Net increase (decrease) in cash...............		###
Cash at beginning of year...............		###
Cash at end of year...............		$###

Operating Activities

A company's income statement reflects the transactions and events that constitute its operating activities. The focus of a firm's operating activities involves selling goods or rendering services. The cash flow from **operating activities** is defined broadly enough, however, to include any cash receipts or payments that are not classified as investing activities or financing activities. For example, cash received from a lawsuit settlement and cash payments to charity are treated as cash flow from operating activities. The following are examples of cash inflows and outflows relating to a firm's operating activities:

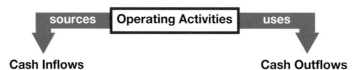

Cash Inflows	Cash Outflows
1. Receipts from customers for sales of goods or services.	1. Payments to suppliers.
2. Receipts of interest and dividends.	2. Payments to employees.
3. Other receipts that are not related to investing or financing activities, such as lawsuit settlements and refunds received from suppliers.	3. Payments of interest to creditors.
	4. Payments of taxes to governmental agencies.
	5. Other payments that are not related to investing or financing activities, such as contributions to charity.

Investing Activities

A firm's **investing activities** include those transactions involving (1) the acquisition or disposal of plant assets and intangible assets, (2) the purchase or sale of stocks, bonds, and other securities (that are not cash equivalents), and (3) the lending and subsequent collection of money.[1] The related cash receipts and cash payments appear in the investing activities section of the statement of cash flows. Examples of these cash flows include:

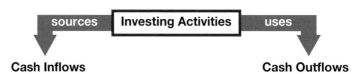

Cash Inflows	Cash Outflows
1. Receipts from the sale of plant assets and intangible assets.	1. Payments to purchase plant assets and intangible assets.
2. Receipts from sales of investments in stocks, bonds, and other securities (other than cash equivalents).	2. Payments to purchase stocks, bonds, and other securities (other than cash equivalents).
3. Receipts from repayments of loans by borrowers.	3. Payments made to lend money to borrowers.

Financing Activities

A firm engages in **financing activities** when it obtains cash from shareholders, returns cash to shareholders, borrows from creditors, and repays amounts borrowed from creditors. Cash flows related to these events are reported in the financing activities section of the statement of cash flows. Examples of these cash flows include:

---

[1] There are exceptions to the classification of these events as investing activities. For example, the purchase or sale of mortgage loans by a mortgage banker, like Bank of America, and the purchase or sale of securities in the trading account of a broker/dealer in financial securities, like Merrill Lynch, represent operating activities for these businesses.

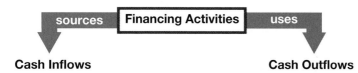

Cash Inflows

1. Receipts from the issuance of common stock and preferred stock and from sales of treasury stock.
2. Receipts from the issuance of bonds payable, mortgage notes payable, and other notes payable.

Cash Outflows

1. Payments to acquire treasury stock.
2. Payments of dividends.
3. Payments to settle outstanding bonds payable, mortgage notes payable, and other notes payable.

Observe that paying cash to settle such obligations as accounts payable, wages payable, interest payable, and income tax payable is an operating activity, not a financing activity. Also observe that cash received as interest and dividends and cash paid as interest are classified as cash flows from operating activities, although cash paid as dividends to a company's stockholders is classified as a financing activity.

IFRS ALERT

Although the statement of cash flows under U.S. GAAP has three activity categories—operations, investing, and financing—this is not the case under International Financial Reporting Standards (IFRS). Under IFRS, the statement of cash flows may have either four or five activity categories: Operations, Investing, Debt Financing, Equity Financing, and sometimes a category called the Effect of Foreign Currency Translation. In essence, IFRS segments the financing activities category into two separate categories relating to financing with debt and financing with equity. The sum of these two categories is exactly equivalent to the single category of financing activities under U.S. GAAP.

An Illustration of Activity Classification Usefulness

The classification of cash flows into the three business activity categories helps financial statement users analyze and interpret a company's cash flow data. To illustrate, assume that companies D, E, and F operate in the same industry, and that each company reported a $100,000 increase in cash during the period. Information from each company's statement of cash flows is summarized below:

	Company		
	D	**E**	**F**
Cash flow from operating activities	$100,000	$ 0	$ 0
Cash flow from investing activities:			
Sale of plant assets	0	100,000	0
Cash flow from financing activities:			
Issuance of notes payable	0	0	100,000
Net increase in cash.	$100,000	$100,000	$100,000

Although each company's increase in cash was exactly $100,000, the source of the cash increase varied by company. This variation affects the analysis of the cash flow data, particularly for potential creditors who must evaluate the likelihood of the repayment of funds loaned to a company. Based only on this cash flow data, a potential creditor would feel more comfortable lending money to Company D than to either Company E or F. D's cash increase came from its operating activities, whereas E's cash increase came from the sale of plant assets, a source that is unlikely to recur, and F's cash increase came from borrowed funds. Company F faces additional future uncertainty when the interest and principal payments on the existing notes become due, and for this reason, a potential creditor would be less inclined to extend additional loans to Company F.

NONCASH INVESTING AND FINANCING ACTIVITIES

Although many investing and financing activities affect cash and therefore are included in the investing and financing sections of the statement of cash flows, some significant investing and financing events do not affect current cash flow. Examples of **noncash investing and financing activities** are the issuance of stock or bonds in exchange for plant assets or intangible assets, the exchange of long-term assets for other long-term assets, and the conversion of long-term debt into common stock. A common feature among each of these transactions is that no cash is exchanged between the parties involved in the transaction.

Noncash investing and financing transactions generally do, however, affect future cash flows. Issuing bonds in exchange for equipment, for example, requires future cash payments for interest and principal on the bonds. On the other hand, converting bonds into common stock eliminates the future cash payments related to the bonds' interest and principal. Knowledge of these types of events, therefore, should be helpful to financial statement users who wish to evaluate a firm's future cash flows.

Information regarding noncash investing and financing transactions is disclosed in a separate accounting schedule. The separate schedule may be placed immediately below the statement of cash flows or it may be placed among the notes to the financial statements.

PRINCIPLE ALERT	**Objectivity Principle**

The *objectivity principle* asserts that the usefulness of financial statements is enhanced when the underlying data are objective and verifiable. Measuring cash and the changes in cash are among the most objective measurements that accountants make. The statement of cash flows, therefore, is the most objective financial statement required under generally accepted accounting principles. This characteristic of the statement of cash flows is welcomed by investors and creditors interested in evaluating the quality of a firm's net income and assets. Financial statement users often feel more confident about the quality of a company's net income and assets when there is a high correlation between, or relationship with, a company's cash flow from operating activities and its net income.

USING THE STATEMENT OF CASH FLOWS

The Financial Accounting Standards Board believes that one of the principal objectives of financial reporting is to help financial statement users assess the amount, timing, and uncertainty of a business's future cash flows. These assessments, in turn, help users evaluate prospective future cash receipts from their investments in, or loans to, a business. Although the statement of cash flows describes a company's past cash flows, the statement is also useful for assessing future cash flows since the recent past is often a very good predictor of the future.

The statement of cash flows shows the cash effects of a firm's operating, investing, and financing activities. Distinguishing among these different categories of cash flow helps financial statement users compare, evaluate, and predict a business's future cash flows. With cash flow information, creditors and investors are better able to assess a company's ability to repay its liabilities and pay dividends. A firm's need for outside financing can also be evaluated using the statement of cash flows. Further, the statement enables users to observe and analyze management's investing and financing policies, plans, and strategies.

The statement of cash flows also provides information useful in evaluating a firm's financial flexibility. **Financial flexibility** is a company's ability to generate sufficient amounts of cash to respond to unanticipated needs and opportunities. Information about past cash flows, particularly cash flow from operations, helps in assessing financial flexibility. An evaluation of a firm's ability to survive an unexpected drop in demand for its goods and services, for example, may include a review of its past cash flow from operations. The larger these past cash flows, the greater will be a firm's ability to withstand adverse changes in future economic conditions.

Some investors and creditors find the statement of cash flows useful in evaluating the "quality" of a firm's net income. Determining net income under the accrual basis of accounting requires many accruals, deferrals, allocations, and valuations. These adjustment and measurement procedures introduce greater subjectivity into a company's income determination than some financial statement users are comfortable with. Consequently, these users can relate a more objective performance measure—a firm's cash flow from operations—to net income. To these users, the higher the relationship between a company's net income and the cash flow from operations, the higher is the quality of the firm's net income.

CASH FLOW FROM OPERATING ACTIVITIES

The first section of the statement of cash flows presents a firm's cash flow from operating activities. Two alternative formats are available to present the cash flow from operating activities: the indirect method and the direct method. Both methods report the same amount of cash flow from operating activities and differ only in how the cash flow from operating activities is presented.

The **indirect method** starts with net income using the accrual basis of accounting and applies a series of adjustments to convert it to net income under the cash basis of accounting, which is equivalent to the cash flow from operating activities. The adjustments to net income do not represent specific cash flows; consequently, the indirect method does not report any detail concerning individual operating cash inflows and outflows.

The **direct method** shows individual amounts of cash inflows and cash outflows for the major operating activities. The net difference between these inflows and outflows is the cash flow from operating activities.

The Financial Accounting Standards Board encourages companies to use the direct method but permits the use of the indirect method. Despite the FASB's preference for the direct method, more than 95 percent of companies preparing the statement of cash flows use the indirect method. The indirect method is popular because (1) it is easier and less expensive to prepare than the direct method and (2) the direct method requires a supplemental disclosure showing cash flow from operating activities prepared under the indirect method.

Popularity of Method for Reporting the Cash Flow From Operations	ACCOUNTING IN PRACTICE

Do you think a direct approach in communicating with financial statement users is best, or should your approach be more indirect? When it comes to reporting the cash flow from operations, companies appear to favor the indirect approach by a wide margin as evidenced by the responses to a survey of 600 large U.S. companies.

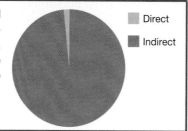

☐ Direct
☐ Indirect

Source: Accounting Trends and Techniques

A Comparison of Accrual-Basis and Cash-Basis Amounts

Accountants calculate net income on the income statement using the accrual basis of accounting. The cash flow from operating activities, presented on the statement of cash flows, represents a company's net income using the cash basis of accounting. There is no necessary relationship between the two numbers. Compared with net income, the cash flow from operating activities may be larger, smaller, or about the same amount. Financial data from past annual reports of three well-known companies— **Chiquita Brands**, **Levi Strauss**, and **Harley-Davidson**—bear this out.

	Net Income or (Loss)	Cash Flow Provided (Used) by Operating Activities
Chiquita Brands Intl. Inc.	$(323,725,000)	$ 8,204,000
Levi Strauss & Co.	$ 229,285,000	$ 224,809,000
Harley-Davidson Inc.	$ 654,718,000	$(684,649,000)

YOUR TURN! 13.1

The solution is on page 514.

Classify each of the cash flow events listed below as either a(n) (1) operating activity, (2) investing activity, or (3) financing activity:

1. Cash received from customers
2. Cash sale of land
3. Cash paid to suppliers
4. Cash purchase of equipment
5. Payment on note payable
6. Cash dividend payment
7. Cash wages paid
8. Purchase of treasury stock
9. Cash sale of investments

The following section on preparing the statement of cash flows uses the indirect method. Appendix 13A uses the direct method. Your instructor can choose to cover either one or both methods. If the indirect method is skipped, then read Appendix 13A and return to the section (8 pages ahead) titled "Analyzing Cash Flows."

PREPARING THE STATEMENT OF CASH FLOWS USING THE INDIRECT METHOD

LO2 **Explain** the preparation of a statement of cash flows using the indirect method.

To prepare a statement of cash flows using the indirect method, the following information is needed: a company's income statement, comparative balance sheets for the current and prior year, and possibly additional data taken from the company's financial statements. **Exhibit 13-2** presents this information for the Bennett Company. We will use this data to prepare Bennett's 2016 statement of cash flows using the indirect method. As will be seen shortly, Bennett's statement of cash flows will explain the $25,000 increase in the company's cash account that occurred during 2016 (from $10,000 at the beginning of the year to $35,000 at the end of the year) by classifying the firm's cash inflows and outflows into the three business activity categories of operating, investing, and financing.

To see that the statement of cash flows can be prepared using only a company's income statement and the changes in its balance sheet accounts, consider the balance sheet equation:

$$\text{Assets (A)} = \text{Liabilities (L)} + \text{Stockholders' equity (SE)} \qquad (1)$$

Separating a firm's assets into its cash (CA) and noncash assets (NCA) gives:

$$CA + NCA = L + SE \qquad (2)$$

And, rewriting the balance sheet equation in changes form yields:

$$\Delta CA + \Delta NCA = \Delta L + \Delta SE \qquad (3)$$

Finally, rearranging the components of the equation shows that the change in cash (which is the end result of the statement of cash flows) can be computed from the change in all of the other balance sheet accounts:

$$\Delta CA = \Delta L - \Delta NCA + \Delta SE \qquad (4)$$

Exhibit 13-2	Financial Data of Bennett Company

BENNETT COMPANY
Income Statement
For Year Ended December 31, 2016

Sales revenue.		$250,000
Cost of goods sold.	$148,000	
Wages expense	52,000	
Insurance expense.	5,000	
Depreciation expense.	10,000	
Income tax expense.	11,000	
Gain on sale of plant assets	(8,000)	218,000
Net income.		$ 32,000

Additional Data for 2016
1. Sold plant assets costing $20,000 for $28,000 cash.
2. Declared and paid cash dividends of $13,000.

BENNETT COMPANY
Balance Sheets

As of December 31	2016	2015
Assets		
Cash	$ 35,000	$ 10,000
Accounts receivable.	39,000	34,000
Inventory.	54,000	60,000
Prepaid insurance	17,000	4,000
Long-term investments	15,000	—
Plant assets	180,000	200,000
Accumulated depreciation	(50,000)	(40,000)
Patent.	60,000	—
Total assets	$350,000	$268,000
Liabilities and Equity		
Accounts payable.	$ 10,000	$ 19,000
Income tax payable	5,000	3,000
Common stock.	260,000	190,000
Retained earnings	75,000	56,000
Total liabilities and equity.	$350,000	$268,000

IFRS ALERT

Currently, both U.S. GAAP and IFRS permit a company to present its statement of cash flows using either the direct method or the indirect method. A topic being considered by the FASB/IASB convergence project would limit the preparation of the statement of cash flows to just the direct method. The direct method is currently preferred by both the FASB and the IASB, although most U.S. firms present their statement of cash flows using the indirect method.

Five Steps to Preparing a Statement of Cash Flows

The process to prepare a statement of cash flows using the indirect method involves five steps. The approach begins by focusing initially only on the balance sheet and then proceeds to integrate a business's income statement through a series of systematic adjustments to a preliminary statement of cash flows derived solely from balance sheet data.

Step One   Using just the beginning and ending balance sheets (see Columns 1 and 2 in **Exhibit 13-3**), calculate the change in each balance sheet account by subtracting the beginning balance sheet amount from the ending amount. The results of this step for the Bennett Company are presented in Column 3 of **Exhibit 13-3**. To simplify this step, the change in the Plant Assets account is combined with the Accumulated Depreciation account—that is, the change in the Plant Assets account is calculated on a net of accumulated depreciation basis.

To verify the accuracy of the Step One calculations, simply compare the sum of the changes in the asset accounts ($82,000) with the sum of the changes in the liability and stockholders' equity accounts ($82,000). These totals must be equal. If the totals are not equal, it indicates the presence of a subtraction error that must be identified and corrected before proceeding to Step Two.

Exhibit 13-3	Preparing a Statement of Cash Flows: The Indirect Method			

BENNETT COMPANY
Balance Sheet
December 31, 2016

	(1) Beginning of Year	(2) End of Year	(3) Change for Year	(4) Cash Flow Classification
Assets				
Cash	$ 10,000	$ 35,000	$25,000	Cash flow increase
Accounts receivable	34,000	39,000	5,000	Operating
Inventory	60,000	54,000	(6,000)	Operating
Prepaid insurance	4,000	17,000	13,000	Operating
Long-term investments	0	15,000	15,000	Investing
Plant assets (net)	160,000	130,000	(30,000)	Investing/Operating
Patent	0	60,000	60,000	Investing/Operating
Total assets	$268,000	$350,000	$82,000	
Liabilities and Equity				
Accounts payable	$ 19,000	$ 10,000	$ (9,000)	Operating
Income tax payable	3,000	5,000	2,000	Operating
Common stock	190,000	260,000	70,000	Financing
Retained earnings	56,000	75,000	19,000	Operating/Financing
Total liabilities and equity	$268,000	$350,000	$82,000	

An important figure identified during Step One is the "bottom line" of the statement of cash flows, namely the change in the cash account. **Exhibit 13-3** reveals that the cash account of the Bennett Company increased by $25,000 from the beginning of the year to the end of the year. Hence, all of the various cash inflows and outflows for the company must aggregate to this figure.

Step Two   Identify the appropriate business activity category—operating, investing, or financing—for each balance sheet account. The cash flow activity classifications are presented in Column 4 of **Exhibit 13-3**.

Although measuring the change in the balance sheet accounts in Step 1 is a straightforward arithmetic activity, there can be some confusion over the correct activity classification for some of the balance sheet accounts in Step 2. The change in accounts receivable, inventory, prepaid insurance, accounts payable, and income tax payable are all easily identified as operating activities because they are associated with the day-to-day operations of a business. The change in common stock, on the other hand, is clearly a financing activity because it is associated with raising capital to finance a business. The change in net plant assets, however, can be both an investing activity and an operating activity. Purchases and sales of plant assets are associated with the capital investment needed to run a business, and thus are an investing activity. However, the depreciation expense associated with plant assets is an operating activity since the depreciation of plant assets is deducted as an expense in the calculation of a company's net income. Similarly, the change in intangible assets such as patents can be both an investing activity and an operating activity because the acquisition or sale of intangibles is an investing activity, whereas the amortization of intangibles is an expense deducted in the calculation of net income, and hence, an operating activity. Finally, the change in retained earnings can be both an operating activity and a financing activity because retained earnings is increased by net income, an operating activity, but decreased by the payment of dividends, a financing activity.

As a general rule, the following cash flow activity classifications apply, although exceptions exist:

Balance Sheet Account	Cash Flow Activity Category
Current assets	Operating
Noncurrent assets	Investing/Operating
Current liabilities.	Operating
Noncurrent liabilities.	Financing
Capital stock	Financing
Retained earnings	Operating/Financing

Examples of exceptions to the above cash flow activity classifications include the following:

■ Marketable securities, a current asset, are an investing activity item.

■ Current maturities of long-term debt, a current liability, are a financing activity item.

■ Employee pension obligations, a noncurrent liability, are an operating activity item.

Step Three Having completed Steps One and Two, you are now ready to build a preliminary statement of cash flows using the calculated increases or decreases in the various balance sheet accounts from Step One and the identified activity classifications from Step Two. The preliminary statement of cash flows for the Bennett Company using the change values from Column 3 of **Exhibit 13-3** and the cash flow activity classifications from Column 4 is presented in **Exhibit 13-4**.

Because a statement of cash flows measures the inflows and outflows of cash for a business, it is important to note that the sign of the asset account changes calculated in Step One must be reversed for purposes of preparing the preliminary statement of cash flows in **Exhibit 13-4**. This can be seen in equation (4) above in which the change in noncash assets has a negative sign. For instance, **Exhibit 13-4** shows that the change in accounts receivable was an increase of $5,000, whereas the change in inventory was a decrease of $6,000. When preparing the indirect method statement of cash flows, a $5,000 increase in accounts receivable represents a subtraction from net income (a cash outflow), and a decline in inventory of $6,000 represents an addition to net income (a cash inflow), to arrive at the cash flow from operations. To illustrate why an increase in accounts receivable must be subtracted from net income to arrive at operating cash flow, consider how sales revenue is initially recorded. Assume that a $2,000 sale of goods is paid for with $1,200 in cash and the remaining amount recorded as an increase in accounts receivable. In this example, net income increases by $2,000, but cash is increased by only $1,200. Therefore, net income must be reduced by the $800 increase in accounts receivable in order to yield the correct cash flow from operations. Hence, when preparing the preliminary statement of cash flows in Step Three, it is important to remember to reverse the sign of the change values for the asset accounts. This is unnecessary for the liability and stockholders' equity accounts as can also be seen from equation (4) above.

Exhibit 13-4	An Illustration of a Preliminary Statement of Cash Flows: The Indirect Method

BENNETT COMPANY
Preliminary Statement of Cash Flows
For Year Ended December 31, 2016

Operating Activities

Retained earnings	$19,000
Accounts receivable	(5,000)
Inventory	6,000
Prepaid insurance	(13,000)
Accounts payable	(9,000)
Income tax payable	2,000
Cash flow from operating activities	0
Investing Activities	
Long-term investments	(15,000)
Plant assets (net)	30,000
Patent	(60,000)
Cash flow for investing activities	(45,000)
Financing Activities	
Common stock	70,000
Cash flow from financing activities	70,000
Change in cash (from the balance sheet)	$25,000

Exhibit 13-4 presents the preliminary statement of cash flows for the Bennett Company. This preliminary statement suggests that the firm's cash flow from operating activities was $0, the cash flow from investing activities was negative $45,000, and the cash flow from financing activities was $70,000. As required, the cash inflows and outflows aggregate to the change in cash from the balance sheet, an increase of $25,000.

Step Four   To this point we have used the balance sheet exclusively to provide the needed inputs to our statement of cash flows. For most businesses, however, cash flow will also be generated by a firm's ongoing operations. Hence, it is now appropriate to introduce the operations related data found on the company's income statement (see **Exhibit 13-2**).

In this step, we accomplish two important actions involving the preliminary statement of cash flows in **Exhibit 13-4**. First, the change in retained earnings from the balance sheet will be replaced by net income from the income statement. For the Bennett Company, the change in retained earnings of $19,000 does not equal net income of $32,000. The difference of $13,000 ($32,000 − $19,000) represents a cash dividend paid to Bennett's shareholders. Thus, when we replace retained earnings of $19,000 with net income of $32,000, it is also necessary to report the $13,000 cash dividend payment as a cash outflow under the financing activities section in **Exhibit 13-5**. Increasing the cash flow from operations and decreasing the cash flow from financing activities by an equivalent amount ($13,000) allows the statement of cash flows to remain in balance with the net change in cash of $25,000.

Second, we adjust the Bennett Company's net income for any **noncash expenses** such as the depreciation of plant assets and the amortization of intangibles that were deducted in the process of calculating the firm's accrual basis net income.[2] These noncash

---

[2] Depreciation expense and amortization expense are called noncash expenses because these expenses do not involve any current period cash outflow. Depreciation expense, for example, represents the allocation of the purchase price of plant assets over the many periods that these assets produce sales revenue for a business. The matching principle requires that the cost of plant assets be matched with the sales revenue produced by these assets, and this is accomplished on the income statement by the deduction of the periodic depreciation charge.

expenses must be added back to net income in the operating activities section to correctly measure the firm's operating cash flow. However, to keep the preliminary statement of cash flows in balance with an increase in cash of $25,000, it is also necessary to subtract equivalent amounts in the investing activities section.

To summarize, the adjustments to the Bennett Company's preliminary statement of cash flows in **Exhibit 13-4** are:

1. Net income of $32,000 replaces the change in retained earnings of $19,000 in the operating activities section. This action adds $13,000 to the cash flow from operating activities. To keep the statement of cash flows in balance with the change in cash of $25,000, it is necessary to subtract $13,000 elsewhere on the statement. Since retained earnings is calculated as follows:

$$
\begin{array}{l}
\text{Retained earnings (beginning)} \\
+ \text{ Net income for the period} \\
- \text{ Dividends declared} \\
\hline
= \text{ Retained earnings (ending)}
\end{array}
$$

the outflow of $13,000 is also reflected as a cash dividend to shareholders under the financing activities section.

2. Depreciation expense of $10,000, a noncash deduction from net income, is added back to net income to avoid understating the cash flow from operations. However, to keep the statement of cash flows in balance with the change in cash of $25,000, a similar amount is subtracted from plant assets under the investing activities section.

Step Five To provide the most useful cash flow data, a final step is required: Make any appropriate adjustments to the operating activities section to calculate a company's operating cash flow. As noted above, a firm's operating cash flow should include only the cash flows from operating activities. Consequently, to calculate the cash flow from operating activities of a business, it is necessary to review a company's income statement to identify and remove the financial effects of any nonoperating transactions included in net income.[3]

To illustrate this point, note that the Bennett Company sold plant assets during the year at a gain of $8,000 ($28,000 sales price less $20,000 cost). This event is an investing activity and therefore properly belongs in the investing activities section. However, the gain of $8,000 is included in net income in the operating activities section. Thus, to correctly assess Bennett's cash flows, it is necessary to subtract the gain from the operating activities section and add it to the change in plant assets in the investing activities section. When combined with the adjustment for depreciation expense from Step Four, the cash flow from plant assets is $28,000 ($30,000 change in plant assets − $10,000 adjustment for depreciation expense + $8,000 adjustment for gain). The adjusted amount of $28,000 is equal to the cash received on the sale of plant assets

Exhibit 13-5 presents the final statement of cash flows for Bennett Company and includes not only the adjustments from Step Four, but also the adjustment to remove any nonoperating gains and losses from the cash flow from operating activities (Step Five). Note that the company's statement of cash flows remains in balance with the change in cash of $25,000 after the adjustments in both of these steps. This result is possible because whatever amount was added to (or subtracted from) net income under the cash flow from operating activities, an equivalent amount was subtracted from (or added to) the investing activities or the financing activities.

---

[3] An exception is interest expense, which most investment professionals view as a financing activity. Regardless, interest payments are required to be included in the cash flow from operating activities.

Exhibit 13-5	Statement of Cash Flows—The Indirect Method

BENNETT COMPANY
Statement of Cash Flows
For Year Ended December 31, 2016

Cash Flow from Operating Activities

Net income		$32,000
Add (deduct) items to convert net income to cash basis		
Depreciation	10,000	
Gain on sale of plant assets	(8,000)	
Accounts receivable increase	(5,000)	
Inventory decrease	6,000	
Prepaid insurance increase.	(13,000)	
Accounts payable decrease	(9,000)	
Income tax payable increase	2,000	
Cash provided by operating activities.		$15,000

Cash Flow from Investing Activities

Purchase of long-term investments	(15,000)	
Sale of plant assets	28,000	
Purchase of patent	(60,000)	
Cash used by investing activities		(47,000)

Cash Flow from Financing Activities

Issuance of common stock	70,000	
Payment of dividends.	(13,000)	
Cash provided by financing activities		57,000
Net increase in cash		25,000
Cash at beginning of year		10,000
Cash at end of year		$35,000

Bennett's statement of cash flows reveals that the cash flow provided by operating activities is $15,000, the cash flow used by investing activities is negative $47,000, and the cash flow provided by financing activities is $57,000. The resulting total cash flow of $25,000 exactly equals the increase in cash on the balance sheet of $25,000, as required.

The following illustration summarizes the five-step process to prepare an indirect method statement of cash flows:

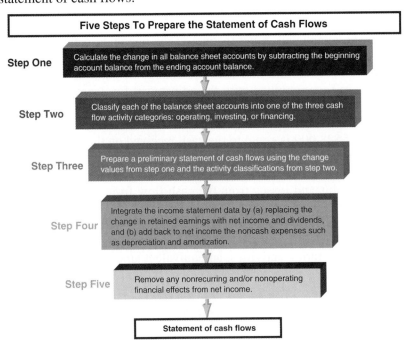

Five Steps To Prepare the Statement of Cash Flows

Step One Calculate the change in all balance sheet accounts by subtracting the beginning account balance from the ending account balance.

Step Two Classify each of the balance sheet accounts into one of the three cash flow activity categories: operating, investing, or financing.

Step Three Prepare a preliminary statement of cash flows using the change values from step one and the activity classifications from step two.

Step Four Integrate the income statement data by (a) replacing the change in retained earnings with net income and dividends, and (b) add back to net income the noncash expenses such as depreciation and amortization.

Step Five Remove any nonrecurring and/or nonoperating financial effects from net income.

Statement of cash flows

According to **Home Depot**, "Our values are our beliefs, principles and standards that do not change over time. Values are the resources we draw on when asked to make decisions. They form the groundwork for our ethical behavior. All that we do at The Home Depot must be consistent with the values of the Company. We believe in *Doing the Right Thing*, having *Respect for all People*, building *Strong Relationships*, *Taking Care of Our People*, *Giving Back*, providing *Excellent Customer Service*, *Encouraging Entrepreneurial Spirit* and providing strong *Shareholder Returns*."

Home Depot believes that "Doing the Right Thing" leads to doing well for all its stakeholders, including its shareholders. As Home Depot states, "We will conduct our business and ourselves in a way that enhances and preserves the reputation of the Company while providing our shareholders with a fair return on their investment." There seems to be a lot of truth in this as Home Depot has managed to stay profitable even as the poor U.S. economy has battered the construction industry. In fiscal years 2008 and 2007, during the height of the construction downturn, the company still managed to produce cash flows from operating activities each year in excess of $5 billion.

Husky Company's 2016 income statement and comparative balance sheets as of December 31 of 2016 and 2015 are shown below:

YOUR TURN! 13.2

The solution is on page 514.

HUSKY COMPANY Income Statement For Year Ended December 31, 2016		
Sales revenue.		$1,270,000
Cost of goods sold.	$860,000	
Wages expense	172,000	
Insurance expense.	16,000	
Depreciation expense.	34,000	
Interest expense.	18,000	
Income tax expense.	58,000	1,158,000
Net income.		$ 112,000

HUSKY COMPANY Balance Sheets	Dec. 31, 2016	Dec. 31, 2015
Assets		
Cash.	$ 22,000	$ 10,000
Accounts receivable.	82,000	64,000
Inventory.	180,000	120,000
Prepaid insurance	10,000	14,000
Plant assets	500,000	390,000
Accumulated depreciation	(136,000)	(102,000)
Total assets	$658,000	$496,000
Liabilities and Stockholders' Equity		
Accounts payable.	$ 14,000	$ 20,000
Wages payable.	18,000	12,000
Income tax payable	14,000	16,000
Bonds payable	260,000	150,000
Common stock.	180,000	180,000
Retained earnings	172,000	118,000
Total liabilities and stockholders' equity	$658,000	$496,000

Cash dividends of $58,000 were declared and paid during 2016. Plant assets were purchased for cash, and bonds payable were issued for cash. Accounts payable relate to merchandise purchases.

Required
Prepare a 2016 statement of cash flows for the Husky Company using the indirect method.

For readers skipping the indirect method, please resume reading here.

ANALYZING CASH FLOWS

LO3 **Define** several ratios used to analyze the statement of cash flows and **explain** their use.

Data from the statement of cash flows are often used to calculate financial measures to evaluate a company's cash flow health. Three such measures include a company's free cash flow, the operating cash flow to current liabilities ratio, and the operating cash flow to capital expenditures ratio.

Free Cash Flow

Free cash flow (FCF) is often used by investment professionals and investors to evaluate a company's cash-flow strength. FCF is an important performance reference point for investment professionals because it is less subject to the accounting trickery that may characterize accrual basis net income of some firms. Free cash flow is calculated as follows:

> **FCF = Cash flow from operating activities − Capital expenditures**

Capital expenditures refer to the required reinvestment in a business's plant and intangible assets necessary to enable a firm to remain a going concern. A firm with strong free cash flow will carry a higher stock value than one with weak (or no) free cash flow.

TAKEAWAY 13.1	Concept ➞	Method ➞	Assessment
	Does a company generate cash flows in excess of its capital expenditure needs?	Statement of cash flows. FCF = Cash flow from operating activities − Capital expenditures	The higher the free cash flow, the greater is a company's ability to generate cash for needs other than capital expenditures.

Operating-Cash-Flow-to-Current-Liabilities Ratio

Two measures previously introduced—the current ratio and the quick ratio—emphasize the relationship of a company's current or quick assets to its current liabilities in an attempt to measure the ability of a firm to pay its current liabilities. The **operating-cash-flow-to-current-liabilities ratio** is another measure of a company's ability to pay its current liabilities. While the current and quick ratios focus on a firm's ability to pay liabilities using existing current or quick assets, the operating cash flow to current liabilities highlights a firm's ability to pay its current liabilities using its operating cash flow. The ratio is calculated as follows:

$$\text{Operating-cash-flow-to-current-liabilities ratio} = \frac{\text{Cash flow from operating activities}}{\text{Average current liabilities}}$$

The cash flow from operating activities is obtained from the statement of cash flows. The denominator is the average of the beginning and ending current liabilities for the year.

The following amounts (in millions of dollars) were taken from the financial statements of the **Gannett Co., Inc.**, a diversified news and information company that publishes *USA Today:*

Cash flow from operating activities	$1,017,186
Current liabilities at beginning of the year	962,163
Current liabilities at end of the year	1,153,141

The operating-cash-flow-to-current-liabilities ratio for the Gannett Co. is calculated as follows:

$$\frac{\$1,017,186}{\left[\frac{(\$962,163 + \$1,153,141)}{2}\right]} = 0.96$$

The higher this ratio, the greater is a firm's ability to pay current liabilities using its operating cash flow. A ratio of 0.5 is considered a strong ratio; consequently, Gannett's ratio of 0.96 would be interpreted as very strong. A ratio of 0.96 indicates that Gannett generates $0.96 of operating cash flow for every dollar of current liabilities.

Concept	Method	Assessment	TAKEAWAY 13.2
Will a company have sufficient cash to pay its current liabilities as they become due?	Statement of cash flows and balance sheet. $\text{Operating-cash-flow-to-current-liabilities ratio} = \dfrac{\text{Cash flow from operating activities}}{\text{Average current liabilities}}$	The higher the ratio, the higher the probability that a company will have sufficient operating cash flow to pay its current liabilities as they become due.	

Operating-Cash-Flow-to-Capital-Expenditures Ratio

To remain competitive, a business must be able to replace, and expand when appropriate, its property, plant, and equipment. A ratio that evaluates a firm's ability to finance its capital investments from operating cash flow is the **operating-cash-flow-to-capital-expenditures ratio**. This ratio is calculated as follows:

$$\text{Operating-cash-flow-to-capital-expenditures ratio} = \frac{\textbf{Cash flow from operating activities}}{\textbf{Annual net capital expenditures}}$$

The numerator in this ratio comes from the statement of cash flows. Information for the denominator may be found in one or more places in the financial statements. Data regarding a company's capital expenditures are presented in the investing activities section of the statement of cash flows. (When capital expenditures are reported in the statement of cash flows, the amount is often broken into two figures—(1) Proceeds from the sale of property, plant and equipment and (2) Purchases of property, plant and equipment. The appropriate "capital expenditures" figure for purpose of calculating this ratio is the net of the two amounts.) Data on capital expenditures are also part of the required industry segment disclosures in the notes to the financial statements. Finally, management's discussion and analysis of the financial statements may identify a company's annual capital expenditures.

A ratio in excess of 1.0 indicates that a firm's current operating activities are providing cash in excess of the amount needed to fund its desired investment in plant assets and would normally be considered a sign of financial strength. The interpretation of this ratio is influenced by the trend in recent years, the ratio being achieved by other firms in the same industry, and the stage of a firm's life cycle. A firm in the early stages of its life cycle—when periods of rapid expansion may occur—may be expected to experience a lower ratio than a firm in the later stage of its life cycle—when maintenance of plant capacity may be more likely than an expansion of plant capacity.

To illustrate the ratio's calculation, **Abbott Laboratories**, a manufacturer of pharmaceutical and health care products, reported capital expenditures (in thousands of dollars) of $1,287,724. Abbott's cash flow from operating activities was $6,994,620. Thus, Abbott's operating-cash-flow-to-capital-expenditures ratio for the year was 5.43, or ($6,994,620/$1,287,724). The following are operating-cash-flow-to-capital-expenditures ratios for other well-known companies:

PepsiCo Inc. (Consumer foods and beverages)	2.98
Lockheed Martin Corporation (Aerospace).	4.77
Norfolk Southern Corporation (Freight transportation services).	1.87
Federal Mogul Corporation (Precision parts)	2.04

ACCOUNTING IN PRACTICE	Know Your Cash Flow
	The expression "Cash is King" certainly holds true for any small business. It is critical for entrepreneurs to understand the difference between net income and cash flow. Cash is what is needed to pay the bills. While earning a positive net income is nice, it is cash and not net income that runs the business. Many small businesses have failed because of a lack of managing cash flows.

TAKEAWAY 13.3	Concept	→ Method →	Assessment
	Does a company generate sufficient operating cash flows to finance its capital expenditure needs?	Statement of cash flows. $$\text{Operating-cash-flow-to-capital-expenditures ratio} = \frac{\text{Cash flow from operating activities}}{\text{Annual net capital expenditures}}$$	The higher the ratio, the higher the probability that a company will generate sufficient operating cash flow to finance its capital expenditure needs.

YOUR TURN! 13.3

The solution is on page 514.

The following selected data were obtained from the financial statements of Blake Enterprises:

Cash flow from operating activities	$40,000
Annual net capital expenditures.	12,500
Average current liabilities	30,000

Calculate the following financial measures for Blake Enterprises:

1. Free cash flow
2. Operating-cash-flow-to-current-liabilities ratio
3. Operating-cash-flow-to-capital-expenditures ratio

COMPREHENSIVE PROBLEM

Terry Company's income statement and comparative balance sheets at December 31, 2016 and 2015, are as follows:

TERRY COMPANY Income Statement For Year Ended December 31, 2016		
Sales revenue.		$385,000
Dividend income.		5,000
		390,000
Cost of goods sold.	$233,000	
Wages expense	82,000	
Advertising expense.	10,000	
Depreciation expense.	11,000	
Income tax expense.	17,000	
Loss on sale of investments.	2,000	355,000
Net income.		$ 35,000

TERRY COMPANY Balance Sheets		
	Dec. 31, 2016	**Dec. 31, 2015**
Assets		
Cash.	$ 8,000	$ 12,000
Accounts receivable.	22,000	28,000
Inventory.	94,000	66,000
Prepaid advertising.	12,000	9,000
Long-term investments	30,000	40,000
Plant assets	178,000	130,000
Accumulated depreciation	(72,000)	(61,000)
Total assets	$272,000	$224,000
Liabilities and Stockholders' Equity		
Accounts payable.	$ 27,000	$ 14,000
Wages payable.	6,000	2,500
Income tax payable	3,000	4,500
Common stock.	139,000	125,000
Retained earnings	97,000	79,000
Unrealized loss on investments	—	(1,000)
Total liabilities and stockholders' equity	$272,000	$224,000

Cash dividends of $17,000 were declared and paid during 2016. Plant assets were purchased for cash, and, later in the year, additional common stock was issued for cash. Investments costing $10,000 were sold for cash at a $1,000 loss.

Required

a.   Calculate the change in cash that occurred during 2016.

b.   Prepare a 2016 statement of cash flows using the indirect method.

Solution

a. $8,000 ending balance − $12,000 beginning balance = $4,000 decrease in cash

b.   1.   Use the indirect method to determine the cash flow from operating activities.

•   The adjustments to convert Terry Company's net income of $35,000 to the cash provided by operating activities of $38,000 are shown in the following statement of cash flows.

2. Analyze changes in remaining noncash asset (and contra asset) accounts to determine cash flows from investing activities.
   - Long-term investments: $10,000 decrease resulted from sale of investments for cash at a $1,000 loss. Cash received from sale of investments = $9,000 ($10,000 cost − $1,000 loss).
   - Plant assets: $48,000 increase resulted from purchase of plant assets for cash. Cash paid to purchase plant assets = $48,000.
   - Accumulated depreciation: $11,000 increase resulted from the recording of 2016 depreciation. No cash flow effect.

3. Analyze changes in remaining liability and stockholders' equity accounts to determine cash flows from financing activities.
   - Common stock: $14,000 increase resulted from the issuance of stock for cash. Cash received from issuance of common stock = $14,000.
   - Retained earnings: $18,000 increase resulted from net income of $35,000 and dividend declaration of $17,000. Cash paid as dividends = $17,000.

   The statement of cash flows (indirect method) is as follows:

TERRY COMPANY **Statement of Cash Flows** **For the Year Ended December 31, 2016**		
Cash Flow from Operating Activities		
Net income	$35,000	
Add (deduct) items to convert net income to cash basis		
Depreciation	11,000	
Loss on sale of investments	2,000	
Accounts receivable decrease	6,000	
Inventory increase	(28,000)	
Prepaid advertising increase	(3,000)	
Accounts payable increase	13,000	
Wages payable increase	3,500	
Income tax payable decrease	(1,500)	
Cash provided by operating activities		$38,000
Cash Flow from Investing Activities		
Sale of investments	9,000	
Purchase of plant assets	(48,000)	
Cash used by investing activities		(39,000)
Cash Flow from Financing Activities		
Issuance of common stock	14,000	
Payment of dividends	(17,000)	
Cash used by financing activities		(3,000)
Net decrease in cash		(4,000)
Cash at beginning of year		12,000
Cash at end of year		$ 8,000

APPENDIX 13A: Preparing the Statement of Cash Flows Under the Direct Method

Although it is quite straightforward to create a direct method statement of cash flows given access to a company's internal accounting records, such access is rarely available to anyone except a company's management team. All that is necessary is to pull the numbers directly off the Cash general ledger account and place them in the appropriate section of the statement of cash flows. This is why the direct method is referred to as "direct." The cash flow from operations is taken directly from the company's general ledger, rather than being indirectly computed from net income. Unfortunately, investment professionals, lenders, and stockholders rarely have access to such proprietary internal data. Thus, it is necessary to be able to create direct method cash flow information using only such publicly available data as the indirect method statement of cash flows.

LO4 Explain the preparation of a statement of cash flows using the direct method.

The process to convert an indirect method statement of cash flows to the direct method requires two steps. First, replace net income (the first line item under the operating activities section of the indirect method statement format) with the line items appearing on a firm's income statement. For instance, Bennett Company's income statement in **Exhibit 13-2** contains the following line items:

Sales revenue.	$250,000
Cost of goods sold.	(148,000)
Wages expense	(52,000)
Insurance expense	(5,000)
Depreciation expense.	(10,000)
Income tax expense.	(11,000)
Gain on sale of plant assets.	8,000
Net income.	$ 32,000

Thus, for the Bennett Company, we begin by replacing the net income of $32,000 under the operating activities section in **Exhibit 13-5** with the seven income statement line items shown above, which aggregate to $32,000.

The second step involves adjusting the income statement line items identified in Step One with the remaining line items from the operating activities section of the indirect method statement of cash flows. **Exhibit 13A-1** summarizes the procedures for converting individual income statement items to the corresponding cash flows from operating activities.

Exhibit 13A-1	Direct Method Conversion Schedule: Adjustments to Convert Income Statement Items to Operating Activity Cash Flows

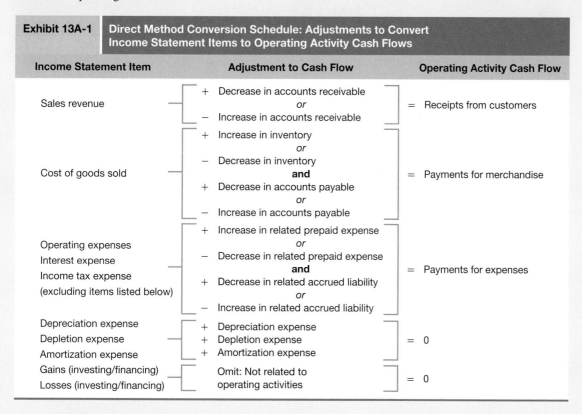

Income Statement Item	Adjustment to Cash Flow	Operating Activity Cash Flow
Sales revenue	+ Decrease in accounts receivable *or* − Increase in accounts receivable	= Receipts from customers
Cost of goods sold	+ Increase in inventory *or* − Decrease in inventory **and** + Decrease in accounts payable *or* − Increase in accounts payable	= Payments for merchandise
Operating expenses Interest expense Income tax expense (excluding items listed below)	+ Increase in related prepaid expense *or* − Decrease in related prepaid expense **and** + Decrease in related accrued liability *or* − Increase in related accrued liability	= Payments for expenses
Depreciation expense Depletion expense Amortization expense	+ Depreciation expense + Depletion expense + Amortization expense	= 0
Gains (investing/financing) Losses (investing/financing)	Omit: Not related to operating activities	= 0

Using Bennett Company's data in **Exhibit 13-5**, those adjustments would appear as follows:

Income Statement Line Items		Operating Activities Line Items		Direct Method Cash Flow	
Sales revenue............	$250,000	Less	**$5,000 accounts receivable**	Cash received from customers	$245,000
Cost of goods sold........	(148,000)	Add	$6,000 inventory	Cash paid for merchandise	(151,000)
		Less	**$9,000 accounts payable**		
Wage expense	(52,000)		**No adjustment**	Cash paid to employees.........	(52,000)
Insurance expense........	(5,000)	Less	**$13,000 prepaid insurance**	Cash paid for insurance..........	(18,000)
Depreciation expense......	(10,000)	Add	$10,000 depreciation		
Income tax expense.......	(11,000)	Add	$2,000 income tax payable	Cash paid for income taxes	(9,000)
Gain on sale of plant		Less	**$8,000 gain on sale of**		
assets	8,000		**plant assets**		
Net income.............	$ 32,000			Cash flow from operations........	$ 15,000

Exhibit 13A-2 presents the Bennett Company's direct method statement of cash flows after undertaking the above two steps. As expected, the direct method cash flow from operating activities of $15,000 is exactly equivalent to the indirect method result of $15,000 as reported in **Exhibit 13-5**. Note that the cash flow from investing activities and the cash flow from financing activities are exactly the same in both **Exhibit 13-5** and **Exhibit 13A-2**. The only difference between the two exhibits is the manner in which the cash flow from operating activities is calculated. In **Exhibit 13-5**, the cash flow from operating activities is calculated by beginning with net income and then adjusting for various noncash expenses (depreciation expense) and nonoperating transactions (gain on sale of plant assets), as well as adjusting for the changes in the various working capital accounts (accounts receivable, inventory, prepaid insurance, accounts payable, and taxes payable). In **Exhibit 13A-2**, net income is replaced with the income statement line items and the noncash expenses and working capital adjustments are disaggregated to the individual line items. But in each case, the operating cash flow is $15,000. A company using the direct method must also separately disclose the reconciliation of net income to cash flow from operating activities prepared using the indirect method.

Exhibit 13A-2	Statement of Cash Flows Under the Direct Method

BENNETT COMPANY
Statement of Cash Flows
For Year Ended December 31, 2016

Cash Flow from Operating Activities		
Cash received from customers		$245,000
Cash paid for merchandise purchased	$(151,000)	
Cash paid to employees..	(52,000)	
Cash paid for insurance..	(18,000)	
Cash paid for income taxes...	(9,000)	(230,000)
Cash provided by operating activities		15,000
Cash Flow from Investing Activities		
Purchase of long-term investments..................................	(15,000)	
Sale of plant assets	28,000	
Purchase of patent...	(60,000)	
Cash used by investing activities....................		(47,000)
Cash Flow from Financing Activities		
Issuance of common stock	70,000	
Payment of dividends...	(13,000)	
Cash provided by financing activities....................		57,000
Net increase in cash..		25,000
Cash at beginning of year		10,000
Cash at end of year		$ 35,000

Husky Company's 2016 income statement and comparative balance sheets as of December 31 of 2016 and 2015 are shown below:

YOUR TURN! 13A.1

The solution is on page 515.

HUSKY COMPANY Income Statement For the Year Ended December 31, 2016		
Sales revenue.		$1,270,000
Cost of goods sold.	$860,000	
Wages expense	172,000	
Insurance expense	16,000	
Depreciation expense.	34,000	
Interest expense.	18,000	
Income tax expense	58,000	1,158,000
Net income.		$ 112,000

HUSKY COMPANY Balance Sheets	Dec. 31, 2016	Dec. 31, 2015
Assets		
Cash.	$ 22,000	$ 10,000
Accounts receivable.	82,000	64,000
Inventory.	180,000	120,000
Prepaid insurance	10,000	14,000
Plant assets	500,000	390,000
Accumulated depreciation	(136,000)	(102,000)
Total assets	$658,000	$496,000
Liabilities and Stockholders' Equity		
Accounts payable.	$ 14,000	$ 20,000
Wages payable.	18,000	12,000
Income tax payable	14,000	16,000
Bonds payable	260,000	150,000
Common stock.	180,000	180,000
Retained earnings	172,000	118,000
Total liabilities and stockholders' equity	$658,000	$496,000

Cash dividends of $58,000 were declared and paid during 2016. Plant assets were purchased for cash, and bonds payable were issued for cash. Bond interest is paid semiannually on June 30 and December 31. Accounts payable relate to merchandise purchases.

Required
Prepare a 2016 statement of cash flows using the direct method.

SUMMARY OF LEARNING OBJECTIVES

Discuss the content and format of the statement of cash flows. (p. 468)

■ The statement of cash flows explains the net increase or decrease in cash and cash equivalents during the period.

■ The statement of cash flows separates cash flows into operating, investing, and financing activity categories.

■ The statement of cash flows also provides a required supplemental disclosure reporting noncash investing and financing activities.

■ The statement of cash flows should help users compare, evaluate, and predict a firm's cash flows and also help evaluate its financial flexibility.

LO1

LO2   **Explain the preparation of a statement of cash flows using the indirect method. (p. 474)**
■   The indirect method of preparing the cash flow from operating activities section reconciles net income to cash flow from operating activities.

LO3   **Define several ratios used to analyze the statement of cash flows and explain their use. (p. 482)**
■   Free cash flow is defined as a company's cash flow from operations less its capital expenditures; the metric provides a measure of a firm's cash flow that can be used to fund business activities beyond the replacement of property, plant, and equipment.
■   The operating-cash-flow-to-current-liabilities ratio is calculated by dividing a company's cash flow from operating activities by its average current liabilities for the year; the ratio reveals a firm's ability to repay current liabilities from operating cash flow.
■   The operating-cash-flow-to-capital-expenditures ratio is calculated by dividing a firm's cash flow from operating activities by its annual net capital expenditures; the ratio evaluates a firm's ability to fund its capital investment using operating cash flow.

LO4   **Appendix 13A: Explain the preparation of a statement of cash flows using the direct method. (p. 487)**
■   The direct method of preparing the cash flow from operating activities section shows the major categories of operating cash receipts and payments.
■   The FASB encourages use of the direct method but permits use of either the direct or the indirect method.
■   A firm using the direct method must separately disclose the reconciliation of net income to cash flow from operating activities.

SUMMARY	Concept	Method	Assessment
TAKEAWAY 13.1	Does a company generate cash flows in excess of its capital expenditure needs?	Statement of cash flows. FCF = Cash flow from operating activities − Capital expenditures	The higher the free cash flow, the greater is a company's ability to generate cash for needs other than capital expenditures.
TAKEAWAY 13.2	Will a company have sufficient cash to pay its current liabilities as they become due?	Statement of cash flows and balance sheet. Operating-cash-flow-to-current-liabilities ratio $= \dfrac{\text{Cash flow from operating activities}}{\text{Average current liabilities}}$	The higher the ratio, the higher the probability that a company will have sufficient operating cash flow to pay its current liabilities as they become due.
TAKEAWAY 13.3	Does a company generate sufficient operating cash flows to finance its capital expenditure needs?	Statement of cash flows. Operating-cash-flow-to-capital-expenditures ratio $= \dfrac{\text{Cash flow from operating activities}}{\text{Annual net capital expenditures}}$	The higher the ratio, the higher the probability that a company will generate sufficient operating cash flow to finance its capital expenditure needs.

KEY TERMS

Cash equivalents (p. 468)
Cash management (p. 468)
Direct method (p. 473)
Financial flexibility (p. 473)
Financing activities (p. 470)

Free cash flow (FCF) (p. 482)
Indirect method (p. 473)
Investing activities (p. 470)
Noncash expenses (p. 478)
Noncash investing and financing activities (p. 472)

Operating activities (p. 470)
Operating-cash-flow-to-capital-expenditures ratio (p. 483)
Operating-cash-flow-to-current-liabilities ratio (p. 482)

Assignments with the ⬤ logo in the margin are available in BusinessCourse.
See the Preface of the book for details.

SELF-STUDY QUESTIONS

(Answers to the Self-Study Questions are at the end of the chapter.)

1. **Which of the following is not disclosed in a statement of cash flows?**   **LO1**
   a. A transfer of cash to a cash equivalent investment
   b. The amount of cash at year-end
   c. Cash outflows from investing activities during the period
   d. Cash inflows from financing activities during the period

2. **Which of the following events will appear in the cash flows from investing activities section of the**   **LO1**
   statement of cash flows?
   a. Cash received as interest
   b. Cash received from issuance of common stock
   c. Cash purchase of truck
   d. Cash payment of dividends

3. **Which of the following events will appear in the cash flows from financing activities section of the**   **LO1**
   statement of cash flows?
   a. Cash purchase of equipment
   b. Cash purchase of bonds issued by another company
   c. Cash received as repayment for funds loaned
   d. Cash purchase of treasury stock

4. **Tyler Company has net income of $49,000 and the following related items:**   **LO2**

Depreciation expense.	$ 5,000
Accounts receivable increase	2,000
Inventory decrease.	10,000
Accounts payable decrease.	4,000

   Using the indirect method, what is Tyler's cash flow from operations?
   a. $42,000   c. $58,000
   b. $46,000   d. $38,000

5. **Free cash flow is a measure of a firm's**   **LO3**
   a. interest free debt.
   b. ability to generate net income.
   c. ability to generate cash and invest in new capital expenditures.
   d. ability to collect accounts receivable in a timely manner.

6. **Which of the following events will not appear in the cash flows from financing activities section of**   **LO1**
   the statement of cash flow?
   a. Borrowing cash from a bank
   b. Issuance of stock in exchange for plant assets
   c. Sales of common stock
   d. Payment of dividends on preferred stock

7. **Taylor Company reports free cash flow of $15,000, total cash of $18,000, net income of $50,000,**   **LO3**
   current assets of $90,000, average current liabilities of $60,000, and cash flow from operating activities
   of $48,000. Compute the operating-cash-flow-to-current-liabilities ratio for Taylor Company.
   a. 0.83
   b. 0.80
   c. 0.30
   d. 1.25

8. **Which of the following is not a cash equivalent?**   **LO1**
   a. Short-term U.S. Treasury bill
   b. Short-term certificate of deposit
   c. Money-market account
   d. IBM common stock

LO2

9. **Which of the following expenses are not added back to net income when using the indirect method to prepare a statement of cash flows?**
   a. Amortization expense
   b. Depletion expense
   c. Interest expense
   d. Depreciation expense

LO4
(Appendix 13A)

10. **Smith & Sons reports interest expense of $90,000 on its income statement. The beginning and ending balances for interest payable reported on its balance sheet are $10,000 and $15,000, respectively. How much cash did Smith & Sons pay for interest expense this period?**
    a. $85,000
    b. $95,000
    c. $100,000
    d. $105,000

LO4
(Appendix 13A)

11. **Which of the following methods will disclose the cash received from customers in the statement of cash flows?**
    a. Indirect method
    b. Reconciliation method
    c. Direct method
    d. Both direct and indirect methods

LO4
(Appendix 13A)

12. **Smith & Sons reports sales revenue of $1,000,000 on its income statement. Its balance sheet reveals beginning and ending accounts receivable of $60,000 and $92,000, respectively. What is the amount of cash collected from customers of the company?**
    a. $1,032,000
    b. $968,000
    c. $1,060,000
    d. $1,092,000

QUESTIONS

1. What is the definition of *cash equivalents?* Give three examples of cash equivalents.
2. Why are cash equivalents included with cash in a statement of cash flows?
3. What are the three major types of activities classified on a statement of cash flows? Give an example of a cash inflow and a cash outflow in each classification.
4. In which of the three activity categories of a statement of cash flows would each of the following items appear? Indicate for each item whether it represents a cash inflow or a cash outflow:
   a. Cash purchase of equipment
   b. Cash collection on loans
   c. Cash dividends paid
   d. Cash dividends received
   e. Cash proceeds from issuing stock
   f. Cash receipts from customers
   g. Cash interest paid
   h. Cash interest received
5. Why is a statement of cash flows a useful financial statement?
6. What is the difference between the direct method and the indirect method of presenting the cash flow from operating activities?
7. In determining the cash flow from operating activities using the indirect method, why is it necessary to add depreciation back to net income? Give an example of another item that is added back to net income under the indirect method.
8. Vista Company sold land for $98,000 cash that had originally cost $70,000. The company recorded a gain on the sale of $28,000. How is this event reported in a statement of cash flows using the indirect method?
9. A firm uses the indirect method. Using the following information, what is its cash flow from operating activities?

Net income.	$88,000
Accounts receivable decrease.	13,000
Inventory increase	9,000
Accounts payable decrease.	3,500
Income tax payable increase	1,500
Depreciation expense.	6,000

10. If a business had a net loss for the year, under what circumstances would the statement of cash flows show a positive cash flow from operating activities?

11. A firm is converting its accrual revenues to corresponding cash amounts using the direct method. Sales revenue on the income statement are $925,000. Beginning and ending accounts receivable on the balance sheet are $58,000 and $44,000, respectively. What is the amount of cash received from customers?

12. A firm reports $86,000 wages expense in its income statement. If beginning and ending wages payable are $3,900 and $2,800, respectively, what is the amount of cash paid to employees?

13. A firm reports $43,000 advertising expense in its income statement. If beginning and ending prepaid advertising are $6,000 and $7,600, respectively, what is the amount of cash paid for advertising?

14. Rusk Company sold equipment for $5,100 cash that had cost $35,000 and had $29,000 of accumulated depreciation. How is this event reported in a statement of cash flows using the direct method?

15. What separate disclosures are required for a company that reports a statement of cash flows using the direct method?

16. How is the *operating-cash-flow-to-current-liabilities ratio* calculated? Explain its use.

17. How is the *operating-cash-flow-to-capital-expenditures ratio* calculated? Explain its use.

18. The statement of cash flows provides information that may be useful in predicting future cash flows, evaluating financial flexibility, assessing liquidity, and identifying a company's financing needs. It is not, however, the best financial statement for learning about a firm's financial performance during a period. Information about a company's financial performance is provided by the income statement. Two basic principles—the revenue recognition principle and the matching concept—work to distinguish the income statement from the statement of cash flows. (a) Define the revenue recognition principle and the matching concept. (b) Briefly explain how these two principles work to make the income statement a better report regarding a firm's periodic financial performance than the statement of cash flows.

SHORT EXERCISES

Use the following information regarding the Seville Corporation to answer Short Exercises 13-1 through 13-3:

Accounts payable increase	$ 9,000
Accounts receivable increase	4,000
Accrued liabilities decrease	3,000
Amortization expense.	6,000
Cash balance, January 1	22,000
Cash balance, December 31	15,000
Cash paid as dividends	29,000
Cash paid to purchase land	90,000
Cash paid to retire bonds payable at par.	60,000
Cash received from issuance of common stock	35,000
Cash received from sale of equipment	17,000
Depreciation expense.	29,000
Gain on sale of equipment	4,000
Inventory decrease.	13,000
Net income.	76,000
Prepaid expenses increase	2,000

LO1, 2   **SE13-1.**   **Cash Flow from Operating Activities** Using the information for the Seville Corporation above, calculate the cash flow from operating activities.

LO1, 2   **SE13-2.**   **Cash Flow from Investing Activities** Using the information for the Seville Corporation above, calculate the cash flow from investing activities.

LO1, 2   **SE13-3.**   **Cash Flow from Financing Activities** Using the information for the Seville Corporation above, calculate the cash flow for financing activities.

The following information for Smith & Sons relates to Short Exercises 13-4 through 13-6:

Cash flow from operating activities	$1,500,000
Capital expenditures	850,000
Current liabilities, beginning of year	300,000
Current liabilities, end of year	360,000

LO3   **SE13-4.**   **Free Cash Flow** Using the above data, calculate the free cash flow for Smith & Sons.

LO3   **SE13-5.**   **Operating-Cash-Flow-to-Current-Liabilities Ratio** Using the above data, calculate the operating-cash-flow-to-current-liabilities ratio for Smith & Sons.

LO3   **SE13-6.**   **Operating-Cash-Flow-to-Capital-Expenditures Ratio** Using the above data, calculate the operating-cash-flow-to-capital-expenditures ratio for Smith & Sons.

LO4
(Appendix 13A)   **SE13-7.**   **Converting Sales Revenue to Cash** Smith & Sons is converting its sales revenues to corresponding cash amounts using the direct method. Sales revenue on the income statement is $1,025,000. Beginning and ending accounts receivable on the balance sheet are $58,000 and $34,000, respectively. Calculate the amount of cash received from customers.

LO4
(Appendix 13A)   **SE13-8.**   **Direct Method** Using the following data for Smith & Sons, calculate the cash paid for rent:

Rent expense	$80,000
Prepaid rent, January 1	10,000
Prepaid rent, December 31	8,000

LO4
(Appendix 13A)   **SE13-9.**   **Direct Method** Using the following data for Smith & Sons, calculate the cash received as interest:

Interest income	$26,000
Interest receivable, January 1	3,000
Interest receivable, December 31	3,700

LO4
(Appendix 13A)   **SE13-10.**   **Direct Method** Using the following data for Smith & Sons, calculate the cash paid for merchandise purchased:

Cost of goods sold	$108,000
Inventory, January 1	19,000
Inventory, December 31	22,000
Accounts payable, January 1	11,000
Accounts payable, December 31	7,000

EXERCISES—SET A

LO1   **E13-1A.**   **Classification of Cash Flows** For each of the items below, indicate whether the cash flow item relates to an operating activity, an investing activity, or a financing activity:

     a.   Cash receipts from customers for services rendered
     b.   Sale of long-term investments for cash
     c.   Acquisition of plant assets for cash
     d.   Payment of income taxes

e. Bonds payable issued for cash
f. Payment of cash dividends declared in previous year
g. Purchase of short-term investments (not cash equivalents) for cash

E13-2A. Classification of Cash Flows For each of the items below, indicate whether it is (1) a cash flow from an operating activity, (2) a cash flow from an investing activity, (3) a cash flow from a financing activity, (4) a noncash investing and financing activity, or (5) none of the above: **LO1**

a. Paid cash to retire bonds payable at a loss
b. Received cash as settlement of a lawsuit
c. Acquired a patent in exchange for common stock
d. Received advance payments from customers on orders for custom-made goods
e. Gave large cash contribution to local university
f. Invested cash in 60-day commercial paper (a cash equivalent)

E13-3A. Cash Flow from Operating Activities (Indirect Method) The Lincoln Company owns no plant assets and had the following income statement for the year: **LO2**

Sales revenue.		$800,000
Cost of goods sold.	$470,000	
Wages expense	120,000	
Rent expense	42,000	
Insurance expense	15,000	647,000
Net income.		$153,000

Additional information about the company includes:

	End of Year	Beginning of Year
Accounts receivable.	$54,000	$49,000
Inventory.	60,000	76,000
Prepaid insurance	8,000	7,000
Accounts payable.	24,000	18,000
Wages payable.	9,000	11,000

Use the preceding information to calculate the cash flow from operating activities using the indirect method.

E13-4A. Statement of Cash Flows (Indirect Method) Use the following information regarding the Lund Corporation to (a) prepare a statement of cash flows using the indirect method and (b) compute Lund's operating-cash-flow-to-current-liabilities ratio.   **LO2, 3**

Accounts payable increase	$ 11,000
Accounts receivable increase	4,000
Accrued liabilities decrease	3,000
Amortization expense.	7,000
Cash balance, January 1	22,000
Cash balance, December 31	16,000
Cash paid as dividends	31,000
Cash paid to purchase land	90,000
Cash paid to retire bonds payable at par.	60,000
Cash received from issuance of common stock	35,000
Cash received from sale of equipment	17,000
Depreciation expense.	29,000
Gain on sale of equipment	5,000
Inventory decrease.	13,000
Net income.	78,000
Prepaid expenses increase	3,000
Average current liabilities.	120,000

LO2 **E13-5A.** **Cash Flow from Operating Activities (Indirect Method)** The Arcadia Company owns no plant assets and had the following income statement for the year:

Sales revenue.		$930,000
Cost of goods sold.	$640,000	
Wages expense	210,000	
Rent expense	42,000	
Utilities expense.	11,000	903,000
Net income.		$ 27,000

Additional information about the company includes:

	End of Year	Beginning of Year
Accounts receivable.	$67,000	$59,000
Inventory.	62,000	86,000
Prepaid rent	8,000	7,000
Accounts payable.	22,000	28,000
Wages payable.	9,000	7,000

Use the preceding information to calculate the cash flow from operating activities using the indirect method.

LO2 **E13-6A.** **Statement of Cash Flows (Indirect Method)** Use the following information regarding the Newcastle Corporation to prepare a statement of cash flows using the indirect method:

Accounts payable decrease.	$ 3,000
Accounts receivable increase	7,000
Wages payable decrease.	9,000
Amortization expense.	16,000
Cash balance, January 1	31,000
Cash balance, December 31	9,000
Cash paid as dividends	6,000
Cash paid to purchase land	100,000
Cash paid to retire bonds payable at par.	69,000
Cash received from issuance of common stock	45,000
Cash received from sale of equipment	11,000
Depreciation expense.	39,000
Gain on sale of equipment	14,000
Inventory increase	11,000
Net income.	94,000
Prepaid expenses increase	8,000

LO3 **E13-7A.** **Cash Flow Ratios** Spencer Company reports the following amounts in its annual financial statements:

Cash flow from operating activities	$45,000	Capital expenditures	$ 31,000*
Cash flow from investing activities.	(35,000)	Average current assets.	80,000
Cash flow from financing activities.	(5,000)	Average current liabilities	60,000
Net income.	22,000	Total assets	180,000

* This amount is a cash outflow

a. Compute Spencer's free cash flow.
b. Compute Spencer's operating-cash-flow-to-current-liabilities ratio.
c. Compute Spencer's operating-cash-flow-to-capital-expenditures ratio.

E13-8A. **Operating Cash Flows (Direct Method)** Calculate the cash flow in each of the following cases:

LO4
(Appendix 13A)

a. Cash paid for advertising:

Advertising expense.	$62,000
Prepaid advertising, January 1.	12,000
Prepaid advertising, December 31.	15,000

b. Cash paid for income taxes:

Income tax expense.	$29,000
Income tax payable, January 1	7,100
Income tax payable, December 31	5,900

c. Cash paid for merchandise purchased:

Cost of goods sold.	$180,000
Inventory, January 1.	30,000
Inventory, December 31.	24,000
Accounts payable, January 1.	10,000
Accounts payable, December 31.	12,000

E13-9A. **Statement of Cash Flows (Direct Method)** Use the following information regarding the cash flows of Mason Corporation to prepare a statement of cash flows using the direct method:

LO4
(Appendix 13A)

Cash balance, December 31	$ 6,000
Cash paid to employees and suppliers	158,000
Cash received from sale of land.	40,000
Cash paid to acquire treasury stock	10,000
Cash balance, January 1	18,000
Cash received as interest.	6,000
Cash paid as income taxes	9,000
Cash paid to purchase equipment.	89,000
Cash received from customers	197,000
Cash received from issuing bonds payable.	30,000
Cash paid as dividends	19,000

E13-10A. **Operating Cash Flows (Direct Method)** Refer to the information in Exercise E13-3A. Calculate the cash flow from operating activities using the direct method. Show a related cash flow for each revenue and expense.

LO4
(Appendix 13A)

E13-11A. **Investing and Financing Cash Flows** During the year, Paxon Corporation's Long-Term Investments account (at cost) increased $25,000, the net result of purchasing stocks costing $90,000 and selling stocks costing $65,000 at a $7,000 loss. Also, the Bonds Payable account decreased by $35,000, the net result of issuing $100,000 of bonds at 104 and retiring bonds with a face value (and book value) of $135,000 at a $9,000 gain. What items and amounts will appear in the (a) cash flows from investing activities and the (b) cash flows from financing activities sections of Paxon's statement of cash flows?

LO2, 4
(Appendix 13A)

EXERCISES—SET B

E13-1B. **Classification of Cash Flows** For each of the items below, indicate whether the cash flow item relates to an operating activity, an investing activity, or a financing activity:

LO1

a. Cash loaned to borrowers

b. Cash paid as interest on bonds payable

     c.   Cash received from issuance of preferred stock

     d.   Cash paid as state income taxes

     e.   Cash received as dividends on stock investments

     f.   Cash paid to acquire treasury stock

     g.   Cash paid to acquire a franchise to distribute a product line

LO1   **E13-2B.**   **Classification of Cash Flows**   For each of the items below, indicate whether it is (1) a cash flow from an operating activity, (2) a cash flow from an investing activity, (3) a cash flow from a financing activity, (4) a noncash investing and financing activity, or (5) none of the above:

     a.   Received cash as interest earned on bond investment

     b.   Received cash as refund from supplier

     c.   Borrowed cash from bank on six-month note payable

     d.   Exchanged, at a gain, stock held as an investment for a parcel of land

     e.   Invested cash in a money market fund (cash may be easily withdrawn from the fund)

     f.   Loaned cash to help finance the start of a new biotechnology firm

LO2, 3   **E13-3B.**   **Cash Flow from Operating Activities (Indirect Method)**   The following information was obtained from Galena Company's comparative balance sheets:

	End of Year	Beginning of Year
Cash.	$ 19,000	$ 9,000
Accounts receivable.	44,000	35,000
Inventory.	55,000	49,000
Prepaid rent	6,000	8,000
Long-term investments	21,000	34,000
Plant assets	150,000	106,000
Accumulated depreciation	(42,000)	(32,000)
Accounts payable.	24,000	20,000
Income tax payable	4,000	6,000
Common stock.	121,000	92,000
Retained earnings	106,000	91,000
Capital expenditures	13,200	

Assume that Galena Company's income statement showed depreciation expense of $10,000, a gain on sale of investments of $7,000, and a net income of $51,000. (a) Calculate the cash flow from operating activities using the indirect method and (b) compute Galena's operating-cash-flow-to-capital-expenditures ratio.

LO2   **E13-4B.**   **Cash Flow from Operating Activities (Indirect Method)**   Cairo Company had a $24,000 net loss from operations. Depreciation expense for the year was $9,600, and a dividend of $5,000 was declared and paid. The balances of the current asset and current liability accounts at the beginning and end of the year are as follows:

	End	Beginning
Cash.	$ 3,500	$ 7,000
Accounts receivable.	16,000	29,000
Inventory.	50,000	53,000
Prepaid expenses.	6,000	9,000
Accounts payable.	12,000	8,000
Accrued liabilities	6,000	7,600

Did Cairo Company's operating activities provide or use cash? Use the indirect method to determine your answer.

LO2   **E13-5B.**   **Cash Flow From Operating Activities (Indirect Method)**   The Smithfield Company owns no plant assets and had the following income statement for the year:

Sales revenue.		$1,120,000
Cost of goods sold.	$770,000	
Wages expense	210,000	
Rent expense.	65,000	
Insurance expense.	45,000	1,090,000
Net income.		$ 30,000

Additional information about the company includes:

	End of Year	Beginning of Year
Accounts receivable.	$74,000	$49,000
Inventory.	70,000	74,000
Prepaid insurance	5,000	7,000
Accounts payable.	26,000	28,000
Wages payable.	11,000	13,000

Use the preceding information to calculate the cash flow from operating activities using the indirect method.

E13-6B.   Statement of Cash Flows (Indirect Method) Use the following information regarding the Fremantle Corporation to prepare a statement of cash flows using the indirect method: **LO2**

Accounts payable increase	$ 14,000
Accounts receivable increase	4,000
Accrued liabilities decrease	5,000
Amortization expense.	26,000
Cash balance, January 1	21,000
Cash balance, December 31	108,000
Cash paid as dividends	49,000
Cash paid to purchase land.	103,000
Cash paid to retire bonds payable at par.	70,000
Cash received from issuance of common stock	75,000
Cash received from sale of equipment	17,000
Depreciation expense.	65,000
Gain on sale of equipment.	14,000
Inventory decrease.	11,000
Net income.	126,000
Prepaid expenses increase	2,000

E13-7B.   Cash Flow Ratios Morgan Company reports the following amounts in its annual financial statements: **LO3**

Cash flow from operating activities	$65,000	Capital expenditures	$ 52,500*
Cash flow from investing activities.	(60,000)	Average current assets.	130,000
Cash flow from financing activities.	(8,500)	Average current liabilities.	90,000
Net income.	37,500	Total assets	225,000

* This amount is a cash outflow

a.   Compute Morgan's free cash flow.
b.   Compute Morgan's operating-cash-flow-to-current-liabilities ratio.
c.   Compute Morgan's operating-cash-flow-to-capital-expenditures ratio.

LO4
(Appendix 13A)

E13-8B. **Operating Cash Flows (Direct Method)** Calculate the cash flow in each of the following cases:

a. Cash paid for rent:

Rent expense.	$62,000
Prepaid rent, January 1	10,000
Prepaid rent, December 31	8,000

b. Cash received as interest:

Interest income.	$16,000
Interest receivable, January 1	5,000
Interest receivable, December 31	3,700

c. Cash paid for merchandise purchased:

Cost of goods sold.	$98,000
Inventory, January 1.	19,000
Inventory, December 31.	22,000
Accounts payable, January 1.	11,000
Accounts payable, December 31.	9,000

LO4
(Appendix 13A)

E13-9B. **Statement of Cash Flows (Direct Method)** Use the following information regarding the cash flows of Gilbert Corporation to prepare a statement of cash flows using the direct method:

Cash balance, December 31	$ 12,000
Cash paid to employees and suppliers	151,000
Cash received from sale of equipment	88,000
Cash paid to retire bonds payable.	70,000
Cash balance, January 1	20,000
Cash paid as interest	7,000
Cash paid as income taxes	24,000
Cash paid to purchase patent	76,000
Cash received from customers	216,000
Cash received from issuing common stock.	35,000
Cash paid as dividends	19,000

LO4
(Appendix 13A)

E13-10B. **Operating Cash Flows (Direct Method)** The Howell Company's current year income statement contains the following data:

Sales revenue.	$775,000
Cost of goods sold.	550,000
Gross profit.	$225,000

Howell's comparative balance sheets show the following data (accounts payable relate to merchandise purchases):

	End of Year	Beginning of Year
Accounts receivable.	$ 71,000	$60,000
Inventory.	115,000	96,000
Prepaid expenses.	3,000	8,000
Accounts payable.	31,000	35,000

Compute Howell's current-year cash received from customers and cash paid for merchandise purchased.

E13-11B. Investing and Financing Cash Flows Refer to the information in Exercise 13-3B. During the year, Galena Company purchased plant assets for cash, sold investments for cash (the entire $7,000 gain developed during the year), and issued common stock for cash. The firm also declared and paid cash dividends. What items and amounts will appear in (a) the cash flow from investing activities and (b) the cash flow from financing activities sections of a statement of cash flows?

LO2, 4
(Appendix 13A)

PROBLEMS—SET A

P13-1A. **Statement of Cash Flows (Indirect Method)** The Wolff Company's income statement and comparative balance sheets at December 31 of 2016 and 2015 are shown below:

LO2, 3

WOLFF COMPANY Income Statement For the Year Ended December 31, 2016		
Sales revenue.		$645,000
Cost of goods sold.	$430,000	
Wages expense	86,000	
Insurance expense.	12,000	
Depreciation expense.	13,000	
Interest expense.	12,000	
Income tax expense.	29,000	582,000
Net income.		$ 63,000

WOLFF COMPANY Balance Sheets		
	Dec. 31, 2016	Dec. 31, 2015
Assets		
Cash.	$ 52,000	$ 8,000
Accounts receivable.	41,000	32,000
Inventory.	90,000	60,000
Prepaid insurance	5,000	7,000
Plant assets	219,000	195,000
Accumulated depreciation	(68,000)	(55,000)
Total assets	$339,000	$247,000
Liabilities and Stockholders' Equity		
Accounts payable.	$ 7,000	$ 10,000
Wages payable.	9,000	6,000
Income tax payable	6,000	7,000
Bonds payable	141,000	75,000
Common stock.	90,000	90,000
Retained earnings	86,000	59,000
Total liabilities and stockholders' equity	$339,000	$247,000

Cash dividends of $36,000 were declared and paid during 2016. Plant assets were purchased for cash and bonds payable were issued for cash. Bond interest is paid semi-annually on June 30 and December 31. Accounts payable relate to merchandise purchases.

Required
a. Calculate the change in cash that occurred during 2016.
b. Prepare a statement of cash flows using the indirect method.
c. Compute free cash flow.
d. Compute the operating-cash-flow-to-current-liabilities ratio.
e. Compute the operating-cash-flow-to-capital-expenditures ratio.

LO2 **P13-2A.** **Statement of Cash Flows (Indirect Method)** Arctic Company's income statement and comparative balance sheets as of December 31 of 2016 and 2015 follow:

ARCTIC COMPANY Income Statement For the Year Ended December 31, 2016		
Sales revenue.		$740,000
Cost of goods sold.	$534,000	
Wages expense	190,000	
Advertising expense.	31,000	
Depreciation expense.	24,000	
Interest expense.	18,000	
Gain on sale of land	(25,000)	772,000
Net loss		$ (32,000)

ARCTIC COMPANY Balance Sheets	Dec. 31, 2016	Dec. 31, 2015
Assets		
Cash.	$ 71,000	$ 28,000
Accounts receivable.	42,000	49,000
Inventory.	107,000	113,000
Prepaid advertising.	10,000	14,000
Plant assets	360,000	222,000
Accumulated depreciation	(80,000)	(56,000)
Total assets	$510,000	$370,000
Liabilities and Stockholders' Equity		
Accounts payable.	$ 17,000	$ 31,000
Interest payable	6,000	—
Bonds payable	210,000	—
Common stock.	245,000	245,000
Retained earnings	62,000	94,000
Treasury stock	(30,000)	—
Total liabilities and stockholders' equity	$510,000	$370,000

During 2016, Arctic sold land for $70,000 cash that had originally cost $45,000. Arctic also purchased equipment for cash, acquired treasury stock for cash, and issued bonds payable for cash. Accounts payable relate to merchandise purchases.

Required
a. Calculate the change in cash that occurred during 2016.
b. Prepare a statement of cash flows using the indirect method.

LO2 **P13-3A.** **Statement of Cash Flows (Indirect Method)** The Dairy Company's income statement and comparative balance sheets as of December 31 of 2016 and 2015 follow:

DAIRY COMPANY Income Statement For the Year Ended December 31, 2016		
Sales revenue.		$700,000
Cost of goods sold.	$460,000	
Wages and other operating expenses	95,000	
Depreciation expense.	22,000	
Goodwill amortization expense	7,000	
Interest expense.	10,000	
Income tax expense.	36,000	
Loss on bond retirement	5,000	635,000
Net income.		$ 65,000

DAIRY COMPANY Balance Sheets	Dec. 31, 2016	Dec. 31, 2015
Assets		
Cash.	$ 22,000	$ 18,000
Accounts receivable.	43,000	28,000
Inventory.	103,000	129,000
Prepaid expenses.	12,000	10,000
Plant assets	360,000	336,000
Accumulated depreciation	(87,000)	(84,000)
Goodwill	43,000	50,000
Total assets	$496,000	$487,000
Liabilities and Stockholders' Equity		
Accounts payable.	$ 32,000	$ 26,000
Interest payable	4,000	7,000
Income tax payable	6,000	8,000
Bonds payable	60,000	100,000
Common stock.	252,000	248,000
Retained earnings	142,000	98,000
Total liabilities and stockholders' equity	$496,000	$487,000

During the year, the company sold for $17,000 cash old equipment that had cost $36,000 and had $19,000 accumulated depreciation. New equipment worth $60,000 was acquired in exchange for $60,000 of bonds payable. Bonds payable of $100,000 were retired for cash at a loss. A $21,000 cash dividend was declared and paid. All stock issuances were for cash.

Required
a. Compute the change in cash that occurred in 2016.
b. Prepare a statement of cash flows using the indirect method.

P13-4A. **Statement of Cash Flows (Indirect Method)** The Rainbow Company's income statement and comparative balance sheets as of December 31 of 2016 and 2015 follow: **LO2**

RAINBOW COMPANY Income Statement For Year Ended December 31, 2016		
Sales revenue.		$750,000
Dividend income.		19,000
		769,000
Cost of goods sold.	$440,000	
Wages and other operating expenses	130,000	
Depreciation expense.	39,000	
Patent amortization expense	7,000	
Interest expense.	13,000	
Income tax expense.	44,000	
Loss on sale of equipment.	5,000	
Gain on sale of investments.	(10,000)	668,000
Net income.		$101,000

RAINBOW COMPANY Balance Sheets	Dec. 31, 2016	Dec. 31, 2015
Assets		
Cash and cash equivalents	$ 25,000	$ 29,000
Accounts receivable	45,000	30,000
Inventory	103,000	77,000
Prepaid expenses	10,000	6,000
Long-term investments—available for sale	—	50,000
Fair value adjustment to investments	—	7,000
Land	190,000	100,000
Buildings	445,000	350,000
Accumulated depreciation—Buildings	(91,000)	(75,000)
Equipment	179,000	225,000
Accumulated depreciation—Equipment	(42,000)	(46,000)
Patents	50,000	32,000
Total assets	$914,000	$785,000
Liabilities and Stockholders' Equity		
Accounts payable	$ 22,000	$ 18,000
Interest payable	6,000	5,000
Income tax payable	8,000	12,000
Bonds payable	165,000	125,000
Preferred stock ($100 par value)	100,000	75,000
Common stock ($5 par value)	379,000	364,000
Paid-in-capital in excess of par value—Common	133,000	124,000
Retained earnings	101,000	55,000
Unrealized gain on investments	—	7,000
Total liabilities and stockholders' equity	$914,000	$785,000

During the year, the following transactions occurred:

1. Sold long-term investments costing $50,000 for $60,000 cash. Unrealized gains totaling $7,000 related to these investments had been recorded in earlier years. At year-end, the fair value adjustment and unrealized gain account balances were eliminated.
2. Purchased land for cash.
3. Capitalized an expenditure made to improve the building.
4. Sold equipment for $14,000 cash that originally cost $46,000 and had $27,000 accumulated depreciation.
5. Issued bonds payable at face value for cash.
6. Acquired a patent with a fair value of $25,000 by issuing 250 shares of preferred stock at par value.
7. Declared and paid a $55,000 cash dividend.
8. Issued 3,000 shares of common stock for cash at $8 per share.
9. Recorded depreciation of $16,000 on buildings and $23,000 on equipment.

Required
a. Calculate the change in cash and cash equivalents that occurred during 2016.
b. Prepare a statement of cash flows using the indirect method.

LO3 **P13-5A.** **Analyzing Cash Flow Ratios** Molly Enterprises reported the following information for the past year of operations:

Transaction	Free Cash Flow $250,000	Operating-Cash-Flow-to-Current-Liabilities Ratio 1.0 times	Operating-Cash-Flow-to-Capital-Expenditures Ratio 3.0 times
a. Recorded credit sales of $7,000			
b. Collected $4,000 owed from customers . . .			
c. Purchased $18,000 of equipment on long-term credit			
d. Purchased $16,000 of equipment for cash .			
e. Paid $5,000 of wages with cash			
f. Recorded utility bill of $1,750 that has not been paid			

For each transaction, indicate whether the ratio will (I) increase, (D) decrease, or (N) have no effect.

P13-6A.   **Statement of Cash Flows (Direct Method)** Refer to the data given for the Wolff Company in Problem P13-1A.   LO3, 4 (Appendix 13A)

Required
a. Calculate the change in cash that occurred during 2016.
b. Prepare a statement of cash flows using the direct method.
c. Compute free cash flow.
d. Compute the operating-cash-flow-to-current-liabilities ratio.
e. Compute the operating-cash-flow-to-capital-expenditures ratio.

P13-7A.   **Statement of Cash Flows (Direct Method)** Refer to the data given for the Arctic Company in Problem P13-2A.   LO4 (Appendix 13A)

Required
a. Calculate the change in cash that occurred during 2016.
b. Prepare a statement of cash flows using the direct method.

P13-8A.   **Statement of Cash Flows (Direct Method)** Refer to the data given for the Dairy Company in Problem P13-3A.   LO4 (Appendix 13A)

Required
a. Compute the change in cash that occurred in 2016.
b. Prepare a statement of cash flows using the direct method. Use one cash outflow for "cash paid for wages and other operating expenses." Accounts payable relate to inventory purchases only.

P13-9A.   **Statement of Cash Flows (Direct Method)** Refer to the data given for the Rainbow Company in Problem P13-4A.   LO4 (Appendix 13A)

Required
a. Calculate the change in cash that occurred in 2016.
b. Prepare a statement of cash flows using the direct method. Use one cash outflow for "cash paid for wages and other operating expenses." Accounts payable relate to inventory purchases only.

PROBLEMS—SET B

P13-1B.   **Statement of Cash Flows (Indirect Method)** The Rural Company's income statement and comparative balance sheets as of December 31 of 2016 and 2015 are shown below: LO2, 3

RURAL COMPANY
Income Statement
For the Year Ended December 31, 2016

Sales revenue.		$645,000
Cost of goods sold.	$376,000	
Wages expense	107,000	
Depreciation expense.	22,000	
Rent expense	28,000	
Income tax expense.	31,000	564,000
Net income.		$ 81,000

RURAL COMPANY
Balance Sheets

	Dec. 31, 2016	Dec. 31, 2015
Assets		
Cash.	$ 41,000	$ 33,000
Accounts receivable.	52,000	60,000
Inventory.	142,000	116,000
Prepaid rent	14,000	10,000
Plant assets	420,000	300,000
Accumulated depreciation	(127,000)	(105,000)
Total assets	$542,000	$414,000
Liabilities and Stockholders' Equity		
Accounts payable.	$ 29,000	$ 17,000
Wages payable.	14,000	7,000
Income tax payable	7,000	8,000
Common stock.	295,000	252,000
Paid-in-capital in excess of par value	72,000	58,000
Retained earnings	125,000	72,000
Total liabilities and stockholders' equity	$542,000	$414,000

Cash dividends of $28,000 were declared and paid during 2016. Plant assets were purchased for cash and additional common stock was issued for cash. Accounts payable relate to merchandise purchases.

Required
a. Calculate the change in cash that occurred during 2016.
b. Prepare a statement of cash flows using the indirect method.
c. Compute free cash flow.
d. Compute the operating-cash-flow-to-current-liabilities ratio.
e. Compute the operating-cash-flow-to-capital-expenditures ratio.

LO2 **P13-2B.** **Statement of Cash Flows (Indirect Method)** The Sweet Company's income statement and comparative balance sheets as of December 31 of 2016 and 2015 are presented below:

SWEET COMPANY
Income Statement
For the Year Ended December 31, 2016

Sales revenue.		$950,000
Cost of goods sold.	$507,000	
Wages expense	207,000	
Depreciation expense.	62,000	
Insurance expense.	13,000	
Interest expense.	12,000	
Income tax expense.	57,000	
Gain on sale of equipment	(16,000)	842,000
Net income.		$108,000

SWEET COMPANY Balance Sheets		
	Dec. 31, 2016	Dec. 31, 2015
Assets		
Cash.	$ 32,000	$ 33,000
Accounts receivable.	68,000	43,000
Inventory.	177,000	126,000
Prepaid insurance	9,000	11,000
Plant assets	887,000	770,000
Accumulated depreciation	(191,000)	(175,000)
Total assets	$982,000	$808,000
Liabilities and Stockholders' Equity		
Accounts payable.	$ 37,000	$ 27,000
Interest payable	5,000	—
Income tax payable	11,000	18,000
Bonds payable	145,000	80,000
Common stock.	660,000	585,000
Retained earnings	176,000	98,000
Treasury stock	(52,000)	—
Total liabilities and stockholders' equity	$982,000	$808,000

During the year, Sweet Company sold equipment for $27,000 cash that originally cost $57,000 and had $46,000 accumulated depreciation. New equipment was purchased for cash. Bonds payable and common stock were issued for cash. Cash dividends of $30,000 were declared and paid. At the end of the year, shares of treasury stock were purchased for cash. Accounts payable relate to merchandise purchases.

Required

a.   Compute the change in cash that occurred during 2016.

b.   Prepare a statement of cash flows using the indirect method.

P13-3B.   **Statement of Cash Flows (Indirect Method)** The Huber Company's income statement and comparative balance sheets as of December 31 of 2016 and 2015 follow: **LO2**

HUBER COMPANY Income Statement For the Year Ended December 31, 2016		
Sales revenue.		$810,000
Cost of goods sold.	$530,000	
Wages and other operating expenses	172,000	
Depreciation expense.	29,000	
Patent amortization expense	6,000	
Interest expense.	18,000	
Income tax expense.	25,000	
Gain on exchange of land for patent	(37,000)	743,000
Net income.		$ 67,000

HUBER COMPANY
Balance Sheets

	Dec. 31, 2016	Dec. 31, 2015
Assets		
Cash..	$ 49,000	$ 16,000
Accounts receivable.......................................	64,000	49,000
Inventory...	85,000	64,000
Land..	117,000	160,000
Building and equipment...................................	441,000	361,000
Accumulated depreciation................................	(122,000)	(100,000)
Patent..	74,000	—
Total assets	$708,000	$550,000
Liabilities and Stockholders' Equity		
Accounts payable..	$ 36,000	$ 26,000
Interest payable	13,000	5,000
Income tax payable	7,000	12,000
Bonds payable..	180,000	75,000
Common stock..	350,000	350,000
Retained earnings	122,000	82,000
Total liabilities and stockholders' equity	$708,000	$550,000

During 2016, $27,000 of cash dividends were declared and paid. A patent valued at $80,000 was obtained in exchange for land. Equipment that originally cost $20,000 and had $7,000 accumulated depreciation was sold for $13,000 cash. Bonds payable were sold for cash and cash was used to pay for structural improvements to the building.

Required
a. Compute the change in cash that occurred during 2016.
b. Prepare a statement of cash flows using the indirect method.

LO2 **P13-4B.** **Statement of Cash Flows (Indirect Method)** The Towne Company's income statement and comparative balance sheets as of December 31 of 2016 and 2015 follow:

TOWNE COMPANY
Income Statement
For the Year Ended December 31, 2016

Service fees earned		$317,000
Dividend and interest income............................		14,000
		$331,000
Wages and other operating expenses	$285,000	
Depreciation expense.....................................	55,000	
Franchise amortization expense	10,000	
Loss on sale of equipment...............................	7,000	
Gain on sale of investments.............................	(17,000)	340,000
Net loss		$ (9,000)

TOWNE COMPANY Balance Sheets		
	Dec. 31, 2016	Dec. 31, 2015
Assets		
Cash..	$ 43,000	$ 33,000
Accounts receivable...................................	13,000	18,000
Interest receivable	—	4,000
Prepaid expenses.....................................	16,000	10,000
Long-term investments—available for sale	—	70,000
Fair value adjustment to investments.................	—	10,000
Plant assets	696,000	655,000
Accumulated depreciation.............................	(237,000)	(185,000)
Franchise	91,000	29,000
Total assets	$622,000	$644,000
Liabilities and Stockholders' Equity		
Accrued liabilities.....................................	$ 12,000	$ 14,000
Notes payable	—	26,000
Common stock ($10 par value)	595,000	535,000
Retained earnings	35,000	59,000
Unrealized gain on investments.......................	—	10,000
Treasury stock	(20,000)	—
Total liabilities and stockholders' equity	$622,000	$644,000

During the year, the following transactions occurred:

1. Sold equipment for $9,000 cash that originally cost $19,000 and had $3,000 accumulated depreciation.
2. Sold long-term investments that had cost $70,000 for $87,000 cash. Unrealized gains totaling $10,000 related to these investments had been recorded in earlier years. At year-end, the fair value adjustment and unrealized gain account balances were eliminated.
3. Paid cash to extend the company's exclusive franchise for another three years.
4. Paid off a note payable at the bank on January 1.
5. Declared and paid a $15,000 dividend.
6. Purchased treasury stock for cash.
7. Acquired land valued at $60,000 by issuing 6,000 shares of common stock.

Required
a. Compute the change in cash that occurred in 2016.
b. Prepare a statement of cash flows using the indirect method.

P13-5B. Analyzing Cash Flow Ratios Molly Enterprises reported the following information for the past   LO3 year of operations:

	Transaction	Free Cash Flow $300,000	Operating-Cash-Flow-to-Current-Liabilities Ratio 1.2 times	Operating-Cash-Flow-to-Capital-Expenditures Ratio 4.0 times
a.	Recorded credit sales of $15,000			
b.	Collected $6,000 owed from customers			
c.	Purchased $45,000 of equipment on long-term credit ...			
d.	Purchased $70,000 of equipment for cash			
e.	Paid $17,000 of wages with cash			
f.	Recorded utility bill of $14,750 that has not been paid ...			

For each transaction, indicate whether the ratio will (I) increase, (D) decrease, or (N) have no effect.

LO3, 4
(Appendix 13A)

P13-6B.   **Statement of Cash Flows (Direct Method)** Refer to the data given for the Rural Company in Problem P13-1B.

Required
a.   Compute the change in cash that occurred during 2016.
b.   Prepare a statement of cash flows using the direct method.
c.   Compute free cash flow.
d.   Compute the operating-cash-flow-to-current-liabilities ratio.
e.   Compute the operating-cash-flow-to-capital-expenditures ratio.

LO4
(Appendix 13A)

P13-7B.   **Statement of Cash Flows (Direct Method)** Refer to the data given for the Sweet Company in Problem P13-2B.

Required
a.   Compute the change in cash that occurred during 2016.
b.   Prepare a statement of cash flows using the direct method.

LO4
(Appendix 13A)

P13-8B.   **Statement of Cash Flows (Direct Method)** Refer to the data given for the Huber Company in Problem P13-3B.

Required
a.   Compute the change in cash that occurred during 2016.
b.   Prepare a statement of cash flows using the direct method. Use one cash outflow for "cash paid for wages and other operating expenses." Accounts payable relate to inventory purchases only.

LO4
(Appendix 13A)

P13-9B.   **Statement of Cash Flows (Direct Method)** Refer to the data given for the Towne Company in Problem P13-4B.

Required
a.   Compute the change in cash that occurred during 2016.
b.   Prepare a statement of cash flows using the direct method. Use one cash outflow for "cash paid for wages and other operating expenses."

EXTENDING YOUR KNOWLEDGE

REPORTING AND ANALYSIS

COLUMBIA
SPORTSWEAR
COMPANY

EYK13-1.   **Financial Reporting Problem: Columbia Sportswear Company** The financial statements for the Columbia Sportswear Company are available on this book's Website.

Required
Answer the following questions:
a.   How much did Columbia Sportswear's cash and cash equivalents decrease in 2014?
b.   What was the largest source of cash and cash equivalents in 2014?
c.   What was the single largest use of cash and cash equivalents in 2014?
d.   How much dividends were paid in 2014?
e.   Why do depreciation and amortization, both noncash items, appear on Columbia's statement of cash flows?

COLUMBIA
SPORTSWEAR
COMPANY

UNDER ARMOUR,
INC.

EYK13-2.   **Comparative Analysis Problem:** Columbia Sportswear Company **vs** Under Armour, Inc. The financial statements for the Columbia Sportswear Company and Under Armour, Inc. are available on this book's Website.

Required
Answer the following questions:
a.   Compute the free cash flow in 2014 for both Columbia Sportswear and Under Armour, Inc.
b.   Compute the operating cash flows to capital expenditures for both Columbia Sportswear and Under Armour, Inc.
c.   Comment on the ability of each company to finance its capital expenditures.

EYK13-3.   **Business Decision Problem** Recently hired as assistant controller for Finite, Inc., you are sitting next to the controller as she responds to questions at the annual stockholders' meeting. The firm's financial statements contain a statement of cash flows prepared using the indirect method. A stockholder raises his hand.

Stockholder: "I notice that depreciation expense is shown as an addition in the calculation of the cash flow from operating activities."

Controller: "That's correct."

Stockholder: "What depreciation method do you use?"

Controller: "We use the straight-line method for all plant assets."

Stockholder: "Well, why don't you switch to an accelerated depreciation method, such as double-declining balance, increase the annual depreciation amount, and thus increase the cash flow from operating activities?"

The controller pauses, turns to you, and replies, "My assistant will answer your question."

Required

Prepare an answer to the stockholder's question.

EYK13-4. **Financial Analysis Problem** Parker Hannifin Corporation, headquartered in Cleveland, Ohio, manufactures motion control and fluid system components for a variety of industrial users. The firm's financial statements contain the following data (Year 3 is the most recent year; dollar amounts are in thousands):

PARKER HANNIFIN
CORPORATION

	Year 3	Year 2	Year 1
Current assets at year-end.	$1,018,354	$1,056,443	$1,055,776
Current liabilities at year-end	504,444	468,254	358,729
Current liabilities at beginning of year	468,254	358,729	345,594
Cash provided by operating activities	259,204	229,382	235,186
Capital expenditures	99,914	91,484	84,955

a. Calculate Parker Hannifin's current ratio (current assets/current liabilities) for Years 1, 2, and 3.

b. Calculate Parker Hannifin's operating-cash-flow-to-current-liabilities ratio for Years 1, 2, and 3.

c. Comment on the three-year trend in Parker Hannifin's current ratio and operating-cash-flow-to-current-liabilities ratio. Do the trends in these two ratios reinforce each other or contradict each other as indicators of Parker Hannifin's ability to pay its current liabilities?

d. Calculate Parker Hannifin's operating-cash-flow-to-capital-expenditures ratio for Years 1, 2, and 3. Comment on the strength of this ratio over the three-year period.

CRITICAL THINKING

EYK13-5. **Accounting Research Problem: General Mills, Inc.** The fiscal year 2014 annual report of General Mills, Inc. is available on this book's Website.

GENERAL MILLS,
INC.

Required

a. Refer to Note 2. How does General Mills define its cash equivalents?

b. What method does General Mills use to report its cash provided by operating activities?

c. What is the change in cash and cash equivalents experienced by General Mills during fiscal 2014? What is the amount of cash and cash equivalents as of May 25, 2014?

d. What is General Mills' operating-cash-flow-to-capital-expenditures ratio for fiscal year 2014?

e. Calculate General Mills' 2014 operating-cash-flow-to-current-liabilities ratio.

EYK13-6. **Accounting Communication Activity** Susan Henderson, the vice president of marketing, was told by the CEO that she needs to understand the numbers because the company's existence depends on making money. It has been a long time since Susan took a class in accounting. She recalls that companies report net income and cash flows in two separate statements. She feels pretty comfortable with the income statement, but is somewhat lost looking at the statement of cash flows. She asks you to help explain this statement.

Required

Write a brief memo to Susan explaining the form and content of the statement of cash flows, along with a short discussion of how to analyze the statement.

EYK13-7. **Accounting Ethics Case** Due to an economic recession, Anton Corporation faces severe cash flow problems. Management forecasts that payments to some suppliers will have to be delayed for several months. Jay Newton, controller, has asked his staff for suggestions on selecting the suppliers for which payments will be delayed.

"That's a fairly easy decision," observes Tim Haslem. "Some suppliers charge interest if our payment is late, but others do not. We should pay those suppliers that charge interest and delay payments to the ones that do not charge interest. If we do this, the savings in interest charges will be quite substantial."

"I disagree," states Tara Wirth. "That position is too 'bottom line' oriented. It's not fair to delay payments only to suppliers who don't charge interest for late payments. Most suppliers in that category are ones we have dealt with for years; selecting these suppliers would be taking advantage of the excellent relationships we have developed over the years. The fair thing to do is to make pro-rata payments to each supplier."

"Well, making pro-rata payments to each supplier means that *all* our suppliers will be upset because no one receives full payment," comments Sue Myling. "I believe it is most important to maintain good relations with our long-term suppliers; we should pay them currently and delay payments to our newer suppliers. The interest costs we end up paying these newer suppliers is the price we must pay to keep our long-term relationships solid."

Required
Which suppliers should Jay Newton select for delayed payments? Discuss.

THE HOME
DEPOT, INC.

EYK13-8. Corporate Social Responsibility Problem The corporate social responsibility highlighted in this chapter (see page 481) mentions that Home Depot believes in giving back. One of the ways the company has done this is through its Team Depot program of employee volunteerism. Under this program, Home Depot employees volunteer their own time to work together on projects that benefit communities in which the company does business. Each year the program provides millions of hours of employee volunteerism.

One of the many programs that benefits from Team Depot is Habitat for Humanity. Do a computer search and report how Team Depot has helped Habitat for Humanity.

EYK13-9. Forensic Accounting Problem Cash larceny involves the fraudulent stealing of an employer's cash. These schemes often target the company's bank deposits. The fraudster steals the money after the deposit has been prepared, but before the deposit is taken to the bank. Most often these schemes involve a deficiency in the internal control system where segregation of duties is not present. The perpetrator is often in charge of recording receipts, preparing the deposit, delivering the deposit to the bank, and verifying the receipted deposit slip. Without proper segregation of duties, the fraudster is able cover up the theft.

In addition to segregation of duties, what internal control procedures might help deter and detect cash larceny?

EYK13-10. Working with the Takeaways For the fiscal year ended February 2, 2014, Home Depot reports (in millions) cash provided by operating activities of $7,628. For the same period, average current liabilities were reported to be $10,749, annual capital expenditures were $1,389, and proceeds from sales of property and equipment were $89. Calculate the free cash flow, operating-cash-flow-to-current-liabilities ratio, and the operating-cash-flow-to-capital-expenditures ratio for Home Depot and comment on the results.

EYK13-11. Analyzing IFRS Financial Statements The 2014 financial statements of LVMH Moet Hennessey-Louis Vuitton S.A. are available on this book's Website. LVMH is a Paris-based holding company and one of the world's largest and best-known luxury goods companies. As a member of the European Union, French companies are required to prepare their consolidated (group) financial statements using International Financial Reporting Standards (IFRS). After reviewing LVMH's consolidated financial statements calculate LVMH's (a) free cash flow, (b) operating-cash-flow-to-current-liabilities ratio (use the year-end current liabilities instead of the average current liabilities), and (c) operating-cash-flow-to-capital-expenditures ratio for 2013 and 2014. What do the ratio results reveal about LVMH? *Hint:* Capital expenditures are classified as "Operating investments" on LVMH Consolidated cash flow statement.

EYK13-12. Preparing a Statement of Cash Flows Kate has just completed her first year running Kate's Cards. She has been preparing monthly income statements and balance sheets, so she knows that her company has been profitable and that there is cash in the bank. She has not, however, prepared a statement of cash flows. Kate provides you with the year-end income statement and balance sheet and asks that you prepare a statement of cash flows for Kate's Cards.

Additional information:

1. There were no disposals of equipment during the year.
2. Dividends in the amount of $1,300 were paid in cash during the year.
3. Prepaid expenses relate to operating expenses.

Required

a. Prepare a statement of cash flows for Kate's Cards for the year ended August 31, 2016, using the indirect method. Hint: Since this was Kate's first year of operations, the beginning balance sheet account balances were zero.

b. Prepare a statement of cash flows for Kate's Cards for the year ended August 31, 2016, using the direct method. (Appendix 13A)

KATE'S CARDS	
Income Statement	
Year Ended August 31, 2016	
Sales revenue.	$135,000
Cost of goods sold.	72,000
Gross profit.	63,000
Operating expenses	
Wages	18,000
Consulting	11,850
Insurance	1,200
Utilities	2,400
Depreciation	3,250
Total operating expenses.	36,700
Income from operations.	26,300
Interest expense.	900
Income before income tax	25,400
Income tax expense.	8,900
Net income.	$ 16,500

KATE'S CARDS	
Balance Sheet	
As of August 31, 2016	
Assets	
Current assets	
Cash.	$12,300
Accounts receivable.	11,000
Inventory.	16,000
Prepaid insurance	1,000
Total current assets	40,300
Equipment	17,500
Accumulated depreciation	(3,250)
Total assets	$54,550
Liabilities	
Current liabilities	
Accounts payable.	$ 6,200
Unearned revenue	1,250
Other current liabilities	1,900
Total current liabilities	9,350
Note payable	15,000
Total liabilities.	24,350
Stockholders' equity	
Common stock.	500
Additional paid-in-capital.	9,500
Preferred stock.	5,000
Retained earnings	15,200
Total stockholders' equity	30,200
Total liabilities and stockholders' equity	$54,550

ANSWERS TO SELF-STUDY QUESTIONS:

1. a, (pp. 468–469)   2. c, (p. 470)   3. d, (pp. 470–471)   4. c, (pp. 474–475)   5. c, (p. 482)
6. b, (pp. 470–471)   7. b, (pp. 482–483)   8. d, (pp. 468–469)   9. c, (p. 479)   10. a, (p. 487)
11. c, (p. 487)   12. b, (p. 487)

YOUR TURN! SOLUTIONS

Solution 13.1

1. Operating
2. Investing
3. Operating
4. Investing
5. Financing
6. Financing
7. Operating
8. Financing
9. Investing

Solution 13.2

HUSKY COMPANY Statement of Cash Flows For the Year Ended December 31, 2016		
Cash Flow from Operating Activities		
Net income.	$112,000	
Add (deduct) items to convert net income to cash basis		
Depreciation.	34,000	
Accounts receivable increase	(18,000)	
Inventory increase	(60,000)	
Prepaid insurance decrease.	4,000	
Accounts payable decrease.	(6,000)	
Wages payable increase	6,000	
Income tax payable decrease	(2,000)	
Cash provided by operating activities		$ 70,000
Cash Flow from Investing Activities		
Purchase of plant assets		(110,000)
Cash Flow from Financing Activities		
Issuance of bonds payable	110,000	
Payment of dividends.	(58,000)	
Cash provided by financing activities		52,000
Net increase in cash.		12,000
Cash at beginning of year		10,000
Cash at end of year		$ 22,000

Solution 13.3

Free cash flow: $40,000 − $12,500 = $27,500
Operating-cash-flow-to-current-liabilities ratio: $40,000/$30,000 = 1.33
Operating-cash-flow-to-capital-expenditures ratio: $40,000/$12,500 = 3.20

Solution 13A.1

Supporting Calculations:

Cash received from customers:

$1,270,000 Sales revenue − $18,000 Accounts receivable increase = $1,252,000

Cash paid for merchandise purchased:

$860,000 Cost of goods sold + $60,000 Inventory increase + $6,000 Accounts payable decrease = $926,000

Cash paid to employees:

$172,000 Wages expense − $6,000 Wages payable increase = $166,000

Cash paid for insurance:

$16,000 Insurance expense − $4,000 Prepaid insurance decrease = $12,000

Cash paid for interest:

Equal to the $18,000 balance in interest expense

Cash paid for income taxes:

$58,000 Income tax expense + $2,000 Income tax payable decrease = $60,000

Purchase of plant assets:

$500,000 Ending plant assets − $390,000 Beginning plant assets = $110,000

Issuance of bonds payable:

$260,000 Ending bonds payable − $150,000 Beginning bonds payable = $110,000

Payment of dividends

$58,000 given in problem data

Other Analysis

Accumulated depreciation increased by $34,000, which is the amount of depreciation expense.

Common stock account balance did not change.

Retained earnings increased by $54,000, which is the difference between the net income of $112,000 and the dividends declared of $58,000.

HUSKY COMPANY
Statement of Cash Flows (Direct Method)
For the Year Ended December 31, 2016

Cash Flow from Operating Activities

Cash received from customers.		$1,252,000
Cash paid for merchandise purchased.	$(926,000)	
Cash paid to employees.	(166,000)	
Cash paid for insurance	(12,000)	
Cash paid for interest	(18,000)	
Cash paid for income taxes	(60,000)	(1,182,000)
Cash provided by operating activities.		70,000
Cash Flow from Investing Activities		
Purchase of plant assets		(110,000)
Cash Flow from Financing Activities		
Issuance of bonds payable.	110,000	
Payment of dividends.	(58,000)	
Cash provided by financing activities		52,000
Net increase in cash.		12,000
Cash at beginning of year		10,000
Cash at end of year		$ 22,000

Analysis and Interpretation of Financial Statements

PAST

In Chapter 13, we examined the statement of cash flows.

PRESENT

In this chapter we complete our study of managerial accounting by looking at the analysis and interpretation of financial statements.

LEARNING OBJECTIVES

1. **Identify** persistent earnings and **discuss** the content and format of the income statement. *(p. 518)*

2. **Identify** the sources of financial information used by investment professionals and **explain** horizontal financial statement analysis. *(p. 522)*

3. **Explain** vertical financial statement analysis. *(p. 527)*

4. **Define** and **discuss** financial ratios for analyzing a firm. *(p. 529)*

5. **Discuss** the limitations of financial statement analysis. *(p. 544)*

6. Appendix 14A: **Describe** financial statement disclosures. *(p. 546)*

PROCTER & GAMBLE

The **Procter & Gamble Company (P&G)** is one of America's oldest companies, dating back to 1837 when candle maker William Procter and soap maker James Gamble combined their small businesses. Over the next few decades the company introduced such well-known products as Ivory soap and Crisco shortening that are still sold today.

P&G has continued to grow, with annual sales of over $80 billion. Not all of the company's growth, however, is the result of internally developed products like Crest toothpaste, Head & Shoulders shampoo, and Pampers diapers. A significant part of P&G's growth has come from mergers and acquisitions. P&G's largest acquisition occurred in 2005 when it acquired Gillette for $57 billion.

Acquisitions, such as the one involving Gillette, are complex transactions. Perhaps the hardest part of any merger or acquisition is to determine the appropriate price to pay—in this case $57 billion. How did P&G determine how much to pay for Gillette? Many factors go into such an analysis, but it often comes down to how much a company like Gillette will be able to add to P&G's future persistent earnings.

In this chapter we explore some of the ways that investment professionals determine how much a company is worth. The process involves analyzing a company's persistent earnings potential as well as the various risks associated with a company's day-to-day operations.

	ANALYSIS AND INTERPRETATION OF FINANCIAL STATEMENTS	
Persistent Earnings		**Analytical Techniques**
• Persistent earnings		• Sources of information
• Discontinued operations		• Horizontal analysis
• Changes in accounting principles		• Trend analysis
• Comprehensive income		• Vertical analysis
		• Ratio analysis
		• Limitations of financial analysis
		• Financial statement disclosures (Appendix 14A)

PERSISTENT EARNINGS AND THE INCOME STATEMENT

LO1 **Identify** persistent earnings and **discuss** the content and format of the income statement.

Net income is the "bottom line" measure of firm performance. It is a measure that depends on such accrual accounting procedures as the revenue recognition and expense matching policies selected by a firm's management. Generally accepted accounting principles have historically emphasized the importance of accounting earnings because past accounting earnings have been found to be a good predictor of a firm's future operating cash flow. Modern valuation theory tells us that the economic value of a company is the present value of the company's future operating cash flows.

Thus, an important role for accounting numbers is their use by investment professionals when assessing the economic value of a company (like Gillette in the feature story).

One of the determinants of the ability of historical accounting earnings to predict future cash flow is the extent to which earnings recur over time, or what is known as *earnings persistence*. Since the value of a share of common stock today is a function of a firm's ability to consistently generate earnings year in and year out, the persistence (or sustainability) of a company's operating earnings is closely linked to its economic value. **Persistent earnings** are also sometimes referred to as *sustainable earnings* or *permanent earnings*, whereas non-persistent earnings are often referred to as **transitory earnings**. In general, transitory earnings include such single-period events as special items, restructuring charges, changes in accounting principle, and discontinued operations.

To assist investors in their assessment of a company's persistent earnings, and hence in assessing a firm's economic value, companies are required under GAAP to classify income statement accounts in a manner that aids a financial statement user in assessing persistent earnings. In this chapter, we discuss a refinement of the classified income statement called the multiple-step or multi-step income statement.

Exhibit 14-1 illustrates the basic format of the multi-step income statement. While a **single-step income statement** derives the net income of a business in one step by subtracting total expenses from total revenues, a **multiple-step income statement** derives one or more intermediate performance measures before net income is reported. Examples of such intermediate performance measures are gross profit, net operating income, and net income from continuing operations before taxes.

The income statement is organized in such a way that items with greater persistence are reported higher up in the income statement, whereas items considered more transitory

Exhibit 14-1	The Multi-Step Income Statement

KALI COMPANY
Income Statement
For Year Ended December 31, 2016

Sales revenue..		$ 500	Usual and frequent
Cost of goods sold....................................		200	Usual and frequent
Gross profit...		300	
Operating expenses..................................		250	Usual and frequent
Net operating income.............................		50	
Other income and expense			
Interest income......................................	25		**Unusual**
Interest expense.....................................	(35)		**Unusual**
Gain on sale of equipment..........................	15	5	**Unusual**
Net income from continuing operations before tax		55	
Income tax...		20	Usual and frequent
Net income from continuing operations..............		35	
Gain from operations of discontinued division (net of tax)............	15		**Infrequent**
Loss on disposal of discontinued division (net of tax)...............	(5)	10	
Net income..		$ 45	
Earning per share (100 shares outstanding)......................		$0.45	

are reported further down in the statement. Thus, accounts representing financial events that are both usual and frequent are reported first. Usual refers to whether an item is central to a firm's core operations, whereas **unusual items** display a high degree of abnormality and/or are unrelated, or only incidentally related, to the normal activities of a business. Frequent refers to how often an item is expected to occur, with infrequent items not reasonably expected to recur in the foreseeable future. Usual and frequent items typically consist of such income statement accounts as sales revenue, cost of goods sold, and other operating expenses. Just below these usual and frequent items are items that are either unusual or infrequent, but not both. Income statement accounts such as interest expense, interest income, and gains on sales of equipment are often frequently recurring items; however, they are not considered part of a firm's central operations and therefore are considered unusual. Examples of infrequent items include such financial events as asset write-downs and restructuring charges. These items are not expected to occur regularly, but are not considered unusual in nature.

Each of the above items is reported as part of a company's continuing operations and is shown before any income tax expense. GAAP, however, requires certain single-period items, or one-time events, to be reported on an after-tax basis. For example, income from discontinued operations, or the part of a business which is being shuttered or sold, are shown net of the financial effect of any applicable income taxes. Reporting discontinued operations on a net-of-tax basis allows the income tax expense reported on the income statement to reflect only the income taxes associated with a firm's continuing operations.

Most believe that the income statement is more useful when certain types of transactions and events are reported in separate sections. For this reason, information about discontinued operations is disclosed separately in the income statement. Segregating these categories of information from the results of continuing operations makes it easier for financial statement users to identify a company's persistent earnings.

The creation of sections within the income statement, however, complicates the reporting of a company's income tax expense. Items affecting the overall amount of income tax expense may appear in more than one section. If this is the case, accountants allocate a company's total income tax expense among those sections of the income statement in which the items affecting the tax expense appear.

Regardless of the format used for the income statement, companies are required to report net income on a per common share basis, called **earnings per share (EPS)**, on the income statement immediately following net income.

IFRS ALERT

Like U.S. GAAP, IFRS encourages companies to use a multi-step income statement when presenting a company's periodic performance. Tesco, the world's third largest retailer, presents its IFRS accounted income statement in its financial statements, which are available on this book's Website. Examining Tesco's income statement reveals that the retailer presents four measures of firm performance: gross profit, operating profit, profit before tax, and profit for the year. These indicators correspond to the four performance measures reported by the Kali Company in Exhibit 14.1: gross profit, net operating income, net income from continuing operations before tax, and net income. The income statements under U.S. GAAP and IFRS are very similar, with only minor labeling differences—like using "profit" instead of "income."

Discontinued Operations

Discontinued Operations

When a company sells, abandons, or otherwise disposes of a segment of its operations, a **discontinued operations** section of the income statement reports information about the discontinued business segment. The discontinued operations section presents two categories of information:

1. The income or loss from the segment's operations for the portion of the year before its discontinuance.

2. Any gain or loss from the disposal of the segment.

This section is reported on the income statement immediately after information regarding a firm's continuing operations.

To illustrate the reporting of discontinued operations, assume that on July 1, 2016, Kali Company, a diversified manufacturing company, sold its pet food division. **Exhibit 14-1** illustrates the income statement for Kali Company, including information regarding its pet food division in the discontinued operations section. From January 1 through June 30, Kali's pet food division operated at a profit, net of income taxes, of $15. The loss, net of income taxes, from the sale of the division's assets and liabilities was $5. Note that when there is a discontinued operations section, the difference between a firm's continuing sales revenues and expenses is labeled net income from continuing operations.

Changes in Accounting Principles

Occasionally a company may implement a **change in accounting principle**—that is, a switch from one generally accepted method to another. Examples include a change in inventory costing method, such as from FIFO to weighted-average cost, or a change in depreciation method, such as from declining balance to straight-line. These changes are permitted when a business can demonstrate that the reported financial results under the new accounting method are superior to the results reported under the replaced method.

Changing accounting principles can present a problem for financial statement users analyzing a company's performance over time because different accounting principles are likely to produce different financial statement results. Consequently, financial statements of prior years, issued in comparative form with current year financial statements, must also be presented using the new accounting principles as if the new method had been used all along.

Consistency Principle

The *consistency principle* states that, unless otherwise disclosed, financial statements use the same accounting methods from one period to the next. A consistent use of accounting methods enhances the comparability of financial data across time. The consistency principle impacts the accounting for a change in accounting principles in several ways. First, to change an accounting principle, a company must be able to justify that the reported results under the new principle are preferable. Second, a company must present its prior year financial statements as though the new principle had been in use all along. In actual practice, only the prior year financial statements presented with the current year financial statements must be presented using the new accounting method. For all financial statements prior to those presented with the current statements, a lump sum adjustment is made to retained earnings on the statement of retained earnings and the statement of stockholders' equity.

Comprehensive Income

Most items that generate wealth changes in a business are required to be shown on the income statement. There are, however, a few items that do not appear as part of the regular content of the income statement and instead are classified under a category labeled **comprehensive income**. A business's comprehensive income includes its net income, any changes in the market value of certain marketable securities, and any unrealized gains and losses from translating foreign currency denominated financial statements into U.S. dollars. This latter topic is covered in more advanced accounting textbooks.

Companies are given some flexibility as to how they report their comprehensive income. They are allowed to utilize two alternative formats under GAAP: (1) appending comprehensive income to the bottom of the income statement; or (2) creating a separate statement of comprehensive income. In addition to comprehensive income for the current period, GAAP requires a company to report accumulated other comprehensive income as part of stockholders' equity on the balance sheet. Accumulated other comprehensive income serves the same role for comprehensive income as retained earnings serves for regular net income—it reports the cumulative amount of comprehensive income as of the balance sheet date.

Pampers and UNICEF

Maternal and neonatal tetanus is a disease that kills 59,000 people annually. **P&G**, through its Pampers product, has teamed up with UNICEF to fight this completely preventable disease. For every purchase of a pack of Pampers, P&G donates one dose of the tetanus vaccine. Pampers' funding has helped protect 100 million women and their babies against maternal and neonatal tetanus (MNT) and has helped eliminate this disease in Myanmar and Uganda. P&G and UNICEF are committed to the elimination of MNT from the face of the earth.

P&G and UNICEF have gone even further in their teamwork. P&G offers its employees in Europe, the Middle East, and Africa, a three-month paid sabbatical to work with UNICEF. The program is aimed at employees who have always wanted to perform humanitarian work but have lacked the financial resources to do so.

YOUR TURN! 14.1

The solution is on
page 580.

Conner Company, a retail company, entered into the following transactions during the year:

1. Sold merchandise to customers
2. Settled a major lawsuit
3. Wrote down the book value of a closed warehouse
4. Paid employee wages
5. Disposed of a line of discount stores
6. Paid income taxes

Required
Classify each of the above items as either persistent earnings or transitory earnings.

SOURCES OF INFORMATION

LO2 **Identify** the sources of financial information used by investment professionals and **explain** horizontal financial statement analysis

Except for closely held companies, businesses publish their financial statements at least annually. Most large companies also issue quarterly financial data. Normally, annual financial statements are attested to by a certified public accountant, and investment professionals carefully review the independent accountant's opinion to assess the reliability of the published financial data.

Companies listed on stock exchanges must also submit financial statements, called a 10-K for the annual report and 10-Q for the quarterly report, to the U.S. Securities and Exchange Commission (SEC). These statements are available to any interested party and are generally more useful than annual reports because they contain greater detail.

Investment professionals may also want to compare the performance of a particular firm with that of the other firms in the same industry. Data on industry norms, median financial ratios by industry, and other relationships are available from such data collection services as Dun & Bradstreet, Moody's, and Standard and Poor's. In addition, some brokerage firms compile industry norms and financial ratios from their own computer databases.

ACCOUNTING IN PRACTICE	**SEC EDGAR Database**

An example of a financial database is **EDGAR**, the Electronic Data Gathering, Analysis, and Retrieval system, maintained by the U.S. SEC (www.sec.gov/edgar.shtml). This computer database aids financial statement analysis by performing automated data collection, validation, indexing, acceptance, and forwarding of submissions by companies and others who are required by law to file forms with the U.S. Securities and Exchange Commission. The primary intent of the SEC in creating EDGAR was to increase the efficiency of the securities market for the benefit of investors, corporations, and the economy, by accelerating the receipt, acceptance, dissemination, and analysis of corporate information filed with the agency. An "efficient" securities market means that investors are able to make the best possible decisions regarding where and when to invest their funds.

Analytical Techniques

The absolute dollar amounts of net income, sales revenue, total assets, and other key data are usually not meaningful when analyzed in isolation. For example, knowing that a company's annual net income is $1 million is of little informational value unless the amount of the income can be related to other factors. A $1 million profit might represent excellent performance for a company with less than $10 million in invested capital. On the other hand, $1 million in net income would be considered meager for a firm that had several hundred million dollars in invested capital. Thus, significant information can be derived by examining the relationship between two or more accounting variables, such as net income and total assets, net income and sales revenue, or net income and stockholders' equity. To describe these relationships clearly and to make comparisons easy, the relationships are often expressed in terms of ratios or percentages.

For example, we might express the relationship of $15,000 in net income to $150,000 in sales revenue as a ten percent ($15,000/$150,000) rate of return on sales. To describe the relationship between sales revenue of $150,000 and inventory of $20,000, we might use a ratio or a percentage; ($150,000/$20,000) may be expressed as 7.5, 7.5:1, or 750 percent.

Changes in selected financial statement items compared in successive financial statements are often expressed as percentages. For example, if a firm's net income increased from $40,000 last year to $48,000 this year, the $8,000 increase related to last year (the base year) is expressed as a 20 percent increase ($8,000/$40,000) in net income. To express a dollar increase or decrease as a percentage, however, the analyst must make the base year amount a positive figure. If, for example, a firm had a net loss of $4,000 in one year and net income of $20,000 in the next, the $24,000 increase cannot be meaningfully expressed as a percentage. Similarly, if a firm reported no marketable securities in last year's balance sheet but showed $15,000 of such securities in this year's statement, the $15,000 increase cannot be expressed as a meaningful percentage.

When evaluating a firm's financial statements for two or more years, analysts often use **horizontal analysis**. Horizontal analysis is a technique that can be useful for detecting an improvement or deterioration in a firm's performance and for spotting trends regarding a firm's financial well-being. The term **vertical analysis** is used to describe the analysis of a single year of financial data.

HORIZONTAL ANALYSIS

The type of horizontal analysis most often used by investment professionals is **comparative financial statement analysis** for two or more years, showing dollar and/or percentage changes for important financial statement items and totals. Dollar increases and decreases are divided by data from the base year to obtain percentage changes. To illustrate, the 2014 and 2013 financial statements of Procter & Gamble (P&G) are presented in **Exhibits 14-2**, **14-3**, and **14-4**. We will use the data in these statements throughout this chapter to illustrate various analytical techniques.

When analyzing financial statements, the investment professional is likely to focus his or her immediate attention on those financial statement items or percentages that are significant in amount. Although percentage changes are helpful in identifying significant items, they can sometimes be misleading. An unusually large percentage change may occur simply because the dollar amount of the base year is small. For example, P&G had a decrease in other non-operating income of $775, from $939 in 2013 to $164 in 2014. This represents a decrease of 82.5 percent, yet the dollar amount of this line item is quite small and insignificant relative to the other reported dollar amounts on P&G's income statement. The financial statement user's attention should be directed first to changes in key financial statement totals: sales revenue, operating income, net income, total assets, total liabilities, and so on. Next, the changes in significant individual items, such as accounts receivable, inventory, and property, plant and equipment should be examined.

P&G's total assets increased 3.6 percent from 2013 to 2014 (see **Exhibit 14-3**), and net sales increased 0.6 percent over the same time period (see **Exhibit 14-2**). (Recall that net sales equals gross sales revenue less any sales returns and allowances and sales discounts.) A small percentage increase in net sales coincided with a larger increase in total assets, reflecting a continued recovery of the economy in 2014, and indicating that P&G undertook certain business strategies to increase capacity to meet increasing demand. One potential note of concern is the relationship between cost of goods sold and net sales. While net sales increased by 0.6 percent, cost of goods sold increased by 2.6 percent, leading to a deterioration in P&G's gross profit margin percentage. P&G was able, however, to reduce selling, general, and administrative expense by 5.8 percent which ultimately helped contribute to an overall increase in net earnings of 2.9 percent in 2014.

Exhibit 14-2	Procter & Gamble Income Statement

THE PROCTER & GAMBLE COMPANY
Consolidated Income Statements

(in millions)	Year Ended 2014	Common-Size	Year Ended 2013	Common-Size	$ Change	% Change
Net sales...................	$ 83,062	100.0%	$ 82,581	100.0%	$ 481	0.6 %
Cost of goods sold............	42,460	51.1%	41,391	50.1%	1,069	2.6 %
Gross profit.................	40,602	48.9%	41,190	49.9%	(588)	(1.4)%
Selling, general, and administrative expense.......	25,314	30.5%	26,860	32.5%	(1,546)	(5.8)%
Operating income.............	15,288	18.4%	14,330	17.4%	958	6.7 %
Interest expense..............	709	0.9%	667	0.8%	42	6.3 %
Other non-operating income	164	0.2%	939	1.1%	(775)	(82.5)%
Earnings from continuing operations before taxes	14,743	17.7%	14,602	17.7%	141	1.0 %
Income taxes on continuing operations	3,178	3.8%	3,391	4.1%	(213)	(6.3)%
Net earnings from continuing operations	11,565	13.9%	11,211	13.6%	354	3.2 %
Net earnings from discontinued operations, net of taxes	78	0.1%	101	0.1%	(23)	(22.8)%
Net earnings.................	$ 11,643	14.0%	$ 11,312	13.7%	$ 331	2.9 %
Earnings per share	4.19		4.04		0.15	3.7 %
Dividends per share	2.45		2.29		0.16	7.0 %

We can see from P&G's statement of cash flows (**Exhibit 14-4**) that even though cash flow from operations declined from 2013 to 2014, P&G decreased its cash outflow used by investing activities to a greater extent. As a result, they were able to increase end-of-year cash from 2013 to 2014. Finally, **Exhibit 14-4** reveals that P&G repurchased its common stock (treasury stock) in both 2013 and 2014, and increased its dividend payments, both of which increased the amount of the cash it returned to shareholders during this period of slow growth.

From this limited analysis of comparative financial statements, an investment professional might conclude that P&G's operating performance for 2014 was slightly better when compared with that of 2013, mostly the result of cost controls in 2014. Further analysis using some of the techniques summarized later in the chapter, however, may cause that opinion to be either affirmed or modified. The foregoing analysis did reveal some concerns, in particular, a deteriorating gross profit margin and a shrinking cash flow provided by operating activities.

PRINCIPLE ALERT	Consistency Principle

Horizontal analysis is a process of analyzing a firm's financial data across two or more years by examining dollar changes, percentage changes, and/or trend percentages. The utility of horizontal analysis, however, is dependent upon the effective implementation of the *consistency principle*. This accounting principle requires that a firm use the same accounting methods from one period to the next or, if a firm finds it necessary (or required) to change an accounting method, that the financial effects of any change be fully disclosed in the financial statements. The consistency principle assures financial analysts that, unless otherwise noted, changes in the accounts over time represent underlying economic changes in a business, and not the result of an accounting method change.

Exhibit 14-3	Procter & Gamble Balance Sheet

THE PROCTER & GAMBLE COMPANY
Consolidated Balance Sheets

(in millions)	2014	Common-Size	2013	Common-Size	$ Change	% Change
Assets						
Current assets						
Cash and cash equivalents..............	$ 8,558	5.9 %	$ 5,947	4.3 %	$2,611	43.9 %
Short-term investments	2,128	1.5 %			2,128	
Accounts receivable....................	6,386	4.4 %	6,508	4.7 %	(122)	(1.9)%
Inventories	6,759	4.7 %	6,909	5.0 %	(150)	(2.2)%
Other current assets...................	7,786	5.4 %	4,626	3.3 %	3,160	68.3 %
Total current assets..................	31,617	21.9 %	23,990	17.2 %	7,627	31.8 %
Property, plant, and equipment, net	22,304	15.5 %	21,666	15.6 %	638	2.9 %
Intangible assets	84,547	58.6 %	86,760	62.3 %	(2,213)	(2.6)%
Other noncurrent assets.................	5,798	4.0 %	6,847	4.9 %	(1,049)	(15.3)%
Total assets........................	$144,266	100.0 %	$139,263	100.0 %	$5,003	3.6 %
Liabilities and Stockholders' Equity						
Current liabilities						
Accounts payable.....................	$ 8,461	5.9 %	$ 8,777	6.3 %	$ (316)	(3.6)%
Other current liabilities	25,265	17.5 %	21,260	15.3 %	4,005	18.8 %
Total current liabilities.................	33,726	23.4 %	30,037	21.6 %	3,689	12.3 %
Long-term debt	19,811	13.7 %	19,111	13.7 %	700	3.7 %
Other noncurrent liabilities...............	20,753	14.4 %	21,406	15.4 %	(653)	(3.1)%
Total liabilities	74,290	51.5 %	70,554	50.7 %	3,736	5.3 %
Preferred stock.......................	1,111	0.8 %	1,137	0.8 %	(26)	(2.3)%
Common stock........................	4,009	2.8 %	4,009	2.9 %	–	0.0 %
Additional paid-in capital	63,911	44.3 %	63,538	45.6 %	373	0.6 %
Treasury stock	(75,805)	(52.5)%	(71,966)	(51.7)%	(3,839)	5.3 %
Retained earnings	84,990	58.9 %	80,197	57.6 %	4,793	6.0 %
Other Stockholders' equity	(8,240)	(5.7)%	(8,206)	(5.9)%	(34)	0.4 %
Total stockholders' equity.............	69,976	48.5 %	68,709	49.3 %	1,267	1.8 %
Total liabilities and stockholders' equity...	$144,266	100.0 %	$139,263	100.0 %	$5,003	3.6 %

TREND ANALYSIS

To observe percentage changes over time in selected financial data, investment professionals often calculate **trend percentages**. Most companies provide summaries of their key financial data for the past five or ten years in their annual reports. With such information, the financial statement user can examine changes over periods longer than just the past two years. For example, suppose an analyst is interested in the trend in sales and net income for P&G for the past five years. The following are P&G's sales revenue and net income figures for 2010 through 2014:

PROCTER & GAMBLE COMPANY
Annual Performance

	2010		2011		2012		2013		2014	
	Millions of Dollars	Percentage of Base Year	Millions of Dollars	Percentage of Base Year	Millions of Dollars	Percentage of Base Year	Millions of Dollars	Percentage of Base Year	Millions of Dollars	Percentage of Base Year
Net sales..............	$75,785	100	$79,385	105	$82,006	108	$82,581	109	$83,062	110
Net income............	12,736	100	11,797	93	10,756	84	11,312	89	11,643	91

| Exhibit 14-4 | Procter & Gamble Statement of Cash Flows | | | |

THE PROCTER & GAMBLE COMPANY
Consolidated Statements of Cash Flows

(in millions)	Year Ended 2014	Year Ended 2013	$ Change	% Change
Operating activities				
Net earnings.	$11,643	$11,312		
Depreciation and amortization	3,141	2,982		
Other adjustments to net income.	304	(479)		
Changes in accounts receivable	87	(415)		
Changes in inventories.	8	(225)		
Change liabilities	1	1,253		
Change in other operating activities.	(1,226)	445		
Net cash flow provided by operating activities.	13,958	14,873	(915)	(6.2)%
Investing activities				
Capital expenditures	(3,848)	(4,008)		
Investments	(544)	(1,605)		
Other cash flows from investing activities	285	(682)		
Net cash flow used by investing activities	(4,107)	(6,295)	2,188	(34.8)%
Financing activities				
Dividends	(6,911)	(6,519)		
Net stock purchases	(6,005)	(5,986)		
Net borrowings.	3,543	1,985		
Other cash flows from financing activities	2,094	3,449		
Net cash used by financing activities	(7,279)	(7,071)	(208)	2.9%
Effect of exchange rate changes	39	4		
Change in cash and cash equivalents	2,611	1,511		
Beginning cash and cash equivalents	5,947	4,436		
Ending cash and cash equivalents.	$ 8,558	$ 5,947		

These data suggest an inconsistent growth pattern for the company, but the pattern of changes from year to year can be determined more precisely by calculating trend percentages. To do this, we select a base year and then divide the data for each of the remaining years by the base-year data. The result is an index of the changes occurring throughout the period. If, for example, 2010 is selected as the base year, all data for 2011 through 2014 will be related to 2010, which is represented as 100 percent.

To create the table of data displayed above, we divide each year's net sales—from 2011 through 2014—by $75,785, P&G's 2010 net sales (in millions of dollars). Similarly, P&G's net income for 2011 through 2014 is divided by $12,736, the company's 2010 net income (in millions of dollars).

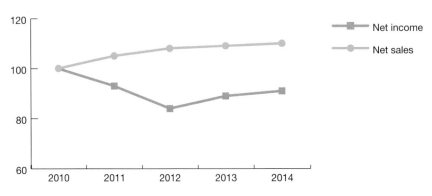

P&G's trend percentages above reveal that the company's growth in net sales outstripped its growth in net income for the entire five-year period. The horizontal analysis of P&G's financial data also reveals that, while sales continued to grow modestly each year, P&G's net income initially declined for two years before recovering the final three years. P&G appeared to have taken steps to counter the adverse impact on its profitability.

It is important to exercise care when interpreting trend percentages. Since all index percentages are related to a base year, it is important to select a good representative base year. For example, if 2010 was an unusual period for the firm, perhaps because of some large transitory items, its use in the trend analysis would be of limited value.

Other data items that an investment professional may relate to sales revenue and net income over multiple years include total assets, a company's investment in plant assets, and its cash flow from operations, among others.

The following data pertain to the Farrow Company:

	2016	2015
Sales revenue.	$800,000	$750,000
Net income.	120,000	100,000
Total assets	300,000	290,000

Calculate both the amount in dollars and the percentage change in 2016 using horizontal analysis and 2015 as the base year.

YOUR TURN! 14.2

The solution is on page 580.

	Concept →	Method →	Assessment	**TAKEAWAY 14.1**
	How does a company's current performance compare with the prior year?	Income statement and balance sheet for current and prior year. The income statement and balance sheet should be compared using the prior year as the base. Percentage changes in financial statement amounts can be computed as the change between years divided by the base year amount.	Significant changes should be analyzed to determine the reason for any change.	

VERTICAL ANALYSIS

The relative importance of various accounts in a company's financial statements for a single year can be highlighted by showing them as a percentage of a key financial statement figure. A financial statement that presents the various account balances as a percentage of a key figure is called a **common-size financial statement**. Sales revenue (or net sales) is the key figure used to construct a common-size income statement, whereas total assets is the key figure used to construct a common-size balance sheet.

LO3 **Explain** vertical financial statement analysis.

A financial statement may present both the dollar amounts and common-size percentages. For example, **Exhibit 14-2** presents P&G's 2014 income statement in dollars and common-size percentages. The common-size percentages show each item in the income statement as a percentage of the company's net sales.

The common-size income statement allows financial statement users to readily compare P&G's ability to manage and control its various expenses while the level of its sales revenue changes over time. For example, P&G's net earnings increased from 13.7 percent of sales in 2013 to 14.0 percent of sales in 2014. We can also observe that there are only small changes in almost all of the line items as a percentage of net sales. Common-size income statements are also useful when comparing across firms, especially when the firms are significantly different in size. We would expect firms of different sizes to report different levels of sales revenues and expenses on a dollar basis. But, we would expect far more similarities when the comparison is done on a common-size basis.

Common-size percentages can also be used to analyze balance sheet data. For example, by examining a firm's current assets and long-term assets as a percentage of total assets, we can determine whether a company is becoming more or less liquid over time. Another use of common-size percentages with balance sheet data is to evaluate the changing sources of financing used by a business. For example, the proportion of total assets supplied by short-term creditors, long-term creditors, preferred stockholders, and common stockholders of P&G are shown in **Exhibit 14-3**.

P&G's common-size balance sheets reveal that P&G is relying slightly more on debt financing than equity financing in 2014 compared to 2013. The primary means that P&G used to make this shift in financing appears to be through an increase in other current liabilities, from 15.3 percent of total assets in 2013 to 17.5 percent in 2014, and an increase in the repurchase of its common shares as treasury stock, from 51.7 percent of total assets in 2013 to 52.5 percent of total assets in 2014. We also see that although P&G experienced an increase in the dollar amount of total assets, the relative composition of those assets remained quite stable between 2013 and 2014.

YOUR TURN! 14.3

The solution is on page 581.

Hint: When preparing common-size income statements, expenses are expressed as a positive percentage of net sales even though they are subtractions on the income statement.

The Sanford Company reported the following income statement in 2015:

SANFORD COMPANY	
Income Statement	
For the Year Ended December 31, 2015	
Sales revenue..	$13,500
Cost of goods sold...	5,400
Gross profit..	8,100
Selling and administrative expenses	1,350
Income from operations..	6,750
Interest expense...	675
Other expense	135
Income before income taxes	5,940
Income tax expense..	2,295
Net income...	$ 3,645

Required

Prepare a 2015 common-size income statement for Sanford Company.

TAKEAWAY 14.2	Concept ⟶	Method ⟶	Assessment
	How do the relationships within a company's income statement and balance sheet compare to those of prior years?	Income statement and balance sheet for current and prior year. Each income statement item should be presented as a percentage of sales revenue and each balance sheet item should be presented as a percentage of total assets. Financial statements in this form are called common-size statements.	The percentages should be analyzed for differences between years and significant changes should be analyzed to determine the reason for any change.

Financial statement analysis is executed, worldwide, in exactly the same way. Common-size financial statements and the financial ratios discussed below are currency neutral and can be effectively used anywhere in the world. Not all ratios are relevant, however, in all countries. For example, in emerging countries that lack the financial infrastructure to support a credit system, ratios involving accounts receivable and accounts payable are likely to be irrelevant since sales transactions in those countries are only executed on a cash basis. Similarly, solvency ratios like the times-interest-earned ratio (discussed shortly) are irrelevant since bank financing in lesser-developed countries is rare (although it is becoming more prevalent with the advent of micro-finance in these countries).

RATIO ANALYSIS

At this juncture, we classify those ratios by their analytical objective and review their analysis and interpretation by calculating them for a single company. P&G's financial statements in **Exhibit 14-2** , **Exhibit 14-3** and **Exhibit 14-4** provide the data for these calculations (all amounts are in millions). Also, representative industry averages are presented for comparison purposes where available. Some of the financial ratios that are commonly calculated by investment professionals, lenders, and managers are presented and explained in **Exhibit 14-5**.

LO4 **Define** and **discuss** financial ratios for analyzing a firm.

Analyzing Firm Profitability

Several ratios assist in evaluating how efficiently a firm has performed in its quest for profits, or what is referred to as firm profitability. These ratios include (1) the gross profit percentage, (2) the return on sales, (3) asset turnover, (4) the return on assets, and (5) the return on common stockholders' equity.

Gross Profit Percentage

The **gross profit percentage** is a closely watched ratio for both retailers and manufacturers, among other industries. The ratio is calculated as:

$$\text{Gross profit percentage} = \frac{\text{Gross profit on sales}}{\text{Net sales}}$$

A.K.A Gross profit is often referred to as *gross margin*.

This ratio shows the effect on firm profitability of changes in a firm's product pricing structure, sales mix, and merchandise costs. **Gross profit**, or **gross profit on sales**, is defined as the difference between net sales and cost of goods sold and reveals the amount of sales revenue remaining after subtracting the cost of products sold.

P&G's common-size income statements (see **Exhibit 14-2**) reveal that its gross profit percentage decreased from 49.9 percent in 2013 to 48.9 percent in 2014. These percentages are derived using the following figures:

	2014	2013
Gross profit.	$40,602	$41,190
Net sales.	83,062	82,581
Gross profit percentage.	**48.9%**	**49.9%**
Industry average.	52.1%	

In addition to the negative trend in P&G's gross profit percentage, we also note that P&G's ratio is below the industry average of 52.1 percent.

Exhibit 14-5	Key Financial Ratios	
Ratio	Definition	Explanation

Analyzing Firm Profitability

Ratio	Definition	Explanation
• Gross profit percentage	$\dfrac{\text{Gross profit on sales}}{\text{Net sales}}$	Percentage of income generated from sales after deducting the cost of goods sold.
• Return on sales	$\dfrac{\text{Net income}}{\text{Net sales}}$	Percentage of net income remaining from a dollar of sales after subtracting all expenses.
• Asset turnover	$\dfrac{\text{Net sales}}{\text{Average total assets}}$	Amount of sales generated from each dollar invested in assets.
• Return on assets	$\dfrac{\text{Net income}}{\text{Average total assets}}$	Rate of return generated on a company's investment in assets from all sources.
• Return on common stockholders' equity	$\dfrac{(\text{Net income} - \text{Preferred stock dividends})}{\text{Average common stockholders' equity}}$	Rate of return generated by a business for its common shareholders.

Analyzing Short-Term Firm Liquidity

Ratio	Definition	Explanation
• Working capital	Current assets − Current liabilities	The difference between a firm's current assets and its current liabilities.
• Current ratio	$\dfrac{\text{Current assets}}{\text{Current liabilities}}$	Amount of current assets available to service current liabilities.
• Quick ratio	$\dfrac{(\text{Cash and cash equivalents} + \text{Short-term investments} + \text{Accounts receivable})}{\text{Current liabilities}}$	Amount of liquid assets available to service current liabilities.
• Operating-cash-flow-to-current-liabilities ratio	$\dfrac{\text{Cash flow from operating activities}}{\text{Average current liabilities}}$	Amount of cash flow from operating activities available to service current liabilities.
• Accounts receivable turnover	$\dfrac{\text{Net sales}}{\text{Average accounts receivable (net)}}$	Number of sales/collection cycles experienced by a firm.
• Average collection period	$\dfrac{365}{\text{Accounts receivable turnover (net)}}$	Number of days required, on average, to collect an outstanding accounts receivable.
• Inventory turnover	$\dfrac{\text{Cost of goods sold}}{\text{Average inventory}}$	Number of production/sales cycles experienced by a firm.
• Days' sales in inventory	$\dfrac{365}{\text{Inventory turnover}}$	Number of days, on average, required to sell the inventory currently on hand.

Analyzing Long-Term Firm Solvency

Ratio	Definition	Explanation
• Debt-to-equity ratio	$\dfrac{\text{Total liabilities}}{\text{Total stockholders' equity}}$	Percentage of total assets provided by creditors.
• Times-interest-earned ratio	$\dfrac{\text{Income before interest expense and income taxes}}{\text{Interest expense}}$	Extent to which current operating income covers current debt service charges.
• Operating-cash-flow-to-capital-expenditures ratio	$\dfrac{\text{Cash flow from operating activities}}{\text{Annual net capital expenditures}}$	The ability of a firm's operations to provide sufficient cash to replace and expand its property, plant, and equipment.

Financial Ratios for Common Stockholders

Ratio	Definition	Explanation
• Earnings per share	$\dfrac{(\text{Net income} - \text{Preferred stock dividends})}{\text{Weighted-average number of common shares outstanding}}$	The net income available to common shareholders calculated on a per share basis.
• Price-earnings ratio	$\dfrac{\text{Market price per share}}{\text{Earnings per share}}$	A measure of the price of a share of common stock relative to the share's annual earnings.
• Dividend yield	$\dfrac{\text{Annual dividend per share}}{\text{Market price per share}}$	The earnings on an investment in stock coming from dividends.
• Dividend payout ratio	$\dfrac{\text{Annual dividend per share}}{\text{Earnings per share}}$	The percentage of net income paid out to shareholders as dividends.

Return on Sales (Profit Margin)

Another important measure of firm profitability is the **return on sales**. This ratio reveals the percentage of each dollar of net sales that remains as profit after subtracting all operating and nonoperating expenses. The return on sales is calculated as follows:

A.K.A Return on sales is often referred to as *profit margin*.

$$\text{Return on sales} = \frac{\text{Net income}}{\text{Net sales}}$$

When common-size income statements are available, the return on sales equals the net income percentage. P&G's common-size income statements in **Exhibit 14-2** reveal that its return on sales increased from 13.7 percent in 2013 to 14.0 percent in 2014. These percentages are calculated using the following figures:

	2014	2013
Net income.	$11,643	$11,312
Net sales.	83,062	82,581
Return on sales.	**14.0%**	**13.7%**
Industry average.	11.6%	

The increase in the return on sales for P&G is encouraging, and as noted above, P&G's increase in its return on sales is mostly attributable to the company's cost control. Additionally, P&G's 2014 return on sales exceeds the industry average.

The return on sales and gross profit percentages should be used only when analyzing companies from the same industry or when comparing a firm's performance across multiple time periods (as we did above) since the ratio may vary widely across industries. Retail jewelers, for example, have much larger gross profit percentages (an industry average of 45.0 percent) than do retail grocers (an industry average of 23.0 percent). Industry averages for the asset turnover ratio, discussed next, would also be expected to vary significantly from one industry to another.

Asset Turnover

The **asset turnover ratio** measures how efficiently a firm uses its assets to generate sales revenue by calculating the amount of sales dollars generated annually for each dollar of assets invested in the company. This ratio is calculated as follows:

$$\text{Asset turnover} = \frac{\text{Net sales}}{\text{Average total assets}}$$

P&G's asset turnover is calculated as (total assets were $132,244 at year-end 2012):

		2014	2013
Net sales.		$ 83,062	$ 82,581
Total assets			
Beginning of year	(a)	139,263	132,244
End of year	(b)	144,266	139,263
Average [(a + b)/2]		141,765	135,754
Asset turnover		**0.59**	**0.61**
Industry average.		0.73	

P&G's asset turnover decreased slightly from 2013 to 2014, indicating that the company is less effective in using its assets to generate sales revenue. Specifically, the company generated $0.59 in net sales for every dollar invested in total assets in 2014, compared to $0.61 in 2013. This ratio result is also below the industry average of $0.73.

Industries that are characterized by low gross profit percentages generally have relatively high asset turnover ratios. Retail grocery chains, for example, typically turnover their assets five to six times per year. By way of contrast, retail jewelers average only one to two asset turnovers per year. These industry differences largely reflect the high cost of products sold by jewelers versus the low cost of products sold by retail grocers.

Return on Assets

The rate of return on total assets, called the **return on assets**, is an overall measure of a firm's profitability. It reveals the rate of profit earned per dollar of assets under a firm's control. The return on assets is calculated as follows:

$$\text{Return on assets} = \frac{\text{Net income}}{\text{Average total assets}}$$

P&G's return on assets is calculated as:

	2014	2013
Net income	$ 11,643	$ 11,312
Average total assets	141,765	135,754
Return on assets	**8.2%**	**8.3%**
Industry average	8.6%	

P&G's return on assets declined from 8.3 percent in 2013 to 8.2 percent in 2014; however the percentage is consistent with the industry average.

The return on asset ratio summarizes the financial impact of two component ratios: the return on sales and asset turnover; that is, the return on assets is the multiplicative product of these latter two ratios, as follows:

Ratio:	Return on sales	×	Asset turnover	=	Return on assets
Ratio calculation:	$\dfrac{\text{Net income}}{\text{Net sales}}$	×	$\dfrac{\text{Net sales}}{\text{Average total assets}}$	=	$\dfrac{\text{Net income}}{\text{Average total assets}}$
P&G:	**14.0 percent**	×	**0.59**	=	**8.3 percent**

Return on Common Stockholders' Equity

The **return on common stockholders' equity** measures the profitability of the ownership interest held by a company's common stockholders. The ratio shows the percentage of income available to common stockholders—that is, net income less any preferred stock dividends—for each dollar of common stockholder equity invested in a business, as follows:

$$\frac{\text{Return on common}}{\text{stockholders' equity}} = \frac{(\text{Net income} - \text{Preferred stock dividends})}{\text{Average common stockholders' equity}}$$

The return on common stockholders' equity for P&G is calculated as (common stockholders' equity was $62,840 at year-end 2012):

		2014	2013
Net income.............................		$11,643	$11,312
Less: Preferred stock dividends.........		253	244
Common stock earnings		11,390	11,068
Common stockholders' equity:			
Beginning of year	(a)	67,572	62,840
End of year	(b)	68,865	67,572
Average [(a + b)/2]......................		68,219	65,206
Return on common stockholders' equity.........		**16.7%**	**17.0%**
Industry average.........................		20.1%	

P&G's return on common stockholders' equity declined by 0.3 percent, from 17.0 percent in 2013 to 16.7 percent in 2014. Unlike the return on assets, P&G's return on common stockholders' equity is well below the industry average.

YOUR TURN! 14.4

The solution is on page 581.

The following data was obtained from the current financial statements for Kelly Corporation:

Net sales..	$30,000
Cost of goods sold...	10,500
Net income..	4,500
Average total assets...	50,000
Average common stockholders' equity	35,000
Preferred dividends	500

Required

Calculate the following ratios for Kelly Corporation:

a. Gross profit percentage
b. Return on sales
c. Asset turnover
d. Return on assets
e. Return on common stockholders' equity

Concept ➡	Method ➡	Assessment	TAKEAWAY 14.3
How much profit is a company generating relative to the amount of assets invested in the company?	Income statement and balance sheet. Calculate the return on assets by dividing net income by the average total assets for the year.	The higher the return on assets, the better a company is doing in terms of generating profits utilizing the assets under its control.	

Analyzing Short-Term Firm Liquidity

A firm's **working capital** is the difference between its current assets and current liabilities. Maintaining an adequate working capital enables a firm to repay its current obligations on a timely basis and to take advantage of any available purchase discounts associated with the timely payment of accounts payable. Shortages of working capital, on the other hand, can force a company into borrowing at inopportune times and unfavorable interest rates. As a consequence, many long-term debt contracts contain provisions that require the borrowing firm to maintain an adequate working capital position. A firm's working capital is calculated as follows:

$$\text{Working capital} = \text{Current assets} - \text{Current liabilities}$$

Analysis of a firm's short-term liquidity utilizes several financial ratios that relate to various aspects of a company's working capital. These ratios are (1) the current ratio, (2) the quick ratio, (3) operating-cash-flow-to-current-liabilities ratio, (4) accounts receivable turnover and average collection period, and (5) inventory turnover and days' sales in inventory.

Current Ratio

The **current ratio** is calculated as a firm's current assets divided by its current liabilities:

$$\text{Current ratio} = \frac{\text{Current assets}}{\text{Current liabilities}}$$

This ratio is a widely used measure of a firm's ability to meet its current obligations and to have funds available for use in daily operations. The following calculations reveal that P&G's current ratio improved from 0.80 in 2013 to 0.94 (or 0.94:1) in 2014:

	2014	2013
Current assets	$31,617	$23,990
Current liabilities	33,726	30,037
Current ratio	**0.94**	**0.80**
Industry average	1.6	

In essence, P&G had $0.94 in current assets for every $1 in current liabilities at the end of 2014.

In the past, a generally accepted rule of thumb was that a firm's current ratio should be approximately 2:1, indicating that a company should maintain twice the dollar amount of current assets as was needed to satisfy its current liabilities. Improved cash flow management techniques and alternate forms of short-term financing (such as bank lines of credit) have reduced the need for businesses to maintain such a high current ratio. Still, many creditors prefer to see a higher current ratio and consider a low ratio as a potential warning sign of short-term liquidity problems.

Evaluating the adequacy of a firm's current ratio may involve comparing it with the recent past (P&G's current ratio improved slightly from 2013 to 2014) or with an industry average (P&G's ratio is below the industry average of 1.6). What is considered an appropriate current ratio varies by industry. A service firm with little or no inventory, such as a car wash service, would be expected to have a smaller current ratio than would a firm carrying a large inventory, such as a hardware retailer. The composition (or mix) of a firm's current assets significantly influences any evaluation of a firm's short-term liquidity. The quick ratio, discussed next, explicitly considers the composition of a firm's current assets when evaluating short-term liquidity.

Quick Ratio

A.K.A. The quick ratio is also referred to as the *acid-test ratio.*

The **quick ratio** reveals the relationship between a firm's liquid, or quick, assets and its current liabilities. Quick assets include cash and cash equivalents, short-term investments, and accounts receivable. The quick ratio omits a company's inventory and prepaid assets, which may not be particularly liquid. Consequently, the quick ratio may give a more accurate picture of a company's ability to meet its current obligations since the ratio ignores a firm's potentially illiquid inventory and prepaid expenses.

Comparing the quick ratio and the current ratio indicates the financial impact of a company's inventory on its working capital. For example, a company might have an acceptable current ratio, but if its quick ratio falls to an unacceptable level, a financial analyst is likely to be concerned about the amount of inventory on hand, and consequently, analyze the company's inventory position more thoroughly.

The quick ratio is calculated as follows:

$$\text{Quick ratio} = \frac{(\text{Cash and cash equivalents} + \text{Short-term investments} + \text{Accounts receivable})}{\text{Current liabilities}}$$

The quick ratio for P&G is calculated as:

	2014	2013
Cash and cash equivalents, short-term investments, and accounts receivable.	$17,072	$12,455
Current liabilities.	33,726	30,037
Quick ratio.	**0.51**	**0.41**
Industry average.	0.28	

P&G's quick ratio increased from 0.41 in 2013 to 0.51 in 2014, and its 2014 quick ratio is well above the industry average of 0.28. P&G's increased quick ratio is mainly due to a large increase in cash and cash equivalents and short-term investments in 2014.

Operating-Cash-Flow-to-Current-Liabilities Ratio

Ultimately, cash will be needed to settle a business's current liabilities. Another ratio indicating a firm's ability to pay its current liabilities as they come due focuses on a company's operating cash flow. The **operating-cash-flow-to-current-liabilities ratio** is calculated as follows:

$$\frac{\text{Operating-cash-flow-to-}}{\text{current-liabilities ratio}} = \frac{\text{Cash flow from operating activities}}{\text{Average current liabilities}}$$

The operating-cash-flow-to-current-liabilities ratio relates the net cash available as a result of operating activities to the average current liabilities outstanding during the period. A higher ratio indicates that a firm has a greater ability to settle its current liabilities using its operating cash flow.

P&G's operating-cash-flow-to-current-liabilities ratio is calculated as (current liabilities at the end of 2012 was $24,907; no industry average is available):

		2014	2013
Cash flow from operating activities		$13,958	$14,873
Current liabilities			
Beginning of year	(a)	30,037	24,907
End of year	(b)	33,726	30,037
Average [(a+b)/2]		31,882	27,472
Operating-cash-flow-to-current-liabilities ratio		**0.44**	**0.54**

P&G's operating-cash-flow-to-current-liabilities ratio declined from 2013 to 2014, a result of a decline in cash provided by operating activities and an increase in average current liabilities.

Accounts Receivable Turnover

The speed with which accounts receivable are collected is of considerable interest to investment professionals when evaluating a firm's short-term liquidity. **Accounts receivable turnover** indicates how many times a year a firm collects its average outstanding accounts receivable, and thus, measures how fast a firm converts its accounts receivable into cash. The quicker a firm is able to convert its accounts receivables into cash, the less cash the company needs to keep on hand to satisfy its current liabilities. Accounts receivable turnover is calculated as follows:

$$\textbf{Accounts receivable turnover} = \frac{\textbf{Net sales}}{\textbf{Average accounts receivable (net)}}$$

Accounts receivable less the allowance for doubtful accounts—that is, the net balance of accounts receivable—is the amount of receivables that the company expects to collect from customers. The accounts receivable turnover for P&G is calculated as (accounts receivable at the end of 2012 were $6,068):

		2014	2013
Net sales.		$83,062	$82,581
Average accounts receivable (net)			
Beginning of year	(a)	6,508	6,068
End of year	(b)	6,386	6,508
Average [(a + b)/2]		6,447	6,288
Accounts receivable turnover		**12.88**	**13.13**
Industry average.		10.12	

The higher the accounts receivable turnover, the faster a company is able to convert its accounts receivable into cash. P&G's accounts receivable turnover decreased slightly from 13.13 in 2013 to 12.88 in 2014. However, P&G's 2014 accounts receivable turnover is well above the industry average of 10.12 for the year.

Average Collection Period

A.K.A. The average collection period is also referred to as the *days' sales outstanding, or DSO.*

An extension of the accounts receivable turnover is the **average collection period**. The average collection period reveals how many days it takes, on average, for a company to collect an account receivable. The ratio is calculated as follows:

$$\textbf{Average collection period} = \frac{\textbf{365}}{\textbf{Accounts receivable turnover (net)}}$$

P&G's average collection period is calculated as:

	2014	2013
Average collection period		
2014: 365/12.88; 2013: 365/13.13.	**28.3 days**	**27.8 days**
Industry average.	36.1 days	

P&G's average collection period increased slightly in 2014. This may have resulted from such actions as P&G relaxing the credit standards they apply to their customers or by extending the allowed credit period. Alternatively, it may reflect that P&G's customers have experienced deteriorating cash flows, and thus they are not able to pay their accounts as promptly. Knowledge of P&G's credit terms would permit a more complete analysis of these results. If, for example, P&G's credit terms are n/20, then an average collection period of 28.3 days indicates that the company has a problem with slow-paying customers. If, on the other hand, P&G's credit terms are n/30, then the 2014 average collection period shows no particular problem with the company's speed of receivable collection.

Inventory Turnover

An analyst concerned about a company's inventory position is likely to evaluate the company's **inventory turnover**. This ratio indicates whether the inventory on hand is disproportionate to the amount of sales revenue. Excessive inventories not only tie up company funds and increase storage costs but may also lead to subsequent losses if the goods become outdated or unsalable. In general, a higher turnover is preferred to a lower turnover. The calculation of inventory turnover is as follows:

$$\text{Inventory turnover} = \frac{\text{Cost of goods sold}}{\text{Average inventory}}$$

P&G's inventory turnover is calculated as (inventory at the end of 2012 was $6,721):

		2014	2013
Cost of goods sold		$42,460	$41,391
Inventory			
Beginning of year	(a)	6,909	6,721
End of year	(b)	6,759	6,909
Average [(a + b)/2]		6,834	6,815
Inventory turnover		**6.21**	**6.07**
Industry average		5.23	

P&G's inventory turnover increased from 6.07 in 2013 to 6.21 in 2014. In addition, the company's 2014 inventory turnover of 6.21 is above the industry average of 5.23.

The cost of goods sold is used in the calculation of inventory turnover because the inventory measure in the denominator is a *cost* figure; consequently, it is appropriate to also use a cost figure in the numerator. By way of contrast, accounts receivable turnover uses net sales in the calculation because accounts receivable is based on sales revenue, which includes a markup for the company's expected profit.

A low inventory turnover can result from an overextended inventory position or from inadequate sales volume. For this reason, an appraisal of a firm's inventory turnover should be accompanied by a review of the quick ratio and an analysis of trends in both inventory and sales revenue.

Days' Sales in Inventory

The **days' sales in inventory** ratio is derived from a firm's inventory turnover ratio and reveals how many days it takes, on average, for a firm to sell its inventory on hand. The ratio is calculated as follows:

$$\text{Days' sales in inventory} = \frac{365}{\text{Inventory turnover}}$$

P&G's days' sales in inventory is calculated as:

	2014	2013
2014: 365/6.21; 2013: 365/6.07	**58.8 days**	**60.1 days**
Industry average	69.8 days	

P&G's days' sales in inventory reveals that the average amount of time required to sell its inventory decreased by 1.3 days from 60.1 days in 2013 to 58.8 days in 2014. Also, P&G's average length of time to sell its inventory is lower than the industry average by eleven days. The improvement in P&G's days' sales in inventory will positively impact the company's profitability due to the related decrease in inventory storage costs and a decrease in its inventory financing costs.

By combining the days' sales in inventory with the average collection period, it is possible to estimate the average time period from the acquisition of inventory, to the sale of inventory, to the eventual collection of cash. The sum of the days' sales in inventory plus the average collection period measures the length of the company's **operating cycle**. Although operating cycles will naturally vary across different industries, a shorter operating cycle is preferred as it is an indicator of the operating efficiency and working capital management of the company. In 2014, for example, it took P&G 87.1 days (58.8 days' sales in inventory + 28.3 days average collection period) to sell its average inventory and collect the related cash from its customers. This operating cycle is significantly better than the industry average of 105.9 days by nearly 19 days and slightly better than P&G's 2013 period of 87.9 days (60.1 days + 27.8 days).

<table>
<tr><td>**YOUR TURN! 14.5**

The solution is on page 581.

</td><td>The following selected data was obtained from the financial statements of Justin Corporation:

Current assets	$ 60,000
Current liabilities for both current and prior year	40,000
Cash flow from operating activities	55,000
Net sales...	100,000
Average accounts receivable..	15,000
Cost of goods sold..	70,000
Average inventory..	9,000

Required
Calculate the following financial measures and ratios for Justin Corporation:

a. Working capital

b. Current ratio

c. Operating-cash-flow-to-current-liabilities ratio

d. Accounts receivable turnover

e. Days' sales in inventory</td></tr>
</table>

TAKEAWAY 14.4	Concept	→	Method	→	Assessment
	How financially capable is a company to pay its current liabilities as they come due?		Income statement, balance sheet, and statement of cash flows.

Calculate the current ratio, the quick ratio, and the operating-cash-flow-to-current-liabilities ratio. | | The higher the ratios, the higher the probability that a company will have the ability to pay its current liabilities as they become due. |

Analyzing Long-Term Firm Solvency

The preceding set of ratios examined a firm's short-term liquidity. A separate set of ratios analyzes a firm's long-term solvency, or its long-term debt repayment capability. Ratios in this latter group include (1) the debt-to-equity ratio, (2) the times-interest-earned ratio, and (3) the operating-cash-flow-to-capital-expenditures ratio.

Debt-to-Equity Ratio

The **debt-to-equity ratio** evaluates the financial structure of a firm by relating a company's total liabilities to its total stockholders' equity. This ratio considers the extent to which a company relies on creditors versus stockholders to provide financing. The debt-to-equity ratio is calculated as follows:

$$\text{Debt-to-equity ratio} = \frac{\text{Total liabilities}}{\text{Total stockholders' equity}}$$

This ratio uses year-end balances for the ratio's components, rather than averages, since we are interested in the firm's capital structure as of a particular point in time. The total stockholders' equity for a business is its total assets minus its total liabilities.

The debt-to-equity ratio gives creditors an indication of the margin of protection available to them (creditors' claims to assets have priority over stockholders' claims). The lower the ratio, the greater the protection being provided to creditors. A firm with a low ratio also has greater flexibility when seeking additional borrowed funds at a low rate of interest than does a firm with a high ratio.

P&G's debt-to-equity ratio is calculated as:

	2014	2013
Total liabilities (year-end)	$74,290	$70,554
Total stockholders' equity (year-end)	69,976	68,709
Debt-to-equity ratio	**1.06**	**1.03**
Industry average	0.66	

P&G's debt-to-equity ratio increased from 1.03 in 2013 to 1.06 in 2014, indicating a small increase in reliance on debt to finance its operations. In addition, the company's 2014 ratio is above the industry average, suggesting an increased risk of insolvency. Still, this ratio is far from a point where it would represent a major concern.

Times-Interest-Earned Ratio

To evaluate the ability of a company to pay its current interest charges from its operating income, an analyst may investigate the relationship between the company's current interest charges and its net income. For example, an extremely high debt-to-equity ratio for a company may indicate extensive borrowing by the company; however, if its operating earnings are sufficient to meet the interest charges on the debt several times over, an analyst may regard the situation quite favorably.

A.K.A. The times-interest-earned ratio is also referred to as the *interest coverage ratio*.

Analysts, particularly long-term credit analysts, almost always consider the **times-interest-earned ratio** of a company with interest-bearing debt. This ratio is calculated by dividing the income before interest expense and income taxes by the annual interest expense:

$$\text{Times-interest-earned ratio} = \frac{\text{Income before interest expense and income taxes}}{\text{Interest expense}}$$

P&G's times-interest-earned ratio is calculated as:

	2014	2013
Income before interest expense and income taxes	$15,452	$15,269
Interest expense	709	667
Times-interest-earned ratio	**21.8**	**22.9**
Industry average	24.7	

P&G's operating income available to meet its interest charges decreased slightly from 22.9 times in 2013 to 21.8 times in 2014. This ratio is below the industry average of 24.7, but still indicates that P&G exhibits an exceptionally good margin of safety for creditors. Generally speaking, a company that earns its interest charges several times over is regarded as a satisfactory risk by long-term creditors.

Operating-Cash-Flow-to-Capital-Expenditures Ratio

The ability of a firm's operations to provide sufficient cash to replace and expand its property, plant, and equipment is revealed by the **operating-cash-flow-to-capital-expenditures ratio**. To the extent that acquisitions of plant assets can be financed using cash provided by operating activities, a firm does not have to use other financing sources, such as long-term debt. This ratio is calculated as follows:

$$\text{Operating-cash-flow-to-capital-expenditures ratio} = \frac{\text{Cash flow from operating activities}}{\text{Annual net capital expenditures}}$$

A ratio of 1.0 indicates that a firm's current operating activities provide sufficient cash to fully fund any investment in plant capacity. A ratio in excess of 1.0 indicates that a company has more than sufficient operating cash flow to fund any needed expansion in plant capacity.

The operating-cash-flow-to-capital-expenditures ratio for P&G is:

	2014	2013
Cash flow from operating activities	$13,958	$14,873
Annual net capital expenditures.	3,848	4,008
Operating-cash-flow-to-capital-expenditures ratio	**3.6**	**3.7**

In 2014, P&G's operating-cash-flow-to-capital-expenditures ratio was 3.6, a slight decrease from 3.7 in 2013. It appears that P&G is generating plenty of operating cash flow to cover its net capital expenditures in each year.

YOUR TURN! 14.6

The solution is on page 581.

The following selected data was obtained from the financial statements for the Hartford Corporation:

Total liabilities.	$180,000
Total stockholders' equity	600,000
Cash flow from operating activities	100,000
Annual capital expenditures.	30,000
Net income.	55,000
Interest expense.	5,000
Income tax expense.	25,000

Required
Calculate the following ratios for Hartford Corporation:
a. Debt-to-equity ratio
b. Times-interest-earned ratio
c. Operating-cash-flow-to-capital-expenditures ratio

Concept ——→	Method ——→	Assessment	TAKEAWAY 14.5
How solvent is a company?	Income statement, balance sheet, and statement of cash flows. Calculate the debt-to-equity ratio, the times-interest-earned ratio, and the operating-cash-flow-to-capital-expenditures ratio.	The higher the times-interest-earned and the operating-cash-flow-to-capital-expenditures ratios, and the lower the debt-to-equity ratio, the greater is a company's solvency.	

Financial Ratios for Common Stockholders

Present and potential common stockholders share an interest with a business's creditors in analyzing the profitability, short-term liquidity, and long-term solvency of a company. There are also other financial ratios that are primarily of interest to common stockholders. These ratios include (1) earnings per share, (2) the price-earnings ratio, (3) dividend yield, and (4) the dividend payout ratio.

Earnings per Share

Because stock market prices are quoted on a per-share basis, the reporting of earnings per share of common stock is useful to investors. **Earnings per share (EPS)** is calculated by dividing the net income available to common stockholders by the weighted average number of common shares outstanding during a year. The net income available to common stockholders is a company's net income less any preferred stock dividends. Preferred stock dividends are subtracted from net income to arrive at the net income available exclusively to a company's common stock stockholders. Thus, earnings per share is calculated as follows:

$$\text{Earnings per share} = \frac{(\text{Net income} - \text{Preferred stock dividends})}{\text{Weighted-average number of common shares outstanding}}$$

Since earnings per share are a required disclosure on a company's income statement, investment professionals do not have to calculate this financial metric. P&G's income statements reveal the following earnings per share (see **Exhibit 14-2**):

	2014	2013
Earnings per share....................................	$4.19	$4.04

P&G's earnings per share increased from $4.04 in 2013 to $4.19 in 2014, an increase of 3.7 percent. This is slightly higher than the 2.9 percent increase in P&G's net income over the same period. The result is due to the small increase in P&G's treasury stock, which reduces the number of common shares outstanding.

Price-Earnings Ratio

The **price-earnings ratio** is calculated by dividing the market price per share of common stock by a company's earnings per share:

$$\text{Price-earnings ratio} = \frac{\text{Market price per share}}{\text{Earnings per share}}$$

A.K.A. The price-earnings ratio is also referred to as the *P/E multiple*.

For many analysts and investors, this ratio is an important tool for assessing a stock's valuation. For example, after evaluating the financial strengths of several comparable companies, an analyst may decide which company to invest in by comparing the price-earnings ratio of each company. Assuming that the companies have equivalent persistent earnings and financial risk profiles, the company with the lowest price-earnings ratio may represent the best investment opportunity.

When calculating the price-earnings ratio, it is customary to use the latest market price per share and the earnings per share for the last four quarters of a company's operations. P&G's price-earnings ratios as of the end of fiscal years 2013 and 2014 are:

	2014	2013
Market price per share (at year-end)	$78.59	$76.99
Earnings per share	4.19	4.04
Price-earnings ratio	**18.8**	**19.1**
Industry average.	22.3	

The market price of a share of P&G's common stock at year-end 2014 was 18.8 times the company's 2014 earnings per share. Since P&G's price-earnings ratio at the end of 2014 is below industry average, this may indicate that the company's shares are undervalued, and thus, that its stock may represent a good investment.

Dividend Yield

Investor expectations vary greatly with personal economic circumstances and with the overall economic outlook. Some investors are more interested in the potential share price appreciation of a stock than in any dividends that a company may pay on its outstanding shares. When shares are disposed of in the future, the capital gains provision of U.S. income tax law generally taxes capital gains at a rate that is lower than the tax rate applied to dividend income. Some investors, on the other hand, are more concerned with dividends than with stock price appreciation. These investors desire a high **dividend yield** on their investments. Dividend yield is calculated by dividing a company's current annual dividend per share by the current market price per share:

$$\text{Dividend yield} = \frac{\text{Annual dividend per share}}{\text{Market price per share}}$$

P&G's dividend yield per common share is calculated as (the dividend per share is disclosed in **Exhibit 14-2**):

	2014	2013
Annual dividend per share	$2.45	$2.29
Market price per share (at year-end)	78.59	76.99
Dividend yield	**3.1%**	**3.0%**
Industry average.	2.8%	

P&G's dividend yield increased from 3.0 percent in 2013 to 3.1 percent in 2014, and is slightly above the industry average of 2.8 percent.

Dividend Payout Ratio

Investors who emphasize the yield on their investments may also be interested in a firm's **dividend payout ratio**—that is, the percentage of net income paid out as dividends to stockholders. The payout ratio indicates whether a firm has a conservative or a liberal dividend policy, and may also indicate whether a firm is conserving funds for internal financing of its growth. The dividend payout ratio is calculated as follows:

$$\text{Dividend payout ratio} = \frac{\text{Annual dividend per share}}{\text{Earnings per share}}$$

P&G's dividend payout ratio is calculated as:

	2014	2013
Annual dividends per share	$2.45	$2.29
Earnings per share	4.19	4.04
Dividend payout ratio	**58.5%**	**56.7%**
Industry average.	50.0%	

P&G's dividend payout ratio increased from 56.7 percent in 2013 to 58.5 percent in 2014. This payout ratio is consistent with the payout ratio for most comparable mature U.S. industrial corporations, but is slightly higher than the industry average for P&G.

Payout ratios for mature industrial corporations vary between 40 percent and 60 percent of net income. Many corporations, however, need funds for internal financing of growth and pay out little (if any) of their net income as dividends. At the other extreme, some companies—principally utility companies—may pay out as much as 70 percent of their net income as dividends.

YOUR TURN! 14.7

The solution is on page 581.

The following selected data was obtained from financial statements for Baylor Corporation:

Earnings per share	$ 4.50
Market price per share of common stock	54.00
Dividends per share of common stock	1.50

Required

Calculate the following ratios for Baylor Corporation:

a. Dividend yield

b. Dividend payout ratio

TAKEAWAY 14.6

Concept	→	Method	→	Assessment
How much dividends are common stockholders likely to receive?		Earnings per share, dividends per share, and market price of common stock. Calculate the dividend yield and dividend payout ratio.		The higher the dividend yield and the dividend payout ratio, the greater the company's dividend distribution policy.

ACCOUNTING IN PRACTICE

Accounting as an Aid to Investing

The days of corporations offering traditional pension plans where the employee is guaranteed certain benefits at retirement are numbered. More and more employers are switching to plans such as a 401(k) where the employee is responsible for deciding what the plan invests in. Having a knowledge of the accounting techniques demonstrated in this chapter can certainly provide a better understanding of the risks and rewards of investing.

LIMITATIONS OF FINANCIAL STATEMENT ANALYSIS

LO5 Discuss the limitations of financial statement analysis.

The ratios, percentages, and other relationships described in this chapter reflect the analytical techniques used by investment professionals and experienced investors. Nonetheless, they must be interpreted with due consideration of the general economic conditions, the conditions of the industry in which a company operates, and the relative position of individual companies within an industry.

Financial statement users must also be aware of the inherent limitations of financial statement data. Problems of comparability are frequently encountered. Companies within the same industry may use different accounting methods that can cause problems in comparing certain key relationships. For instance, inventory turnover is likely to be quite different for a company using LIFO than for one using FIFO. Inflation may also distort certain financial data and ratios, especially those resulting from horizontal analysis. For example, trend percentages calculated from data unadjusted for inflation may be deceptive.

Financial statement users must also be careful when comparing companies within a particular industry. Factors such as firm size, diversity of product line, and mode of operations can make firms within the same industry dissimilar in their reported results. Moreover, some firms, particularly conglomerates, are difficult to classify by industry. If segment information is available, the financial statement user may compare the statistics for several industries. Often, trade associations prepare industry statistics that are stratified by size of firm or type of product, facilitating financial statement analysis.

FORENSIC ACCOUNTING

It is generally considered more difficult to deter financial statement fraud than it is to deter other types of fraud such as embezzlement. The best approach to fraud deterrence is to put into place a strong set of internal controls. Unfortunately, senior management, such as a firm's CEO and CFO, are the most likely employees to commit financial statement fraud. These individuals are able to use their position of authority to override most internal controls. Thus, it is important to consider alternative approaches to fraud deterrence. Potential alternative approaches are based on the fraud triangle concept, in which fraud is related to the interaction of three factors: (1) pressure, (2) opportunity, and (3) rationalization.

The fraud element of pressure can be reduced by avoiding the practice of setting unachievable financial goals and utilizing compensation systems that are considered fair but which do not create excessive incentives to commit fraud. Although internal controls may be circumvented by senior management, it is still important to maintain a strong system of internal controls and to establish clear and uniform accounting procedures with no exception clauses. In addition, a strong internal control department reporting to the board of directors provides further deterrence. Finally, the creation and promotion of a culture of honesty and integrity throughout an organization makes the rationalization of financial statement fraud much more difficult.

Knox Instruments, Inc., is a manufacturer of various medical and dental instruments. Financial statement data for the firm follow:

(thousands of dollars, except per-share amount)	2016
Sales revenue.	$200,000
Cost of goods sold.	98,000
Net income.	10,750
Dividends	4,200
Cash provided by operating activities	7,800
Earnings per share	3.07

KNOX INSTRUMENTS, INC. **Balance Sheets**		
(thousands of dollars)	Dec. 31, 2016	Dec. 31, 2015
Assets		
Cash.	$ 3,000	$ 2,900
Accounts receivable (net).	28,000	28,800
Inventory.	64,000	44,000
Total current assets	95,000	75,700
Plant assets (net)	76,000	67,300
Total Assets	$171,000	$143,000
Liabilities and Stockholders' Equity		
Current liabilities.	$ 45,200	$ 39,750
10% Bonds payable.	20,000	14,000
Total Liabilities	65,200	53,750
Common stock, $10 par value.	40,000	30,000
Retained earnings	65,800	59,250
Total Stockholders' Equity.	105,800	89,250
Total Liabilities and Stockholders' Equity	$171,000	$143,000

Required

a. Using the given data, calculate the nine financial ratios below for 2016. Compare the ratio results for Knox Instruments, Inc., with the following industry averages and comment on its operations.

Median Ratios for the Industry

1.	Current ratio	2.7
2.	Quick ratio	1.6
3.	Average collection period	73 days
4.	Inventory turnover	2.3
5.	Operating-cash-flow-to-current-liabilities ratio	0.22
6.	Debt-to-equity ratio	0.50
7.	Return on assets	4.9 percent
8.	Return on common stockholders' equity	10.2 percent
9.	Return on sales	4.1 percent

b. Calculate the dividends paid per share of common stock. (Use the average number of shares outstanding during the year.) What was the dividend payout ratio?

c. If the 2016 year-end market price per share of Knox's common stock is $25, what is the company's (1) price-earnings ratio and (2) dividend yield?

Solution

a.

1.   Current ratio = $95,000/$45,200 = 2.10
2.   Quick ratio = $31,000/$45,200 = 0.69
3.   Average collection period:
     Accounts receivable turnover = $200,000/($28,800 + $28,000)/2 = 7.04
     Average collection period = 365/7.04 = 51.8 days
4.   Inventory turnover = $98,000/($44,000 + $64,000)/2 = 1.81
5.   Operating-cash-flow-to-current-liabilities ratio = $7,800/($39,750 + $45,200)/2 = 0.18
6.   Debt-to-equity ratio = $65,200/$105,800 = 0.62
7.   Return on assets = $10,750/($143,000 + $171,000)/2 = 6.8 percent
8.   Return on common stockholders' equity = $10,750/($89,250 + $105,800)/2 = 11.0 percent
9.   Return on sales = $10,750/$200,000 = 5.4 percent

Although the firm's current ratio of 2.10 is below the industry median, it is still acceptable; however, the quick ratio of 0.69 is well below the industry median. This indicates that Knox's inventory (which is omitted from this calculation) is excessive. This is also borne out by the firm's inventory turnover of 1.81 times, which compares with the industry median of 2.3 times. The firm's average collection period of 51.8 days is significantly better than the industry median of 73 days, while the operating-cash-flow-to-current-liabilities ratio is close to the industry median. Knox's debt-to-equity ratio of 0.62 indicates that the firm has proportionately more debt in its capital structure than the median industry firm, which has a debt-to-equity ratio of 0.50. Knox's operations appear efficient as its return on assets, return on common stockholders' equity, and return on sales all exceed the industry medians.

b.   Average number of shares outstanding = (4,000,000 + 3,000,000)/2 = 3,500,000 shares.
$4,200,000 dividends/3,500,000 shares = $1.20 dividend per share.
Dividend payout ratio = $1.20/$3.07 = 39.1 percent.

c.   Price-earnings ratio = $25/$3.07 = 8.1.
Dividend yield = $1.20/$25 = 4.8 percent.

APPENDIX 14A: Financial Statement Disclosures

LO6 **Describe** financial statement
disclosures.

Disclosures related to a company's financial statements fall into one of three categories: (1) parenthetical disclosures on the face of the financial statements, (2) notes to the financial statements, and (3) supplementary information. Most disclosures amplify or explain aggregated information contained in the financial statements. Some disclosures, however, provide additional information.

Parenthetical Disclosures

Parenthetical disclosures are placed next to an account title or other descriptive label in the financial statements. Their purpose is to provide additional detail regarding the item or account. An example of parenthetical disclosures indicating the amount of the allowance for doubtful accounts follows:

	2016	2015
Accounts receivable, less allowances for doubtful accounts (2011—$7,545; 2010—$7,098)...	$351,538	$300,181

Instead of using a parenthetical disclosure, companies may choose to present the additional detail in the notes to the financial statements.

Notes to the Financial Statements

Although much information is gathered, summarized, and reported in a company's financial statements, the financial statements alone are limited in their ability to convey a complete picture of a company's financial status. *Notes* are added to the financial statements to help fill in these gaps. In fact, over time, accountants have given so much attention to the financial statement notes that the notes now consume more page space in the annual report than the financial statements themselves. Notes may cover a wide variety of topics. Typically, they deal with significant accounting policies, explanations of complex or special transactions, details of reported amounts, commitments, contingencies, business segments, quarterly data, and subsequent material events.

Significant Accounting Policies

GAAP contains a number of instances for which alternative accounting procedures are equally acceptable. For example, there are several generally accepted depreciation and inventory valuation methods. The particular accounting policies selected by a company affect the financial data presented. Knowledge of a firm's specific accounting principles and methods of applying these principles helps users more fully understand a company's financial statements. Accordingly, these principles and methods are disclosed in a **summary of significant accounting policies**, which is typically the first note to the financial statements.

For example, the annual report of the **Columbia Sportswear Company** contains the following description of its inventory policy:

> Inventories are carried at the lower of cost or market. Cost is determined using the first-in, first-out method. The Company periodically reviews its inventories for excess, close-out or slow moving items and makes provisions as necessary to properly reflect inventory value.

Explanations of Complex or Special Transactions

The complexity of certain transactions means that not all important aspects are likely to be reflected in the accounts. Financial statement notes, therefore, report additional relevant details about such transactions. Typical examples include notes discussing the financial aspects of pension plans, profit-sharing plans, acquisitions of other companies, borrowing agreements, stock option and other incentive plans, and income taxes.

Transactions with related parties are special transactions requiring disclosure in the financial statement notes. Related party transactions include transactions between a firm and its (1) principal owners, (2) members of management, (3) subsidiary companies, or (4) affiliate companies.

Details of Reported Amounts

Financial statements often summarize several groups of accounts into a single aggregate dollar amount. For example, a balance sheet may show one asset account labeled *Property, Plant, and Equipment,* or it may list *Long-Term Debt* as a single amount among the liabilities. Notes report more detail, presenting schedules that list the types and amounts of property, plant, and equipment and long-term debt. Other items that may be summarized in the financial statements and detailed in the notes include inventories, other current assets, notes payable, accrued liabilities, stockholders' equity, and a company's income tax expense.

The notes to Columbia Sportswear Company's 2014 annual report contain several examples of financial statement items that are detailed, including accounts receivable (**Note 6**), property, plant, and equipment (**Note 7**), short-term borrowing and credit lines (**Note 9**), accrued liabilities (**Note 10**), other long-term liabilities (**Note 12**), and income taxes (**Note 11**).

Commitments

A firm may have contractual arrangements existing as of a balance sheet date in which both parties to the contract still have acts yet to be completed. If performance under these **commitments** will have a significant financial impact on a firm, the existence and nature of the commitments should be disclosed in the notes to the financial statements. Examples of commitments reported in the notes include contracts to purchase materials or equipment, contracts to construct facilities, salary commitments to executives, commitments to retire or redeem stock, and commitments to deliver goods.

Columbia Sportswear Company reports the following commitments in its annual report:

> During its normal course of business, the Company has made certain indemnities, commitments and guarantees under which it may be required to make payments in relation to certain transactions. These include (i) intellectual property indemnities to the Company's customers and licensees in connection with the use, sale and/or license of Company products, (ii) indemnities to various lessors in connection with facility leases for certain claims arising from such facility or lease, (iii) indemnities to customers, vendors and service providers pertaining to claims based on the negligence or willful misconduct of the Company, (iv) executive severance arrangements and (v) indemnities involving the accuracy of representations and warranties in certain contracts. The duration of these indemnities, commitments and guarantees varies, and in certain cases, may be indefinite. The majority of these indemnities, commitments and guarantees do not provide for any limitation of the maximum potential for future payments the Company could be obligated to make. The Company has not recorded any liability for these indemnities, commitments and guarantees in the accompanying Consolidated Balance Sheets.

Contingencies

If the future event that would turn a contingency into an obligation is not likely to occur, or if the liability cannot be reasonably estimated, the **contingency** is disclosed in a note to the financial statements. Typical contingencies disclosed in the notes include pending lawsuits, environmental cleanup costs, possible income tax assessments, credit guarantees, and discounted notes receivable.

Under Armour, Inc. reports the following regarding contingencies in its annual report:

> The company is, from time to time, involved in routine legal matters incidental to its business. The company believes that the ultimate resolution of any such current proceedings and claims will not have a material adverse effect on its consolidated financial position, results of operations or cash flows.

Segments

Many firms diversify their business activities and operate in several different industries. A firm's financial statements often combine information from all of a company's operations into aggregate amounts. This complicates the financial statement user's ability to analyze the statements because the interpretation of financial data is influenced by the industry in which a firm operates. Different industries face different types of risk and have different rates of profitability. In making investment and lending decisions, financial statement users evaluate risk and required rates of return. Having financial data available by industry segment is helpful to such evaluations.

The FASB recognizes the usefulness of industry data to investors and lenders. Public companies with significant operations in more than one industry must report certain financial information by industry **segment**. Typically, these disclosures are in the financial statement notes. The major disclosures by industry segment are sales revenue, operating profit or loss, identifiable assets (the assets used by the segment), capital expenditures, and depreciation.

Other types of segment data may also be disclosed. Business operations in different parts of the world are subject to different risks and opportunities for growth. Thus, public companies with significant operations in foreign countries must report selected financial data by foreign geographic area. The required data disclosures include sales revenue, operating profit or loss (or other profitability measure), and identifiable assets. Also, if a firm has export sales or sales revenue to a single customer that are ten percent or more of total sales revenue, the amount of such sales revenue must be separately disclosed.

Note 19 to Columbia Sportswear's financial statements in its annual report illustrates segment disclosures by foreign versus domestic segments.

Quarterly Data

Interim financial reports cover periods shorter than one year. Companies that issue interim reports generally do so quarterly. These reports provide financial statement users with timely information on a firm's progress and are useful in predicting a company's annual financial results. The SEC requires that certain companies disclose selected quarterly financial data in their annual reports to stockholders. Included among the notes, the data reported for each quarter include sales revenue, gross profit, net income, and earnings per share. **Quarterly data** permit financial statement users to analyze such things as the seasonal nature of operations, the impact of diversification on quarterly activity, and whether the firm's activities lead or lag general economic trends.

The Columbia Sportswear Company provides quarterly financial information as supplemental data in its annual report.

Subsequent Events

If a company issues a large amount of securities or suffers a casualty loss after the balance sheet date, this information should be reported in a note, even though the situation arose subsequent to the balance sheet date. Firms are responsible for disclosing any significant events that occur between the balance sheet date and the date the financial statements are issued. This guideline recognizes that it takes several weeks for financial statements to be prepared and audited before they are issued. Events occurring during this period may have a material effect on a firm's operations and should be disclosed. Other examples of **subsequent events** requiring disclosure are sales of assets, significant changes in long-term debt, and acquisitions of other companies.

For example, Under Armour, Inc. reported the following subsequent event in its annual report:

> In February 2012, 150.0 thousand shares of Class B Convertible Common Stock were converted into shares of Class A Common Stock on a one-for-one basis in connection with a stock sale.

Supplementary Information

Supplementing the financial statements are several additional disclosures—management's discussion and analysis of the financial statements and selected financial data covering a five- to ten-year period along with possible other supplementary disclosures that are either required of certain companies by the SEC or recommended (but not required) by the FASB.

Management Discussion and Analysis

Management may increase the usefulness of financial statements by sharing some of their knowledge about a company's financial condition and operations. This is the purpose of the disclosure devoted to the management discussion and analysis. In this supplement to the financial statements, management identifies and comments on events and trends influencing a company's liquidity, operating results, and financial resources. Management's position within a company not only provides it with insights unavailable to outsiders, but also may introduce certain biases into the analysis. Nonetheless, management's comments, interpretations, and explanations should contribute to a better understanding of a company's financial statements.

A.K.A. The management discussion and analysis is also referred to simply as the *MD&A*.

Comparative Selected Financial Data

The analysis of a company's financial performance is enhanced when financial data for several years are available. By analyzing trends over time, it is possible for a financial statement user to learn much more about a company than would be possible by analyzing only a single year of data. Year-to-year changes may give clues as to a firm's future growth or may highlight areas for concern. Corporate annual reports to stockholders present complete financial statements in comparative form, showing the current year and one or two preceding years. Beyond this, however, the financial statements are supplemented by a summary of selected key financial statistics for a five- or ten-year period. The financial data presented in this historical summary usually include sales revenue, net income, dividends, earnings per share, working capital, and total assets.

SUMMARY OF LEARNING OBJECTIVES

Identify persistent earnings and discuss the content and format of the income statement. (p. 518)   LO1

- Persistent earnings are earnings that are likely to recur, while transitory earnings are unlikely to recur.
- The continuing income of a business may be reported in a single-step format or in a multiple-step format.
- Gains and losses from discontinued operations are reported in a special income statement section following income from continuing operations.
- The effect of most changes in accounting principle requires restatement of prior financial statements as if the new method had been applied all along.
- Companies are required to report other comprehensive income in addition to regular income in their financial statements.

Identify the sources of financial information used by investment professionals and explain horizontal financial statement analysis. (p. 522)   LO2

- Data sources for investment professionals include published financial statements, filings with the U.S. Securities and Exchange Commission, and statistics available from financial data services.
- A common form of horizontal analysis involves analyzing dollar and percentage changes in comparative financial statements for two or more years.
- Analyzing trend percentages of key figures, such as sales revenue, net income, and total assets for a number of years, related to a base year, is often useful.

Explain vertical financial statement analysis. (p. 527)   LO3

- Vertical analysis deals with the relationship of financial statement data for a single year.
- Common-size statements express financial statement items as a percentage of another key item, such as expressing income statement items as a percentage of sales revenue and balance sheet items as a percentage of total assets.

Define and discuss financial ratios for analyzing a firm. (p. 529)   LO4

- Ratios for analyzing firm profitability include the gross profit percentage, the return on sales, asset turnover, the return on assets, and the return on common stockholders' equity.

- Ratios for analyzing short-term firm liquidity include the current ratio, quick ratio, operating-cash-flow-to-current-liabilities ratio, accounts receivable turnover, average collection period, inventory turnover, and days' sales in inventory.
- Ratios for analyzing long-term firm solvency include the debt-to-equity ratio, the times-interest-earned ratio, and the operating-cash-flow-to-capital-expenditures ratio.
- Ratios of particular interest to common stockholders include a company's earnings per share, the price-earnings ratio, dividend yield, and the dividend payout ratio.

LO5 **Discuss the limitations of financial statement analysis. (p. 544)**

- When analyzing financial statements, financial statement users must be aware of a firm's accounting methods, the effects of inflation, and the difficulty of currently identifying a firm's industry classification.

LO6 **Appendix 14A: Describe financial statement disclosures. (p. 546)**

- Parenthetical disclosures on the face of the financial statements provide additional detail regarding the item or account.
- Notes to the financial statements provide information on significant accounting policies, explanations of complex or special transactions, details of reported amounts, commitments, contingencies, segments, quarterly data, and subsequent events.
- Supplemental information includes the management discussion and analysis, and comparable selected financial information.

SUMMARY OF FINANCIAL STATEMENT RATIOS

Analyzing Firm Profitability

$$\text{Gross profit percentage} = \frac{\text{Gross profit on sales}}{\text{Net sales}}$$

$$\text{Return on sales} = \frac{\text{Net income}}{\text{Net sales}}$$

$$\text{Asset turnover} = \frac{\text{Net sales}}{\text{Average total assets}}$$

$$\text{Return on assets} = \frac{\text{Net income}}{\text{Average total assets}}$$

$$\text{Return on common stockholders' equity} = \frac{(\text{Net income} - \text{Preferred stock dividends})}{\text{Average common stockholders' equity}}$$

Analyzing Short-Term Firm Liquidity

$$\text{Current ratio} = \frac{\text{Current assets}}{\text{Current liabilities}}$$

$$\text{Quick ratio} = \frac{(\text{Cash and cash equivalents} + \text{Short-term investments} + \text{Accounts receivable})}{\text{Current liabilities}}$$

$$\text{Operating-cash-flow-to-current-liabilities ratio} = \frac{\text{Cash flow from operating activities}}{\text{Average current liabilities}}$$

$$\text{Accounts receivable turnover} = \frac{\text{Net sales}}{\text{Average accounts receivable (net)}}$$

$$\text{Average collection period} = \frac{365}{\text{Accounts receivable turnover (net)}}$$

$$\text{Inventory turnover} = \frac{\text{Cost of goods sold}}{\text{Average inventory}}$$

$$\text{Days' sales in inventory} = \frac{365}{\text{Inventory turnover}}$$

Analyzing Long-Term Firm Solvency

$$\text{Debt-to-equity ratio} = \frac{\text{Total liabilities}}{\text{Total stockholders' equity}}$$

$$\text{Times-interest-earned ratio} = \frac{\text{Income before interest expense and income taxes}}{\text{Interest expense}}$$

$$\text{Operating-cash-flow-to-capital-expenditures ratio} = \frac{\text{Cash flow from operating activities}}{\text{Annual net capital expenditures}}$$

Financial Ratios for Common Stockholders

$$\text{Earnings per share} = \frac{(\text{Net income} - \text{Preferred stock dividends})}{\text{Weighted average common shares outstanding}}$$

$$\text{Price-earnings ratio} = \frac{\text{Market price per share}}{\text{Earnings per share}}$$

$$\text{Dividend yield} = \frac{\text{Annual dividend per share}}{\text{Market price per share}}$$

$$\text{Dividend payout ratio} = \frac{\text{Annual dividend per share}}{\text{Earnings per share}}$$

SUMMARY	Concept ⟶	Method ⟶	Assessment
TAKEAWAY 14.1	How does a company's current performance compare with the prior year?	Income statement and balance sheet for current and prior year. The income statement and balance sheet should be compared using the prior year as the base. Percentage changes in financial statement amounts can be computed as the change between years divided by the base year amount.	Significant changes should be analyzed to determine the reason for any change.
TAKEAWAY 14.2	How do the relationships within a company's income statement and balance sheet compare to those of prior years?	Income statement and balance sheet for current and prior year. Each income statement item should be presented as a percentage of sales revenue and each balance sheet item should be presented as a percentage of total assets. Financial statements in this form are called common-size statements.	The percentages should be analyzed for differences between years and significant changes should be analyzed to determine the reason for any change.
TAKEAWAY 14.3	How much profit is a company generating relative to the amount of assets invested in the company?	Income statement and balance sheet. Calculate the return on assets by dividing net income by the average total assets for the year.	The higher the return on assets, the better a company is doing with respect to generating profits utilizing the assets under its control.
TAKEAWAY 14.4	How financially capable is a company to pay its current liabilities as they come due?	Income statement, balance sheet, and statement of cash flows. Calculate the current ratio, the quick ratio, and the operating-cash-flow-to-current-liabilities ratio.	The higher the ratios, the higher the probability that a company will have the ability to pay its current liabilities as they come due.
TAKEAWAY 14.5	How solvent is a company?	Income statement, balance sheet, and statement of cash flows. Calculate the debt-to-equity ratio, the times-interest-earned ratio, and the operating-cash-flow-to-capital-expenditures ratio.	The higher the times-interest-earned and the operating-cash-flow-to-capital-expenditures ratios, and the lower the debt-to-equity ratio, the greater is a company's solvency.
TAKEAWAY 14.6	How much dividends are common stockholders likely to receive?	Earnings per share, dividends per share, and market price of common stock. Calculate the dividend yield and dividend payout ratio.	The higher the dividend yield and the dividend payout ratio, the greater the company's dividend distribution policy.

KEY TERMS

Accounts receivable
  turnover (p. 536)
Asset turnover ratio (p. 531)
Average collection period
  (days' sales outstanding, or
  DSO) (p. 536)
Change in accounting
  principle (p. 520)

Commitments (p. 547)
Common-size financial
  statement (p. 527)
Comparative financial
  statement analysis (p. 523)
Comprehensive income (p. 521)
Contingency (p. 548)
Current ratio (p. 534)

Days' sales in inventory (p. 537)
Debt-to-equity ratio (p. 539)
Discontinued
  operations (p. 520)
Dividend payout ratio (p. 542)
Dividend yield (p. 542)
Earnings per share
  (EPS) (p. 520, 541)

Gross profit (Gross margin) (p. 529)

Gross profit on sales (p. 529)

Gross profit percentage (p. 529)

Horizontal analysis (p. 523)

Inventory turnover (p. 537)

MD&A (p. 549)

Multiple-step income statement (p. 518)

Operating-cash-flow-to-capital-expenditures ratio (p. 540)

Operating-cash-flow-to-current-liabilities ratio (p. 535)

Operating cycle (p. 538)

Persistent earnings (p. 518)

Price-earnings ratio (P/E multiple) (p. 541)

Quarterly data (p. 548)

Quick ratio (acid-test ratio) (p. 534)

Return on assets (p. 532)

Return on common stockholders' equity (p. 532)

Return on sales (profit margin) (p. 531)

Segment (p. 548)

Single-step income statement (p. 518)

Subsequent events (p. 548)

Summary of significant accounting policies (p. 547)

Times-interest-earned ratio (interest coverage ratio) (p. 539)

Transitory earnings (p. 518)

Trend percentages (p. 525)

Unusual items (p. 519)

Vertical analysis (p. 523)

Working capital (p. 533)

Assignments with the logo in the margin are available in BusinessCourse.
See the Preface of the book for details.

SELF-STUDY QUESTIONS

(Answers to the Self-Study Questions are at the end of this chapter.)

1. Assume that an income statement contains each of the three sections listed below. Which will be the last section presented in the income statement?   **LO1**
   a. Gross profit
   b. Income from continuing operations
   c. Discontinued operations

2. When constructing a common-sized income statement, all amounts are expressed as a percentage of: **LO3**
   a. net income.
   c. net sales.
   b. gross profit.
   d. income from operations.

Questions 3–9 of the Self-Study Questions are based on the following data:

HYDRO COMPANY Balance Sheet December 31, 2015			
Cash	$ 40,000	Current liabilities	$ 80,000
Accounts receivable (net)	80,000	10% Bonds payable	120,000
Inventory	130,000	Common stock	200,000
Plant and equipment (net)	250,000	Retained earnings	100,000
Total Assets	$500,000	Total Liabilities and Stockholders' Equity	$500,000

Sales revenues for 2015 were $800,000, gross profit was $320,000, and net income was $36,000. The income tax rate was 40 percent. One year ago, accounts receivable (net) were $76,000, inventory was $110,000, total assets were $460,000, and stockholders' equity was $260,000. The bonds payable were outstanding all year and the 2015 interest expense was $12,000.

3. The current ratio of Hydro Company at 12/31/2015, calculated using the above data, was 3.13 and the company's working capital was $170,000. Which of the following would happen if the firm paid off $20,000 of its current liabilities on January 1, 2016?   **LO4**
   a. Both the current ratio and working capital would decrease.
   b. Both the current ratio and working capital would increase.
   c. The current ratio would increase, but working capital would remain the same.
   d. The current ratio would increase, but working capital would decrease.

4. What was the firm's inventory turnover for 2015?   **LO4**
   a. 6.67
   c. 6
   b. 4
   d. 3.69

LO4   5. **What was the firm's return on common stockholders' equity for 2015?**
      a. 25.7 percent   *c.* 17.1 percent
      b. 12.9 percent   *d.* 21.4 percent

LO4   6. **What was the firm's average collection period for 2015?**
      a. 36.5 days   *c.* 35.6 days
      b. 37.4 days   *d.* 18.3 days

LO4   7. **What was the firm's times-interest-earned ratio for 2015?**
      a. 4   *c.* 5
      b. 3   *d.* 6

LO4   8. **What was the firm's return on sales for 2015?**
      a. 4.0 percent   *c.* 5.0 percent
      b. 4.5 percent   *d.* 5.5 percent

LO4   9. **What was the firm's return on assets for 2015?**
      a. 6.0 percent   *c.* 7.5 percent
      b. 7.0 percent   *d.* 8.0 percent

LO2   10. **When performing trend analysis, each line item is expressed as a percentage of:**
      a. net income.   *c.* the prior year amount.
      b. the base year amount.   *d.* total assets.

LO5   11. **Recognized limitations of financial statement analysis include each of the following except:**
      a. companies in the same industry using different accounting methods.
      b. inflation.
      c. different levels of profitability between companies.
      d. difficulty of classifying by industry conglomerates.

LO6
(Appendix 14A)   12. **Financial statement disclosures include each of the following except:**
      a. notes to the financial statements.   *c.* supplementary information.
      b. parenthetical disclosures.   *d.* promotional giveaways.

QUESTIONS

1. What is the difference between a single-step income statement and a multiple-step income statement?

2. Which of the following amounts would appear only in a multiple-step income statement?
    a. Income from continuing operations
    b. Income from discontinued operations
    c. Gross profit on sales
    d. Net income

3. What is a business segment? Why are gains and losses from a discontinued segment reported in a separate section of the income statement?

4. How do horizontal analysis and vertical analysis of financial statements differ?

5. "Financial statement users should focus attention on each item showing a large percentage change from one year to the next." Is this statement correct? Why?

6. What are trend percentages and how are they calculated? What pitfalls must financial statement users avoid when preparing trend percentages?

7. What are common-size financial statements and how are they used?

8. What item is the key figure (that is, 100 percent) in a common-size income statement? A common-size balance sheet?

9. During the past year, Lite Company had net income of $5 million, and Scanlon Company had net income of $8 million. Both companies manufacture electrical components for the construction industry. What additional information would you need to compare the profitability of the two companies?

10. Under what circumstances can the return on sales be used to assess the profitability of a company? Can this ratio be used to compare the profitability of companies from different industries? Explain.

11. What is the relationship between asset turnover, return on assets, and return on sales?

12. Blare Company had a return on sales of 6.5 percent and an asset turnover of 2.40. What is Blare's return on assets?

13. What does the return on common stockholders' equity measure?

14. How does the quick ratio differ from the current ratio?

15. For each of the following ratios, is a high ratio or low ratio considered, in general, a positive sign?
    a. Current ratio
    b. Quick ratio
    c. Operating-cash-flow-to-current-liabilities ratio
    d. Accounts receivable turnover
    e. Average collection period
    f. Inventory turnover
    g. Days' sales in inventory

16. What is the significance of the debt-to-equity ratio and how is it computed?

17. What does the times-interest-earned ratio indicate and how is it calculated?

18. What does the operating-cash-flow-to-capital-expenditures ratio measure?

19. Clair, Inc., earned $4.50 per share of common stock in the current year and paid dividends of $2.34 per share. The most recent market price per share of the common stock is $46.80. What is the company's (a) price-earnings ratio, (b) dividend yield, and (c) dividend payout ratio?

20. What are two inherent limitations of financial statement data?

SHORT EXERCISES

Use the following financial data for Hi-Tech Instruments to answer Short Exercises 14-1 through 14-10:

2016 (Thousands of Dollars, except Earnings per Share)	
Sales revenue	$210,000
Cost of goods sold	125,000
Net income	8,300
Dividends	2,600
Earnings per share	4.15

HI-TECH INSTRUMENTS, INC.
Balance Sheets

(Thousands of Dollars)	Dec. 31, 2016	Dec. 31, 2015
Assets		
Cash	$ 18,300	$ 18,000
Accounts receivable (net)	46,000	41,000
Inventory	39,500	43,700
Total Current Assets	103,800	102,700
Plant assets (net)	52,600	50,500
Other assets	15,600	13,800
Total Assets	$172,000	$167,000
Liabilities and Stockholders' Equity		
Notes payable—banks	$ 6,000	$ 6,000
Accounts payable	22,500	18,700
Accrued liabilities	16,500	21,000
Total Current Liabilities	45,000	45,700
9% Bonds payable	40,000	40,000
Total Liabilities	85,000	85,700
Common stock, $25 par value (2,000,000 shares)	50,000	50,000
Retained earnings	37,000	31,300
Total Stockholders' Equity	87,000	81,300
Total Liabilities and Stockholders' Equity	$172,000	$167,000

Industry Average Ratios for Competitors	
Quick ratio	1.3
Current ratio	2.4
Accounts receivable turnover.	5.9 times
Inventory turnover	3.5 times
Debt-to-equity ratio	0.73
Gross profit percentage	42.8 percent
Return on sales	4.5 percent
Return on assets	7.6 percent

LO4 **SE14-1.** **Quick Ratio** Calculate the company's quick ratio for 2016 and compare the result to the industry average.

LO4 **SE14-2.** **Current Ratio** Calculate the company's current ratio for 2016 and compare the result to the industry average.

LO4 **SE14-3.** **Accounts Receivable Turnover** Calculate the company's accounts receivable turnover for 2016 and compare the result to the industry average.

LO4 **SE14-4.** **Inventory Turnover** Calculate the company's inventory turnover for 2016 and compare the result to the industry average.

LO4 **SE14-5.** **Debit-to-Equity Ratio** Calculate the company's 2016 debt-to-equity ratio and compare the result to the industry average.

LO4 **SE14-6.** **Gross Profit Percentage** Calculate the company's 2016 gross profit percentage and compare the result to the industry average.

LO4 **SE14-7.** **Return on Sales** Calculate the company's return on sales for 2016 and compare the result to the industry average.

LO4 **SE14-8.** **Return on Assets** Calculate the company's return on assets for 2016 and compare the result to the industry average.

LO4 **SE14-9.** **Dividends per Share** Calculate the company's dividend paid per share of common stock. What was the dividend payout ratio?

LO4 **SE14-10.** **Earnings per Share** If the company's most recent price per share of common stock is $62.25, what is the company's price-earnings ratio and dividend yield?

LO1 **SE14-11.** **Persistent Earnings** Identify each of the following items as either (P) persistent, or (T) transitory.

    a. Sale of merchandise
    b. Settlement of a lawsuit
    c. Interest income
    d. Payment to vendors
    e. Loss from expropriations of property by a foreign government

LO2 **SE14-12.** **Horizontal Analysis** Total assets were $1,000,000 in 2016, $900,000 in 2015, and $950,000 in 2014. What was the percentage change from 2014 to 2015 and from 2015 to 2016? Was the change an increase or a decrease?

LO3 **SE14-13.** **Common-Size Income Statement** A partial common-size income statement for Prag Company for three years is shown below.

Item	2016	2015	2014
Net sales.	100.0	100.0	100.0
Cost of goods sold.	60.5	63.0	62.5
Other expenses	21.0	19.0	20.5

Did Prag's net income as a percentage of net sales increase, remain the same, or decrease over the three-year period?

SE14-14. Financial Statement Analysis Limitations Which of the following is not considered a limitation of financial statement analysis?   **LO5**

    a. Firms may use different accounting methods.

    b. Firms may be audited by different auditing firms.

    c. Inflation may distort trend analysis.

    d. It may be difficult to classify large conglomorate firms by industry.

SE14-15. Financial Statement Disclosures Which of the following is not a common form of financial statement disclosure?   **LO6**
(Appendix 14A)

    a. Notes to financial statements

    b. Supplemental information

    c. Parenthetical disclosure

    d. Bullet points

EXERCISES—SET A

E14-1A. Income Statement Sections During the current year, Dale Corporation sold a segment of its business at a gain of $210,000. Until it was sold, the segment had a current period operating loss of $75,000. The company had $850,000 income from continuing operations for the current year. Prepare the lower part of the income statement, beginning with the $850,000 income from continuing operations. Follow tax allocation procedures, assuming that all changes in income are subject to a 35 percent income tax rate. Disregard earnings per share disclosures.   **LO1**

E14-2A. Earnings per Share Lucky Corporation began the year with a simple capital structure consisting of 240,000 shares of outstanding common stock. On April 1, 5,000 additional common shares were issued, and another 30,000 common shares were issued on August 1. The company had net income for the year of $589,375. Calculate the earnings per share of common stock.   **LO4**

E14-3A. Comparative Income Statements Consider the following income statement data from the Ross Company: **LO2**

	2016	2015
Sales revenue	$550,000	$450,000
Cost of goods sold	336,000	279,000
Selling expenses	105,000	99,000
Administrative expenses	60,000	50,000
Income tax expense	7,800	5,400

    a. Prepare a comparative income statement, showing increases and decreases in dollars and in percentages.

    b. Comment briefly on the changes between the two years.

E14-4A. Common-Size Income Statements Refer to the income statement data given in Exercise E14-3A.   **LO3**

    a. Prepare common-size income statements for each year.

    b. Compare the common-size income statements and comment briefly.

E14-5A. Ratios Analyzing Firm Profitability The following information is available for Buhler Company: **LO4**

Annual Data	2016	2015
Net sales	$8,600,000	$8,200,000
Gross profit on sales	3,050,000	2,736,000
Net income	567,600	488,000

Year-End Data	Dec. 31, 2016	Dec. 31, 2015
Total assets	$6,500,000	$6,000,000
Stockholders' equity	4,000,000	3,200,000

Calculate the following ratios for 2016:

a.   Gross profit percentage

b.   Return on sales

c.   Asset turnover

d.   Return on assets

e.   Return on common stockholders' equity (Buhler Company has no preferred stock.)

LO4   **E14-6A.**   **Working Capital and Short-Term Liquidity Ratios**   Bell Company has a current ratio of 3.00 on December 31. On that date the company's current assets are as follows:

Cash...	$ 29,000
Short-term investments	49,400
Accounts receivable (net)...................................	170,000
Inventory..	200,000
Prepaid expenses...	11,600
Current assets	$460,000

Bell Company's current liabilities at the beginning of the year were $140,000 and during the year its operating activities provided a cash flow of $60,000.

a.   What are the firm's current liabilities on December 31?

b.   What is the firm's working capital on December 31?

c.   What is the quick ratio on December 31?

d.   What is Bell's operating-cash-flow-to-current-liabilities ratio?

LO4   **E14-7A.**   **Accounts Receivable and Inventory Ratios**   Bell Company, whose current assets at December 31 are shown in Exercise E14-6A, had net sales for the year of $900,000 and cost of goods sold of $550,000. At the beginning of the year, Bell's accounts receivable (net) were $160,000 and its inventory was $195,000.

a.   What is the company's accounts receivable turnover for the year?

b.   What is the company's average collection period for the year?

c.   What is the company's inventory turnover for the year?

d.   What is the company's days' sales in inventory for the year?

LO4   **E14-8A.**   **Ratios Analyzing Long-Term Firm Solvency**   The following information is available for Antler Company:

Annual Data	2016	2015
Interest expense..	$ 90,000	$ 82,000
Income tax expense.......................................	203,500	185,000
Net income..	496,500	400,000
Capital expenditures	320,000	380,000
Cash provided by operating activities	425,000	390,000

Year-End Data	Dec. 31, 2016	Dec. 31, 2015
Total liabilities..	$2,400,000	$1,900,000
Total stockholders' equity	4,000,000	3,800,000

Calculate the following:

a.   2016 debt-to-equity ratio

b.   2016 times-interest-earned ratio

c.   2016 operating-cash-flow-to-capital-expenditures ratio

E14-9A. **Financial Ratios for Common Stockholders** Kluster Corporation has only common stock out- standing. The firm reported earnings per share of $5.25 for the year. During the year, Kluster paid dividends of $2.10 per share. At year end the current market price of the stock was $63 per share. Calculate the following: **LO4**

    a.   Year-end price-earnings ratio
    b.   Dividend yield
    c.   Dividend payout ratio

E14-10A. **Financial Statement Limitations** You have been asked to perform financial statement analysis on the Patton Company. The Patton Company is a large chain of retail outlets that sells a wide range of household items. Last year the company introduced its own credit card and is pleased that profit from this financing activity now accounts for over twenty percent of the company's total profit. As part of your analysis you have chosen to compare the Patton Company to Johnson Stores, a much larger chain of stores. Johnson Stores sells household items and groceries, but it does not have its own credit card. Your analysis includes both horizontal trend analysis and vertical analysis. Identify some of the limitations from the description above.   **LO5**

E14-11A. **Financial Statement Notes** The notes to financial statements present information on significant ac- counting policies, complex or special transactions, details of reported amounts, commitments, con- tingencies, segments, quarterly data, and subsequent events. Indicate which type of note disclosure is illustrated by each of the following notes: **LO6**
(Appendix 14A)

    a.   The company has agreed to purchase seven EMB-120 aircraft and related spare parts. The ag- gregate cost of these aircraft is approximately $41,250,000, subject to a cost escalation provi- sion. The aircraft are scheduled to be delivered over the next two fiscal years.

    b.   The company has deferred certain costs related to major accounting and information systems enhancements that are anticipated to benefit future years. Upon completion, the related cost is amortized over a period not exceeding five years.

    c.   The company has guaranteed loans and leases of independent distributors approximating $27,500,000 as of December 31 of the current year.

    d.   An officer of the company is also a director of a major raw material supplier of the company. The amount of raw material purchases from this supplier approximated $410,000 in the current year.

EXERCISES—SET B

E14-1B. **Income Statement Sections** During the current year, Newtech Corporation sold a segment of its business at a loss of $225,000. Until it was sold, the segment had a current period operating loss of $200,000. The company has $750,000 income from continuing operations for the current year. Pre- pare the lower part of the income statement, beginning with the $750,000 income from continuing operations. Follow tax allocation procedures, assuming that all changes in income are subject to a 40 percent income tax rate. Disregard earnings per share disclosures.   **LO1**

E14-2B. **Earnings per Share** Ewing Corporation began the year with a simple capital structure consisting of 35,000 shares of common stock outstanding. On May 1, 10,000 additional common shares were issued, and another 10,000 common shares were issued on September 1. The company had a net income for the year of $468,000. Calculate the earnings per share of common stock.   **LO4**

E14-3B. **Comparative Balance Sheets** Consider the following balance sheet data for Great Buy Co., Inc., an electronics and major appliance retailer, at February 26, 2016 and February 27, 2015 (amounts in thousands):   **LO2**

	Feb. 26, 2016	Feb. 27, 2015
Cash and cash equivalents	$ 59,872	$ 7,138
Accounts receivables	52,944	37,968
Merchandise inventories	637,950	249,991
Other current assets	13,844	9,829
Current Assets	764,610	304,926
Property and equipment (net)	172,724	126,442
Other assets	15,160	7,774
Total Assets	$952,494	$439,142
Current Liabilities	$402,028	$186,005
Long-term liabilities	239,022	70,854
Total Liabilities	641,050	256,859
Common stock	2,087	1,149
Additional paid-in-capital	224,089	137,151
Retained earnings	85,268	43,983
Total Stockholders' Equity	311,444	182,283
Total Liabilities and Stockholders' Equity	$952,494	$439,142

a. Prepare a comparative balance sheet, showing increases in dollars and percentages.
b. Comment briefly on the changes between the two years.

LO3 **E14-4B.** **Common-Size Balance Sheets** Refer to the balance sheet data given in Exercise E14-3B.

a. Prepare common-size balance sheets for each year (use total assets as the base amount for computing percentages).
b. Compare the common-size balance sheets and comment briefly.

LO4 **E14-5B.** **Ratios Analyzing Firm Profitability** The following information is available for Crest Company:

Annual Data	2016	2015
Sales revenue	$6,600,000	$6,000,000
Cost of goods sold	4,006,400	3,800,000
Net income	310,000	264,000

Year-End Data	Dec. 31, 2016	Dec. 31, 2015
Total assets	$2,850,000	$2,500,000
Common stockholders' equity	1,900,000	1,800,000

Calculate the following ratios for 2016:

a. Gross profit percentage
b. Return on sales
c. Asset turnover
d. Return on assets
e. Return on common stockholders' equity (Crest Company declared and paid preferred stock dividends of $25,000 in 2016.)

LO4 **E14-6B.** **Working Capital and Short-Term Firm Liquidity Ratios** Favor Company has a current ratio of 2.15 on December 31. On that date its current assets are as follows:

Cash and cash equivalents	$ 28,000
Short-term investments	87,000
Accounts receivable (net)	125,000
Inventory	178,500
Prepaid expenses	11,500
Current assets	$430,000

Favor Company's current liabilities at the beginning of the year were $195,000 and during the year its operating activities provided a cash flow of $33,830.

    a.   What are the firm's current liabilities at December 31?

    b.   What is the firm's working capital on December 31?

    c.   What is the quick ratio on December 31?

    d.   What is the firm's operating-cash-flow-to-current-liabilities ratio?

E14-7B.   **Accounts Receivable and Inventory Ratios** Favor Company, whose current assets at December 31 are shown in Exercise E14-6B, had net sales for the year of $580,000 and cost of goods sold of $345,900. At the beginning of the year, accounts receivable (net) were $121,000 and inventory was $154,650.   **LO4**

    a.   What is the company's accounts receivable turnover?

    b.   What is the company's average collection period?

    c.   What is the company's inventory turnover?

    d.   What is the company's days' sales in inventory?

E14-8B.   **Ratios Analyzing Long-Term Firm Solvency** The following information is available for Percy Company: **LO4**

Annual Data	2016	2015
Interest expense.	$170,000	$166,000
Income tax expense.	126,000	117,000
Net income.	294,000	275,000
Capital expenditures	435,000	350,000
Cash provided by operating activities	247,000	223,000

Year-End Data	Dec. 31, 2016	Dec. 31, 2015
Total liabilities.	$3,500,000	$2,900,000
Total stockholders' equity	2,200,000	1,900,000

Calculate the following:

    a.   2016 debt-to-equity ratio

    b.   2016 times-interest-earned ratio

    c.   2016 operating-cash-flow-to-capital-expenditures ratio

E14-9B.   **Financial Ratios for Common Stockholders** Henshue Corporation has only common stock outstanding. The firm reported earnings per share of $2.00 for the year. During the year, Henshue paid dividends of $0.85 per share. At year end, the current market price of the stock was $35.15 per share.   **LO4**

    Calculate the following:

    a.   Year-end price-earnings ratio

    b.   Dividend yield

    c.   Dividend payout ratio

E14-10B.   **Financial Statement Limitations** You have been asked to perform financial statement analysis on the Anderson Company. The Anderson Company is a large manufacturer of construction machinery and vehicles. Last year the company closed down a segment of the business that produced mining equipment because it was not providing an adequate return on assets. This segment represented fifteen percent of the company's total assets. As part of your analysis you have chosen to compare the Anderson Company to Bertran, Inc., a much smaller manufacturer of equipment, although Bertran, Inc. also performs contract repairs for many other brands of equipment. Your analysis includes both horizontal trend analysis and vertical analysis. Identify some of the limitations from the description above.   **LO5**

E14-11B.   **Financial Statement Notes** Notes to the financial statements present information on significant accounting policies, complex or special transactions, details of reported amounts, commitments, contingencies, segments, quarterly data, and subsequent events. Indicate the type of note disclosure that is illustrated by each of the following notes: **LO6**
(Appendix 14A)

    a.   Sales by the Farm and Equipment segment to independent dealers are recorded at the time of shipment to those dealers. Sales through company-owned retail stores are recorded at the time of sale to retail customers.

    b.   Members of the board of directors, the advisory board, and employees are not charged the vendor's commission on property sold at auction for their benefit. (From the notes of an auctioneer company.)

    c.   Sales to an airline company accounted for approximately 45 percent of the company's net sales in the current year.

    d.   The company's product liability insurance coverage with respect to insured events occurring after January 1 of the current year is substantially less than the amount of that insurance available in the recent past. The company is now predominantly self-insured in this area. The reduction in insurance coverage reflects trends in the liability insurance field generally and is not unique to the company.

PROBLEMS—SET A

LO1   **P14-1A.**   **Income Statement Format** The following information from Belvidere Company's current operations is available:

Administrative expenses	$ 73,000
Cost of goods sold	464,000
Sales revenue	772,000
Selling expenses	87,000
Interest expense	10,000
Loss from operations of discontinued segment	60,000
Gain on disposal of discontinued segment	40,000
Income taxes:	
Amount applicable to ordinary operations	60,000
Reduction applicable to loss from operations of discontinued segment	24,000
Amount applicable to gain on disposal of discontinued segment	16,000

Required

    a.   Prepare a multiple-step income statement. (Disregard earnings per share.)

    b.   Prepare a single-step income statement. (Disregard earnings per share.)

LO4   **P14-2A.**   **Earnings per Share** Leland Corporation began the year with 150,000 shares of common stock outstanding. On March 1 an additional 10,000 shares of common stock were issued. On August 1, another 16,000 shares of common stock were issued. On November 1, 6,000 shares of common stock were acquired as Treasury Stock. Leland Corporation's net income for the calendar year is $516,000.

Required

Calculate the company's earnings per share.

LO1, 4   **P14-3A.**   **Earnings per Share and Multiple-Step Income Statement** The following summarized data relate to Bowden Corporation's current operations:

Sales revenue	$760,000
Cost of goods sold	450,000
Selling expenses	65,000
Administrative expenses	72,000
Loss on sale of equipment	5,000
Income tax expense (not allocated)	42,000
Shares of common stock	
Outstanding at January 1	20,000 shares
Additional issued at May 1	7,000 shares
Additional issued at November 1	2,000 shares

Required

Prepare a multiple-step income statement for Bowden Corporation for the year. Assume a 25 percent income tax rate. Allocate income tax expense within the income statement. Include earnings per share disclosure at the bottom of the income statement.

P14-4A. **Trend Percentages** Net sales, net income, and total asset figures for Vibrant Controls, Inc., for five consecutive years are given below (Vibrant manufactures pollution controls): LO2

	Annual Amounts (Thousands of Dollars)				
	Year 1	Year 2	Year 3	Year 4	Year 5
Net sales..........................	$71,500	$79,800	$85,275	$88,400	$94,700
Net income........................	3,200	3,650	3,900	4,250	4,790
Total assets	42,500	46,200	48,700	51,000	54,900

Required

a. Calculate trend percentages, using Year 1 as the base year.
b. Calculate the return on sales for each year. (Rates above 2.8 percent are considered good for manufacturers of pollution controls; rates above 6.4 percent are considered very good.)
c. Comment on the results of your analysis.

P14-5A. **Changes in Various Ratios** Presented below is selected information for Brimmer Company: LO4

	2016	2015
Sales revenue..	$920,000	$840,000
Cost of goods sold.....................................	575,000	545,000
Interest expense.......................................	20,000	20,000
Income tax expense....................................	27,000	30,000
Net income..	61,000	52,000
Cash flow from operating activities	65,000	55,000
Capital expenditures	45,000	45,000
Accounts receivable (net), December 31	126,000	120,000
Inventory, December 31................................	196,000	160,000
Stockholders' equity, December 31.....................	450,000	400,000
Total assets, December 31.............................	750,000	675,000

Required

a. Calculate the following ratios for 2016. The 2015 results are given for comparative purposes.

		2015
1.	Gross profit percentage	33.5 percent
2.	Return on assets	8.3 percent
3.	Return on sales	6.2 percent
4.	Return on common stockholders' equity (no preferred stock was outstanding).............................	13.9 percent
5.	Accounts receivable turnover.....................................	7.50
6.	Average collection period...	48.7 days
7.	Inventory turnover	3.61
8.	Times-interest-earned ratio	4.80
9.	Operating-cash-flow-to-capital-expenditures ratio	1.22

b. Comment on the changes between the two years.

P14-6A. **Ratios from Comparative and Common-Size Data** Consider the following financial statements for Waverly Company. LO2, 3, 4

During 2016, management obtained additional bond financing to enlarge its production facilities. The company faced higher production costs during the year for such things as fuel, materials, and freight. Because of temporary government price controls, a planned price increase on products was delayed several months.

As a holder of both common and preferred stock, you decide to analyze the financial statements:

WAVERLY COMPANY Balance Sheets (Thousands of Dollars)	Dec. 31, 2016	Dec. 31, 2015
Assets		
Cash and cash equivalents	$ 19,000	$ 12,000
Accounts receivable (net).	55,000	43,000
Inventory.	120,000	105,000
Prepaid expenses.	20,000	14,000
Plant and other assets (net)	471,000	411,000
Total Assets	$685,000	$585,000
Liabilities and Stockholders' Equity		
Current liabilities.	$ 91,000	$ 82,000
10% Bonds payable.	225,000	160,000
9% Preferred stock, $50 Par Value	75,000	75,000
Common stock, $10 Par Value.	200,000	200,000
Retained earnings	94,000	68,000
Total Liabilities and Stockholders' Equity	$685,000	$585,000

WAVERLY COMPANY Income Statements (Thousands of Dollars)	2016	2015
Sales revenue.	$820,000	$678,000
Cost of goods sold.	545,000	433,920
Gross profit on sales.	275,000	244,080
Selling and administrative expenses	175,000	149,200
Income before interest expense and income taxes	100,000	94,880
Interest expense.	22,500	16,000
Income before income taxes	77,500	78,880
Income tax expense.	22,900	21,300
Net income.	$ 54,600	$ 57,580
Other financial data (thousands of dollars)		
Cash provided by operating activities	$ 65,200	$ 60,500
Preferred stock dividends.	6,750	6,750

Required

a. Calculate the following for each year: current ratio, quick ratio, operating-cash-flow-to-current-liabilities ratio (current liabilities were $77,000,000 at January 1, 2015), inventory turnover (inventory was $87,000,000 at January 1, 2015), debt-to-equity ratio, times-interest-earned ratio, return on assets (total assets were $490,000,000 at January 1, 2015), and return on common stockholders' equity (common stockholders' equity was $235,000,000 at January 1, 2015).

b. Calculate common-size percentages for each year's income statement.

c. Comment on the results of your analysis.

LO4 P14-7A. Constructing Statements from Ratio Data The following are the 2015 financial statements for Omicron Company, with almost all dollar amounts missing:

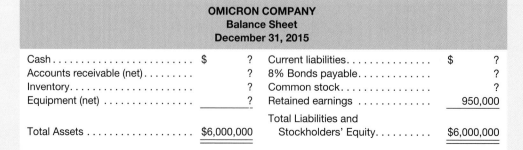

OMICRON COMPANY Balance Sheet December 31, 2015				
Cash.	$?	Current liabilities.	$?
Accounts receivable (net).	?	8% Bonds payable.	?
Inventory.	?	Common stock.	?
Equipment (net)	?	Retained earnings	950,000
		Total Liabilities and	
Total Assets	$6,000,000	Stockholders' Equity.	$6,000,000

OMICRON COMPANY Income Statement For the Year Ended December 31, 2015		
Sales revenue.	$	?
Cost of goods sold.		?
Gross profit.		?
Selling and administrative expenses		?
Income before interest expense and income taxes		?
Interest expense.		80,000
Income before income taxes		?
Income tax expense (30%).		?
Net income.		$580,000

The following information is available about Omicron Company's financial statements:

1. Quick ratio, 0.95.
2. Inventory turnover (inventory at January 1 was $924,000), 5 times.
3. Return on sales, 8.0 percent.
4. Accounts receivable turnover (accounts receivable (net) at January 1 were $860,000), 8 times.
5. Gross profit percentage, 32 percent.
6. Return on common stockholders' equity (common stockholders' equity at January 1 was $3,300,000), 16 percent.
7. The interest expense relates to the bonds payable that were outstanding all year.

Required

Compute the missing amounts, and complete the financial statements of Omicron Company. *Hint:* Complete the income statement first.

P14-8A. **Ratios Compared with Industry Averages** Because you own the common stock of Phantom Corporation, a paper manufacturer, you decide to analyze the firm's performance for the most recent year. The following data are taken from the firm's latest annual report: **LO4**

	Dec. 31, 2016	Dec. 31, 2015
Quick assets.	$ 700,000	$ 552,000
Inventory and prepaid expenses	372,000	312,000
Other assets.	4,788,000	4,200,000
Total Assets	$5,860,000	$5,064,000
Current liabilities.	$ 724,000	$ 564,000
10% Bonds payable.	1,440,000	1,440,000
8% Preferred stock, $100 par value.	480,000	480,000
Common stock, $10 par value.	2,700,000	2,160,000
Retained earnings	516,000	420,000
Total Liabilities and Stockholders' Equity	$5,860,000	$5,064,000

For 2016, net sales amount to $11,280,000, net income is $575,000, and preferred stock dividends paid are $42,000.

Required

a. Calculate the following ratios for 2016:
   1. Return on sales
   2. Return on assets
   3. Return on common stockholders' equity
   4. Quick ratio
   5. Current ratio
   6. Debt-to-equity ratio

b. Trade association statistics and information provided by credit agencies reveal the following data on industry norms:

	Median	Upper Quartile
Return on sales	4.9 percent	8.6 percent
Return on assets	6.5 percent	11.2 percent
Return on common stockholders' equity.	10.6 percent	17.3 percent
Quick ratio	1.0	1.8
Current ratio	1.8	3.0
Debt-to-equity-ratio	1.08	0.66

Compare Phantom Corporation's performance with industry performance.

LO4 **P14-9A.** **Ratios Compared with Industry Averages** Packard Plastics, Inc., manufactures various plastic and synthetic products. Financial statement data for the firm follow:

	2016 (Thousands of Dollars, except Earnings per Share)
Sales revenue.	$825,000
Cost of goods sold.	540,000
Net income.	50,500
Dividends	15,000
Earnings per share	4.25

PACKARD PLASTICS, INC. Balance Sheets (Thousands of Dollars)	Dec. 31, 2016	Dec. 31, 2015
Assets		
Cash.	$ 4,100	$ 2,700
Accounts receivable (net).	66,900	60,900
Inventory.	148,000	140,000
Total Current Assets.	219,000	203,600
Plant assets (net)	215,000	194,000
Other assets.	13,900	3,900
Total Assets	$447,900	$401,500
Liabilities and Stockholders' Equity		
Notes payable—banks.	$ 31,000	$ 25,000
Accounts payable.	27,600	23,000
Accrued liabilities	25,100	24,800
Total Current Liabilities.	83,700	72,800
10% Bonds payable.	150,000	150,000
Total Liabilities	233,700	222,800
Common stock, $10 par value (12,500,000 shares).	125,000	125,000
Retained earnings	89,200	53,700
Total Stockholders' Equity	214,200	178,700
Total Liabilities and Stockholders' Equity	$447,900	$401,500

Required

a. Using the given data, calculate items 1 through 8 below for 2016. Compare the performance of Packard Plastics, Inc., with the following industry averages and comment on its operations.

	Median Ratios for Manufacturers of Plastic and Synthetic Products
1. Quick ratio	1.2
2. Current ratio	1.9
3. Accounts receivable turnover.	7.9 times
4. Inventory turnover	7.8 times
5. Debt-to-equity ratio	0.95
6. Gross profit percentage	32.7 percent
7. Return on sales	3.5 percent
8. Return on assets	6.3 percent

b. Calculate the dividends paid per share of common stock. What was the dividend payout ratio?

c. If the most recent price per share of common stock is $50.25, what is the price-earnings ratio? The dividend yield?

P14-10A. Financial Statement Notes: Quarterly Data Quarterly data are presented below for Company A and Company B. One of these companies is Gibson Greetings, Inc., which manufactures and sells greeting cards. The other company is Hon Industries, Inc., which manufactures and sells office furniture. Both companies are on a calendar year basis.   **LO2, 4**

	(Amounts in Thousands)				
	First Quarter	Second Quarter	Third Quarter	Fourth Quarter	Year
Company A					
Net sales.	$186,111	$177,537	$203,070	$213,608	$780,326
Gross profit.	55,457	53,643	64,024	69,374	242,498
Company B					
Net sales.	$ 84,896	$ 83,796	$142,137	$235,336	$546,165
Gross profit.	53,900	52,983	66,018	104,961	277,862

Required

a. Compute the percent of annual net sales generated each quarter by Company A. Round to the nearest percent.

b. Compute the percent of annual net sales generated each quarter by Company B. Round to the nearest percent.

c. Which company has the most seasonal business? Briefly explain.

d. Which company is Gibson Greetings, Inc.? Hon Industries, Inc.? Briefly explain.

e. Which company's interim quarterly data are probably most useful for predicting annual results? Briefly explain.

PROBLEMS—SET B

P14-1B. Income Statement Format The following information from Tricon Company's operations is available: **LO1**

Administrative expenses	$ 145,000
Cost of goods sold	928,000
Sales revenue	1,650,000
Selling expenses	174,000
Interest expense	14,000
Loss from operations of discontinued segment	120,000
Gain on disposal of discontinued segment	90,000
Income taxes	
Amount applicable to ordinary operations	115,000
Reduction applicable to loss from operations of discontinued segment	68,000
Amount applicable to gain on disposal of discontinued segment	30,000

Required

a. Prepare a multiple-step income statement. (Disregard earnings per share amounts.)

b. Prepare a single-step income statement. (Disregard earnings per share amounts.)

LO4 **P14-2B.** **Earnings per Share** Island Corporation began the year with 50,000 shares of common stock outstanding. On May 1, an additional 12,000 shares of common stock were issued. On July 1, 20,000 shares of common stock were acquired as treasury stock. On September 1, the 6,000 treasury shares of common stock were reissued. Island Corporation's net income for the calendar year is $230,000.

Required

Compute earnings per share.

LO1, 4 **P14-3B.** **Earnings per Share and Multiple-Step Income Statement** The following summarized data are related to Garner Corporation's operations:

Sales revenue	$2,216,000
Cost of goods sold	1,290,000
Selling expenses	180,000
Administrative expenses	142,800
Loss from plant strike	95,000
Income tax expense	204,000
Shares of common stock	
Outstanding at January 1	65,000 shares
Additional issued at April 1	17,000 shares
Additional issued at August 1	3,000 shares

Required

Prepare a multiple-step income statement for Garner Corporation. Assume a 40 percent income tax rate. Include earnings per share disclosure at the bottom of the income statement. Garner Corporation has no preferred stock.

LO2 **P14-4B.** **Trend Percentages** Sales of automotive products for Ford Motor Company and General Motors Corporation for a five-year period are:

	Net Sales of Automotive Products (Millions of Dollars)				
	Year 1	Year 2	Year 3	Year 4	Year 5
Ford Motor Company	$82,879	$81,844	$72,051	$ 84,407	$ 91,568
General Motors Corporation	99,106	97,312	94,828	103,005	108,027

Net sales for Pfizer Inc. and Abbott Laboratories for the same five years follow:

	Net Sales (Millions of Dollars)				
	Year 1	Year 2	Year 3	Year 4	Year 5
Pfizer Inc....................................	$5,672	$6,406	$6,950	$7,230	$7,478
Abbott Laboratories.........................	5,380	6,159	6,877	7,852	8,408

Required

a. Calculate trend percentages for all four companies, using Year 1 as the base year.

b. Comment on the trend percentages of Ford Motor Company and General Motors Corporation.

c. Comment on the trend percentages of Pfizer Inc. and Abbott Laboratories.

P14-5B. Changes in Various Ratios Selected information follow for Cycle Company: LO2, 4

	2016	2015
Sales revenue...	$680,000	$520,000
Cost of goods sold.......................................	407,700	310,000
Interest expense...	20,000	14,000
Income tax expense......................................	6,200	5,100
Net income...	26,000	20,300
Cash flow from operating activities	29,500	26,500
Capital expenditures	42,000	25,000
Accounts receivable (net), December 31	182,000	128,000
Inventory, December 31..................................	225,000	180,000
Stockholders' equity, December 31.......................	205,000	165,000
Total assets, December 31...............................	460,000	350,000

Required

a. Calculate the following ratios for 2016. The 2015 results are given for comparative purposes.

		2015
1.	Gross profit percentage	40.4 percent
2.	Return on assets	6.5 percent
3.	Return on sales	3.9 percent
4.	Return on common stockholders' equity (no preferred stock was outstanding)................................	14.2 percent
5.	Accounts receivable turnover......................................	4.77
6.	Average collection period...	76.5 days
7.	Inventory turnover	2.07
8.	Times-interest-earned ratio	2.81
9.	Operating-cash-flow-to-capital-expenditures ratio	1.06

b. Comment on the changes between the two years.

P14-6B. Ratios from Comparative and Common-Size Data Consider the following financial statements for Vega Company. LO2, 3, 4

During the year, management obtained additional bond financing to enlarge its production facilities. The plant addition produced a new high-margin product, which is supposed to improve the average rate of gross profit and return on sales.

As a potential investor, you decide to analyze the financial statements:

VEGA COMPANY Balance Sheets (Thousands of Dollars)	Dec. 31, 2016	Dec. 31, 2015
Assets		
Cash..	$ 22,000	$ 16,100
Accounts receivable (net)......................	39,000	21,400
Inventory.....................................	105,000	72,000
Prepaid expenses.............................	1,500	4,000
Plant and other assets (net)....................	463,500	427,500
Total Assets.................................	$631,000	$541,000
Liabilities and Stockholders' Equity		
Current liabilities.............................	$ 77,000	$ 46,000
9% Bonds payable............................	187,500	150,000
8% Preferred stock, $50 par value.............	60,000	60,000
Common stock, $10 par value..................	225,000	225,000
Retained earnings	81,500	60,000
Total Liabilities and Stockholders' Equity	$631,000	$541,000

VEGA COMPANY Income Statements (Thousands of Dollars)	2016	2015
Sales revenue...............................	$850,000	$697,500
Cost of goods sold...........................	552,000	465,000
Gross profit on sales.........................	298,000	232,500
Selling and administrative expenses	231,000	174,000
Income before interest expense and income taxes....	67,000	58,500
Interest expense.............................	17,000	13,500
Income before income taxes	50,000	45,000
Income tax expense..........................	14,100	12,500
Net income..................................	$ 35,900	$ 32,500
Other financial data (thousands of dollars):		
Cash provided by operating activities	$ 30,000	$ 25,000
Preferred stock dividends......................	5,000	4,800

Required

a. Calculate the following for each year: current ratio, quick ratio, operating-cash-flow-to-current-liabilities ratio (current liabilities were $40,000,000 at January 1, 2015), inventory turnover (inventory was $68,000,000 at January 1, 2015), debt-to-equity ratio, times-interest-earned ratio, return on assets (total assets were $490,000,000 at January 1, 2015), and return on common stockholders' equity (common stockholders' equity was $265,000,000 at January 1, 2015).

b. Calculate common-size percentage for each year's income statement.

c. Comment on the results of your analysis.

LO4 **P14-7B.** **Constructing Statements from Ratio Data** The following are the financial statements for Timber Company, with almost all dollar amounts missing:

TIMBER COMPANY
Balance Sheet
December 31

Cash..........................	$	?	Current liabilities................	$?
Accounts receivable (net)..........		?	10% Bonds payable.............	144,000
Inventory......................		?	Common stock..................	?
Equipment (net)		?	Retained earnings	50,000
			Total Liabilities and	
Total Assets	$576,000		Stockholders' Equity...........	$576,000

TIMBER COMPANY
Income Statement
For the Year Ended December 31

Sales revenue..	$?
Cost of goods sold..	?
Gross profit on sales	?
Selling and administrative expenses	?
Income before interest expense and income taxes.......................	?
Interest expense..	?
Income before income taxes	?
Income tax expense (30%)...	?
Net income..	$70,200

The following information is available about Timber Company's financial statements:

1. Quick ratio, 1.75.
2. Current ratio, 3.0.
3. Return on sales, 8.0 percent.
4. Return on common stockholders' equity (common stockholders' equity at January 1 was $340,000), 20 percent.
5. Gross profit percentage, 30 percent.
6. Accounts receivable turnover (accounts receivable (net) at January 1 were $97,200), 12 times.
7. The interest expense relates to the bonds payable that were outstanding all year.

Required
Compute the missing amounts, and complete the financial statements of Timber Company. (*Hint:* Complete the income statement first.)

P14-8B. **Ratios Compared with Industry Averages** You are analyzing the performance of Lumite Corpora- LO4
tion, a manufacturer of personal care products, for the most recent year. The following data are taken
from the firm's latest annual report:

	Dec. 31, 2016	Dec. 31, 2015
Quick assets..	$ 385,000	$ 350,000
Inventory and prepaid expenses	950,000	820,000
Other assets.......................................	4,165,000	3,700,000
Total Assets	$5,500,000	$4,870,000
Current liabilities......................................	$ 600,000	$ 500,000
10% Bonds payable....................................	1,300,000	1,300,000
7% Preferred stock	900,000	900,000
Common stock, $5 par value.............................	1,900,000	1,800,000
Retained earnings	800,000	370,000
Total Liabilities and Stockholders' Equity	$5,500,000	$4,870,000

In 2016, net sales amount to $8,800,000, net income is $680,000, and preferred stock dividends paid
are $65,000.

Required

a. Calculate the following for 2016:
   1. Return on sales
   2. Return on assets
   3. Return on common stockholders' equity
   4. Quick ratio
   5. Current ratio
   6. Debt-to-equity ratio

b. Trade association statistics and information provided by credit agencies reveal the following data on industry norms:

	Median	Upper Quartile
Return on sales	3.7 percent	10.6 percent
Return on assets	5.8 percent	14.2 percent
Return on common stockholders' equity	18.5 percent	34.2 percent
Quick ratio	1.0	1.8
Current ratio	2.2	3.7
Debt-to-equity ratio	1.07	0.37

Compare Lumite Corporation's performance with industry performance.

LO4 **P14-9B.** **Ratios Compared with Industry Averages** Avery Instruments, Inc., is a manufacturer of various measuring and controlling instruments. Financial statement data for the firm are as follows:

	2016 (Thousands of Dollars, except Earnings per Share)
Sales revenue	$220,000
Cost of goods sold	125,000
Net income	8,000
Dividends	2,600
Earnings per share	4.25

AVERY INSTRUMENTS, INC. Balance Sheets (Thousands of Dollars)	Dec. 31, 2016	Dec. 31, 2015
Assets		
Cash	$ 18,500	$ 18,000
Accounts receivable (net)	46,000	43,000
Inventory	39,500	43,700
Total Current Assets	104,000	104,700
Plant assets (net)	52,600	51,500
Other assets	15,600	13,800
Total Assets	$172,200	$170,000
Liabilities and Stockholders' Equity		
Notes payable—banks	$ 6,000	$ 6,000
Accounts payable	22,700	18,700
Accrued liabilities	16,500	24,000
Total Current Liabilities	45,200	48,700
9% Bonds payable	40,000	40,000
Total Liabilities	85,200	88,700
Common stock, $25 par value (2,000,000 shares)	50,000	50,000
Retained earnings	37,000	31,300
Total Stockholders' Equity	87,000	81,300
Total Liabilities and Stockholders' Equity	$172,200	$170,000

Required

a. Using the given data, calculate ratios 1 through 8 for 2016. Compare the performance of Avery Instruments, Inc., with the following industry averages and comment on its operations.

		Median Ratios for Manufacturers of Measuring and Controlling Instruments
1.	Quick ratio	1.3
2.	Current ratio	2.4
3.	Accounts receivable turnover.	5.9 times
4.	Inventory turnover	3.5 times
5.	Debt-to-equity ratio	0.73
6.	Gross profit percentage	44.3 percent
7.	Return on sales	4.5 percent
8.	Return on assets	7.6 percent

b. Calculate the dividends paid per share of common stock. What was the dividend payout ratio?
c. If the most recent price per share of common stock is $63, what is the price-earnings ratio? The dividend yield?

P14-10B. Financial Statement Notes: Quarterly Data Quarterly data are presented below for Company C and Company D. One of these companies is Toys "R" Us, a children's specialty retail chain. The company's fiscal year ends on the Saturday nearest to January 31. The other company is the Gillette Company prior to its acquisition by Procter & Gamble. Gillette manufactures and sells blades, razors, and toiletries. Gillette was on a calendar year basis.

LO2, 4

	(Amounts in Thousands)				
	First Quarter	Second Quarter	Third Quarter	Fourth Quarter	Year
Company C					
Net Sales	$1,216.6	$1,237.3	$1,339.7	$1,617.2	$5,410.8
Gross profit.	753.1	773.6	839.0	1,000.8	3,366.5
Company D					
Net Sales	$1,172.5	$1,249.1	$1,345.8	$3,401.8	$7,169.2
Gross profit.	362.5	384.6	423.2	1,030.3	2,200.6

Required

a. Compute the percentage of annual net sales generated each quarter by Company C. Round to the nearest percent.
b. Compute the percentage of annual net sales generated each quarter by Company D. Round to the nearest percent.
c. Which company has the most seasonal business? Briefly explain.
d. Which company is Toys "R" Us? The Gillette Company? Briefly explain.

EXTENDING YOUR KNOWLEDGE

REPORTING AND ANALYSIS

EYK14-1. Financial Reporting Problem: Columbia Sportswear Company The financial statements for the Columbia Sportswear Company are available on this book's Website.

COLUMBIA
SPORTSWEAR
COMPANY

You are considering an investment in Columbia Sportswear after a recent outdoor trip in which you really liked some of the clothes you purchased from the company. You decide to do an analysis of the company's financial statements in order to help you make an informed decision.

Required

a. Using the five-year selected financial data reported in the annual report, produce a five-year trend analysis, using 2010 as a base year, of (1) net sales, (2) net income, and (3) total assets. Comment on your findings.

b. Calculate the (1) gross profit percentage, (2) return on sales, and (3) return on assets for 2013 and 2014. Comment on Columbia Sportswear's profitability. (2012 total assets = $1,458,842,000)

c. Calculate the (1) current ratio, (2) quick ratio, and (3) operating-cash-flow-to-current-liabilities ratio for 2013 and 2014. (2012 current liabilities = $252,059,000) Comment on Columbia Sportswear's liquidity.

d. Calculate the debt-to-equity ratio for 2013 and 2014. Comment on Columbia Sportswear's solvency.

EYK14-2. **Comparative Analysis Problem:** Columbia Sportswear Company vs Under Armour, Inc. The financial statements for the Columbia Sportswear Company and Under Armour, Inc. are available on this book's Website.

Required

Based on the information from the financial statements of each company, do the following.

a. Calculate the percentage change in (1) net sales, (2) net income, (3) cash flow from operating activities, and (4) total assets from 2013 to 2014.

b. What conclusions can you draw from this analysis?

EYK14-3. **Business Decision Problem** Crescent Paints, Inc., a paint manufacturer, has been in business for five years. The company has had modest profits and has experienced few operating difficulties until this year, 2016, when president Alice Becknell discussed her company's working capital problems with you, a loan officer at Granite Bank. Becknell explained that expanding her firm has created difficulties in meeting obligations when they come due and in taking advantage of cash discounts offered by manufacturers for the timely payment of the company's accounts payable. She would like to borrow $50,000 from Granite Bank. At your request, Becknell submits the following financial data for the past two years:

	2016	2015
Sales revenue.	$2,000,000	$1,750,000
Cost of goods sold.	1,320,000	1,170,000
Net income.	42,000	33,600
Dividends.	22,000	18,000
December 31, 2014, data.		
Total assets	1,100,000	
Accounts receivable (net).	205,000	
Inventory.	350,000	

CRESCENT PAINTS, INC. Balance Sheets		
	Dec. 31, 2016	Dec. 31, 2015
Assets		
Cash.	$ 31,000	$ 50,000
Accounts receivable (net).	345,000	250,000
Inventory.	525,000	425,000
Prepaid expenses.	11,000	6,000
Total Current Assets.	912,000	731,000
Plant assets (net)	483,000	444,000
Total Assets.	$1,395,000	$ 1,175,000

(continued)

(continued from previous page)

CRESCENT PAINTS, INC. Balance Sheets	Dec. 31, 2016	Dec. 31, 2015
Liabilities and Stockholders' Equity		
Notes payable—banks.....................................	$ 100,000	$ 35,000
Accounts payable..	244,000	190,000
Accrued liabilities.......................................	96,000	85,000
Total Current Liabilities...............................	440,000	310,000
10% Mortgage payable	190,000	250,000
Total Liabilities	630,000	560,000
Common stock...	665,000	535,000
Retained earnings	100,000	80,000
Total Stockholders' Equity	765,000	615,000
Total Liabilities and Stockholders' Equity	$1,395,000	$1,175,000

Calculate the following items for both years from the given data and then compare them with the median ratios for paint manufacturers provided by a commercial credit firm:

		Median Ratios for Paint Manufacturers
1.	Current ratio	2.5
2.	Quick ratio	1.3
3.	Accounts receivable turnover................................	8.1
4.	Average collection period....................................	44.9 days
5.	Inventory turnover	4.9
6.	Debt-to-equity ratio	0.78
7.	Return on assets	4.8%
8.	Return on sales	2.4%

Required

Based on your analysis, decide whether and under what circumstances you would grant Becknell's request for a loan. Explain the reasons for your decision.

EYK14-4. Financial Analysis Problem Listed below are selected financial data for three corporations: Honeywell International, Inc. (environmental controls), The Dow Chemical Company (chemicals and plastic products), and Abbott Laboratories (health care products). These data cover five years (Year 5 is the most recent year; net income in thousands):

HONEYWELL
INTERNATIONAL,
INC.

THE DOW
CHEMICAL
COMPANY

ABBOTT
LABORATORIES

	Year 5	Year 4	Year 3	Year 2	Year 1
Honeywell International, Inc.					
Net income.........................	$278,900	$322,200	$246,800	$331,100	$381,900
Earnings per common share	$2.15	$2.40	$1.78	$2.35	$2.52
Dividend per common share	$1.00	$0.91	$0.84	$0.77	$0.70
The Dow Chemical Company					
Net income.........................	$938,000	$644,000	$276,000	$942,000	$1,384,000
Earnings per common share	$3.88	$2.33	$0.99	$3.46	$5.10
Dividend per common share	$2.60	$2.60	$2.60	$2.60	$2.60
Abbott Laboratories					
Net income*.........................	$1,399,100	$1,239,100	$1,088,700	$965,800	$859,800
Earnings per common share*............	$1.69	$1.47	$1.27	$1.11	$0.96
Dividend per common share	$0.68	$0.60	$0.50	$0.42	$0.35

*Before accounting change

Required

a. Calculate the dividend payout ratio for each company for each of the five years.

b. Companies may differ in their dividend policy; that is, they may differ in whether they emphasize a constant dividend amount per share, a steady growth in dividend amount per share, a target or constant dividend payout ratio, or some other criterion. Based on the data available, identify what appears to be each of the above firm's dividend policy over the five-year period.

CRITICAL THINKING

EYK14-5. **Accounting Research Problem: General Mills, Inc.** The fiscal year 2014 annual report of General Mills, Inc. is available on this book's Website.

Required

a. Calculate (or identify) the following financial ratios for 2013 and 2014:
   1. Gross profit percentage
   2. Return on sales
   3. Asset turnover (2012, total assets = $21,096.8 million)
   4. Return on assets (2012, total assets = $21,096.8 million)
   5. Return on common stockholders' equity (2012, total stockholders' equity = $6,882.7 million)
   6. Current ratio
   7. Quick ratio
   8. Operating-cash-flow-to-current-liabilities ratio (2012, current liabilities = $3,843.2 million)
   9. Accounts receivable turnover (2012, accounts receivable = $1,323.6 million)
   10. Average collection period
   11. Inventory turnover (2012, inventory = $1,478.8 million)
   12. Days' sales in inventory
   13. Debt-to-equity ratio
   14. Times-interest-earned ratio
   15. Operating-cash-flow-to-capital-expenditures ratio
   16. Earnings per share
   17. Price-earnings ratio (Use year-end adjusted closing stock price of $53.81 for 2014 and $48.98 for 2013.)
   18. Dividend yield
   19. Dividend payout ratio

b. Comment briefly on the changes from fiscal 2013 to fiscal 2014 in the ratios computed above.

EYK14-6. **Accounting Communication Activity** Pete Hollingsworth is currently taking an accounting course and is confused about what his professor told the class about analyzing financial statements. Pete would like you to lead a study session on the topic. In order to help everyone out, you decide to write a short memo describing some of the key points.

Required

Include the following items in your memo:

a. What is meant by trend analysis and how is it helpful?

b. How are common-size statements constructed and what are their uses?

c. What are a few common profitability, liquidity, and solvency ratios and how are they interpreted?

d. What are some limitations of financial statement analysis?

EYK14-7. **Accounting Ethics Case** Chris Nelson, the new assistant controller for Grand Company, is preparing for the firm's year-end closing procedures. On December 30, 2016, a memorandum from the controller directed Nelson to make a journal entry debiting Cash and crediting Long-Term Advances to Officers for $1,000,000. Not finding the $1,000,000 in the cash deposit prepared for the bank that day, Nelson went to the controller for a further explanation. In response, the controller took from her desk drawer a check for $1,000,000 payable to Grand Company from Jason Grand,

chief executive officer of the firm. Attached to the check was a note from Jason Grand saying that if this check were not needed to return it to him next week.

"This check is paying off a $1,000,000 advance the firm made to Jason Grand six years ago," stated the controller. "Mr. Grand has done this every year since the advance; each time we have returned the check to him in January of the following year. We plan to do so again this time. In fact, when Mr. Grand retires in four years, I expect the board of directors will forgive this advance. However, if the firm really needed the cash, we would deposit the check."

"Then why go through this charade each year?" inquired Nelson.

"It dresses up our year-end balance sheet," replied the controller. "Certain financial statement ratios are improved significantly. Further, the notes to the financial statements don't have to reveal a related-party loan. Lots of firms engage in year-end transactions designed to dress up their financial statements."

Required

a. What financial statement ratios are improved by making the journal entry contained in the controller's memorandum?

b. Is the year-end handling of Jason Grand's advance an ethical practice? Discuss.

EYK14-8. **Corporate Social Responsibility Problem** The chapter highlighted one way in which the Procter & Gamble Company demonstrates its commitment to being a good corporate citizen (see Page 521). Go to Procter & Gamble's Website and navigate to the section on sustainability. From there you can download their annual sustainability report. The report contains a section on social responsibility. In addition to the joint effort with UNICEF, what are some other ways that P&G demonstrates its commitment to being a good corporate citizen?

PROCTER
& GAMBLE
COMPANY

EYK14-9. **Forensic Accounting Problem** Accrual accounting is based on the principle that revenue should be reported when earned and that expenses associated with that revenue should be matched against the revenue in the same period. Some financial statement frauds violate this fundamental concept in order to overstate net income in the current year. Provide an example of how this may be accomplished.

EYK14-10. **Working with the Takeaways** Below are income statements and balance sheets for the Fango Company for 2016 and 2015:

FANGO COMPANY Income Statement For the Years Ended December 31, 2016 and 2015		
(in millions)	2016	2015
Sales revenue.	$10,000	$9,500
Cost of goods sold.	5,500	5,200
Gross profit.	4,500	4,300
Selling and administrative expenses	2,800	2,700
Income from operations.	1,700	1,600
Interest expense.	300	250
Income before income taxes	1,400	1,350
Income tax expense.	420	400
Net income.	$ 980	$ 950

FANGO COMPANY **Balance Sheet** **December 31, 2016 and 2015**		
(in millions)	**2016**	**2015**
Assets		
Current assets		
Cash and cash equivalents	$ 200	$ 400
Accounts receivable	900	800
Inventory	700	650
Other current assets	400	250
Total current assets	2,200	2,100
Property, plant, & equipment (net)	2,600	2,500
Other assets	5,700	5,900
Total assets	$10,500	$10,500
Liabilities and Stockholders' Equity		
Current liabilities	$ 3,000	$ 2,900
Long-term liabilities	5,000	5,400
Total liabilities	8,000	8,300
Stockholders' equity—common	2,500	2,200
Total liabilities and stockholders' equity	$10,500	$10,500

Required

Calculate the following ratios for the Fango Company for 2016 and 2015 and discuss your findings:

1. Profitability
   a. Return on sales
   b. Return on common stockholders' equity (common stockholders' equity was $2,000 on December 31, 2014)
2. Liquidity
   a. Current ratio
   b. Accounts receivable turnover (accounts receivable was $780 on December 31, 2014)
   c. Inventory turnover (inventory was $620 on December 31, 2014)
3. Solvency
   a. Debt-to-equity ratio
   b. Times-interest-earned ratio

EYK14-11. Analyzing IFRS Financial Statements The 2014 financial statements of **LVMH Moet Hennessey-Louis Vuitton S.A.** are available on this book's Website. LVMH is a Paris-based holding company and one of the world's largest and best-known luxury goods companies. As a member of the European Union, French companies are required to prepare their consolidated (group) financial statements using International Financial Reporting Standards (IFRS). After reviewing LVMH's consolidated financial statements, calculate the following for 2014 and 2013:

   a. Current ratio
   b. Quick ratio
   c. Accounts receivable turnover
   d. Inventory turnover
   e. Debt-to-equity ratio
   f. Times-interest-earned ratio (*Hint:* Interest expense is called "Cost of net financial debt.")
   g. Return on sales
   h. Return on assets
   i. Return on common stockholders' equity

EYK14-12. Kate is very pleased with the results of the first year of operations for Kate's Cards. She ended the year on a high note, with the company's reputation for producing quality cards leading to more business than she can currently manage. Kate is considering expanding and bringing in several employees. In order to do this, she will need to find a larger location and also purchase more equipment. All this means additional financing. Kate has asked you to look at her year-end financial statements as if you were a banker considering giving Kate a loan. Comment on your findings and provide calculations to support your comments.

KATE'S CARDS Income Statement Year Ended August 31, 2016	
Sales revenue.	$135,000
Cost of goods sold.	72,000
Gross profit.	63,000
Operating expenses	
Wages	18,000
Consulting	11,850
Insurance	1,200
Utilities	2,400
Depreciation.	3,250
Total operating expenses.	36,700
Income from operations.	26,300
Interest expense.	900
Income before income tax	25,400
Income tax expense.	8,900
Net income.	$ 16,500

KATE'S CARDS Balance Sheet August 31, 2016	
Assets	
Current assets	
Cash.	$12,300
Accounts receivable.	11,000
Inventory.	16,000
Prepaid insurance	1,000
Total current assets	40,300
Equipment	17,500
Accumulated depreciation	3,250
Total assets	$54,550
Liabilities	
Current liabilities	
Accounts payable.	$ 6,200
Unearned revenue	1,250
Other current liabilities	1,900
Total current liabilities	9,350
Note payable	15,000
Total liabilities.	24,350
Stockholders' equity	
Common stock.	500
Additional paid-in-capital.	9,500
Preferred stock.	5,000
Retained earnings	15,200
Total stockholders' equity	30,200
Total liabilities and stockholders' equity	$54,550

KATE'S CARDS Statement of Cash Flows Year Ended August 31, 2016	
Cash flow from operating activities	
Net income	$16,500
Add depreciation	3,250
Increase in accounts receivable	(11,000)
Increase in inventory.	(16,000)
Increase in prepaid expenses.	(1,000)
Increase in accounts payable.	6,200
Increase in unearned revenue.	1,250
Increase in other current liabilities	1,900
Cash provided by operating activities	1,100
Cash flow from investing activities	
Purchase of equipment.	(17,500)
Cash used by investing activities.	(17,500)
Cash flow from financing activities	
Proceeds from bank note	15,000
Issuance of common stock.	10,000
Issuance of preferred stock	5,000
Cash dividends.	(1,300)*
Cash provided by financing activities	28,700
Net increase in cash.	12,300
Cash at beginning of year	0
Cash at end of year	$12,300

*Kate issued cash dividends on both the common stock and the preferred stock. There are 50 preferred shares outstanding and 500 common shares outstanding. The dividends that Kate paid were $6 per share on the preferred shares and $2 per share on the common shares.

ANSWERS TO SELF-STUDY QUESTIONS:

1. c, (p. 520) 2. c, (p. 528) 3. c, (p. 534) 4. b, (p. 537) 5. b, (p. 533) 6. c, (p. 537)
7. d, (p. 540) 8. b, (p. 531) 9. c, (p. 532) 10. b, (p. 526) 11. c, (p. 544) 12. d, (p. 546–549)

YOUR TURN! SOLUTIONS

Solution 14.1
1. Persistent
2. Transitory
3. Transitory
4. Persistent
5. Transitory
6. Persistent

Solution 14.2

	Increase in 2016	
	Amount	**Percent**
Sales revenue.	$50,000	6.7 percent [($800,000 − $750,000)/$750,000]
Net income.	20,000	20.0 percent [($120,000 − $100,000)/$100,000]
Total assets	10,000	3.4 percent [($300,000 − $290,000)/$290,000]

Solution 14.3

SANFORD COMPANY Income Statement For the Year Ended December 31, 2015		
	Amount	**Percent**
Sales revenue.	$13,500	100.0
Cost of goods sold.	5,400	40.0
Gross profit.	8,100	60.0
Selling and administrative expenses	1,350	10.0
Income from operations.	6,750	50.0
Interest expense.	675	5.0
Other expense	135	1.0
Income before income taxes	5,940	44.0
Income tax expense.	2,295	17.0
Net income.	$ 3,645	27.0

Solution 14.4

a. Gross profit percentage = ($30,000 − $10,500)/$30,000 = 65.0 percent
b. Return on sales = $4,500/$30,000 = 15.0 percent
c. Asset turnover = $30,000/$50,000 = 0.60
d. Return on assets = $4,500/$50,000 = 9.0 percent
e. Return on common stockholders' equity = ($4,500 − $500)/$35,000 = 11.4 percent

Solution 14.5

a. Working capital = $60,000 − $40,000 = $20,000
b. Current ratio = $60,000/$40,000 = 1.5
c. Operating-cash-flow-to-current-liabilities ratio = $55,000/$40,000 = 1.375
d. Accounts receivable turnover = $100,000/$15,000 = 6.67 times
e. Days' sales in inventory = 365/($70,000/$9,000) = 46.9 days

Solution 14.6

a. Debt-to-equity ratio = $180,000/$600,000 = 0.30
b. Times-interest-earned ratio = ($55,000 + $5,000 + $25,000)/$5,000 = 17.0 times
c. Operating-cash-flow-to-capital-expenditures ratio = $100,000/$30,000 = 3.33 times

Solution 14.7

a. Dividend yield = $1.50/$54.00 = 2.8 percent
b. Dividend payout ratio = $1.50/$4.50 = 33.3 percent

Appendix

Accounting and the Time Value of Money

LEARNING OBJECTIVES

1. **Describe** the nature of interest and **distinguish** between simple and compound interest. *(p. A-2)*

2. **Calculate** future values. *(p. A-3)*

3. **Calculate** present values. *(p. A-6)*

TIME VALUE OF MONEY CONCEPT

Would you rather receive a dollar now or a dollar one year from now? Most people would answer "a dollar now." Intuition tells us that a dollar received now is more valuable than the same amount received sometime in the future. Sound reasons exist, however, for choosing the option of receiving the money sooner rather than later, the most obvious of which concerns risk. Because the future is always uncertain, some event may prevent you from receiving the dollar at a later date. To avoid this risk, we choose the earlier date.

LO1 **Describe** the nature of interest and **distinguish** between simple and compound interest.

A second reason for choosing the earlier date is that the dollar has a **time value**—that is, the dollar received now could be invested such that one year from now, you could have not only the original dollar but also the interest income on the dollar for the past year. **Interest** is a payment for the use of money, much like a rent payment for the use of an apartment. Interest is calculated by multiplying an interest rate, usually stated as an annual rate, by a principal amount for a period of time. The **principal** amount represents the amount to be repaid. The amount of interest can be computed as either a simple interest amount or a compound interest amount.

Time Value of Money: Simple Interest Model

Simple interest involves calculating interest on only the principal amount owed without considering any interest already earned. Simple interest is calculated using the following well-known formula:

$$\textbf{Interest} = \textbf{p} \times \textbf{i} \times \textbf{n}$$

where

> p = principal (total amount)
> i = interest rate for one period
> n = time (number of periods)

For example, if you borrow $3,000 for four years at a simple interest rate of six percent annually, the amount of simple interest would total $720, calculated as $3,000 × .06 × 4.

Time Value of Money: Compound Interest Model

Compound interest differs from simple interest because it is calculated on both the principal and any previously earned interest that has not been paid. In other words, compound interest involves computing interest on interest, along with the principal amount.

As we can see in **Exhibit A-1**, simple interest only uses the original $3,000 principal to compute the annual interest in each of the four years. In contrast, compound interest uses the entire principal balance, including both the original $3,000 principal and the accumulated interest to date, to compute the next year's interest. This results in increasing interest each year, with the result in **Exhibit A-1** for compound interest yielding a larger ending balance by $67.43.

Because almost all businesses use compound interest, we will assume the use of compound interest in all of the illustrations in this appendix. Simple interest is generally only used in short-term credit arrangements, typically lasting less than a year.

Exhibit A-1	Illustration Comparing Simple Interest to Compound Interest						
	Simple Interest Model			**Compound Interest Model**			
	Interest Calculation	Simple Interest	Principal Balance		Interest Calculation	Compound Interest	Principal Balance
Year 1..	$3,000.00 × 6%	$180.00	$3,180.00		$3,000.00 × 6%	$180.00	$3,180.00
Year 2..	$3,000.00 × 6%	$180.00	$3,360.00		$3,180.00 × 6%	$190.80	$3,370.80
Year 3..	$3,000.00 × 6%	$180.00	$3,540.00		$3,370.80 × 6%	$202.25	$3,573.05
Year 4..	$3,000.00 × 6%	$180.00	$3,720.00		$3,573.05 × 6%	$214.38	$3,787.43
		$720.00		→ $67.43 difference ←		$787.43	

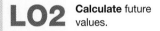

FUTURE VALUE OF AN AMOUNT

LO2 **Calculate** future values.

The **future value** of a single sum is the amount that a specified investment will be worth at a future date if invested at a given rate of compound interest. For example, suppose that we decide to invest $6,000 in a savings account that pays six percent annual interest, and that we intend to leave the principal and interest in the account for five years. Assuming that interest is credited to the account at the end of each year, the balance in the account at the end of five years is determined using the following formula:

$$FV = PV \times (1 + i)^n$$

where

FV = future value of an amount
PV = present value (today's value)
i = interest rate for one period
n = number of periods

The future value in this case is $8,029, computed as [$6,000 × (1.06)⁵] = ($6,000 × 1.33823).

It is often easier to solve time value of money problems with the aid of a time diagram, as illustrated in **Exhibit A-2**. Time diagrams are drawn to show the timing of the various cash inflows and outflows. Note in **Exhibit A-2** that our initial $6,000 cash inflow (the amount deposited in a savings account) allows us to withdraw $8,029 (a cash outflow) at the end of five years.

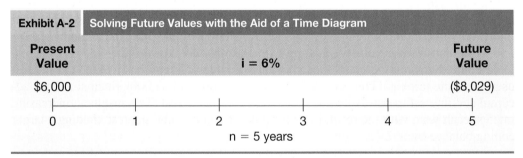

Exhibit A-2	Solving Future Values with the Aid of a Time Diagram

Present Value	i = 6%	Future Value
$6,000		($8,029)

| 0 | 1 | 2 | 3 | 4 | 5 |

n = 5 years

We can also calculate the future value of a single amount with the use of a table like **Table I**, which presents the future value of a single dollar after a given number of time periods. Simply stated, future value tables provide a multiplier for many combinations of time periods and interest rates that, when applied to the dollar amount of a present value, determines its future value.

Table I	Future Value of $1											
Period	**1.0%**	**2.0%**	**3.0%**	**4.0%**	**5.0%**	**6.0%**	**7.0%**	**8.0%**	**9.0%**	**10.0%**	**11.0%**	**12.0%**
1	1.01000	1.02000	1.03000	1.04000	1.05000	1.06000	1.07000	1.08000	1.09000	1.10000	1.11000	1.12000
2	1.02010	1.04040	1.06090	1.08160	1.10250	1.12360	1.14490	1.16640	1.18810	1.21000	1.23210	1.25440
3	1.03030	1.06121	1.09273	1.12486	1.15763	1.19102	1.22504	1.25971	1.29503	1.33100	1.36763	1.40493
4	1.04060	1.08243	1.12551	1.16986	1.21551	1.26248	1.31080	1.36049	1.41158	1.46410	1.51807	1.57352
5	1.05101	1.10408	1.15927	1.21665	1.27628	1.33823	1.40255	1.46933	1.53862	1.61051	1.68506	1.76234
6	1.06152	1.12616	1.19405	1.26532	1.34010	1.41852	1.50073	1.58687	1.67710	1.77156	1.87041	1.97382
7	1.07214	1.14869	1.22987	1.31593	1.40710	1.50363	1.60578	1.71382	1.82804	1.94872	2.07616	2.21068
8	1.08286	1.17166	1.26677	1.36857	1.47746	1.59385	1.71819	1.85093	1.99256	2.14359	2.30454	2.47596
9	1.09369	1.19509	1.30477	1.42331	1.55133	1.68948	1.83846	1.99900	2.17189	2.35795	2.55804	2.77308
10	1.10462	1.21899	1.34392	1.48024	1.62889	1.79085	1.96715	2.15892	2.36736	2.59374	2.83942	3.10585
11	1.11567	1.24337	1.38423	1.53945	1.71034	1.89830	2.10485	2.33164	2.58043	2.85312	3.15176	3.47855
12	1.12683	1.26824	1.42576	1.60103	1.79586	2.01220	2.25219	2.51817	2.81266	3.13843	3.49845	3.89598
13	1.13809	1.29361	1.46853	1.66507	1.88565	2.13293	2.40985	2.71962	3.06580	3.45227	3.88328	4.36349
14	1.14947	1.31948	1.51259	1.73168	1.97993	2.26090	2.57853	2.93719	3.34173	3.79750	4.31044	4.88711
15	1.16097	1.34587	1.55797	1.80094	2.07893	2.39656	2.75903	3.17217	3.64248	4.17725	4.78459	5.47357
16	1.17258	1.37279	1.60471	1.87298	2.18287	2.54035	2.95216	3.42594	3.97031	4.59497	5.31089	6.13039
17	1.18430	1.40024	1.65285	1.94790	2.29202	2.69277	3.15882	3.70002	4.32763	5.05447	5.89509	6.86604
18	1.19615	1.42825	1.70243	2.02582	2.40662	2.85434	3.37993	3.99602	4.71712	5.55992	6.54355	7.68997
19	1.20811	1.45681	1.75351	2.10685	2.52695	3.02560	3.61653	4.31570	5.14166	6.11591	7.26334	8.61276
20	1.22019	1.48595	1.80611	2.19112	2.65330	3.20714	3.86968	4.66096	5.60441	6.72750	8.06231	9.64629
25	1.28243	1.64061	2.09378	2.66584	3.38635	4.29187	5.42743	6.84848	8.62308	10.83471	13.58546	17.00006
30	1.34785	1.81136	2.42726	3.24340	4.32194	5.74349	7.61226	10.06266	13.26768	17.44940	22.89230	29.95992
35	1.41660	1.99989	2.81386	3.94609	5.51602	7.68609	10.67658	14.78534	20.41397	28.10244	38.57485	52.79962
40	1.48886	2.20804	3.26204	4.80102	7.03999	10.28572	14.97446	21.72452	31.40942	45.25926	65.00087	93.05097
50	1.64463	2.69159	4.38391	7.10668	11.46740	18.42015	29.45703	46.90161	74.35752	117.39085	184.56483	289.00219

Future value tables are used as follows. First, determine the number of interest compounding periods involved (five years compounded annually are five periods, five years compounded semiannually are ten periods, five years compounded quarterly are 20 periods, and so on). The extreme left-hand column indicates the number of periods covered in the table.

Second, determine the interest rate per compounding period. Note that interest rates are usually quoted on an annual or *per year* basis. Therefore, only in the case of annual compounding is the quoted interest rate the interest rate per compounding period. In other cases, the rate per compounding period is the annual rate divided by the number of compounding periods in a year. For example, an interest rate of ten percent per year would be ten percent for one compounding period if compounded annually, five percent for two compounding periods if compounded semiannually, and 2 ½ percent for four compounding periods if compounded quarterly.

Finally, locate the factor that is to the right of the appropriate number of compounding periods and beneath the appropriate interest rate per compounding period. Multiply this factor by the number of dollars involved.

Note the logical progression among the various multipliers in **Table I**. All values are 1.0 or greater because the future value is always greater than the $1 present amount if the interest rate is greater than zero. Also, as the interest rate increases (moving from left to right in the table) or the number of periods increases (moving from top to bottom), the multipliers become larger.

Continuing with our example of calculating the future value of a $6,000 savings account deposit earning 6 percent annual compound interest for five years, and using the multipliers from Table I, we solve for the future value of the deposit as follows:

$$\text{Principal} \quad \times \quad \text{Factor} \quad = \quad \text{Future Value}$$
$$\$6,000 \quad \times \quad 1.33823 \quad = \quad \$8,029$$

The factor 1.33823 is in the row for five periods and the column for six percent. Note that this factor is the same as the multiplier we determined using the future value formula in our calculation above.

Suppose, instead, that the interest is credited to the savings account semiannually rather than annually. In this situation, there are ten compounding periods, and we use a three percent rate (one-half the annual rate). The future value calculation using the **Table I** multipliers is as follows:

$$\text{Principal} \quad \times \quad \text{Factor} \quad = \quad \text{Future Value}$$
$$\$6,000 \quad \times \quad 1.34392 \quad = \quad \$8,064$$

FUTURE VALUE OF AN ANNUITY

Using future value tables like **Table I**, we can calculate the future value of any single future cash flow or series of future cash flows. One frequent pattern of cash flows, however, is subject to a more convenient calculation. This pattern, known as an **annuity**, can be described as *equal amounts equally spaced over a period.*

For example, assume that $100 is to be deposited at the end of each of the next three years as an annuity into a savings account. When annuity cash flows occur at the end of each period, the annuity is called an **ordinary annuity**. As shown below in **Exhibit A-3**, the future value of this ordinary annuity can be calculated from **Table I** by calculating the future value of each of the three individual deposits and summing them (assuming eight percent annual interest).

Exhibit A-3	Future Value of an Ordinary Annuity					
Future Deposits (ordinary annuity)				**FV Multiplier (Table I)**		**Future Value**
Year 1	Year 2	Year 3				
$100			×	1.16640	=	$1.1664
	$100		×	1.08000	=	1.0800
		$100	×	1.00000	=	1.0000
				Total future value		$324.64

Present Value			**Future Value**
	$100	$100	$100
0	1	2	3

Table II, on the other hand, provides a single multiplier for calculating the future value of a series of future cash flows that reflect an ordinary annuity. Referring to **Table II** in the three periods row and the eight percent interest column, we see that the multiplier is 3.24640, equal to the sum of the three future value factors in **Exhibit A-3**. When applied to the $100 annuity amount, the multiplier gives a future value of $324.64, or $100 × 3.2464. As shown above, the same future value is derived from several multipliers of **Table I**. For annuities of 5, 10, or 20 years, numerous calculations are avoided by using annuity tables like **Table II**.

Table II	Future Value of an Ordinary Annuity of $1 per period											
Period	1%	2%	3%	4%	5%	6%	7%	8%	9%	10%	11%	12%
1	1.00000	1.00000	1.00000	1.00000	1.00000	1.00000	1.00000	1.00000	1.00000	1.00000	1.00000	1.00000
2	2.01000	2.02000	2.03000	2.04000	2.05000	2.06000	2.07000	2.08000	2.09000	2.10000	2.11000	2.12000
3	3.03010	3.06040	3.09090	3.12160	3.15250	3.18360	3.21490	3.24640	3.27810	3.31000	3.34210	3.37440
4	4.06040	4.12161	4.18363	4.24646	4.31013	4.37462	4.43994	4.50611	4.57313	4.64100	4.70973	4.77933
5	5.10101	5.20404	5.30914	5.41632	5.52563	5.63709	5.75074	5.86660	5.98471	6.10510	6.22780	6.35285
6	6.15202	6.30812	6.46841	6.63298	6.80191	6.97532	7.15329	7.33593	7.52333	7.71561	7.91286	8.11519
7	7.21354	7.43428	7.66246	7.89829	8.14201	8.39384	8.65402	8.92280	9.20043	9.48717	9.78327	10.08901
8	8.28567	8.58297	8.89234	9.21423	9.54911	9.89747	10.25980	10.63663	11.02847	11.43589	11.85943	12.29969
9	9.36853	9.75463	10.15911	10.58280	11.02656	11.49132	11.97799	12.48756	13.02104	13.57948	14.16397	14.77566
10	10.46221	10.94972	11.46388	12.00611	12.57789	13.18079	13.81645	14.48656	15.19293	15.93742	16.72201	17.54874
11	11.56683	12.16872	12.80780	13.48635	14.20679	14.97164	15.78360	16.64549	17.56029	18.53117	19.56143	20.65458
12	12.68250	13.41209	14.19203	15.02581	15.91713	16.86994	17.88845	18.97713	20.14072	21.38428	22.71319	24.13313
13	13.80933	14.68033	15.61779	16.62684	17.71298	18.88214	20.14064	21.49530	22.95338	24.52271	26.21164	28.02911
14	14.94742	15.97394	17.08632	18.29191	19.59863	21.01507	22.55049	24.21492	26.01919	27.97498	30.09492	32.39260
15	16.09690	17.29342	18.59891	20.02359	21.57856	23.27597	25.12902	27.15211	29.36092	31.77248	34.40536	37.27971
16	17.25786	18.63929	20.15688	21.82453	23.65749	25.67253	27.88805	30.32428	33.00340	35.94973	39.18995	42.75328
17	18.43044	20.01207	21.76159	23.69751	25.84037	28.21288	30.84022	33.75023	36.97370	40.54470	44.50084	48.88367
18	19.61475	21.41231	23.41444	25.64541	28.13238	30.90565	33.99903	37.45024	41.30134	45.59917	50.39594	55.74971
19	20.81090	22.84056	25.11687	27.67123	30.53900	33.75999	37.37896	41.44626	46.01846	51.15909	56.93949	63.43968
20	22.01900	24.29737	26.87037	29.77808	33.06595	36.78559	40.99549	45.76196	51.16012	57.27500	64.20283	72.05244
25	28.24320	32.03030	36.45926	41.64591	47.72710	54.86451	63.24904	73.10594	84.70090	98.34706	114.41331	133.33387
30	34.78489	40.56808	47.57542	56.08494	66.43885	79.05819	94.46079	113.28321	136.30754	164.49402	199.02088	241.33268
35	41.66028	49.99448	60.46208	73.65222	90.32031	111.43478	138.23688	172.31680	215.71075	271.02437	341.58955	431.66350
40	48.88637	60.40198	75.40126	95.02552	120.79977	154.76197	199.63511	259.05652	337.88245	442.59256	581.82607	767.09142
50	64.46318	84.57940	112.79687	152.66708	209.34800	290.33590	406.52893	573.77016	815.08356	1163.90853	1668.77115	2400.01825

If we decide to invest $50 at the end of each six months for three years at an eight percent annual rate of return, we would use the factor for 6 periods at four percent, as follows:

Periodic Payment × Factor = Future Value
$50 × 6.63298 = $331.65

PRESENT VALUE OF AN AMOUNT

We can generalize that (1) the right to receive an amount of money now—its **present value**—is normally worth more than the right to receive the same amount later—its future value; (2) the longer we must wait to receive an amount, the less attractive the receipt is; and (3) the difference between the present value of an amount and its future value is a function of interest (Principal × Interest Rate × Time). Further, the more risk associated with any situation, the higher the appropriate interest rate.

LO3 Calculate present values.

We support these generalizations with an illustration. What amount should we accept now that would be as valuable as receiving $100 one year from now ($100 represents the future value) if the appropriate interest rate is ten percent? We recognize intuitively that with a ten percent interest rate, we should accept less than $100, or approximately $91.

We base this estimate on the realization that the $100 received in the future must equal the present value (100 percent) plus ten percent interest on the present value. Thus, in our example, the $100 future receipt must be 1.10 times the present value. Dividing $100 by 1.10, we obtain a present value of $90.91. In other words, under the given conditions, we would do as well to accept $90.91 now as to wait one year and receive $100. To confirm the equality of a $90.91 payment now with a $100 payment one year later, we calculate the future value of $90.91 at ten percent for one year as follows:

$$\textbf{\$90.91} \times \textbf{1.10} \times \textbf{1 year} = \textbf{\$100 (rounded)}$$

Thus, we calculate the present value of a future receipt by discounting (deducting an interest factor) the future receipt back to the present at an appropriate interest rate. We present this schematically below:

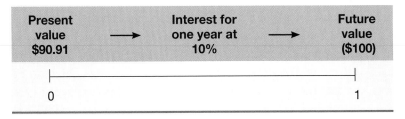

The formula for calculating the present value of a single amount is determined using the following formula:

$$\textbf{PV} = \textbf{FV} \times [\textbf{1} \div (\textbf{1} + \textbf{i})^{\textbf{n}}]$$

where

PV = present value of an amount
FV = future value
i = interest rate for one period
n = number of periods

As can be seen from this formula, if either the time period or the interest rate is increased, the resulting present value would decrease. If more than one time period is involved, compound interest calculations are appropriate. **Exhibit A-4** illustrates the calculation of the present value of a single amount.

Exhibit A-4	**Present Value of a Single Amount**

How much must be deposited in a savings account today in order to have $1,000 in four years if the savings account pays 12 percent annual interest?

$$PV = \$1,000 \times [1 \div (1.12)^4] = (\$1,000 \times 0.63552) = \$636$$

Present Value		**Discounted for 4 years at 6%**		**Future Value**
$636				($1,000)
0	1	2	3	4

Table III can be used to calculate the present value amounts in a manner similar to the way we previously calculated future values using **Tables I** and **II**. As with the future value tables, present value tables provide a multiplier for many combinations of time periods and interest rates that, when applied to the dollar amount of a future cash flow or annuity, determines its present value.

Table III	Present Value of $1											
Period	**1%**	**2%**	**3%**	**4%**	**5%**	**6%**	**7%**	**8%**	**9%**	**10%**	**11%**	**12%**
1	0.99010	0.98039	0.97087	0.96154	0.95238	0.94340	0.93458	0.92593	0.91743	0.90909	0.90090	0.89286
2	0.98030	0.96117	0.94260	0.92456	0.90703	0.89000	0.87344	0.85734	0.84168	0.82645	0.81162	0.79719
3	0.97059	0.94232	0.91514	0.88900	0.86384	0.83962	0.81630	0.79383	0.77218	0.75131	0.73119	0.71178
4	0.96098	0.92385	0.88849	0.85480	0.82270	0.79209	0.76290	0.73503	0.70843	0.68301	0.65873	0.63552
5	0.95147	0.90573	0.86261	0.82193	0.78353	0.74726	0.71299	0.68058	0.64993	0.62092	0.59345	0.56743
6	0.94205	0.88797	0.83748	0.79031	0.74622	0.70496	0.66634	0.63017	0.59627	0.56447	0.53464	0.50663
7	0.93272	0.87056	0.81309	0.75992	0.71068	0.66506	0.62275	0.58349	0.54703	0.51316	0.48166	0.45235
8	0.92348	0.85349	0.78941	0.73069	0.67684	0.62741	0.58201	0.54027	0.50187	0.46651	0.43393	0.40388
9	0.91434	0.83676	0.76642	0.70259	0.64461	0.59190	0.54393	0.50025	0.46043	0.42410	0.39092	0.36061
10	0.90529	0.82035	0.74409	0.67556	0.61391	0.55839	0.50835	0.46319	0.42241	0.38554	0.35218	0.32197
11	0.89632	0.80426	0.72242	0.64958	0.58468	0.52679	0.47509	0.42888	0.38753	0.35049	0.31728	0.28748
12	0.88745	0.78849	0.70138	0.62460	0.55684	0.49697	0.44401	0.39711	0.35553	0.31863	0.28584	0.25668
13	0.87866	0.77303	0.68095	0.60057	0.53032	0.46884	0.41496	0.36770	0.32618	0.28966	0.25751	0.22917
14	0.86996	0.75788	0.66112	0.57748	0.50507	0.44230	0.38782	0.34046	0.29925	0.26333	0.23199	0.20462
15	0.86135	0.74301	0.64186	0.55526	0.48102	0.41727	0.36245	0.31524	0.27454	0.23939	0.20900	0.18270
16	0.85282	0.72845	0.62317	0.53391	0.45811	0.39365	0.33873	0.29189	0.25187	0.21763	0.18829	0.16312
17	0.84438	0.71416	0.60502	0.51337	0.43630	0.37136	0.31657	0.27027	0.23107	0.19784	0.16963	0.14564
18	0.83602	0.70016	0.58739	0.49363	0.41552	0.35034	0.29586	0.25025	0.21199	0.17986	0.15282	0.13004
19	0.82774	0.68643	0.57029	0.47464	0.39573	0.33051	0.27651	0.23171	0.19449	0.16351	0.13768	0.11611
20	0.81954	0.67297	0.55368	0.45639	0.37689	0.31180	0.25842	0.21455	0.17843	0.14864	0.12403	0.10367
25	0.77977	0.60953	0.47761	0.37512	0.29530	0.23300	0.18425	0.14602	0.11597	0.09230	0.07361	0.05882
30	0.74192	0.55207	0.41199	0.30832	0.23138	0.17411	0.13137	0.09938	0.07537	0.05731	0.04368	0.03338
35	0.70591	0.50003	0.35538	0.25342	0.18129	0.13011	0.09366	0.06763	0.04899	0.03558	0.02592	0.01894
40	0.67165	0.45289	0.30656	0.20829	0.14205	0.09722	0.06678	0.04603	0.03184	0.02209	0.01538	0.01075
50	0.60804	0.37153	0.22811	0.14071	0.08720	0.05429	0.03395	0.02132	0.01345	0.00852	0.00542	0.00346

Exhibit A-5 illustrates calculations of present values using the factors in **Table III**.

Exhibit A-5	Present Value of a Single Amount Using Present Value Tables

Calculate the present value of $1,000 four years hence, at twelve percent interest compounded annually:

   Number of periods (one year, annually) = 4
   Interest rate per period (12%/1) = 12%
   Multiplier = 0.63552
   Present value = $1,000 × 0.63552 = $636
   (This result agrees with our earlier illustration.)

Calculate the present value of $116.99 two years hence, at eight percent compounded semiannually:

   Number of periods (two years, semiannually) = 4
   Interest rate per period (8%/2) = 4%
   Multiplier = 0.85480
   Present value = $116.99 × 0.85480 = $100 (rounded)

PRESENT VALUE OF AN ANNUITY

We can also use present value tables like **Table III** to calculate the present value of any single future cash flow or series of future cash flows. For example, assume $100 is to be received at the end of each of the next three years as an annuity. As shown in **Exhibit A-6**, the present value of this ordinary annuity can be calculated from **Table III** by calculating the present value of each of the three individual receipts and summing them (assuming five percent annual interest).

Exhibit A-6	Present Value of an Ordinary Annuity					
Future Receipts (ordinary annuity)				**PV Multiplier (Table I)**		**Future Value**
Year 1	**Year 2**	**Year 3**				
$100			×	0.95238	=	$ 95.24
	$100		×	0.90703	=	90.70
		$100	×	0.86384	=	86.38
				Total present value. . . .		$272.32

Table IV, on the other hand, provides a single multiplier for calculating the present value of a series of future cash flows that represent an ordinary annuity. Referring to **Table IV** in the three periods row and the five percent interest column, we see that the multiplier is 2.72325, equal to the sum of the three present value factors in **Exhibit A-6**. When applied to the $100 annuity amount, the multiplier gives a present value of $272.32.

Table IV	Present Value of an Ordinary Annuity of $1 per period											
Period	1%	2%	3%	4%	5%	6%	7%	8%	9%	10%	11%	12%
1	0.99010	0.98039	0.97087	0.96154	0.95238	0.94340	0.93458	0.92593	0.91743	0.90909	0.90090	0.89286
2	1.97040	1.94156	1.91347	1.88609	1.85941	1.83339	1.80802	1.78326	1.75911	1.73554	1.71252	1.69005
3	2.94099	2.88388	2.82861	2.77509	2.72325	2.67301	2.62432	2.57710	2.53129	2.48685	2.44371	2.40183
4	3.90197	3.80773	3.71710	3.62990	3.54595	3.46511	3.38721	3.31213	3.23972	3.16987	3.10245	3.03735
5	4.85343	4.71346	4.57971	4.45182	4.32948	4.21236	4.10020	3.99271	3.88965	3.79079	3.69590	3.60478
6	5.79548	5.60143	5.41719	5.24214	5.07569	4.91732	4.76654	4.62288	4.48592	4.35526	4.23054	4.11141
7	6.72819	6.47199	6.23028	6.00205	5.78637	5.58238	5.38929	5.20637	5.03295	4.86842	4.71220	4.56376
8	7.65168	7.32548	7.01969	6.73274	6.46321	6.20979	5.97130	5.74664	5.53482	5.33493	5.14612	4.96764
9	8.56602	8.16224	7.78611	7.43533	7.10782	6.80169	6.51523	6.24689	5.99525	5.75902	5.53705	5.32825
10	9.47130	8.98259	8.53020	8.11090	7.72173	7.36009	7.02358	6.71008	6.41766	6.14457	5.88923	5.65022
11	10.36763	9.78685	9.25262	8.76048	8.30641	7.88687	7.49867	7.13896	6.80519	6.49506	6.20652	5.93770
12	11.25508	10.57534	9.95400	9.38507	8.86325	8.38384	7.94269	7.53608	7.16073	6.81369	6.49236	6.19437
13	12.13374	11.34837	10.63496	9.98565	9.39357	8.85268	8.35765	7.90378	7.48690	7.10336	6.74987	6.42355
14	13.00370	12.10625	11.29607	10.56312	9.89864	9.29498	8.74547	8.24424	7.78615	7.36669	6.98187	6.62817
15	13.86505	12.84926	11.93794	11.11839	10.37966	9.71225	9.10791	8.55948	8.06069	7.60608	7.19087	6.81086
16	14.71787	13.57771	12.56110	11.65230	10.83777	10.10590	9.44665	8.85137	8.31256	7.82371	7.37916	6.97399
17	15.56225	14.29187	13.16612	12.16567	11.27407	10.47726	9.76322	9.12164	8.54363	8.02155	7.54879	7.11963
18	16.39827	14.99203	13.75351	12.65930	11.68959	10.82760	10.05909	9.37189	8.75563	8.20141	7.70162	7.24967
19	17.22601	15.67846	14.32380	13.13394	12.08532	11.15812	10.33560	9.60360	8.95011	8.36492	7.83929	7.36578
20	18.04555	16.35143	14.87747	13.59033	12.46221	11.46992	10.59401	9.81815	9.12855	8.51356	7.96333	7.46944
25	22.02316	19.52346	17.41315	15.62208	14.09394	12.78336	11.65358	10.67478	9.82258	9.07704	8.42174	7.84314
30	25.80771	22.39646	19.60044	17.29203	15.37245	13.76483	12.40904	11.25778	10.27365	9.42691	8.69379	8.05518
35	29.40858	24.99862	21.48722	18.66461	16.37419	14.49825	12.94767	11.65457	10.56682	9.64416	8.85524	8.17550
40	32.83469	27.35548	23.11477	19.79277	17.15909	15.04630	13.33171	11.92461	10.75736	9.77905	8.95105	8.24378
50	39.19612	31.42361	25.72976	21.48218	18.25593	15.76186	13.80075	12.23348	10.96168	9.91481	9.04165	8.30450

CALCULATIONS USING A CALCULATOR AND A SPREADSHEET

While present value tables can provide a handy method to solve some time value of money problems, they are not suitable for many real-world situations. For example, many real-world interest rates are not even integers like those appearing in **Table I** through **Table IV**, nor are many problems limited to the number of time periods appearing in the tables. While it is still possible to solve these problems with the provided formulas, financial calculators and spreadsheet programs provide a much quicker solution. Financial calculators can be distinguished from other calculators by the presence of dedicated keys for present and future values, along with keys for the number of periods, interest rates, and annuity payments. There exists many brands of financial calculators; however, all of them work in much the same way.[1] We illustrate time value of money calculations using a calculator and a spreadsheet in Appendix 12A at the end of Chapter 12.

---

[1] It is usually necessary to do some preliminary setup on a financial calculator before performing time value of money calculations. For example, the HP 10BII calculator has a default setting of monthly compounding. This may need to be changed if the problem calls for a different number of compounding periods, such as annual. In addition, the calculator assumes annuity payments occur at the end of each period. This will need to be changed if the problem requires beginning of period payments. See your calculator manual to determine how to make these setting changes.

SUMMARY OF LEARNING OBJECTIVES

Describe the nature of interest and distinguish between simple and compound interest. (p. A-2)   **LO1**
- Interest is payment for the use of money over time.
- Simple interest is computed only on the principal.
- Compound interest is computed on the accumulated principal including any earned interest that has not been paid.

Calculate future values. (p. A-3)   **LO2**
- The future value of a single amount is the amount that a specified investment will be worth at a future date if invested at a given rate of compound interest.
- The formula for calculating the future value of a single amount is $PV = FV \times (1 + i)^n$.
- Future value tables provide a multiplier for many combinations of time periods and interest rates that, when applied to the dollar amount of a present value, determines its future value.
- An annuity represents a special case of a pattern of cash flows where the cash flow amounts are of equal amounts and equally spaced over time.
- A separate table is available that provides a multiplier for the future value of an annuity rather than using separate multipliers from the future value of $1 table.

Calculate present values. (p. A-6)   **LO3**
- The right to receive an amount of money now—its present value—is normally worth more than the right to receive the same amount later—its future value.
- The formula for calculating the present value of a single amount is $PV = FV \times [1 \div (1 + i)^n]$.
- A separate table is available that provides a multiplier for the present value of an annuity rather than using separate multipliers from the present value of $1 table.

GLOSSARY OF KEY TERMS

Annuity (p. A-5)	**Interest** (p. A-2)	**Principal** (p. A-2)
Compound interest (p. A-2)	**Ordinary annuity** (p. A-5)	**Simple interest** (p. A-2)
Future value (p. A-3)	**Present value** (p. A-6)	**Time value** (p. A-2)

Assignments with the ⓜ logo in the margin are available in my BusinessCourse.
See the Preface of the book for details.

SELF-STUDY QUESTIONS

(Answers to Self-Study Questions are at the end of this appendix.)

LO2   **1. Calculate the future value of each of the following items.**
   a. $50,000 deposited in a savings account for ten years if the annual interest rate is
      1. Twelve percent compounded annually.
      2. Twelve percent compounded semiannually.
      3. Twelve percent compounded quarterly.
   b. $5,000 received at the end of each year for the next ten years if the money earns interest at the rate of four percent compounded annually.
   c. $3,000 received semiannually for the next five years if the money earns interest at the rate of eight percent compounded semiannually.
   d. $1,000 deposited each year for the next ten years plus a single sum of $15,000 deposited today if the interest rate is ten percent per year compounded annually.

LO3   **2. Calculate the present value of each of the following items.**
   a. $90,000 ten years hence if the annual interest rate is
      1. Eight percent compounded annually.
      2. Eight percent compounded semiannually.
      3. Eight percent compounded quarterly.
   b. $1,000 received at the end of each year for the next eight years if money is worth ten percent per year compounded annually.
   c. $600 received at the end of each six months for the next fifteen years if the interest rate is eight percent per year compounded semiannually.
   d. $500,000 inheritance ten years hence if money is worth ten percent per year compounded annually.
   e. $2,500 received each half year for the next ten years plus a single sum of $85,000 at the end of ten years if the interest rate is twelve percent per year compounded semiannually.

EXERCISES—SET A

LO1   **EA-1A. Simple and Compound Interest**
   a.   For each of the following notes, calculate the simple interest due at the end of the term.

Note	Principal	Rate	Term
1	$10,000	2%	6 years
2	$10,000	4%	4 years
3	$10,000	6%	3 years

   b.   Compute the amount of interest due at the end of the term for each of the above notes assuming interest is compounded annually.

LO2   **EA-2A. Future Value Computation** At the beginning of the year you deposit $3,000 in a savings account. How much will accumulate in three years if you earn 8% compounded annually?

LO2   **EA-3A. Future Value Computation** You deposit $3,000 at the end of every year for three years. How much will accumulate in three years if you earn 8% compounded annually?

LO3   **EA-4A. Present Value Computation** You will receive $3,000 in three years. What is the present value if you can earn 8% interest compounded annually?

LO3   **EA-5A. Present Value Computation** You receive $3,000 at the end of every year for three years. What is the present value of these receipts if you earn 8% compounded annually?

LO2   **EA-6A. Future Value Computation** What amount will be accumulated in five years if $10,000 is invested today at 6% interest compounded annually?

EA-7A. Present Value Computation You are scheduled to be paid $10,000 in five years. What amount today is equivalent to the $10,000 to be received in five years assuming interest is compounded annually at 6%?   **LO3**

EA-8A. Future Value Computation What amount will be accumulated in five years if $10,000 is invested every six months beginning in six months and ending five years from today? Interest will accumulate at an annual rate of 10% compounded semiannually.   **LO2**

EA-9A. Future Value Computation You are scheduled to receive $10,000 every six months for ten periods beginning in six months. What amount in five years is equivalent to the future series of payments assuming interest compounds at the annual rate of 8% compounded semiannually?   **LO2**

EA-10A. Present Value Computation Zazzi, Inc., believes it will need $100,000 in five years to expand its operations. Zazzi can earn 5%, compounded annually, if it deposits its money right now. How large of a deposit must Zazzi make in order to have the necessary $100,000 in five years?   **LO3**

EA-11A. Future Value Computation Peyton Company deposited $10,000 in the bank today, earning 8% interest. Peyton plans to withdraw the money in five years. How much money will be available to withdraw assuming that interest is compounded (a) annually, (b) semiannually, and (c) quarterly?   **LO2**

EA-12A. Future Value Computation Sam Smith deposited $5,000 in a savings account today. The deposit will earn interest at the rate of 8%. How much will be available for Sam to withdraw in three years, assuming interest is compounded (a) annually, (b) semiannually, and (c) quarterly?   **LO2**

EA-13A. Present Value Computation Pete Frost made a deposit into his savings account three years ago, and earned interest at an annual rate of 8%. The deposit accumulated to $25,000. How much was initially deposited assuming that the interest was compounded (a) annually, (b) semiannually, and (c) quarterly?   **LO3**

EA-14A. Future Value Computation Kumari Jennings has decided to start saving for his daughter's college education by depositing $2,500 at the end of every year for 18 years. He has determined that he will be able to earn 6% interest compounded annually. He hopes to have at least $70,000 when his daughter starts college in eighteen years. Will his savings plan be successful?   **LO2**

EA-15A. Present Value Computation Kerry Bales won the state lottery and was given four choices for receiving her winnings.   **LO3**

1. Receive $400,000 right now.
2. Receive $432,000 in one year.
3. Receive $40,000 at the end of each year for 20 years.
4. Receive $36,000 at the end of each year for 30 years.

Assuming Kerry can earn interest of 8% compounded annually, which option should Kerry choose?

EXERCISES—SET B

EA-1B. Simple and Compound Interest   **LO1**

a. For each of the following notes, calculate the simple interest due at the end of the term.

Note	Principal	Rate	Term
1	$8,000	8%	8 years
2	$8,000	12%	5 years
3	$8,000	4%	2 years

b. Compute the amount of interest due at the end of the term for each of the above notes assuming interest is compounded annually.

LO2   **EA-2B.** **Future Value Computation** At the beginning of the year you deposit $2,500 in a savings account. How much will accumulate in four years if you earn 6% compounded annually?

LO2   **EA-3B.** **Future Value Computation** You deposit $2,500 at the end of every year for four years. How much will accumulate in four years if you earn 6% compounded annually?

LO3   **EA-4B.** **Present Value Computation** You will receive $2,500 in four years. What is the present value if you can earn 6% interest compounded annually?

LO3   **EA-5B.** **Present Value Computation** You receive $2,500 at the end of every year for four years. What is the present value of these receipts if you earn 6% compounded annually?

LO2   **EA-6B.** **Future Value Computation** What amount will be accumulated in six years if $5,000 is invested today at 5% interest compounded annually?

LO3   **EA-7B.** **Present Value Computation** You are scheduled to be paid $5,000 in eight years. What amount today is equivalent to the $5,000 to be received in eight years assuming interest is compounded annually at 6%?

LO2   **EA-8B.** **Future Value Computation** What amount will be accumulated in five years if $3,000 is invested every six months beginning in six months and ending five years from today? Interest will accumulate at an annual rate of 4% compounded semiannually.

LO2   **EA-9B.** **Future Value Computation** You are scheduled to receive $5,000 every six months for eight periods beginning in six months. What amount in four years is equivalent to the future series of payments assuming interest compounds at the annual rate of 8% compounded semiannually?

LO3   **EA-10B.** **Present Value Computation** Zumi, Inc., believes it will need $150,000 in nine years to expand its operations. Zumi can earn 6%, compounded annually, if it deposits its money right now. How large of a deposit must Zumi make in order to have the necessary $150,000 in nine years?

LO2   **EA-11B.** **Future Value Computation** Triton Company deposited $9,500 in the bank today, earning 8% interest. Triton plans to withdraw the money in five years. How much money will be available to withdraw assuming that interest is compounded (a) annually, (b) semiannually, and (c) quarterly?

LO2   **EA-12B.** **Future Value Computation** Sally Smithton deposited $2,000 in a savings account today. The deposit will earn interest at the rate of 12%. How much will be available for Sally to withdraw in three years, assuming interest is compounded (a) annually, (b) semiannually, and (c) quarterly?

LO3   **EA-13B.** **Present Value Computation** Raul Gomez made a deposit into his savings account four years ago, and earned interest at an annual rate of 12%. The deposit accumulated to $40,000. How much was initially deposited assuming that the interest was compounded (a) annually, (b) semiannually, and (c) quarterly?

LO2   **EA-14B.** **Future Value Computation** Herman Lee has decided to start saving for his daughter's college education by depositing $3,000 at the end of every year for 18 years. He has determined that he will be able to earn 6% interest compounded annually. He hopes to have at least $90,000 when his daughter starts college in eighteen years. Will his savings plan be successful?

LO3   **EA-15B.** **Present Value Computation** Kelly Zales won the state lottery and was given four choices for receiving her winnings.

1. Receive $1,000,000 right now.
2. Receive $1,040,000 in one year.
3. Receive $150,000 at the end of each year for eight years.
4. Receive $57,500 at the end of each year for 30 years.

Assuming Kelly can earn interest of 4% compounded annually, which option should Kelly choose?

ANSWERS TO SELF-STUDY QUESTIONS:

1. *a.* 1. $ 50,000 × 3.10585 = $155,293
      2. $ 50,000 × 3.20714 = $160,357
      3. $ 50,000 × 3.26204 = $163,102
   b. $ 5,000 × 12.00611 = $ 60,031
   c. $ 3,000 × 12.00611 = $ 36,018
   d. $ 1,000 × 15.93742 = $ 15,937
          $ 15,000 × 2.59374 = $ 38,906
                                $ 54,843

2. *a.* 1. $ 90,000 × 0.46319 = $ 41,687
      2. $ 90,000 × 0.45639 = $ 41,075
      3. $ 90,000 × 0.45289 = $ 40,760
   b. $ 1,000 × 5.33493 = $ 5,335
   c. $ 600 × 17.29203 = $ 10,375
   d. $500,000 × 0.38554 = $192,770
   e. $ 2,500 × 11.46992 = $ 28,675
          $ 85,000 × 0.31180 = $ 26,503
                                $ 55,178

INDEX

S

T

U

V